# The
# Legacies
## of
# Literacy

# The
# LEGACIES

## CONTINUITIES AND CONTRADICTIONS

INVITA NIL PROFICIES, DISCESVE MINERVA·

# of
# LITERACY

IN WESTERN CULTURE AND SOCIETY

Harvey J. Graff

INDIANA UNIVERSITY PRESS

BLOOMINGTON AND INDIANAPOLIS

For Allan Sharlin
(1950–1983)

The strength of his
life lives on in
his memory.

Frontis: Early modern attitudes toward literacy, print, reading and their uses, from Johann Theodor de Bry, *Emblemata secvlaria mira et livcvnda*, 1611 (Case W 1025.1268), emblem 69. *Courtesy of The Newberry Library, Chicago.*

Manufactured in the United States of America

**Library of Congress Cataloging-in-Publication Data**

Graff, Harvey J.
   The legacies of literacy.

   Includes bibliographical references and index.
   1. Literacy—History.   I. Title.
LC149.G63   1986          302.2          85–46029
ISBN 0–253–14733–6


I   2   3   4   5   90   89   88   87

# Contents

## Part Three: An Old World and a New World

## Part Four: Toward the Present and the Future

# PREFACE

The subject of literacy is immense and complex. This book attempts to clarify that it is also a subject with continuities and contradictions at its very core. That may surprise some readers, for discussions of literacy are typically considerations of change.

How simple are our notions about literacy. How directly and linearly we conceive its consequences. How stark and inflexible are our assumptions and expectations about it. And, how deeply we hold our faith in its powers. What a great burden we place on a single attribute. Literacy has come to assume many meanings and to carry within its own fragile status the power of a cultural symbol, as well as of social and economic reality. The condition of literacy in a given society is often questioned, but seldom is our faith in its provenance subjected to critical view. That is especially glaring at a moment in history such as we inhabit now, in which we confront many crises, and a "crisis" of literacy is claimed to be one of the most threatening.

Now is the time for a synthetic and systematic account of literacy's history to be attempted. If my argument, that literacy can be understood *only* in terms of its historical development, is correct, then the approach to understanding and meaning offered here is required for us to comprehend the present and face the future. That is no small undertaking. Consequently, I seek no complete success. Although long, this book is not intended to be definitive. The nature of the subject precludes any such delusions. What follows is a highly interpretive synthesis based on my re-conceptualization of a tremendous amount of research.

This work is offered as one student's guide to thinking about literacy. I hope it stimulates discussion and controversy and many efforts to revise its own explicit revisionism. Much is at stake—not only our comprehension but also our confronting the present and framing options for tomorrow. It is to the future that this book is dedicated. In this respect, we must heed well these poignant words of author Nadine Gordimer:

> The kind of education the children've rebelled against is evident enough; they can't spell and they can't formulate their elation and anguish. But they know why they're dying. You were right. They turn away and screw up their eyes, squeal 'Eie-na!' when they're given an injection, but they kept on walking towards the police and the guns. You know how it is they understand what it is they want. You know how to put it. Rights, no concessions. Their country, not ghettos allotted within it, or tribal 'homelands' parcelled out. The wealth created with their fathers' and mothers' labour and transformed into a white man's dividend. Power over their lives instead of a destiny invented, decreed and enforced by white governments—Well, who among

those who didn't like your vocabulary, your methods, has put it as honestly? Who are they to make you responsible for Stalin and deny your Christ?*

HARVEY J. GRAFF

*A note on documentation*: This book is a critical, selective synthesis of a great deal of research. No complete body of references can therefore be appended. The notes are full but hardly a complete guide to my research and reading. They are mostly illustrative. A fuller approach to citations would have made a lengthy book prohibitively long. Readers who are interested in further documentation and bibliography should consult my *Literacy in History: An Interdisciplinary Research Bibliography* (New York: Garland Publishing, 1981). For additional efforts at relating the past, present, and future of literacy, see my *Literacy and Social Development in the West* (Cambridge: Cambridge University Press, 1981); Robert F. Arnove and Graff, eds., *National Literacy Campaigns: Historical and Comparative Perspectives* (New York: Plenum Publishing Co., 1987); and my collection of essays, *The Labyrinths of Literacy* (Sussex: Fulmer Press, 1987).

---

*Rosa Burger's imaginary conversation with her dead father during 1976 Soweto School children's riots. Nadine Gordimer, *Burger's Daughter* (Harmondsworth: Penguin, 1980), p. 349.

# ACKNOWLEDGMENTS

Even attempting a project of this scope represents a challenge not only to one's own literacy but to the limits of an individual's knowledge and understanding. For one such as I, primarily a student of comparative modern social history, even to contemplate such an enterprise required the assistance and support of many people and institutions. I want them all to recognize and accept my gratitude, even though doing so in no way implicates them in my sins of commission and omission. Without their assistance and encouragement, this project could not have been completed. For those whom I neglect to mention here, I offer my apologies; this acknowledgment is as complete as memory and notes permit. All who contributed in one or another way to *The Literacy Myth: Literacy and Social Structure in the Nineteenth-Century City* (1979) and *Literacy and History: An Interdisciplinary Research Bibliography* (1981) also assisted, at least indirectly, in the preparation and completion of this book; to them also go my thanks.

For financial assistance, I acknowledge the important contributions of the American Council of Learned Societies, the Newberry Library, the National Endowment for the Humanities, the National Academy of Education, and the Spencer Foundation. Most of this book was written during a two-year period of residence at the Newberry Library, Chicago, which provided an almost ideal atmosphere. Bill Towner and Dick Brown deserve the gratitude of numerous scholars who have benefited from the library's collections, staff, support, and community of fellows and users. They certainly have mine. During much of my stay, an incredibly learned and collegial group helped in countless ways, including Barbara Hanawalt, Gordon Whatley, Hank Dobyns, Steven Foster, John Tedeschi, John Aubrey, George Huppert, John Riker, Dick Frost, Fritz Jennings, Dan Smith, Jon Butler, Richard Jensen, Hugh Ormsby Lennon, Ellen Dwyer, Jeffrey Huntsman, and Jim Wells. In particular, Jan Reiff and Harriet Lightman helped me professionally and personally in too many ways to mention. The remainder of this book was written while I was a visiting professor at Simon Fraser University, Burnaby, British Columbia, where the staff, students, and faculty extended numerous courtesies and kindnesses, and where Jerry Zaslove and David Wallace merit special thanks, and at the University of Texas at Dallas. Librarians at these and other institutions greatly eased the burdens of research and reference checking.

Among the others who contributed to my research and/or welfare during the long period in which this study was in formation were fellow literacy students Ed Stevens and Lee Soltow, Bill Gilmore, David Cressy, Dan Resnick, David Levine, Egil Johansson, Ken Lockridge, Michael Clanchy, Elizabeth Eisenstein, Roger Schofield, Peter Laslett, M. J. Maynes, Shirley Heath, Jeffrey Brooks, Ben Eklof, Susan Noakes, Dick Venezky, Eric Havelock, Bob Arnove, Natalie Davis, Roger Farr, Armando Petrucci, Attillio Langeli Bartoli, and John Craig. Fellow participants at the March 1980 Leicester University History of Literacy special seminar, wonderfully led by Joan and Brian Simon; the July 1980 Library of Congress and National Institute of Education Literacy in Historical Perspective Conference, organized by Dan Resnick and John Y. Cole; and the summer 1981 Simon Fraser University SITE program also receive my thanks.

I should also like to thank Alison Prentice, Chad Gaffield, Jim Turner, Charles Tilly, Irving Bartlett, Jim Crouse, Paul Mattingly, Maurice Careless, Margery Murphey, Nancy Fitch, Lew Erenberg, Susan Hirsch, Jerry Soliday, Paul Monaco, Allan Sharlin, Bob Black, Elliot Werner and Dan Orlovsky for their friendship and support. As in all my historical work, Michael Katz merits a special note of gratitude. He made much of that possible through his tutelage and friendship.

A number of panels and audiences patiently listened to different parts or versions of this book. My ideas were challenged, tested, sharpened, and revised by these encounters. I wish to acknowledge their interest and their helpful reactions: Social Science History Association meetings, 1979 and 1981; Seminar on the History of Literacy in Post-Reformation Europe, Leicester University, 1980; Library of Congress Literacy in Historical Perspective Conference, 1980; Annenberg School of Communications and Graduate School of Education Communications Colloquium, University of Pennsylvania, 1980 (thanks to Dell Hymes, George Gerbner, and Robert Shayon); University of Chicago History of Education Workshop, 1979 and 1980 (thanks to John Craig); Newberry Library Fellows Seminar, 1980; American Antiquarian Society Conference on Printing and Society in Early America, 1980; Bard College Conference on Crisis in Literacy: Cultural Hard Times (thanks to Paul Swift, Leon Botstein, and Michael Simpson); History of Education Society meeting, 1981; Tenth World Congress of Sociology, Mexico City, 1982 (thanks to Shirley Heath); the Wellcome Institute Conference on Medicine in the Renaissance, 1982. Thanks, too, to groups at the Ontario Institute for Studies in Education and the University of Toronto, 1980 and 1985; the Transformation of European Society Conference, Bellagio, 1984 (thanks to Konrad Jarausch); the University of Delaware, 1980; Fairleigh Dickinson University, 1981; Indiana University, 1981; Illinois State University, 1981; Emory University, 1981; and the University of Massachusetts at Boston, 1981, among others who heard me speak on literacy.

Among those who assisted directly and ably in the various phases of manuscript preparation, special thanks go to Carole Loverde, Katy Smyser, Kathleen Mooney, Hollie Hunnicutt, John Bodé, Lauren Bryant, Jill Millong, the Indiana University Press production staff, and Vicki Graff. The contributions of Jane Shelly and Bob Mandel are incalculable.

As in all my work, there is a cast in the background whose larger role is often closer to center stage. In this respect, I want especially to thank my parents, my brother, and, incomparably, Vicki Graff. Last of all, a word for Harrison, who succeeded more than anyone else in taking me away from the typewriter and redirecting my frustrations during the final stages.

# The
# Legacies
## of
# Literacy

# PART ONE

# Setting the Stage

Classical legacies of learning and literacy, from Achille Bocchi, . . .
*Symbolicarvm qvaestionvm. . .*, 1574 (Case *W 1025.091), emblem CCXII. *Courtesy of The Newberry Library, Chicago.*

# Introduction: Literacy's Legacies

In the popular imagination, literacy is the most significant distinguishing feature of a civilized man and a civilized society. Expressions of these attitudes are readily culled from the popular press. . . . The assumption that nonliteracy is a problem with dreadful social and personal consequences is not only held by laymen, it is implicit in the writings of academics as well.[1]

Since popular literacy as earlier noted depends not alone on that alphabet but on instruction in the alphabet given at the elementary level of child development, and since this is a political factor which varies from country to country, the alphabetized cultures are not all socially literate.

. . . for whereas historians who have touched upon literacy as a historical phenomenon have commonly measured its progress in terms of the history of writing, the actual conditions of literacy depend upon the history not of writing but reading. In dealing with the past, it is obviously much harder to be certain about the practice of reading, its conduct and extent, than about writing. For the latter can simply exist in an artifact. . . . [Literacy] is a social condition which can be defined only in terms of readership.[2]

Not long ago anthropologists equated civilization with literacy. Many archaeologists working in the Near East still believe that writing is highly likely to develop as a data-storage technique when a given level of complexity is reached. This seems to be supported, for example, by the apparently extensive use of writing for bureaucratic purposes in ancient Egypt. . . . Yet, the evidence from Africa and the New World reveals that complex societies can exist without fully-developed (initially logosyllabic) writing systems and that those early civilizations that lacked writing were of comparable complexity to those that had it . . . there is no obvious reason why some of these should have developed writing systems and not the rest.[3]

Literacy is for the most part an enabling rather than a causal factor, making possible the development of complex political structures, syllogistic reasoning, scientific enquiry, linear conceptions of reality, scholarly specialization, artistic elaboration, and perhaps certain kinds of individualism and of alienation. Whether, and to what extent, these will in fact develop depends apparently on concomitant factors of ecology, intersocietal relations, and internal ideological and social structural responses to these.[4]

For certain uses of language, literacy is not only irrelevant, but is a positive hindrance.[5]

THESE STATEMENTS MAY SEEM SWEEPING and vast, but they are important examples of correctives and revisions only now beginning with respect to understanding the presumed impacts and consequences of literacy.[6] Until recently, scholarly and popular conceptions of the value of the skills of reading or writing have almost universally followed normative assumptions and expectations of vague but powerful concomitants and effects presumed to accompany changes in the diffusion of literacy. For the last two centuries, they have been intertwined with post-Enlightenment, "liberal" social theories and contemporary expectations of the role of literacy and schooling in socioeconomic development, social order, and individual progress. These important conjunctures constitute what I have come to call a "literacy myth."

Along with other tenets of a world view dominant in the West for most of the past two centuries, the "literacy myth" no longer serves as a satisfactory explanation for the place of literacy in society, polity, culture, or economy.[7] Given the massive *contradictions* that complicate our understanding of the world we inhabit, it is hardly surprising that a perceived "crisis" and "decline of literacy" rank among the other fears of our day. Now is the time to ask new questions that may lead to new views about literacy and its roles. If the present teaches us nothing else, we must heed the lesson that the presumed places of literacy and schooling are neither sacrosanct nor well understood. That awareness can be tremendously liberating, and is, I think, what is urgently required.

I

Literacy is *profoundly misunderstood*. That is as true for the past as for the present. This misconstrual of the meanings and contributions of literacy, with the revealing contradictions that result, is not only a problem of evidence and data but also a failure in conceptualization and, even more, epistemology.

Discussions about literacy are surprisingly facile, whether they come from the pen of a Marshall McLuhan or a contemporary social and educational critic such as Paul Copperman, author of *The Literacy Hoax*. I find that virtually all such discussions founder because they slight efforts to formulate consistent and realistic *definitions of literacy*, have little appreciation of the *conceptual complications* that the subject presents, and ignore the vital role of *sociohistorical context*. The results of such failures surround us. They preclude our knowing even the dimensions of qualitative changes in popular abilities to read and write today.[8]

Discussions about literacy levels rarely pause to consider what is meant by literacy. Part of the inattention to context, this failure invalidates most discussions at their outset and permits commentators to use the evidence of changes in such measures as Scholastic Aptitude Tests, undergraduate composition abilities, Armed Forces Qualifying Tests, and random written or textual evidence as appropriate representations of literacy. Whereas the evidence of such measures should not be ignored, these indicators reveal little directly about the skills of literacy: *the basic abilities to read and write*.

To study and interpret literacy, to the contrary, requires three tasks. The *first* is a consistent definition that serves comparatively over time and across space. *Basic or primary levels of reading and writing* constitute the *only* flexible and reasonable indications that meet this criterion; a number of historical and contemporary sources, while not wholly satisfactory in themselves, can be employed (see Table I.1), including measures ranging from the evidence of written documents, sources that reveal proportions of signatures and marks, the evidence of self-reporting, responses to surveys and questionnaires, and test results.[9] Only such basic but systematic and direct indications meet the canons of accuracy, utility, *and* comparability that we must apply consistently. Otherwise, quantitative and qualitative dimensions and changes cannot be known, and only confusion and distortion result. Some may question the quality of such data; others argue that tests of basic skills are too low a standard to apply.

To counter such common objections requires moving to a *second* task in defining literacy—to stress that it is above all a *technology or set of techniques for communications and for decoding and reproducing written or printed materials*. Writing *alone* is not an ''agent of change''; its impact is determined by the manner in which human agency exploits it in a specific setting. Moreover, literacy is an acquired skill, in a way in which oral ability or nonverbal, nonliterate communicative modes are not. As I will explain later, we need to be wary of drawing overly firm lines between the oral and the literate.[10]

Literacy is conceived sometimes as a skill, but more often as representative of attitudes and mentalities. That is suggestive. On other levels, literacy ''thresholds'' are seen as requirements for economic development, ''take-offs,'' ''modernization,'' political development and stability, standards of living, fertility control, and on and on. The number of asserted consequences and ecological correlations is literally massive. The evidence, however, is much less than the expectations and presumptions, as a review of the literature quickly reveals.

One major contradiction in the literacy-as-a-path-to-development enterprise is the disparity between theoretical assumptions and empirical findings. When they are attempted, second, the results of macro-level, aggregative, or ecological studies are usually much less impressive than the normative theories and assumptions. Schuman, Inkeles, and Smith's ingenuous effort to account for this disparity is revealing: ''Rather than finding literacy to be a factor which completely pervades and shapes a man's entire view of the world, we find it limited to those spheres where vicarious and abstract experience is essentially meaningful. The more practical part of a man's outlook, however, is determined by his daily experiences in significant roles.''[11] The conclusion is that literacy in the abstract is at most viewed as a technique or set of techniques, a foundation in skills that can be developed, be lost, or stagnate; at worst, it is meaningless.

Hence, understanding literacy requires a *further*, *large* step: into precise, historically specific materials and cultural contexts. As psychologist M. M. Lewis recognized, ''The only literacy that matters is the literacy that is in use. Potential literacy is empty, a void.''[12] The first two points are preparations for the main effort, reconstructing the contexts of reading and writing: how, when, where, why, and to whom the literacy was transmitted; the meanings that were assigned to it; the uses to which it was put; the demands placed on literate abilities; the degrees to which they were met; the changing extent of social restrictedness in the distribution and diffusion of literacy; and the real and symbolic differences that emanated from the social condition of literacy among the population. To be sure, answers to such questions are not easy to construct; nevertheless, an awareness of their overriding importance is only beginning to appear in some research and discussion. The meaning and contribution of literacy, therefore, cannot be *pre*sumed; they must themselves be a distinct focus of research and criticism.

Important new research suggests that the environment in which students acquire their literacy has a major impact on the cognitive consequences of their possession of the skill and the uses to which it can be put. For example, formal school education may result in a different set of literacy skills from those obtained through informal learning.[13]

Few research areas suffer more than literacy studies from the obstruction to understanding that rigid dichotomizing represents. Consider the common phrases literate *and* illiterate, written *and* oral, print *and* script. None of these polar opposites usefully describes actual circumstances; all of them, in fact, preclude contextual understanding. The oral-literate dichotomy is the best example. Despite decades of scholars' proclaiming a decline in the pervasiveness and power of the "traditional" oral culture, it remains equally possible and significant to locate the persisting power of oral modes of communication.[14]

Oversimplifying a complicated and sophisticated sociocultural process of interchange and interaction, we can say that Western literacy was *formed*, *shaped*, and *conditioned* by the oral world that it penetrated. In earliest times, literacy was highly restricted and a relatively unprestigious craft; it carried little of the association with wealth, power, status, and knowledge that it later acquired. It was a tool, useful firstly for the needs of state and bureaucracy, church, and trade. This "triumvirate" of literacy and writing, although reshaped with the passage of time, has remained incredibly resilient in its cultural and political hegemony over the social and individual functions of literacy and schooling. Yet, it was established and continued in a world in which communications consisted overwhelmingly of the oral and the aural.

As reading and writing began to spread sporadically among the population, their links with the larger cultural world of speech and hearing, and seeing, too, were articulated ever more elaborately. Writing was used to set down speech and to facilitate patterns of thought and logic that were exceedingly difficult without its technology. Even with the encroachment of literacy, the ancient world remained an oral world. This tradition continued from the classical era through the 1,000 years of the Middle Ages and beyond; it is not dead today and may well have been reinforced by the impact of the newer electronic media.

The oral and the literate, like the written and the printed, need not be opposed as simple choices. Human history and human developments did not occur in that way. Rather, they allowed a deep, rich process of reciprocal interaction and conditioning as literacy gradually gained acceptance and influence. The poetic and dramatic word of the ancients was supplanted, if not replaced, by a new *Word*: a religion of Christ rooted in the *Book*, but propagated primarily by oral preaching and teaching. Analogously, education long remained an oral activity. The written and then printed word were spread to many semiliterates and illiterates via the oral processes, and far more widely than purely literate means could have allowed. For many centuries, reading itself was an oral, often collective activity and not the private, silent one we consider it to be.

**TABLE I.I**
**Measures of Literacy**

| Source | Measure of literacy | Population | Country of availability | Years of availability | Additional variables |
|---|---|---|---|---|---|
| Census | Questions: read and write, read/write Signature/mark (Canada 1851, 1861 only) | Entire "adult" population (in theory): ages variable, e.g., over 20 years, 15 years, 10 years | Canada, United States | Manuscripts: Nineteenth century | Age, sex, occupation, birthplace, religion, marital status, family size and structure, residence, economic data |
| Wills | Signature/mark | 20–50% of adult males dying; 2–5% of adult females dying | Canada, United States, England, France, etc. | Canada, eighteenth century on, U.S. 1660 on, others from sixteenth–seventeenth century on | Occupation, charity, family size, residence, estate, sex |
| Deeds | Signature/mark | 5–85% of living landowning adult males; 1% or less of females | Canada, United States | Eighteenth century on | Occupation, residence, value of land, type of sale |
| Inventories | Book-ownership | 25–60% of adult males dying; 3–10% of adult females dying | Canada, United States, England, France, etc. | Seventeenth–eighteenth century on (quantity varies by country and date) | Same as wills |
| Depositions | Signature/mark | Uncertain: potentially more select than wills, potentially wider Women sometimes included | Canada, United States, England, Europe | Seventeenth–eighteenth century on (use and survival varies) | Potentially, age, occupation, sex, birthplace, residence |
| Marriage records | Signature/mark | Nearly all (80%+) young men and women marrying (in England) | England, France, North America | From 1754 in England; 1650 in France | Occupation, age, sex, parents' name and occupation, residence (religion—North America) |

| Source | Measure | Population | Geography | Period | Data available |
|---|---|---|---|---|---|
| Catechetical examination records | Reading, memorization, comprehension, writing examinations | Unclear, but seems very wide | Sweden, Finland | After 1620 | Occupation, age, tax status, residence, parents' name and status, family size, migration, periodic improvement |
| Petitions | Signature/mark | Uncertain, potentially very select, males only in most cases | Canada, United States, England, Europe | Eighteenth century on | Occupation or status, sex, residence, political or social views |
| Military recruit records | Signature/mark or question on reading and writing | Conscripts or recruits (males only) | Europe, esp. France | Nineteenth century | Occupation, health, age, residence, education |
| Criminal records | Questions: read, read well, etc. | All arrested | Canada, United States, England | Nineteenth century | Occupation, age, sex, religion, birthplace, residence, marital status, moral habits, criminal data |
| Business records | Signature/mark | 1. All employees 2. Customers | Canada, United States, England, Europe | Nineteenth, twentieth century | 1. Occupation, wages 2. Consumption level, residence, credit |
| Library/mechanics institute records | Books borrowed | Members or borrowers | Canada, United States, England | Late eighteenth, early nineteenth century | Names of volumes borrowed, society membership |
| Applications (land, job, pensions, etc.) | Signature/mark | All applicants | Canada, United States, England, Europe | Nineteenth–twentieth century | Occupation, residence, family/career history, etc. |
| Aggregate data sources *a* | Questions or direct tests | Varies greatly | Canada, United States, England, Europe | Nineteenth–twentieth century | Any or all of the above |

*a* Censuses, educational surveys, statistical society reports, social surveys, government commissions, prison and jail records, etc.

*Source:* Harvey J. Graff, *The Literacy Myth* (New York: Academic Press, 1979), Appendix A, pp. 325–27. Note: this is a modified and greatly expanded version of Table A in Kenneth A. Lockridge, *Literacy in Colonial New England* (new York: Norton, 1974).

One point of special significance may be raised at this juncture. It is a question of chronology: the comparatively *late* invention of alphabetic literacy and the striking recency of the invention of moveable typographic printing, despite the sanctity with which we hold them. The chronology is devastatingly simple: *homo sapiens* as a species is about 1,000,000 years old. Writing dates from approximately 3000 B.C., so is about 5,000 years old; Western literacy from about 700–600 B.C., making it roughly 2,600 years old; and printing from the 1450s, now aged a mere 430 years.[15] The numerical exercise may appear frivolous, but a reflection upon this time sequence and its implications assists us in placing literacy in a larger, proper context.

The history of literacy is typically conceived and written in terms of *change*. The assumption is that literacy, development, growth, and progress are inseparably linked. Literacy becomes one of the key elements in the larger parcel of characteristics and processes that remade a traditional, premodern world into the modern West.[16] Most studies ignore the first 2,000 years of Western literacy—before the so-called advent of printing—despite the major insights that the historical experience provides for us.

My argument is that this perspective is unduly limiting and distorting. Its simplicity and linearity obstruct and complicate understanding. The reconceptualization that underlies this book emphasizes *continuities* and *contradictions* in the history of Western society and culture, especially with respect to the place of literacy, and considers the extent of change, and discontinuity, in that framework. On one hand, the approach is a corrective to the long-standing interpretation that slights the roles of continuities and traditions, the legacies of literacy, as I call them. On the other hand, it constitutes a mode of analysis and a set of theoretical assumptions that seem to explain literacy's complex history more fully and effectively than the former approach has done.[17]

*Continuity*, as a historical concept, has an impressively broad meaning and applicability, despite historians' traditional abhorrence of this aspect of change and development. Among the insidious dichotomies that confuse more than they instruct, change versus continuity ranks highly. To focus on continuities does not require neglecting changes or *dis*continuities. Concepts of continuity involve comparisons over time, as well as awareness of the need to determine the relationship between elements of change and continuity simultaneously operating in any historical moment or situation. It is useful to employ the language of continuity and its implications when describing circumstances in which development and change tend to be more gradual than rapid. Such is the case with respect to the history of literacy.

Particularly impressive within the *longue durée* of literacy's full history is the role of traditions and legacies. The use of elementary schooling and learning one's letters began in the Greek city-states during the fifth century B.C. and constitutes a classical legacy regularly rediscovered and reinterpreted by persons in the West: during the late Middle Ages, the Renaissance, the Reformation, and the Enlightenment, and again during the great institutional reform movements of the nineteenth century. (For a summary of key points in the history of literacy, see Table I.2.)

Recognizing this series of continuities, or legacies of literacy, is not reductive. It allows us to consider the similarities and differences in rates of literacy, schooling configurations, practical and symbolic uses of literacy, and the like that accompany renewed recognition of the positive value of expanded popular literacy within the

TABLE I.2

**Key Points in the History of Literacy in the West**

| | |
|---|---|
| ca. 3100 B.C. | Invention of writing |
| ca. 3100–1500 B.C. | Development of writing systems |
| ca. 650–550 B.C. | "Invention" of Greek alphabet |
| ca. 500–400 B.C. | First school developments, Greek city-states, tradition of literacy for civic purposes |
| ca. 200 B.C.–200 A.D. | Roman public schools |
| 0+ | Origins and development of Christianity |
| 800–900 | Carolingian language, writing, and bureaucratic developments |
| 1200+ | Commercial, urban "revolutions," expanded administration and other uses of literacy and especially writing, development of lay education, rise of vernaculars, "practical" literacy, Protestant heresies |
| 1300+ | Rediscovery of classical legacies |
| 1450s | Advent of printing, consolidation of states, Christian humanism |
| 1500s | Reformation, spread of printing, growth of vernacular literatures, expanded schooling (mass literacy in radical Protestant areas) |
| 1600s | Swedish literacy campaign |
| 1700s | Enlightenment and its consolidation of tradition, "liberal" legacies |
| 1800s | School developments, institutionalization, mass literacy, "mass" print media, education for social and economic development: public and compulsory |
| 1900s | Nonprint, electronic media |
| late 1900s | Crisis of literacy . . . and other things. . . . |

differing social or economic contexts. In the words of Alexander Gerschenkron, "To say continuity means to formulate a question or a set of questions and to address it to the material."[18] In other words, this conceptualization provides an appropriate model with which to approach and reinterpret the history of literacy in culture and society.

We can also point to the issue of the oral and the literate in Western culture. An exaggerated emphasis on change and discontinuity, in addition to the excesses of radical dichotomization, is principally responsible for the neglect of the important contribution of oral communications and traditions to the penetration of reading and writing. Third is the equally impressive power of the "trinity" of literacy's primary uses: for reasons of state and administration, theology and faith, and trade and commerce. The priority of these demands for and uses of literacy has remained, regardless of the degree of social restrictiveness that regulated the supply curve of popular diffusion. They also have played vital roles in determining the degree of restriction, the opening and closing of opportunities for the transmission and acquisition of the skills of reading and writing. Commerce and its social and geographical organization, for example, stimulated rising levels of literacy from the twelfth century onward in advanced regions of the West.

The significant link between literacy and religion forms one of the most vital legacies. It is perhaps the best example of the intricate role of continuities and contradictions in the nearly three millennia of Western (alphabetic) literacy. The sixteenth-century Reformations are the most striking examples, but the religious impulse to read for the propagation of piety and faith long predated that time. Its history is closely tied to the history of Western Christianity, and the contradictions within one are often those of the other. Within the religious traditions, the dialectic between the oral and the written has played a major part, with different balances being struck in different periods, places, and sects.

Literacy served to record for time immemorial the Word, but for centuries its influence and diffusion came overwhelmingly through oral means of teaching and preaching. Still, many nonclericals learned their letters through the universal medieval Christian church. The Reformation, however, constituted the first great "literacy campaign" in the history of the West, with its social legacies of individual literacy as a powerful social and moral force and its pedagogical traditions of compulsory instruction in public institutions specially created for the purposes of indoctrinating the young for explicitly social ends. One of the great innovations of the German or Lutheran Reformation was the recognition that literacy, a potentially dangerous or subversive skill, could be employed—if controlled—as a medium for popular schooling and training on a truly unprecedented scale. The great reform was hardly an unambiguous success in its time, but it may well have contributed more to the cause of popular literacy than to that of piety and religious practice.[20]

We see the workings of *contradictions* in social, economic, and cultural development at the core of the processes that shaped the historical movement of literacy in the West. Some contradictions are order-threatening or destructive; others are embedded within the ongoing processes of development. They are present regardless of the extent of continuity, or discontinuity, although outcomes certainly differ.[21] To understand literacy means that contradictions should be expected to result from the ongoing processes and developments within culture, polity, economy, and society. These are neither ironic nor paradoxical, as some call them, but fundamentally *historical*.[22]

Literacy's relationships with the processes of economic development provide one of the most striking examples of patterns of contradictions. Contrary to popular and scholarly wisdom, major steps forward in trade, commerce, and even industry took place in some periods and places with remarkably low levels of literacy; conversely, higher levels of literacy have not proved to be stimulants for "modern" economic development. More important than high rates or "threshold levels" of literacy have been the educational levels and power relations of key persons, rather than of the many; the roles of capital accumulation, "cultural capital," technological innovations, and the ability to put them into practice; or the consumer demands and distribution-marketing-transportation-communication linkages.

Major "take-offs," from the commercial revolution of the Middle Ages to eighteenth-century protoindustrialization in rural areas and even urban factory industry, owed relatively little to popular literacy abilities or schooling. The demands of early industrialization upon the labor force were rarely intellectual or cognitive. In fact, industrialization often reduced opportunities for schooling, and, consequently, rates of literacy fell as it took its toll on the "human capital" on which it fed.

In other places, later in time, higher levels of popular education and literacy *prior* to the advent of factory capitalism may have made the process different by contributing to a rapid but smoother transition to the market and factory. Literacy, by the nineteenth century, became vital to the process of "training in being trained." Finally, it may also be that the "literacy" required for the technological inventiveness and innovations that made the process possible was not a literacy of the alphabetic sort at all, but rather a more visual, experimental one.[23]

There are many kinds of "literacies." One need distinguish not only between basic or elementary kinds of literacy and higher levels of education, but also among alphabetic, visual and artistic, spatial and graphic, mathematical, symbolic, technological, and mechanical literacy. An understanding of any one type requires care in qualifying terms and specifying what precisely is meant by reference to "literacy." These many "literacies" are all conceptually distinct, but nonetheless interrelated. Our primary focus will be on alphabetic literacy.

2

The concept of *social and cultural hegemony* also underlies the analytic and interpretive framework of this book. It provides the most useful approach toward understanding the many uses and the patterns of literacy. Considering literacy's usefulness as a means for creating and maintaining hegemony at and among various levels of social hierarchies makes sense not only interpretively and empirically, but also in escaping dichotomies.[24]

Literacy's many roles and meanings require a subtle and sophisticated approach. Antonio Gramsci's formulation of a concept of hegemony permits us to escape the crudities of social control theories, modernization and enlightenment notions, ideas of overt coercion, and excessively voluntaristic interpretations. As this book attempts to show, none of these approaches is as fruitful as an explicit use of the idea of social and cultural hegemony in a framework that emphasizes the roles of continuities and contradictions.[25]

According to his recent student Walter Adamson, Gramsci's concept of "hegemony" has two related definitions. "First, it means the consensual basis of an existing political system within civil society. Here it is understood in contrast to the concept of 'domination'. . . ." Gramsci noted that only weak states rely on force for their power and control. Stronger states and institutions rule and cohere through hegemony. Literacy is not a likely technique for domination or coercion; for hegemony, however, it has proved a much more viable option and often a successful tool. "Schooling," in common values, attitudes, and norms, as well as in skills and common languages, has long been grasped as especially useful.

Hegemony is especially relevant to the concerns of this book because of its intrinsic relationship to literacy, schooling, and education. Hegemonic relationships have historically involved processes of group and class formation, recruitment, indoctrination, and maintenance at all levels of society. For most of literacy's history, these functions have centered upon elite groups and their cohesion and power. For them, the uses of literacy have been diverse but have included common education, culture, and language (such as Latin); shared interests and activities; control of scarce commodities, such as wealth, power, and even literacy; and common symbols and badges, of which literacy could be one.

Throughout the history of alphabetic literacy, efforts have been made to expand its distribution. The process has been uneven and often slow. Literacy and schooling have been seized increasingly as a tool for establishing and maintaining social and cultural hegemony.

Typically, the process of schooling has sought, in Gramsci's conception, to develop assimilation and control. Since the Reformation, schooling and analogous hegemonic activities have sought to secure the *consent* of the masses in response to "the direction imposed on social life by the dominant fundamental group." Hegemony derives from consent, "the spontaneous loyalty that any dominant social group obtains from the masses by virtue of its social and intellectual prestige and its supposedly superior function in the world of production."[26]

Just as the classes over whom hegemony was sought have changed, so too have the institutional modes and patterns. In diverse ways, various reformers have sought through literacy and education to establish or maintain hegemony. Its development, they learned, depended on a "level of homogeneity, self-consciousness, and organization" reached by a social class. Neither narrowly economic nor crudely imposed or conspiratorial, their actions derived from a recognition of the needs of society and of the perceptions of the unity of social interests, and the identification of their own requirements with those of others. Schooling and literacy for more and more persons, eventually for all, became an instrument for stability and cohesion.[27]

Although literacy as a skill was often important and highly valued, its moral bases have been historically more dominant. The inculcation of values, habits, norms, and attitudes to transform the masses, rather than skills alone or per se, was the developing task of schooling and its legitimating theme. Literacy properly was to serve as an instrument for training in a close and mutually reinforcing relationship with morality; that was to be, at least in theory, the source of cohesion and order, and with time became the concern of increasing numbers of people throughout the Western world.

3

The history of literacy shows clearly that there is no *one* route to universal or mass literacy. In the history of the Western world, one may distinguish the roles of private and public schooling in the attainment of high rates of popular literacy, as well as the operation of informal and formal, voluntary and compulsory education. Mass literacy was achieved in Sweden, for example, without formal schooling or instruction in writing. High rates of literacy have followed from all of these approaches in different cases and contexts. The developmental consequences are equally varied.

Historical experiences furnish a better guide to the contributions of basic literacy to the economic and individual well-being of persons in different socioeconomic contexts, and to the circumstances under which universal literacy can be achieved. The costs and benefits of the alternative paths can be discerned, too. Thus, the relationships between literacy and commercial development, a favorable one, and literacy and industrial development, often an unfavorable one, offer important case studies and analogs for analysis. If nothing else, the data of the past strongly suggest that a simple, linear, modernization model of literacy as a prerequisite for development and development as a stimulant to increased levels of schooling, will not do. Too many periods of lags, backward linkages, setbacks, and contradictions existed to permit such cavalier theorizing to continue without serious challenge and criticism.

The example of Sweden is perhaps most important in this respect. As shown by the pioneering research of Egil Johansson, near-universal levels of literacy were achieved rapidly and permanently in Sweden in the wake of the Reformation. Under the joint efforts of the Lutheran church and the state, reading literacy was required under law for all persons from the seventeenth century. Within a century, remarkably high levels of literacy existed—without any concomitant development of formal schooling or economic or cultural development that demanded functional or practical employment of literacy, and in a manner that led to a literacy defined by reading and not by writing.

Urbanization, commercialization, and industrialization had nothing to do with the process of making the Swedish people perhaps the most literate in the West before the eighteenth century. Contrary to the paths of literacy taken elsewhere, this campaign, begun by King Charles XI, was sponsored by the state church. By legal requirement and vigilant supervision that included regular personal examination by parish clergy, the church stood above a system rooted in home education. The rationale of the literacy campaign, one of the most successful in Western history before the last two decades, was conservative; piety, civility, orderliness, and military preparedness were the major goals. The former was as important as the other reasons, and in the end it was the decisive one.

Significantly, the home and church education model fashioned by the Swedes not only succeeded in training up a literate population, it also placed a special priority on the literacy of women. Sweden also marched to its impressive levels of reading diffusion without writing; it was not until the mid-nineteenth century and the erection of a state-supported public school system that writing became a part of popular literacy and a concern of teachers. The only other areas to so fully and quickly achieve near-universal levels of literacy before the end of the eighteenth century were places of intensely pious religion, usually Protestant: lowland Scotland, New England, Huguenot French centers, and places within Germany and Switzerland.[28]

Other important examples are literacy's relationships to economic and social development. In this case, we again discover a history of continuities and contradictions. From the classical period forward, leaders of polities and churches have recognized the uses of literacy and schooling. Often they have perceived unbridled, untempered literacy as a potential threat to social order, political integration, economic productivity, and patterns of authority. But, increasingly, they concluded that literacy, if provided in carefully controlled, formal institutions, could be a useful force. For our purposes, the Reformations of the sixteenth century represented the first great educational campaigns. As the Swedish case reminds us, they were hardly homogeneous efforts, in either design or degree of success. Nonetheless, they were precedent-setting and epochal in their significance for the future of Western social and educational development. In their own times, many of wealth and power still doubted the efficacy of schooling the masses.

With the Enlightenment and its heritage came the final ideological underpinnings for the "modern" and "liberal" reforms of popular schooling and institution building that established the network of educational, social, political, and economic relationships central to the dominant ideologies for the past 150 years. Prussia, revealingly, took the lead, and provided a laboratory that United States, Canadian, English, French, and Scandinavian school promoters and reformers regularly came to study. North Americans and Swedes followed in Prussia's wake, and, in time and in their own ways, so did the English, French, and Italians.

A final issue focuses on the question of the *quality* of literacy. Because of the nature of the evidence, virtually all historical studies have concentrated on measuring the extent and distributions of reading and writing; the level of and abilities to use the skills themselves have not attracted much attention. What research has been conducted, however, suggests that qualitative abilities cannot be deduced simply or directly from quantitative levels of literacy's diffusion, and that there is a significant disparity between levels of possession of literacy and the usefulness of those skills. In Sweden, for example, many persons who had attained high levels of *oral* reading skill did not have comparable abilities in *comprehension* of what they read.

The implications of such findings are *enormous*. First, measuring the distribution of literacy in a population may in fact reveal relatively little about the uses to which such skills could be put. Second, it is also possible that increasing rates of popular literacy did not bring ever-rising qualitative abilities. Third, and potentially most important today, such evidence places the often-asserted contemporary decline of literacy in a new and distinctive context, leading to the possibility that mass levels of ability to use literacy may have, over the long term, lagged behind the near-universality of literacy rates. For some, such as blacks, great progress has occurred. The recent decline, so often proclaimed but so ineffectively measured and little understood, may be *much less a major decline than we are told*. We should perhaps pay more attention to longer-term trends than those of a decade or two, and to changes in popular communicative abilities and compositional effects among students, than to "competency examinations" and SAT scores.[29] That, however, does not mean that real, even grave, problems do not exist. They are perhaps *not* so new.

CHAPTER ONE

🜲

# The Origins of Western Literacy

> Graeco-Roman Egypt presents us with the spectacle of a society
> very different in kind, living in quite other presuppositions and
> with purposes remote from those of our day. That society was both
> pre-technological and pre-democratic. We shall find that it made
> a large place for illiteracy. The illiterate person was able to function
> in a broad variety of occupations, to be recognized as a respectable
> member of his class, to attain financial success, to hold public
> office, to associate on equal terms with his literate neighbors.
>
> —H. C. YOUTIE, "The Social Impact of Illiteracy in Graeco-
> Roman Egypt"

THE SKILLS OF READING AND WRITING ARE commonly taken to constitute
the characteristics of literacy, and as such they have come to be highly valued in
Western society. To understand their significance, one must imagine a time almost
wholly without reading or writing, as well as times in which their employment and
social distribution were so restricted as to function almost totally differently from
their place in the modern world. Literacy, in other words, *has a history*; and without
reference to this history it cannot be properly or realistically understood.

The first fact about literacy is its *recency*. That is very hard for modern men and
women to recognize, given our equation of literacy with civilization itself. Over
the millennia of human evolution and existence, however, literacy's history is rather
a short one.[1] The development of a technique of writing (symbolization) or reading
(phoneticization) based on an alphabet that we can recognize as one of the foundations of Western society and culture did not occur until the last one or two thousand
years before the common era.

A second fact is the *lack of evidence* about literacy before the recent past. The
sources, when they exist, tend to provide evidence of writing (commonly a signature)
and not of reading, though both attributes must be encompassed in any measure of
literacy, and the relationships between them in any study. Nevertheless, as Eric
Havelock has commented, "the actual conditions of literacy depend upon the history
not of writing but of reading."[2] As a consequence, historical attempts to discover
the distribution of literacy at any point in time or its changes over time can be only
approximate at best.

A third fact that cannot be neglected is the *restricted nature* of literacy historically
considered.[3] In much of the Western world, only in the nineteenth and twentieth

centuries have rates of literacy approached universality (with a few important exceptions). History has not witnessed a simple and linear progress in literacy rates.

A final preliminary fact is the *complexity of the relationship between the oral and the written cultures and traditions*. Students of literacy have hopelessly confused the issues as they have sought to separate these modes of communication and discourse into sharp dichotomies in which one mechanism must dominate over the others. We stress the oral origins of literacy, the persistence and perspicacity of oral communications, and the continuing interactions of these two primary modes.

The very bases of modern Western literacy are found in the centuries before our own era. The origins of writing as a technology of communications; the invention of the Greek alphabet, the first to allow a truly useful and popular literacy based in readership; and the origins of formal institutions in which instruction in literacy was provided date from these centuries. Even more fundamentally, the wellsprings of reading and writing, rooted in political authority and administrative needs, theology and religion, and the requirements of commerce and trade, are found in early civilizations and predate the evolution of alphabetic literacy. These three motives provide perhaps the most powerful elements of continuity in all of Western history. Traditions that we commonly associate with the recent period, such as the uses of literacy as bases for popular government and for effective citizenship, derive from the years before the birth of Christ. Remarkably high levels of popular literacy were possible without compulsion, state control of schooling, or the technologies of print and papermaking. We also confront evidence of the central contradictions that lay at the heart of literacy's roles, and the inequalities that have always been tied to the distribution and the uses of literacy, whether in fifth-century Athens or late-twentieth-century America.

## 1. From Writing to Literacy

The prehistory of literacy spans the ages of pictures, or of "no writing"; the forerunners of writing, from pictographic elements simplified for transmission of information to symbols used to help record or identify things for posterity by memory aids; and the development of full writing, or phonography. The earliest systems were, on one hand, bound by the traditions of art and rooted in the need to remember and identify an object or a being. Their aims, on the other hand, were not to describe or establish a correspondence between symbols and objects, nor were they directed at conventionalizing the relationships between object and marks.

From these first developments came the discovery that words could be expressed in written symbols and that better methods of human intercourse would result. Recognition that symbols or signs could correspond directly with words or expressions led toward more complete systems of word writing, or logography; the completeness achieved by such evolving systems, however, is uncertain.[4] Phonetization, the most important single step in the history of writing and of preliteracy, arose from the need to express words and sounds that could not be indicated by pictures or their combination. It developed by associating words that are difficult to express in writing with signs resembling the words in sound that were easy to make. Fol-

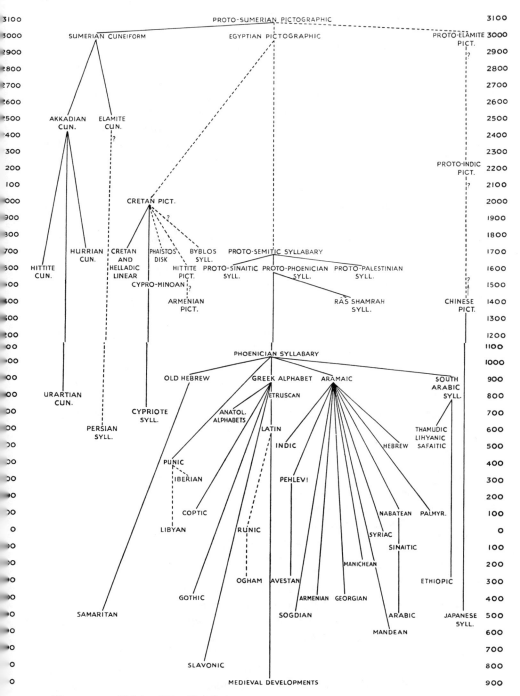

**Figure 1.1.** Origin of the Alphabet
*Source:* J. J. Gelb, *A Study of Writing* (Chicago: University of Chicago Press, 1963), pp. x–xi.

lowing the rapid spread of this principle came the development of fuller standardization and conventionalization: in forms of signs, in correspondence of signs with words and meanings and of signs with syllabic values, and in the orientation of signs and the direction, shape, and order of the lines of script. School tablets mark this progress.

The Sumerians achieved this advance. The reasons ascribed for it are of inestimable importance. Requirements of state and economic organization made keeping records of movement of goods imperative. A full word-syllabic system grew out of this identifying-mnemonic one, allowing the Sumerians to break entirely from the hampering conventions of descriptive-representational devices. This breakthrough dates from only about 3100 B.C.E. in southern Mesopotamia. It influenced over the next centuries Egyptian writing, which then spread westward to stimulate Cretan writing around 2000 and shortly thereafter Hittite writing. (With the Chinese, four word-syllabic systems developed by the second millennium.)

For the first time, the written expression of all the words of a language was permitted. It was encouraged by the need to record personal names and foreign words. The signs of logograms that served as standardized representations of the things signified by particular words permitted added devices and culminated in the ability to express much wider ranges of meaning. Writing, on the phonetic principle, was achieved.

Before the development of the syllabaries, and finally the Greek alphabet, these systems failed to carry through a systematic application of their phonetic advances. Incompletely phonetic (nonphonemic) writing systems were too awkward and complicated to foster widespread literacy. The number of signs was very large. For example, at least six hundred would have had to be learned for simplified Assyrian cuneiforms or Egyptian hieroglyphics. A writing system that has signs substitute directly for objects must be very complex. Although it did not lead to literacy in the Near East or the Mediterranean, logographic or word writing did constitute an effective basis for advanced developments and widespread literacy in China and India.[5]

The creation of syllabic writing systems was the next step, with major simplifications in the conventions of communicative technology, by four heterogeneous peoples (the Elamites, West Semites, Cypriotes, and Japanese). Most important for Western civilization was the Palestinian and Syrian Semites' acceptance from the Egyptians only of the principle of writing monosyllables without indicating differences in vowels. From the West Semitic syllabary later came developments that in little over a thousand years would culminate in the Greek alphabet. The major difference separating a syllabary from an alphabet is that the former is a writing in which a sign normally stands for one or more *syllables* of the language, whereas the latter is one in which a sign corresponds to one or more *phonemes* of the language. That was the step taken by the Greeks in the first millennium.

Although several attempts were made to indicate vowels in the Egyptian and Semitic syllabaries during the second millennium, none succeeded in creating a fully vocalic writing. The syllabaries, despite a basic advance that made writing easier, were far from simple. They were commonly combined with logograms and pictographs, and mainly restricted to elites, whether by necessity or tradition. Writing was seized upon as an aid to memory rather than an independent mode of communication; it was often considered a divine instrument. Writing, therefore, neither quickly nor independently changed the habits of the population or displaced the oral tradition.[6] Oral instruction, communication, and memory were dominant, and writing most often stood in their support.[7]

For the great early civilizations of Babylonia and Egypt, the religious, political, and economic importance of writing is clear. In the most general sense, writing developed partly out of the need to keep accounts and insure property rights. The demand for effective accounting had a double origin: as a result both of new conditions engendered by the accumulation of economic surplus and of the growth of groupings larger than a family, which raised the question of ownership.

Urban centers and social consolidation, standardization, power, and control overlapped in this historical use of writing. Given the hierarchical nature of these societies and the expanding, complex writing systems, writing was restricted largely to elite and scribal requirements and control. With no impetus to increase popular participation in protoliteracy, only those with wealth and power had the need, leisure, and inclination for formal education.[8]

Temple priests claimed that they alone held the right to teach reading, limiting access to the secrets of religion. The concept of the divine origin and character of writing is found in many societies and cultures. Belief in the sacred character of writing tends to be especially strong where knowledge of writing is restricted to a special class or caste of priests.[9]

As others than priests learned to write, they too became committed to the ruling and property-owning classes. Those who knew writing were generally quickly imbued with an outlook priestly and aristocratic. More practical learning (mathematics, science, law) also evolved but was taught very slowly. Preliteracy did not disrupt earlier ways, nor did it supplant the power of oral culture.[10] In such a context, schoolmasters and scribes were not accorded high status, and there was no question of mass education.

In Egypt, the requirements stimulated by agricultural surplus and the need for a trained class of priests and clerks were similar in consequence to those in Sumer and Babylonia. The centralization stemming from the single monarchy seems to have delayed the rise of temple priests, whereas it aided the unification and systemizing of literary traditions and created an atmosphere of order and slow technical advance in which formal instruction for the few could develop.[11]

As the work of Harold A. Innis, in particular, makes clear, the uses of writing in Sumer, Babylonia, and Egypt were all closely tied to the exigencies of the state and empire. Examples include: legitimation and reproduction; order, control and regulation; administration and centralization; command and communication; commerce and law; and the transmission of belief. The motivating factors of religion, politics, and economics, and the perpetuation of the dominance of oral traditions and the systems of belief rooted in them were interdependent: "Oral traditions were written down and literature became the bond slave of religion."[12]

It was the Greeks who, accepting the forms of the West Semitic syllabary, developed a system of vowels that reduced the syllables to simple consonantal signs when attached to the syllabic signs, therefore creating the first full alphabetic system

The Uses of Writing in Mesopotamia[13]

| | |
|---|---|
| I Recording data for future use | a. administrative purposes |
| | b. codification of law |
| | c. formulations of a sacred tradition |
| | d. for annals |
| | e. and ('eventually') for scholarly purposes |
| 2 Communication of data on a synchronic level | a. letters |
| | b. royal edicts |
| | c. public announcements |
| | d. texts for training scribes |
| 3 Communication with gods | secret texts, amulets, etc. |

of writing.[14] The development of a full Greek alphabet, expressing single sounds of language by means of consonant and vowel signs, Gelb insists, is the last important step in the history of writing. "This is the alphabet that conquered the world."[15]

The classical age predates the onset of full literacy. That culture began its flowering as pre-or protoliterate. The polis, geometric art, early temple architecture, and poetry preserved in the Homeric hexameter all developed in the preliterate context. Greek culture was not primitive, however; a highly developed mechanism was available for the regular transmission of religious, political, legal, and familial customs, codes, and beliefs. The mechanism was a complex of oral practices, mainly "poetic," with a language controlled by rhythm, words shaped and placed in syntax fixed by rhythmic order, and the rhythms of verbal meter wedded to those of melody. Mnemonic needs were satisfied by techniques characteristic of oral cultures. The social functioning of cultural transmission was effective because memories were shared; oral poetry was performed regularly before audiences who participated in its memorization. Private communication of preserved information, by contrast, is possible only with developed literacy.[16]

The writing that existed was narrowly restricted. The syllabaries were "too clumsy and ambiguous to allow fluency or encourage general literacy." Their idiom lacked the power to change the broader idiom of oral communication, and was forced to reproduce it. Several centuries were required for the advent of the alphabet to lead to literacy. During those centuries, to the sixth or probably the fifth B.C., the alphabet, as it developed, was applied not to the transcription of vernacular statements but to the materials of the oral tradition. The *Odyssey* and *Iliad* of Homer are the most renowned cases, as the new Greek alphabetic literacy seized first upon the poetic literature composed according to the oral rules of memorization for recording.[17]

Though books and the alphabet were present, Greek culture at the beginning of the fifth century B.C.E. was essentially oral.[18] The encroachment of literacy was under way, but it was very gradual. A progress from restricted or craft literacy to semiliteracy marked the transitional period, circa the 700s to the 400s. Not until the fifth century did the signs of literacy become fully significant.

Oral verse was an instrument of cultural training and a powerful tool. Orally preserved communication operated in legal and political transactions, including the issuance of directives that accumulated as precedents; the constant retelling of history, emphasizing the behavior of ancestors as a guide for the present; and the continual indoctrination of the young, who were required to listen and repeat as part of their training. Power in the oral context was within the domain of the more cultivated members of the community. This world had its technological and intellectual limits. But its achievements without literacy were great.[19] Organized instruction in reading at the primary level does not seem to have been introduced in Athens until the last third of the fifth century, becoming standard within a century thereafter.[20]

Until the fifth century, the principal users—and perhaps the inventors—of the alphabet were craftsmen and traders. This stage can be termed "craft literacy." Certainly the leisured classes acquired their letters with time, but it is unclear to what extent. Their motives must have been minimal until the middle of the fifth century. Craftsmen's children, by contrast, went to work in the shops before adolescence, and learned their letters there, if at all. The upper-class boy, with a leisurely and lengthy schooling, mastered the "polite arts," which do not seem to have included reading.

From the seventh to the end of the sixth century, craft literacy slowly replaced preliteracy. The Greek alphabet, the foundation of Western literacy, evolved, but its spread was slow, and it led at first to no more than a restricted literacy of experts. During the latter part of the sixth and first half of the fifth centuries, literacy began to embrace more of the free male population, although the use of the written word remained restricted. Not until the late fifth and fourth centuries does literacy seem to have been achieved or do authors begin to take it for granted,[21] and even then its use was most often in support of the culturally dominant modes of communication.

The developing modern alphabet had to meet a number of new social and intellectual conditions. First, it had to cover a large number of linguistic sounds and a sufficient number or character of visible shapes to trigger a reader's memory of the distinctive sounds (or phonemes); second, this requirement had to be met unambiguously, without guesses or choices. Next, the number of signs or shapes had to be limited to avoid overburdening the memory.

Meeting these conditions was difficult. The Greek alphabet, the first in the West to allow full literacy, was created only after ca. 700 B.C.E., and only in Greece; several hundred years were required for it to lead to literacy in a mode recognizable to us. The Greeks followed the Semites in cutting the number of signs to twenty-two but were alone able to solve the problem of ambiguity: in moving from syllables to phonemes as the irreducible basis of linguistic *and* alphabetic sound units. The Greek alphabet reduced syllables to acoustic components, distinguishing vowels from consonants and, thus, creating an efficient reading instrument. Only then was the transition from restricted, elite literacy to full, popular literacy possible.[22] The literacy transition of ancient Greece was not immediate. The new alphabetic literacy created the possibility and potential for development and change; it took place in a context that made for important continuities with traditional cultural patterns.

## 2. Literacy's First Legacies: From Athens . . .

The first question is why alphabetic literacy was achieved and "democratized" in the Greek city-states of the mid-first millenium. Obviously, one must be wary of overly deterministic and functional solutions, of ascribing causality to Hellenic spirit, genius, or brilliance.[23] Recall the gradual nature of the coming of alphabetic literacy, and that "for the great mass of the Greek people literary communication [oral transmission] continued for generations, even after the coming of writing and its general adoption for official and business purposes," after the advent of literacy.[24]

The social ecology and the economy of the Ionian peninsula were critical factors, providing the physical conditions in which the great transition occurred. The rise in importance of writing and the invention of the alphabet took place in a period of great economic activity and the revival of trade and exchange with the East. This activity brought material prosperity, technological advance, and the Semitic-Phoenician syllabary writing system, which was adapted by the Greeks. Trade with Egypt stimulated the importation of papyrus, making writing easier and less expensive. As a result, writing returned to the Greeks (it had disappeared following the twelfth-century collapse of Mycenea) by the end of the eighth century B.C.E., in a modified Semitic alphabet.[25]

Greek writing throughout the classical period remained relatively difficult to decipher, as it was awkward and spaced irregularly on a page. The alphabet and scripts were not yet standardized. Literacy does not seem to be presumed by contemporaries until the fifth and fourth centuries.[26]

To these factors are added the roles of social stability, decentralization, population size and density, social structure, and perhaps also political flexibility. These are also the foundations of the city-state or polis, the specific sociopolitical environment in which the invention and adoption of literacy took place. The potential for literacy was further reinforced by the powerful collective cultural memory, emphasis on civil life, and sociocultural gatherings with widespread participation. In many ways, the conditions of oral preliteracy, on one hand, paved the way for a literacy evolving by economic and commercial need and deriving from intercultural communication. On the other hand, in these circumstances, the oral tradition virtually determined the early uses of literacy and the ends to which it was put.[27]

In the historical case of Athens and poleis like it, the oft-described revolutionary intellectual advances stemming from the adoption of literacy were never dominant. The full vernacular was not the first source to be transcribed, and the alphabet was not early put to the service of regular human intercourse.[28] The spread of writing led to its employment in recording the most valued products of the culture, the orally performed poems that carried the canons of the civilization and served to indoctrinate the young and to reinforce, by constant repetition, the memories of the entire population. The cultural impulse or dynamic, in other words, was powerfully present at the moment at which technology (writing), economy, and society created the conditions for writing to develop into literacy: a rare point in the history of the Western world.

By the sixth century, intellectual breaks with the past began to occur. Before the achievement of either the democratic city-state or full literacy, a "situation of compulsory originality" developed: in lyric poetry, public architecture, Hesiod, philosophy, and politics. It took place under conditions of pre- and semiliteracy; the results of new thinking and new literary creations were presented publicly, as was the production of the arts. As literacy "conquered" classical society, its products could be consumed only through the mechanisms of the oral culture.[29]

The fifth century brought a new level of political sophistication, which resulted in oligarchies and democracies. New freedoms became possible for citizens and free men based on economic independence. Religion developed into a more public and state function; temples were visible signs of growing prosperity and political maturity. With developing literacy, religion continued to be based in myth, accessible to all, not in "theology." Belief, despite the diffusion of literacy and writing, persisted in its oral transmission; witness the *ora*cles of Delphi and elsewhere. It was the eve of the classical flowering of the city-states.

In the fifth century, the polis assumed a variety of sizes and governing forms. Even in democracies, great variation of rules of conduct and social organization was the norm. In Athens, popular participatory democracy meant that only a minority of the resident population constituted the community proper and political. The nonparticipatory and subject majority included noncitizens, slaves, and women. The free, male citizens, who in theory and practice composed the community will, were becoming more often, and perhaps more highly, literate by the fifth and fourth centuries. Their direct participation at the Assembly, on the Council of 500, and on juries was the key to Athenian democracy. The Assembly, Council, and juries, however, did not demand a high degree of literacy. Their business was conducted by voice, and they were dominated by skilled, trained orators. Nevertheless, the Western tradition of an educated electorate, schooling in literacy as preparation for citizenship, and the equation of literacy and democracy were born here.

Inscriptions and public notices were among the most commonly cited support for claims of nearly universal literacy in Athens by the fifth and fourth centuries. Following the reforms of Solon, laws had to be posted in public.[30] The constitutions of the city were also made available to the citizens. We cannot conclude that these were indicators of anything but a people becoming increasingly able to read them; at the same time, without more direct evidence (which does not exist for this time), there is no reason to conclude that universal literacy of a high quality existed by the fifth or even fourth century. The notices could have been read aloud.

With trade and business, the issues seem clearer. Merchants and craftsmen had recourse to some use of literacy during the stage of "craft literacy," but it was probably not a highly developed skill.[31] There is no doubt that by the fourth century, Greeks who traded in Athens put some of their contracts into writing; those who handled money kept accounts, some apparently made lists of items for sale, and traders who needed to correspond with partners in distant cities wrote. More generally, letters were sent, memoranda were jotted, and wills were made.[32] What is not certain is whether these activities were restricted to a small group or were shared in by a larger number. It simply is impossible to know how much use a hypothetical average Athenian male made of writing or reading.

Plato, an astute observer of the advent of Greek literacy, criticized the use of writing as a medium for carrying thought and values. Although he also criticized the oral medium and its abuses, he objected to writing's inherent shallowness, believing that only a dialectical approach could result in the essential principles of truth. He also objected to its superficiality, since reading could give a specious sense of wisdom, which could be gained only from oral queries and responses. He feared that men would come to rely on writing and would cease to use memory. Plato considered oral transmission of the cultural tradition to be more effective and permanent than written transmission, despite his own use of literacy as a tool in criticism and philosophic abstraction. He found oral instruction, with opportunities for dialectical exchange, superior to a static written tract.[33]

The social conditions of reading are especially interesting. To the increasingly literate Athenians, reading was not yet a silent, internalized activity. Overwhelmingly, it was a social and an *oral* one.[34] Ancient reading, privately and publicly, was habitually reading aloud.

Oral performances of poetry and new dramas continued after they began to be recorded. There is abundant evidence that audiences "knew" these works with a familiarity akin to that of habitual readers. But their awareness, in a culture so close to its time of immemorial memory and that still stressed recitation and recall, does not mean that they read habitually or were able to do so. Greek drama was composed for the theater, not for readers: to be seen and heard and felt by an audience with a commonality of experience, values, and reactions. As this practice persisted, literary forms developed that were more and more often written. The importance of oratory also continued, even as speeches began to be written for presentation, planned, and memorized.

Change did slowly occur. Thucydides wrote down his histories—not for an immediate audience, he maintained, but for posterity. Thus the spoken word was reduced to writing. Plato also wrote, in spite of his mixed views about writing's effects, although his teachings were chiefly oral. Socrates did not write, but his teachings were written down after his death. Readers and libraries did not come to the fore until the age of Aristotle. A very small number of Greeks achieved a higher, somewhat liberating literacy; most did not. Despite the obvious uses of literacy in recording and calculating, little critical or inquisitive scientific inquiry developed.

Before the late fifth century B.C.E., formal Greek education seemingly was principally of two kinds. There was the traditional upper-class "finishing" and cultivating, nonalphabetic schooling, which heavily stressed military training and physical culture.[35] There was apparently also a kind of craft or vocational schooling of scribes and secretaries. Primary school began, it seems, in the fifth century B.C. In Greek regions generally, the children—males, at least—of all freemen gained some schooling; by the fourth century, primary school existed throughout the Hellenistic world.[36]

Also developing, according to Pomeroy, was a new attitude favoring the education of women, at least from the fourth century. Opportunities were expanding. At about the age of seven, children left home daily for primary schooling, although the poorer youngsters seem to have started several years later and attended with less regularity and duration. The primary schools were concerned almost exclusively with reading, writing, and arithmetic, all at a relatively rudimentary level. Schools were ungraded, containing a mixture of those aged seven to eleven or twelve. Teaching was apparently a humble and somewhat despised occupation; the post required no special qualifications. Primary schools had no special responsibility for ethical, moral, or civic training such as they gained later and have assumed ever since.[37]

Rote learning, repetition, and recitation were the mainstays of classroom procedure, as the pupils were slowly taught their letters first, then the syllables and the words, before they confronted texts. Innovations were few, and discipline was apparently brutal.[38] Reading and writing were taught together and in the same manner. Pupils learned first to trace their letters in sand or on wax tablets, later advancing to papyrus but also using fragments of pottery. The principle was the imitation of the teacher.

Counting was also taught. Pupils learned to say and read numbers, to count on their fingers, and to perform calculations and handle fractions. They were not instructed in addition, subtraction, multiplication, and division.

Even the secondary school, which far fewer attended, stressed oral, expressive reading, memorization, and recitation. Cultured men (and sometimes women) studied the poets, the great prose writers, and, naturally, the orators. Mastery of this material was central to the training of those who were able to proceed through secondary schooling, those whose high place in society was assumed. Such was the proper literary, cultural, ethical, and rhetorical preparation for their expected future roles.[39]

While the curriculum of the primary school was resolutely functional and practical, it was not at all vocational. Apprenticeship, training at home, and intergenerational skill transmission remained the dominant modes of work preparation. Some sons of the poor and the laboring class may have been taught only by their parents.[40] Greece's strong emphasis on moral and religious training was not yet a part of formal schooling. For the sons of the upper class, the "pedagogue," often a trained and trusted slave, who chaperoned the children and was with them all day, taught proper conduct and behavior; the teacher was more a technician. "For the Greeks the decisive factor was the surroundings in which the child grew up—the family, with its servants, and friends." The system of morality, ethics, and conduct of life, so valued, was not a part of the early curriculum, although it was introduced for those able to acquire advanced education. It was based firmly upon tradition.[41]

It is likely that most male citizens in places such as Athens were literate. Mass literacy was, however, never a highly skilled one; it was socially, sexually, and geographically stratified. Athenians achieved a higher degree of popular literacy than elsewhere. Primary training in reading and writing was certainly more common than in Sparta, although the extent of Spartan illiteracy has been too often maligned. Elsewhere in the Hellenic world, similar educational emphases and results are found, if somewhat less frequently.[42]

Manuscript trade and publication were poorly developed in Athens. Books were expensive and rare, although they were becoming more common. Libraries were private and small. Books at this time were hand-copied manuscripts, consisting of rolls of papyrus sheets, nine or ten inches high and up to thirty-five feet long. A work usually appeared in two or more rolls.

Books typically varied in quality, size, shape, style, and script. They were produced by individual scribes, usually in single copies on demand; this early book trade had a relatively private, or individual, basis. Books were sold and exchanged in the market place in Athens, where literary men gathered to read their work. Here are found the beginnings of Western literary culture.[43]

## 3. . . . to Rome, and Beyond

Continuity paved the path that led from Athens to Rome. The orality that permeated Athenian culture continued in the Roman, reinforced in many ways through the direct influence of the Greeks. In Athens, developments in the oral tradition stimulated the adaptation of writing and its evolution and the invention and diffusion of alphabetic literacy. The new literacy was conditioned and shaped by the dominant oral culture; literacy, in turn, began to have an impact on that culture. Reading was practiced aloud; the oration and the epic were the two great verbal arts of oral and "residually oral" society in the West. Verbalization in theory and practice was deeply affected.[44]

The origins of writing in Italy remain obscure. No Latin literature is found much before the third century. Nothing resembling a literary culture within the society can fairly be claimed until the end of the Punic Wars, the time of the "Hellenization" of Roman intellectual production. Education grew up in the wake of Greek teaching, based on Greek textbooks; the new Latin literature developed on Greek models.[45]

By the second century, Rome began to develop its first system of educational institutions. Prior to this time, home education had been the norm; education was practical and oriented to one's expected place in the social and occupational structure. Much of this informal training consisted of memorizing stories, songs, ballads, and the laws; learning was a result more of informal socialization processes than of instruction per se. Greek ways were quickly and thoroughly adopted, following Roman victory in war; Rome's lack of distinct educational institutions aided the absorption of Greek models and acceptance of the Hellenic influence.[46]

From the Greeks, Rome inherited structures and methods of primary education and a positive emphasis on fairly widespread popular literacy. The elementary schools that developed, apparently rapidly, in the second and first centuries B.C.E. were direct copies of those in Athens. They replaced home education for many youngsters, teaching reading, writing, and calculation in the "traditional" manner. School teachers gained little remuneration and even less stature and respect. The curriculum was modest. Children began with the alphabet and the names of the letters in their correct order. After the letters came the syllables, then single words or names. Before progressing to continuous passages, children recited and memorized short moral sayings of one or two lines each.[47]

Writing was taught simultaneously with reading. Children wrote the letters, word, or passage that they were learning to read on writing tablets. Either the masters guided pupils' hands in making the shapes of the letters until they became accustomed to the shapes, or letters were imprinted into the waxen surface of a tablet, with children following the outlines with their "prickers." (The latter method may have been Roman in origin.) Both reading and writing were taught through exercises dictated by the teacher.[48]

Recitation was the mainstay of this pedagogy. Pupils learned their letters, syllables, words, and passages by heart; they learned literacy and trained their memories at once. This regimen was backed up by harsh discipline and constant reinforcement by repetition. Such instruction may not have resulted in very useful literacy skills.

Overall, instruction was aimed at a low level of proficiency, paced painfully slowly, and conducted in a thoroughly unexciting manner. Instruction was highly passive. Reading aloud and oral instruction dominated the classrooms. Competition, too, was encouraged; its benefits were apparently held to outweigh the inherent moral dangers. Herein we may find the origins of the most common Western pedagogical traditions, in method, discipline, and curriculum, as well as major reinforcement of the positive evaluation of literacy and the ways in which it was transmitted to the young.

Several important changes occurred. First, some girls may have attended at least elementary school with boys, but their numbers are impossible to estimate.[49] Second, and much more significant, is the special recognition given to the schools by a number of Roman emperors, including direct state funding of schools.[50] A hierarchical system of state-supported schooling was developing by the second and third centuries of the common era. Emperors from the first century onward made attempts to extend schooling to a wider social and geographic spectrum, showing that they favored training in literacy and realized its usefulness to the polity. A new stress on civic morality was created. Schooling was not available to the children of the poor; it seems that the Roman society was more unequally stratified than the smaller Greek polis, and that much more of the free population was poor.[51]

Despite the efforts of successive emperors to finance a system of state schools, the literacy rate in Rome was at best no higher than that in Athens. Even with an expanding elementary system, there were not enough schools to reach everyone.[52] Secondary education was reserved for the sons of the wealthy, the aristocracy, and the well-to-do. It stressed grammar and rhetoric, the skills valued by the elite of society. Oratory, as in Athens, persisted as the chief public art and sociopolitical skill. On one hand, education stressed character; on the other, in stages, it offered tutelage in grammar and then rhetoric. This instruction was limited in its audience to a selective character that a still-distrustful oligarch had imposed on it.

As with the Greeks, Roman grammarians taught reading, along with recitation and sometimes music. Reading at this stage meant more than simply recognizing words; voice control, expression, philology, morphology, and explication were stressed. The quality of the oral rendition was the valued result, not the intellectual or critical development that might take place during the learning process.

Rhetoric completed what existed of "higher education" at this time. Public assemblies had lost most of their powers, but as the law grew more complicated, opportunities for forensic speaking by trained lawyers widened, as did imperial work in the provinces.[53]

The full significance of this tradition of "applied" grammar and rhetoric lies in the continuing "habit of giving and hearing public readings and recitations, which was the absorbing occupation and perpetual distraction of cultivated Romans. . . ."[54] Despite the political, social, and cultural changes that separated Roman society from Greek, the role of oral culture remained well in place through the first centuries of the common era.

Nothing like a bookmaking or -selling business developed during the classical period. An author made copies of his work and distributed them to friends. Novices aired their prose and verse in public recitations, seeking to create a reputation or attract patronage, and also to foil book merchants who "pirated" editions or evaded payment to authors. Public readings were important and popular in Rome during the first centuries after Christ. Symbolized by the Atheneum, traditions reinforced the use of oral settings for producing literature.[55] In time, literature, caught between literacy and orality in this situation, drawing on but limited by both, lost its dignity and seriousness of purpose.[56] The power of the spoken word and the written word could not be realized; authors and public, readers and writers all suffered.

Early in the new era came new methods and achievements in publishing, which permit us to speak for the first time of a book trade and a "publishing industry," and public libraries. Atticus, viewed in almost legendary terms in the annals of publishing history, initiated the "mass production" of books in manuscript by converting his own copying studio into a large-scale concern, with a small army of scribes making multiple copies of sections of texts, which were then collated. This procedure stimulated the rise of a Roman book trade by the first century after Christ. At the same time, Caesar established the first Roman state library, giving the manufacturer a steady demand for his products, including editions of Seneca, Caesar, Virgil, and Horace, sometimes produced in script "runs" of 500 copies or more. The Ptolemies' Alexandrian Museum and Institution provided the seminal example.

Book merchants came into their own in the first and second centuries. Their teams of trained slave scribes produced editions that were sold for high prices. Payment came from patrons, or from an author if he was unknown. No system of royalties existed; no protection was available to authors, and most earned very little through their writings. It was a buyers' market, controlled increasingly by merchants rather than authors.[57] As an early publishing business grew, reading became a more common habit.

Publishing and bookmaking declined sharply in the fourth and fifth centuries, as the empire declined. As the Christian church gained in influence and power, it increasingly restricted the spread of pagan literature. The precedents of early publishing were not carried continuously into the Middle Ages.

The rising use of vellum and parchment was an important step in the first centuries of the new era. With this trend came the shift from the roll to the codex. Parchment and vellum were more flexible than papyrus and could be folded into sheets to make a book that was more easily managed and contained more writing. Christian literature propelled this seminal shift; pagan writings were much more slowly produced in the codex format.

Nevertheless, books were limited in supply and in the audience they could reach. Most buyers were libraries, schoolmasters, and wealthy patrons. There is no evidence of a mass market comparable to that for hearing works of literature; some books may have been acquired more for their decorative or status value than for their literary merit. The active reading population was small. Most people still did not habitually use literacy for literary culture.[58]

In one aspect, Roman society stimulated uses of literacy that, while not novel, were precedent-setting in their extent and consequence. They constituted the widespread use of writing for meeting the needs of the state and empire and those of trade and commerce. The emergence of state intervention in education was one attempt to meet those requirements. As the republic passed into the empire and the empire grew, its need for competent civil servants became ever more urgent. One solution was to educate slaves or employ highly educated persons who were later enslaved in bureaucratic posts; that apparently was done relatively frequently up to the time of Claudius and again through the reign of Traijan.[59] For obvious reasons that could not be a complete and satisfactory solution to the problems of statecraft.

Numerous developments in government, law, and commerce required the use of writing; these seem to have increased after 150 or 100 B.C.E. Publication of court and senate proceedings was initiated. A literate tradition, within the still-pervasive orality of the society and culture, developed within the engines of the state.[60]

The growth of trade and commerce also contributed to the increasing use of literacy. The wealthy used slaves as skilled workers: as clerks, accountants, messengers, and operatives. They were apparently preferred to the native lower classes.[61] Businessmen needed accounting and corresponding that could be satisfied only by the use of literacy; credit records, banking and exchanges, money lending, and tax accounts all required it. The skill demanded by most of these was not sophisticated and was likely satisfied by the abilities taken from the primary classrooms. Overwhelmingly, it was the larger businesses and the corporations that grew up under the conditions of increasing (and unequally distributed) wealth, conquest, and imperial expansion who needed more.[62] The few, rather than the many, relied on extensive use of literacy in their occupations, as in their daily lives and their sociocultural affairs. Such men could acquire the highly trained, but highly priced, slaves or employ others with the requisite talents. For most men, a little literacy was probably quite sufficient to satisfy their needs, and that, it seems, most could obtain while young.

As we begin to look toward the future of Western society and culture, we cannot neglect the early impact of Christianity and Judaism. Christianity, we now assume, is one of the religions of the Book, as are other of the great religions.[63] But religions of the Word, which developed into religions of the Book, did not begin that way. As Ong has made clear, early Christianity was an oral-aural "theology of the Word of God." The oral preceded the written. Though they were relatively quickly recorded and disseminated widely through writing, the Gospels, Testaments, and Scriptures, in their competing versions, were not "fixed" for some time.[64] Literacy and reading were not central to early Christianity. They were media that could be and were seized upon in the struggle for human souls and peoples' faith. The Jewish tradition provided one model. Writings, as they were made and valued, attracted fascination as the vital, living monument to the spoken word of the Creator and the Savior. They took on the power and mass appeal of magical sacred texts.[65] "While the earliest Christians were without schools of their own and were largely illiterate, their religion itself served as an education."

Increasingly, Christian opposition grew to the worldly, pagan culture of the Graeco-Roman world. On one hand, distinctly Christian schools began to develop; on the other, many Christians withdrew from Roman schools. Finally, the Edict of Justinian of 529 sought to close all the pagan schools in the empire as it became a part of Christendom.[66] This goal was apparently never achieved, as evidence of lay schools' and perhaps the Roman public schools' persistence through the first millennium of the new era has been found for Italy and southern France.

A new tradition, of Christian schooling, dates from these early centuries after the birth of Christ, a tradition pregnant for moment through the Middle Ages and into the modern era, one different from that of Eastern Christianity. In part, it was the tradition of *lectio divinia*: the centrality of reading the Holy Scriptures, reflecting that aspect of Christianity's origins that stressed the word as written and building on the Greek and Roman achievements in alphabetic literacy and in its popular dissemination. At the heart of this impulse was the inseparable connection of schooling with morality, which constitutes a major legacy.

Often neglected in quests to comprehend the Western religions of the Book are their oral origins and traditions. For Jews, the Torah, often the oral Torah, was central. Quite early, distinct but not separated oral and written aspects of the authoritative sacred traditions were recognized.

Written Torah as an object of study is called "reading," and is learned by heart; oral Torah as an object of study is called "repetition." Written notes were used to assist private repetition, but in teaching, preaching, and legal proceedings, Torah had to be repeated from memory. The oral and written interrelated complexly in the practice of the faith.[67] Distinctions were made; yet they were much more relative than absolute as they intersected in education and cultural continuity.

With the barbarian invasions of the sixth century and the final decline of the Roman Empire, the new Christian schools came to play a critical role in preserving classical literature, transmitting literacy, and maintaining scholarly activities. Monastic schools were important educational institutions during the early Middle Ages. Also born in the sixth century was the tradition of teaching parish priesthoods, although it would be centuries before their contribution was influential. The Second Council of Vaison, in 529, declared that all parish priests were "to gather some boys round them as lectors, so that they may give them a Christian upbringing, teach them to read the Psalms and the lessons of Scripture and the whole law of the Lord and so prepare worthy successors to themselves." Not the "birth of the modern" ordinary village school, as Marrou and others have claimed, but an important step, a goal that would occupy the clergy for centuries.

By the sixth century, the foundations of the medieval school system were just taking outline. The first presbyterial or bishops' schools were established to train future priests, presenting opportunities for some sons of peasants to be educated alongside the sons of the nobility. In part this practice was a continuation from Roman times, when cultivation was a mark of the upper class and partly a matter of practical necessity. The opportunities for schooling were undoubtedly fewer than under the Romans and Greeks, and the quality may have suffered, too. Much of the schooling that survived the onset of the so-called "Dark Ages" was "very much a technical education for one particular purpose, involving reading and writing, knowing the Bible, or at least the Psalms by heart, with a certain basic minimum of doctrinal, canonical and liturgical knowledge." Some teachers tried to insulate their charges from pagan culture, meaning the classics; monastic education had its obscurantist and antiliterary aspects. There was a new, unprecedented religious emphasis in formal schooling, as the Christian schools rarely separated their teachings from their religious instruction in dogma and morality.[68]

# PART TWO

# Before the Printing Press:
# The Middle Ages

The power of the book, the pen, and the
sword, from Jacob a Bruck, *Emblemata
politica*, 1618 (Case W 1025.117), p. 29.
*Courtesy of The Newberry Library, Chicago.*

CHAPTER TWO

🦂

# The Light of Literacy in the "Dark Ages"

IN THE MIDDLE AGES, THE REPLACEMENT of one civilization with another, the rise of Christianity and of Latin as a universal language for cultural communication, and the long years of invasion, epidemics, and high mortality dramatically influenced the history of reading and writing. Levels of literacy fell from the achievements of Greece and Athens, and of Rome, too. Literacy became much more restricted but certainly never disappeared. We find a series of variations in efforts to limit or to widen the dissemination of reading if we are sensitive to the contradictions of the period's developments; in equally important ways, we find continuities from the pre-Christian era, too.

Levels of literacy rose strikingly after the tenth century, gaining through the fifteenth, but not in linear patterns. As before, the significance of economic, political, and religious factors is paramount; they are impressive engines of change and continuity. Among the lessons of the premodern age, the achievements of literacy without print and without mass educational institutions, the persistence and even dominance of orality in a period with an impressively high circulation of literacy, and the role of bilingualism stand out. Literacy was related to development, socially and economically. But the relationships are rarely clear and simple; the patterns of possession and use were complex and sometimes contradictory.

Medieval notions of literacy were totally different from the ideas of today. *Litteratus* does not equal literate: it speaks of a higher degree of erudition, or at least schooling, in grammar, theology, and perhaps rhetoric, not in the vernacular of a state or region but in Latin, the universal language of the educated and of international communications. Nevertheless, "when explaining medieval ways of thought it is correct to say that all laymen were considered illiterate, yet it would be mistaken to conclude from that proposition that in any particular time or place all non-churchmen were unable to read or write. Scholastic axioms differ from real cases."[1]

For studies of literacy in the early modern and modern periods, historians use the presence or absence of a signature as a sign of the achievement or absence of a minimal degree of literacy. That is admittedly a rough measure,[2] and for the medieval era it is less valid. "The automatic coupling of reading with writing and the close association of literacy with the language one speaks are not universal norms, but products of modern European culture." Writing largely remained a craft and a skill, often highly valued but not taught conjointly or sequentially with reading. It was a skill distinct from reading, in part because parchment and quills made it difficult. Similarly, the traditional emphasis on the spoken word caused reading to be linked more often with speaking.[3]

This example is one of the clearest cases of continuity with the ancient and classical periods. It also complicates problems of evidence. Writing leaves its remains; it is an artifact. Reading is not. Data pertaining to reading are much more infrequent and uncertain.[4] Scholars, officials, and ecclesiastics were also most likely to have scribes and secretaries; they themselves may seldom have had the need to put pen to parchment or vellum.

Contemporary assessments are likely to mislead. They concentrate on levels of maximum abilities rather than the distribution of basic skills. Literacy cannot be conceptualized as monolithic. Michael Parkes emphasizes that the typical contemporary uses of the terms for literacy "are too restricted to be profitable in an investigation into an age that is characterized by the emergence of written vernacular literature," among other developments. He distinguishes three kinds of literacy: that of the professional reader, the literacy of the scholar or man of letters; that of the cultivated reader, the literacy of recreation; and that of the pragmatic reader, the literacy of one who has to read or write in transacting business.[6] These are not necessarily the best categories for considering medieval patterns of literacy, but thinking about literacy in such terms assists us.

Definitions of literacy, associated expectations, and the resulting prejudices that led to the official denigration of those with lower skills; distinctions between reading and writing and between knowledge of Latin and the vernaculars; and the role of scribes must be grasped. Recognition of these allows greater flexibility in considering the evidence. In understanding that people of the medieval past could be quite literate while still being viewed as lay and *illitteratus*, we gain a new perspective on the age.[7]

### I. Fifth–Seventh Centuries

In and after the sixth century, as the empire declined and disappeared, we find evidence of the persistence of its schools, especially in Italy, but also in a number of regions of Gaul (France).[8] The collapse of Rome did not culminate in the simultaneous disappearance of its educational institutions.[9] Lay and classical schools persisted, and in Italy may have remained continuously open throughout the "Dark Ages." J. W. Thompson concluded that the laity were not as ignorant of Latin as is generally supposed, and that in every century of this period, a number of literate men and women were found outside ecclesiastical confines. There is evidence that even some barbarians acquired a fair knowledge of Latin.[10]

During the fifth century, the Romans evidently retained confidence in their educational arrangements. Rome apparently did not plan for a popular intellectual tradition to develop; no real "democratization" of culture took place. Still, the achievements, in popular levels of literacy and in higher levels for the few, were impressive. After the Roman conquest, "the written word . . . reached countries which had previously known only oral traditions. To learn to read and write had become an obligation for all who wished to participate in the activities of *Romania*."

Literacy surely expanded with the establishment and some funding of schools. Nothing resembling the levels of literacy of Athens or Rome itself could have been achieved; much of Rome's concern was directed to the secondary schooling of the children of the elite and those likely to become civil servants. With this imperial strategy, Rome sought to preserve its strength and prestige.[11] These schools were in place at the dawn of the Middle Ages.

New modes of Christian schooling were developing. During the third through fifth centuries, classical lay schooling was not always viewed as a threat to the education of Christians. Augustine, who was often critical of the influences of pagan and literary instruction, indicated in his *De Doctrina Christiana* how Christians could use skills learned in secular schools to deepen their appreciation of religious culture. He never proclaimed the need for separate parochial schools.[12] To him and to others, the Roman schools remained sufficient, *if* supplemented by catechizing in the faith. Such men recognized the context of higher learning for the few, including clerics of the church. They also "assumed that many would remain illiterate. They were to be taught the rudiments of Christian doctrine orally, and they had to accept them on faith."[13]

Another approach to education was also evolving: the new ideal of spiritual asceticism, or monasticism. This force, which would play a powerful if contradictory role during the Middle Ages, rejected literary and secular culture. In theory, it claimed no place for worldly knowledge. For literacy, there was room for young pupils and for adult monks. Reading, while often required for a fixed period each day, as part of an order's rules, was narrowly and rudimentarily focused in practice.[14] Lay and noble children were accepted in many Western monasteries for schooling, even when there was no intent for a clerical future. Their later use of literacy and their support of schooling could be significant.

The state of elementary instruction is far less clear. Whereas most evidence pertains to Roman grammar and rhetoric schools, monastic schools, and the occasional ecclesiastical or episcopal school, it is likely that there was also primary instruction. Some of the nobility and the wealthy also educated their sons and some of their daughters at home. On the eve of the empire's collapse, established educational arrangements—which provided regular schooling for the children of the well-to-do and higher, some chances of primary instruction for those of lesser families, and maintenance of Graeco-Roman educational traditions—remained. Some of these arrangements survived barbarian migrations and invasions.

The situation was decidedly mixed. It is wholly inappropriate to term the state of literacy as anything more than restricted.[15] To conclude that levels of literacy had fallen since the achievements of Greece and Rome is inescapable, given the new conditions. Levels of wealth, commerce, cultural and political order and unity, and urban prominence declined, and with them arrangements responsible for high rates of literacy and pragmatic necessities. To consider the result a "nadir of civilization" or a period of darkness is not accurate. Not all barbarians were opposed to schooling in literacy or illiterate themselves, nor did the church and its training schools maintain a monopoly on the transmission of literacy and learning.

It is possible that levels of literacy across the West in the sixth through eighth centuries did not diverge radically from those that preceded them. Oral patterns continued to be pervasive and instrumental, interacting with and conditioning the uses of literacy. Literacy was still used, especially for political and administrative needs, religion, and commerce.

The values and modes of socialization of the barbarians differed from those of Roman Europeans. Education seems to have been overwhelmingly oral; physical training, military preparedness, and indoctrination in the traditions of warriors, the myths of oral legends, and the morality of nature's power and force formed its core. "Intellectual training was foreign to them. While Germanic writing—runic script—did exist, its knowledge was reserved for the priest, and its use was magical." Even with destruction and defeat, Romans clung to their educational system and culture; outside the regions completely given over to the barbarians (Britain, northern Gaul, Germany), as well as in Italy and southern Gaul, schools remained open. In fact, a Romanization of the barbarians slowly began.[16]

The written word and the organized transmission of literacy were not lost. During the first third or more of the sixth century, those with the means continued to obtain instruction as before. At Rome and Ravenna, the public posting of documents continued. Elementary education, furthermore, seems to have survived in and outside the cities.[17]

Roman Latin culture also influenced the barbarians. As early as the fifth century, Latin had become the official language of the Burgundian and Visigothic courts. Latin culture did well, apparently, in Ostrogothic Italy and Visigothic Spain and among the Franks in eastern areas of the former empire. Among the Merovingians, too, Latin early became the language of the court; most Merovingian kings were probably able to write: all were able to sign administrative documents. According to Pirenne, lay instruction was not limited to the royal families but was prevalent among the lay aristocracy.

Levels of literacy were maintained in large part as a result of the interaction of state administrative needs, cultural continuity of the old Roman families, and the impact of Roman ways upon barbarians. The evidence of many lives illustrates the continuing existence of lay public schools in sixth- and seventh-century Merovingian society.[18] The barbarians employed Romans, especially trained lawyers, and encouraged the instruction of their own bureaucrats to meet expanding administrative needs. Their literacy was more pragmatic and technological than classical.[19]

Like the Romans and Greeks before them, the Frankish aristocracy retained educated servants to read aloud to them and to assist them with literary activities. Clerks and merchants needed some degree of literacy to do their work. Illiterate merchants apparently employed literates to assist them. A knowledge of Latin was "undoubtedly indispensable" in the commercial world of sixth-century Italy. Some freemen apparently also gained schooling.[20]

The balance between lay and clerical instruction is unclear. Relatively, it was shifting toward the church. Opposition to classical culture and literature was increasing among Christians; many found it profane, sensual, misleading, and conducive to doctrinal deviation. Problems were experienced in recruiting clerics, and the demands for increasing their numbers led to a minimum of time for training and testing.

On the other hand, classical education and literature continued in some of the schools initiated and sponsored by the church, in the training that some bishops and clerical leaders obtained (sometimes in lay schools before assuming the cloth), and in the invaluable service rendered by monasteries in preserving and reproducing manuscript literature. Neither ironic nor paradoxical, this consequence is the necessary contradiction of the early medieval church and the development of Christian education and culture in its context. Its criticism of pagan classicism and fears cannot be minimized, but that is not the entire situation. To understand these developments means to recognize not one standard for literacy, but several.

Monastery schools remained an important agency for the transmission of reading and writing during the early Middle Ages. Many accepted children who were not destined for a life in the orders. Youngsters learned to read at least Biblical texts, and sometimes the skill of writing in order to copy manuscripts. Considerable time and attention were dedicated to reading; some learned to write at the same time.[21] Older, unlettered monks were also encouraged to learn.

This literacy was for the few. Students were destined for a thoroughgoing and uniquely religious culture, not to be confused with classical or lay cultures. Nor, in most cases, should such literacy be viewed as "Christian learning." Psalmody, based in the rote memorization of the Psalter and sometimes the Gospels, occupied a primary place; monastic rules linked the learning of letters to the Psalms. The stress of monastic primary instruction on memory and repetition was shared by ancient and much later elementary curricula.

Reading was overwhelmingly oral; educated persons either read a text aloud or had it read to them. Monastic rules also demanded several hours daily of personal reading. It was a task more ritual and spiritual than intellectual, an ideal perhaps more than reality.[22]

Far more children were educated in lay clerical schools. Episcopal and parish schools predated the end of the empire. Their main purpose was to train clerics, but literacy was also provided to many youngsters who did not assume a clerical career. Until the second half or even last one-third of the Middle Ages, these schools were a major force for the transmission of literacy in the West.

First in the Ostrogothic kingdom, schools were established at the parish level to secure and instruct future priests. Apparently, they were successful in Italy, although their extent is unknown. Their necessity and endorsement came from the Council of Vaison, in 529, which proclaimed that each rural parish priest should take in lectors and teach them the Psalter, the holy texts, and divine law.

The parish schools were too irregular and varied to be considered a system. In some places they did not replace Roman public schools. Intended as secondary training, they developed in some areas into primary schools instead of or in addition to the former function, depending on the abilities and interest of the regular clergy and on local alternatives. Their recruits undoubtedly came from a broader range of society than those of the episcopal schools; they offered a chance for education and mobility to the lower orders.[23]

The remaining years of the sixth and the first four decades of the seventh centuries are "darker," at least as far as the evidence of literacy and schooling is concerned. Although the balance may well have continued to shift from secular schools to the church, public and classical schools did not completely disappear. Justinian restored

the privileges of teachers' salaries and reorganized schools; his empire needed
trained functionaries and had to maintain some forms of schooling.[24]

Gregory the Great, pope of Rome at the turn of the sixth to the seventh century,
also supported a Christian compromise and cooperation with ancient schooling.
Seeking the conversion of his fellows to the superior wisdom of the sacred texts
as had Paul, Augustine, and Cassiodorus, he tolerated profane culture—*if* appro-
priated for and subordinated to higher purposes.[25] In Italy, support for schooling,
lay and clerical, continued through the sixth and onset of the seventh centuries.

Elsewhere in the West, in regions south of the Loire, Roman culture and civilization survived the sixth and early seventh centuries. There is evidence of a great
deal of writing. Literacy was restricted, yet it was regularly employed by some.
Written documents were used in property transactions, wills and dowries, adoption
of children, and manumission of slaves. Documents were carefully preserved and
registered, as in Rome and Ostrogothic Italy. Urban society also survived, supporting schools and the sorts of exchanges that put a priority on literacy and writing.
In formal exchanges, oral and written procedures interacted. Rights to property,
payments of fines, loans, and sworn oaths were oral events witnessed and com-
memorated by making and preserving documents in manuscript. Gregory of Tours
provides evidence of the persistence of Roman habits and the use of writing in
southern and eastern Gaul.

A line of differentiation distinguished this region from the lands north of the
Loire and the Langres plateau. Barbarian influence predominated above this cultural-
political boundary. In Barbarian Gaul, in contrast to Roman Gaul to the south, the
Franks are held to have eradicated the earlier Roman contribution. With the previous
educational and literate traditions largely unknown and little evidence of literacy
or learning in the sixth and seventh centuries, the extent of decline remains an open
question.

In Province and Burgundy to the south, however, Roman civilization was prolonged. Numerous scholars and other elite figures achieved a notable degree of
classical learning. Clerics, aristocrats, and even a slave were "men of letters"—
with knowledge of the liberal arts and writing gained from education in the classical
tradition. Such examples hint at the presence of lay and public schools. For some
laymen, learning and literacy were available, and were used in trade and the law.

· In cities, at least, preachers sermonized in Latin. The vulgar Latin was the tongue
of the masses, but both the literary and the vulgate were used. A decline in linguistic
quality can easily be exaggerated. Those formally educated learned the former,
often with Virgil as their model; scholars read the classical texts available to them;
elementary education probably changed little.[26]

## 2. Seventh Century

The period after the mid-seventh century is often considered the time of the loss
of the classical tradition. Riché, for example, asserts that in Italy the surviving
institutions and interest in "traditional" culture were "converted" toward a more
religious orientation; Merovingian Latin, to the north, was in the process of be-

coming a spoken but not written language, moving increasingly away from the Roman toward the basis for a vernacular. A fundamental shift, though long delayed, may well have been under way. The problem is that the arguments are from the *lack* of evidence rather than its presence.

Nevertheless, schools—clerical schools, at least—existed. Training future clerics and some laymen, they instructed youths of nonaristocratic origin. As municipal schools became scarcer, children of the nobility once again were taught at home. Even without lay schools, some young persons were kept in touch with classical traditions. In the long run, however, the lack of institutions led to a gradual degradation of learning. The anarchy that plagued the Merovingian kingdom apparently had this impact in southern Gaul. Nevertheless, education and literacy did *not* disappear.

To the north, with the greater dominance of the barbarian Franks, conditions changed. Urban schools cannot be found. Nevertheless, Roman culture did not disappear suddenly. In an important sense, barbarian chiefs were also influenced by Roman culture from the south in the seventh and eighth centuries. King Clovis and his descendants borrowed political institutions, inscriptions, financial arrangements, and tax roll revisions. Despite the conquest, uses and arrangements for literacy developed in ways that may have been novel to the region, ironically. Among the Franks, written royal documents, Roman legal practices, willmaking, contracts, and acts of sale were used, as the use of and appreciation for writing increased; writing, in fact, began to sanction oaths and payment of the *wergeld*.

Royal agents needed some instruction to perform their increasingly formal duties. In the seventh century, writing was found in the German lands. Public scribes, a notariate, and the recording of the law all marked the emergence of an apparently new, if surely highly restricted, literacy in places where there apparently had been little or none before. Similarly, Frankish aristocrats, like those of Gothic and Burgundian background, did not abolish the oral procedures and symbolic rites that accompanied legal actions as they grasped the usefulness of written documents. Some of the early uses of writing, for inscriptions, property marks, and magical signs and religious talismans, strikingly parallel the earliest uses of writing before the invention of alphabetic literacy. But even as writing and limited literacy made headway, illiteracy was the condition of virtually all.

A process of assimilation to literacy had begun, however. It started among the Frankish aristocracy, with evidence of learning in letters, including by some women, in the second half of the sixth century but more frequently during the next. Letters and verses have been discovered that show elements of both classical *and* religious culture. The slow spread of literacy to the Franks stemmed from the joint effects of the two Western traditions of learning, each of which had developed agencies for the transmission of literacy. Thus, literacy spread to new areas in the West.

Increasingly, the Frankish aristocracy received some modicum of instruction. Reading and writing, to accompany their new uses of writing as well as their adoption of the Christian religious culture, became a part of socialization. Most of the higher-born, though, continued to use scribes and secretaries, as elsewhere, although signatures became more common among this class by the latter half of the seventh century.[27]

The Merovingian court can be considered an early educational center. Youths gained entry through kinship and were literally apprenticed to their future work. Largely learning their letters before arrival, they were trained for literate-based labors as officers and bureaucrats. Future officials learned stenography; some had to master administrative practices and the law. This literacy was functional and practical; it was also enjoying increased distribution and usage. In contrast with the Romans, it was the aristocrat, rather than slaves or ambitious young men from classes below them, who came to court and office to learn the skills and use them pragmatically—another indication of the narrowing and increased restrictiveness that had taken place. Although we are describing the spread of literacy to places previously largely illiterate, it is important to find its utilitarian concentration in different social levels from those in which it was found when the aristocracy primarily had been cultural users. The church was not the agency for those from the middle and lower ranks of society to gain literacy and letters.

Visigothic Spain, like Roman Gaul, had preserved much of antique culture and education, including some Greek influences. Much evidence of writing has been located in Spain: letters, bills of sale, donations, wills, registry offices, and personal archives. In the cities, at least, writing was used among laymen, although most could not write. In contrast to Gaul, there seem to be no regions in Spain in which writing was totally absent. Clerical and monastic schools contributed to the preservation of lay education; some monks and clerics placed themselves in private homes to tutor children who were not preparing for a religious career. A rich cultural life surrounded the Spanish Visigothic court, as kings and princes adhered more closely to classical traditions than did the Merovingians. Grammar and rhetoric instruction continued, although both kings and laymen were actively involved in religious culture, too.[28]

This period saw great church activity in the political and economic life of Gaul, but little cultural production. It was a time of building and administrative development, rather than of scholarly vitality; writing consisted largely of reproducing manuscripts of Patristic writings. Clerics rarely acceded to episcopal power. Kings preferred men who were able to administer the diocese and collaborate with the courts; "bishops, as a result, behaved like judges and legislators." As members of the aristocracy, they had received instruction more classical than clerical; many had been provided with schooling that stressed erudition, poetry, and rhetoric. To them, the Bible was one classic among many. These lettered clerics were often erudite scholars who might well delight in displays of learning. They did not denounce the baleful influences and dangers of classics, or convert to a religious culture. Since so little religious culture developed, little owed to these influences.

In Spain, by contrast, the religious culture of the clerics flowered. The lettered clerics of Spain were rarely former laymen. There the renewal of theological studies was tied to the development of ecclesiastical schools.

In Gaul, the parish or presbyterial schools spread rapidly in Roman and barbarian regions after the first half of the sixth century. As they expanded, they more often included day schools to which children could go, and which laymen could attend beside future clerics. About Spanish elementary education we have little information. From the sixth century, however, schools opened whenever rural parishes were initiated. In both Gaul and Spain, studies were based on the Psalter and chant; study of Scripture and hagiography followed. These schools are deemed modest and often classified as elementary; they probably incorporated primary instruction, heavy with rote learning and memorization, with a religious training alien to earlier elementary curricula.

Pupils who desired clerical studies had to turn to the episcopal school. Not only did it provide the religious training required for the priesthood, but it also trained certain youths to assist the bishops in administering their often sizable bureaucracies and their written work. Instruction was wholly religious; there were no literary studies, regardless of the uses to which pupils later put their reading and writing. The church provided an increasingly common opportunity for learning literacy, especially for boys for whom there were no other alternatives.[29]

Monasteries also grew in number and size. At the dawn of the seventh century in Gaul, there were at least 200, incorporating a bewildering variety of residents: exiles, political prisoners, and children without real vocations, as well as monks. Some few remained centers of study and learning. The training and regimen for most were rooted in asceticism, with a minimum of ecclesiastical culture. Monks read their Psalters, the Scriptures, and the rules; they copied manuscripts, but few went further with their reading and writing. In Spain, sacred culture seems to have been more profound than in Gaul. Extensive reading, as well as discussion, was required, and despite their lack of Greek, the major monasteries and episcopal centers were uniquely developed institutions of religious culture and learning. In both Spain and Gaul, the monasteries provided one of few agencies for the provision of literacy. Their service in preserving and reproducing valuable manuscripts was unique; in them lay the main source of care and "publication" for the first half of the Middle Ages.[30]

By the late sixth and seventh centuries, evidence permits a northward glance, to the lands that would become England. Here the history of literacy and the relationship between classical traditions and clerical circumstances were different. In the first half of the fifth century, the Romans evacuated their legions and administrators from Britain; in the second half, barbarians occupied the land, forcing the Celts to the west. The Germanic invaders, unlike the Goths, Vandals, or Burgundians to the south, took little care to save the substance or symbols of Roman culture. As one consequence, little information about previous educational or cultural affairs survived.

In the fifth century, perhaps Latin was still used in the west. Only in the Celtic church did Latin culture find a refuge, in institutions developing from the fourth century, largely around monasteries—centers that were virtually urban. These monasteries were primarily rigorous schools of asceticism, whereas those in Wales emphasized classical culture and liberal learning. By the sixth century, the Irish monasteries had become important study centers, which soon influenced Britain, as well as the Continent. The Roman schools of the first four centuries of the common era had completely disappeared before the long, gradual rise of literacy and learning that commenced in the sixth and seventh centuries.[31]

In barbarian Britain, the first schools did not appear much before the beginning of the seventh century. They followed the arrival of Roman missionaries to the south *and* Irish monks to the north of the island. Missionaries migrated with the intent of converting the pagans to Christianity; with this hope came the wellsprings of literacy and education, the first since the loss of earlier Roman institutions. With designs for the spiritual conquest of the heathen came needs for training priests to take the word to the people and education in Christianity to kings and the aristocracy. The model for the distribution of literacy became one that stemmed from the top (in several senses) downward.

By the first third of the seventh century, religious schools were functioning at Canterbury and Dunwich. By mid-century, schools also accompanied the establishment of cathedrals at London, Rochester, and Dorchester. These developments were slow; the soldiers of Christ had to combat warfare among the kingdoms as well as paganism, and the distance from Rome made it difficult to supply the schools with books. Training at these schools focused on reading sacred texts and learning chants.

Conditions in the north proved somewhat more hospitable for the rooting of clerical education. In 625 King Oswald, who had been raised among Celts, called Aidan, an Iona monk, to establish a monastery at Lindisfarne. This center became a renowned site of culture and education. With the education of clerics as its goal, it also received aid from other Anglo-Saxons and initiated a double monastery for men and women at Whitby. These and related houses brought to northern England a culture similar to the Irish, although few of the new houses could rival the Irish centers.[32]

These monastic schools made a larger contribution to literacy and schooling than many on the Continent. Given the traditions of Saxon socialization and the lack of alternatives, converted aristocrats who desired schooling in Christian letters for their children had no choice but to send them there, which they could do without intending them for holy orders. Leaders so educated were likely to support the church's efforts to evangelize, convert, and further develop schooling. A momentous linkage was initiated, furthering lay literacy at the top of society and committing powerful support to the expansion of clerical schooling and literacy.

Irish monks were "exported" to the Continent—to Gaul—where they stimulated religious scholarship and learning. This late-sixth- and seventh-century invigoration from the north began with the legendary Columban, who led a dozen monks to establish a school near Luxeuil in Burgundy. Columban insisted on an ascetic, rather than a scholarly, training; no provision for reading periods was made. Irish practice of literary studies was apparently unnecessary, because "Columban found young men in Gaul who were semiliterate but who knew enough Latin to read the sacred text and thus did not need to study the grammarians as had the Irish." If that was so, these young men were more than semiliterate: the result of educational provision in (northern) Gaul. We capture a revealing glimpse of one of the most common and valued *uses* of literacy at this time.

Columban, despite an apparent desire to the contrary, became a missionary among the unconverted; his institution at Luxeuil was the training school for his foot soldiers, whose tasks included the education of the masses to the Word: through oral preaching mainly, but also through the instruction in letters of some new priests. Literacy, and religion, were thus spread. Not all lay converts entered the monastery.

In the home education observed by the aristocracy, more children were faced with the task of learning letters, if holy ones, than before. The Merovingian court also felt the impact of Columban's clerical and educational reforms. The movement won supporters at a time at which the religious culture of the secular clergy had begun to wane. A source of schooling for some few was maintained, drawing together elements of the divergent cultures of Ireland, Gaul, and Italy.[33]

With time and settlement, Romanization and Latinization among Lombard leaders and aristocrats also gradually replaced barbarian traditions and customs. Literacy, in part through Christianity, accompanied this transformation during the seventh century. Under Rothari's rule (636–643), for example, customs were recorded in Latin as well as the Germanic Language. Written documents began to be used, although traditions and oral culture remained strong. Under the early influences of Catholicism, literacy first appeared at the court.

During the first centuries of the Middle Ages, a new beginning was made. Restricted elite and clerical literacy could now be found where none had existed previously, and elsewhere literacy was undoubtedly on the rise, albeit neither sharply nor rapidly. The pendulum had swung to the church as the keeper and producer of culture and the primary agent for the transmission of literacy.[34] But the classical tradition and antique education influenced the church, as did pagan traditions. And in some areas, lay schooling disappeared. Literacy, within its restrictions of class and largely clerical culture, was beginning its long and slow increase through the remaining centuries of the Middle Ages. A new basis for the medieval West had been created.

### 3. Eighth Century

The latter half of the seventh century marks a point of development. It is portrayed as a time of "renaissances." But what do they signify for the history of literacy in the West?

The production and illumination of manuscripts in the scriptoria of monasteries increased by the end of the seventh and first decades of the eighth centuries. Religious leaders began to revitalize their houses and to organize them for a much greater production of culture: for the glory of God. By the end of the seventh century, for example, scribes and illustrators were active at Corbie, Luxeuil, and Soissons, and writers at Corbie, Nivelles, Rebais, Fontenell, Remiremont, and Laon. Burgundy experienced a revival of canon law; Lyon and Aquitaine an intellectual renewal, with reading of classical as well as ecclesiastical literature. England witnessed new interest in classical learning, with the Roman Hadrian and the Greek Theodore as leaders. Italy saw a revival of interest in Greek and grammar. The temporary end of political anarchy and instability in the West underlay these developments; their preconditions in literacy and learning derive from the previous development. It had taken time to develop institutions, build foundations, and establish wealth and security. Currents of personal exchange and communication throughout Europe also favored intellectual and artistic unity and renewal.[35]

A cultural flowering took place in England. Theodore arrived in Kent, reorganized the school, imported and produced manuscript books, and expanded the secondary and higher curricula. In Wessex, as well, literary education advanced, making it unnecessary for Anglo-Saxons to go to Ireland for education. Among the lesser centers, Benedict Biscop (Bede's teacher) impressed the new spirit of learning in Northumbria: establishing important clerical schools; collecting and copying books; adopting a Roman spirit in studies of history, science, and especially scripture; and establishing libraries in monasteries. Poetry and chant grew more common.

This rebirth represented neither a rediscovery of liberal arts nor a revival of classical education. Both clerics and lettered Anglo-Saxons were hostile to secular learning.[36] Grammar, of course, was studied, in order to appreciate properly the Bible; it was "Christianized," as was the classical literature that was studied out of context, but not rhetoric or dialectic. Herein lay one of the pillars of medieval Christian culture and schooling.

Moreover, the audience for instruction was not altered. The Anglo-Saxon intellectual renewal touched only an elite, and not even all clerics and monks in these centers were literate. There is no reason to expect that literacy was increasing as a result of these intellectual currents. The major forces that influenced its levels were felt before these times.

Most laymen were strangers to Latin. Their literary culture came not from written literature per se but rather from the Celtic and Anglo-Saxon oral lore, of poems, myths, legends, epics, romances, and morals. Not until the seventh and eighth centuries did this apparently vast literature begin to be recorded, showing the interaction of the pagan with the Christian and the vernacular with Latin. Christian poetry dated to the sixth century, and apparently was received warmly. Clerics contributed to the writing, and much poetry was influenced by Christian teaching. The timeless lore was to a large extent Christianized, and it was certainly influenced by Latin themes and meters.

The church also contributed to the formation of a national culture in a way that did *not* occur elsewhere in the West, not only through this writing but also by individual priests' bringing poetry and poets into their chapels and monasteries. To combat this activity, the church itself encouraged the creation of poems in the vernacular to attract both clergy and laity from other pagan poems. A blending of cultures, with the tiny elite's production of literate Latin materials but the mass's adaptation of the traditional oral with the Latin and the clerical into a Christianized, broadly based culture, sometimes written but most often transmitted orally, is as fine a summary of the condition of popular literacy and cultural learning for the late-eighth-century English as can be presented.[37]

In Italy, monastic culture did not attain the level of the Anglo-Saxons in the first half of the eighth century. The only sign of intellectual life is found at Bobbio, the center founded by Columban where study and copying went on.[38] For developments in literacy and learning, we must look to the past: to the towns of the north and to their traditions of schooling.

At the end of the seventh and beginning of the eighth centuries, towns and commerce were growing. Town administration and commercial dealing demanded instruction. Notables knew at least how to sign the documents that their scribes drew up; those who could not sign placed a cross. Something of a notary system was in operation. Surviving records do not indicate whether schools were lay or clerical, although some writing evidently came from clerical scriptoria, such as that of Verona.

Many laymen, whose wealth and status are evident from their occupations, learned their letters in clerical institutions. Other evidence shows that some received elementary training from a priest, *outside* either episcopal or rural schools; clerical notaries may also have taught their lay colleagues. Regardless of agency, a functional or utilitarian level of literacy existed in Italy. Connected with towns and trade, it suggests a minimal range of distribution, as well as the nonclerical, nonroyal, or aristocratic needs that were met for some persons in the seventh and eighth centuries.[39]

Lombard kings were often literate. Their courts were considered centers of culture, and their administrations made regular use of writing. Princes and dukes organized their offices in terms of Roman traditions; the Carolingians copied Roman notarial procedures when attempting to reorganize their own.

Clerical education revived in Rome by the late seventh century, with the reestablishment of papal sovereignty and the defeat of the Byzantine heresy. Although Greek learning was rapidly renewed, no other innovations took place. Nothing occurred to carry literacy outside the clergy; education was strictly religious. Among the aristocracy, family education probably persisted. There were also elementary schools that taught children their letters.[40]

To the north, in Frankish Gaul, seventh-and eighth-century developments were fewer. Amid problems and invasions, the Merovingian dynasty ended, which posed a severe threat to the cultural renewal of the late seventh century. The traditional refuges of culture, Aquitaine, Provence, and Burgundy, stood victims to civil war and foreign invasion, by Arabs as well as Carolingians, as Roman Gaul was brutally reincorporated into the *regnum Francorum* at the cost of its culture and much of its literacy. The early Carolingians were perhaps less often literate than their Merovingian predecessors. A new nobility replaced the old Romano-Frankish aristocracy, abandoning certain Roman traditions, including educating their children. In the transformation of bureaucratic practice, it fell to clerics and their writing ability to maintain registers and draw up documents. Laymen and lay literacy were replaced in the notariate.

During the first half of the eighth century, the Merovingian monasteries suffered. A secularization occurred, with laymen heading abbeys and a dilution of the religious culture and schooling, though the revival of monastic culture continued. All active scriptoria were north of the Loire, where monastic activity continued—in contact with other centers. Fine illuminated manuscripts were produced. Yet, the activities of the scriptoria cannot be taken as a sign of literary activity or of extensive literacy or schooling. "Monks could be calligraphic artists and painters without being lettered . . ."; in only a few instances does copying seem to have accompanied literary work in poetry or lives of saints. A few abbots attempted to turn their houses into cultural centers amid this generally retrogressive atmosphere among laity and clergy.[41] Levels of literacy fell even lower by mid-century.

To the east, in Germany, Frankish lands remained the scene of repeated battles and conquests. Little social or cultural development took place until the end of the seventh century, when Irish and Anglo-Saxon missionaries arrived to essay a deeper Christianization. As in England a century before, conversion stemmed from the monasteries; monastic schools were established to train up a cadre of clergy to preach to the populace.

In German areas, the monastic houses became the first centers of culture and agencies for the spread of the limited literacy; they also established scriptoria and began to produce and reproduce manuscripts. This influence led in time to the enrichment of education, cultural awareness, and support at the Frankish court: the prelude to the Carolingian Renaissance under Charlemagne. That was foreshadowed when Charles Martel, Charlemagne's grandfather, chose to have his son Pepin instructed by the monks of Saint Denis, a step away from Merovingian tradition and toward Anglo-Saxon princes' patterns of the seventh century. No rush to found schools followed, however; literacy outside the court and monasteries could not have been touched. At court, though, legal activities using writing began to develop in new ways. Beginnings toward a society in which writing and literacy would become more important were stimulated. The "renaissance" had begun.[42]

Without exception, this cultural event of the eighth and ninth centuries is seen as a shining beacon of light in the darkness. In large measure, the revival of learning stemmed from early Carolingian developments and the impact of earlier English activities on the Continent, stimulated by Boniface at Fulda. The seminal figure was the English cleric and schoolmaster Alcuin, Archbishop of York, who responded to Charlemagne's call to direct studies at his court and stimulate clerical learning. Charlemagne's major concerns were the education of his children and grandchildren and the insurance that the clergy should get at least some necessary instruction, to provide the church with a satisfactory *libri catholic*. He also hoped to further the spread of Christianity.

The renaissance under Charlemagne was essentially clerical. It represented the culmination of early medieval developments rather than a new direction or a boost to more extensive schooling or literacy outside the aristocratic and clerical scope. It very likely led to a qualitative increase in skills within an established context, but not to a breaking of restrictions or established boundaries.[43]

As head of the palace school and doctrinal advisor to the king, Alcuin's major work consisted of reforming Latin grammar and spelling and assisting the development of a uniform, legible script for manuscript writing and copying—the Carolingian miniscule, which subsequently evolved into Gothic script in the twelfth and thirteenth centuries. This important work by a scholar-cleric more pedantic than brilliant promoted greater uniformity in Latin usage and writing throughout the West. He also edited a number of ecclesiastical texts, including the Christian liturgy and a complete, ordered Bible. Alcuin's classification of grammar, correction of texts, and simple, legible writing all contributed to the spread of Christian education, but without corresponding changes in the agencies for transmitting literacy, they could not affect levels and uses of reading and writing for some time.

The reforming activities of Charlemagne and Alcuin had only a narrow impact on schooling. They concentrated on three types of educational institution: the palace school, in which the royal and aristocratic children would receive a thorough Christian schooling, and the episcopal and monastic schools. With the former, these efforts resulted in making learning more prestigious and desirable to the nobility. With the latter two, improvement took place within the clerical tradition. Reading, singing, and ecclesiastical computation continued to dominate. Carolingian schools had limited aims and limited clientele; in students and content they were largely ecclesiastical. "Even after Charlemagne's reforms most of his lay functionaries could not read administrative orders."[44] Within a very limited scope, lay literacy among the highest classes increased, while the masses understood and spoke only Vulgar Latin or the Teutonic vernacular; they read and wrote neither. Among the laity, the ability to write was probably less common than in the preceding age.[45]

Manuscript book production was further stimulated. In the ninth century, there are many signs of the circulation and reproduction of vernacular as well as clerical writings, largely from the monastic scriptoria. The level of activity in copying, of corrected religious and classical texts, was unprecedented. Manuscript copying was an ascetically disciplined activity. Within the monastic rules it represented a part of the required physical labor.[46] It constituted "publication" and distribution of written literature at least until the twelfth century.

Charlemagne's reforms reveal one additional important use of literacy. An important aspect of his desire for an effective palace school derived from the need for efficient record keeping and document production for the administration of the realm: a fundamentally utilitarian side to the renewal of learning among the Carolingians. Written documents became basic to the act of royal authority. The decisions were still pronounced *orally* by the king with all due ritual; the subsequent writing in his name and circulation might serve as proof that the decision had been taken, as a means of publication, or as a memorandum to the agents responsible for its execution. Under Charlemagne, the use of documents designed to furnish or facilitate proof of individual rights increased; existing laws of both church and state were collected and published, new ones were promulgated, and written evidence became more common in judicial matters.

These developments took place in an essentially oral environment, wherein writing represented *an extension* in time and space of the spoken word—*not* its replacement. Charlemagne's memoranda and other written orders reinforced instructions given orally. The extensive use of written material under Charlemagne and several of his successors was not a full exploitation of literacy. In many areas there was apparently no extended use of writing.[47]

Most children received all the training they would get, and perhaps require, from their families, friends, and neighbors. In theory, the parish church and local cleric contributed to moral training, as education was supposed to suppress all evil tendencies. We do not know how often the children went to church or how well the cleric instructed them. For an increasing number of persons, faith and belief were an admixture of traditional and Christian lore, of new Christian magic with the old popular magic, as the church gradually won its place, a partial and ritualistic one, among them. Their culture remained oral but was influenced by the impact of the sacred texts and, indirectly, literacy.

The number of laymen who were instructed in schools—primarily ecclesiastical ones by this time—was very small; most were from the highest classes. The religious culture that reached the majority found them through symbol, image, ritual, and, above all, oral communication. Contact with the church and clergy occurred most often in the symbolic ceremonies such as baptism and other rites of the life cycle that slowly drew in the people. In lieu of literacy, bishops hoped that important prayers would be learned by memory and repeated at the correct moments without the need for a text.[48]

Teaching was through preaching. That is, it was oral: heard and listened to, not seen and read. Preaching, some recognized, must also be adapted to the language and level of the audience. Bishops and abbots constantly criticized the clergy's inappropriate use of language. Sometimes interpreters were used; more often priests used their native tongue or had to learn the vernacular, if they hoped for any chance of success. Prayers and Gospels were translated for their use. Scripture reading and explication and moral stories constituted most sermons.

The use of images was increasingly employed to familiarize the faithful with the Bible. Pope Gregory the Great recommended that the sacred representations used to decorate church walls not be suppressed " 'so that the illiterate will at least read by looking at the walls. . . .' " Similarly, clerics often brought song and dance, which were stamped as offensive, pagan, and erotic by church leaders, into their churches. They were far more likely to adapt and Christianize than to suppress these practices.[49]

Religious education and whatever degree of popular participation was achieved came through the ears, the eyes, and the voice. The culture was a spoken and, to a lesser extent, a seen one; it was also collective. Literacy played virtually no direct role. Nevertheless, it contributed to these efforts. The priests read, to some degree, in Latin and/or the vernacular; their learning from texts, even if rote, was transmitted to their audiences. Adherents responded by word, spoken and sung. The word was of record, and it was fixed in writing. It permeated, if superficially, the popular culture, affecting traditional "literature" too—taming it, frequently but not completely, to Christianity. Literacy, as it slowly spread, represented an increasing, although often muted and indirect, presence.

Only the few received schooling in letters. Classroom equipment and methods had changed little from those in ancient elementary schools. The first step in learning to read was still the alphabet. After the letters were mastered, the child progressed to syllables and then nouns, learning and memorizing each in turn. Sometimes the syllabary was abandoned, and the children proceeded directly to reading the Psalter.[50]

Oral reading was the classroom norm. Outside the schoolroom, however, personal and silent reading was becoming more common. It was imposed in the monasteries, but perhaps to reduce the volume of the drone that reading monks produced. Chant and computation of the clerical calendar completed the primary curriculum. When examined, the child would recite his lesson orally and in writing. Laymen often learned their reading with scant attention to writing.

"It is difficult to assess the results of elementary education. To learn to read, write, chant, indeed to count, must have required a tremendous effort. We can be sure that many clerics and monks [and lay persons] never went beyond this level," concludes Riché. To many, this level probably represented a literacy more rote than useful. We cannot be sure that many were able, were required, or even needed to use or develop their skills for other purposes. What remained in their memories may have lingered longer than the skills of literacy themselves. Even in secondary or ''higher'' instruction, docility and submission to the master were not conducive to forming a critical mind.[51] That was not a pedagogical goal of the times or of the institutions that provided the tools of literacy. Literates were rare in the first centuries of the Middle Ages, the time in which the foundations for medieval education and culture were laid. The eighth- and ninth-century renaissance did little to change the situation.

## 4. Ninth–Tenth Centuries

From the mid-eighth through much of the ninth centuries, new waves of invasions and destruction rocked the West and struck down these levels of literary and cultural achievement. England, perhaps the most severely threatened, only slowly recovered from the ninth-century Danish conquests. The important terms of this revival are among the best-documented of contemporary developments. The state of English literacy compared favorably with that found on most of the Continent by the first half of the century. The fierce invasions of the Danes changed that, to the point at which King Alfred, famed for his literary and educational zeal, could lament, probably with some hyperbole, ''There are only a few on this side of the Humber, and indeed not many across it, who could understand the Divine Service or who can explain a Latin letter in English.''[52] The Danish warriors burned the centers at Lindisfarne, Jarrow and Wearnmouth, Whitby, Croyland, Medehampsted (Peterborough), Ely, and Abingdon, among other houses of learning; both books and inmates met their end.

Alfred's place in the history of literacy and education results in large part from his own writings. He offered three periods of educational development: a golden age of English ecclesiastical and secular scholarship in the second half of the seventh century; a period of decay preceding his own time in the late ninth century; and a time of regeneration and new beginnings during his reign, with his royal support. In the first period, he drew upon Bede's references to Theodore, Hadrian, and Benedict Biscop. But why did they not translate their learning into English? he wondered. ''Those good and wise men never expected that men would become so heedless as to permit learning to decay; they were unwilling to translate, because they desired that in this country learning should increase as the knowledge of languages increased.'' Clearly, Alfred romanticized, exaggerating the level of achievement and removing it from its seventh-century context.

In Alfred's second period, the time of degeneration, his description is influenced by chronological proximity and the conditions of his time. He saw this period as a time of slaughter by the heathen Danes, culminating in a disorganized church and the frustration of learning. This low bench mark preceding his own activities caused him to lament and romanticize the golden age; it also created the needs he felt for his own program. Especially problematic to him was that even before the loss of books and manuscripts, ''a great number, too, of God's servants, derived small benefit from them since they were not written in their own language." These clergy were not totally illiterate, he indicated; more had some proficiency in the vernacular than in Latin. Alfred suggested that reading knowledge of English had spread beyond the clergy, even if that of Latin had declined.

Alfred's comments on the state of literacy cannot be confirmed. We have good reason to qualify his quantitative allusions about the earlier distribution of Latin and the contemporary diffusion of English literacy. He affirmed that literate persons existed, then and previously, in some number, and that more attained some level of proficiency in English than in Latin. He thus pointed to the route that much of the future of literacy would travel in the second half of the Middle Ages. Alfred was pleased with the revitalization of Latin learning in the last third of the ninth century, but in recognizing the state of his world, he was not confident that it would continue in the future.

To mute his fears, he sponsored and personally aided the translation into English of important works: "such books as 'are most needful to be known of all men'." He began to translate the *Shepherd's Book*, or *Pastoralis*, and to distribute one copy to each bishopric. He also created versions of Pope Gregory's *Pastoral Call*, Boethius's *Consolation of Philosophy*, and Orosius's *Seven Books of History against the Pagans*.

Alfred had another, even more prescient plan: "to ensure that 'all youth of free men now in the English people, having the means to apply themselves, should be committed to learning, while they have no strength for other employments, until they are able to read English well'." Some would progress to Latin. That goal was not attained in Alfred's time; yet Alfred's goals are still noteworthy. First, he foreshadowed, and apparently recognized, that a more popular literacy depended on structures of schooling that embraced all the children who had the "means" for elementary instruction. It is not clear whether he meant the intellectual or the material wherewithal, but the latter was one major obstruction to many. There were probably social restrictions in his term, too. Second, he pointed to the fact that a greater diffusion of literacy depended upon literary training in the language of daily life, the vernacular.

Alfred combated a situation in which many clerics had obtained some small, but inadequate, tutelage in Latin, but English was the language in which they did their teaching and preaching.[53] The church's linguistic need to reach the people helped, perhaps unwittingly and contradictorily, to assist the development of vernaculars and eventually popular literacy. Alfred's support and his preparation of English texts had perhaps little immediate impact. Nevertheless, they were important, even seminal, precedents.

Literacy was also stimulated by the expanding needs of state and trade.[54] Alfred sought to make his subjects literate in order to make them wiser—a tradition rather new to the ninth century. Literacy was linked with Christian and moral knowledge: the beginning of a tradition that has maintained its power ever since. At Alfred's time, it was sought only among the elite few who ruled and assisted the rulers.[55]

Equally impressive is the vitality of the native language. A considerable body of Anglo-Saxon poetry was still available, the best-known of which included *Beowulf*, *The Dream of the Road*, and the religious verse of Cynewolf. Alfred's translations

were addressed to those who read this literature. The developing vernacular made
great strides in the tenth and eleventh centuries, as it entered almost all aspects of
secular and religious life. Vernacular literature and writing were becoming more
common and important; that did not indicate significant increases in lay literacy,
however. It surely reached a larger public by being read or recounted orally to those
who could not read it themselves. Its popularity expanded with only a small change
in levels of lay literacy; more important for the future were the beginning of translations and the recording of the oral poems and stories.[56]

Book production was increasing, but ownership was not common even among
the higher classes. Books owned tended to be religious, spiritual, or moralistic; the
link between literacy and religious morality was firm and persisting.[57]

Literacy in England on the eve of the Norman Conquest reached a small number
of persons. The nobility and monarchs were more often literate to some degree.
Lay literacy, while tightly restricted, had increased during the first five centuries
of the medieval experience. There was some variety in the uses of and demands
for literacy. The church dominated the transmission of reading and writing; clerics
provided by far the most teachers, pupils, and, consequently, persons able to read
and/or write in some fashion. To suggest that religious reasons were the most
significant for possession of literacy skills would hardly be an exaggeration. Increasingly, society used writing, but literacy remained restricted in its social condition and its state of development. Orality still dominated society and culture. The
medieval approach began to take form.[58]

CHAPTER THREE

🦩

# New Lights of Literacy and Learning: From the Tenth–Eleventh to the Thirteenth Centuries

At all levels of society, the majority of the population of Europe between the fourth and fifteenth centuries was, in some sense, illiterate. Yet medieval civilization was a literate civilization; the knowledge indispensable to the functioning of medieval society was transmitted in writing: the Bible and its exegesis, statutory laws, and documents of all kinds. The need for writing that served a wide variety of purposes is evident in the development of the *ars dictaminis*.

—FRANZ H. BAUML, "Varieties and Consequences of Medieval Literacy and Illiteracy"

THE TENTH-ELEVENTH THROUGH the thirteenth centuries constitute a period of fundamental importance. That is apparent in several ways, significant both in themselves and in terms of what they represent for the future: that critical transition from the medieval to the early modern period. Literacy's history is a part of that history, if often a missing one.

From the late tenth century until the mid- to later thirteenth, new currents swept through the West.[1] Not suprisingly, these forces of development influenced some of the major changes in literacy. The important precedents in the transmission of literacy, its social distribution, and the uses to which it was put force us to reconsider both the extent of literacy and the roles that it played.

Literacy rates grew to new levels, although we lack the statistical evidence to document this fact. Lay as well as clerical schooling changed. The church's quasi-monopoly on learning was reduced, as more nonclericals gained access to its tutelage and more lay opportunities became available. Although secularization did occur, with new attention to the individual, the ecclesiastical and the secular should not be dichotomized.

Literacy remained restricted, but its distribution shifted, incorporating more of the clergy, certainly, but also more of the laity: virtually all of the nobility and royalty and more administrators and larger merchants, as well as their clerkly assistants and associates. Changes in procedures of government and commerce and increasing levels of town and city living were critical. The professions also expanded in parts of Europe. The beginnings of lay copying of manuscripts were important, too. It is likely that the church began to recruit more of its clerics from lower in the social structure. In some small ways, literacy began to be associated with limited opportunities for social mobility and changes in position. It became more useful for more persons, although in an absolute sense few required it for their livelihoods and welfare.

Changed material conditions, prosperity in agriculture leading to surpluses and marketing, population increases, economic diversification, growth of towns and secular governments better able to reduce private warfare and conflict, and major changes in administrative and judicial functions of the church were concentrated in the period spanning the late tenth to mid-thirteenth centuries. As Lerner notes, "These changes allowed momentous changes in the history of education. With greater wealth and population, education became much less a luxury."[2]

Most of the educational institutional development was concentrated in the towns and cities that grew up in this three-century era. It included more and probably larger, higher-quality schools in the cathedrals and collegiate churches, private instruction by clerics, and the first town schools of the Middle Ages proper. Instruction continued largely in Latin, but we also witness further development of the vernaculars of Europe and an increase in the number of persons who could read and/or write them.

In recognizing this fact, we must neither lose the medieval context nor neglect the powerful forces of continuity. The contradictions of increasing numbers of literate men and some women with increasing uses for their literacy in a largely non- or restricted literacy context were sharpened. The culture that affected the greatest numbers of men and women and was closest and most vital to daily life remained oral. As before, it did not exist in isolation from the developing written or literate culture, nor did the latter expand without a continuing conditioning and adaptation to the traditional means of communication and sociocultural discourse. The changes that took place were significant ones that prepared the way for the future in many respects; the context in which they occurred, and that influenced the consequences and the impacts felt, however, remained firmly connected with the present and the past.

## I. Italy and Commercial Revolution

Paradigmatic eleventh-century Italy exemplifies the general case of a commercial revolution-expanding literacy linkage. The relations tying urban life, commerce and trade, and at least a fair degree of elementary schooling span the history of the West. The strength of the linkage is variable; it was increasing in this period.[3]

Italy's medieval foundations helped to prepare the way; the maintenance of even low levels of town life, commercial trading, lay literacy, and lay education was crucial for the eleventh-century "take-off."[4] Of course, only in conducting fairly large-scale trade was literacy truly required.[5] Many commercial activities can proceed with a minimal level of even pragmatic literacy. If the levels in Italy exceeded such a minimum, then other than functional or deterministic factors were at work.

The commercial revolution depended on lay literacy and encouraged expanding levels of popular, if stratified, educational preparation for commercial reading and writing. Lawyers and civil administrators, as well as participants in the growing volume of trade, were prominent; the medieval social foundations, with a legal tradition inherited from Rome, stressed their importance. The trained lawyers were the most highly educated laymen. Unlike the early merchants, who were often itinerant, they normally resided in the main centers of administration, where their talents were drawn upon by city communities.[6]

Lawyers were major actors in the development of economy, polity, culture, and society in Italy. Later, they were instrumental in the spread of education to higher levels. Their contribution was felt by the church as well as civil society. In the late twelfth and thirteenth centuries, the advent of the *popolo* and the expansion of bureaucratic activity created even greater opportunities for them throughout communal Italy.

This stimulus for a "new" learning was not concentrated in higher education; much of the demand for professional and commercial training focused on lower levels, especially clerks and notaries, for whom literacy proficiency was essential. Notarial schools and the formation of a guild (almost a class) of notaries were central to this process. Entry into the profession depended partly on attendance in schools created specifically for notaries, which stressed technical uses of writing and reading. Business quickly found notaries indispensable, and as a result, they developed political and social strength as a group of literate men who had attained administrative experience for use in business and politics.[7] Above them, literacy was virtually certain; below them, it was sporadic, although it probably was spreading by the thirteenth century. Italian communes led the West in the distribution of literacy, especially lay literacy, in these centuries.[8]

By the thirteenth century, a new connection was emerging: a practical application of learning to civil life and a corresponding assumption of the usefulness of education for participation, service, and power. This tradition stands firmly among the legacies of literacy. School as an approach to social problems was much more a novelty then than it would later become.[9] That fact alone underscores the significance of this new role for literacy and schooling. Concentrated now in the middle and upper ranks of society, in time it filtered down the social structure.

During these centuries, commerce was transformed, and with it the social characteristics of mercantile groups. Literacy, though stratified, became more common at all levels. Wealth, power, *and* schooling were differentially distributed, however, as larger merchants, those participating in interregional and intercontinental commerce, banking, credit and finance, and related affairs, dominated. Circumstances of their business affairs virtually demanded literacy, as well as employees with some degree of it. The primary uses of literacy included the very stuff of trading (inventories, correspondence, bills and invoices, credit letters, and the like), details of banking and finance that were being created, legal matters such as contracts, the workings of the evolving arrangements and institutions for credit, and the increasing volume of paperwork and documentation, from letters of credit and commercial correspondence to bills of exchange.[10] The emergence, testing, revision. and evolution of these developments are the urban and commercial history of the eleventh through thirteenth centuries. Towns were the "nerve centers" of expansion; in them schools and literacy spread. A tradition of urban-rural differentials in rates of literacy, sharper than ever before, accompanied this social change.

It is unclear whether much of the impact of the shifts in distribution affected the smallest traders and crafts workers. Some increase in the middle ranks is much more likely. A differential by language of literacy also followed: lower in the social hierarchy, writing and reading in the vernacular were much more common than Latin literacy. Moving up the social structure into the better schools, we find the opposite path of development: Latin literacy, but also the increasing use of the vernacular—leading to a literary movement of massive moment by the end of the thirteenth century.

Commercial literacy was not a higher literacy in a classical or modern sense, and certainly not in the strict sense of the Middle Ages. It required some Latin for legal dealings and international trading and the ability to write letters (or to dictate them to a clerk or secretary), count, make lists, and keep books and ledgers. Many skills could be gained in practical experience or apprenticeship. The increasing distinction by class and group in terms of schooling had much to do with the cultural correlates of class and position that were emerging.[11] Cultural changes impinged on, and largely followed from, those of rank or class and wealth; extended classical-style schooling with emphases on culture and literature rather than on functional, professional, or pragmatic training was one concomitant of Italian commercial development, especially in the later twelfth and thirteenth centuries.[12]

Elsewhere in the West, similar forces were beginning. Transformations occurred first and developed furthest in Italy because of the peculiar circumstances of history, traditions, and resources and geographic location. A set of forces propelling achievements in literacy in Italy took lay literacy to the highest development and the closest connection with daily lives in the West. These developments occurred to a smaller extent, or before long found parallels, elsewhere in Europe, especially in the north and in England.

The trend was under way as the eleventh century flowed into the twelfth and thirteenth, as Europe prospered. For the small traders and dealers, the ability to read and write was little needed and therefore rare.[13] For the larger regional traders, it was more useful, and more attained it. Many, however, prospered or declined regardless of their achievement of schooling or writing. Other factors, of economics, society, and politics, were more important. One did not need literacy to engage in an early "money economy."

From the second half of the twelfth century, and increasingly in the thirteenth, towns began to open their own municipal schools. Although usually taught by a cleric, these institutions were lay-controlled. The church long resisted this development, as lay and clerical interests began to divide. Merchants began to seek out and initiate convenient schools for training their children and for mercantile preparation of clerks and other employees. Notaries began their own schools; before the end of the Middle Ages, commercial and business education, distinguished from other types of curricula, was emerging.[14]

Pirenne argued that most merchants engaged in international trade by the thirteenth century had acquired a "more or less advanced degree of instruction." Literate they no doubt were, and, if their families had prepared their paths, a solid and "classical" kind of training was more commonly becoming their childhood and adolescent experience. Significant, too, "it was certainly largely as a result of their initiative that the vulgar tongues took the place of Latin in private instruments." A knowledge of foreign languages was also becoming more widespread among the larger merchants, among many of whom French took the role that English later acquired. With linguistic development and potential for contradiction, Latin continued to fulfill the role of an international language.[15]

The key Italian development was the early emergence of *professional* laymen: teachers, lawyers, notaries, and physicians, whose business in life made it necessary for them to be educated, especially in Latin. In the north of Europe, professions that in Italy were in lay hands either did not yet exist or were present only to a small degree; otherwise, they were held by clerics. Virtually all teachers in the north, for example, were clergy, and Latin was not taught outside the schools of the church. In Italy, lay schools existed in addition to church schools. The number of private teachers apparently was comparatively large. By the twelfth century, monastic schools had been eclipsed, in quantity and quality of instruction, by cathedral and collegiate church schools; the monasteries declined for the remainder of the Middle Ages. Among the lay nobility and upper classes, literacy was far more common in the vernacular, although most had at least some familiarity with Latin. Education was well on its way toward becoming a normative experience for these classes, and in a formal sense, education at this time meant the learning of Latin.[16]

## 2. The Church, Papacy, and Schools

Much of the activity that occupied the universal Catholic church in the initial years of this period stemmed from the need to reform the institution and its clerical representatives. Efforts to remake the operations and, in an important sense, the "public relations" of the church affected literacy and schooling both directly and indirectly.

The creation of an administrative machine and regular governmental bureaucratic structure within the papacy was central.[17] It shows the place of literacy to a significant degree, and it parallels changes in civil administration by cities and states. The reform of the clergy was equally important. Levels of literacy were raised to new plateaus. Clerical illiteracy became less frequent, and the church's schools led the intellectual renaissance of the twelfth century.

A number of developments central to a reformed, reforming, and interventionist papacy led to new demands on literacy. An active, more independent pope required extensive written communications. He also required notaries and secretaries to handle the growing production and receipt of writing. A higher literacy was required for the clerical scholars added to the staff and councils to study, review, revise, and amend the laws of the church and to review the reports of civil and religious behavior among the "faithful." The growing finances of the emerging papal state also required oversight, accounting, and expenditure. Money lending and employing armed forces were only two of the many new responsibilities of the church that demanded an increasing number of trained literate clerics. A substantial part of the church's effort to achieve independence and ecclesiastical dominion related to its success in creating and maintaining an administrative structure. This success not only assisted the church's thrusts, it also made consolidating its victories quicker and firmer. These endeavors, based in literacy, occurred in the context of an emerging "feudal" papal monarchy and state, a political papacy, and its central place in the machinations and struggles of the monarchies of the West.

The papacy sought powers in wars that used paper to an unprecedented extent. Writs of excommunication and removal from office and threats and punishments decreed in Rome were not only communicated to the civil or clerical person under penalty but also transmitted orally to larger numbers throughout Western Christendom. The popes of these years sometimes backed their "paper promises" with physical force by their liegemen's armies or by their own forces of soldiers. Nevertheless, the extended use of written correspondence and official notices was new and forward-looking.[18]

Important precedents for administration and finance flowed from the innovations established by the medieval papacy. The uses of writing expanded and increased in bureaucratic complexity. The written word, supported by papal voice and person, in its oral transmission to more and more people touched new parts of the West. The major impact on popular knowledge was more indirect than direct. Only a few persons' literacy and learning were influenced directly by these developments. For those few, literacy was important; for some, the acquisition of its skills brought individual mobility and success within clerical confines. This use of literacy remained important, gaining in value with time.

In sharp contrast to the *absolutely* few persons directly involved in the uses of literacy for administration are the *relatively* many more whose lives were touched by another institution of the universal Christian church of the medieval West: the school. Throughout this period, despite the impressive increases in lay-controlled and initiated schools, most institutions for the transmission of literacy were part of the church. Teachers in the lay schools were usually church-educated clerics. Without the church, provisions for schooling and literacy in the West would have been incredibly reduced, and the number of available teachers would have been tiny. A relative shift to lay schools and an absolute increase in lay literacy occurred in the context of persisting ecclesiastical domination of schooling. The period from the eleventh through the thirteenth centuries saw a shift to cathedral or episcopal schools as the centers for Latin literacy and away from the role of the monasteries. The regular church schools grew in number, regularity, and quality of instruction.[19]

The episcopal schools led in the organized learning of the West until their partial eclipse by the new universities in the late twelfth century. The twelfth-century renaissance was based in these great churches, especially those of France. Much more the providers of secondary and higher education than of primary, they focused on the liberal arts (the Latin trivium and quadrivium), although, with the grammar schools of the dioceses, they continued to teach grammar and rhetoric to schoolboys and theology to most of the diocesan clergy.

The eleventh and twelfth centuries brought to fruition the hopes enunciated by Charlemagne and others in the eighth and ninth centuries for a strengthened system of religious schools. The expansion of the schools was marked, and no doubt fostered literacy, by an increase in the number of schoolmasters. Teachers gained new appreciation and social recognition; these schools grew into well-developed, structured institutions with staffs of their own. In the dioceses, other grammar schools became more frequent, although the right of teaching remained a strict monopoly, guarded increasingly against the challenges of urban laity who sought to found schools of their own.[20]

The cultural currents that rose to new levels in the twelfth century are typically termed a "renaissance." Literacy had risen to new levels among the clergy and laity, although it was still restricted.[21] It is important not to confuse the cultural flowering called a renaissance with a further increase in lay literacy. While rising rates of literacy may have been one of the many factors that stimulated this development, they were not the major one. Rather, both resulted in part from changed material and political conditions and advances over the preceding years. Conditions of relative stability, wealth, and increased numbers of teachers underlay both.

In several areas of Europe, particularly in France, learning and teaching gained new prestige in the twelfth century. France and Italy, especially, saw the emergence of perhaps the first class of professional teachers in the West and the origins of institutions that began to regularize and systemize this teaching. Philosophy and theology in France and law and theology in Italy dominated in the development of new schools and universities, which also led to a shift in the centers of book production and copying away from the monasteries to new circles of scribes and booksellers clustering around and under the supervision of the universities.[22] For the unprecedented numbers attracted to studies, knowledge gained new prestige, and careers from and in education rose to new levels: in the clergy, in state and church law, as clerks at courts, and in medicine.[23] This development reveals the founding of a new tradition and a legacy for education and literacy that became a powerful force in Western society and culture.

Society and culture were beginning to shift toward the secular, but schooling and learning remained overwhelmingly religious. The "renaissance" saw renewed attention to the classics and theology; philosophy, as it grew into a full-blown scholasticism, was stretched but did not break from religion. There was a new professional interest and a practical side to the demand for teachers and higher schools, but the advancement that occurred had firm bases in the past and was limited contemporarily.[24]

For literacy, the twelfth-century development was a continuation of the forces set in motion by the eleventh. Most scholarly and intellectual endeavors were distinct from those aspects of social change and cultural development that stimulated popular literacy. Apart from its impact on professional studies in which a demand was being met, its influence and causes were at best indirectly connected to the trends in the history of literacy per se.

## 3. Patterns of Literacy

As significant as these developments are to the cultural and intellectual history of the West, their relevance to the history of literacy is not major. The increase in both lay and clerical literacy was only one of the currents that led to the twelfth-century flowering of schools and learning. The demands for more literacy did not result directly in these developments of higher learning; their influence on literacy per se was, conversely, indirect.[25] Levels of literacy, although restricted, were almost certainly increasing in these centuries, both inside and outside the church.

## A. Germany

The late tenth- and early eleventh-century German kings were apparently literate to some extent in Latin and supporters of clerical learning. Some of their spouses also learned to read and write Latin: "Of the five kings of the Saxon house, only one, Henry I, seems to have been entirely illiterate." "The illiteracy of the masses can be taken for granted," as is commonly the case elsewhere.[26] What about the remainder of the laity? A complete disparagement of the state of learning and culture is no longer in order. Wallach, for example, maintains that "the process of education was never completely interrupted." Established monastic, episcopal, and rural schools continued to function. Educational institutions were built in the newly missionized sections of the Slavic East and in southeastern Europe.[27]

The institutions for education of the church, with some place for the laity in them, were most important; a specifically lay education does not seem to have developed in Germany in the first two or more centuries of the period. Firmly in the hands of the church, the training obtained was largely for clerics. Learning was associated closely with the needs of monasteries, cathedrals, and rural churches.

Schools seem to have been held in any convenient location, although an ordinance prohibited them from private homes or unauthorized places. Apparently, even under the control and supervision of the church, things could get out of hand! Schools were urged to take in poor scholars. Many of the institutions and scholars apparently achieved a high level of intellectual activity—in a variety of ecclesiastical settings. Yet, it was a rare community in which cultural and intellectual activities played more than a minor role. That is indicative not of popular literacy but rather of a developing scholarly life, based around the church and including mainly men of nonlocal origins.[28]

The church's cultural leadership was consistently stronger than its political leadership in these times of regular struggle between the emperors of the Holy Roman Empire and the emerging papal state. The schooling that existed under this arrangement was perhaps more "traditional" than in other parts of Europe. It consisted of the liberal arts, although few schools taught all seven arts and many did not progress much beyond grammar or rhetoric. In the tenth and eleventh centuries, schooling was advanced by the "renewal" of the church and the state. The use of literacy increased in both throughout the period. In addition, a more rudimentary grammar training was available under parish priests in rural schools of dioceses, and perhaps in some parishes as well. Lay participation never stopped, but in the tenth century it must have been quite low.[29]

In Germany as elsewhere, a growing number of persons, although probably a minute number, were becoming literate in the native tongues. For a more formal training in Latin literacy, we must concentrate on the upper classes of the laity: "There seem to be numerous indications that among the upper classes a liberal education was more common than is generally supposed."[30] In addition to the Latin writing produced in tenth-century Germany intended for ecclesiastics, there was also a literature more popular in nature and directed much to lay persons. By the last half of the twelfth century, the increase in writing in the vernacular, for literacy and documentary purposes, "breached the link between literacy and Latin, and vernacular literature from the oral tradition made its appearance in written form."

During these centuries, the extent of literacy, dependency on literacy, and the vernacular were simultaneously increasing. By the last half of the twelfth century, vernacular literature from the oral tradition began to appear in written form.[31] At first, an audience's experience and expectations for written literature were conditioned by Latin literature. Latin was learned for reading and writing; it was largely a literary language. Increasingly, it was used for specific communicative functions— as a learned language. Early vernacular literature developed in the same context, conditioned by Latin standards and expectations. The situation changed, partly because of structural differences between languages and their implications for use and partly because of the nature of written narrative.

Oral reading presented written texts to more illiterates, who gained familiarity with and some dependence on writing. They thus came to rely on and be partially oriented by literacy. But at this time, the experience was limited. The social stratification of literacy was only one of the contradictions that shaped changing communications and modes of literacy production.[32]

How did upper-class lay persons acquire their letters? There is evidence for tenth-century court schools, but it is unclear if a permanent or regular educational organization existed. Some decline in Latin schooling and literacy may have occurred, it has been surmised. It is also possible that positive developments in the ecclesiastical schools may have been temporally concomitant with negative ones, or perhaps a failure to improve, in lay literacy levels. That possibility reinforces the view that few laymen were sharing in the church's schools. Even more interesting is Thompson's observation that "throughout the Middle Ages a knowledge of liturgical Latin seems to have been more common among women than among men." Their knowledge was mostly elementary, and probably stressed rote memorization more than useful reading skills; nevertheless, it points to circumstances and motivations that could lead to improvement in female levels of literacy in these rather narrow social circles. Overall, there is little sign of much learning among the upper circles of German laity before the eleventh century.

By the twelfth century, an increase in lay literacy among the nobility and upper classes is indicated. Both cathedral and court schools probably were available to those lay families who could afford the expense and luxury. At the same time, those associated with court circles and the wealthy were beginning to urge the king to issue an edict that all rich men should see that their sons were educated in letters and law. That may have been an attempt to promote education for sons *not* destined for careers in the church; it also may have stemmed from the needs of a developing secular administration and government to secure trained bureaucrats to supplement or, in the context of empire-papal conflicts, supplant trained clerics in the chancellery.

Also developing was a knightly or chivalric culture no longer inimical to letters and literacy or a literature rooted in them. The tension that marked this transition is seen in Stephen of Limburg's statement on education: "a knowledge of letters is in no way detrimental to one who intends to become a knight, although it is of greater profit to one who intends to foresake the world." Stephen's tutelage of noble youths apparently included some instruction in letters, which suggests an increasing knowledge of literacy and Latin among the upper laity in the early twelfth century.

Even before the twelfth-century renaissance in Germany, the literacy of the upper ranks of the laity was not as low as it is often depicted, although Germany was clearly not among the front rank in the West. Lay education, perhaps permeating outward and downward from the courts, was attracting attention. It stimulated a new type of school, primarily in the towns, intended chiefly for instructing the laity in secular subjects. Education was no longer solely dependent upon Latin; the vernacular was emerging literarily.[33]

At work were forces that would eventually reshape the social structures of literacy. By the thirteenth century, with the development of trade and commerce in the towns of Germany, lay schools for the children of the commercial classes were being added to the educational landscape. This shift was only in the process of developing; as yet it influenced comparatively few. German educational development related to political and commercial development, rising in the twelfth and early thirteenth centuries and declining with the political dissolutions of the mid- to later thirteenth. This factor influenced "higher learning" perhaps more than the newly emerging literacy of the laity. The later, and probably more uneven, development of the economy was one important factor in the slower and later changes in literacy.[34] Germany's moment, in attempting to seize the Western leadership in literacy and learning, came three centuries later.

### B. France and Flanders

In the tenth century, after a brief time of intellectual emphases in the court of Charles the Bald at the end of the ninth century, a "long period of darkness in the history of lay literacy" fell upon France. Outside Aquitaine and Anjou, where the nobility maintained a tradition of culture and learning, rarely did laymen possess a knowledge of Latin. The traditional Vulgar Latin of Gaul had so changed by this time, on its way to becoming Old French, that it was fundamentally a different language from Latin. Latin remained the language of learning and literacy, in a strict sense, but was no longer used in ordinary speech. In general, few lay persons had either time or opportunity to gain their letters. Sons of the nobility intended for secular lives had little literacy training; their education stressed less bookish characteristics of feudal and early chivalric culture. Letters were considered the concern primarily of the clergy. Nevertheless, in the early tenth century, at least a few lay nobles were literate, whether educated privately by tutors at court or by an early stay in a monastery or bishop's household. The average lay person in France and the Low Countries was almost certainly illiterate.

In the south of France, literacy and learning apparently continued among at least a few upper-class families, most likely through private teaching, by parents or tutors at home. Latin was at least a bit more common than in the north, where the vernacular sufficed. French kings or nobility apparently were not instructed in Latin letters until the time of Robert II (the Pious) at the turn of the eleventh century (996–1031). In the later eleventh through the thirteenth centuries, literacy and some appreciation of learning were becoming common in the highest circles of the laity.[35]

As Latin literacy became the norm at this level, lay education was further developing, especially by the thirteenth century. Ironically, the vernacular was not only maturing and becoming more popular for literature, songs, and communication, it also was making deeper inroads into lay education even at the highest levels. As literacy was spreading, the status of *illitteratus* remained, confusing for the sources and complicating for the historian. Translation from Latin to the vernacular supported this development.

At the top of the social order, an impressive transition took place, from a tenth-century lack of schooling, representing perhaps a decline from the Carolingian and Merovingian accomplishments, to the eleventh century, in which it became more common for sons of the nobility to receive some instruction in letters. In the later eleventh and twelfth centuries, the well-to-do and higher-ranking lay families' children probably shared in the flourishing condition of French cathedral schools that contributed to the renaissance of the twelfth century. This process occurred in Flanders, too. Before the twelfth century, signs point to progress toward a higher level of lay literacy. A growing number of professionally educated laymen appeared, beginning to resemble their peers in Italy. Schooling opportunities were apparently increasing for at least the upper ranges of the laity. Teachers became more common, some of whom never took clerical orders; Paris attracted many of them.[36]

With the rise of these wandering scholars and teachers came a shift from cathedral schools to early university life, especially in Paris. Associated with the intellectual renaissance was also a gradual increase in the number of laymen who were interested in letters in their own right, aside from any utilitarian purpose. The situation changed by the next century, with rising interest in learning and increased numbers of masters and students. In some ways this progress was a consequence of economic prosperity and commercial development in France. "It was precisely these unattached and wandering clerks who contributed most heavily to the increase in literacy among the laity."[37] Simultaneously, French was also growing in significance as a language of cultured laymen.

The level of instruction provided and the level of social structure reached by this newly numerous group of teachers are unknown. L'Abbé Allain, writing in 1881, claimed evidence of rural parish schools in the twelfth century, as well as the presence of lay pupils in exterior schools of monasteries. If that is true, teachers in ecclesiastical vows could well have contributed to their numbers. Allain, however, exaggerates the extent of rural schools, although they may have been increasing by the thirteenth century; he also confuses diocesan with parochial schooling.[38] Even he finds the distribution of elementary instruction to be class-biased and stratified.

Latin instruction for the children of the lay upper classes was the primary area for the contribution of these teachers. However, it is unclear from how far down in the social order their pupils came and if they taught literacy in French as well as Latin. Since more and more lay persons were desirous of obtaining some degree of literacy, there was a demand for teachers' services. Not all of this demand would have been for Latin learning; a lower level of Latin and/or French literacy would have satisfied the needs of those seeking careers in commerce and trade and, indeed, some of those planning to enter the schools of the church or higher education at the expanding university centers in cities and towns.

The example of merchant education is revealing here. Some of the wealthiest merchants' sons had private training at home; others attended monastic and cathedral schools.[39] Where literacy was needed, apparently those most in need found it. Their means remain unclear, for it is not until the thirteenth century that city and town schools, outside the structures of clerical education, appear.

In the Low Countries, at least one town school is documented before the thirteenth century: at Gand, where the burghers took advantage of a fire in the church and opened a school of their own. Not surprisingly, these Flemish actions led to controversy and conflict between the laity and the church; the burghers of Ypres were excommunicated in the mid-thirteenth century for contesting the church's educational monopoly.[40] By this time, town schools, commonly taught by clerics but often controlled by merchants or a guild, were becoming more frequent. Much of their training was in Latin and stressed grammar. They were apparently also active in providing instruction in the vernacular and the skills required in commerce.[41]

These schools remain relatively unstudied. We do not know their extent in numbers or in pupils taught, or how far down the social ladder they reached. Their presence by the thirteenth century is documented for Italy and Flanders, the commercial leaders of the West; there may have been others. They broke at least partially with the classical grammatical Latin tradition and included at least some instruction in the vernacular and in manuscript writing. The rest of their curriculum, however, is unknown. Given the paucity of evidence, their association with the wealthy and the larger commercial trading centers, and their apparent concentration in Italy and Flanders, we should not exaggerate their impact on popular, lay rates of literacy before the fourteenth century, at the earliest. Their precedent did look forward.[42]

This development reflects again upon the declining use of Latin among the French and Flemish laity in the twelfth and early thirteenth centuries. Although it exacerbates the problem of determining the course of literacy, it should *not* be confused with a decline in the condition of lay culture. The opposite is closer to reality.

For the French, the second half of the twelfth century was a period of intense literary productivity, especially in epics and romances. When not derived from Celtic themes, their material was in large part drawn from classical sources. The romances were popular stories in vernacular literary form for the entertainment of laymen unable to understand Latin.[43] The vernacular literatures drew upon a variety of lay, classical, and religious influences. The developing lay culture, in France as in Italy, began to share with the church the guardianship of history, myth, and tradition; no longer did the authority of the church stand alone.[44]

In the centuries immediately preceding this period, Catholicism had incompletely penetrated the minds and behavior of the masses. The parish clergy were too few and unfit, intellectually and morally, for their work. Preaching, passing the Word orally, was the only potentially effective means given the conditions of mass illiteracy. It, however, was irregularly and ineffectually practiced. Clerical training and preaching, including some use of the vernaculars (a highly problematic area for the church), undoubtedly improved during this period. Popular religious practices probably improved as a result, but it is doubtful that they ever reached the complete "Christianization" of the people desired by the higher clergy.[45]

With literacy, people were probably brought somewhat closer to the official canons of the faith and the words of the sacred and holy books. Their beliefs and observations probably became more inflexible and correct. For some, literacy brought the ability to see the Word for themselves and to question the practices of the clergy and the church. Most people, however, were not reached directly by literacy; the church made a greater impact in their social and moral training and religious practices than before but hardly transformed them into the ideals that it sought to form. Their illiteracy was, in all probability, not the major reason for the church's incomplete victory and control.

The prominent dualism, or bilingualism, of the Middle Ages was another problem. In the eleventh through thirteenth centuries, contradictorily perhaps, both the vernaculars and Latin were flourishing, and changing. Both were revived and attended to; both seemed to be spreading, with literacy in them increasing. For the highly educated, Latin speech allowed special fluency. For educated priests and monks, and more laymen than previously, the old language retained a function in oral communication. Its role in writing was even more important.

Simultaneously, the vernaculars—Romance and Germanic tongues—were increasingly distinguished from Latin and from one another. The situation is curious, the results contradictory. Latin was not the only language in which instruction was offered, but it was the only language that was taught. The advance of linguistic separation and differentiation was complex; it was also in flux.[46]

New to society in the twelfth and thirteenth centuries was the beginning of literacy on a significant (though still restricted) scale in the vernacular among the laity, accompanied by the rise of literary works in the vernaculars. This sociolinguistic phenomenon was a major development in the history of literacy and culture. As they developed, regional differences were beginning to be reduced, although hardly erased.[47] National languages and cultures were developing, gradually touching more of the populations and tying people culturally and linguistically together. At the same time, this development had the impact of separating peoples by language and culture. The dynamic logic inherent in this contradiction became one of the engines of Western history, as nation-states emerged and conflicted with one another.

The use of Latin as the official, legal language for documents and writing also had the effect of disguising for the record the mode of expression in which business was transacted or documents received. Language, in other words, functioned to camouflage and distort the realities of both speech and writing. The currents of the twelfth and thirteenth centuries helped to resolve some of these problems, and the maturation of the vernaculars was in part a response to the imprecisions of Latin for self- and contemporary expression.

Language and literacy developed a close relationship with class or rank, wealth, and cultural levels. With the newer concern for literacy and learning among royalty and nobility came a stronger association than ever before, and one connection that would persist thereafter. The upper laity's earlier neglect of education was replaced by the twelfth century with a stress on education, for both pragmatic and cultural motivations.[48]

## C. England

The Norman invasions and conquest of the early to mid-eleventh century were clear obstructions to the further development of schooling and literacy in England. The promises of Alfred and his time were lost. English educational development lagged behind that of others in the West. The coming of the Normans led to the underdevelopment of the Anglo-Saxon and older English languages. With William and his successors, the French language came to prominence, bringing a period effectively of trilingualism, with the obvious complications. And with the Normans, Thompson argues, came *no* firm tradition of even a lettered nobility: even William's own literacy, in Latin, is in doubt.[49]

A new, gradually emerging tradition of education and Latin letters for the nobility and royalty began with William's children. The contribution of his wife, Mathilda, was instrumental. She was apparently familiar with Latin and may have wanted the same for her sons. Of the Conqueror's children, Adela and Henry I (called Beauclerk or the Scholar, though not until the fourteenth century) were well educated for their time and place. At least one of Henry's children, his natural son Robert, Earl of Gloucester, merits the reputation of a student and patron of letters. Other noblemen, and women, too, joined their numbers by the first half of the twelfth century. Henry II was apparently without peer as a patron of letters and learning for his time, but the Latin of his queen, Eleanor of Aquitaine, seems to be lacking. There is no doubt about their children. By the twelfth century, education for the royal family was the norm.[50]

The nobility were more acquainted with Latin letters than is typically assumed. However, a decline in the frequency of Latin literacy among the highest laity is suggested by the end of the century. The chief reason behind this apparent decline, which took place at the time of expanding grammar schooling for those somewhat lower, is probably the rise of the vernacular as a literary vehicle. That signifies the permeation of French, the language of the Anglo-Saxon aristocracy, among the English nobility, a strength it never held among the population at large.[51]

As elsewhere, the period from the end of the tenth through the thirteenth centuries was one of major transitions and transformations. Levels of literacy rose within the context of social restrictedness among the laity and clergy; town and commerce played their parts; the vernaculars developed and contributed to the spread of literacy; and a structure of agencies for education emerged. An England that lagged behind much of Europe at the onset of the period may well have risen to near the highest levels of literacy by the end of the thirteenth century.

The oral context that informed the use of written records slowed the progress of writing as a useful mode for record keeping. For example, for centuries the function of the Doomsday Book was symbolic rather than practical; legal questions were answered not by consulting it but by asking a jury of twelve knights to give *oral* testimony. The practice of consulting and ultimately depending on documents was established only gradually. For most of the period, memory remained in control of record keeping, with writing spreading but still the preserve of few persons.

Objects served as agents of mnemonic recording, symbolizing the business transacted. Symbolic mementoes were recognized as signs of recorded evidence until the early thirteenth century. The shift "from memory to written record" occurred, within sharp limits, between the times of William the Conqueror and Edward I: the growth of reliance on writing and the normal use of writing for government business and titles to property.[52] For some persons, literacy developed into new habits and uses, from recording to revising and storing for reuse. This development influenced the lives of many more, and pointed firmly to the future.

The first "triumph" of literacy was in the administration of the royal government, probably at the time of Henry II. It involved the extension of learning to those of knightly rank and modest fortune, on one hand, and, on the other, the desire and use of secular rulers to have the written word reshape the arts of governing. Richardson and Sayles argue that for this class and for administrative development, the twelfth century was critical. By that time, it may be presumed that a man of noble birth would have had the opportunity to learn Latin letters in his youth. Laymen who exercised offices demanding the use of written instruments were literate, as were clerks called upon to exercise an office in the church. At the same time, no great learning, ease of reading, or extensive Latin needed accompany this literacy.

> In a population that cannot have exceeded, even if it attained, two millions, some hundreds of literate laymen would suffice to do all the business that professed clerks did not perform. . . . It would seem, however, that while, in the second half of the twelfth century, a command of Latin implied a command of French, there were those who could write in the vernacular but who were ignorant of Latin. For the requirements of public administration such a limited qualification was inadequate. At the same time, the Latin vocabulary, even of royal clerks, might be very limited and might need to be eked out, on occasion, with French.

This conclusion, if not generalized beyond the upper laity, nobility, and knights, marks a civilization newly conditioned by literacy. Literacy was now required more often by administration; noble and knightly educational habits were changing; and the two came together in a greater frequency of literacy in these ranks and a larger utility for a functional, pragmatic literacy.[53]

Below this level were the lower officials, bailiffs, sheriffs, and other laymen who came to account at the exchequer and would be in increasing contact with written documents in the twelfth and thirteenth centuries. Literacy, it seems, had begun to be diffused into these ranks, and more were literate in the twelfth and thirteenth centuries, although the diffusion was probably not yet complete. What remains important, however, is that clerical tasks shifted from clerics to laymen, without divided loyalties to church and state.[54] No universality in lay literacy was required for this achievement; a firm and significant increase, within the medieval context of restricted literacy, was sufficient, and by no means diminishes its importance.

Manuscript production at this time was largely the preserve of scribes. After the twelfth century, it shifted from monasteries to royal bureaucracies, urban notaries, and university centers. Manuscripts were expensive, primarily because they were produced by hand and not because the cost of parchment was high. Paper did not appear in England much before the fourteenth century.

Different scripts were used for different documents. Cursive script and new layouts developed to meet new demands. The trend was away from elaborately copied manuscripts, and toward documents written economically and legibly. Books became smaller; portability and readability became a greater concern. Silent reading was spreading, too.[55]

Latin and French were largely the languages of written record in this period; not until the thirteenth and especially the fourteenth centuries did English begin to make headway in contemporary writing, although it was the most common spoken language. Eleventh- through thirteenth-century England witnessed a rich trilingualism. The future of English as a written language was assured not by scribes but by writers who promoted various forms of spoken English to the status of a literary language. Written and spoken language differed radically. The former usually derived not from the speech of the majority of people, but from tradition, political authority, and social status. "Those who read or wrote had to master a variety of languages. They passed from English to French or Latin, and some to Hebrew as well, frequently without comment and perhaps without effect."[56] *Mass* literacy does *not* result from a trilingual context.

By the thirteenth century, literacy had undoubtedly increased. Royalty, nobility, knights, merchants, and clergy were overwhelmingly literate. Among artisans, literacy was probably more common, but it was nowhere near universal. Among the peasantry, it must have remained a rarity, but not a complete implausibility.[57] Nevertheless, the rise of literacy to these new levels took place in a context that owed much to tradition and oral culture. "For the people at large, the irreducible minimum of Christian teaching—namely the Lord's Prayer and the Creed—was to be recited in Latin, while sermons, homilies and the like were expressed in the vernacular." Memory and memorization, listening and learning constituted this education. The growth in lay literacy was real, and it was not stimulated overly by recreational or self-improvement motivations.

The relationship between literate and oral culture was dialectical. Oral ways persisted, slowed, and shaped the impact of literacy, and were in turn influenced by written culture. Preliterate habits continued long after written records had become common. Spoken words continued to be considered better evidence than written ones; bureaucratic and diplomatic procedures developed to incorporate the evidence and the force of the two together. Only slowly and cautiously was the written word accepted. Much business was still conducted orally; documents were certain to remain relatively rare until printing made reproduction simpler and quicker. New laws and regulations were usually published by proclamation—a quick and efficient mode of communication in crowded places such as London, but its efficacy in the countryside could be different. Rural resistance and ignorance were one result. Publication by public reading incorporated the vernacular as well as the Latin. Only in time did the written gain equal status with the oral; a much lengthier period was required for it to gain the upper hand.[58]

Listening remained for most people the road to information and to learning. Literacy could supplement it, directly or indirectly, but not in this period supplant it. Reading itself remained oral, and often social, for many literates. Whole books were "published" by reading them aloud; most literature was received orally. Latin punctuation developed to assist such readers. Writing meant dictating first, and copying second. Reading aloud and dictating permitted the nonliterate or the semi-literate a fuller participation in the use of documents and the transmission of culture than reading and writing in the modern silent sense ever do.[59]

In England, as elsewhere, economic prosperity and the development of trade and commerce also contributed to the extension of literacy, especially in towns and cities, and to changes in the structure of schooling. The factors responsible for this development included international trade in some cases; the needs of localities were instrumental in many others.[60]

With urban and commercial development came the need and demand for schooling. New forms of organization among first merchants and later artisans and craftspersons, the guilds that began to ask for and then to receive some authority over trade and urban government also began to develop educational functions. They established schools for merchants' children, lay schools, and in some cases began to open them to other children in the towns. Starting gradually in the twelfth century, this function became more important, and the guilds were almost ubiquitous by the thirteenth.[61]

For this reason and others, "presumably the standard of lay literacy was always higher in the towns than in the country." This level only increased between the eleventh and thirteenth centuries. Towns, by Reynolds's assessment, were relatively well provided with schools; by 1180, for example, London had enough pupils to engage in public disputations. These schools, however, were often not well established or stable.[62]

The increasing scale of urban government added to the engine of royal and commercial needs in creating demand and need for literacy among some urban residents. The scope of municipal government was regulated by the liberties a town could secure from the king. Civil jurisdiction, including the law merchanra, registration of deeds and wills, probate of wills, wardship and widow supervision, and nuisance cases, provided much business for town courts and administrations. These could take up a good deal of time, and demanded at least a minimal use of literacy by an increasing number of laymen. So did correspondence. As towns struggled for greater autonomy, to control trade and protect town traders and consumers against outside competition and exorbitant tolls, needs for civil literacy skills and for administration grew.[63]

As elsewhere, merchants and financiers "could not have pursued their calling on any large scale without the use of written instruments," which either they or their clerks had to write and read. Town schools, along with church schools, contributed to meeting these newer needs. Some schools of *ars notaria*, virtually commercial training schools, may have developed before the fourteenth century to teach letter and legal document drafting, accounting, and some law.[64]

The English legal profession also emerged during the thirteenth century. Although it did not become well organized for another two centuries, the achievement of a fair ability of literacy was obviously required. From the mid-thirteenth century, numerous books for legal reference and memoranda for law and administration became common. Legal reporting also dates from the last years of the thirteenth century. Outside the cities, treatises on estate management date from the end of the century.[65]

The work of schooling the children and youth progressed in schools of various kinds and levels.[66] If studies can be trusted, some elementary training in letters (chiefly in Latin, but increasingly in English) went on in a surprisingly wide range of agencies, including *grammar schools* (of cathedral churches, monasteries, collegiate churches; hospital, guild, and town schools; and the debated chantries), which "flowered" in medieval England but stressed the liberal arts; the *parish primary schools*, which met irregularly (in elementary chantry schools, churches, and priests' homes), were poorly documented, and varied with the ability and interest of the instructor; *specialized schools* (song schools, writing schools, reading schools, and ABC schools); and *informal opportunities*.

Literacy learning took place in circumstances that owed most to the past; few curricular or pedagogical innovations took place during these centuries. Although books—in manuscript—and texts became somewhat more widely available in the twelfth and thirteenth centuries, they seem to be decidedly secondary to the oral and rote bases of literacy instruction in the classrooms. Certainly their contribution to elementary education was minor. Primary schooling, which was the basis for the transmission of literacy, remained the least efficient, least organized, and most irregular aspect of the evolving system of schools.

The most important development of this period, which occurred within *both* clerical and lay educational circles, was the growth—in number of institutions, their apparent quality, and the size of their audiences—that took place before the fourteenth century.[67] In medieval England, as elsewhere in the West, schools were only one small part of the larger educational socialization of the people; they touched only a minority of the children. Nevertheless, although often informal, tiny, and irregular, they seem to have been the main means for learning literacy even then.

The most numerous opportunities for basic instruction in letters are, necessarily, the most obscure. These were the irregular, often casual schools held in parish churches and in the homes of parish clergy. Instruction was aimed at preparing children for grammar schooling and clerical careers. A fairly impressive number of students who desired and could afford the time and leisure probably gained their literacy in this way. Some went on to lay or clerical grammatical training, while others went no further.[68] Neither systemized nor organized, this instruction represented an incontestable foundation for the educational arrangements of the period.

Despite strident criticism, the song and reading schools were also important elements in the basic layers of school provision. Among schools that appear in the records, their presence is stronger, documentarily, than that of the parish schools; they therefore *seem* more common and have been interpreted by most as the lowest or elementary form of schooling. These schools were continuous throughout the period, and may have been among the most important types of elementary agencies before the Reformation.[69]

ABC schools also grew in number in this period, and especially in the next. Much of the instructional work, such as it might be, fell to the parish clerk, the sexton, clerical students in minor orders, or, in a small rural parish, the priest himself; that seems as true for reading schools and ABCs as it was for song schools and parish elementaries. Teaching was undoubtedly simple in most instances, and probably in the first two was relatively free from overlapping with the elements of grammar and preparation for clerical careers. Nonetheless, some advantaged children progressed into grammar schools, while some few fortunate youngsters from poorer families found further schooling possible through selection for a career in the church. Here luck, in the form of a kindly or searching parish priest, was probably more important than a pupil's ability or intentions.[70]

Writing schools, emphasizing notarial and secretarial skills over reading, are almost impossible to locate before the fourteenth century. Writing was not automatically coupled with reading as a part of elementary training. It was more a part of later elementary or more commonly secondary or grammar schooling, and more a part of the curriculum of the newer lay schools in the towns and cities than of the more traditional church-sponsored schools that dominated educational opportunities. Writing was still seen first as a technology, the "scrivener's art." A specialized craft, it was associated with commerce, church administration, monastic copying, and civil administration rather than with general education.[71]

Before 1300, and even later, there was no rigid division separating song, reading, and grammar schools. Separate and established elementary schools became common only toward the end of the medieval period, especially with foundations and endowments from the fourteenth and early fifteenth centuries to the Reformation.

According to the extant records, most places with a school had but one, and that was a grammar school (in the towns, at least).[72] These schools were found in cathedral and collegiate churches, in some monasteries that continued to admit lay children, and by the thirteenth century in towns and cities under lay control. Their numbers were increasing from the twelfth through the fifteenth centuries.[73]

To understand the evident increase in literate persons in this period in England, on one hand, and the increase in educational institutions (which need not in itself imply the former), on the other, we must flexibly approach the existing configuration of agencies for instruction. While pointing to the parish schools, informal education, and reading, song, and ABC schools that existed and are underrepresented in the evidence, we must also allow for elementary training that took place in institutions that appear to be secondary or higher schools. Well-studied cathedral schools, the declining monastery schools (which instructed the youths of nobles and some poorer students in almonry schools), collegiate church schools, town and guild schools, and hospital schools (of which few examples have been found, especially before the fourteenth century) must be noted. Excepting the monastery schools, which increasingly discouraged admission of lay students, the others were increasing in number, and perhaps also in quality, during the twelfth and especially the thirteenth centuries; they continued to multiply in the next period.

Within the cathedral schools, for example, were chantries and song schools that taught "the rudiments of a general education" as well as chanting. Almonries, infirmaries, and hospitals, as parts of cathedral centers, sometimes also included provision for schooling, often for poorer boys seeking entry into the clergy.

Collegiate church schools were numerous and increasing. Although of a distinctly clerical character, these schools were open to lay pupils. The liberal arts, divinity, and preparation for both constituted the curricula. Little is known about hospitals (typically almshouses for the poor), especially their frequency. With numerous but small schools, grammar was a part of their studies, but the fate of the school depended totally upon that of the institution.[74]

In these schools, as well as those of towns and guilds, opportunities for the local laity were not unusual. Their instruction was encouraged by papal decrees and episcopal urging. Much of it was elementary. A strict division by pupil levels or firm prerequisites of grammar education were neither fundamental nor universal. Despite an official stress on Latin learning in the tradition of the liberal arts and the religious orientation and general control of studies, "many people who studied grammar . . . were less interested in its linguistic and literary aspects than in its practical uses in the administrative and commercial spheres of life. . . ." Even a short period spent learning only elementary Latin could be useful and in demand.[75]

For elementary studies, the alphabet was the first task confronted. Learning the letters, it seemed, had progressed pedagogically remarkably little from the ancient and earlier medieval methods. Instruction was overwhelmingly oral and repetitive. A procedure of harshly disciplined, rote, and oral memory learning for grammar was, if anything, worse at the elementary level. With few texts, and primers or hornbooks rare, the letters were drummed individually into the pupils' minds; when the letters were committed to memory, they began on the syllables, finally advancing to whole words. After an arduous, unexciting, and invariant process, they began to confront passages, phrases, and sentences.

Students cut their reading teeth on a diet of religious miscellany. Whether wholly by rote, or from cardboard and primer, they read aloud repeatedly the basic prayers and elements of the faith. Later, reading was practiced from the available church service books.[76] This method was not an effective way to develop good reading abilities, useful skills, or a desire for further reading. Obstacles to learning to read were many; learning in a language that differed from the one the child spoke was just one of the many difficulties.[77]

Although seven years was the "standard" age for beginning one's schooling, some favored children began earlier, with instruction in letters at home by parents or tutor, or other informal means of preschooling. Others were not so advantaged: "many people, whose need, desire or opportunity for education came only in later life, must have learnt their first letters at a much later age."

Girls and women appear very rarely in the records that relate to learning. Women, with important exceptions, stood with most of the peasantry, laborers, the poor, villeins and serfs, and many of the craftsmen, artisans, and lesser traders, outside the restricted opportunities for schooling. Although the nunneries were inferior in wealth and numbers, they remained the single most important source for female literacy and learning, among women in orders and noble daughters who attended their schooling. Some of their products were distinguished.

Among the laity beyond the nobility, only the wives and daughters of the wealthy and well-born enjoyed the leisure and surplus wealth that allowed some education. For those able to gain some schooling, reading allowed many religiously inclined ladies to pursue their piety in holy writings; others indulged more directly and individually in poetry and romances. Those with property or with family in commerce and trade could assist or substitute for a spouse in managing affairs, corresponding, and the like.[78] Those who did not gain their literacy in the nunneries either learned informally from chaplains or other literate persons in their company or attended one of the elementary schools (some of the latter apparently included a few girls at times). Female schooling, when available, seldom included as much of Latin or the liberal arts as was open to boys; socially, it was even more highly restricted and hierarchically stratified.[79]

In England, by the eve of the fourteenth century, impressive developments in literacy and schooling had taken place. Royal administration, greater efforts among the clergy, growth of trade, commerce, and towns, and spread of the vernacular all contributed to this increase. Developments in society, polity, and economy were reciprocally related to those in literacy.

The context of the medieval period was not, however, broken. Despite the emergence of a new lay interest in literacy and lay supervision of schools, which led them into conflicts with the church, education remained more religious than not. Public, secular schools of towns and guilds were almost invariably taught by clerics, often in explicit compromise with the local bishop or head of a collegiate church or monastery. The ecclesiastical bases of education remained dominant; neither the shifting role of the vernacular nor lay initiatives or commercial and administrative needs led to a new breakthrough. The church no longer held a monopoly, but its role was still commanding. There was no hint of the passing of that role. Demand was only beginning to shift away from the church's traditional and almost total presence among those who sought and used literacy and education; the laity, in a variety of ways, were moving toward new uses and starting to seek new agencies to meet their needs.

This period saw the budding of new ideas that would develop into additional legacies of literacy. For the time being, literacy and schooling, with all their expansion during this era, remained restricted.[80]

For most of the population, of England and elsewhere, literacy was not required for their lives, well-being, or even religious observations. "Religious instruction was less a stimulus to thought or skill than an addition to ritual invocation. . . ."[81] For most, the written message diffused orally into their culture of sound and sight. In the church or chapel, images no doubt stimulated their minds more than Latin services. Few children, especially from rural villages, reached any school. Few had much use for literacy. That fact is as significant in understanding the parameters of medieval literacy as the impressive increases that took place. If it contradicted the concurrent fact that "medieval civilization was a literate civilization; the knowledge indispensable to the functioning of medieval society was transmitted in writing," that was inherent in the nature of the historical reality.[82]

### 4. Thought, Theory, and Practice

In its rather rigidly hierarchical conception of society, rooted in estates seen as venerable and lasting, ordained by the Lord and static in its immobility, much of the thinking of the times was out of touch with the evaluation within society, polity, and economy. Scholastic theologians and philosophers, representatives of state and church, took great pains to include within their mental boundaries a world in transition and flux.[83] The results were not always consistent or satisfactory, either to contemporaries or to later observers.

In this conception of society, there was little attention to schooling. Most of what there was came relatively late in the medieval era, and was addressed to the education of princes, nobility, and the wealthiest of laymen—those who required schooling to prepare them for the best use of their offices, their decision making, and their cultural standing. This schooling was education in Christian character building, in intellectual cum moral thought and understanding: "moral education in gradual development is to be attended to all the time." The scholastic side of mental training stressed not gaining information but "the quickness of intellect which logic or dialectic would bring." Scripture and its study typically took first place over literature. The vernacular literatures slowly made their entry. Early schooling did not as yet receive the attention that higher studies did.[84]

Only in contrast to its silence was medieval social thought confronted with the development of lay education, more pragmatic sorts of schooling, and training for those in the middle or even lower ranks in society. The dearth of thought about lay and functional literacy and schooling indicates that thinkers thought very little about schooling outside the upper laity and the clergy. England had laws that forbade those bound to a lord of the manor to send their children to school without paying a fine or dues. This prohibition reflects efforts to socially control the masses and restrict freedom of movement for labor force needs, but it also reveals a state of mind that saw no reason for such persons to attend schools and learn letters. The exceptions were those who were able to secure priestly training to rise above their origins into the clergy and those who migrated to towns, gaining some literacy there. Conflicts between merchants and guilds in the towns and cities and the medieval church are but one sign of the assumptions of social thought held by the clergy confronting new ideas arising out of commerce and social needs. Other factors, including the monopolistic rights of local churches and clerical schoolmasters over the supply of teaching, were important, too.

The clergy and nobility required education, increasingly more of it, to perform their clerical and civil tasks: protecting the church, augmenting the faith, defending the people, maintaining public prosperity, combating violence and tyranny, and confirming peace.[85] The rest of the people apparently did not. One key question is: How far did the extension of literacy contradict social ideas? Lay and pragmatic training, which aimed at neither professional labors for church nor state and was outside the control of the church, certainly did. How far down the ranks of the social structure it permeated, we cannot be certain. Within the fundamentally religious thought, conceptions, and spiritually ordered universe that shaped medieval thinking, the new developments had little place. It is surprising that no more conflict is recorded. That, of course, came later, along with new theories and social thought that accorded a more prominent place to the education of the people. Here again, we see the restrictedness and the limits of the Middle Ages, despite their achievements.[86]

꙾

# CHAPTER FOUR

# Ends and Beginnings: The Fourteenth and Fifteenth Centuries

FROM THE LATE THIRTEENTH THROUGH the mid- to late fourteenth centuries, renewed forces of destruction came to the West. Economic stagnation set in; war broke out all over the Continent; food shortages were very real and severe. The great plague of the Black Death swept over Europe, leaving massive population loss, lowered labor productivity, and deep scars on the minds of millions. Heresy was rife. The Great Schism tore the universal church in two from 1378 until 1416. Popular revolts became common. Recovery was slow until the fifteenth century. For most of the period between the 1270s and 1470s, stability and prosperity were swept away. This context naturally affected the courses of literacy and schooling; both educational agencies and the transmission of literacy were challenged, but the mechanisms for improving levels of literacy withstood the pressure. Contradictorily, outpourings of piety and searchings for faith stimulated educational expansion. In fact, by the last part of the fifteenth century, when printing was just beginning to have an impact and the origins of a postmedieval world were gradually fitting themselves into place, education and literacy may well have reached new levels.[1]

After the great disasters, Europe was a smaller community in 1500 than it had been in 1300, but per capita productivity was probably higher. By the fifteenth century, recovery and new prosperity for many, renewed development of trade and commerce, expansion of the European world system, and a new context for educational development and literacy had been created.[2]

The consequences for the state of education and literacy were important yet surprisingly contradictory. Over the two centuries literacy and educational levels undoubtedly increased, but development was hardly simple or linear. The impact of war, plague, famine, and death was immediate and direct. Educational opportunities decreased; nevertheless, literacy rates may actually have risen. The greatest losses from the disasters were felt among the poor, the laboring classes, and the rural populations—those for whom educational opportunities and literacy were least frequent; conversely, those more likely to be literate were more likely to have survived. The result of this complex situation may actually have been a relative increase in the proportion of literates in the population of survivors, even though the absolute numbers of both literates and illiterates certainly fell.

The great human wastage claimed the lives of many literate persons in clerical, municipal, or royal administrative positions. Teachers, lawyers, clerks, and other literates needed to be replaced. The church, in its efforts to combat lay learning and, especially, heresy and popular bewilderment over the disasters and plagues, required more, and better-educated, clergy. For others, such as the Italian humanists, education was seen as a necessity for finding the path to a virtuous and good life. With per capita incomes rising and governmental and ecclesiastical bureaucracies increasing in size and in their use of writing at all levels, "new jobs called for more men who could at least read and write, and the numbers of the educated continued to swell. . . ."[3]

Urban life continued with little interruption. With greater demands for labor and higher wages, more families could at least consider some schooling for their children. With renewed urban growth came more lay schools. Three developments whose origins we can place in the twelfth and, especially, the thirteenth centuries came increasingly to the fore in fueling new levels of schooling and literacy: education in the vernaculars; schooling of an appreciable number of students whose families were not "wealthy"; and greater secularization of learning. Although the shifts in progress were gaining strength and significance, they were not surpassing the clerical and Latin orientation of medieval education. A monumental transition was under way; its progress is best seen as more relative than absolute. Most learning was firmly regarded as an underpinning of Christianity. A large share of the contributions to the church that resulted from the human response to dearth and death went to support education, including endowed schools, especially grammar schools; song schools; chantries and colleges.

From the context of contradictions and continuities that moved Western society from the thirteenth into the declines and suffering of the fourteenth century and the recoveries of the later fourteenth and fifteenth centuries came first a decline in institutions and opportunities for literacy and education, then a rise to new levels.[4] The "one thousand years" that constituted the history of medieval Western civilization culminated in the last half of the fifteenth century. The West stood between the Middle Ages and (early) modernity. Continuities were strong, contradictions persisted, and novelties were present. An important end was approaching; new beginnings were at hand.

Restrictions of class, sex, wealth and status, region, and technology and culture were being dented, but overall they held strongly. Some few "enlightened" thinkers began to speak about mass schooling, but such epochal reforms were well in the future. Cultural continuities continued to be important; educational transitions, new levels of lay literacy and vernacular instruction, and the impact of the printing press took place in a context shaped by them. Lines of differentiation developed among regions and states; these national differences influenced the histories of literacy and education.

### 1. Humanism and the Italian Renaissance

In the early fourteenth century the city state of Florence was the proverbial jewel at a time at which economic and cultural development in the cities and towns of Italy stood at the pinnacle of Western achievements. Its merchants and bankers led in the vast expansion of the Italian economy.[5] Dominated by an upper bourgeoisie, the arts and culture were highly patronized; high culture flourished.

Literary and commercial educations were available to boys.[6] There were also lay schools of rhetoric. Canon law may have been taught in the cathedral school of S. Giovanni, and some civil law in notarial schools. Private instruction in Latin certainly had a long tradition in the city, and notarial schooling dates at least to the thirteenth century. Teachers, including women, appear in the records well before the fourteenth century, and included elementary and classical grammar instructors. At the turn of the fourteenth century, a new enthusiasm for the classical authors and a distinct cultural advance occurred. Much of the educational development resulted from the efforts of secular teachers. Religious schools, with their monopoly on elementary and higher instruction, also increased their influence.[7]

A series of structures for schooling was articulated in Florence by the late thirteenth and early fourteenth centuries. With humanism also came expanded opportunities for some girls.[8] A variety of kinds of training, from devotional to theological or lay and commercial, was available to an impressively large number of persons.

The rate of adult literacy was probably in the range of 25 to 35 percent, with sharp differentials by sex, status, wealth, and occupation. There was no emphasis placed on literacy for women, but daughters of well-to-do families could secure some schooling (or home instruction). (See table 4.1 for basis of estimates.)[9] The great expansion in lay literacy and educational participation struck strongly at those in the middle ranks of society, whose own careers and those of their male children could be facilitated by literacy: in trade, commerce, and finance; church and clerical administration; or public and civic administration. Women are rarely included in these expanding numbers of literacy-related occupations. If it were possible to correct for these biases of class and sex, the (potential) male literacy rate would be higher, the female correspondingly lower. For the time, the levels of schooling and literacy were very impressive achievements.[10]

Literacy was seen increasingly as a commodity with functional and economic value in the commercial context of fourteenth-century Italy. This attitude, of investing in education in hopes for future success, was spreading throughout the West. A new legacy had been founded.

Educational opportunities on such a scale played other roles in Florence. The size, quality, and variety of educational arrangements, including apprenticeship, helped to draw talented and ambitious persons from other areas. Florence's attraction for men with professional training is seen in the flow of petitions from lawyers, notaries, and physicians from elsewhere who desired Florentine citizenship. The city's underwriting, through patronage and forms of public recognition, brought and held many persons of intellectual and artistic ability.

This flowering of art and literature accompanied the achievements of literacy and schooling. However, such a relationship is neither sufficient nor necessary. Intellectual achievements of a high level are not a direct or simple consequence of a large amount of primary or even secondary training. Intellectual flowerings may occur with a low rate of literacy or schooling; conversely, mass literacy and education are no guarantees of high-quality literacy production, artistic achievements, or scientific or technical advances. Artistic, scientific, and technical progress depend

TABLE 4.1
## School Enrollment Levels, Florence, 1339, after Villani

| | |
|---|---|
| Boys and girls learning to read | 8,000–10,000 |
|     Midpoint | 9,000 |
| Total population | 90,000 |
| Those learning to read as a percentage of the total population | 10% |
| 0–14 year-olds as a percentage of the total population* | 38.7% |
| 6–7 to 11–12 year-olds as a percentage of the 0–14 years old cohort | 50% |
| Those learning to read (6–7 to 11–12 years old) as a percentage of the total population | 19–20% |
| Those learning to read as a percentage of those aged 6–7 to 11–12: *Elementary enrollment rate* | 50% |
| | |
| Those continuing on to commercial training | 1,000–1,200 |
|     Midpoint | 1,100 |
|     As a percentage of those who learn to read | 12.2% |
|     As a percentage of boys (assuming parity at elementary level and only boys continuing) | 24.4% |
| | |
| Those continuing on to Latin schooling (grammar) | 550–600 |
|     Midpoint | 575 |
|     As a percentage of those who learned to read | 6.4% |
|     As a percentage of boys (assuming parity at elementary levels and only boys continuing) | 12.8% |

*This percentage is derived from data presented in David Herlihy and Christine Klapisch-Zuber, *Les Toscans et leur families*, p. 375. It is for Florence in 1427.

on many factors other than literacy and schooling. In fact, it has been argued that their "literacies" are distinctive and not very comparable to those of letters.[11] To understand the educational and cultural achievements of early Renaissance Italy in Florence and in other cities requires proceeding beyond the system of schooling. Economic development explains much of the progress in lay schooling.

A large proportion of the population lived in towns and cities, despite the primarily agrarian nature of the economy. Most persons worked on the land; yet, the character of society and culture was heavily influenced by urbanization. Within the cities, four principal classes constituted the social hierarchy: the lower class— the peasantry and urban proletariat of the great towns, "enjoying a primitive folk culture of song and story, but largely untouched by the higher culture of the age"; the lesser bourgeoisie, artisans and shopkeepers, "who, despite a constant struggle to maintain their economic position, could sympathize with some at least of the Italian literature of the day, and who produced from their ranks some of the best-known artists of the time"; the upper bourgeoisie, with a wide range of status and income; and the aristocracy. The sentiments and intellectual background of the latter two classes were similar. There was frequent intermarriage between them and imitation of aristocratic modes of life by the bourgeoisie.[12] That involved the cultural development of the upper classes, with a use of education and literacy distinct from its pragmatic employment for commercial or administrative purposes.

The upper bourgeoisie dominated Italy, shaping the most important aspects of society and giving the greatest patronage to the arts. Reading and writing were only one aspect of this larger, more rational ordering of life. The latter included *portolan* maps, double-entry bookkeeping, and the mechanical clock.[13]

Literacy took its place among a larger constellation of emergent transformations. Its role was less causal than were the changing effects of larger social forces. Rationality and enterprise became by the fourteenth century major forces that would expand Europe well beyond its territorial boundaries and remake the world, with the West dominant. Literacy contributed to these forces; its uses were many. That is one aspect of its new secular roles.

Literacy also related to the late medieval cultural and intellectual movements of humanism and the Renaissance. The consequences for literacy from these movements, however, are less clear than typically mentioned and are differentiated between these two cultural currents. An analytic and conceptual distinction should be maintained between humanism (whose origins date from the late thirteenth century) and the Italian Renaissance, which was stimulated in large part by humanism (which emerged by the mid-to later fourteenth and fifteenth centuries).

Humanism, the historian Lauro Martines asserts, was "A Program for Ruling Classes."[14] As an intellectual development predating the mid-fourteenth century, humanism implied not a specific outlook but an area of study: the intensive study of the classics and the world of antiquity. Philosophically, it focused on man in society and strongly emphasized civic consciousness. Humanists studied grammar, rhetoric, poetry, history, and moral philosophy from Latin and, less frequently, Greek texts.[15] From late-thirteenth-century developments in France, which stemmed from medieval Latin studies, humanism began to "take off" in the next generation, becoming a central element in the Italian cultural scene.

In the fourteenth century, local political events in the city-states resolved important questions about the allocation of power. Political life regained stability, and the ruling classes became more secure. At this point, elites turned to cultural and intellectual programs that seemed attuned to their positions. Humanists, largely men outside the elites and with middling origins, were able to win positions and patronage; they could gain for themselves and also establish their idealistic program in the social and political structures of the day.[16]

Just as humanism was developing its base within Italian high culture, the mid-century crises came. Plague followed famine; the population declined; production in agriculture, commerce, and industry fell. Economic decline stimulated political instability and conflict. Up to at least 1380, profound pessimism and renunciation of life were not infrequent human emotional expressions. Many turned to religion. Provision of education and literacy for the many could not be sustained. The lack of records about elementary instruction and the number learning to read is revealing. That is impressive testimony to change, and most likely decline, since there is so much evidence about other kinds of intellectual activities.[17]

The enthusiasm for humanism, as "the program for ruling classes," during the middle decades of the fourteenth century is not difficult to understand. Government demanded skills in expression: elegance in diplomatic correspondence, propaganda, and orations at state occasions. In councils and courts, speeches had to carry the force of conviction. For these purposes, the style and manner of the ancient world exercised a strong attraction, especially in times of uncertainty and loss of leaders from death. In the first half of the century, humanists in Venice and Verona were taking skilled places in government service.[18] The close relationship between classical study and style and social prestige and power grew rapidly from the second half of the fourteenth century through the mid-fifteenth.

Francesco Petrarch (1304–1374) was the principal in its consolidation, expansion of disciplines, and promotion. Others modified and extended his ideals, but it was Petrarch who established the classical world as model and ideal. Humanism was seen as neither exclusively an applied field nor a sedentary scholarly one. Nevertheless, it was *not* one for the popular classes or closely related to changes in literacy. Interest in the Roman past was not isolated among scholars. During the second half of the thirteenth and first half of the fourteenth centuries, a large number of translations from the classics into the Italian vernacular were made. These translations reflected popular interest in the past and stimulated an even more widespread fascination. Even friars, with a concern for public taste, "laced their sermons with popularised classical knowledge."[19]

This aspect of humanism was secondary. Humanism envisioned a specific course of study and a particular kind of citizen; it was meant neither for pure contemplation or prayer nor for the urban community writ large. its orientation was that of practical life in society, and as such it was intended for the men most likely to hold positions of leadership. Most of all, it was an educational idea for the well-placed. The educational thrust of humanist teachers was traditional as well as innovative. Latin grammar was the fundamental discipline on which all learning and doctrine depended. Latin remained the medium for educated men—and in this sense, education was *not* synonymous with literacy.

The educational assumptions of humanism that underlay much of the Renaissance not only were closely associated with an urban sociopolitical elite, they were also allied with that elite's ideology. A complete humanistic schooling required support of the student at least until the age of seventeen. This relatively expensive and lengthy period of leisure and nonproductivity limited the numbers and class for whom such a training was possible. For even in the households of rich merchants, boys usually entered the family business at the age of thirteen or fourteen, unless they were intended for the church; in lower-middle-class and artisanal families, sons began to learn their trades at the ages of seven or eight. Not all of those able to afford or to benefit from a humanist education secured it.[20]

Rhetoric was the humanists' highest aim: in writing as well as speech. The perfect orator united virtue and wisdom and achieved classical heights of grandeur and virtuosity. Regardless of the requirements of private men, public men had to learn the art. On the humanists' agenda, rhetoric represented the pinnacle in "applied humanities."

History was important, too. The humanists' attitude toward it was elitist, selective, self-interested, and linked to values of worldly success. Their hierarchy of interest is revealing: first came classical Rome and especially Greece, then the history of one's own city and recent-contemporary history. All other historical subjects, except certain historical sections of the Bible, found no place. History presented examples of virtue and vice; it offered the outline for a science of politics. In the classical past, the humanists sought images of themselves and their own world, and guides for their actions. Thus, they focused on urban life, orators, and public men.

Florentine humanists were unequivocally committed to oligarchical republicanism. Consequently, they applauded the literary and political lives of republican Rome and traced the origins of Florence to that time. The Roman principiate attracted even greater praise. "All humanists, whatever their stripe, made a candid alliance with power. . . ."[21] After the mid-fifteenth century, as conditions changed, they stressed more positively the value of a contemplative life. Whatever their priority, humanists and their moral-civic visions remained overwhelmingly aristocratic. "In short, the highest humanist good resided with the happy few, with those who had the political rank for grand action or the virtues and economic resources for leisurely study."

Thus, humanism was indeed "a program for the ruling classes." Its relevance to the history of literacy or popular learning was secondary at best. Humanists themselves saw little relationship for their ideals as preparation even for the professions of law and medicine, which they tended to scorn as "mere money-making pursuits." The impact of humanism, with implications for the Renaissance to follow, was felt among a select few. As an educational or intellectual endeavor, the overlapping connection with power and privilege could not be broken.

As the pursuit of eloquence became a way of life, it went beyond a technical skill and also encompassed philosophy and logic. Rhetoric could reproduce the subtleties and technicalities of philosophers in more ordinary speech. It drew precepts, pointers, and examples from poetry, history, and civil experience, and used them in discourse. Aiming "to move, persuade, excite, or educate listeners and readers . . . , it was turned toward the practical and recreational needs of people in civil society." Most of all, it became a powerful instrument of social, political, and cultural force, used to change people's minds, to manipulate.

Although based on a high level of literacy, and a lengthy educational indoctrination, the applied power of this learning was channeled largely through the oral medium, the most traditional of vehicles. This use of learning, and its connection to influence, derived from that context; in this way, literacy, directly and indirectly, underlay the exercise of power. Supported by the ruling class and turned to their gain, without that interest and endorsement, "it could be no more than a bookish desire." Not a popular use of literacy or of speech, it was for those with advantages in birth and citizenship, time and leisure, and disposable income or wealth.

Humanist goals and emphases underlay the Italian Renaissance of the fifteenth and sixteenth centuries. Its orientation was equally educational, but its contribution to literacy and learning was carefully and narrowly circumscribed. Classical letters, manly worldliness, versatility, accomplishments, and polish were the concerns of the small elite. With their high regard for a powerful and rich degree of literacy, "they stressed the habit of reading aloud, to help pupils develop self-confidence in public speaking." When some few humanist educators spoke of teaching the talented sons of the poorer families, they were not deviating from this program. They knew the value of a small degree of sponsored mobility through education in maintaining the hegemony of the elite.[22]

The Florentine contribution to the Renaissance was extraordinarily broad. It included painting; sculpture, architecture, craft and artisanal products; technological innovations; classical studies in history, poetry, and moral philosophy; legal writing; medical advances; theological work; and a wide range of original writings in Latin and the vernacular, combining "the Graeco-Roman-Christian tradition, universal in scope, hierarchical and authoritarian in structure; and the vernacular tradition, which gave expression to the particular attitudes and values of this Tuscan community." The former was based upon the Latin language, principles of Roman law, and concepts from Greek antiquity reformulated throughout the medieval ages. It underlay the training and values of theologians, lawyers, notaries, and rhetoricians; its agencies were the grammar schools, the *studia*, and the universities. The vernacular, in contrast, was flexible and unstructured. "Its modes of communication were largely oral and visual; its written form was not yet bound by rules of grammar and orthography." The former embraced the classical and legal culture of humanists, certain artists, learned priests and monks, lawyers, and notaries; the latter was more associated with the mercantile, noble, occult, heretic, and street or popular cultures.[23]

The most significant aspect of fifteenth-century Florentine intellectual life was *not* its variety or complexity but "the unusually close rapport between these cultural traditions." Central to this interplay were the flexibility of the social structure and the precedent-shaping contribution of Dante, who fused ideals of the classical Christian tradition with more parochial interests and values of the local context, writing some of his most important work in the Tuscan vernacular. Boundaries circumscribed this social-structural flexibility but did not preclude it.[24]

The roles of the literate and the oral crossed and enriched one another in influencing the Florentine cultural climate. *Convegni*, informal gatherings of clerics, humanists, scholars and writers, doctors and lawyers, and patricians, were common in the early fifteenth century and were central to this process of communication. Absence of a clerical monopoly of education and ecclesiastical hegemony over culture, as well as an active condition of secular learning, were important aspects of this intellectual environment. Humanism thrived along with other traditions.

Widespread literacy and schooling indicate the value of education and literacy in the Florentine commercial economy. The schools were one factor that attracted migrants and talented persons to the city. The relationship between literacy and the Renaissance remains indirectly causal; cultural, economic, and sociopolitical forces stimulated both developments.

Between about 1380 and 1450, the central theme in this cultural history was the emergence of classical antiquity as the source, focus, and inspiration of intellectual and artistic life. Classical interests expanded from literary sources to include architecture, sculpture, music, mathematics, and physical science. An interest in antiquity and familiarity with its literature were not unprecedented; medieval Europe had never lost its fascination with the Latin language and Latin texts.

An education in the Latin classics was the realm of the few. In the central concerns of the Renaissance, and in its major cultural *impacts felt in its own time and terms*, the influences left the populace and provision for literacy far behind. Both humanism and the Renaissance had implications for the larger society and culture. They have had long-lasting consequences for culture and schooling in the West. To a significant extent, however, these were not among the major contemporary consequences.[25]

As the fourteenth century passed into the fifteenth, the relatively new legacy of a close connection between learning and power gained in scope. That was as true for social ideals as it was in the social world itself.[26] This striking undergirding of a tradition, a legacy related to literacy, was enormously important over the next centuries. Based in assumptions, expectations, *and* social realities, it took on a power of its own and was applied in significant, if contradictory, ways—sometimes in support of extending literacy and popular education, more often in terms of maintaining (or recreating) restrictions and elite patterns of schooling. A major endorsement came from the world of Renaissance humanism and the city-states and republics of fourteenth- and fifteenth-century Italy.[27]

A point of even greater importance is suggested about the relationships of literacy. Studies of the Renaissance often associate the intellectual and cultural "take-offs" with achievements in schooling and printing. The influences of literacy and print were undeniably significant, yet they have commonly been exaggerated. The activities of the Renaissance were well developed *before* the invention of moveable typography. The contribution of printing to the Renaissance, while important, was relatively late and specific. More important was a transition from a primarily oral culture to one more literary and visual. The place of literacy is continuous, if also contradictory. But this position is not complete.[28]

First, visual literacy, related to artistic, architectural, and even technological developments, must be distinguished from alphabetic literacy. Peter Burke found a clear differentiation in the origins of writers and humanists compared to artists and architects (the former tended to be sons of nobles, merchants, and professionals, the latter of artisans and shopkeepers), which may relate to different dimensions of literacy.[29] As Burke makes clear, the social context furthered creative and intellectual activities along these lines: "a talented but well born child might be unable to become a painter or a sculptor because these occupations were considered beneath him. . . . At the other end of the social scale, it was difficult for the sons of peasants to become artists and writers because they would not know about these occupations, or could not easily acquire the necessary training. . . ." In many urban centers, the necessary concentration of artisans undergirded artistic developments. These were the circumstances in Italy and the Netherlands, where the greatest contributions to art were made.

A full explanation for the underlying mechanisms of this unprecedented level of activity and creativity is beyond our scope. Yet its relevance is inescapable. "To produce the necessary concentration of artisans, towns had to be oriented towards craft-industrial production, rather than towards commerce or services." These forms of wealth generation should not be rigidly separated, but places with industrial development, such as Florence, did contribute more to the arts than places less industrially oriented, such as Rome and Naples. If artisanal concentration was a necessary condition, it was not a sufficient one. Wealth, patronage, education for an appreciation of the arts among the elite, time for leisure, and opportunities for training were more important than numbers.

Differences in education, in *forms* of literacy, and in the uses to which those kinds of literacy were put underlay these distinctions. Artists received an education unlike that of writers, humanists, and scientists, as well as a different orientation— from family and environment, craft, career, and outlets for creativity and production. By the late fourteenth and fifteenth centuries, both had achieved an elementary training that included reading and writing, so that a base of elementary literacy was shared and cannot in itself explain much else.

"Training, like recruitment, shows that artists and writers were in fact two cultures." Painters and sculptors were trained as craftsmen, by apprenticeship. Scientists, humanists, and writers tended to acquire some form of advanced education. The distinction lies in a lengthy classical and humanistic training that emphasized a deep orientation toward the word, alphabetic literacy, and writing. Renaissance humanist schooling represented, in the context of Western civilization, a highly traditional attitude toward alphabetic literacy in Latin. That it produced scholars and writers in a "classical" mode is not surprising. That they valued the word and left a profound legacy for learning and scholarship in the history of Western education and literacy is only appropriate.[30]

For artists, training and literacy were different, regardless of such exceptional examples as Michelangelo or da Vinci. On-the-job education was lengthy and detailed: learning all branches of a craft. The process could last as long as thirteen years. Painters began early, sometimes before their teen years. They did not have time for many years of schooling in reading or writing literature.[31]

The implications of these divergences are key aspects of the history of literacy. Of the methods of symbolic communication, those by pictures and words are among the most useful and important. Both words and pictures have been known immemorially. Nevertheless, their differences are essential:

> All words need definitions, in the sense that to talk about things we have to have names for them. Verbal definition is a regress from word to word, until finally it becomes necessary to point to something which we say is what the last word in the verbal chain of definition means. Frequently the most convenient way of pointing is to make a picture. The word then receives definition. . . .[32]

The crucial distinctions relate to the development and differentiation between the writer and the artist and their modes of education, practice, and even styles of cognition.

In a path-breaking perspective on technological development, Eugene Ferguson attempts to grasp the cognition of innovators and inventors by exploring their "nonscientific" modes of thought. "Many features and qualities of the objects that a technologist thinks about cannot be reduced to unambiguous verbal descriptions; they are dealt with in his mind by a visual, nonverbal process," Ferguson discovers. Illustration and pictorial representation played a key role in Renaissance design and invention. Ferguson stresses the influence and paramount position of nonverbal, nonscientific, and nonliterary reasoning, cognition, and representation. Illustrations predominate over words and texts, he finds in a review of technological literature in manuscript and printed forms. He also notes the role of "object" teaching, and the persistence of this form of thought and practice from the fifteenth and sixteenth centuries. The significance of this perspective cannot be exaggerated. Distinct forms of literacy exist; they relate to and underlie different forms of thought and different kinds of creative and intellectual production.[33]

The Renaissance period thus had another important role in the history of Western literacy. Developments advanced in alphabetic *and* visual literacy—before the printing press, which would influence their further development. The emphasis on the written word and its separation from the visual and the oral increased during the late fourteenth and fifteenth centuries. Parallel developments occurred in pictorial, or visual, literacy. While the oral tradition and the oral bases of the popular—and to an important extent the literate—culture did not become less pervasive, a fateful increase occurred in the distinctions between these modes of cognition and communication. Differentiation in popular literacies and means of interchange and discourse advanced more than ever before, and precisely at a time at which levels of popular literacy were achieving their pre- or early modern pinnacles: the contradictions of literacy's social and cultural history. The importance of alphabetic literacy was more generally felt, but its full realization and utility remained restricted quantitatively and qualitatively. Even alphabetic literacy was not a constant or universal cultural skill or force. And it still played its part in a universe largely oral.

Culture was becoming increasingly visual, but literature still had very strong oral elements. Poetry, for example, was more closely associated with music than it is now. It was meant to be intoned. Reading prose was becoming more and more a private activity; but it was still often read aloud in company. The Renaissance rediscovery of ancient texts, which were often written to be read, led to much oral and aggregate reading.

In the fourteenth century, an oral emphasis worked toward a larger audience for authors, and may have increased chances for their work to come to the attention of a potential sponsor or patron. No less significant, illiterates were exposed to some great works.[34] The spread of the vernacular by some of the greater writers of the day facilitated this process. Modes of composition remained profoundly oral, despite the changes in distribution and uses of literacy. "Writing was used a great deal, but in connection with oral expression. . . . always, writing was subordinated to the oral. . . ." The mode of structuring thought was the dialectic, and rhetoric its expression; dialectic was as central to thought of the Middle Ages as was rhetoric to the Renaissance.[35] The spread of reading and writing took place in these orally conditioned environments. The uses of reading and writing were shaped by this force.

Even by the fourteenth and fifteenth centuries, patterns of reading and writing among those most involved in literate lives reflected earlier currents. Private readings to circles of friends were more common than set performances.[36] Personal, private, and individualized silent reading was becoming more common, but oral reading was not disappearing. The style of totally silent reading developed slowly and probably with some difficulty.[37]

The auditory and the visual "memory" complemented one another. Medievalists note with awe the power of the memory of intellectuals and the educated, as well as that of oral performers in past societies with a strong oral tradition. Typically, a dichotomy of conflicting senses and emphases is presumed. But the situation is more complex and interesting. With an increase in literacy, on one hand, and a rising number of written materials, on the other, in a context in which oral reading, performances, and communicative modes were essential means of relationship and communications, they interrelated rather than conflicted.[38]

The new emphasis on preaching and sermonizing within the church added to the need for memory, as did the transformation of oratory. It was not until the effective end of the era, in the sixteenth century, that emphases changed and memory declined from its central place: "killed by the printed book, unfashionable because of its mediaeval associations, a cumbrous art which modern educators are dropping." The art was taken up again in the occult tradition, expanded into new forms, and infused with a new life.[39] In the seventeenth century, it became an aid for investigating the encyclopedia and the world with the object of discovering new knowledge; it survived as a factor in the growth of scientific method.[40] This shift, and memory's decline, were not an inevitable consequence of the diffusion of printing.

Memory's art had another, more obscure but more popular dimension—its use by storytellers, singers, chanters, and other entertainers who formed a major component of popular and elite culture throughout the period. Their ways and methods no doubt derived from the same traditions and followed many of the same techniques as the more elite, literary, and intellectual lines. Sound and sight were highly developed senses distinct from reading and writing. This oral and visual world represented to most persons the dominant mode of cultural and interpersonal communication. Increases in literacy and the reinforcement of the legacy of literacy's primacy and significance that were boosted in these centuries were shaped, in diverse ways, by this cultural context.

Religion illustrates the dialectic relating the oral and the written, representing an aspect of sociocultural life that touched far more people.[41] The church capitalized on an audience beyond readers in its efforts to evangelize and gain popular acceptance. Preaching and sermons, increasingly in the vernacular, provided one mechanism; visual imagery, music, ritual and ceremony, and drama also served. The church produced and disseminated an ever-larger amount of devotional literature, but its channels for reaching more of the masses included a number of means beyond reading.[42]

The fourteenth century saw a rise in Florentine piety and its manipulation for public order and control. Responsibility for care of the indigent, infirm, aged, orphaned, starving, dying, and dead shifted to the state. Guilds and fraternal societies administered pious works and charities. Florentine wealth provided an opportunity for the requisite benevolence. With a rise in literacy and, for some, wealth came a secularization not away from organized religion but rather to a greater expression of civic and social piety.

The combined force of political exigencies and the wishes of a large number of the laity to participate in charitable activities, to enhance their own worthiness in the eyes of God, underlay this thrust. Ritual shaped their actions. Collective action, often through confraternities, in contradistinction to the forms of behavior typically associated with movements in literacy and approaches toward modernity, represented the major forms of philanthropy. Religion and civic responsibility did not conflict dichotomously; they "interlaced" as the laity took a place within the "frame of a sacred community." Within those collective acts of giving were, undoubtedly, benefits to schooling, too, one further irony.[43]

Training in literacy came increasingly to include socialization in social piety. While hardly an unprecedented aspect of schooling, this highly significant connection predated the sixteenth-century Reformations, which so deeply emphasized the relationship. Florentine evidence suggests that by the fourteenth century, instruction in social piety was not yet formalized. Parents who sought moral training for their sons outside the home had few choices. Adult confraternities provided the only education for secular Florentine youth in both piety and grammar. In the next century, special confraternities for the young were created; they aimed at adolescents and grew in number and size by the quattrocento.[44]

By the mid-fifteenth century, other schools for moral education appeared, located in cathedral and Medici parish churches and under mixed secular-ecclesiastical direction. Ritual and instruction in grammar and song were their main purposes; the former was very extensive. They aimed at securing priests, but may not have been used in that way by parents and youngsters. Youth received moral and pious training along with their literacy; at the same time they were socialized into adult social patterns. Important social functions were fulfilled in a manner that gave new scope to formal schooling and left important legacies to the future.

Humanist education supported much of this development. The humanist pedagogue was a school cum moral family all in one, combining the best features of mother and ideal father. Orderliness and docility were held essential to intellectual progress; religion and piety contributed to this intellectual orientation. Humanistic training also provided tutelage in normative social and intellectual graces. Spontaneity of expression or behavior was not desirable, in physical conduct or in speech or writing. The results expected from such a preparation were hardly conducive to the upbringing of independent and creative persons. They "could not help but be a consolation to civil society at large." With the humanists, educational personnel were decidedly laymen.[45]

Humanist education and the new urban confraternities shared social goals and methods and tone and content, despite the differences in audiences, status, and costs. Both sought to produce young persons who would contribute to civil order, pious behavior, and moral regeneration of family and society. Their methods were also similar: avoiding solitude or contacts with older boys, systematically utilizing leisure time, and training in gesture, expression, acting, and oration. There is an echo of monastic regulations, but regardless of precedent, this training looked and contributed to the future. In the process, the social and Christian fascination with children and youth and the moral regeneration of society through them became ever more deeply embedded in the culture of the West.[46]

One area in which literacy was contributing to an unprecedented extent was trade and commerce, in both Latin and the vernacular. The needs and results of the "commercial revolutions" played an important function in the increasing use of reading and writing. By the fourteenth century, merchants were producing a voluminous amount of writing—account books, letters, and documents. The activities and advice literature of merchants, the increasing production of books (still before printing), and the behavior of humanists reflected the growing habits of literacy. Praise of the book as the companion to the lonely appeared as a new commonplace in literature.[47] The mental cast of a society becoming literate was emerging, leaving a deep legacy for Western culture.

The fourteenth and fifteenth centuries witnessed an expansion of copying, loaning, and selling of manuscript texts,[48] but full publishing had not yet emerged. Manuscripts were presented to the patrons who financed them, who were then free to do with them as they pleased. Patrons were probably under some obligation to circulate the works—to loan them or allow copies to be made—but once in public, a work was beyond its author's control. Unauthorized publication stood high among a writer's concerns.

Before formal publication, a work might be read and criticized by friends. Corrections and revisions were made informally. The author of nonscholastic works was literally his own publisher; he secured scribes, oversaw their work, and distributed copies. The professional booksellers, *stationarii* and *librarii*, served as agents and commissioners of copies.[49]

By the fourteenth century, independent booksellers began to appear. The larger firms assumed responsibility for all operations of book manufacture, and some also led in printing. Some other merchants, such as silk dealers, also might include manuscripts among their merchandise.[50] The high cost of even small and unimportant volumes limited their dissemination somewhat, but the availability of paper meant that books were becoming cheaper to produce. Paper also made the act of writing easier.[51] Collectors tended to prefer volumes in the more durable parchment or even more expensive vellum, however. Nevertheless, the increase in literacy and the rise of materials in the vernacular led to more publishing and more reading.

Libraries grew tremendously in these last centuries before printing. The ancient monastic and cathedral libraries were the most significant, but royal libraries and, gradually, university libraries also increased in size and importance. Most of the books in these collections pertained to theology and philosophy; people with other interests had to collect their own.[52] Private collections were relatively small and usually consisted almost entirely of books related to the owner's profession and/or of those of a religious and devotional character. Only the exceptional household, even by 1400, possessed any books at all.

Far more important for the history of literacy was the major new use of the vernacular, which aided the expansion of opportunities for elementary schooling and new demands for some degree of literacy. A wide range of literature was produced and disseminated, and much of this literature reached nonreaders orally. With Latin literature, the audience narrowed tremendously, to a small, well-educated class of the elite, some clerics, and professional men. Degrees of utility and quality of literacy existed among the Latin-trained, and it is likely that the level and quality of much humanist learning increased the distinctions between popular and elite culture (both in Latin and the vernacular), reduced the potential reading public for much literature, and reinforced the distinction between written literature for the educated and leisure class and patterns of popular culture.[53]

The "language question" intensified during these centuries, becoming fiercer in the late-fifteenth- and sixteenth-century crises of Italian society. Was a polished Latin or an Italian vernacular the appropriate language for literature and imagination, and if a vernacular, then which one? The terms of the debate, and its resolution—in favor of the wishes of courts and oligarchies—reveal that cultural and class values and styles dominated over concerns either academic or functional.

Humanists preferred the Latin of the Augustan age; few of them wrote in Italian. They were able to spread their values to a select section of the upper classes, receiving in return patronage and acceptance for their educational program. "At the same time, however, in the same circles, a strong interest persisted in vernacular literature." Dante, Boccaccio, and Petrarch were read often during the fifteenth century. Despite grumbles and snobbery, no formal debate broke out until the end of the century. By that point, some argue, literature was turning more and more toward the vernacular.[54]

As late as the 1520s, some literati continued to defend Latin as the language of gentility. The dominant view, however, stood in favor of Italian as equal or even superior to Latin for imaginative literature and learned discourse. But which of the vernaculars was best? Some favored a cosmopolitan courtly language; some the archiastic one advanced by Pietro Bembo, whose standard was the language of Petrarch and Boccaccio; and some that of the Tuscans, who favored the current Florentine or Tuscan. Each represented class and ideological interests, as well as regional divisions—united only in a search for a single consciousness for a common Italian identity in the face of foreign invasion.

Nationalism, a powerful if often incomplete force in cultural consciousness and literary-linguistic consolidation, represented a significant attitude. The concerns of the masses, the needs of administration or commerce, and popular accessibility to the written text were seldom raised as issues. Without other forms of centralization, in contrast to developments elsewhere, linguistic nationalism was insufficient protection against further splintering of views. That two cultural Italies resulted is not surprising. There was an Italy of many dialects but no true literature, and an Italy of courtiers, oligarchies, and the learned, with one language and one great literature. The society's social divisions were mirrored in the realities and the debates of language.[55]

In many aspects, the onset of the Italian decline is found by the middle of the fifteenth century. Literacy and education fell from their earlier impressive levels. There were major political and economic changes. During the middle decades of the quattrocento, Florentine and other ruling families were gradually giving up the substance of power for its form; they were not aware of the contradictions. A single family, the Medici, came to dominate Florence and Tuscany.[56]

The severe military and political problems that confronted Italy in the later quattrocentro were produced by a general social and economic crisis. Economic development was arrested, while the state became, for a few, a profitable business. Lavish expenditure for luxuries, including great sums in patronage of the arts, replaced developmental efforts. Business failures and withdrawals from commerce were no longer replaced by the rise of new firms or the entry of new men and families.[57]

In this context, the courtier began to replace the humanist, and "civic humanism" decayed. A "flight from the world," often to a life of contemplation, became a new goal of the educated, replacing the earlier primacy on civic responsibilities. Mentions of achievements in education and popular literacy became scarce by the late fifteenth century; illiteracy may even have increased. With time and the contradictions of development, the Italian achievements could not be sustained. Neither literacy nor school opportunities had increased in Florence by the first third of the fifteenth century; in Venice, documents from 1450 and 1463 indicate that illiteracy held steady at a level of around 60 percent.[58]

### 2. Continental Conditions in Literacy

Despite some important developments and a probable (and parallel) increase in schooling and diffusion of literacy, changes on the continent outside the Italian peninsula were relatively smaller, in terms of contemporary circumstances and traditions or legacies for the future. Perhaps as a result, there seems to be far less documentation. Progress in literacy took place, but largely in a context whose origins owed a greater debt to changes initiated before the fourteenth century.

In the *German lands*, as in England and France, the agricultural crisis of the fourteenth and fifteenth centuries caused major dislocations in rural society. Massive abandonment of the land occurred, prices for grains fell sharply, and, in the fourteenth century, labor became scarce as demographic crises thinned the population and reduced migration levels. In the south, the cloth industry developed rapidly, seeking outlets to replace plague-stricken and money-scarce former markets of the north and northwest. Development in the east offset some of the losses but was not sufficient to replace the older industries. Not until well into the fifteenth century were former levels of prosperity and international trade and production regained. The north of Europe was only beginning to transform itself into the economic spearhead of the West; the fulfillment of its promise, and its replacement of Italy in economic leadership, lay ahead.[59]

The effects on schooling and literacy could only be negative, at least in the short run. However, among the results was almost certainly an immediate shortage of educated workers, which increased demands for literate persons in commerce, clergy, and civil administration, and pious support of the cause of learning. The advances of the urban (or commercial) "revolution" of the twelfth and thirteenth centuries came to abrupt halts, but probably resumed before the end of the fourteenth. There is, for example, evidence of children learning to read and write under private teachers, and during the fourteenth and fifteenth centuries, needs of commerce and industry stimulated young persons to learn to read, write, and cast accounts. German cities established "German Schools" during the fourteenth century, at the same time that the earliest German universities (Prague, Vienna, Heidelberg, Cologne, and Erfurt) began. The vernacular became a part of education, and its fuller development was supported. By the fifteenth century, there were a number of vernacular schools in Germany.[60]

Throughout the West, schools were being founded by individuals, guilds and/or corporations, and towns. Most teaching remained part of the organization of the church; schools, even those outside official ecclesiastical control, were commonly taught by clerics. In Germany, a number of towns established elementary schools in the second half of the thirteenth century, but German developments were late.[61] Agricultural areas were hit harder than the towns by fourteenth-century destruction, and their recovery was slower; they surely ended the period at a much lower level of literacy and schooling. Although historians often speak of a striking line of differential diffusion of literacy and schooling between the northern and southern parts of the German territories, significant differences do not seem likely before the end of the fifteenth century.

Similar trends occupied the *Low Countries*. Holland and, especially, Flanders made substantial progress before the fourteenth century. As towns and industry developed, Flanders initiated town schools relatively early. With demands for clerks to write and calculate, significant educational developments came to this densely urban region. The Low Countries were noted for their high extent of literacy.[62]

The formal ecclesiastical provisions for education and transmitting literacy were becoming more inadequate for the needs of the population and the new demands for literacy skills. Such needs were met, at least in part, in the Low Countries, southern Germany, and the Rhineland by a new religious order, the Brethren of Common Life.

The Brethren of Common Life were an outgrowth and institutional development of the religious sentiments and evangelical cum educational activities of Gerard Groote (1340–1384) and Florent Radewyns (1350–1400), which came to be known as the "Devotio Moderna," the New Devotion.[63] After a period of monasticism, Groote emerged to "go out among the people and preach" the gospel of repentance throughout the Low Countries. His zeal, conviction, and personality apparently attracted many urban residents to imitate the life of Christ, as they called it; he preached from town to town, gathering up followers in his wake. Reform and closer relations between religion and learning were his goals. Toward that end, he realized the need, on one hand, for popular literacy—for people to read the Bible and decide the right path for themselves—and, on the other, for translations of the Bible and hymns, to further that effort. The movement Groote initiated continued long after his own demise.[64]

Beginning as popular preachers, the Brethren gradually entered the field of teaching. Their instruction emphasized character training, and many towns welcomed their religious influence.[65] In several places, they reproduced their own schoolbooks, and later innovated in printing religious and educational materials. Some of the boarding houses and schools that they established lasted into the eighteenth and even nineteenth centuries. Some became organs of the Counter Reformation; others turned to the Reform cause.[66]

A number of scholars have assigned the Brethren of Common Life a powerful role in influencing literacy in the late-fourteenth- and fifteenth-century revival of learning.[67] Emphasis on morality and character building of children and youth as a formal component of the school program, while not unprecedented, received renewed endorsement in their activities. Providing something of a parallel with the humanist educators' stresses, the Brethren concentrated not on the often private instruction of the high-born and wealthy but on the schools as they existed. They extended this emphasis to the middle and even the lower ranks. This focus was expanded in the educational programs of the sixteenth-century Reformation, as well as in the Counter Reformation's response. The increasingly close association of literacy and learning with morality derived support from such efforts.

The order's emphasis lay in the translation of holy writings to make them accessible to more lay persons. The Brethren considered the reading of sacred writings—as long as they contained no errors or heresy, were easy to understand, and did not contradict canonical writings—to be permissible and praiseworthy, despite clerical objections. They argued that the Bible should be studied by everyone.

In their intellectual work, the Brethren stressed reading, taught through dictation of extracts in the classroom. The stress was on memory and oral transmission, even with the focus on literacy and reading. In this way, they were able to educate religiously the pupils of their grammar schools, encourage evangelization, and add to the stock of written texts among the population. The focus and methods spread throughout fifteenth-century Europe and were influential among students and teachers. The schools were attractive to many, and they were generous in their support of poorer pupils; they were profitable, as well.[68]

Before the origin of moveable typography in the mid-fifteenth century, the production and circulation of writing were more limited in Germany than in Italy or England. Among the upper classes and the nobility, there was less interest in and less disposable wealth to expend on "literary luxuries." Only after printing did German cities become centers for the distribution of literature. University curricula were narrower and the classical revival slower than in Italy; monastery scriptoria and university booksellers remained the main producers. That resulted in complete and accurate texts, but it also left the imprint of stricter controls and narrower selections. The trade was increasing, however, in the fifteenth century.

Without great demand and especially a supply of books beyond the universities and ecclesiastics, the work of the Brethren of Common life in the vernacular served to meet the needs of many. They served as both instructors and book dealers, and were "important influences in helping to educate the lower classes of Northern Germany to read, if not necessarily . . . to think for themselves." In this underdeveloped context, the work of school teachers was closely connected with that of producers and sellers of manuscripts. Teachers not infrequently built manuscript businesses.

By the fifteenth century, changes were occurring that marked an increase in the supply of, and probably demand for, written literature. Princes and nobles began to show greater interest in books, and fairs and annual markets were held for the manuscript trade. The changes reflected an increased interest in the written word and related, at least temporarily, to increased provision of instruction in the vernacular, if often for moral and religious reasons.

In the Netherlands, the trade was more highly developed and had a greater influence on popular education. Books were produced outside university circles; the greater wealth of the commercial class made literature more accessible. In Germany, the signs of an organized and developing book trade are found after 1400: a rising interest in literature and a wide array of popular works in the vernacular.

The introduction of paper assisted circulation, as did the firmer link emerging among the vernacular, religion, and education. Scribes slowly moved from the special, restricted work of universities to a place among the hand workers and dealers of the larger cities.[69]

Literacy and reading in Germany and the Low Countries were reaching new levels. The relationship between these developments and the rise of printing, on one hand, and the spread of the Reformation with its impact on literacy and education, on the other, constitute major questions and issues.

Emmanuel LeRoy Ladurie's *Montaillou*, the "cultural archaeology" of a small village, yields a rare view of the function of literacy in fourteenth-century French society. It illustrates revealingly the relationship between literacy and cultural transmission, using as an example the transmission of heresy. The evidence indicates that heretical (and other) ideas were passed on not directly from books and literacy but through the primacy of oral transmission and its interaction with the written.

Books, including heretical works, were produced on a small scale in Montaillou. The village was overwhelmingly illiterate (246 out of the 250 inhabitants), so dissemination of ideas from books was primarily oral. The contents of these few books were spread more widely by the goodmen, wandering heretical preachers. "So there were some links between learning and popular culture, and these were helped by the circulation of a few books. . . ." Literacy and the book had an important role in spreading heresy, but it was not a direct role: the fact that an intermediary (the goodman) was required; the "infection" of many by the literacy of a few; the association of books with magic and power; and the oral culture were more important. More than solitary reading by the few literate persons was required for the "word" to be spread.

Social life revolved around village gatherings. "Convivial evenings in Montaillou were *devoted to words* rather than wine." The traditional culture and oral transmission, and sometimes a very small extent of reading among a few, were sufficient for heresy, and other information and ideas, to circulate widely. Words the villagers knew and respected; they valued oral skills and listened well. For them, words did not require personal familiarity with the written texts.[70]

France was struck by social and economic forces similar to those in other areas of northwestern Europe, with pronounced regional variations. In the towns, impacts from economic dislocation and price increases were differential by class and rank, but trade, commerce, and industry recovered, and the new residence of formerly rural landowners stimulated some activity. Written records were kept, but not as extensively as in the south. Often, vital occupations in which financial skill was required were dominated by foreign specialists, notably Italians.

French commerce was growing, but its relatively underdeveloped condition created less demand for literacy. State and church administrative requirements added to the uses of and needs for reading and writing. Trade and commercial needs increased by the fifteenth century, with the end of wars and a relative shift in economic dominance from southern to northern Europe.[71] Some forces acted to stimulate levels of literacy, but, in all probability, they were less than those in Italy, the Low Countries, or the leading German centers.

In consequence, provision of literacy and educational opportunities showed no

sudden shifts or major new dimensions in France. The church continued to supply
most schooling, in parish schools and cathedral/collegiate church grammar schools.
Lay schooling and town schools were present and probably growing in size and
number, but not to the extent found elsewhere.

Grammar schooling probably attracted most educational energies and funds. At
the beginning of the fourteenth century, "every great town had at least one grammar
school, and a knowledge of grammar, dialectic, and rhetoric was widespread." The
Hundred Years' War reduced this activity until the second half of the fifteenth
century. That may have been even truer of elementary education and literacy training
than of higher schooling, although some rural clergy operated schools.[72]

The use and development of the vernacular continued to advance. The languages
of the West were taking on much more of their later forms; people were beginning
to write in the language that they spoke. This period, concurrently, produced an
abundant and rich literature in each of the European languages.[73]

As late as the thirteenth century, each region had its own well-marked dialect or
dialects, although the greatest distinction was between the north and the south: the
*langue d'oil* and the *langue d'oc*. The language of Paris and its vicinity was becoming *the* language of France.[74] It had been raised to preeminence since the
eleventh century by the presence of the king and the court. And from the mid- to
late thirteenth century, this form of French, strongly influenced by Latin, began to
appear in the official records. Its use became more frequent, and in the fourteenth
century it began to equal and then predominate over Latin as the language of
documentary use. Official use reflected the practices mainly of the official and upper
classes. France is distinctive for the early date, the wide interest, and the dissemination of its chronicles in the native tongue.[75]

Not only did the progress in the national vernacular mark the spread of a more
popular and non-Latin literacy, it also served to stimulate that literacy. Yet, linguistic
developments alone, in the context of slower educational and economic development
and the strong persistence of regional dialects, were not sufficient to place France
among the leaders in Western literacy.

The development of manuscript publishing and the book trade in France was
closer to that in Germany than that in Italy. Through much of the fourteenth century,
the universities retained control and supervision of book dealers. The center was
Paris, where the market was controlled by university authorities. *Stationarii* and
*librarii* were unable to obtain privileges of their own. Paris was also a European
center of theological books.

By 1411, references to books in French as well as Latin are found. The regulations
controlling the book trade were becoming more flexible. That "seems to have been
an attempt to widen the range of the book trade, while reference to books in the
vernacular indicates an increasing demand for literature outside of the circles of
instructors and scholars." More nobles and their families showed a heightened
interest in literature, which stimulated the production and reproduction of manuscripts.[76]

The small role accorded to individual reading in late medieval religious practices
is impressive, as is how far the "word" could be spread by a tiny number of readers
principally through the oral medium. Family and kin were central to popular reli-

gious behavior. Clerical forces attempted to combat this popular orientation: "to convert the mass from a public ritual offered by those present for themselves and the whole community of Christians, into a private ritual offered by the priest for the benefit of a specific group of individuals, living or dead." Progress was slow, paralleling modernizing changes. That did not detract from popular religious observances, regardless of how much it disturbed many clerics. Parish priests' main contributions were more in terms of keeping peace and settling conflicts than in preaching or teaching.[77]

### 3. The English Example

English literacy reached a level before the sixteenth century that not only was impressively high but may have approximated in some areas the peaks of Florence, similar Italian cities, and the Low Countries. While still socially and culturally restricted, it reached this level before the "educational revolution" of the mid-sixteenth century, the impact of the printing press, and the English Reformation.[78] It is not coincidental that English economic activity emerged most fully by the end of the period, that the epochal shift in economic advantage and capitalist development from southern to northern Europe was under way, or that the English were successful in their foreign-policy and war making.[79]

The fourteenth-century crises that swept across the West struck England with force. Plague, subsistence crises, depopulation, falling agricultural yields, and decline were manifest during the early and middle decades of that century. Rural conditions were not conducive to supporting very high levels of literacy.[80] Urban places fared somewhat better, although trade ebbed and flowed, declining in most years. Overall, though, recovery was quicker and easier, the level of disorder and dislocation less, and relative stability easier to regain. The wool trade benefited the towns, as did the growth of other rural industries. Town, and rural, life changed economic course by the second half of the fifteenth century: part of a larger northern European pattern.

After the mid-fifteenth century came a period of recovery, which included population growth, new sources of wealth, increasing agricultural production, and industrial expansion.[81] The resurgence in economic activity, commerce, town and city life, and the like underlay the emergence of education and literacy from the effects of fourteenth- and fifteenth-century declines. They make the sixteenth-century postprinting and Reformation currents especially interesting. The parts of the West in which literacy and education were reaching new, impressively high levels by 1500 tended to be those in which recovery and new economic developments proceeded furthest: England and the Low Countries, and to a lesser extent Germany and France.[82]

With respect to literacy and education in fourteenth- and fifteenth-century England, all indications point to the role of cities and towns. Centers of population, institutions, wealth, and piety, they were also places in which the need and demand for literacy were greatest. They were probably selective of migrants with some previous schooling or with a strong interest in attaining that after arrival. A few fifteenth-century towns had lending libraries; many had elementary or grammar schools by the fourteenth century. Foundations multiplied in the fifteenth.[83]

The increased evidence of writing and record keeping has direct implications for the social meaning of literacy. The facts of more literacy, its wider diffusion, its increased employment, and, most likely, its higher evaluation did not lead in themselves to new uses of writing.

Town histories illustrate educational developments, showing the connection between commerce and educational development. In York, for example, the wealthy trading class founded grammar schools and built or rebuilt cathedrals and churches. Most educational work was under church control. Apparently, that did not stop the merchant and commercial class from supporting schooling (as was common elsewhere in initiating or maintaining lay schools). Three significant factors intermingled: outpourings of piety after the plagues and destruction of the fourteenth century, support for the institutional church, and support and endorsement of educational growth required for commerce and administration. Thus, York had an ancient grammar school at the cathedral and two additional grammar schools attached to hospitals. Parish and chantry priests organized elementary schooling, sometimes including girls, who were also taught at home. Friars also conducted "educational welfare work."[84]

Books were not plentiful. In this area, most copying was conducted by the monasteries. "Instruction was given as a rule orally, but also by means of pictorial art and drama." Instruction in crafts and manual skill was the work of the masters of the crafts under the supervision of guilds. This training was often highly technical and skilled, not much influenced by formal classroom work or a primacy on reading and writing.

York was not a typical town. Long an important administrative, commercial, and market center, it had a tradition of educational possibilities and intellectual vitality from at least 1300 through the mid-sixteenth century. Opportunities were increasing, especially in the fifteenth century. The town housed a variety of educational agencies, including virtually all known types of schools. At the grammar-school level, York served as the regional center for the north, maintaining this position despite the city's economic and demographic decline. At the elementary level, the dioceses experienced an increase in parish reading and song schools. There was no comparable increase in grammar schools until the sixteenth century. Elementary schooling was beginning to emerge as a distinct entity.

With an increase in educational institutions came an increase in the supply of texts, for both grammar and elementary schooling. Reading and writing were not necessarily learned together or within the same school. A number of scriveners apparently provided private lessons for those in need of the craft of writing. Books also existed in fair supply. As a result of changing needs for literacy and the surprisingly varied and large extent of schooling, literacy levels were impressive. However, news and information were still transmitted primarily orally.[85]

These sketches from York are complemented by those of other towns.[86] The context, the modes of vocational training, the restricted nature of literacy and schooling, and the oral world of society and information owed as much to the past as to the present. Literacy grew in influence, value, and utility in this world. The oral culture shaped the effects of literacy, while literacy progressed. Only a few lives were now heavily shaped by reading or writing, but more and more were touched by it.

The urban merchant class of England was most likely to support education and to be literate. Mixed motives underlay the education of many among the laity; religious reasons stood high among them. In London, to take an example, almost all secondary education, in Latin, was under the control of the church. Ostensibly, the reason behind this monopolistic control was the preservation of high standards of learning. In contrast, elementary and commercial training had an open field.

Despite its expansion, literacy was still a socially restricted accomplishment and skill. The rate of literacy among male Londoners was around 40 percent, impressive testimony to the spread of reading and/or writing. But there was a "fringe of ignorance" among middle-ranking citizens.[87] (See table 4.2.)

The support underlying literacy among urban workers came in many instances from the guilds. Some required that apprentices be able to read and write, at least in the vernacular, and some even sent illiterate apprentices to school. It was only later, however, that apprenticeships commonly carried educational requirements. The ironmongers, in 1498, required only that apprentices register their names

TABLE 4.2
**London Literacy, 1467–1476**

| Occupation | Literate | Illiterate | Occupation | Literate | Illiterate |
|---|---|---|---|---|---|
| Baker | | 3 | Haberdasher | 1 | 1 |
| Barber-surgeon | 4 | 5 | Hosier | 1 | |
| Bargee | | 1 | Ironmonger | 1 | 2 |
| Bladesmith | 1 | | Joiner | | 2 |
| Brazier | 1 | | Laborer | | 3 |
| Brewer | 1 | 5 | Mercer | 2 | |
| Broiderer | 2 | | Merchant | 2 | |
| Butcher | | 1 | Ostler | | 2 |
| Butler (mayor's) | 1 | | Patenmaker | | 2 |
| Capper | 1 | 2 | Pewterer | 3 | 1 |
| Cook | | 1 | Pinner | 1 | |
| Cooper | | 1 | Saddler | | 1 |
| Cordwainer | | 1 | Salter | 1 | |
| Cutler | | 1 | Shearman | 5 | 2 |
| Dauber | | 1 | Skinner | 2 | 4 |
| Draper | 4 | 1 | Smith | | 4 |
| Dyer | | 1 | Sourrier | | 1 |
| Founder | 1 | 2 | Tailor | 6 | 9 |
| Fuller | | 1 | Tiler | | 1 |
| Glover | | 1 | Tinner | 1 | |
| Goldbeater | 1 | 2 | Whitetawyer | | 1 |
| Goldsmith | 1 | 1 | | | |
| Graytawyer | | 2 | | | |
| Grocer | 4 | | Totals | 48 | 68 |

" 'with theire owne handes, yf they can write' ''; brewers' wardens decided in
1422 to keep their records in English, rather than continue with Latin: none of the
members could read them in Latin, but some read and wrote in the vernacular.
Other evidence suggests that literacy was not required for skill in a craft or entry
into a guild or company, and that poorer citizens were not attaining literacy. The
poor needed their children in the workshop, or saw no advantage in schooling. The
school fees were beyond the means of most; there was little free education, which
reflected the social and political fact that despite the spread of schooling, the lower
class and the poor were not encouraged to attend or to become literate; if anything,
the opposite was the case.[88]

In these circumstances, schooling for some was less religious than pragmatic,
and for some it was delayed until apprenticeship. No graded, hierarchical structure
for schooling existed. A mixed elementary education, required for most persons
who desired some literacy, could be gained from small, private schools attached
to grammar schools or operated independently by priests or scriveners. The latter
offered the most functional, commercially oriented instruction of all: in theory, at
least, a curriculum stressing reading and writing, arithmetic, and some French—
in preparation for a London apprenticeship.

Circumstances were changing in many merchants' families. The first generation's
schooling had been exceptional but somewhat haphazard and irregular. For the
second generation, a more thorough schooling was received: an education informed
by more than solely commercial interests. "Parents were genuinely anxious for
their sons to be initiated into that world of Latin learning over which the church
presided"; parents in various occupations left legacies for sons' schooling.[89]
Wealthier merchants' families, like the more cultivated gentry, sought a more formal, "classical," and lengthy schooling for their sons.

Many of the gentry had more formal schooling than the merchants, but successful
merchants were probably as knowledgeable about law and politics. Merchants
formed an important portion of the country's small lay book-owning public; professional men were the only other group with marked attachment to books. An "in-
terpenetration of culture" between the merchants and the gentry occurred. Education
among at least a segment of the merchant class had status-symbolic, elite cultural,
and surplus, conspicuous-consumptive aspects, in addition to religious and utilitarian functions. Literacy, at various levels, had a variety of meanings.

Nevertheless, few men in the merchant class stayed in school past the age of
sixteen; those who attended longer likely went into one of the professions. All the
men read English, and most had some training in Latin. "Intelligent" women
probably found a way to learn at least how to read and write English. The question
is whether these skills were used except in handling business transactions and
following the liturgy.

Lack of common use of literacy beyond the mundane requirements of commerce
and religious practice does not attest to a high value of literacy for nonutilitarian
functions. Few merchants owned many books, and those that they did own were
primarily liturgical and devotional. There was little patronage of literature. Merchants' use of literacy and education was not often turned to intellectual ends.

The intellectual life in this environment was religiously oriented. There was also an interest in history. Merchants patronized and encouraged the writers who composed the custumals and chronicles, and thus had influenced the interpretation of the city's political experience and its relationship to the nation. There was apparently little other patronage of literature. The use of their literacy and education was not often turned to intellectual ends.

The education in London's grammar schools was traditional. Church schools stressed virtue and moral discipline along with instruction in grammar. The child received religious instruction and lessons in deference and obedience to elders and superiors, good manners, and sensitivity to social differences. Proper behavior had a moral aspect, adding to personal dignity and sense of place. Self-restraint and self-control were to be learned early and thoroughly, regularly reinforced in schooling and at home.

Schooling for girls differed. Their education was to make them grow up useful, but gentle and amenable to male authority at the same time. Among the wealthiest, a governess or mistress was engaged until the time of marriage, or a daughter might be entrusted to nuns. Among the poorer classes, it was common for girls to learn a trade. Since illiteracy could have hampered efficiency in business matters, girls were seen as needing some elementary education. They were admitted to the elementary schools, but not to grammar schools. "This evidence is not enough to show whether education was actually as general among women as it was among the men of the merchants class, but one may infer that it was quite commonly within their reach."[90] Here may be the pinnacle of female literacy in the medieval world of the West.

Education and the social condition of literacy among the merchant class of London provide a valuable entry into the issues of literacy and schooling in the larger society and culture. Not only do they reveal the sociocultural portrait of a leading and expanding class, they also set the outer limits for the examination of the extent, transmission, uses, and meanings of literacy. With the exception of the clergy and the small number of professionals and scholars, this class and the gentry were the most literate and most likely to have some need and desire for reading and writing.[91]

The level of literacy for the entire society of adult males was nowhere as high as the possible 40 percent among merchants. It may have been less than one-half to one-fourth that proportion—a high and expanding rate, nonetheless. Increasing literacy came in tandem with increased use of English, translations from French and Latin, and new levels of writing. Pragmatic and middle-class uses are especially evident.[92]

Two trends were critical to contemporary education: the continuation of the earlier expansion of schools and the development of new kinds of schools (e.g., the famed proprietary and independent grammar schools and writing and reading schools), and formidable patterns of giving to a wide variety of schools, largely in the cause of piety and charity. This age was one of patronage and endowment. In the confluence of these currents lie the bases for the extent of literacy that constitutes our theme.[93] The period also saw the rise of the vernacular as a language of instruction, the development of business studies, and education beyond the compass of this formal network, in the family, from the church, and in the trades. Progress in English education marked the era. New opportunities for schooling and new levels of literacy were highly stratified and unequal; there was no equality of opportunity, as some commentators have benignly suggested.[94]

The events of the fourteenth through early fifteenth centuries affected schooling. Mortality differentials likely raised slightly the overall rate of literacy, but they also created demand for educated persons to replace those who had died, for example, clergy who were qualified to serve as schoolmasters. The plagues may also have contributed to the passing of French as the language of scholars. The rising level of contributions to education constitutes a further effect.[95]

The key institutional agencies for formal learning, although often attached to grammar schools, were the parish primary schools (elementary chantries, church or priests' home schools) and the so-called specialized schools (song schools, writing and/or reading schools, ABCs). Most, perhaps all, of these forms of schooling were expanding during this period.[96] Primary factors for much elementary schooling included the priests' interest, education, and pedagogical abilities (some parish clergy were poorly trained and unfit for their pedagogical tasks); the local demand for primary schooling; and the state of the local economy. Tremendous regional and interregional variation must have been the norm.

A great deal of elementary literacy and schooling probably took place under the aegis of the parish system, in the elementary chantries and, especially, the local priests' or their clerks' schools and song schools. Many of the newly literate persons of late medieval England had their only exposure to schooling through such agencies as these. They continued to instruct the youth of England through the next century and later.[97]

The chantries constituted an important, if debated, part of the school system of the late Middle Ages. Essentially contributions to the cause of religion, they were to support chapel and prayer in most cases, but founders usually desired to benefit the community, too. In many cases, education was regarded highly and so specified. In more than a few instances, the aid of a chantry allowed another priest or a clerk in lower orders to be retained to provide the educational services that parishes were, in theory, to supply. Some chantries were dedicated to grammatical instruction; others were elementary or no more than primary. Chantry priests played an important role in providing educational facilities and transmitting literacy in England.[98]

In addition to the parish elementaries, song schools continued, expanding into the next two centuries. Not all of them were directly attached to church institutions; in some, the scope was wider. Similar to reading and writing schools, many song schools provided instruction in these elementary subjects, providing a relatively full primary curriculum. Others, whose pupils had already learned to read, focused more narrowly on song and music. Their main purpose, of course, was not to provide literacy but to train choristers for the services. Nevertheless, they added to the numbers of youths attaining some literacy in the late Middle Ages.[99]

Next at the elementary level came writing and reading schools. There were presumably also schools aimed at commercial preparation, as well as those in small villages taught by the parish priest. By the later fourteenth and fifteenth centuries, some of them offered instruction in the vernacular.[100]

Reading and writing were seen as separate skills in the medieval period. But evidence of such schools, along with the contemporaneous development of apprentice schooling in guild and town schools and the emergence of commercial education, suggests that a major change in elementary (and other) curricula was beginning.[101]

The ABC schools were the most diffuse and informal elementary institutions. They were probably independent or private, relatively informal, and perhaps irregularly conducted. Their importance lay in their simplicity of instruction and low cost. In some ways, they might be seen as the precursors of the petty schools.[102]

The extent of elementary forms of schooling in fourteenth- and fifteenth-century England is impressive. The number of children able to obtain some rudimentary training in literacy in this extensive but hardly formalized or integrated network of schools must have been considerable, and to their number should be added those few who learned in monastic and almonry schools,[103] at home, and elsewhere. An impressive network of schooling apparently was turning out an impressive number of literate persons from all levels of the social structure, but opportunities were far from equal.

It is unlikely that a truly useful level of reading ability commonly resulted from elementary instruction. With the oral emphasis and the stress on memory, rote learning predominated strongly over concern with understanding or comprehension. Materials were comparatively rare and highly traditional, mostly of a religious variety. Much reading was a pious act of meditation and reflection.[104] We cannot assume, for a world of little writing and little reinforcement of skills learned in schools, that high levels of literacy were commonly achieved from the processes of instruction.

The curriculum provided a firm grounding in popular morality and normative socioreligious values. Religion and morality were the central purposes of schooling. In the pedagogy, the pupils did not even need to be able to read the words for themselves in order to receive the lessons. The oral style, rote learning and memorization, and constant repetition all reinforced them.

The expansion of town and guild schools was another marked feature of the period. Despite their ancient roots, town and city guilds began to shift more effort into school provision. The value of education was increasingly realized, and the duty of providing for education was no longer regarded as exclusively the function of the church. The emergence of schools from the bounds of the church was a major, long-term movement, which perhaps had less impact on the substance of schooling than might be supposed.[105]

An expansion of education and schooling largely within the medieval mold occurred. Few new precedents were set; in all likelihood, schooling looked somewhat more to the past than to the future in its institutions, networks, and content. In the real expansion of schools and students, the role of lay endowments, the shift toward more secular sponsorship and control, the new place of the vernacular, and schooling for commerce and trade, important advances were made.

These centuries witnessed an expansion in the use of English, in translations from French and Latin, original writings in the vernacular, and commercial and administrative usage.[106] It rose to new prominence and took on new uses, supplanting French and making major inroads on Latin, except in the church and scholarship. Administrative uses of English increased in the fourteenth century, as it virtually became the norm. Beginning in 1362, Parliament was opened with a speech in English by the chancellor. By the mid-fourteenth century, English was the native language of all classes.

This reorientation occurred first and fastest in the spoken language. For much of the fourteenth and part of the fifteenth centuries, a three-way contest took place between English, French, and Latin as the language of written record. English began to predominate by 1450. Ironically, the statute requiring the use of English in the courts was written in French and required that judgments be enrolled in Latin. Literates were divided into those who knew only the vernacular and those who had access to more than one language of record. Literacy, even if more persons had it, did not guarantee an equality or universality among them; the differences in access to documents, books, and the authority attached to them continued and perhaps increased.

In lower official circles, English advanced into documentary use earlier, though perhaps slowly. A rich national literature was also emerging; the fourteenth century was undoubtedly a great period for English literature.[107] By the middle of the fifteenth century, the vernacular was used in every phase of national life and literature.

The popular functions that the vernacular played are seen in the relationship between politics and poetry. There was a considerable volume of contemporary verse; much of it had an important association with political and social subjects. By the fifteenth century, almost all of it was in English.

Political verse needed to be disseminated publicly to be effective. One means was through scribal copies. Some political poems were also oral. V. J. Scattergood argues that there was a considerable reduction in the amount of oral verse in the fifteenth century, when political topics began to be treated more frequently in sophisticated courtly songs. He also asserts that the "undoubted increase in literacy in the fifteenth century must have been an important factor in the decline of oral literature." While this increase is real and significant, we must be hesitant in assuming its causal role in the decline of oral forms. Among the effects of writing is its heightened use to turn the oral record into a written one and to introduce new literate bias into cultural perceptions, both acting to distort the evidence of the oral culture. The decline of the oral is easily exaggerated.

Written verse was posted on walls and gates, and handbills were sometimes used, but a high rate of public literacy is not necessarily indicated: a few readers were sufficient for a much greater number to *hear* their contents. In the cities, where adult male literacy could be as high as 25 percent, female literacy much less, and in rural areas, where literacy levels were considerably lower, transmission of all kinds of information took place largely through the oral medium.[108]

Concomitant with these developments were changes in the production and distribution of written literature. Without technological innovation or major changes from the earlier period, the production, reproduction, and circulation of manuscripts increased, in fair measure a response to the demand of the more often literate middle and upper classes. Before the mid-fourteenth century, most literature had been transmitted orally; now the number of translations and English compositions increased. Books remained expensive and rare, but their cumulative frequency rose. Of the small number of privately owned books, most were in Latin; the few vernacular books consisted mainly of works of piety and devotion. Libraries were also infrequent, but growing in number and scope, especially among kings, nobles, scholars, and leading clerics.[109]

All the problems and complexities of the process of publication that we found in Italy were also present in England. Some authors read their work with friends or members of an informal literary circle. They were more or less helpless once a copy of their work left their possession. It was impossible to insure that revised manuscripts actually replaced earlier versions, or to prevent unauthorized circulation. Most commonly, works were put into circulation through professional scriveners; a large number of books were "shop made." In some cases, that led to a seriously contaminated product, because of scribal copying errors. A writer was quite literally at the mercy of his copyists.[110]

The increasing demand for books was occasionally met by employing an individual scribe to make copies. More commonly, books were purchased from the growing number of booksellers in the towns and cities, or at fairs. Traveling peddlers also sold manuscript books. In the university towns of Oxford and Cambridge, *stationarii*, appointed by and under the supervision of the university, supplied books. In 1403, the rise and extent of the book trade were marked by the chartering of the Stationers Company in London as a permanent guild. English dealers were freer to buy and sell than their confreres in Italy, Germany, or France.[111] The trade grew rapidly and went at least part way toward meeting the rising demands of the reading population.

There was an important relationship between literacy and Lollardy (and medieval heresy in general).[112] Most of the common people remained illiterate; the movement was supported and taken to the countryside by a plethora of wandering preachers, who spread the "Word" orally. John Wyclife's strategy involved translating the Bible from the Latin Vulgate into easy vernacular English and disseminating it to the people. By 1400, English translations from the Latin Bible were becoming common.[113]

Lollards placed great emphasis on reading the Bible. Aware of the state of popular schooling, they prepared translations and encouraged persons who could read very little and not understand much. The learneds' mastery over the Scriptures needed to be erased. The Lollards established a tradition of Biblical study and vernacular learning that resisted all efforts to destroy it.

The heretics valued their books. Many of them were book owners, but not all of those who possessed texts were able to read them. For many, familiarity with books remained totally oral, and rote learning and listening substituted for reading. While some of the literate or semiliterate Lollards were clerks, more were artisans or even laborers. The family circle was probably the most common group in which some level of literacy was learned.

The vernacular literate movement of the Lollards brought them persecution. A general ecclesiastical obsession about the dangers of *all* works written in English, if read by the wrong sort of people, developed in the fifteenth century. The real grounds for concern lay in the heretics' preaching against the failures of orthodoxy. It is possible that official reaction to the Lollards arrested the development of orthodox usage of the vernacular, so that no printed editions of the Bible in the vernacular appeared in the fifteenth century.

For most of the next three centuries, a deep distrust remained of popular schooling and mass literacy. This stance battled, fairly successfully until the late eighteenth and early nineteenth centuries, with a more progressive one, that literacy and school-ing, if properly and safely transmitted, could insure tranquility and social order and promote social and economic discipline.[114]

Popular religion for most persons remained within the conventional bounds of orthodoxy, if not always within the goals of the church. Religion was important, and it permeated life. Literacy was not required for popular religious observation. The clergy were certainly more educated than the mass of their congregants, but what use was that education in the face of restricted literacy, general lack of con-nection between literacy and daily life, and popular beliefs that freely mixed su-perstition with church doctrine?[115]

Religion, as it came from the church's priests, consisted of mostly oral, and sometimes visual, means of communication: the mass, sermon, and confessional, and the rites of baptism, confirmation, communion, extreme unction, and the holy days. Literacy related little to these practices. The daily mass, unintelligible and uninteresting to the illiterate, was a distant and rote experience to most congregants. The fifteenth-century translations into English of primers and the Gospels did little to change the situation. The church was aware of this difficulty, and it attempted to meet lay needs with pictures, imagery, and symbolism. That had some impact on even the poorest and most illiterate congregants. It probably helped to present the liturgy a bit more understandably, but much of it must have remained incom-prehensible.

Through sermons, religious instruction was provided more directly. Preaching was the chief means used to instruct the laity. Many of the clergy lacked the skills or interest to practice this "art" successfully, and many did not rank its importance highly enough. Some, however, knew how to reach the people; they were skilled in oral expression and were able to adapt to the context of their audience. Using parables drawn from daily life to emphasize their messages, they played upon the emotions and minds of their listeners and used well the popular oral culture.[116]

At this time, in contrast to later, the church was somewhat tolerant of popular notions and superstitions. It was selective in its struggle against popular opinion. The superstitions and the doctrine interacted, as did the literate and the oral. Through these and other interrelations came a foundation of popular religion that owed to, and depended on, more the oral and the traditional than the written and the church's rationality.[117]

Within a largely medieval and "premodern" context, the fourteenth and fifteenth centuries built upon the earliest medieval foundations and stimulated a significant expansion of literacy and schooling. Literacy, while expanding, did not break the bounds of restrictedness. The impressive achievement of the culmination of the one thousand years of medieval history, with its legacies from the more distant past and newer ones of its own, must be grasped without exaggeration or scorn, in its historical context. The role and contribution of the church persisted throughout the period; despite the shift, its authority certainly did not wither away by 1500.[118] The minority status of literates, the highly variable quality of literacy, the distinction between the possession and the uses of reading and writing, and the oral cultural context must be emphasized. The social condition of literacy is found in the interaction of such factors. For the society remained—literally and figuratively—only partially literate and partially numerate. Most persons did not require literacy for their lives and livelihoods. The literacy needs of the medieval community may have been rather well met.[119]

The *clergy* were probably the most literate social group. Although not all were well educated, and many fell below ecclesiastical and popular expectations, virtually all acquired some ability to read and write. Many of their duties involved reading and memorizing liturgical texts in Latin. But too much learning and literacy might not have been the best route to communication with parishioners. It seems certain that clerical literacy underwent a real increase during the medieval period.[120]

Several centuries earlier, the literacy of *kings* and their sons, at least, had ceased to be a matter of concern. Even if relatively few princes were schooled to the standards that scholastic schoolmasters, moralists, and humanists held, their literacy was assured long before the fifteenth century. Commonly their literacy was in Latin, and their education typically included morality and physical and social education, in addition to literacy studies. The degree of learning advanced with time.[121]

Below the kings came the *upper ranks* of laypersons, from members of the royal family to the great magnates, knights, and gentry, and their families. Many of their children were sent to schools to be trained for ecclesiastical, legal, and administrative careers. Their training often included a military ethos and physical culture, but it increasingly came to include more literary and social skills. By the fourteenth and fifteenth centuries, literacy was virtually certain—and much more often for daughters in this class, at least in English. Literature became more important to their leisure. Some noble youths began to attend universities, while others trained in the church or the law.[122]

Among *administrators and lawyers*, literacy—in Latin—was becoming necessary before the fourteenth century. Some used only a low level of literacy; some had greater need for numeracy than for alphabetic literacy; others needed only the vernacular; and a smaller number possessed and used a fuller Latin literacy. With the development and expansion of government and the ecclesiastical state, more literate persons were required to fill positions. It is more difficult to be certain about the literacy skills of those who retained clerks to assist them and those in lower, local administrative levels. Illiterates were becoming less common.

Gradually, laymen were replacing clerics in administrative posts in the upper hierarchies. Administrative work demanded a working knowledge of Latin among the higher ranks, and until the early fifteenth century a knowledge of French, as well. The law's requirements were similar, as English made a relatively later entrance into formal legal matters.[123] Literacy, at least in the vernacular, was nearly universal in the upper ranks and classes of English society by the end of the fifteenth century.

The next levels—*merchants*, *craftspersons*, and *artisans*—are the ranks into which literacy penetrated farthest during these centuries. Administrative needs and commercial requirements insured that the larger merchants and the burgher class would be virtually universally literate, at least in English. At this level, literacy was required, and it brought a stimulus, certainly in the vernacular and perhaps not uncommonly in Latin. Merchants used their literacy in record keeping and correspondence. The largest establishments employed clerks; literate servants and apprentices might assist. Little Latin was required for trade, banking, or international commerce. There were limitations on the use of literacy even by London merchants. The literacy of this class meant mostly the ability to read and write in English, and occasionally in French. Less common was knowledge of Latin and grammar.

While larger merchants were almost universally literate, those in *lower-class occupations* were more likely to be illiterate than not, and the level for the entire group was about 40 percent. This sample included only men. Thus, for the mercantile work force of the leading city, literacy of *employed males* would not exceed the 25 to 30 percent range, at best. Outside London and other leading towns and outside the ranks of those most likely to leave wills, appear as witnesses, or make similar appearances in the records, literacy was likely to be less common. *Urban male adult* literacy for the nation could not have exceeded 15 to 20 percent; that may be an overly optimistic estimate.

The records indicate that some persons in virtually every class or occupation acquired literacy. They were able to spread information and lend the skill to other persons. Their presence as literates cannot be taken as representative of their class or occupation. Literacy, even as it grew impressively in the towns, remained restricted socially, and its restrictions pivoted especially around class, wealth, and status.[124]

The largest group in the population, those who *worked and resided on the land*, are the most difficult about whom to generalize. As with urban workers, some persons among all ranks and levels had become literate before the sixteenth century. Schooling was not available in all rural areas of the country, and even where it was present, many could not afford to send their youngsters. Some of them did not have sufficient motivation for the loss of family income and labor in the expected returns and utility of the results. The social superiors of yeomen, farmers, rural craftsmen, and agricultural laborers by no means encouraged schooling. Class and resources, as well as popular ideas and values, played large roles.[125]

With the addition of these numbers, the great majority of whom remained illiterate—and with the inclusion of women, relatively few of whom achieved literacy—conclusions can be offered.[126] Though literacy in the countryside and among women expanded, the rate of growth must have been far less than in urban places and among the upper social levels. If urban male literacy is put at about 25 percent maximum, national male literacy could not have been more than one-half of that, and probably closer to one-fourth. Female literacy could not have exceeded one-half that, and probably less. Given the lack of systematic information and direct evidence, such estimates are the best we are likely to possess.

I urge that we do not underestimate the meaning of this achievement. An achievement of even 5 to 10 percent male literacy before the events of the next century—printing's diffusion, the Protestant Reformation, and the like—in the context of medieval social structures and institutions constitutes a major achievement. The major developments of the late Middle Ages underlay this change in literacy levels: the emergence of the vernacular, the education of appreciable numbers of lay students who came from families that were not all wealthy, and the beginnings of secularization in schooling and learning. While granting that "in 1500 Europe had just begun to traverse the road to full literacy,"[127] a foundation for the future was laid.

# PART THREE

# An Old World and
a New World

A nineteenth-century French colporteur bringing print to
the people. Reprinted from Robert Escarpit, Pierre Or-
rechioni, and Nicole Robin, *Les loisirs: La vie populaire
en France du Moyen Age a nos jours*, 2 (Paris: Editions
Diderots, n.d.), p. 315.

CHAPTER FIVE

🐦

# Print, Protest, and the People

COMMENTATORS ON THE CULTURAL and social development of the West have long considered the mid-fifteenth-century invention of printing to mark an epochal shift in the history of Western humanity. The date is commonly taken to signify a "great divide": between medieval and modern, oral and literate, script and print, pretechnological and technological. The associations transcend the social and cultural, to encompass the material, the economic, and the trans-European. They include entrepreneurial capitalism, mass literacy and educational systems, the Reformation, much of the Renaissance, the rise of modern science, the spirit of critical inquiry and scholarship, and major cognitive shifts in the minds and mentalities of Western men and women. This situation constitutes no less than a "printing myth," to rest beside the "literacy myth."[1] Despite the undoubted significance of the onset of printing, its place in Western history is often distorted. Printing represented continuities and contradictions, socially and culturally, as well as the oft-cited changes.

The fifteenth and sixteenth centuries are of the utmost importance in the history of literacy. Not only did the invention of printing, the spread of humanism and Renaissance thought, and the Reformation all occur within a relatively short span, but the Western-dominated world system, the structure of modern states, and the inter- and trans-European relations of capitalism all expanded to significant new levels. These were times of change and reordering of traditional social, political, and economic relationships, although critical continuities remained. As one result, sociocultural contradictions are especially important to note and understand. Of these, literacy provides one important example.

## 1. The Advent and Impact of Print

Books were not exceptionally rare items during the manuscript period.[2] There was even something of an organized scheme of production and exchange. In a general sense, the real growth in the supply of books *before* the age of print was associated with the growth of lay literacy during the latter part of the medieval period. "The coming of the book" did not await the mid-fifteenth-century invention of moveable type.

Well before that point, the demand for books had outrun the capacities of the monastic scriptoria. Professional scriveners and copyists expanded to meet the demand. By the thirteenth century, a distinction developed between the work of authors and that of scribes.

Books produced by hand were susceptible to human errors in copying and transcription. With fundamental texts such as the Scriptures, efforts were made constantly to correct and emend, and a general accuracy could be maintained. With other books, however, manuscript copies tended to become progressively less authentic with successive reproduction. Carelessness, incompetence, and a deterioration in the quality of handwriting increased under lay scriveners and secular literary copying. The "average" manuscript book could be rather sloppy, unattractive, and difficult to read, especially when contrasted with similar writings of the eleventh or twelfth centuries. While deficient by modern standards, "publishing" and trading were sufficient by the end of the period for books to circulate widely throughout much of the West and for something of a reading public to develop.[3]

By the time of the invention of moveable typographic printing, literacy levels were relatively high, literacy was spreading, and books were known and widely distributed. The list of books in circulation before the mid-fifteenth century is long and includes the main writers of classical antiquity. From these texts a huge literature of commentary and creativity was produced; Roman and Greek ideas interplayed with and challenged the Hebrew Scriptures and Christian New Testament. These elements also mixed with the scholarship and science of the Arab world. Medieval writers and scholars tended to produce digests, anthologies, and *florilegia*. Glosses and expounding on texts, with the conviction that a scholastic dialectic would lead them to the truth, were raised to an art.

Most medieval manuscripts were composed and reproduced in Latin. The vernaculars that developed in this period were used increasingly for legal, administrative, and commercial recording, but written literature in them was negatively viewed as secular, popular, and more or less frivolous.[4] Yet, vernacular writing was coming into its own.

Thus was the stage set for the "rise of printing." Change was not swift; the press was received suspiciously by some. It was shaped for decades by traditions and continuities.

Mechanical book production in Europe began in Mainz, Germany, in 1447, in the printing office of Johann Gutenberg, Johann Fust, and, later, Peter Schoeffer. The availability of paper, the development of block printing, the invention of a suitable ink, and the adaptation of the press for printing paved the way for moveable typography. The next step, usually associated with Johann Gutenberg, was the development of metal type. Die casting was the key to the development of type founding. The process was first conducted on a major scale in Mainz.

Early printing was not a simple operation. Highly developed artisanal skills were required to cast type, and an enormous amount of time was spent simply in manufacturing basic elements for imprinting. Huge numbers of types were in use at any one time, all of which were set by hand. Setting one page took perhaps a day. It is estimated that the famous Gutenberg Bible, completed in 1455, required two years for the typesetting alone.[5]

The origin of the mechanical process was only a first step. Development also required time and trials to "learn to accept the technological limitations of typography and to exploit its pecularities."[6] Nevertheless, efforts to understand the impact of printing continue to be plagued by assumptions about an autonomous role of print and its diffusion. A myth of printing and the book has grown up with the literacy myth.[7]

Printing, the book, and literacy have had an enormous impact. The authors of one of the important revisionist studies in the history of printing, Lucien Febvre and Henri-Jean Martin, noted this fact when they wrote that "the printed book was . . . a triumph of technical ingenuity, but was also one of the most potent agents at the disposal of western civilization in bringing together the scattered ideas of representative thinkers." Books, by creating new habits of thought, underlay the development of much of the future.[8]

A sharp distinction between an age of manuscripts and a subsequent era of early printed materials should not be made. With increased production and distribution of hand-copied books and, especially, the introduction of paper, with its sharply lowered costs and increasing supply, it was "possible to satisfy, more or less, the new requirements for books expressed by a steadily growing number of clients." Yet, paper's role was not deterministic; parchment and vellum were in good supply from the second half of the fourteenth century, though printing could not have developed as it did without abundant stocks of paper. As impressive as the production and trade in manuscripts was, it was *not* sufficient to meet all needs of readers and students.[9]

The earlier development of block printing had made possible the multiple reproduction of religious pictures. It was enormously successful at a time at which religious observance was at the center of spiritual and intellectual life, the church was dominant, and culture was still essentially oral. In this context, a graphic technique for the mass reproduction of devotional images must have seemed more important than moveable typographic printing.

Woodcuts depicted legends or saints vividly enough to attract the imagination. In them people could "see the miracles of Christ or scenes from the Passion, feel the Biblical characters come to life in their hands, be reminded of the ever-present fact of death or see the fight between angels and demons for the soul of a dying man." The need for such simple visual items was felt, and responded to, long before that for printed literary, theological, or scientific works, interest in which was much more restricted. Other printed products, such as the spectacularly popular playing cards, quickly developed for the market. Similar production took place in satirical posters, commercial prospectuses, and calendars—in which text began to take precedence over picture.

An entire literature produced by block printing soon grew up. Consisting of the most popular moral and religious tales of the day, in its pages text came to be nearly as important as images and illustration. Not only did these books provide poor and isolated clergy with models for sermons and religious teaching, but their price and format put them within reach of many more people. "Those who could not read could at least grasp the sense of a sequence of pictures, and those who had some rudimentary knowledge of reading . . . could follow the texts much more easily because they were in the vernacular." But block prints had their limits. The difficulty of cutting letters in wood with enough precision to register cleanly was an inescapable restriction. For that reason, the printed book, while influenced by block printing, represents more than a simple refinement, especially in its dependence on metal founding.

The first books (usually termed *incunabula*) *looked just like manuscripts.* Some have suggested that that was to deceive the buyer who distrusted the new mechanical process, or that it was an effort to "pass off" printed books as manuscripts to avoid arousing the unwelcome attention of copyists and their guilds who feared for their monopolies.[10] But the use of the new printing processes did not signify any sudden change in the appearance of the book; printed books looked to contemporaries as books were expected to look. Their acceptance was accomplished directly through their accommodation to the manuscript ideal.

Early types were designed to resemble handwriting. Four basic styles of script were current: the gothic of scholastic texts (traditional "black letter"); the larger-sized gothic or missal letter of ecclesiastical books; "bastard" gothic, used in luxury manuscripts in the vernacular and some Latin texts; and "littera antiqua," the humanist or roman script inspired by the Carolingian miniscule and made popular by Petrarch and his followers. A cursive script was also associated with the roman— the Cancelleresca, based on the writing of the Vatican chancellery—and represented the origin of italic. These were the models for printers. In keeping with tradition, there was a conventional type for each kind of book and reader, just as there was a handwriting.[11]

Within the first century of printing, types became more uniform and standard. Material reasons related to costs of fonts were important, but cultural forces such as the association of humanist texts with roman and italic type and script are at least as significant. A modernizing change took place, shaped, however, by forces of traditions and continuity. Regional styles began to disappear, and, much more slowly, the major forms of script were standardized, until the newer roman type "triumphed" in most of the West.

Other continuities and traditions kept the pace of uniformity slow, and nearly a century passed before roman was used throughout Europe. Only in the third decade of the sixteenth century did roman begin to replace the gothic bastarda in vernacular texts; university professors in France and Germany continued to prefer black letter, which long remained in liturgical texts. Not until the second half of the sixteenth century did popular printers acquire the roman type that the public was coming to expect, when their gothic fonts had to be replaced.

In the fifteenth and even the sixteenth centuries, readers were not greeted by title pages containing author, title, place of publication, publisher, and date; most of the publication information was found at the end of the book in the "colophon"— a residue from manuscripts—including the printer's name, the place of publication, and, perhaps, the title and name of the author.

One new element accompanied the shift from script to print, however: an identifying sign, the printer's mark, made with a woodcut and included with either an incipit or a colophon. By the end of the fifteenth century, the mark had been moved to the title page. Such changes slowly transformed a printed tome from the manuscript model to one more familiar.

The text and format of the book also evolved gradually. Slowly, books left behind

the marks of manuscripts and became simpler, more uniform in design and production. Formatting, spacing, pagination, and size of line shifted to standard, accurate, and more legible dimensions. Lines became more spacious, spelling more
uniform, pages more often set in one column of type than two; greater clarity was
sought; and chapter headings were more clearly indicated. Books began to be smaller
for portability and readability. More in the middle ranks began to collect them.[12]
The invention of typography had no immediate impact on illustrations. Illuminators
and miniaturists continued to work after the advent of printing, painting *on the
printed page* as they had on the handwritten. The method was costly, slow, and,
in general, totally unsuitable for mass book production. Block printing met the need
for mechanical reproduction. A woodcut was easily inserted in a form alongside
the text, and simultaneous printing of picture and text was quickly adopted. This
process originated in Germany.

Many of the illustrations in books were religious images and pictures, a clear
and necessary link with the age of manuscripts and block books. Iconographic
themes were widely diffused. The most popular books in the fifteenth century were
devotional works, most often in the vernacular. Book illustration met a practical
as well as an artistic need: "to make graphic and visible what people of the time
constantly heard evoked."[13] Illustrated books represented one way to instruct those
too uneducated to read the text for themselves.

For technical and financial as well as cultural, reasons, early editions were small
and produced in limited script runs. The market was limited, and regular sales could
be expected for only a few books: the Bible, Donatus's grammar, prayer books,
and the like. The possibility of mass production did not revolutionize the supply
or demand for books.[14]

Typography brought no change in the uncertainty of the livelihood or modes of
compensation of authors. Many new books were printed at the expense of the author
or a patron. If an author was becoming well known, a printer might share in the
costs; if the author was famous, the printer might bear all costs.[15] There was still
no protection or copyright; nothing prevented other publishers or printers from
reprinting without the author's or original printer's knowledge. Pirated editions
were more the norm than exceptions.[16] Only in the seventeenth century did authors
begin to be paid in cash for their work, and only a century later did larger sums
accrue immediately for publication rights. Not until the nineteenth century were
recognizable relations of writers and publishers more or less complete as we know
them.[17]

The advent of printing did represent change. Significant new trends were created
in the wake of the ensuing technological revolution. Yet, of at least equal import
is how little major change took place *at first*. The lines joining the age of manuscripts
to that of printed books and moveable typography were strong and firm. Regardless
of its potential for sociocultural transformation, typographic printing was introduced
to a largely receptive public and was shaped and conditioned by the manuscript
traditions.[18] To find this development contradictory is to understand how historical
change takes place. Innovation is seldom revolutionary in the short term. The
realization of books' possibilities came only with time.

The process of growth and diffusion of printing, important in itself, is a step toward assessing printing's relevance for the spread of humanism, Renaissance currents, and religious reform, on one hand, and the relationship of all four topics to conditions of literacy and schooling, on the other. Related is the issue of printing's impact during its first two centuries.[19]

The first master printers were Germans—either apprentices of Gutenberg and Schoeffer or workmen who learned from those apprentices. This small group of artisans is as noteworthy for their enterprise and spirit of adventure and risk taking as for their technical skills. They established printing across Europe, and sought the capital and a town in which to establish themselves permanently and successfully. Mobile, migratory printers, largely Germans, taught the craft to much of the West.[20]

The church's role in the creation, preservation, and reproduction of manuscript writings was long central to the culture of the West. In this tradition, many in the church turned rapidly to printing when it became available: bishops, monastics, and groups such as the Brethren of Common Life. For a number of years, ironically it turned out, the Roman church was strongly supportive of the new art industry.[21] Printers were commissioned, and supported, by the church to provide church books to meet a large demand; some churchmen and monks initiated their own presses.[22]

The demand for liturgical works was greatest. To assist theologians and clerics in their work, the Scriptures and other theological materials were commonly published; texts of classical antiquity and others for student use were produced for educational purposes. Above all, works of more popular piety in the format of tracts and manuals were common. The press seemed best suited to serve the needs of scholarship, education, and popular devotion. Churchmen were among the leaders of press support.[23] Support for printers also came from individual and institutional efforts reflecting diverse motivations, from the sacred to the scholarly. Channels for interest and patronage reflected a process of laicization (a term more appropriate than *secularization*) and diffusion that was under way long before printing began to replace hand copying.

Printers faced a problem in locating and developing a market for their new commodity. The successful early printers published works for which the most demand existed, books beyond those for the relatively restricted academic market. They also had to seek out the more popular market; so in addition to works for libraries and scientific use, they printed devotional literature and little books at cheaper prices, in large numbers, with a market large enough to demand more and more copies. With time, diversification within the trade became the norm for the larger, more successful printers.[24] The need to reach a "mass," nonlatinate reading public was imperative for survival. Reading had become a ritual in properly run merchant households; family and collective reading habits helped to shape the market. The problem for printers was to bring their wares to the attention of potential purchasers.

With the availability of printing causing a gradual shift in buying habits from used to new books, assessing demand was now an entirely different matter; failure led to the end of many printing businesses. Book buyers' habits were shaped by the manuscript market. An educational effort was required for the potential of print to be realized by readers with sufficient resources to expend. One response, apparent in Italy before the sixteenth century and perhaps later elsewhere, was the use of peddlers and middlemen dealers and sellers to bring books to potential buyers, to help develop a market and better balance demand and supply. Printers also began to avoid specialization, finding it more prudent to publish a variety of titles to promote sales and reduce risks. Overdiversification was also risky. Vernacular and popular religious publishing were stimulated in this way. There were several reading publics, and tapping them was one key to success.[25]

Presses tended to prosper in university and scholarly centers. Ecclesiastical and secular administrative centers also attracted and sustained early printing businesses. A century after the initial spread of printing, new universities were being created, especially in Protestant areas; they provided new markets for printers. In much of Catholic Europe, however, and even in some reformed places, economic crises and savage competition reduced opportunities for many. Censorship, in lands Protestant and Catholic, was also increasing. Declining university markets impelled printers to search for stable markets in lesser towns and in producing posters, official announcements, and pamphlets. They also benefited from the seventeenth-century growth of bureaucracy.[26]

Educational developments, typically associated with expansion of schooling and the increase in literacy in the Reformation and post-Reformation years, also stimulated demand for printing work. The Jesuits, like the Brethren before them, were active in this field, as were humanist educators and grammar masters. Their efforts and the colleges they founded provided work and attracted printers to towns. Other professionals, especially lawyers, and prospering merchants added to demand, as the bourgeoisie and some successful artisans sought to amass their own collections. Reflected in these trends is the major shift from the famed humanist printers to the jobbers and printers of more ordinary materials. From the "golden age" of printers came the more "modern" work—which had a far greater impact on the course of literacy, schooling, and nonelite culture.

Despite all comments about the slow spread of printing, its progress, for its time, was surprisingly rapid. By 1480, a quarter-century after the first important books were printed, presses were operating in more than 110 towns in Western Europe. Several German and Italian firms had grown to a point at which they had trading contacts in much of the West; in Italy, no town of importance was without a press, and some towns rivaled the great German centers. By the early 1480s, the balance had shifted, and Venice had become the printing capital. As a result of its geographical location, wealth, and intellectual life, great support for printers led to tremendous growth. Mainz had lost some of its initial significance, and Italy claimed more numerous, productive printers and centers.[27]

A reading public existed outside humanist circles, within the middle class and largely preprofessional and professional. Their interest was in learning the classical languages as preparation for professional training, not in the ideas of the ancients. The books available reflected the large number of religious and theological titles. Sermons, liturgy, pastorals, and devotionals were popular works.[28]

Personal piety and religiosity were central in late quattrocento Italy. Printed *vernacular* books were the "best sellers" of the day. Moral treatises, confessional manuals, lives and passions of Christ and the Virgin, and the like appealed to many

## TABLE 5.1
### Incunabula Production by Country

|                    | Actual No. | | Percentage | | Projected No. | |
|                    | GKW[a] | Lenhart[b] | GKW | Lenhart | GKW | Lenhart |
|--------------------|-------|-------|------|--------|--------|--------|
| Italy              | 3,386 | 9,766 | 37.5 | 41.9   | 15,000 | 16,816 |
| Germany            | 2,752 | 6,876 | 30.4 | 29.5   | 12,160 | 11,845 |
| France             | 1,478 | 3,639 | 16.3 | 15.6   | 6,520  | 6,275  |
| Netherlands        | 714   | 1,955 | 7.9  | 8.4    | 3,160  | 3,368  |
| Switzerland:       |       |       |      |        |        |        |
|   German | 261   |       | 2.9  |        | 1,160  |        |
|   French | 36    |       | 0.4  |        | 160    |        |
| Spain and Portugal | 270   | 605   | 3.0  | 2.6    | 1,200  | 1,054  |
| England            | 109   | 274   | 1.2  | 1.2    | 480    | 472    |
| Other Countries    | 29    | 193   | 0.4  | 0.8    | 160    | 116    |
| Total              | 9,035 | 23,308 |     |        | 40,000 | 39,946 |

[a]Carl Wehmer, "Inkunabelkunde," *Zentralblatt fuer Bibliothekswesen*, 57 (1940): 214–32.
[b]John M. Lenhart, *Pre-Reformation Printed Books: A Study in Statistical and Applied Bibliography*, vol. 14: *Franciscan Studies* (New York: Joseph F. Wagner, 1935), p.26.
Source: L.V. Gerulaitus, *Printing and Publishing in Fifteenth-Century Venice* (Chicago: American Library Association, 1976), p.60.

among the literate and their illiterate relations and coresidents at the time. Authors on occasion addressed women as well as men, and sometimes seem to have anticipated broader diffusion among illiterates and servants.[29] Professional and religious literature dominated in this period; printing was only in very small part concerned with the spread of humanist ideas.[30]

Thus was the printing business founded, and thus did it begin to expand and develop. This growth continued into the next century, as presses were founded regularly in towns and cities, and as it became an industry under the control of wealthy capitalists and a big international business.

The expansion of printing was rapid in Germany and France in the sixteenth century. The Italian book trade, though, became less active by the turn of the century. Conditions there, with local strife, economic decline, and foreign invasion, were not conducive to expansion. Real decline marked the trend, even in Venice, by the third and fourth decades of the sixteenth century. England, in sharp contrast, developed an independent trade rapidly. Its partial isolation from the Continent during the Reformation was a major stimulus to production at home, which the Tudors aided with protectionist economic policies.[31]

As small as the earliest editions were, many more volumes were produced than scribes could write. The potentials for mass reproduction were of great significance.[32] Some contemporaries saw great value in print, but that value was realized only gradually over time. Continuities and contradictions accompanied, and helped to shape, the changes that took place.[33]

Elizabeth Eisenstein's *The Printing Press as an Agent of Change* is a monumental work dealing with the impact of printing.[34] It is concerned primarily with the effects of printing on written records and on the views of already literate elites, and it makes some important points. Eisenstein argues that the shift from script to print revolutionized all forms of learning. She attempts to relate this shift to significant historical developments, focusing on the advent of printing and the resulting "communications revolution." She regards dissemination, standardization, reorganization, data collection, preservation, and amplification and reinforcement as the six seminal features that constituted an "initial" shift.

In regard to dissemination, Eisenstein believes that the increased access to books caused something of a "knowledge explosion" among late- fifteenth- and sixteenth-century intellectuals. Printing fostered greater cross-cultural exchange; master printers gathered around them circles of intellectuals whose labors were essential to their work, but whose presence and mutual stimulation resulted in "forms of combinatory activity which were social as well as intellectual" and were "conducive to cross-fertilization of all kinds." Scholarly and pious activity both increased.[35]

The capacity to produce uniform images and typography made possible by early printing methods represented a great leap forward. Affecting a wide range of cultural characteristics, standardization has had a major and long-term impact. Among other things, it influenced awareness of differences, including regional customs, styles, and languages.

The reorganization of texts and reference guides—rationalizing, codifying, and cataloguing data—is another important element. Eisenstein postulates that early printers' editorial decisions about format "probably helped to reorganize the thinking of readers." She speculates that "basic changes in book format might well lead to changes in thought-patterns." The encouragement that printed reference works gave to "repeated recourse to alphabetic order" may not be so unprecedented and revolutionary. For example, reading instruction had been initiated from the days of antiquity forward through the memorization of the letters of the alphabet; more recent reformers have questioned the usefulness of mere rote learning of "meaningless symbols and sounds."

With printing and its greater volume and accessibility of books came a larger need for and more frequent recourse to the ordering of the alphabet. More systematic cataloguing and indexing became not only feasible but desirable. Analogously, a "rationalization of format helped to systematize scholarship in diverse fields." Too much can be made of the "alphabetization" of Western humanity; the documentable consequences, in organization of knowledge and work habits, are sufficiently important in themselves. New, logical, rationalized formats for various kinds of data and information served many purposes, such as law and science; their full effects deserve far greater attention than presumptive speculations.[36] And, in time, they too were recognized as limiting and obstructive.

Printing also brought the technology to continually improve and correct successive editions of a work, especially a large reference work. The new medium made errors and inconsistencies more visible to learned men; the association of some printers with scholars accelerated and emphasized this use of the new technology's potential. Sixteenth-century publishers "created vast networks of correspondents [and] solicited criticism of each edition. . . ." Such data collection brought new modes of research and new standards, which influenced efforts in natural and human sciences and humanistic scholarship that led, in turn, to further interchanges and new investigations. The collection of more data stimulated more refined classification. The process took more than two centuries of print to achieve; it was not a simple or direct result of the new mechanical invention.[37]

Preservation may be the most important of print's duplicative powers. Increased copying of manuscripts often resulted in corruption and error, and using and storing materials caused damage and disintegration. With printing, durability was not as important. Paper, one of the keys to the successful diffusion of printing, was abundant and could be discarded without thought, but, ironically, it was less durable and permanent than parchment and vellum and led to the development of new techniques for preservation. In some ways, the preservative powers of print had to be learned; they were not automatically adopted.

Printing accelerated the decrease in Latin and the increase in vernacular usage. Some regional vernaculars emerged dominant as national tongues, whereas others died out or survived orally. Barriers of language were reinforced between peoples by print; and between geographical-linguistic areas, homogenization was more rapidly achieved. National literary cultures developed more quickly in the sixteenth and seventeenth centuries through the contributions of the printing press. Schools and governments also worked toward unifying national languages, but printing played a key role, and printers seeking markets for their wares encouraged the uses of the vernacular.

Printers were key figures in the standardization of spelling, grammar, and vocabulary. "By encouraging production in the national languages for economic reasons, the book trade was in the end fostering the development of those languages— and bringing about the decline of Latin. . . ." Whereas they underlay and encouraged the spread of literacy and aided the creation of mass and class cultures, such developments also contributed to political fragmentation. As they facilitated national unity and social cohesion, they also contributed to internal differentiation. The uses of printing, language, and literacy are diverse and contradictory.[38]

With increased print came increased repetition (creation of typologies, archetypes, and stereotypes), reinforcing and amplifying the messages.[39] This impact was gradual and uneven, especially with the slow progress of literacy and the uneven distribution of printed books. Reinforcement was also the norm of earlier culture and learning.

Any "initial shift from script to print" directly affected only a small portion of the population. Print did not produce deterministically or mystically readers and literates without intermediate steps, such as schooling. The level of literacy was not raised rapidly by printing.

One must distinguish between literacy and habitual reading. Not all of those who learned to read and write became book readers. The oral focus in reading instruction persisted, and apprenticeship learning (learning by seeing and doing) and the use of mnemonic devices and memory reliance continued. Important uses of older ways apparently remained sufficient among the "already literate elites" of Western Europe; some were "rediscovered."

The role of imagery and its relationship to print and literacy are complex. If a movement from images to words took place, it was an exceptionally slow process.

It seems more likely, as the use of illustrations and the development of new reproduction techniques suggest, that images continued even as words increased. Their
role may have shifted; in special contexts, as in the arts and scientific inventions,
a different form of literacy from alphabetic mental processes was at work. A dichotomy should not be drawn between the two.

The oral and the written continued to interact. In many cases, spoken words were
conveyed but not replaced by print. Printed sermons and orations continued to be
delivered orally. How these forms of discourse were affected by "new possibilities
of silent publication" remains an important question. That the recording of, say,
parliamentary debates, the printing of poems, plays, and songs, or the preparation
of speeches for print rather than delivery changed them and their culture speaks of
accelerations from the impact of writing rather than unprecedented impacts. Literary
culture continued to be assimilated by the ear as well as by the eye.[40]

Different groups were affected differentially. Rural villagers did not relate to
print in the same way as many urban residents, but what they heard had, in many
instances, been transformed by printing; they were also read to directly. Bookshops,
coffee houses, and reading rooms provided new gathering places; "even while
communal solidarity was diminished, vicarious participation in more distant events
was also enhanced; and even while local ties were loosened, links to larger collective
units were being forged." Ties could remain relatively firm and solid while the
other trends were gaining, we are beginning to understand.[41]

It is likely that the availability of printed materials did increase the level of
readership in places where readers and schools were present. Supply does not result
automatically in demand and use; nor does an increase in reading materials lead
simply and directly to more readers. But it was most likely the new readers, groups
who previously had had little access to books, who were most strongly affected by
the new printing method.

Rudolph Hirsch presents fascinating evidence on what some writers expressed
to and about their readers. Most statements seem to be simple moralisms or homilies,
but some go beyond formal formulisms. Books were identified by authors as intended for specific audiences, usually by age, gender, or social status. Revealing
is the 1484 comment by Lanzkranna in his *Himmelstrasse* [Heavenly Road]: "I
have put this book into concise form and I have used simple words to show how
men should live; I have done so for the sake of the poor and the ignorant, the
intemperate and the lazy, the cross, the forgetful and the simple." One part recognition of readers' skills, perhaps, to several parts hope for sales and pious intentions. Other books, as for centuries afterwards, stressed the moral value of
reading.[42] Hirsch writes:

> These and other passages prove authors' and printers' concern with readers and though
> it was obviously in their interest to recommend their books to as many people as
> possible, and especially to the new reader (the common man), this form of advertising
> presupposes the ability of "rude" men and women to read their recommendations.
> To teach how to read was the natural concern of schoolmen, sometimes of the clergy,
> and late of reformers.

After some decades of printing had passed, educators saw the potential for a
literate population in building a moral, godly, trained, and civil society. With the

aid of the printing press and its capabilities for mass reproduction, mass literacy could be sought in a manner never before attempted, and maintained through moral reading. The press was a tool, but the ideas came not from its agency but from humanists and reformers of religion and society.[43]

The enormous increase in the printing of elementary grammars not only made the study of grammar somewhat more accessible, it also gave those who learned some Latin a firmer grounding. More standard and uniform writing resulted. The classics, translated into the vernacular *and* circulated more fully, were brought to the eyes *and* ears of many more persons. Both Latin language and literature study and vernacular learning benefited.[44] Mass communication was newly possible, as was standardization of grammar, orthography, vocabulary, and diction. To emphasize that several additional centuries were required for their fuller effects is not to reduce printing's role.

Finally, printing, for the few, it seems, had more immediate and direct impact. In the case of commercial arithmetics or the Ramist method, printing's products were important, although even in these relatively clear-cut examples, printing's impact required more than half a century to be felt.

Peter Ramus, a sixteenth-century scholar, promoted the use of method as a formal, conscious part of logical scholarly procedure. He attempted to extend the idea of the economy of an "art" to the whole of discourse, which he considered fundamentally a means of "teaching," ruled by a topical logic. He struggled for a method to guide his search for principles that would enable a student to construct a demonstration of the cause or reason for a fact.[45]

Printing contributed by furthering the shift in the relationship between space and discourse. Ramus thought of speech in terms not of sound but of space; he asserted that the elements of words are not sounds but letters—which have sound only when combined with other "oral" letters. With printing, books began to be regarded as objects, and no longer as bits of speech.

Ramus was encouraged by ways of organizing thought according to spatial models. Printed textbooks enabled teachers to focus on the spatial arrangement of material. Directives such as "Look at page seven, line three, the fourth word" became routine. "Millions of schoolboys were inducted into an understanding of language and of the world around them by making their way conjointly through individual texts arranged in identical spatial patterns."[46]

Ramus's method affected the commercial world of artisans and merchants, in whose schools such a curricular approach was strong. It was congenial to the bourgeois mentality; merchants and artisans, as "dealers in physical wares," were concerned with commodities, things visible, definite, and commanding itemization and inventory control. The Ramist method appealed to the desire for order; it was a technique for organization that offered a more or less objective view.

Printing was associated with artisans and commerce in a way that scribal copying was not. Printers could set type without having to be able to pronounce or even understand the words. Books were increasingly regarded as products of crafts, as commodities. Thus the word was reified—a prelude to *selling* it, rather than subjecting it to formal analysis. Ramus's concept of method has been compared to the printing process itself, in that "it enables one to impose organization on a subject by imagining it as made up of parts fixed in space much in the way in which words are locked into a printer's form.''[47]

The similarity apparently lies between the process of "methodizing" materials for study and analysis spatially by Ramists and the setting up of type taken from a font. Analogously, Ramus's textbooks were organized for visual, not auditory, assimilation, through the use of headings, tables, and diagrams. The organization of subjects according to "method" may have been an accommodation to the mentality of the merchant and artisan. Knowledge lost some of its mystery and became something more manageable.

Merchants' needs for and use of accounting principles and techniques were paralleled and reinforced by the Ramist vision of knowledge. "A young boy taught the principles of method could feel assured in advance of control of any body of knowledge which might come his way.''[48] Thus, some merchants and artisans found Ramist approaches advantageous to their work and suited to their world views.

The authors of the sixteenth-century French arithmetics, which applied mathematical techniques to business, focused on method and technique, avoiding any mention of religion or morality. "The implied or explicit suggestion was that necessary business practice was the ordinary guide to behavior." They thus attempted to enhance the prestige of business, showing the merchant as an important, patriotic, cultivated man.[49] Printing helped to circulate such materials in quantity to relevant audiences.

In Renaissance Florence, formal professional training in commercial subjects became important for sons of the patriciate. Following elementary schooling and training in basic literacy, boys were sent to *scuola d'abbaco* for three or four years of commercial education. Commercial arithmetic played a major part in this schooling. From the thirteenth century, when the formal institutions were founded, the curriculum emphasized instruments, manuals, and methods. In school as in texts, method played a central part. A logico-spatial bias is obvious in teachers and texts, attention to organization and method, and the formats that such calculations obviously required.[50] With the merchants, a strong, if presumptive, case is presented for the importance of printing's influence.

Printing's role was not simple, independent, or linear. It was used for many purposes, new and old, forward- and backward-looking; it was employed as an agent for many different ends. Its roles were complex, and their relevance for humanism, religion, Renaissance, Reformation, and literacy and schooling has but been hinted. In these complex and mutually reinforcing contexts, printing had vastly important implications.

## 2. Renaissance(s) Revisited

Among the connections that dominate early modern European history is the stereotypical assertion of the links tying humanism or the Renaissance, with its educational component, to the advent and diffusion of printing. More is involved than the fact that printing resulted in a greater volume and circulation of humanistic texts and writings and that leading humanists were closely associated with scholarly printers/ entrepreneurs.

The more "revolutionary" impact of printing lay in the increase in extant texts.[51] Printers first contributed not by marketing new works but by providing greater quantities of the old. Increased production changed patterns of book consumption. The literary fare of a sixteenth-century reader was qualitatively different from that of his or her fourteenth-century predecessor. The role that printing played influenced both the continuities and the changes that occurred.[52]

Although travelers and translators had communicated humanist currents outside of Italy, printing made a difference. Fewer trips were made; printed materials reduced the reliance on personal encounters. The spread and reception of Renaissance humanist ideas were conditioned by the process of migration. As the transformation of Italian ideas into something of a Christian humanism shows, "It would be a mistake to separate classical and Christian traditions too sharply," the northern from the southern renaissances.[53]

Printing made possible a more "permanent" Renaissance. Here is an important if easily exaggerated example of the preservative power of print. For Eisenstein, the classical revival was reoriented during this period of transition and transformation. The shift, related to print, involved a new sense of a fixed distance between the living present and the past (a sense of history), distinction between the activities of the ancients and the moderns, correcting and clarifying rather than retrieving old texts, and, eventually, a struggle for originality. Print's role was significant, but it was likely facilitating and contributing rather than cognitively shaping. Printing was a useful tool in furthering the recovery process and the development of techniques for investigating the past. It shaped the process, but it neither determined it nor possessed a dynamic of its own.

Eisenstein adds a shift toward "modern forms of consciousness" to the transformations. She cites publicity efforts by authors and printers and associates the press with a heightened recognition of individual achievement. The process of making private thoughts public was not fully realized until authors began to address an audience of silent and solitary readers.

An enhanced recognition of singularity seems to result from typographical standardization, or at least from its mass reproductive potential. Apparently influencing visual artistic as well as literary production, it represents another aspect of the consequences that may derive from the preservative powers of print.[54]

A veritable avalanche of treatises aimed at a variety of forms of self-help and improvement, from praying to singing and accounting, rolled from sixteenth-century presses.[55] Potential was being created for self-instruction. Its implications for the future, rather than for the sixteenth century, were a point of origin for another of literacy's legacies. Its roots in the development and diffusion of printing are significant, even if several centuries and an enormous increase in popular schooling and literacy were required for its realization.

The use of self-instruction for personal religion in the sixteenth century was obviously of tremendous consequence. Progress was made in some areas of literature and scientific invention, but self-learning had little impact on crafts and artisanal skilled work; rather, more training programs began to insist on some schooling in literacy (and morality, of course) as part of apprenticeship requirements. Masters taught, as well as teachers.[56] The proliferation of new technical and vocational literature was *a source* of change, but it did not immediately stimulate new patterns of training or new career lines.

Medical self-help was one area affected by new printed works. The medical profession, with its rituals of training and quasi-medical trade secrets and reliance on Latin, long resisted individual action. There are other "professional" fields in which some of the possibilities for individualized learning created by printing were discouraged, as well. Yet, printing began to create new possibilities and to allow some to engage them. Memory reliance and prompters were gradually reduced in importance, but visual images remained essential, perhaps underlying a nonalpha-betic literacy for artists, artisans, or inventors. The interactions between printed text and printed image are elusive and complex, as are those between the uses of applied technological knowledge and scholarly theories. Much more than either printing or literacy is involved.

New interchanges between persons, traditions, and developing disciplines were enormously enriching—at least for the few. "Publication programs launched from urban workshops in many regions made it possible to combine and coordinate scattered investigations on a truly unprecedented scale."[57] Printing's part was spe-cial.

The process of change was hardly swift or smooth. "Mysteries" of the past were not suddenly shed. The emergence of printing did not erase centuries of transmission of trade skills by ritual and initiation; "thus when 'technology went to press' so too did a vast backlog of occult practices and formulas and few readers were able to discriminate between the two." The printing of traditional crafts and lore reflected the traditions and the historical context of their amplification in type. Magic may well have increased in popularity as one result of printing's impact.[58]

The most important aspect of the advent of printing in respect to humanism and scholarly work was its potential for technological mass reproduction. "Successive printed editions of sixteenth-century reference works became easier to use and more useful. . . . the data contained in early editions were supplemented, clarified, codi-fied, and surpassed by later ones."[59] But for the time being, printing and humanism contributed little to schooling and literacy. Humanism was not a *mass* movement. Its educational impact was important, but it was circumscribed. In the later fifteenth through the sixteenth centuries, comparatively few went to school, although im-portant transitions occurred. Comparatively few of the schools in operation or the new foundations relied heavily upon humanistic texts, pedagogies, or philosophies. For too long have a few great texts, manifestoes, or schoolmasters been taken as representing major shifts and large-scale trends. Yet, with humanism, and also "Christian humanism," came new ideas, goals, and standards for schooling. While their immediate impact did not permeate very far, in time they had a more mo-mentous meaning. From humanism came significant legacies of literacy.

The humanists had a great deal to say about the typical practices of their day. Little was complimentary. Their solutions were not addressed often to the ordinary or poorer child; rather, they proposed most of their reforms at the grammar school or university level, not the elementary level that was the only sort of schooling that most children were likely to obtain. Humanist pedagogues had remarkably little to say about primary schooling for the masses, except to stress morality and religion.[60]

For most families in early modern Europe, schooling of any sort was relatively rare and expensive. If some schooling was possible, such youth were unlikely to encounter an institution or instructor familiar with the reforms promoted by the humanists. Many grammar schoolmasters were more hostile than friendly to the "new learning," with the child closer to its center, comprehension stressed above memory, complete study of complete texts, cults of eloquence, and quests for total individual development.[61] Humanistic influence for more was felt in other ways.

If R. R. Bolgar is correct, humanistic educational reform in the north did not represent a great advance over scholastic modes of schooling. In the sixteenth century, some educators found answers to pedagogical problems by considering the role of factual information. But the mainstream of sixteenth-century Protestant reformers believed that "a teacher's first duty was to inculcate sound religious and moral principles." Toward this end, the classics and the arts of expression were subordinated to the goals of piety and morality, which required detailed instruction in Latin and restricted reading. That was one way in which humanism was felt in education in the later fifteenth and sixteenth centuries. Its effectiveness in Italy was declining, however.[62]

In Italy, there may have been little direct connection between the growth of Renaissance humanism and that of literacy and schooling. The platform of the essentially educational humanism was never directed toward a broad audience, regardless of its own impressive breadth. Historical materials and studies indicate that a "declension" in both literacy and humanistic education took place by the late fifteenth century and continued into the sixteenth.[63]

Another form of elementary, lay-sponsored education was developing in Italy at this time: schooling for the poor, one aspect of charity and care for the poor for which institutions developed in both Catholic and Protestant states in the fifteenth and sixteenth centuries. These developments were linked to humanism—not the more rarefied classical humanism of the higher studies, but a Christian humanism, with a new attitude toward the poor and the importance of proper social conduct. That became the new basis for charity, as the state as well as higher ecclesiastical authorities began to assume greater responsibilities toward the poor.

Schooling was one of a variety of efforts initiated in the sixteenth century. Unlike contemporary philanthropy in Reformation England, with its increasing endowments of schools and promotion of secondary education, schooling efforts in Venice centered on extensive provision for orphaned and poor children. Institutions emphasized religious training but also provided instruction in literacy and numeracy. Education stressed Christian doctrine, conduct, trade schooling, or other skill provisions that would reduce poverty and dependency. Poor laws moved in similar directions. More general educational efforts were apparently not attempted. Venice, along with other places in Italy, also established an extensive Sunday school movement, "which aimed at raising the general level of literacy, because literacy was the key to Christian knowledge. Ostensibly, this movement . . . probably drew more heavily on the poor than on the genteel."

Power, control, and a form of hegemony over the poor were central aspects of this educational charity. Education—training in literacy as a means to moral, religious, and civil ends—was one form of social, cultural, and economic power. While not unprecedented, this use of education was novel in its application to larger numbers and those in the lower ranks of the social structure.[64]

For the sixteenth century, efforts such as these were common throughout the West. They brought accessibility to literacy to some who had little chance of attaining its skills otherwise. This literacy was never neutral or functionally conceived. Long noted for Protestant areas, and seen as a marked differential between geo-religious regions, this evidence argues for a less simplistic interpretation. Religion was only one important factor. We are just beginning to see the multiple interactions that determined levels of schooling and rates of literacy. New provision for schooling the poor was initiated in Catholic Italy, but it is unlikely that collective levels of literacy changed much as a result. That does not diminish the significance of the institutions and their efforts.[65] The uses of literacy and the motives for provision of training are as interesting as the rates themselves.

Moving from southern to northern Europe, another dimension is added: "Christian humanism." Present in the Italian strain of humanism increasingly by the late fifteenth and sixteenth centuries, Christian considerations were never wholly absent. The difference is more a matter of timing, emphasis, and local circumstances.[66]

"That humanists should combine one self-appointed role, the schoolmasters of secular Europe, with another as the re-educators of Christendom, was a foregone conclusion," writes J. R. Hale. It accompanied their desire to reestablish the original texts of the civilization, including not only Plato, Aristotle, and Cicero, but also the establishment of the Christian church. A consequence of their attack on scholasticism was an attack on attitudes toward religion, scholastic method, and the type of priest produced by theology faculties. They found wanting the neglect of sources, rote learning, uncritical acceptance of bad authorities, and stress on form rather than content. They criticized religious practices that underemphasized Christ but stressed the worship of saints and rote repetition of unknown and unfelt prayers.[67]

Within this movement were the seeds of its own failure to capture mass support, to lead to reforms that might have prevented the divisive Reform and counter reforms. Some humanists lost any hope of acceptance by seeing themselves literally as living in the world of the ancients. Others stressed wisdom and ethics at the expense of the miraculous and revelatory, weakening the sense of conviction and surrender needed for a widely felt regeneration of Christianity. Eclecticism was also a factor. Humanist scholarly curiosity, on one hand, and the emphasis on moral philosophy that led them to a wide variety of source materials that they thought relevant to the study of religious life, on the other, led them far from liturgy and matters of the pulpit. Writing in Latin, lacking institutional influence, and without corps of preachers, "inevitably it could act only as a very slow leaven within the spiritual life of Europe as a whole."[68] Similarly, its impact on schooling and literacy was limited.

In *pre-Reformation Germany,* a heavily leavened Christian humanism became a force of significance among the highly educated groups and played an important part in the road to Reformation. That is important, but it does not constitute a case for the direct and large-scale impact of humanism on mass schooling or popular literacy. German humanists, like others elsewhere, had goals that extended beyond the more narrow intellectual circles and schools that served as their personal and professional boundaries, but these were seldom extended, their impact rarely felt outside in a direct way. For example, their spirit was not that of the churchliness of popular religiosity.[69]

German humanists were deeply concerned about education. Their concern, however, was seldom aimed at lower levels or popular schooling. Their aim was higher than one that might have influenced the broader courses of literacy and instruction for the many. In the end, those who broke with their ranks, most particularly Luther, found that they had to reject the Renaissance synthesis of the problem of religion and culture. While humanists maintained their program of classical studies within the secondary and university curricula and gradually reverted to synergisms and a spiritualized view of the Sacrament, those who sought actively to reform the church and the world "clarified the theological picture by commissioning regenerate man to build a truly Christian culture as a work of love, not as an exaltation of self nor as a work of justification before God."[70]

Perhaps the best example of this complex, contradictory set of beliefs was the professional scholar Desiderius Erasmus, the "Prince of Christian Humanism."[71] Born in 1466, he was educated by the Brethren of Common Life. His formal education included a variety of religious, monastic, and secular schools, and his diverse experience colored his views on schooling and pedagogy. His intellectual interactions took him not only throughout the Low Countries and the German lands but also to Italy, France, and England.[72]

Erasmus spent a great deal of his time in cooperative work with printers. Much of his work served to produce standard editions of texts of the New Testament and the Christian fathers. He was also concerned with the state of education. His educational goals were directed toward raising the standard of religion and conduct in the community.

Erasmus dealt prominently with state and community service. In accord with classical ideals, parents were urged to teach their children citizenship, responsibility, courtesy, and good manners: qualities of properly schooled members of society. Even with their ancient roots, these qualities are forward-looking. They became an end to which the properly controlled transmission of literacy was devoted. Vocational training was never ranked above social, literary, or individual aims.

Erasmus's humanistic educational aims are significant, but they had special limits. For all his psychological theorizing and sweeping statements, Erasmus's program was limited first by the clientele whose schooling needs he wished to improve. With other humanists, he was concerned with the relatively few who were expected to advance to secondary and university education.

Only the classical languages were permitted for instructional purposes, eliminating "purely national elements in education" and substituting for them "a universal culture." "The popular speech has, and ought to have, no claim to be regarded as a fit instrument of literary expression." Modern languages lacked the fixity, definiteness, and uniformity that the ancient ones possessed. Erasmus held popular stories, folklore, and traditional tales of national heroes in contempt, especially deprecating their use with young children. He stressed that the only material suited for instruction was that of the ancients. Arguing that only thus could mind come into contact with mind, he felt that subsequent inquiry had added nothing to their wisdom and claimed that outside of them no organized secular knowledge existed.[73]

Erasmus was an astute critic of much that ailed classical and theological instruction. His censures were influential, but his intentions and writings remained limited. In key respects, the humanists were too restricted for some of their own stated ends. To assert their contributions for schooling and literacy more widely is distorting to them. There were exceptions, however, principally in England. Their goals were approached only gradually. For the moment, they were incorporated into the evolving traditions of the legacies of literacy, to which humanism contributed.

Development in *France* was little different. The benefits of French peace and security in the beginning of the sixteenth century were reaped by the men of the middle class, "above all because the modern state was taking shape bit by bit, with its specialized bureaucracy, basic services, and need for informed and technically trained people in law, administration, diplomacy, and finance." Learning was one tool for success, and printing was a fine way to assist this new demand for learning: religious materials, schoolbooks, practical literature, classics. Classical ideas became attractive, and some of the currents of medieval thought and mind were left behind. With relatively few humanist teachers and institutions, a tremendous struggle was required for advancing in one's education.

French Renaissance persons quested for knowledge and beauty, but they remained Christian and faithful. For most, religion was more a part of life than a formal belief or a thing taught. All were to go to church; all had the right to feel their place there, regardless of their rank, wealth, or station. Still, the majority spoke only their regional tongue, and few could read in any language. Mass was said in Latin, and prayers were "incomprehensible incantations." The people felt a sense of obligation to attend church, but their minds were undoubtedly "in the fields, the woods, the moors, and with the fairies, spirits, and other objects of traditions and superstitions that constituted the stuff of belief." They clung to obscure, independent traditions, the surviving traditions of a latent paganism.[74] In this context, as in Germany, a late medieval outpouring of piety took place.

Above the masses were the few who had been taught formally. These men discussed and disputed and nourished their faith with dogmatic and theological arguments. They were mostly middle-class people who "knew the value of education and the power of human knowledge." The world of the masses was different, a world in which formal doctrines and dogmas seldom penetrated and in which written texts were rare.[75]

Scholarly concerns did not affect most people. In the cities, ideas and texts did circulate more widely, but within social and literary limits. Their relevance to most lives was restricted, and overlaps were most likely with the practical ones of merchants and artisans, with links to Ramist classifications. Humanist intellectual life was in practice more narrowly confined to smaller numbers of upper middle and upper class. "The intellectuals who lived in the first thirty or forty years of the sixteenth century embodied an ideal of human progress. They were able to communicate to others their faith and hope. . . ."[76] Humanists, as elsewhere, were first scholars, writers, editors, and teachers. Insofar as they were popularizers, it was of the classics and the wisdom that they derived from their studies of the ancients; it was not of and for the people.

Men such as Guillaume Budé led the French humanist scholars. A classicist and learned man, he was also a zealous Catholic; he was a Christian humanist, subscribing to a view of life that justified both his religion and his scholarly activities. He was also a monarchist, an advocate of the rule of law, an opponent of war and waste, and a patriot. Budé was concerned about the education of princes, but he was more interested in classical studies. His writings stress the cultivation of reason and eloquence, especially through the study of classical literature.[77]

The town grammar schools in Renaissance France encapsulated the educational program of this humanism. A new kind of school, they were established quickly and widely for the bourgeoisie, under the control of municipalities. The celebration of learning and letters became an intellectual fashion and a cultural trait of this class, as well as a "passport to honors." The *collèges* were the creation and the mark of the higher bourgeoisie in their quests for status, culture, and training. Their pupils included children of the nobility, but also those of merchants and others "who are being prepared to live without working in a workshop or countinghouse, to live off their *rentes*, to become, if they are not already, *nobles hommes*." In the *collège* they were taught not only to despise manual labor and commerce, but also the idle life of the *gentilshommes*. A number of new virtues were inculcated, and a lifestyle founded on books and learning was presented. The social process was the nurturing of a new social class; the classics formed the core of this experience.[78] Here was a clear, if limited and higher, form of literacy and schooling.

A further perspective on humanism in France is its connection with poor relief. Studies of poor-relief institutions during the sixteenth century reveal striking similarities from place to place in Europe, regardless of religious differences. They isolate the role of Christian humanism in early welfare reform.

In early-sixteenth-century Lyon, traditional causes of urban poverty intersected with population growth, greatly increasing the problems of city life. Townspeople complained of the numbers of starving poor, especially the young, on the streets. The presence of children was one important factor in welfare reform, and in humanist interest in poor relief. Coincident with a hardening of attitudes toward the poor, the conditions led Protestants as well as Catholics to consider new forms of charity. The lines between religious support and criticism of charity or between compassion and fear were indistinct for prominent Lyonese. Poverty was threatening not only physical and spiritual health, but also property and power within the city. In this context, the shift in 1534 toward an institutional solution was precedent setting.

The plan that was finalized included training and education for poor children. The welfare system sought to fulfill the hope that " 'a greater number of boys and girls would learn in their youth some art or skill which would keep them from becoming bums and beggars.' " Here was the humanist welfare model in operation. With its conviction that education can mold and improve character, it represented contemporary efforts.[79]

Before the Henrican Reformation of the 1530s and 1540s, the context of humanism in *England* was remarkably similar to that to the south. Northern Christian humanism blossomed, with a limited, but important, impact upon higher levels of schooling, an impact upon charity and welfare reform, and a foreshadowing of notions about expanded schooling, the direct effects of which were felt later. The arrival of the Renaissance late in the fifteenth century reflected the combination of cultural communications, as individuals and their journeys throughout the West remained the key to cultural correspondence and exchange; by this time, the impact of printing was also felt. During the century, change was slow but steady.

Humanism in England centered on the widest range of classical studies and activities. Economic, political, and social factors underlay scholarly and intellectual developments. By 1485, humanism was recognized in administrative and academic circles, the Latin secretaryship had become an official post, and a royal librarian appeared among court officials. Humanists began to lecture regularly in the universities, and their status began to assume signs of the transition from amateur to professional.[80]

The larger effect and growth of humanism did not take hold until around the turn of the century. In one way, they were the cultural consequences of governmental actions. In another they reflected the ''thrusting ambitions'' of the small landowners who increasingly sent their children to school—not with a clerical career in mind, but to learn about law and arithmetic or to prepare for the new opportunities for literate laity. A new ideal of devotion accompanied this development.

A new school foundation developed, ''public'' schooling, and was apparently well received by the middling gentry. The establishment of a cadre of talented humanist scholars and teachers, and their involvement with translations and preparation of printed editions, educational institutions, and governmental decision making and operations, contributed greatly to the spread of humanism.[81]

The thrust of English humanism was scholarly and educational. Classical studies and their interpretation within Christian cultural concerns constituted the major focus. The first enthusiasm derived from Italy, through direct and indirect communications and personal acquaintances. Greek studies marked a major component in the humanists' interests; their orientation was, however, much more influenced by theology and philosophy than was often the case in the south.

Like his contemporaries, John Colet was dissatisfied with the dullness of traditional modes of learning and the shortcomings of clerical institutions. He journeyed directly to Italy in his search for a spiritual community. Colet's ''continental learning was turned primarily not to literary or scholarly objectives, but to the evangelical work of preaching and lecturing on the text of the Bible.'' He took as his forum the traditional media of school and pulpit, rather than the printing press.

Colet's pupils in his humanist school at St. Paul's were to combine pure style with pure doctrine. They were schooled in the faith by vernacular learning in the catechism, Creed, and Ten Commandments; they were expected to obey the rules of Latin prosody even as they knelt at the sound of the sacring bell. The church fathers and the great Romans stood together in the curriculum.[82] Yet Colet was conscious of a possible conflict between style and doctrine. The books he selected for his pupils omitted some of the best Latin literature.

The issue of language symbolized the best and the worst within humanism. Humanism could have but little direct impact on the course of schooling and literacy

within its self-imposed, if much lauded, confines. It was inhibiting the full development of the European vernaculars and the increasing diffusion of literacy, dependent on native tongues. The future, and with the Reformation the near future,
turned against the values underlying humanism, sometimes reluctantly and contradictorily. Needs and demands were such that the vernaculars were seized increasingly, and quickly, for the pursuit of a number of ends.[83]

English humanism was also tied to contemporary social issues. One of the most
important links was the declining prejudice of the gentry toward education by the
end of the first quarter of the sixteenth century. In a time in which educational
opportunities for them were expanding, that resulted in their sons' more often
attending formal schools and finding their talents and learning rewarded more often
by an expanding, active Tudor state that needed trained persons. Such men were
often introduced to the Greek and Latin classics of theology and literature in grammar
schools and increasingly in universities, but few of them were scholars. Their
accession to positions was nevertheless a definite sign of success in terms of humanistic goals.[84] The humanistic Christian leader, who would in every way distinguish himself honorably from those beneath, not only was the best possible leader,
he was also an example of the good life to those in his charge.

This development of "a specifically humanistic ethos" was unparalleled elsewhere in northern Europe. During the sixteenth century, English humanists evolved
a doctrine with which they tried to defend and improve the existing social structure.
They used knowledge of the classics to justify the aristocratic order. They were
especially concerned that rulers should also be the "best" men. Opportunities for
government service and for schooling were both expanding; these factors intertwined, as the gentry supplied the crown some of its most able servants. "Humanistic
ideas thus became a powerful element in the predominant sixteenth-century belief
in a social hierarchy which it was the duty of the ruler and of the aristocracy to
maintain and in which every man had his place, high or low."

As Stone has argued, this time was also one of tremendous social mobility, and
of educational and religious flux. The economy was becoming commercialized; the
society was assuming new shapes. The state and its institutions were evolving and
becoming more centralized. It required men trained in the arts of government and
administration. The newly educated began to displace the "aristocracy of the
sword." That was where the humanists injected their ideas.

This demand met a broad and favorable response. Among the diverse elements
within the humanists' appeal was the fact that they were able to illustrate one way
in which the position of the aristocracy (and the gentry) could be preserved in a
time of social change, in part because they replaced outmoded criteria with new,
more requisite standards. Humanists' deep concern about education and its improvement, and the audience for which their reforms and instruction were intended,
overlapped neatly with social and political tendencies of the period. Rather than
being conspiratorial or conniving, "inherited position and an illustrious ancestry
could be joined with learning and virtue. . . ."[85]

Thomas More, in *Utopia*, a thinly disguised attack on contemporary European
societies, made the major statement of Christian humanistic educational ideals and
arrangements. "Utopia" was a state in which material goods and most political

issues were expressly subordinated to learning and knowledge as pleasures to all. The rulers would be the most erudite of men. Appropriately, More detailed the education for those with natural intellectual ability and who showed signs of future leadership qualities. When it came to liberal education for all children, which he endorsed, and adult education, the description was less full and complete. More, nevertheless, was an important early voice for universal, free education, a proposal in which he was not alone but in which he was literally centuries ahead of his day. That reflects another legacy of literacy.

All Utopians, both boys and girls, went to school. Their education did not stop when they started working: lectures apparently began a little after four in the morning, ending just before nine, when daily labor commenced; despite the hours, Utopians flocked to them and continued self-improvement efforts by reading, orally examining the young, and engaging in music and educational games throughout the day. Utopians received instruction in agriculture and trades, and also studied the humanities and sciences, but the aim of their schooling was neither technical nor cultural. Teaching emphasized virtue and good conduct.

Such is the function that More holds up for education in the best possible commonwealth: central to the creation of the state is that of the citizen; central to the making of the citizen is education. Properly educated persons get along well, require few laws, and are productive and peaceful. Instruction and institutions, together, provide the foundation of the best state.

A tenet held by many humanists was a preoccupation with reform of life and society through education; it would become one of the tenets of progressive or liberal Western thought and a goal whose attainment was a prerequisite for social progress and equality. More's views seem less ambiguous, less equivocal, than those of many of his peers. In them, we recognize especially clearly a legacy of literacy and a force to be understood in future centuries.

Schooling, including literacy, is seen as a means to a larger, social end. The good and godly society must be composed of good and godly men and women; education would produce them if it was itself good and godly. That brings us to a point of puzzlement: when the humanists wrote with any detail about schooling, pedagogy, or curricula, it was all but exclusively in terms of grammar-level and higher studies and education for primarily the upper ranks of society. They did not tell how a proper Christian humanist schooling might be adapted to universal instruction. Perhaps *only* in a "Utopia" could such an effort be more than contemplated. With other great humanists, More was an educator, and his *Utopia* was an educational tract, an ideal, a challenge, a rebuke to an imperfect world. This utopia reveals at once the brilliance and promise of the humanist imagination *and* its limitations.

An impressive faith in the reforming power of words is an act of faith, that is, *without* a Utopia. Later developments revealed that faith without compulsion, institutions, and an active role of the state would be insufficient to establish universal literacy and schooling, let alone a Good Society. Neither the classics nor humanism has proved sufficient to attain those ends.[86] The Reformation released a religious force that made possible versions of Utopias; no Utopias resulted from those efforts, however.

Thomas More's general educational aims are more significant than a basis in a classical curriculum. They are more revealing about humanistic thinking about general social education. More wrote that learning is to be pursued not for its own sake or for the attainment of personal accomplishments but for more practical reasons. Utility was social, not functional, in more recent conceptual terms; in *Utopia*, the priests of education instruct the young in learning, but also in virtue and good manners. There is no doubt that this emphasis, the society, its order, and finding through education one's proper place within it were the chief beneficiaries of education. For those not to be scholars, philosophers, statesmen, or teachers, the virtues of Christian citizenship are supreme. Literacy and literature are the means to those ends. Means, for the masses, received less than their measure of attention from humanists, who did not hesitate in their views on proper ends.[87]

At all levels of education, privileged children advanced at the expense of less privileged peers. "Access to education and opportunities within the educational system were severely constrained by social, economic, and ideological limitations." That was as true of educational institutions as of the ideas of educational thinkers. Humanist ideals were compromised by the demands of social order. Social stratification and the persisting restrictedness of literacy continued and expanded from the mid-sixteenth through the later seventeenth centuries. The theorists of sixteenth-century humanist schooling, regardless of their hopes for the improvement of the social order, endorsed the social hierarchy, maintained deep concern about orderliness, and hesitated about education for all, despite their pious pleas, on occasion, for universal schooling.[88]

As on the Continent, in England welfare and poor-law reform were an area in which humanist opinion was important and in which the bounds of intervention were sometimes stretched below that of other educational reforms. That constitutes a vital precedent and legacy for the future. English welfare legislation and the stances taken toward the poor in the first three or four decades of the sixteenth century reveal the currents of humanism.

By the early sixteenth century, many humanists were appalled by the social and cultural changes that surrounded them. They criticized the luxurious living and irresponsibility of the well-to-do and the surliness of the able-bodied poor. From their perspective, justice and harmonious social relations among the social classes had declined dangerously. Education for the poor in social and moral values was at root the cause of social malaise. For social reform to take place, scholastic dogmas had to be replaced by the renewal of classical and scriptural studies. Properly trained persons, embodying Christian virtue in their lives, would then be prepared to assume leadership and assist ordinary persons in finding the truth. Thus would human errors be escaped and social behavior be ameliorated. Reform would flow from the top down: through the best teaching and best examples.

Juan Vives was directly interested in education and social ethics. He too was convinced that human nature was moral but that "this propensity could be brought to useful fruition only through careful, practical, and moral education." He wrote at some length about welfare and treatment of the poor, and designed under commission a plan for Bruges in 1525–1526, *De subventione pauperum*. Vives's plan stressed laicization and rationalization; it called for the cessation of begging and the appointment of censors to examine the real needs of the poor and dispense relief funds. The municipal officials were charged with treating the poor humanely.

Christian humanistic ideas and values permeate Vives's proposals: the emphasis on rescuing persons from moral degradation and restoring them to usefulness and virtue, the faith that wise and humane public servants must use government and the law to show the population the proper path to greater love and respect, and the importance of education to the well-being of the community. Schools were required to teach poor children "letters, morals, Christian duty, and proper values." At the end of the treatise, Vives made clear the ends he felt should follow from the adoption of such a policy: a decrease in crime, deeper civil harmony, improved urban health, and a more pleasant life. The goals were social rather than individual. " 'So many citizens [would be] made more virtuous, more law-abiding, more useful to the country.' "[89]

Only in terms of reform of welfare and the poor did humanists become more concrete about the institutionalization of education below the level of the elite, and were they able, on occasion, to influence the making of public policies. In these ways humanism did have direct application for the present, but its greater impacts lay in the future.

### 3. Print, Reform, and Reformation

In the history of the West, the Protestant Reformation is said to be one of the greatest positive forces toward the spread of literacy and schooling. It can easily be viewed as an educational reform movement: "The basic assumptions of the reformers were that one must start with the young, that indoctrination is necessary for religious and moral improvement . . . , that this indoctrination must be done in public schools. . . ."[90] The Reformation involved factors far beyond the religious and theological. Its roots lay in the Middle Ages; economic, political, cultural, and social issues inextricably intertwined to give rise to a deep and bitterly divisive mass movement. Its conflicts lasted through much of the sixteenth and seventeenth centuries; the reformation of social life was a long-term endeavor in Western society and culture, to which literacy was often central.

Ecclesiastical reform movements were the central cause of the Reformation, which was triggered by the "publication" of Martin Luther's ninety-five theses in 1518. Increasing dissatisfaction with the church and papacy resulted in a slow, but steady, development of active dissent in the first half of the sixteenth century.

The major reform movements that helped to shape the context for the Reformation shared a common concern with moral criteria and a common approach: except for the "Devotio Moderna," the movements all looked to secular authorities for aid, took arguments and inspiration from the Bible, and appealed to the early church. They sought the reaffirmation of community, the reorganization of lay piety and religion, and the reintegration of the outer and inner self. The Northern Renaissance, with its central current of humanism, was probably the most important. Humanism benefited from such new factors as the role of printing, the urban and articulate commercial classes, and the increasingly literate laity; it offered an optimistic, progressive reform program.[91]

Early-sixteenth-century humanism appealed to the educated laity in their search for more religion and a more active piety. But the impact of the doctrines of the religious reformers went beyond theology alone; in addition, political changes in the territorial states necessitated major social and economic adjustments. Some turned to the new Protestantism, others toward Catholicism and the church. Towns-people, nobility, and even the peasants responded to the calls for reform or counter reform.

Martin Luther's own reform began as a university-based effort to transform the curriculum, replacing Aristotle and scholasticism with the Bible and St. Augustine. He was aware of the sensitive nature of his theses and made his challenge patiently through official channels. When no response arrived, he sent handwritten copies of the theses to some friends for clarification. Those copies were reproduced and circulated, and were even translated into German. They spread widely, and soon all of Germany, and then all of Christendom, had been aroused by Luther's theses.[92]

Two of the most significant developments of the Reformation were the contri-bution of the printing press and the use of the vernacular. These seminal currents were especially relevant to the history of literacy, yet their contributions were not always direct or immediately recognized. Neither Luther and his theses, the church's hierarchy, the social context, the printing press, nor any single factor or development *caused* the events that permanently split the world of Western Christendom and firmly ended the Middle Ages.

The contribution of moveable typography to the religious revolution of the six-teenth century is easily exaggerated. At the beginning of the century, traditional moral and religious books were popular, but newly developing literary forms were also being published before the Reformation, including collections of sermons and the works of the church fathers. A large number of religious works were being published, but they constituted a smaller percentage of the total production. They may not have reached a larger public after the turn of the century than before.

The situation changed rapidly in Germany by 1517. Religious issues quickly took on the utmost importance. The first propaganda campaign with the help of the printing press was conducted, as the power of the press to influence public thought and opinion was realized. An attempt was made "to place within the reach of everyone and in the vernacular the Holy Writ which provided the basis of the reformed and restored religion."

The printing press did not determine the Reformation, for it had been techno-logically prepared for some time. Pious materials had been printed for many years— Bibles, books of simple piety, posters, handbills, and broadsheets. The press, rather, prepared the coming of the Reformation, providing a tried and tested vehicle for both reformers and their opposition to spread their ideas.

Leaflets and, especially, posters helped to keep the public informed. Illiterates could receive the message by having a poster read to them. The availability of printed matter did not cause an increase in literacy; it increased the flow of com-munications and raised the probability of more and more persons' receiving infor-mation. The use of printing insured that Luther's theses and later writings were rapidly and widely circulated.[93]

The contribution of print was dramatic. Notices posted on walls, church doors, and gateways were read with interest. Luther's own writings were in demand, and he and his colleagues produced more and more literature in the vernacular, hoping to reach the widest audience possible. In support and response came pamphlets caricaturing the church fathers and monks. More important, the number of books printed in Germany rose quickly. The presses of Germany were kept busy with the business of the Reformation until well past mid-century.

Colporteurs and book peddlers carried Reformation propaganda into the country-side. In this way, printing was a direct influence in the Peasants' Revolt of 1524–1525. That revolt marked a watershed in the Lutheran Reformation, as reform leaders recognized dangers to social order and drew back in their calls for mass participation. A greater effort at formal, more cautious institutional and religious change was made—more directed and controlled. The number of pamphlets and polemical works declined as printing became a more controlled measure of prop-aganda. Reform-related printing became more narrowly religious and theological, but publishing in the vernacular remained a major preoccupation.[94]

Luther continued his translation of the Bible into German, and it was a great success. Some buyers were probably unable to read or comprehend it for themselves; to many it was more a symbol of faith, piety, and, perhaps, status. Despite a relatively high rate of literacy in urban areas, the ensuing educational campaign of the Reformation indicates that popular reading habits and skills were far from satisfactory.

Recognizing that rising lay literacy was one of the preconditions for the reform and that the struggles for reform depended upon print, and hence reading, requires no determinism about their roles. They were vehicles among many others; their larger importance was realized through the interactive potentials of print and literacy. Some readers could "enlighten" many others; high levels of literacy were hardly a requirement for embracing the Scriptures and making faith real. The roles of literacy and print, in a popular rather than an intellectual or theological sense, must be placed in sixteenth-century sociocultural settings.

The ideas of the Reformation were spread through various channels. One way was through personal contact. Luther and his supporters were responsible for some of the diffusion, but more significant were itinerant middlemen—preachers, sales-men, and journeymen. Print and literacy surely contributed here.

The message was also disseminated through print and writing—the distribution of books, manuscripts, pictures, personal letters, and songs. More was involved than literacy alone; sales of Reformation literature could yield high profits, and as this literature was bought in one place and reprinted and sold to other towns and cities, Lutheran ideas were spread without direct personal contact. Illiterates were attracted to Luther's ideas through visual devices (woodcuts and copperplates) and oral communications.

Institutions, including universities and political administrations, also helped to circulate evangelical ideas, supplementing and reinforcing personal contacts. Pro-fessors and students frequently returned to their home areas after their university studies and spread the new gospel through preaching, official service, or active citizenship. Other institutional contributions came from servants in imperial and territorial city administrations and similar agencies. Literacy and print acted in concert with personal and institutional contacts and exchanges to spread the Reformation. The sermon movement and preachers played an important role. From this basis, we begin to grasp the fuller nature of communications linkages and the mixture of media in sixteenth-century society. Print and literacy, while important, were parts of a larger whole. Personal relations, printing and writing, oral communications, institutions: each played a part, separately and interactively. The meaning of literacy to the reform effort, and its opposition, lies precisely in the nature of these relationships.[95]

The roles played by print and other media and channels were not exceptional to Germany. Similar processes within the international reform movement occurred in France, Switzerland, England, the Low Countries, and Scandinavia. The Reformation was brought to the New World by colonists.[96]

On a different level, among intellectuals and churchmen, the advent of printing had an important, contradictory impact. The use of printing assisted the movement for reform within the church, advanced the standardization of texts and observances within liturgical practices, influenced habits of sermonizing, and duplicated all sorts of literature, new and old. While changed by print, none of that was new. On the other hand, these uses of the press were not determined in advance; virtually all of them worked toward the efforts of the church or its critics. Printed texts could standardize church practices and improve them; or they could reveal, to literates at least, the gap between official doctrine and clerical practice. ''With typographical fixity, moreover, positions once taken were more difficult to reverse. Battles of books prolonged polarization, and pamphlet wars quickened the press.''

Despite the many claims advanced for the powers of ''typographical fixity,'' that force has stopped few writers from changing their minds or positions in print, revising their work, or even, knowingly or unknowingly, contradicting themselves. Many of the reformers, from Luther on, did so. The battles of words, on printed pages, had a force that earlier, manuscript debates did not. Reducing face-to-face debates and disputations, they carried the issues, the divisions, the vehemence far beyond that possible in the age of script. Printing made propaganda, in a modern sense, possible; the Reformation was an early example, although perhaps not the first. Humanists and the church had engaged in such pursuits before the first international age of reform erupted.

One of the principal eruptions centered on the vernacular Bible, which the church was unwilling to countenance. One of the most important innovations furthered by the Reformers, it was a principal use of print. A tremendous incentive for literacy and a great boost to the vernacular followed. Yet, it is necessary to distinguish Bible study as scholarly exegesis from Bible study as lay Bible reading. Protestantism supported both; Catholicism promoted only the former.

Thus, Protestant doctrines stressing Bible reading for salvation generated special incentives toward literacy. That is a stereotypical view now, almost a myth, and *almost* true. Protestantism *was* a vital force toward the propagation of literacy among the populace in the West. But Catholicism has suffered a too negative, too unilaterally condemnatory press on this issue.[97] The written texts of the Bible had been a sacred and extraordinarily highly valued part of Christianity from its earliest days. It was Christianity more generally, long before Protestantism, that stressed the need to circulate *written* versions of the Bible despite the fact that severely restricted educational opportunities and literacy prevented the overwhelming number of adherents from confronting the great book for themselves. For this reason—and the fact that the Bible was not withheld from adherents who mastered Latin—comparisons with the Koran, on one hand, and strict Protestant-Catholic dichotomies, on the other, misrepresent realities that are more complex and interesting. The Bible was never restricted to a set of holy priests who recited it in the ways of the Koran and Islam; the Catholic church did not forbid the learned lay person from access to the Scriptures. Other issues were more central.

Post-Tridentine (Council of Trent, 1546) policies differed from those of the medieval church. A dramatic hardening of policy occurred, with vernacular Bibles prohibited, removing the Holy Scriptures from the direct access of virtually all adherents—an access marked by ability to read and perhaps even understand it. The Scriptures long assumed the qualities of sacred untouchable symbols to the Catholic laity. Trent curiously endorsed some forms of educational advancement and lay learning, but proscribed direct access to the Bible through the vernacular languages. The consequences were many. Not only were lay congregations further removed from clergy and texts, but an end was put to serious translations by Catholics for almost two centuries. Venetian printers were severely hit by the loss of some of their most salable products. Only in countries in which the Roman Catholic church was threatened by Protestant traditions was publication of vernacular Bibles permitted.[98]

In contrast, vernacular Bibles, prayer books, and catechisms were adopted by all the reformed and reforming churches. These materials, more traditional than innovative, served as a basis for schooling and literacy instruction, now in the native tongue. Educational and religious promotion were combined and reciprocally reinforced. Linguistic uniformity, as a part of nation building, was also advanced.[99]

The difference in support for public or popular schooling and promotion of literacy between lands Catholic and Protestant is often exaggerated, and the peculiar mix of local factors unexplored. Protestant promotion of literacy had social morality and secularized religious concerns at its core, rather than individualized, liberating, independent, self-advancement goals. The individual applications of literacy, of course, could not always be controlled, although the promoted ones were often dominant. Contrary to many generalizations, neither printing *alone* nor Protestantism *alone* shaped outcomes during the sixteenth century or the early modern period. Just as one should not be divorced from the other, neither should either be removed from its context or special mix of factors, local and national, that gave it meaning and shaped its use.

In this respect, it is important to note that by the second half of the sixteenth century, the post-Tridentine Catholic church had successfully and consciously mobilized printers for its counter-reform offensive. They, too, used print for proselytizing, produced devotional materials for clerics and laity, and contributed to printers' profits. In England, "Catholic printers proved as skillful as their Puritan counterparts in handling problems posed by the surreptitious printing and the clandestine marketing of books." Although their limits differed and their enthusiasm was restrained by a greater ambivalence, Catholic reformers had to promote lay literacy to combat the Protestants and struggle for their place in the new religious pluralism.[100] Printing comprised issues religious, economic, *and* political; so did literacy and its provision.

## 4. Reforming Literacy Provision

Protestant reforms often aimed at family and household. Many of them were explicitly educational, including, in addition to moral and religious schooling and, in places such as Sweden and New England, literacy training, moral regulation of marital relations, sanctioning of clerical marriage, renewed dignification of the marital state, and use of the family as a pillar of the civil cum moral community and state. The need for at least a literate household head was a plank in the Protestant platform for social reform. Consequently, much printed literature was produced for the family, including advice literature as well as prayer books.[101]

Protestant reformers found the household basis *insufficient* in most areas for achieving their educational ideals. In early modern Sweden, however, nearly universal levels of literacy were attained by the early eighteenth century, largely through a household mode of literacy instruction for religious purposes and a key role for women: all under the strict control of the Lutheran state church. And in early New England, where migrants were impressively literate for the mid-seventeenth century, church and home combined to sustain the level of literacy until more extensive schooling was possible.[102]

### A. Germany (with a note on Poland)

The Reformation set new educational goals:

> It embarked on a conscious and, for its time, remarkably systematic endeavor to develop in the young new and better impulses, to implant inclinations in consonance with the reformers' religious and civic ideals, to fashion dispositions in which Christian ideas of right thought and action could take root, and to shape personalities capable of turning the young into new men—into the human elements of a Christian society that would live by evangelical principles.

The total population was the target. To reach them, "instruments of indoctrination" and "techniques of conditioning" were fashioned: to reveal God's truth and teach people to live by it. Education was itself a pious work. Attempting to combine religious and humanistic traditions into a program for all children constituted a new effort in the history of the West. Success was probably less than we have been led to expect, but in many ways that was of secondary importance. What marks the Lutheran educational reformation is the organized attempt to establish an institutional and compulsory schooling program and the assumption that all children required formal education for the good of society and for themselves, and that literacy training was one key vehicle for this activity. In this way, the Protestant Reformation left a tremendous legacy for the future.[103]

Luther's first ideas on Christian education differed from the resulting institutional and legal configuration. His model was based on instructional preaching, set in a larger context of household education. Those most in need of education, he felt, could not be reached easily by preachers' teaching; it was through the moral education of the householder that their needs would be met. To guide household heads, Luther composed a number of manuals for the "simple layman," ending with the 1529 Greater and Shorter Catechisms.

Academic subjects were for learning in school, not the home. In the early period, reformers felt that popular support and governmental goodwill were sufficient for voluntary and locally supported programs of Christian and academic education. However, the early enthusiasm for education began to wane because of the costs involved. It became clear to Luther and his colleagues that schools were disintegrating and that parents were neglecting their duties at home. More debilitating were the religious and social disturbances that were occurring. The people seemingly could not be entrusted with the freedom that Luther's theology and social program gave them; it was becoming progressively obvious that only firm control could reestablish order and promote the Christian state.

Philip Melanchthon, the pedagogical philosopher of Reform, stated in 1525 that schools were needed more than ever before " 'so that young people may be raised to be peaceful and decent.' " He looked to the legal and moral authority of government for help in indoctrinating the masses against dangerous thoughts and influences. Luther endorsed the shift to public, compulsory, institutional education. He agreed that the decline in schools resulted from antiintellectualism among the people and required intervention. He reminded parents that their children belonged first to God, and only second to them; child rearing was no longer solely a private issue.

Increasingly, reformers found that civil compulsion was required to effect their ends; the Reformation, they felt, must be institutionalized formally. Working together, reformers and governments prepared school ordinances and established policies for teaching and learning. These were often central parts of comprehensive ecclesiastical constitutions for cities and states placing educational work at the center of creating the civil and religious life of the community. Luther wrote of " 'schools where children are trained in the liberal arts, in Christian discipline, . . . faithful service to God, . . . to become responsible men and women who can govern churches, countries, people, households, children, and servants.' " At this stage, the training of society at large was not yet the central goal; first was required the education of leaders for the next generation. Only after a competent and skilled group of social, political, and religious elites was in place could the full program of social reform and regeneration through education be tackled.

By the end of the 1520, the foundation for political control of education was being put into place. The control over conduct and morality so basic to the political mentality of the times and the perceived need for order and cohesion—respect and obedience to the law—would be secured through proper schooling under the aegis of the state. "No one saw a conflict in this fusion of religious and secular objectives," and governments were quick to respond to the reformers' appeals.[104]

The concrete result was a large number of school ordinances in the 1530s. The reformers participated actively in framing the first city regulations; these stood as examples and models for later documents. Although successful achievement of their objectives varied by place and time, school legislation produced major changes in the manner of teaching and learning. Governments were expected to make education available, and they eagerly complied. Citizens were encouraged to cooperate by paying most of the costs and sending their children as pupils. Their reluctance to do so led to an extension and tightening of school regulations.

It was mandated that all places should have schools, even the smallest villages. Larger towns should have graded five-form institutions, small places at least one grade school in which children should stay until they learned to read and write. The brightest pupils could proceed to higher schools in other places. Special concern was addressed to the need for uniformity and common examinations.

Instruction was aimed at giving the ablest a foundation for higher studies and at instilling discipline and the fear of God. Boys learned obedience, respect for elders and betters, and modesty in speech, dress, and behavior. Parents were to insure attendance and observe conduct, but teaching professionals were to form the minds and characters of the young. To safeguard the entire operation, ordinances called for supervision by teams of school inspectors, including pastors and three other "learned men" from each town or village. Inspections consisted of monthly visits and quarterly examinations of all pupils.

Reform also included German schools for the education of the general public. During the 1530s, conflicts between German and Latin schools were commonly settled in favor of the academic training of the latter. The former were seen as a threat by appealing to overly utilitarian parents. A supervised system of vernacular schools became less objectionable as reform continued and seemed advisable by the late 1550s. Civil officials and clerical agents of reform realized that many people did not educate their own children; German schools staffed by trained and licensed teachers were needed if the young were to be brought up literate in basic religion. These schools taught reading, writing, and "above all other things" the fear of God through committing the catechism to memory. Girls were to be taught, and, as in the Latin schools, discipline was to be strict, but not cruel.

Little more than literacy was expected of the teachers. Although they were engaged by the community, they were not appointed without " 'prior examination [by the *Kirchenrat*] for honest birth, life, and conduct,' also for orthodoxy of belief, legible handwriting, and a thorough understanding of the catechism."

According to the visitation records, such schools were common in villages and small towns and seem to have performed tolerably well. True, there were problems—with buildings, teachers, enrollments, and, especially, money—but in a sixteenth-century context, the Reformation educational accomplishment is impressive.

The system being erected led the superior student to an advanced secondary school, usually a *Gymnasium* (the favored humanist term) or *Paedagogium*, which stressed Latin, Greek and Hebrew, and theology. At the bottom of the system, and most important for most people, were the German schools. Evidence is less munificent about them; debates about their timing and place in reformation efforts continue. If early reformers were ambivalent about fostering literacy and book learning at the village level, their successors became more convinced. "Other impulses were at work, notably the wish for literacy shown by small-town and village folk themselves. . . . the impetus for extending schools into the countryside came from below as well as from above.[105]

Mass provision of literacy had become desirable from both sides by mid-century. For government and church officials, the spread of literacy—if it was tied to the system of indoctrination and control of the ecclesiastical constitutions—served important purposes. It was seen as a way to reach the greatest number of persons in towns and rural parishes, in order to shape their religious and civil behavior, and to achieve uniformity in practice and belief. Reading and writing were of secondary importance as skills in and for themselves.

Questions concerning literacy run through most discussions of the reforms. "Reformers and their governments seem to have taken it for granted that nearly every head of household could read . . . with fluency and expression." Mass illiteracy would have made the Lutheran effort to promote domestic instruction useless. "It could therefore be reasonably argued that the reformers' ceaseless efforts to involve the family—at least among the urban and rural well-to-do—in Christian instruction constitute . . . a kind of proof of extensive literacy." Protestant mandates and visitation directives also assume literacy as more the norm, illiteracy more the exception. Mandates and directives were based upon regular examination of the populace in vernacular catechetical reading; citizens were expected to be able to read that much. This evidence is insufficient to "prove" the point or to establish any numerical level of literacy, but it points to levels of literacy that, while not high by modern standards, were impressive for the immediate postmedieval period: literacy diffused widely throughout the population but was stratified by location, class, wealth, occupational needs, sex, and age.

Among Protestants, reading was seen as a primary means of implanting evangelical faith. Regardless of the extant levels of literacy, reform was conducted in a manner and on a scale that required literacy and its provision systematically to the young *on a scale never before attempted*; a high rate of success should not be expected. Authors of domestic instruction books also spoke of a sizable readership. "They appealed to their readers to employ their reading skill in the service of the reforming enterprise, above all to use it in doing their duty to children and other dependents in their homes." Of course, that was not always or often done; the shift from the home to the school model of education suggests that it was not common practice. When people settled into routines of established orthodoxy, indifference became much more common.

The catechism was central to the elementary educational experience of the young. Knowledge of it was the expected outcome of tutelage in basic literacy. Instruction in the catechism quickly became the regular mode in which to indoctrinate the young in their religious culture. School regulations, and church rules, fixed the frequency of its reading and recitation. The emphasis placed on catechetical learning is revealed in numerous ways, but particularly as a central part of the school experience.[106]

Examinations of pupils and parishioners were used regularly to reinforce learning. Results varied widely but were rarely satisfactory: examinations were not always well attended, schoolchildren came only by force, and students and their elders were not always well prepared. That convinced preachers and teachers of the value of uniformity and administrative order.

To establish uniformity and orderliness, regulations and directives became more and more rigid. Governments promoted the use of the catechism and the provision of literacy because they accepted its power as a conditioning instrument for the proper upbringing and training of future citizens. Literacy as a tool of social and religious learning was endowed with a deep faith and accorded a great power. In the public ritual of catechetical recitation was found a communal testament of loyalty, with the young setting an example for others. The community, in theory and in ceremony, gave affirmation of its allegiance to the established order.

Focusing on the young was an important shift in policy. Adults depended on sermons for their knowledge of the faith or were seen as unreachable. The hopes of the pedagogical reformers now lay with the young. If even their lowest expectations were fulfilled, a significant change in popular religious practice and morality would follow. This point is crucial to understanding the meaning of literacy in this form of education; mass memorization of the catechism was itself beneficial. No high level of literacy was required for it. That low level of literacy and learning—especially regarding the ability to understand—is all that a sixteenth-century mass literacy campaign would hope to achieve. The faith in literacy and catechetical learning was not based on hopes for a high degree of literacy or the ability to use that literacy. It was also a valued tool of propaganda: for the Reformation and against Catholics and their ways.

Pedagogically, minimal literacy and knowledge of the catechism were an appropriate mode of schooling. The suitability of the catechism to oral instruction was explicitly valued. Despite the decided emphasis on reading for reformation, reformers recognized that many of their purposes could be achieved without literacy or with only a low level. As the pedagogical program reveals, reformers and teachers did not make a hard and fast distinction between oral and literate ways; they sought to use them both, and to use the former to transmit the latter. This schooling was the way in which most persons who achieved literacy, or at least rote knowledge of the catechism and related values, gained their learning for centuries to come. But in the end, rote memorization was not sufficient for the more important purposes of moral reformation. It was often unconnected with knowledge or feeling.

A conclusion about the state of literacy from such an educational experience is easier to draw than one about the success or failure of the Reformation itself. "The rote memorization encouraged by this procedure seems to have left many youngsters less than fluently literate . . . ," in German or Latin. Children listened to sentences spoken by their teacher and repeated them aloud as they looked at the printed syllables in their ABC book or traced the letters on wax tablets or scraps of paper. But did this minimal degree of learning contribute some of the expected results in regard to conduct and morality? With these the pupils were literally bombarded, from texts and oral messages; some effect must have taken hold.

The encouragement of reading among the population and a campaign to increase the literacy levels of the whole populations were central goals of the Reformation. Magistrates and rulers had their reasons for encouraging this movement, and elementary schools expanded during the second half of the sixteenth century. Educational laws gave concrete endorsement to official efforts to promote literacy. Literacy, in consequence—for the first time on this scale—was becoming regarded as a normative and desirable skill.

Literacy was increasingly regarded as necessary for occupations associated with trade, commerce, and exchange. For that reason, more parents wanted it for their children, and more young persons wanted it for themselves. The reports of those seeking to establish or maintain vernacular schools in their communities are over-whelmingly from the artisanal orders and lower middle ranks. Functional, work-related needs held the first priority, although the pleasures of reading and books as sources of knowledge were also mentioned in the local battles for their schools.[107]

Equally revealing, religious motives were seldom presented among reasons to become literate, despite clerical promotion of reading. The reformers' and the peo-ple's desires for literacy—for different ends—overlapped in the promotion of ver-nacular lay literacy through the German schools. Different motives operated toward different ends (although many among the middle ranks may also have valued literacy for religious and pious reasons), but they met in support for local schools and the desire to spread literacy. As a result, vernacular schools proliferated in Protestant, and many Catholic, areas during the sixteenth century. The local elite was the element most important for the presence or absence of schools in any given locality. Local social and economic conditions had a major impact on the educational de-cisions of villagers and townspeople.[108]

On the eve of the Reformation, literacy levels were rising. By the mid-sixteenth century, literacy was taken for granted in the highest ranks; that was not a direct result of the Reformation. Literacy was increasingly valued, as useful to their work and probably also for religious reasons; it was becoming more common but was not yet a normal attainment. As for the peasantry and rural residents, literacy there, too, was probably rising. Among the rural and urban "proletariat," landless laborers and manual workers without skill or trade, illiteracy was normal. Other evidence shows that printed literature was also spreading, and could be found in the homes of the lowly as well as the well-to-do. Larger and more prosperous towns offered greater incentives to their residents learning literacy, as well as more opportunities for institutional provision.

In terms of providing institutional means for the mass promotion and instruction of literacy for the people of Reformed Germany, the Reformation can be termed a success. On the level of facilitating access to instruction in and raising popular levels of literacy, it was also partly successful. Both these achievements are im-pressive. But in regard to the more encompassing goal of reforming the character and conduct of the people, and through them the community and the larger society, the Lutheran Reformation was not so successful. The levels of godly behavior, religiosity, and zeal equivalent to successful social and moral reform were more often lacking than present, it seems. Success came mainly in the systematic use of constraints over the populace of a small territory; coercion and close supervision were the keys.[109]

The Reformation's educational program had another side, paralleling non-Prot-estant activities:. welfare reform and schooling for the poor.[110] Control of social welfare shifted to the hands of the laity; almost every reform created new institutions to centralize and coordinate activities. High among reformers' activities was school-ing for all, including the poor, and welfare for the poor and needy. Reformed cities in Germany continued the evolution of relief that began in the Middle Ages, but with social change and disruption came increased problems of the poor, destitute, and beggars. In many of his writings and sermons, Luther urged the taking of measures to eliminate begging and almsgiving and to have each city support its own poor. Many cities followed his advice.[111]

The work of the Reformation in the heart of the West, Germany and Switzerland, is clear. Its importance to literacy and learning was crucial—for the present and more so for the future. New traditions were created; a new primacy on reading and mass schooling was put into place. Most important in understanding this great historical process is seeing the transitional role of the Reformation: how it served to connect the past and present to the direction of the future. Herein lies its major significance for the history of literacy. Currents that began in the classical age, in Rome and Greece, and in the long medieval era came together in the sixteenth century. The legacies of literacy, rooted in continuities and contradictions, reached an epochal culmination in the Reformation era. Its goals were not all realized, but a program for the future had been set forth, one that would occupy Western society and polity for the next centuries and that would undergo many transformations.

Before turning west and north, the availability of exceptional evidence on literacy in sixteenth-century Poland merits a note. Two studies, based on early signatory legal records, have been conducted that give an outline of the social distribution of basic literacy for southern Poland. For the period 1564–1565, Wyczanski found impressively high levels of signing for advantaged groups of nobles, bourgeois, and priests. The evidence points to a perhaps surprising extent of literacy for this place and time. As elsewhere in the West, this period was one of cultural development.

In Poland, a national literature was emerging; intellectual, artistic, religious, and political life were intense. It was also a time of educational expansion: in the provinces of Lithuania and Ruritania, estimates suggest a ratio of one parish school for each 1,300 inhabitants. Nevertheless, it remains doubtful that the literacy rate for Poland exceeded 10 percent.[112]

### B. France (with a note on Spain)

The Reformation and Protestantism did not have the significance for literacy, education, or social change in France that they had elsewhere.[113] Numbers of schools, extent of reform thought and institutional activities, and literacy rates that began to be possible by the last third of the sixteenth century all point to this conclusion. Traditional views point to the relative educational backwardness of France as it entered the (early) modern era, the sharp Protestant/Catholic and urban/rural distinctions, and the depressing role of Catholicism on the popular levels of schooling.

School opportunities and literacy remained restricted throughout this period. Schools were concentrated in the towns; some poorer children were included, but education was generally reserved for the upper classes. Literacy levels were differentiated between places urban and rural. Most villagers were literate, as were small merchants, craftsmen, and some semiskilled workers in the cities (and their wives). However, "the floating mass was just illiterate; and . . . the only reader to whom they listened with any regularity was the town crier ordering them to show up for work. . . ."

Widespread poverty and a lack of schools caused rural literacy to remain low, although its level and impact were increasing. Virtually no rural women knew letters. Maybe 3 percent of agricultural workers and 10 percent of more well-to-do peasants could sign their names. In sharp contrast to the residents of towns, rural inhabitants were distinguished by their *il*literacy. One must be guarded in accusing them of ignorance and lack of culture, for there was the powerful oral world, which also brought to them some aspects of the written.[114]

In the areas north and southwest of Paris, where the language was French, literacy rates were somewhat higher, and rural schools were present in several places. Pupils came from exceptional families and/or were intended for nonagricultural occupations. Most farmers, even some prosperous ones, apparently did not need the ability to read and write. Itinerant scribes and notaries could perform the necessary services (land sales, marriage contracts, wills, etc.) for the peasants.

Those rural youth who gained a reasonable education were most likely to depart for the cities, to apprentice for crafts or train for the priesthood, or in very exceptional cases to attend a university. Literacy and migration were tied, as throughout the past centuries. When such persons came home to visit, they apparently did not leave their books in their villages. Peasants' inventories made scant mention of books. That was not wholly a result of lack of funds or unavailability of books for purchase; even literate laborers in parts of France might never encounter a bookseller or an itinerant peddler. Books available might also be written in a language that peasants had difficulty understanding; little printing was done in vernaculars other than French. More important, few peasants felt any need or desire for written materials.[115]

Local tradition and experience, the oral world, and the contributions of traveling players were primary influences in the rural world. Print, in the context of limited penetration and low rates of literacy, could not compete. Village life was rich with tradition, festivals, and rituals, including *veillées*, at which community members came together to work, recreate, sing, flirt, and tell tales. A literate man might read a book aloud to the others. Printed texts were transformed in this setting; the reader turned them into oral materials and into a dialect that his listeners could understand. A process of translation and editing mediated the interaction between the written and oral cultures.

By the 1530s, some *veillées* were being introduced to a book that was new and potentially disruptive to traditional pattern: the vernacular Bible. The literalness of this text was important. It "could not be 'edited' or reduced to some formulaic magic. It had to be understood, and there were probably no pictures to help." The inroads of the written Scriptures were made by evangelical peddlers, working the countryside systematically. Yet, the Calvinist spirit never gained major support in the countryside: "For most peasants, the religion of the book, the Psalms, and the Consistory gave too little leeway to the traditional oral and ritual culture of the countryside, to its existing forms of social life and social control." Reformed materials were harder for the ill-skilled readers to understand, and Protestant calendars stripped the agricultural year of its basic meanings. Such books were not suited to their intended audience. Although new books, especially almanacs, began to circulate in rural areas by the later sixteenth century, "we have no *sure* evidence that any of these books addressed to a rural public ever actually reached a peasant audience."

Despite the increased circulation of print material, the consequences of printing and literacy for peasants remained limited. A few new lines of communication were created; these expanded gradually. "Expectations were higher by 1600 that a printed book might come into the village and be read aloud at the veillée, . . . but oral culture was still so dominant that it transformed everything it touched. . . ."[116] Information was still imparted mainly by word of mouth for virtually all levels of the society and culture. Even enthusiastic readers, such as humanists, read aloud, *hearing* the text.

One important factor making for the primacy of hearing and nonliterate visuality was religious: the Word of God was the supreme authority of the church. The ears were the most important sensory organ for Christians; sight, in a way that diverges from the use of the eyes in reading, was also central in this world of nature and visual imagery. Thus the enormous attraction of clerical art and of woodcuts and printed imagery.[117] Print and literacy were increasing their penetration into this slowly changing world, but in the sixteenth, and even seventeenth, centuries, their roles were far from dominant.

In the cities, printing brought greater changes. Literacy rates had long been higher in the towns and cities, especially among urban artisans and tradesmen. The gap apparently widened, with economic, religious, and educational changes, during this period—for males, at least. Choirboy schools continued to serve some sons of artisans and petty traders, and the number of vernacular school teachers increased.[118] Simple instruction was provided by municipal orphanages, and a variety of primary schools were open to many. Occupation and wealth, rural and urban residence, school opportunities, religion, and perception of needs were among the chief factors determining the social distribution of literacy. No one factor was independent or all-powerful; rank or class and resources were probably most significant.[119]

Except in special contexts, male rates were well above those of females. For example, Protestantism offered women a new option: "women like their husbands (indeed *with* their husbands), could be engaged in the pure and serious enterprise of reading and talking about Scripture." Of course, not all Protestant women became literate; "the Protestant path was not a way to express their new literacy but a way finally to associate themselves with that surge of male literacy. . . ." Protestant women also included more than a "random" number of widows, employed women, and distinctive women. The reform movement apparently did not attract "genuinely learned" women in the city.

Literacy was not in itself determinative. In most cases, reformed women gained their letters as part of the educational impulse of the churches. After 1562, the French Calvinist church began special catechism classes in French for women; towns under Huguenot control tried to encourage literacy, among the poor in the orphanages as well as the more well-to-do. Some literate husbands began to teach their wives to read. Regardless, women's literacy remained on the whole well below that of men, except for some Calvinists and those in families of lawyers, merchant-bankers, and publishers.[120]

In the towns and cities, not only was literacy more common, easier to acquire, and more desirable for reasons religious and economic, but understanding of French was also more common. Migrants from rural areas spoke local patois, and urban speech was influenced by regional dialects. Yet, the maturation of the national vernacular, and especially its use by the royal government and increasing commonness in commerce, led to its rising frequency among the people.

The record of book ownership, as revealed in wills and inventories, suggests that literacy was not often employed for the regular reading that resulted in the purchase and keeping of printed materials. Books were especially uncommon among artisans. The few books owned included primarily vernacular Bibles and other religious books. Artisans also possessed technical works, such as pattern books, for which little literacy was required. The literate apparently took little advantage of the fruits of printing, but that does not mean that they were not in contact with the messages of printed media. Books were cheaper than manuscripts, but with prices commonly equivalent to the cost of one-half to one loaf of bread, economic reasons limited their purchase, as did means of access and lack of desire or need for them.

Artisans "bought a book, read it until they were finished, or until they were broke or needed cash, and then pawned it with an innkeeper or more likely sold it to a friend or a *librairie*." Books represented relatively liquid assets, less likely to depreciate than many other personal commodities and therefore useful for exchange purposes. It is also likely that only especially valued books were kept and that literate artisans and shopkeepers lent and traded books with one another. Most important, books were also shared in reading groups that brought, and tied, the literate and illiterate together.

Desires for literacy and the uses to which it might be put complemented one another at times and conflicted at others. Among reforming Protestants, for example, imposition of literacy served perceived and instructed needs of the people. In lands where orthodoxy dominated, religious drives for literacy were seen as, and sometimes were, threats to the sociocultural order. Traditionally, literacy had been highly restricted; during the Middle Ages, this legacy began to crumble. Its full demise did not come in much of the West until the nineteenth century. Where it did decline earlier, the reasons were primarily socially conservative and pious—quite apart from the popular uses to which literacy might be put. The long legacies of social restriction of literacy and schooling were declining, but it was a lengthy fall, replete with new fears of the masses and their schooling as threatening to order. This renewed theme began to compete with the humanist and Reformation spirit of bringing schooling to virtually all men (occasionally to women, too).

Some artisans, tradesmen, and women began to compose a few of the books they read; some such persons had composed manuscripts in the fourteenth and fifteenth centuries, but these authors did not become well known or have their works reproduced by the presses. The advent of printing was not the sole cause of this new widening of authorship, but it gave their works a new permanence. The uses of the written and printed word were incredibly diverse. Groups of common persons could speak more or less collectively to the public through the press, sometimes even attempting to influence opinion on political issues.

The development of pamphlet literature, another omen for the future of literacy and reading, as well as for politics and influence, was an important step. Although most of the early polemical literature flowed downward and outward from the political and religious opinions of those at the center, some people on the edge of power recognized that the press could be used to respond. Adding printed pamphlets to the traditional means for spreading news increased the people's knowledge of national events. Such writing attracted both favorable and unfavorable attention—within its own circles and without.

The agencies of church and state attempted to silence these voices of political and religious dissent. But censorship could not stop the new relations evolving between reading, listening, and talking. After the 1570s, for example, a French Bible, a Catholic revision of the Genevan Scriptures, was approved legally and began to circulate. This edition, popular among urban Catholic laity, was successful, and undoubtedly stimulated people to acquire literacy. The authorities perceived the dangers of print and of individual, unmediated access to the holy writ. Their answer was to make the text safe; that was attempted by wrapping it in orthodox exposition, in which the Jesuits were especially active. They attempted to fix the meaning of devotional works by accompanying them with standardized religious illustrations. Catholic lay people were permitted an increasing amount of spiritual literature "in which the eye was guided by exposition and illustration." Medical knowledge presented a parallel but less intense problem.[121]

Literacy was coming—slowly, haltingly, and not without ambivalence—to the people of post-Reformation France, with its unreformed majorities. The contexts and results differed from those in reformed countries, although Calvinists' efforts paralleled those of reformers elsewhere. The similarities, especially in the social and geographic distribution of literacy, the conditions into which print was received and shaped by traditional popular culture, and the people's uses of literacy, are as important as the equally instructive differences. Orthodoxy and counter reform, while hesitant, were not totally hostile to reading and writing. Internal differences are just as revealing. The countryside was changed little by print and literacy for the first one hundred and more years of printing.[122]

Although the evidence is fragile, it seems that schooling and literacy expanded in France during the sixteenth and seventeenth centuries. The major stimulus was the efforts of Protestant schools and, in Catholic areas, the perseverance of the Roman clergy. It was often the bishops, agents of the institutionalized Counter-Reformation, who were involved in education. Some bishops inspected village schools during their pastoral visits, checking on schoolmasters and student attendance. By the end of the seventeenth century, this activity began to show results in schooling and literacy at elementary levels.

Literacy was gradually becoming a part of the life of more and more persons. Class differentials remained, but large-scale tenant farmers, who had been mainly illiterate a century before, often were able to read and write by the beginning of the eighteenth century. "The farmers now knew a little reading, writing, and arith-

metic and could thus market their produce in the most favorable circumstances.''
Many more literate persons were also available to the great noble and ecclesiastical
landowners in their efforts by the end of the seventeenth century to manage their
estates more effectively.[123]

The most impressive general figures available (which of course mask huge variations by geography, sex, and social class) are the results of Louis Maggiolo's 1877
survey. He found, impressively, that during the years 1686–1690, 29 percent of
grooms and 14 percent of brides were able to sign their names.[124] Real progress
in literacy had been achieved, despite sharp regional variations.

The development of primary education through the auspices of the church was
a major motor driving this change. The role of Protestantism, among the Huguenots,
is clear. Municipal schools were also important. Less noticed has been the role of
the Catholic church and the Counter Reformation.[125] Education, broadly speaking,
was central to the reforms emanating from Trent. Faithful Catholics were to attend
Mass and receive sacraments and the eucharist regularly from the parish priests.
The state of rural popular piety meant that this massive effort of reform required
new education for priests and the people. The colleges and academies that grew
up, especially those initiated and run by the new order of the Jesuits, were concerned
largely with priests; schooling the people represented another question.

Education was central to the struggles of Christianization. A campaign of schooling ''arose in part from the miserable state of popular religious instruction; without
dramatic improvements in this field, habits of church attendance and sacramental
practice would never express more than . . . a 'sheep-like conformism.' '' The
strength of the oral tradition is revealed in this form of indoctrination and instruction,
as is potential for tremendous local and regional variation in attempts and rates of
success and failure. Such obligations were more easily imposed than accepted or
met; for example, private enterprise could play an important role, one fulfilled more
easily in towns than in countryside. In some places, schools were created to meet
the perceived needs. After 1650, all French dioceses seem to have had legislation
imposing catechism as a duty on parish priests and parents.

Children learned their catechism by memorizing small books written in question-
and-answer form. These children were not comprehending and understanding what
they read, but, in a way, this was literacy (albeit a rather low and not especially
useful level), the product of common schooling experiences. The models for these
books were sixteenth-century Jesuit catechisms, indebted to Luther and in general
use in Germany and Italy, with many volumes composed by French bishops or their
appointed authors. A child's exposure to them was expected to produce a great
change in popular religious understanding; ''yet they were a dubious introduction
to a truly Christian life.'' After a more ambitious and imaginative beginning, they
became a set of scholastic formulae, a set of chilling moral imperatives, all presented
as the ''duties of the Christian religion.''

Regardless of the difficulties and contradictions involved in the uses of the catechism as a tool of religious *and* literacy training, there can be no doubt about its
contribution to promoting primary education, especially in the countryside. A foundation in literacy, along with the more important elements of the faith, came to
more and more children. Gradually, French bishops began to help hard-worked

priests by encouraging the presence of a schoolmaster in parishes. Weekday schooling supplemented Sunday and holy-day instruction, at least for male children among the better-off in rural society. By 1704, there was a schoolmaster in every parish, and one child was being given some sort of schooling among every two or three families.[126]

Currents in Spanish education and literacy are relatively unknown. A recent analysis of signatures in the records of the Tribunals of the Inquisition in Toledo and Cordova by Rodriguez and Bennassar provides a brief glimpse into trends in literacy levels. Interestingly, Rodriguez and Bennassar discover that over the period 1525–1817, 45 percent were literate and 47 percent were unable to read or write or sign. Fully 87 percent of women were illiterate, compared to 37 percent of men (of whom 4 and 53 percent respectively were literate). Not surprisingly, urban residents were more often literate than country people. These are impressive levels.

The population of those represented in the inquisitional records is heavily biased toward higher social levels. Nevertheless, it gives an indication of gross social differences. In each group, male literacy rates exceeded female. The lines of social distinction that ruled the processes of literacy's transmission in this Catholic region are clear; most dramatic is that separating the clergy, nobility, literati, professionals, officials, and merchants from the rest. We note, too, that the largest social group, the peasantry, is largely absent; illiteracy was their common condition. Chronologically, literacy was definitely increasing, here as elsewhere. The increase, however, was not equally shared by the sexes, rural residents, or the social classes.[127]

### C. Sweden and the North

The Reformation and Lutheran Protestantism stimulated the Swedish Lutheran literacy movement, one of the most impressive and successful literacy campaigns in the Western world. The Swedish example is special for the rapid progress to near-universal levels of literacy, and for the context in which that progress occurred: teaching on a household basis, supervised and reinforced by the parish church and clergy, with regular compulsory examinations. Such an experiment largely failed in Germany. In Sweden, it took place mostly *without* formal institutional schooling or instruction in writing, in a land of widespread poverty. Egil Johansson writes:

> It is still difficult for foreign observers to understand what has happened in Sweden, owing to the special nature of the Swedish and Finnish reading tradition. . . . people were persuaded to learn to read by means of an actual campaign initiated for political and religious reasons. . . . The social pressure was enormous. Everybody in the household and in the village gathered once a year to take part in examinations in reading and knowledge of the Bible. The adult who failed these examinations was excluded from both communion and marriage.

Luther's goal of compulsion was successfully achieved. The purposes of literacy provision were socially conservative, rooted in political and religious motives. At least as important, literacy neither followed from nor stimulated economic development.

The ideas of the Reformation were put into effect by a united effort of virtually the entire nation. The Swedish nation was rebuilding after a long period of wars of conquest and defeat; national reconstruction came to include extensive education of the people, under laws of state and church. The Church Law of 1686 included rulings about general literacy; it stated that children, farmhands, and maid-servants should "learn to read and see with their own eyes what God bids and commands in His Holy Word." Here was the Protestant influence. The goal was to promote individual consciousness of Christian faith and life; the method was exposure by individual literacy—reading by and for oneself.

The link between church and household, under the influence and protection of the state, was the literacy connection. The service, with its sermons, was the scene of collective instruction and questioning (including formal examinations); the household was the place in which daily instruction, especially of the young, was to take place. Psalm books and Biblical texts were to be used daily for family prayers; the old were to conduct the young in their programmed learning, based on the Lutheran catechism. The master was the teacher in the household, responsible for devotion, instruction, and examination of those who resided there. Church services and home instruction were highly complementary in the villages. Reading was taught in this manner: herein was the "reading movement." And through learning in literacy, the religious, social, and political ideologies were transmitted to virtually all persons.

With priestly supervision and regular examinations, the reading campaign brought mass literacy without formal schooling. Parents were primarily responsible for teaching their children. Children learned the alphabet and spelling thoroughly before proceeding to basic reading. Memorization exercises stressed learning verbatim. Clarity and comprehension in reading were emphasized, and the children were required to be able to paraphrase what they had read.

Strong social pressures furthered the spread of reading ability and knowledge of the catechism. People who could read were expected to teach those who could not. However, more than compulsion was at work in the Swedish reading movement; many persons came to feel a religious need as a result of village reading and family prayers.

A system of regular examinations was established by the church to test reading and catechetical knowledge. Examination records indicate the timing of the coming of literacy. By the late seventeenth century, there was a clear differentiation by age; almost all young Swedes were able to read—an indication of the results of a purposeful literacy campaign. The older persons were educated primarily by oral instruction and memorization; the younger learned by reading and therefore were able to progress further through the catechism's articles and Luther's explanations of them. Female literacy was rising equally with male; a special stimulus was the centrality of the mother as domestic teacher.

Reading was learned in Sweden principally for purposes of religion and spirituality, although values conducive to citizenship and social conduct were also important. This literacy was *not* of a high qualitative level, nor was it a skill especially useful or valued for economic reasons or for personal achievement. That is one of the factors that lay behind the success of the reading campaign in seventeenth-century Sweden.[128]

## D. England and the Isles

England, as elsewhere, built upon late medieval developments, including progress in literacy and education. Its Reformation was in some ways an educational one, too. Most interesting, its reforms lay somewhere between the Counter Reformation and the Lutheran and Calvinist Reformations.

The rising tide of lay literacy, printing, and English language usage during the fifteenth and early sixteenth centuries interplayed with the religiocultural changes associated with the English Reformation. Reform was also influenced, not uniquely, by lay piety, humanist critiques and programs, and the perceptions and needs of the Crown. In association with the increase in literacy that preceded the reform, the oral culture was strong and persistent; it remained so despite changes in the distribution of literacy or the supply of books. Much of the Reformation's effort to renew the faith seized upon the traditional processes of communication. Changes and new relationships between communicative media were in the making, however.[129]

As on the Continent, the English Reformation grew out of the condition of late medieval piety and religiosity and the grievances that more and more persons felt against the established church, grievances that reform by and within the church proved unable to resolve. The pre-Reformation church was central to national and parochial life.[130] It was also an international institution. Its significance and its troubles were deeply rooted. Deriving in part from its dual role as the spiritual representative of God on earth and material, worldly power, the late medieval English church was a bundle of contradictions. The church was its own major critic, but that was insufficient to prevent an irrevocable schism from dividing it. The problems facing the church and the laity by 1500 were numerous. Clerical training and the condition of the monasteries were areas of special complaints and real problems. By 1535, a definitive move toward Protestantism had been made.

Printing increased the potential impact of criticism and unsatisfied piety and religiosity, especially at a time when literacy was rising and the message of the printed text was diffusing more widely through the oral media. Although most early books were orthodox books of devotion, printing made it easier to circulate more subversive materials and facilitated the critical examination of religious as well as classical texts to seek their original meanings. Here, the contributions of Erasmus, Colet, and More were especially important.[131]

Among the early achievements that had an impact on literacy were the production and distribution of an English Bible. Orthodox opinion distrusted the availability of vernacular scriptures, and the appearance of an official English translation was long delayed. By 1538, all parish churches were ordered to equip themselves with an English Bible for public readings. In 1539, an official translation, the "Great Bible," was published.

The new availability of the Scriptures for reading in church and of cheaper editions for private reading was an undoubted spur to lay literacy. On one hand, it gave the literate new material, essential texts, on which to work their skills of reading; on the other, its presence and popularity among the populace stimulated others to acquire the tools of literacy. In the few, but increasing, households that owned books, the Bible and other devotional literature were among the most common.[132]

Another significant development within the Reformation was the dissolution of the monasteries. Conducted in the spirit of ecclesiastical reform, it was done to fill the dangerously low royal coffers. At the same time, the government also conducted a more general assault of the church's wealth and on popular superstitions. In addition to bringing needed wealth to the crown, the dissolution vested the interest of more laymen in the new order being created.

The increased reading and disputation of the Bible by the lower classes led to an unsuccessful prohibition in 1543, and protests in response. Bringing Reformation and Protestantism to England was not the act of tailors or shepherds. "The fact that the gentry and the middle classes continued to read the Bible mattered far more than the fact that poor men suffered a temporary restraint." The Crown and the hierarchy could not remove the Bible from the groups active in intellectual, political, or religious affairs, regardless of wishes to do so. What was growing during the early Reformation period was not only lay literacy, but also a "New Learning" comprising Biblicism, Erasmian reformism, and Protestant beliefs.[133]

Despite the so-called revolution, literacy remained restricted. Perhaps most revolutionary were changes in the incidence of formal schooling at the grammar, university, and other higher educational levels. Literacy levels did increase, but the growth did not touch all classes equally. Also, the changes that occurred were not wholly unprecedented. If change accelerated after the mid-sixteenth century, it was because of earlier transformations.

Reformation educational developments were firmly rooted in the ideas and programs of the humanists, who saw educational reform as a way to turn people away from the evils of the day and toward virtue and religion. All aspects of education were discussed, but the major concern was *not* the masses. When mass schooling was raised as an issue, the terms were revealing. Much of the talk was by churchmen, and involved the development of prescribed catechisms and primers. Reforming bishops, for example, advocated an extension of schooling; elementary teaching in the vernacular, not as unprecedented as some have thought, received a boost. In 1537, Latimer urged the clergy and chantry priests to accept their duty of teaching children to read in English, so they might " 'the better learn how to believe, how to pray and how to live to God's pleasure.' "

The course of the political reformation limited efforts to achieve immediate reforms, but the refounding of schools began well before 1560. Royal injunctions of 1559 required the licensing of teachers by bishops and ordered clerical incumbents who were not licensed to preach to teach reading and writing to the children in their parishes.[134] Something of a system of schools—under control of state and church—was beginning to appear by the end of the century.

English educational opportunity was, and remained, socially stratified, even as expansion occurred. At all levels, privileged children made progress at the expense of others. Humanist goals were contradicted by the forces for social order. Reformers and some statesmen grasped that schooling could be a cure for social problems, but their practices were more limited. Despite much hope and even more rhetoric through the time of the Cromwellian Commonwealth, educational expansion *never* achieved fulfillment to embrace the masses. The availability of schooling was long determined by private philanthropy and local requirements.

In fact, the advocates of universal schooling in Tudor and Stuart England never were concerned primarily with opening up mass opportunities. Social mobility from increased education was anathema to most of the theoreticians; even the progressive Comenius stressed that he sought moral and religious growth rather than social or economic change. Education was to be expanded, indeed revolutionized, but without risk to the orders of society. Many, including some who clamored for reform and expansion, felt that the social order was endangered when educational opportunities increased. That was one reason why most expansion and reform took place at the higher levels of the educational hierarchy. [135]

There was a significant increase in educational philanthropy in the post-Reformation period. However, more apparently was said about educating the poor than was done about it. Surviving school admission registers and roll books support the contention that educational opportunities were more limited than is usually asserted—and perhaps more restricted than the philanthropists had desired. The evidence from the institutions themselves shows that education was the preserve of the wealthy and never was readily available to poor persons who desired it, despite pious intentions and rhetoric. [136]

Illiteracy in early modern England, as measured by the individual ability to sign one's name, was widespread but distributed unevenly.

> Pre-industrial England was a partially literate society encompassing a broad range of literate skills. Some people, we have no way to discover how many, could have been able to read without knowing how to write or even to sign their names. The existence of this semi-literate segment of the population, whose literacy was passive rather than active, is suggested by the conventional ordering of the curriculum in Tudor and Stuart elementary education.

There were a wide variety of ways in which to acquire literacy. A fair, and increasing, number took advantage of these opportunities. They were limited by social class and wealth, as well as familial evaluation of the need for such training, pupil interest, costs, and competence of instruction. Instructional skills varied, poor teaching and low-level learning were common, and useful degrees of literacy skills were difficult to transmit. For many, high-level skills did not follow from primary educational experiences.

Literacy was sharply stratified by occupational class and social and economic position (see tables 5.2 and 5.3). Rare among shopkeepers, men of commerce, and the elite, illiteracy was more common among skilled craftsmen and was almost the normal condition of the laboring class. Clergymen, lawyers, and schoolmasters were universally literate; that was a requirement of their professions. The gentry were normally literate. Their literacy, in almost all cases, was one appropriate to their needs. The literacy rate of yeomen was significantly beneath that of the gentry, but, equally important, it was considerably above that of husbandmen and poor country persons.

Tradesmen and craftsmen possessed literacy rates similar to those of yeomen.

TABLE 5.2
**Illiteracy of Social Groups in the Diocese of Norwich, 1580–1700**

| Group | Number sampled | % illiterate | 95% confidence interval |
|---|---|---|---|
| Clergy and professions | 332 | 0 | – |
| Gentry | 450 | 2 | ±1 |
| Yeomen | 944 | 35 | ±3 |
| Tradesmen and craftsmen | 1,838 | 44 | ±2 |
| Husbandmen | 1,198 | 79 | ±3 |
| Labourers | 88 | 85 | ±7 |
| Women | 1,024 | 89 | ±2 |

Source: L.V. Gerulaitus, *Printing and Publishing in Fifteenth-Century Venice* (Chicago: American Library Association, 1976), p.60.

TABLE 5.3
**Illiteracy of Tradesmen and Craftsmen in the Diocese of Norwich, 1580–1700**

| Occupation | Number sampled | % illiterate | 95% confidence interval |
|---|---|---|---|
| Grocers | 49 | 6 | ± 7 |
| Haberdashers | 11 | 9 | ±17 |
| Merchants | 25 | 12 | ±13 |
| Bakers | 33 | 27 | ±16 |
| Tanners | 36 | 31 | ±15 |
| Wheelwrights | 16 | 31 | ±23 |
| Innkeepers | 25 | 36 | ±19 |
| Maltsters | 22 | 36 | ±20 |
| Brewers | 32 | 41 | ±17 |
| Weavers | 225 | 42 | ± 6 |
| Glovers | 25 | 44 | ±19 |
| Tailors | 139 | 44 | ± 8 |
| Blacksmiths | 49 | 45 | ±14 |
| Butchers | 60 | 48 | ±13 |
| Shoemakers | 79 | 58 | ±11 |
| Sailors | 27 | 59 | ±19 |
| Carpenters | 91 | 64 | ±10 |
| Millers | 20 | 70 | ±20 |
| Gardeners | 11 | 73 | ±26 |
| Masons | 21 | 76 | ±18 |
| Bricklayers | 24 | 88 | ±13 |
| Shepherds | 10 | 90 | ±16 |
| Thatchers | 33 | 97 | ± 6 |

Source: David Cressy, "Levels of Illiteracy in England, 1530–1730," *Historical Journal* 20 (1977): 1–23, p.5.

## TABLE 5.4
### Illiteracy in the Diocese of Norwich by Decade, 1580–1700

| | Yeomen | | Husbandmen | | Tradesmen | |
|---|---|---|---|---|---|---|
| Decade | No. | % | No. | % | No. | % |
| 1580s | 78 | 55 | 94 | 93 | 98 | 61 |
| 1590s | 112 | 38 | 121 | 87 | 161 | 55 |
| 1600s | 89 | 39 | 108 | 79 | 151 | 48 |
| 1610s | 84 | 38 | 91 | 77 | 126 | 44 |
| 1620s | — | — | — | — | — | — |
| 1630s | 90 | 32 | 84 | 86 | 140 | 39 |
| 1640s | 36 | 28 | 23 | 78 | 90 | 52 |
| 1650s | — | — | — | — | — | — |
| 1660s | 37 | 24 | 82 | 71 | 176 | 33 |
| 1670s | 24 | 12 | 56 | 82 | 149 | 35 |
| 1680s | 42 | 45 | 38 | 89 | 174 | 44 |
| 1690s | 33 | 18 | 40 | 82 | 125 | 30 |
| 1720s | 46 | 26 | 39 | 87 | 104 | 34 |

Source: David Cressy, "Levels of Illiteracy in England, 1530–1730," *Historical Journal* 20 (1977): 1–23, p.11.

Artisans and outside workmen were often illiterate, whereas shopkeepers and merchants commonly signed their names. Many of these tradespeople could read, even if they could not write.

Farm laborers and building workers were not expected to be able to read or write; typically they could not. The massive illiteracy of this majority of the population meant more than lack of educational opportunities. They neither were encouraged nor had the means to acquire literacy; normally, they had little use for it. There is no doubt, however, that they were active participants in the oral culture, communicating with others and sharing tales, jokes, and news. They were in touch, through reading in church or other places, with some of the messages of the print media. Those few who could read were able to share the results with their fellows.

Most women were unable to sign their names. If educated at all, women in Tudor and Stuart England normally were not taught to write, although some learned to read. Their education was primarily in domestic skills, a learning that did not involve literacy. In London, however, where literacy levels were higher than elsewhere, female literacy gained rapidly after the Revolution, and by the end of the seventeenth century, city women's literacy rates compared well with those of men in other parts of the country.[137]

The progress of literacy fluctuated irregularly over time (see table 5.4 and figure 5.1). The literacy levels of gentlemen and clergy at the top of the social scale and women and laborers at the bottom remained stable between 1580 and 1700, but there was considerable instability among the rates of yeomen, husbandmen, and tradesmen. If the availability of schooling was changing during the period with the

**Figure 5.1.** Illiteracy of Social Groups, Diocese of Norwich, 1530–1710
*Source*: David Cressy, "Levels of Illiteracy in England, 1530–1730." *Historical Journal* 20 (1977):1–23, p. 13.

political and religiopolitical events, it is likely that the groups in the middle of society were most susceptible to fluctuating opportunity structures. Those at the top were most secure; those at the bottom were seldom included regardless.

From 1500 to 1700, there was a sharp reduction in illiteracy. The lowest in social and economic standing, husbandmen, gained the least. Relatively, they fell behind, as did laborers, whose literacy was scarcely influenced by these currents of change. Equally significant major improvement took place in the sixteenth century—*not* in the seventeenth. The Reformation and its enactment of reform for religious and political reasons were more important than what followed. The later periods saw progress turn much more sluggish and uneven. "The overall pattern shows none of the gradual elimination of illiteracy which might have been expected."

Schooling, within limits, was expanding on the eve of the Henrican Reformation. The relationship between schooling and literacy was not quite a one-to-one correspondence. Time lags, varying ages and different rates of learning of children, irregular attendance, and alternative needs of child labor were among the complications. Also, "enthusiasm for educational expansion contested with fears that widespread learning would endanger religion, the State and the entire social order." Neither ideas nor institutional developments proved a reliable guide to the realities of school participation and literacy learning.

The 1530s were a time of slumping educational philanthropy. A reduced rate of giving continued into the 1540s, but charity improved measurably in the 1550s. Literacy, however, improved in the 1530s but fell in the 1550s. That is no surprise, given that the best-documented endowments were not charitable, but were aimed at grammar school foundations. "Even if educational bequests did contribute to the reduction of illiteracy a time lag would be expected between the date of an endowment and the time of its impact.'' The last factor might account for the cyclical phenomenon and the periods of increasing giving, followed by increasing literacy one and two decades later. The political events of the period may be more important than reduced support for education at the time of declining levels of literacy. As it brought advancement in literacy and schooling at higher levels, the Reformation also brought confusion.

Literacy did not make constant forward progress after the Reformation. The revival stopped on the onset of civil war, which ushered in a time of collapse for elementary education. Schoolmasters left posts or were ejected. The revolutionaries' educational hopes could not be confronted until the relative calm of the 1550s. New progress followed the restoration of the monarchy, perhaps ironically, but the end of the seventeenth century was a period in which literacy levels fell once again. With illiteracy associated with idleness and vice, a new attempt was then made to reinvigorate popular education: charity schools to socialize the poor, produce " 'honest and industrious servants,' " and spread literacy.[138]

As in any nation, there was tremendous regional variation in literacy within England. Religious and political leadership, community size, and, especially, educational opportunities and economic development contributed to the differentiation. In the preindustrial north, for example, illiteracy was much higher than in the south, an indication of the region's backwardness and cultural impoverishment. Neither literacy nor schooling developed homogeneously within the realm.[139]

In the village of Terling in Essex, to take one example, the "educational revolution" was highly selective socially in its impact. Many families could afford neither the money nor the time for education for their children, and not all valued or sought it. Schooling affected primarily the middle and upper ranks; those lower were little touched outside the metropolis.

Literacy had the potential to open up the world and free persons from their dependence on priests and other intermediaries. It could also enrich and expand the oral culture. However, a rigid distinction should not be made between the literate and oral cultures of the period. Some literates used their skills only in an instrumental way, continuing to root their attitudes and perceptions in the traditional culture. And some illiterates were touched by the influences of the literate culture even though they could not participate in it directly. Beyond its religious uses, literacy could give people more direct access to sources of information, news, and knowledge.

Essex County had been centrally involved in the school development of the period; the end of the century brought increases in licensed schoolmasters and in their qualifications. Although this growth was later reversed, a permanent decline in illiteracy remained. The level of adult male literacy varied within the county; by the end of the 1640s it was 30 to 40 percent, and by the 1690s 45 to 50 percent.

By the end of the sixteenth century, gentlemen and larger farmers were literate, and the levels were rising for yeomen and wealthy craftsmen. By 1640 the literacy level of yeomen was 70 percent, of husbandmen 30 percent, and of trades- and craftsmen over 60 percent. Male illiteracy declined steadily through the late seventeenth century; female illiteracy remained high until the last decades of that century. The laboring poor also remained overwhelmingly illiterate until the end of the seventeenth century, when their incomes increased enough for some of them to consider schooling for their children.

Literacy was seen as a practical skill in Terling. Reading and writing were regarded as important preparation for future occupations. Yeomen, husbandmen, and trades- and craftsmen found increasing need for the ability to read and write. Will making was also critically important; the ability to write and check wills was highly valued.

Literacy also had uses for those involved in local government. With time, it may have become a prerequisite for parish office. On the one hand, literacy was becoming increasingly associated with status, wealth, reputation, and positions of power and prominence; on the other, the written and printed word were penetrating the local community more regularly and deeply.[140]

Well-to-do villagers were beginning to evidence a real desire to acquire literacy for themselves and/or for their children. Economic reasons were not yet a driving force for literacy; the requirements of farming and most crafts demanded little familiarity with reading and writing. Schooling developments only partially explain the trends in popular literacy. Major, and deep, cultural imperatives and pressures were at work, selectively and differentially touching the lives of more men and women. Any explanation must include unrecorded means of acquiring literacy outside formal educational channels and usual ages for primary learning. Schools were important, but they were not determinative or all-pervasive. Popular literacy must also be understood in the textures of popular life, that is, in the confluence of forces from above, largely conservative forces of church and state and sometimes economy, and pressures from below—both working for the expansion of literacy. Neither were constant or unambiguous in their support for mass literacy; contradictions were commonplace.

Some exceptional individuals left autobiographies that recount their acquisition of literacy and their uses of it.

> Four points emerge from the study of the educational experiences of the poor. Learning to read and write was not a distinct activity undertaken during a compact period in one's life but part of a process which might go on from early childhood well into adulthood. Smatterings of these skills might be acquired as the opportunity and the necessity arose so that the process was organically related to the rest of life. Teaching literacy was a task divided between parents, relatives, friends, local old men and women who kept small and highly informal schools and occasionally by masters in endowed or charity schools. Finally, there were ample opportunities to use literacy skills whether for work, for religious edification or for leisure.

These books show the processes that enabled persons to acquire the skills and the varying mixtures of religious, economic, political, and social or recreational motivations for and uses of literacy. "To the extent that literacy was part of the structure of popular culture, it was a skill required not for any one special task or reason but in order to participate [more] fully in that culture." In some cases, a culture grounded in a religion committed to the principle of democratic access to scripture formed one imperative.[141]

From above and below, cultural and political forces brought more and more people to closer relations with the holy text. The sixteenth-century translation of the Bible and its dissemination were crucial; equally important was the wide distribution of the Book of Common Prayer and catechism. The increasing probability of more active congregational and individual religious participation was enhanced under Anglicanism, and much more so under Puritanism. Those who could not read listened to readings.

For literate and illiterate alike, religious literature came increasingly to be within the access of the common folk. Among records of books printed and books owned, religious material stands out.[142] With increasing literacy, the culture was more influenced by writing and print, and people joined, more or less, the literate culture. "In every village there were some who simply wanted to read," mainly the Bible.

Associated with the campaign to spread literacy was the beginning of efforts to enforce a stricter religious conformity. From the 1580s, the church courts actively prosecuted those lacking in religious observation. This mounting offense in the cause of a visible practice of faith was aimed at persons low in the social hierarchy. Regular church attendance was not a habit for many; other beliefs and superstitions interacted with their parochial forms of Christianity. As with literacy, so with religious conduct and conformity; the reformation of morality and behavior was an active campaign of Protestants and Puritans alike. This pressure was largely but not exclusively from the top down. Yeomen, whose own literacy had risen, led the campaign.

Under these forces, local culture did change, although traditional ways did not disappear. Some parishioners were drawn into the religious culture, but some moved on for themselves. In part, "a popular culture of communal dancing, alehouse sociability, and the like had retreated before a more sober ideal of family prayer, neighborly fellowship, and introspective piety." This process took place within a social structure that was relatively unchanged.

The outcome was largely molded by persisting structures of wealth, status, and power. Illiteracy had been erased only at the top of the social scale. Religious innovation descended from the parish leaders, with only a limited impact on the village poor. Occurring within conjoint processes of change and continuity was a growing offense against the conduct and customs of the poor—an effort to reshape them. But these developments also saw an increasing gap between the standards and customs of the rich and the poor. Social distance was growing, just as the leaders of the parish consciously attempted to impose on the community a new social discipline that would insure social order, while also reforming the conduct of the people.[143] A struggle began that lasted for centuries.

The growth of literacy also influenced political life, to a limited degree. Local government and popular political protest made increasing use of the written or printed word. Writing was becoming more of a symbol as well as substance of popular protest, although that was as much a growth from the late medieval era as it was a novelty. Much of this incipient political culture was, and continued to be, based in the oral exchange and the oral amplification and dissemination of the political message. Radical artisan and middle-class culture was, however, linked to literacy.

There was a new market by the seventeenth century for ballads, posters, almanacs, and chapbooks. They were wares for the people, printed in London and distributed by itinerant peddlers or chapmen. This material was mundane but relevant: ballads and stories of unrequited love, strange occurrences, religion, contemporary events, folk heroes, and the like. It also interacted with the oral culture. "In these printed materials folk culture and national history co-existed; through literacy they became increasingly linked."[144]

The popular culture of seventeenth-century London shows the process of change and continuity, of literate culture and oral culture in their interchange. Much of the city's culture of and for ordinary residents involved traditional rituals and festivals, some involving magic and witchcraft, other marking the seasonal calendar. London by the seventeenth century was one of the most literate cities in the West, but many of the ongoing cultural affairs of its common people were hardly touched by the encroachment of literacy. Religion and the Reformation, however, struck down the number of festivals and rituals. A new popular culture was in the process of developing. Professional, permanent kinds of entertainment, especially the theater, were one indication. Alongside entertainers were men trying to build a new religious and political culture.

Entertainment was becoming more professional, and, as one result, the audience was expected to be more passive and restrained. Religion, in contrast, was becoming deprofessionalized, with opportunities for popular participation opening up. The spread of literacy, as well as the persistence of the oral culture, related to both sorts of developments. The same is true of the emergent political culture and consciousness within the city. Popular culture, in print and orally, increasingly confronted the issues of the day, in impressively creative ways. Pageants addressed, mocked, and satirized major contemporary issues; their audiences included all ranges of classes and all levels of society, from the "rude and unlettered" to the rich and learned.

The relatively new popular culture of print was one part of this changing cultural universe. In the seventeenth century, there was a great increase in the amount of cheap printed literature available; a variety of broadsides, pamphlets, newspapers, and chapbooks took their place among the media of culture. Few people could avoid at least the broadsides; even without personal literacy, their messages must have been communicated to virtually all.[145] Here was one of the most common points of exchange and intersection between the media. London, of course, was exceptional: in its levels of literacy, its availability of print, and the penetration of literacy. It represented one extreme in England, indeed in the West; elsewhere things were different. Yet, even in this "literate London," much of the popular culture was not much shaped or determined by print or literacy.[146]

A high level of literacy was unlikely to be taken from many, if not most, educational settings—especially by those who would progress no further. Highly useful skills of reading and writing were probably *not* the norm. Rote learning, memorization, drill, and repetition were meant to dent pupils' skulls, rather than raise their skills or enlighten and enliven their intellects. That was also the case in many grammar schools. It was mainly students from families with social and economic advantages who reached the secondary and higher levels.

One of the major shifts in education in the sixteenth century was the activism of the state and the diminishing role of the church. By the close of Henry's reign, a wholesale transfer of rights over the established schools to the Crown had occurred, bringing to a climax a lengthy process of secular encroachment on ecclesiastical power over education. This shift was not accompanied by a concerted, coherent program of reform and refoundation. The period was one of confusion and uncertainty in the schools. Under Edward and, especially, Elizabeth, renewed progress took place, partly reflecting a new awareness of the potential dangers from below within the land. Popular schooling was trumpeted by reformers, within and without the government structures. It was recognized, for example, that the yeoman class was "so pressed [by economic forces] that they could no longer keep their sons in school and thus could destroy the realm," especially if these sons were not instructed in the religion and the civil faith. Here, literacy reached, though it did not touch, all the members of the popular classes.

Over the decades from the troubled reign of the young Edward to the exciting first period of Elizabeth's rule, schools were refounded and founded throughout the country, and the clergy were strengthened, all within the design of the central authority in London. A systematic approach was attempted, including schools for the poor. Religion and morality were central to the curriculum of the schools; that is reflected in the charters, the pedagogical tracts and treatises, and the materials produced for the students' use.

In the petty school, a typical middle-class or fairly well-to-do schoolboy would begin his studies around the age of five. Early studies would concentrate not on grammar but on reading and writing English. The hornbook was the primary aid to learning: a wooden tablet covered with parchment on which were printed the alphabet, basic syllables for English words, and the Paternoster in English, covered with a transparent sheet of horn. The pupil might advance to an ABC book with a catechism; a volume including the Paternoster, the Creed, the Ten Commandments, and short catechetical exercises on the fundamentals of the faith; and a primer, a devotional book with prayers and metrical versions of the Psalms. Girls sometimes joined their brothers, though they rarely advanced to the grammar school. For several years, they learned reading and writing, the rudiments of spelling, and the basics of the authorized religious beliefs. In market towns and some villages, the petty school was sometimes an appendage of the local grammar school. Many others were small, private, and irregular.

Catechism and other religious materials formed the core of the elementary curriculum. Their meaning was stressed, in the hope that the children might understand morality and the code of conduct, and assimilate into their values this message. The character of the teacher was also a major concern; he was the immediate agency of indoctrination. Teaching for children, preaching for adults and the young—these were the major pedagogical paths to social and religious reform. Literacy was one part of the large campaign, a controlled, conservative use of literacy.[147]

Like other small, intensely reforming areas in the period, Scotland despite its poverty managed some success at founding schools and diffusing literacy among its people under John Knox and Calvinism. During the seventeenth century Scottish literacy increased more rapidly than English, passing England's achievement before 1700 and outdistancing it throughout the next century and a half. The improvements took place mostly in the South or lowlands, however (they were mirrored across the border in districts in the north of England), and can easily be exaggerated. It has often been said that lowland Scotland joined with Sweden, parts of the Low Countries, and Germany, New England, and Switzerland in leading the march in the West toward universal male literacy. This is a major case of a ''literacy myth,'' as Houston shows.[148]

It proved impossible completely to control the development of education, although the expansion of schooling was rarely in itself a threat to the social order. The benefits were not shared by all. That was neither surprising nor wholly distinct from educational promoters' expectations, given the ambivalence of their thought. Expansion was one thing; equal opportunities and universal schooling were quite another, for the times and for the resources expended.

For many, education was perceived as more important than ever before; demand rose, and so did supply. In the process, opportunities for literacy increased, especially in the petty schools. ''Local schools began, therefore, to provide an education for the earliest stages, though there were evidently many small private schools, sometimes little dame schools. . . .'' The safeguards on a complete freedom of opportunity and mobility proved far too many. Indeed, few wished anything like that result. School reform and expansion helped in diverse ways to further differentiate the social ranks, to facilitate the formation of self-conscious classes, and perhaps to instruct the people properly. Grammar schools, for example, helped to mold the habits and speech of the middle and upper middle classes; a lack of schooling increasingly became a stigma of ignorance and low breeding.[149]

In goals such as bringing literacy and reformed manners and beliefs to the people, the reform in England was only a partial achievement. Relative to more radical, intense Protestant efforts, the English case was no world–shaping achievement.[150] It was still impressive, and it was apparently enough of a success to help propel England into world leadership in other realms. The partial success on one measure and larger accomplishment on the other are more than coincidentally related.

Another aspect of schooling merits notice, especially in this regard. That is apprenticeship, the major training in skilled work during this period. It supplied not only training in manual skills but also practical and theoretical knowledge. Civil and moral training were principal components, and reading and writing were increasingly taught.

It seems that the more prestigious the craft or trade, the higher the standards for literacy and education on entry and during the service period. Thus, literacy was becoming more a part of the training of prospective craftsmen; it was also among larger concerns about proper moral, social, and religious training. ''Unlike training in a business or skill, or the formal extensive education offered by household, gild, and parish, formal education was only minimally a part of the apprenticeship years.'' Examples of apprenticeship contracts indicate that ''school'' was usually no longer than a year of instruction in reading, writing, and doing accounts. Most often, it was the responsibility of the master and mistress to send the apprentice to school; occasionally, his own father did so.[151]

Puritan strongholds were among the most education-conscious and literate centers in England. In their intense piety and concern about individual access to the Word, Puritans expected their adherents to learn to read. Household and schoolhouse, as well as pulpit and chapel, were centers of schooling. Puritans were for their day a reading people, even if their tastes were often narrow. To an impressive degree, they effected an educational revolution. They also sought to bring their Word to other corners of the land, and to the colonies they established in North America in the seventeenth century.

Puritans had truly grand plans for the educational reform of the realm and beyond. Advocates of universal schooling, they desired to educate the poor, to uplift them, and to train them for socially safe, useful, and productive lives. They recognized the neglect of the poor by the educational institutions of the time, and how earlier reforms had barely touched those low in the social order. Their intended resolution was not an egalitarian or leveling expansion of education, but rather a training for the lower class, to school them properly morally and civically, on one hand, and for their stations, on the other. Room should be made even in the universities for the talented, but for most, a technical agricultural training was best. Literacy—to gain the holy literature for oneself and to participate in worship fully—should come to all.[152]

The Puritans did not succeed in their aims.[153] If anything, levels of schooling and of literacy declined from the onset of the civil war to the time of the Restoration. A time of war, division, and bitterness is not a time to refashion a network of schools or to provide literacy to the masses. Their intentions, if properly understood and not separated from their context or their contradictions, need not be questioned. It is their results, in England as in New England, that have been unduly exaggerated.

### E. North America

Contrary to historical stereotype, North American colonial settlers were born neither modern nor universally literate. Their origins were European, primarily English.[154] American students of American history, in stressing the exceptionality and uniqueness of these "plantations" of the Old World, have distorted the transatlantic connection that the colonists themselves held so dearly. A new, more contextually accurate and sophisticated understanding has recently developed, seeing the colonists as linked to the world in which the first generation was born and socialized and to a culture that shaped not only their lives but the lives of their children. Attitudes toward education, values of literacy, and notions about institutions, as well as the larger cultural universe, were brought from one side of the Atlantic to the other with the immigrants, but changes also occurred in the process of founding and developing a society in the wilderness of the North Atlantic coastal regions.[155]

The literacy levels of seventeenth-century colonists were relatively high. The rate of male literacy in New England was around 60 percent, as compared to a rate in contemporary England of no higher than 40 percent.[156] Puritanism was one reason. A religion of the Word and of the Book, it had a dynamic propelling its adherents toward literacy. This impetus was complex; in some ways it played a direct, almost linear, role in increasing rates and uses of literacy.[157] But more than Puritanism was responsible for the level of literacy among the first generation. Migratory selectivity was most important; persons more likely to be literate for religious, familial, occupational, demographic, geographic, or economic reasons, and/or from places with higher-than-average rates of literacy, were more likely to migrate over the long transatlantic distance. Both kinds of selectivity joined to constitute a population of movers whose ability to sign was perhaps (among males) one and one-half times the level at home—and possibly even higher.[158]

The situation of early French settlers in Quebec was similar. During the second half of the seventeenth century, migrants from the old country had relatively high levels of literacy. Marriage registers show that of those born in France and marrying between 1657 and 1715, 38 percent of men and 32 percent of women were able to sign. In contrast to British North American colonies, formal parish schooling was satisfactorily initiated. Of marriage partners born in the colony, 46 percent of grooms and 43 percent of brides signed, higher rates but also less differentiated by gender. The second generation progressed in this urban place in a way that was far more difficult in more rural, agrarian areas, whether in Quebec or in the English colonies. Here, too, schooling was traditional, and it was distinguished by class, gender, and geographic locale.[159]

For many English persons, especially Puritans, education, schooling, and literacy were acquiring a new importance by the early seventeenth century. That this value was transported with the colonists should be expected. English Protestant concern with schooling intersected with the Puritan stress on the importance of individual access to the Book and the Word among the New England settlers. Within a relatively few years of settlement in the Massachusetts colonies, the famous school laws were enacted requiring schooling for all children. An expression of piety, not a fearful reaction to the colonial wilderness, the laws derived from traditional Puritan motives, which were instrumental in raising literacy rates in England and which, when compulsory, seemed a powerful force for education. Literacy was a universal prerequisite to spiritual preparation, the central duty of the covenant about which Puritans were deeply concerned.[160]

Colonial New England witnessed a rise in literacy from little more than one-half of males to almost all men between the mid-seventeenth century and the end of the eighteenth. In the seventeenth century, literacy's progress was slow and uneven. Overall, levels of literacy barely moved during the lifetime of the second generation, those dying around the year 1710 and educated during the 1660s. The rise of high levels of literacy, part of a trend in much of the West, came only after a slow start. The success of New England's literacy campaign, largely through local, town, or parish schools (the English model), came mainly in the eighteenth century.[161]

Women's literacy was also relatively high in colonial New England. About one-third of the women who died prior to 1670, and who left wills, could sign their names. This rate, about one-half that of males, may have been about one and one-half times that of women in England, the same proportional advantage as among the men. However, the seventeenth century was not a time of opportunities for schooling; not until the eighteenth century does it seem that the teaching of literacy to girls as well as boys was frequently attempted. The literacy of a woman's parents had no effect on her own literacy. Church membership was the only variable significantly related to women's literacy. A traditional Puritan concern with religion was felt on the individual as well as the societal level. The only families in which

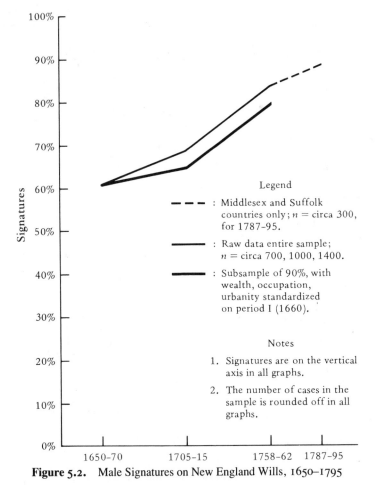

**Figure 5.2.** Male Signatures on New England Wills, 1650–1795

daughters were literate in most cases had two parents who were full members of the church. Familial wealth was not related to daughters' literacy, as it was for sons. For women, not even elite status was a guarantee of literacy.[162]

The desired rise in literacy, a skill not practically useful to most settlers, took place primarily after the turn of the eighteenth century. The increasing level of signatures most likely resulted from a rising inclination *and* ability of families to send their children, especially sons, to schools, and from the increasing availability of schools, due in large part to population density and the processes of social development. With rising levels of commercialization and urbanization came for more men a need for and advantages from reading and writing. In this way, social development intersected with original intentions to drive the rates of literacy from about two-thirds of men to almost all men. This progress was more conservative than revolutionary or "liberating," and was essentially a movement among previously less literate peoples and regions that began to negate the traditional association of literacy with social status but not with economic standing.

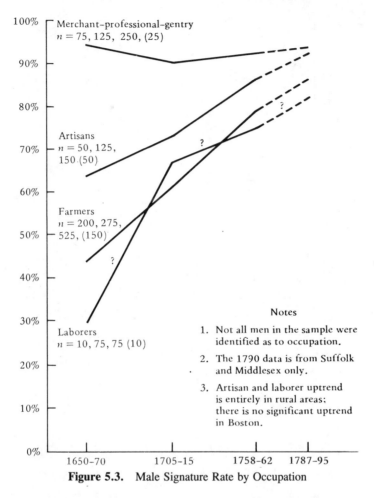

**Figure 5.3.**   Male Signature Rate by Occupation

In the seventeenth century, the social and geographic distribution of literacy was much more "traditional" than it would become. The more urban residents and higher-ranking persons, as in the Old World, were much more likely to be literate than lower-ranking and rural persons. As in England, literacy was linked directly to social standing. Social status, in wealth, occupation, deference, and the like, was brought with the settlers; it shaped literacy levels.

A number of historians have implied that literacy was instrumental to the formation of modern personality characteristics in the new colonies: activism, participation, optimism, awareness, cosmopolitanism, and larger loyalties. The presumed result was a more rational, planning, and calculating sort of person.[163] With regard to charitable behavior, however, studies have shown no modernization of attitudes occurring in colonial New England. Rather than literate men showing an increasing tendency to give to the needs of society, especially outside their families; to give to abstract causes and institutions rather than to persons; to give beyond their home villages and towns; or to give to rehabilitate rather than to

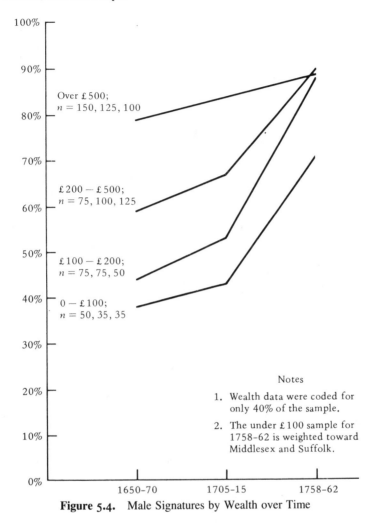

**Figure 5.4.** Male Signatures by Wealth over Time

alleviate, the analysis of charitable gifts revealed no such pattern, either for all givers or as a distinction between literate and illiterate givers. Literates, with their greater wealth, tended to give more often than illiterates, but when wealth is controlled, virtually no distinction existed.

The reason for charitable giving was usually traditional, to aid the poor or to further religion. Very few gifts were meant to rehabilitate the poor or turn religion to constructive secular needs; hardly any went to educate men or improve society. Literacy, it seems, did not press mightily upon men's beliefs or attitudes.[164]

Literacy did equip men with a skill that could be useful. But the quality of literacy and the environment limited and restrained its uses. In the seventeenth century many persons were not literate, but a high level of universal literacy was not required. Most transactions were localized and personal contacts; Puritans had a strong oral culture that shaped and received their value of the importance of individual access

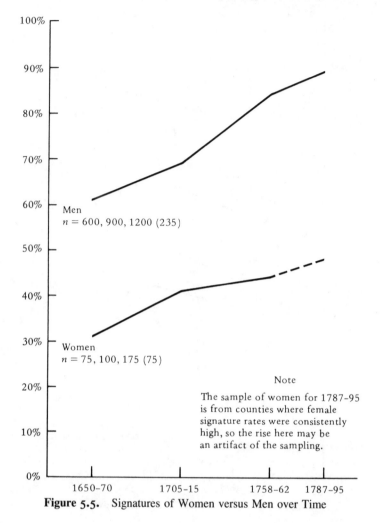

**Figure 5.5.** Signatures of Women versus Men over Time

to the Book and the Word. Reading and writing were not often required in daily affairs outside the needs of devotion and piety. Land was obtained from towns by grant, and deeds were usually registered locally by clerks. "The gap between the literacy of the population and the functional demands of the society was not great."[165] High levels of literacy did not assist colonial New Englanders in dealing with the confusion that regularly plagued their social and cultural maturation and road to revolution.

As in England, the oral and the literate culture intertwined. The oral medium was employed to disseminate much of print culture. Illustrations in books helped to carry ideas to illiterates, as did books designed to be read aloud. The substance of the world of print was transmitted and broadcast well beyond the relatively narrow boundaries of the individual, silent reader.[166]

Printing existed in New England from 1630, a year after the first press arrived.

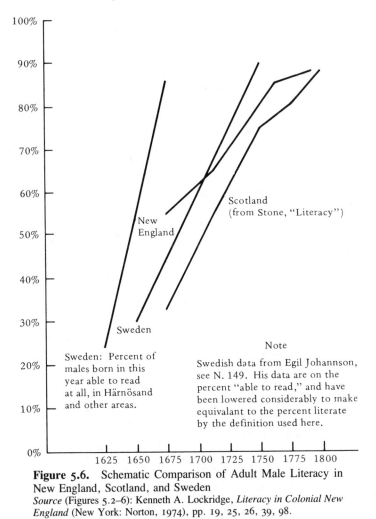

**Figure 5.6.** Schematic Comparison of Adult Male Literacy in New England, Scotland, and Sweden
*Source* (Figures 5.2–6): Kenneth A. Lockridge, *Literacy in Colonial New England* (New York: Norton, 1974), pp. 19, 25, 26, 39, 98.

The establishment of this press, in Cambridge, Massachusetts, probably was influenced by events at home, especially the extension of control over the press from censorship within England to pressure over publishing of Puritan works in the Netherlands. The presses started out slowly; most production was religious or administrative. Booksellers peddled their wares gradually. Their books were primarily religious; they also sold popular almanacs, medical manuals, and some literature—classics, histories, and other practical books. Other books were brought directly by the wealthiest or most educated settlers, who had the most important private libraries in seventeenth-century New England.[167] Primarily, only college graduates had collections that justified the label of library. The print culture of the early settlers, the limited evidence suggests, was not a vibrant, lively, and enlivening secular culture. Most print material related to religion.

The history of schooling in New England belongs more to the end of the sev-

enteenth and the eighteenth centuries than to this period. The evidence of literacy
and the limited reconstruction of educational activities join in suggesting that schooling, in a fairly systematic, regularized, and institutional way, came *after* initial
plantation founding and society building. The social structure of literacy, for the
seventeenth century, tended to vary mainly with the literacy levels of the founders
themselves; levels of population concentration, wealth, commercialization, and
"institutional maturity" related more closely to the presence of schools than did
the facts of settlement per se. That English men and women brought English and
Puritan motives, values, and plans for schooling with them is clear; it is also likely
that they were not able to erect many schools at first. The compulsory schools
required by the laws do not seem to have been established.[168] More developed
areas and towns were able to sustain schools, but many simply were not.

The schooling that took place was traditional and religiously oriented. Children
learned much as they had in England, from hornbooks and/or primers, either in
schoolhouses under a schoolmaster or from their pastors. Catechisms were central
to the curriculum. Primers, such as the famous *New England Primer*, were filled
with religious material. Moral and religious training and knowledge were the most
prized accomplishments of schooling.

Education was to begin as soon as the child was able to absorb it. The very young
were to be prepared by oral instruction and moral comments on their actions. The
household's piety and morality were to condition the child from the earliest moments
of awareness. As the child grew, more formal instruction was to replace informal
socialization. Other teaching took place in the church, and when possible in a school.
At school, training was more intellectual, to provide the pupil with the tools, such
as literacy, for acquiring religious knowledge. By the age of five, boys might be
attending reading or dame schools. These elementary schools of colonial New
England supplemented the lessons of the church.[169] As soon as they were old
enough, children were taken regularly to church, to learn their religious knowledge
from the pulpit. In theory, all aspects of education and literacy aimed at one central
lesson.

In the Southern colonies of Virginia and Maryland, the male literacy rate in the
seventeenth century was around 50 percent, again indicating the literacy selectivity
of the generation migrating to the North American colonies. The rich were almost
all literate, but only about half of the farmers and a third of the poor could sign.
The level rose to about two-thirds by the middle of the eighteenth century, then
stopped, at the same time that New England was achieving near-universal rates of
male literacy.

A lack of intense Protestantism and the resulting school laws contributed to this
stagnation, but other factors were equally important. The Puritan connection between individual literacy and reading the Scriptures was absent here. Piety and
devotion were of interest, but education was viewed as academic and practical, as
a means of teaching trades to boys and of giving domestic training to girls. An
academic education was based on an ability "to read distinctly in the Bible"; pupils
learned how to make a living and gained firsthand knowledge of the Bible at the
same time. Schooling was also clearly class-biased. The paucity of formal education
in the Colonial South was also due partly to the low population density, but more

to the short life expectancy of the settlers. Parents often did not live long enough to see to their children's education.

Education of children in this area had little bearing on their success as adults. Literacy was not necessary for economic prosperity; occupation and age were more important. "The wealth differences between literates and illiterates among those engaged in agriculture and common laboring pursuits indicate that society did not provide much economic incentive for literacy for those people."

Although there were persistent desires for schools, and the early laws of each colony called for schooling of all children, few institutions followed. Literacy rose slightly through the period, but mainly through selective migration streams; the progress of educational development was slow.[170]

One problem in places such as Virginia and Maryland was that the dispersed nature of geographic settlement required for the land- and labor-intensive plantation system greatly reduced the possibilities of formal schools' being founded and maintained. In huge parishes, some as large as a hundred square miles, churches reached only a portion of the population. "And, with residences scattered across the countryside, schools became uneconomical, for lack of both funds and scholars. Indeed, even the formal education of communal life was missing. . . ." Some Virginians hoped that towns, concentrating settlement and resources, would solve some of the problems, but for all their administrative, economic, and cultural importance, towns never played this role on a level sufficient for mass schooling.

Despite conviction, interest, and intention, schools remained restricted in the Southern colonies. That is as true for free and charity schooling for the poor as for other formal educational foundation. Little institutional progress took place until the second century of development. Education for the elite and wealthy was more successful before 1700 than were plans and desires for more inclusive schooling, with the exception of a handful of bequests for free and charity schools. Apprenticeship apparently developed on the English model, but fulfillment of its educational requirements proved a constant source of complaints and litigation.[171] The systematic program that came with time in the Puritan areas never developed in the Southern colonies.

Books and other elements of print culture were imported with the Southern colonists. Tastes were largely traditional, with major interests in religious literature, followed by a diversity of other materials. Indigenous printing developed more slowly than in New England; English products were even more pervasive. Book ownership and libraries were limited overwhelmingly to elites.

On this note of traditions, of legacies of literacy, this chapter ends. We have moved from the dawn of moveable typographic printing in the mid-fifteenth century in the workshops of Mainz, through the Northern Renaissance and Christian humanism, the Reformations of the sixteenth century, the development of new attitudes toward the extension and uses of schooling and literacy, the growth of literacy, and the transit of English and European civilization to the North American colonies. It has been a lengthy journey, taking us through two and one-half centuries, encompassing the West and spanning the Atlantic. It is a critical story, whose significance for its own time and for the future cannot be doubted. We appreciate the role of the new technology of printing while we see its continuities with the medieval past;

we grasp the manner in which literacy was endorsed to a major new extent for reasons of religion and politics as well as practical utility, while seeing the earlier precedents.

The emphasis on continuities and contradictions and on the legacies of literacy is a major innovation. Placing the history of literacy in a new context, seeing its possibilities as well as its limitations and restrictions, opens a new order of understanding. This conceptual orientation is especially striking for the dawn of the early modern era. This time in Western history is best viewed as transitional: the founding age of the modern West. To grasp its complexities requires seeing its roots in the earlier history of the Western world. The early modern experience of literacy must be examined by looking backwards as well as forwards—studying continuities as well as changes, and the contradictions that so often connect them.

Before we turn to a new era in literacy's history, the age of Enlightenment— another seminal period—the diversity of the early modern Western experience should be emphasized: the number of different paths in which efforts were made to increase levels of literacy; the many different factors and motives that intersected, sometimes smoothly but sometimes more raggedly or contradictorily, in the changing levels of literacy; and the number of different agencies and institutions that played major roles in this activity. That is part of the larger story, with lessons for the present and the future as well as from the past.

CHAPTER SIX

🦅

# Toward Enlightenment/
# Toward Modernity: 1660–1780

> From prime minister down to the last peasant, it is good for every-
> one to know how to read, write, and count.
>
> —Diderot's advice to Catherine II

> The necessary change in human life can easily be effected. Edu-
> cation will provide the key; teach the young to associate virtue
> with happiness and vice with misery and the problem will be
> solved. Let man, who is a rational being, behave in a manner
> suitable to his nature, and the turbulence which disrupts society
> will be completely curbed. Man will then behave as he should.
>
> —GERALD R. CRAGG, *Reason and Authority in the Eighteenth
> Century*

IN THE HISTORY OF LITERACY AND EDUCATION, the eighteenth century in
the West has an assured place. The century of Enlightenment laid a foundation for
the future: an ideology and a program for the nineteenth and twentieth centuries.[1]
It was at once a traditional century, with crucial continuities with its predecessors;
an irrevocable time of transition; and a beginning of transformation.

Hopes for social and moral betterment were increasingly associated with notions
about schooling. Literacy was more often seen as the root of schooling for the
populace. The increased interest in education in the West resulted from various
causes, some new, others carried forth from efforts initiated earlier. There was an
increased recognition of childhood as a critical life-cycle stage. The attention was
hardly directed to *all* children, but was mainly a middle- and upper-class development. Still, a new awareness of the distinctiveness of childhood as a developmental stage had obvious educational implications; it stimulated interest in
education.

The eighteenth century was also a time of psychological thinking. Many leaders
of the Enlightenment hoped along with John Locke that "through education human
progress, including moral progress, might be promoted."[2] Moral education often
formed a central plank in reform platforms, as moral and intellectual developments
intertwined. The idea of creating useful members of society accompanied these

moral reform hopes. Utility took many forms: from the training of professionals, civil servants, and economic innovators—a higher educational dimension—to the schooling of the masses, for nationality, homogenization, productivity, and social control—all in the name of citizenship training. The latter often led to an increased, and sometimes new, role for the state in promoting and controlling education.[3]

Not all persons of influence, power, or record shared the excitement of the promoters of education. Many were haunted by fears of too much education: that it would weaken society by alienating people from manual labor, threaten the natural social order, promote social mobility. They advocated a hierarchy of schools paralleling the social structure and more restricted training for the masses.[4] Instructively, a tiny amount of education—for example, the ability among servants to read masters' or mistresses' letters—was considered by some too much! The fear of a schooled population abated gradually, but lingered in much of Europe (though less in North America) into the next century.

Historians concur that the eighteenth century was an age of progress. The emphasis in recent years has swung to the "modernity" of the century. Stressing the final passing of the lineages of the Middle Ages, historians now claim for the period's transition a passage from an "early modern" era to a modern age. Its relationship to what would follow is now taken as a key point of departure, rather than its association with that which came before.[5]

Especially relevant is the role that modernization interpretations accord to education. In stressing the philosophes' concern for integration of diverse elements of the populace and fuller participation, a distinctive role is assigned to schooling.

> Another subject of serious concern in modernization theory is that of education. "Education, related as it is to civic training, on the one hand, and functional skills for particular occupations, on the other hand, is perhaps the most sensitive indicator of the structure of a society in terms of the history of power and prestige."

In modernization theory, the state is accepted as an impersonal, final arbiter of human affairs. The philosophes stressed the need for secular control in public education and emphasized that education was the concern of the nation.[6]

However, the modernization perspective remains either presumptive or dramatically incomplete. Surely the developments of the century and the Enlightenment itself deserve better. If they are to be understood, they require greater attention to context and relationship with the past, as well as the present. In making a case for novelty and modernity, and especially in arguing for a "pagan" Enlightenment that broke with traditional religious beliefs, recent historians remove the thinkers of the Century of Light from their grounding in time and space.

To the contrary, we must recognize the period's emergent leanings toward the future and modernity but *also* note its relationship to, and place within, a "world we have lost." With the history of literacy and schooling, that is especially important. Their understanding requires analysis of change and progressive development *within* a context that flexibly is anchored in attention to continuities and contradictions: a framework that makes clear that the dynamics of change—irregular and uneven as they are—consist of forces of historical continuity and the process of contradiction at their very center.

The discovery of the centrality of education in eighteenth-century thought and society is nonetheless important. Although concern with schooling was not a novel element by this late date in the history of Western civilization, the attention accorded to pedagogy sets it off from its predecessors and links it to the next period. The Enlightenment was an educational movement. To the philosophes, the overwhelming illiteracy and lack of autonomy among the masses obstructed reform and freedom. "There was only one realistic way of accepting the world of the present without sacrificing the possibilities of the future—education. This was the logic of enlightenment: if most men are not yet ready for autonomy, they must be *made* ready for it. The great political dilemma of the Enlightenment could be resolved only through time."[7] Thus, education had to form a component of reform schemes.

The philosophes were never quite secure in their faith in the "common" people, and not all of them shared confidence in the efficacy or even the possibility of educating all men and women. Voltaire, for one, believed that enlightening the people often seemed at best hopeless and at worst dangerous. More direct and forthright than most, he generally was suspicious of institutional attempts to bring literacy or "reason" to the people, although he admitted that " 'the low people will certainly be worth much more when the principal citizens cultivate wisdom and virtue; they will be contained by example, which is the most beautiful and greatest of virtues!' " To him, institutionalized dissemination of enlightenment was hopeless; the best path to popular improvement was through the example of *honnêtes gens'* reading and understanding the new philosophy, on one hand, and the tempering of superstition as a result, on the other. He also feared that institutionalized public instruction would result in fewer workers: " 'I think it proper that some children learn to read, write, and calculate, but that most, especially the children of laborers, know only how to cultivate, because you need only one pen for every two or three hundred arms.' " Yet, Voltaire was an exceptional estate owner who educated his peasants.[8]

Popular schooling was not an affordable luxury made possible by stability or relative prosperity, as some historians have argued. Not only did hostility to popular schooling persist, but there are also the facts of economic, demographic, political, and military history. Frequent warfare, agricultural problems, and revolutions are hardly the stuff of stability. But changes that revolutionized the literacy of the masses were not to be in this period.[9] In many ways, social, political, and economic developments propelled new interest in the condition of the people, which in turn suggested the need and utility for more schooling for moral, social, economic, and political reasons. But the realities of the Ancien Regime simultaneously limited much of that change.

The increasing interest in schooling needs to be seen in a larger context, one determined neither by an exclusive focus on legal decrees, expression of thought, or utopian schemes, nor by the often harsh realities of existence of the popular classes. As the years of the eighteenth century passed, interest in education grew only slowly. By the 1760s, concern reached new levels. Education was one of a much larger set of institutional changes propounded, and sometimes established, during an important transitional era.

In the process, more and more persons were achieving their literacy outside the

formal institutions often proposed and sometimes actually erected. Informal schooling, from charity schools to dame schools, individual tuition, and self-teaching,
was the avenue for some persons for literacy and education. The institutional aspects
and the philosophes' or states' programs were distinct,[10] although one may well
have influenced the other.

## 1. Thinking about Literacy and Schooling

It is easy, yet important, to recognize the prominence of educational interest and
concern in the eighteenth century. At the same time, the amount of attention that
education has received by students of the period is surprisingly small. Either the
recent awareness of education's place in the thought and goals of the period is
misplaced, or other factors have led to this paradox. Several are striking.

First is the huge gap between developments within education and efforts to put
programs into practice, and the spread of educational ideas and ideology, especially
in the second half of the century. Second is the evolution of educational thought
during the century. Although signs of interest in education were present from the
end of the seventeenth century, attention was hardly consistent.

Because of a number of factors, greater interest developed in the second half of
the century. Stimulated on the Continent in small part by the expulsion of the Jesuits,
that was one thread of the larger Enlightenment and humanitarian movement that
grew rapidly after mid-century. This timing, amounting to an explosion of writings
and debates about virtually all levels of schooling, is significant. The first half of
the century saw a comparatively small and somewhat rarefied discussion of education. But with the exception of the beginnings of a charity school movement in
England, for example, the greatest interest was in elite and specialized schooling.
This interest never died out, even with the relative shift by the 1760s. Concern with
moral education developed more slowly, but increased, as well, in the second half
of the century. It intersected, in interesting ways, with the notions of the philosophes,
although their goals were not the same. Social and economic factors underlay much
of this change in sentiment.[11]

Overall, one can argue that educational opportunities and structures remained
more like those of the past than those of the future. More novel were *thoughts* and
*goals* for mass schooling and educational reform.

> By 1780, monarchs in most European nations had issued decrees that looked forward
> to some form of universal instruction. The Roman Catholic Church accelerated its
> efforts, begun after Trent, to spread village schools across the countryside of all
> nations within its fold. These efforts were matched by the less centralized efforts of
> Pietists in Germany, humanitarians and evangelicals in England, economic societies
> in Spain, and seigneurs in France. The concern for reaching the people through
> schooling had multiple roots. For religious leaders, the logic remained the same: to
> win the minds of the masses. For humanitarians, such as the leaders of the charity
> school movement in England, instruction might provide economic skills and moral
> cultivation. For monarchists, the expulsion of the Jesuits in France, Spain, and Austria
> during the 1760s appeared to open new doors to kings who saw in public instruction
> a means of political consolidation.

To grasp the variety of influences and goals at work and their coming together in the third quarter of the century requires remembering the cessation of war in the early 1750s, a period of relative demographic and economic growth, political stability, and national consolidation. Specific factors, such as the end of the Jesuitical domination of instruction, the beginnings of industrialization, commercialization of agriculture, new elements in economic as well as psychological thought, and further secularization and bureaucratization of the state, added their impact.[12]

Especially important were the philosophes. Coalescing as an intellectual tendency by the 1760s, they had many reasons for turning toward educational solutions for what they saw as social problems. As religion faded as a legitimate social sanction, instruction took its place as its counterpart. The new epistemology, which stressed the power of environment and education, enhanced the hope that instruction was the way to enlighten the lowest orders.

In France, the Physiocrats were among the first to urge widespread popular education. Their motives were perhaps more narrow and utilitarian than others'; their conception of public education was often limited to its offering economic opportunity to the nation. Physiocrats, meeting resistance to their advocacy for free markets in grain, turned toward public instruction to influence popular minds and habits.

Advocates in other nations also found economic arguments compelling, either in the form of curricula related to work or in the general argument that minimally educated workers are more open to new techniques and ideas. Economic arguments, while relatively novel and "modern," gained popularity in the context of ongoing social and economic changes. A consensus was beginning to form, and part of it was economic: the people needed schooling; "progress," economic growth, and social stability required it. Fear was spreading that *without* the security of mass education, social order, morality, and productivity were increasingly threatened. An epochal shift was beginning.[13]

During the 1760s and 1770s, members of philosophic circles promoted plans for popular education. The Physiocrats, for example, demanded a secular schooling supervised by the state that included reading, writing, and arithmetic, as well as the basics of morality. In an age in which the duties of governments, states, and rulers were often debated, intellectuals began to argue that popular education was the duty of the state. Enlightened, benevolent despots in Europe began to listen.

Other French philosophes picked up threads of the Physiocratic educational plank. Turgot, for one, drafted in 1775 a "Mémoire sur les municipalitiés" with Dupont de Nemours. This typical document had for its first proposal a system of public education, which was "put forward with an easy optimism which knows no bounds." Existing educational establishments were criticized for being too technical and academic—inadequate for training the citizens. Turgot proposed the creation of a Council of Public Instruction to draft a curriculum of social education, provide a schoolmaster in every parish, and arrange for textbooks dealing with the duties of citizenship. More advanced education was to be provided in colleges and universities, from which teachers would be drawn, with opportunities open to all with talent. Within ten years, the nation " 'would not be recognizable.' "[14]

By the 1770s, the philosophes, and their patrons and supporters, quickly adopted public education as a major goal. Their impact was widespread. Efforts toward some form of popular schooling were discussed and sometimes attempted by several Central European monarchs. Minimal literacy was considered necessary even for peasants, to spread new agricultural ideas. Demands for public instruction were heard even in Basque country and the papal states.[15]

In proposing legislation, the new proponents of education often turned to the model of the church. Ironically, but not surprisingly given the church's prominence in schooling during the preceding era, reformers sought to move beyond the clerical foundations while reorienting and expanding the bases of tutelage.[16] A number of schemes drew upon existing patterns of religious education, with a role for priests as teachers, albeit supplemented by lay instructors. Turgot and Dupont de Nemours's proposed national instructional council would assume control of all educational facilities, teaching social morality with the uniformity of the religious model as its example. Many philosophes were anticlerical, however, and sought to remove the church's hand. No one sought to dispense with a firm moral basis to schooling, as moral and intellectual development together were equated with progress.[17]

Two developments joined in this increase in educational interest: the realization that the populace could not be ignored if reform was to be achieved, and the emergence of a concept of public schooling with morality as its core but separate from the church. For all their imputed liberalism or toleration, the philosophes had at best an ambiguous relationship with the masses (and with religion). Many of their writings and letters show them as despising the people as little higher than animals, because they were illiterate and unable to reason. That was not a base on which to build a new enlightened social order. The philosophes realized increasingly that the people were undeniably the base on whose labor and behavior the larger society depended. Since the peasantry and laboring classes were useful, and a part of society, they needed fairer treatment. If governed by the right legislation, taxed equitably, and provided with some measure of proper schooling, they could assume a more responsible and reasoning position in the society.[18]

Education for the masses was based in a useful literacy, but above all, instruction in the duties of their social position, their estate, was most important. This process of increasing attention to the people represented a revision of the philosophes' orientation and a slight revision of their estimation of popular capabilities. "The new advocates of public instruction were forced to attribute to all men some modest ability to comprehend and accept abstract truths."[19] As their programs developed, the recognition of the need to reach the masses increased. Optimism and cautiousness divided the philosophes. The common stress on the moral aspects of schooling joined them.[20]

This morality was primarily social and civic. The goal was to produce persons concerned about their own and their families' welfare, the condition of society, obedience to the state, and patriotism. Society was the beneficiary of morally trained persons residing within it. To bring up a nation of such persons required national, public schooling that began early and had a moral and ethical core. Reward and punishment reinforced the lessons, as moral training permeated the entire curriculum. All subjects could be taught in ways that produced moral impacts upon the pupils: from grammar to history.[21]

To the philosophes, only the truly enlightened few would understand the moral and social order and take an advanced role in learning and leading. Many, if properly instructed, could learn the rules of social order; they need not understand the intellectual bases of morality. The new schools of the state and the catechisms would teach the people what they needed to know to lead better lives and contribute to society. Schools for citizens were the most explicit goal of all. Formal instruction would become part of a systematic effort to make government a means of schooling the population in sociability and citizenship.

The philosophes' proposals did not ignore existing social differences. They tried to reconcile the people to their estate rather than create a critical intelligence that might stimulate the desire and means to escape it. Instruction would provide skills and moral perspective for people to perform social functions peaceably and productively. Reading, writing, and arithmetic would provide an adequate and necessary background for all work. Beyond that, instruction would emphasize performing one's roles.

Educational programs allocated limited access for the masses' children for secondary schooling, although the philosophes claimed that public service should be open to competition through education. Few of them believed that virtue, talent, and genius were to be found among many of the peasants and workers. A small number of scholarships for secondary education would meet the needs of the talented from below. The far greatest number would assume laboring positions.[22] Still, the philosophes wished to discover special ability among the commonality. The educational system envisioned was to teach most their duties and basic skills but also to locate the exceptional man among the many.[23]

Economic and social realities and contemporary opinion limited Enlightenment educational plans. Given the needs for children's labor and the limited resources for national systems of public education, even broadening the base of educational accessibility was asking a great deal. Questions of the educability of the masses and the wisdom in teaching them also worked to restrain proposals, and to limit schooling. Many feared that expanding education would lead to the loss of labor and the rise of dissatisfaction among the people. The philosophic promoters of education wanted a nation of minimally educated, virtuous, and peaceful farmers and workers. That would be a major step toward the new society of a population capable of being well-governed. A properly educated people would understand and accept its place in life and society.[24]

Only on occasion were these imposed limits passed in philosophes' thinking. Adam Smith urged the state's sponsorship of public education. All citizens, he stated, should be required to learn the skills of reading, writing, and counting— for economic reasons. He also felt that the deadening of daily drudgery in manual labor might be counteracted by education. Mirabeau, on the other hand, thought that morality and citizenship through universal schooling might help to unify a fragmented society. Education could bind together diverse members of a society without eradicating the facts of class or social differences. The progress of society and the improvement of the life of the masses might both be furthered. That was the educational logic of the Enlightenment: the dream of the eighteenth century, which has held power for many who followed it.[25] Therein lay one key use for literacy.

Condorcet, the major promoter of schooling, was the principal sponsor for educational schemes during the revolutionary period. His famous Report on Education was presented to the Legislative Assembly in April 1792. A true statement of the age, it comprised five philosophic treatises on education and a full curriculum for each grade and type of schooling. Condorcet began with a prototypical enunciation of faith: " 'Public education is a duty that society owes to all citizens.' " In creating a national system of schooling, the goal, accordingly, was " 'to assure to each one the opportunity of making himself more efficient in his work; of making himself more capable of performing his civic functions; and of developing, to the highest degree, the talents one has received from nature, thereby establishing among the citizens actual equality in order to make real the political equality decreed by law.' " Here was a program to put the logic of Enlightenment into practice—a logic that the eighteenth century was not capable of realizing, but one that the next century would confront.

The assumptions implicit throughout the report are suggestive. Condorcet implied that education was principally a public, rather than a private, activity. The Ancien Regimes' private schools, catering to the rich, corresponded to a rigid social structure in which education was a mark of wealth and status. In building a new, more egalitarian society in which greater opportunities were available to the many, the state must act to reduce the inferiority of ignorance. The state, through public, universal, and free schooling, could reduce the impact of social inequality by providing some schooling opportunities to every person. To Condorcet, ignorance not only led to poverty, but it was also a form of poverty itself, because it led to dependence on the educated. Not everyone needed the same degree of education; each person required enough to guarantee that he or she could enjoy his rights.

Condorcet especially abhorred the presence and power of an educated class. Regardless of their talent and learning, they hindered social progress. Progress would be advanced, materially and spiritually, with the addition of the gifted among the masses to the pool of talent within the state. One of education's tasks was to discover meritocratically the most able few from all classes. Only through education could a turbulent, unruly, superstitious people be changed into an orderly, enlightened, and self-sustained population. Education was a requirement for democracy; how otherwise would the populace know their rights and be capable of fulfilling their duties? " 'Diffusion of knowledge enables a people to establish good laws, a wise administration, and a truly free constitution.' "[26]

Education had other uses. It was vital in promoting economic advancement. Individual progress would occur, as prosperity became general; the wealth of a few men would be of little consequence. With the beginnings of industrialization and the emergence of mechanization, Condorcet grasped that education was a requirement if the minds of manual workers were not to be destroyed by the monotony of daily tasks. Education would give them the means of counteracting the stultifying impact of the "machine age" and the industrial division of labor.

With his predecessors and peers, he claimed that education was also a natural right for women. Women were citizens, too, and needed education to know their rights and fulfill their duties. Programmatically, Condorcet favored coeducation in elementary schooling; that developed camaraderie between the sexes and stimulated emulation.

Condorcet was strongly opposed to religious instruction in the public school. The young of all faiths and opinions could meet and mix in the public schools. Moral education lay at the heart of his curriculum, but a moral schooling separated from religious ritual and dogma. His morality was a more intellectual, rationalist variety than that which he felt was offered by the schools of the Ancien Regime and the church.

The second half of the report presented a full plan of instruction for a national system. Four grades constituted the system: primary, secondary, institutes, and lycées, all free and coeducational. The compulsory primary schools would be established in each district of France. A four-year course, this element taught the three Rs and the basics of geometry, geography, and agriculture. "Moral instruction was to be given in the form of stories to arouse sympathy for all living things." There would also be instruction in the rights and duties of citizens. Every village of 400 was to have a school; efforts to make them available to rural children would be made. The secondary school, also four years in length, would be maintained in the major city of each district (4,000 or more residents). It would offer instruction in sciences, commerce, languages, and social science. All teachers would be trained and certified.

Together the first four grades represented an open system, at least in theory. To eradicate illiteracy, all children would attend the primary level to receive the minimum of education. The other grades, while open and free, were closed to parents who required their children's labor or could not afford to maintain a child at school away from home. Condorcet hoped that a scholarship program would erase the burdens for at least some of the poor. The greatest number of future citizens would leave the system after the first four years. For them, adult education, on Sundays, with lectures and reading courses, would continue moral and civic education. Farmers would be taught scientific agriculture, parents the care and training of children, and so on.[27]

The report, a great summation of enlightened pedagogical ideals, was presented to the Legislative Assembly in April of 1792. Instructively, it was never adopted. Fifteen months later, in July 1793, a new Committee of Public Instruction reported. A plan for a state-monopolistic elementary system, not at all like Condorcet's, was accepted in December. Attendance was free and compulsory for boys and girls; children had to attend for three years. The state paid the salaries of the teachers, but at a rate in proportion with the number of students taught. Members of religious orders could also teach, but with other teachers, they had to have a certificate of civics. The pupils were to be instructed in the ideas of the Declaration of the Rights of Man and the Citizens.

Even those more limited ends of publicly supported schooling were not attained. Lack of funds and time constituted one set of limitations, along with more pressing concerns for the government. The lack of acceptance of this form of schooling by a large proportion of the population further reduced its efficacy. Never in the decade of the 1790s was schooling at any level made compulsory.

By 1795, in its final moments, the convention passed a new public education act. More conservative views came to the fore. Pupils now had to pay for their own schooling, although up to one-fourth might be exempted on grounds of poverty. Central administrative authority was reduced.

The act of October 1795 was far more successful in its initiatives at the non-elementary levels than below. A significant secondary school system was created. Special schools for medicine, veterinary medicine, music, fine arts, natural history, and instruction of the deaf and blind also were established. Basic and continuing aspects of a national system were built in a normal school, a polytechnic, school of mines, military school, school of highways and bridges, a series of museums, the Bibliothèque Nationale, and national and departmental archives. Virtually all of these grew from roots in the Ancien Regime, now renovated and expanded to a larger population. Advancement of the literacy and morality of the masses was another issue, one that was not furthered despite the powerful legacy of the philosophes and their many schemes.[28]

## 2. Patterns of Literacy; Paths to Literacy

Throughout the century, traditional school arrangements remained generally in place in most of Europe. Until the end of the century, the few enlightened reforms that were made could not have greatly influenced popular levels of schooling or literacy.[29] Literacy levels, however, insofar as we can reconstruct them, were rising during the course of the eighteenth century in France, England, and North America, and probably also in Scandinavia and the German states, which began the century with high levels. The extent of change was not regular or constant, and progress was uneven and sporadic.

Popular perceptions and behavior are among the most crucial elements for understanding the patterns of literacy and schooling. Mary Jo Maynes, author of an important comparative history of education in Germany and France, reminds us not only of the contributions of local or communal factors, but also of the roles of families:

> For apathy toward schooling was a rational stance for most early modern families. Agricultural families everywhere relied heavily upon seasonal child labor. There was little free school available, so sending a child to school meant strain upon often marginal family budgets. Economic payoff from schooling was minimal for most peasant families, although elementary education was undoubtedly becoming more relevant with growing commercialization of the rural economy.[30]

That reminds us of the contrast at the heart of educational developments. Thinkers and legislators turned increasingly to large-scale institutional and bureaucratic notions about public schooling for virtually all the people, whereas many of the people themselves had not come to share such an evaluation of the place of formal schooling in their lives.

The world remained largely traditional for most residents. The opprobrium of the phrase *Ancien Regime* too easily masks the continuities of ongoing life and its close connectedness with the past. Such is the case for most persons who inhabited rural areas, despite the social, economic, and demographic changes that were beginning to transform their world. For city folk, too, life had not yet been transformed irrevocably. The ways in which people responded to the forces of change—commercialization of agriculture, protoindustrialization, migration, urbanization, and the like—reveal the manner in which traditional customs and actions informed human responses to novel developments.[31]

With regard to education, patterns were not so different. "Education in the old, traditional world, the 'world we have lost,' did not take place in the school." Example, imitation, and action were central; formal schooling was decidedly secondary. The Bible was the major textbook.[32]

Whether literate, largely for religious purposes, or not, the world of the eighteenth century did not demand a high level of literacy from most persons. Few occupations or lifestyles required reading and writing. Oral culture and communication supplied most, if not all, needs of the majority of the population. Life for literates was little different from that of illiterates. The great increase in books and printed materials did not affect all persons uniformly, nor were nonreaders excluded from their content. Books and printed matter were beginning to influence more lives and shape the popular culture to a greater extent than previously. Tradition, nonetheless, remained strong.[33]

## A. Germany

The German lands had a strong literate tradition from the Reformation era. Compulsory educational legislation emerged in the eighteenth century. It was enacted first in Prussia, in 1717, in Saxony in 1772, and in Bavaria just after the turn of the century, in 1802. Yet nowhere was it enforced regularly. The new laws had but a slight impact on educational behavior.

In Prussia, the towns remained much the same as they had. Different patterns of education divided the burgher classes. Sons of craftsmen were trained at home and by apprenticeship. Since the Reformation, every town and parish was to have a school, and in theory, attendance was compulsory. Church ministers were to be inspectors.

The decrees were not, and really could not be, enforced. Many children were put to work, in towns and in the countryside. School buildings were in ill repair; there often were no separate classes or grading of the pupils by level of achievement. Attendance in both town and village schools was irregular. Teachers were a special problem; most were incompetent, and many were so poorly paid that they had to hold other jobs. The limited curriculum included reading, writing, some arithmetic, and religion. The Bible and the catechism were the primary reading matter. Licensed private schools were common in the towns, but they were no better than the public schools; they generally lacked proper schoolbooks and trained teachers.

The reform of enlightened intentions and state expansion was deeply concerned about this situation. Nevertheless, "such of its energies as were not absorbed in theoretical discussion only influenced the better placed middle class." Those who could afford it either taught their youngsters themselves or secured private tutors. Preparation of the future middle class was assisted by the town grammar or Latin schools, which provided a classical education and sound religious training along traditional lines. Some pupils went on to the universities; most, sons of officials, shopkeepers, and successful craftsmen, did not. More practical education, in the *Realschules*, was only beginning by mid-century. The lower class benefited little from traditional forms or the slowly developing innovations. "Education, it will be seen, would not be likely to modify seriously the general view of life current in the class from which the pupil came. It was intended of course to conserve it."

Actions such as Prussia's were one aspect of the enlightened reform of benevolent despots. Frederick the Great, for example, did not always consider education an integral aspect of state policy, although he maintained a lively interest in it. He found ridiculous the upper-class notion that popular education would make absolute government more difficult. Influenced by the philosophes, he considered education to be practical. Its aim should be to fit people better for their work, not to move them beyond their stations. For peasants, that was "a little reading and writing," and the moral commandments of Christian religion, which Frederick summarized as " 'Do not do anything to others that you do not want to have done to yourself.' "[35]

Despite Enlightenment rhetoric and legislation, relatively little was accomplished, especially in elementary (or literacy) education, during Frederick's lifetime. In 1763 he issued legislation calling for compulsory school attendance, no fees for the poor, specific qualifications for teachers, graded classes, and uniform schoolbooks, but it proved ineffective, and he subsequently lost interest in education. Well aware of the contradiction between his theory of the natural equality of men and the actual situation of the peasants, Frederick did nothing to change or alleviate it.[36] Theory and practice were not integrated during the time of the Enlightenment.

Major educational development in Prussia did not follow the adoption of enlightened sentiments. It seems that more schools were established in villages and towns, providing the basis for an increasing level of popular literacy. Evangelicalism was one force. But compared with the hopes and rhetoric, no educational revolution occurred.

The most thoroughgoing changes were superstructural, rather than basic. Schools were drawn into the scope of the state; methods of supervision were established; some support for teacher training institutions was provided; ideas evolved. But the quantity and quality of instruction changed much less. Frederick and his peers "saw no need for rooting the life of the state deeply in a common civilization. Education was to provide the individual with a set of moral rules and equip him with the practical knowledge necessary in his occupation."[37]

The upper-class and aristocratic conservatives campaigned against virtually all of the "modern" institutional and bureaucratic developments. Popular literature and newspapers and other elements seen by some as related to human progress were held as principal sources of recent or expected social and political troubles. Such people opposed the expansion of popular education:

> Our forefathers never had occasion to quarrel with their illiterate serfs: an illiteracy which did not prevent fields from being cultivated at least as well as they are today, and manners being unquestionably purer. Today many peasants cannot only read and write, but they also begin to master arithmetic; some even start to read books. Does this make them better men? do their lives become less dissolute? have they become more obedient subjects, or better cultivators of the soil? On the contrary: is it not true that manners have visibly declined? and the lords experience far more difficulty in maintaining authority over their serfs than they did when the latter were still

illiterate? . . . the most uncouth and ignorant peasant will invariably make the best
soldier. He can be treated as if he were a machine, and when he is so treated one
can rely on him absolutely.

The conservatives, perhaps, had less to fear than such opinions suggest. Nevertheless, they were aware that the spread of popular education and literacy was not
to be stopped by complaints and worries, regardless of how loudly they deplored
it. Their task was to propagate the conservative viewpoint to instill moral safeguards
to counter the potential impact of liberal reforms. They wrote and disseminated a
number of popular statements of conservative religious and political principles from
the 1780s onward. The target audience of lower-class readers was urged to abide
by traditional Christian virtues and told that it was to their temporal and spiritual
advantage to do so.[38]

The dominant impression gained from a review of the Prussian schools is of the
contrast between rhetoric and goals of reform *and* the facts of schooling. Frederick
William I initiated the process of Prussian school reform in 1713. At that time,
schools were under the aegis of the church. He began gradually to place them under
the state. His first enactment stressed that piety and religion ranked among the
highest purposes of the school; the second affirmed the need for inspection. In 1717,
the king ordered attendance to be compulsory: parents must send their children to
school regularly between the ages of five and twelve (or until they were considered
sufficiently prepared in religion, reading, writing, and arithmetic). This order was
not enforced because of parental poverty and landlords' opposition.

As a result of monarchial interest, a number of new schools were established and
much legal and rhetorical support was provided. Still, the reality of the schools
contrasted strikingly with the spirit of endorsement and these enactments. The wars
that ravaged much of the Continent during the 1740s and 1750s also may well have
destroyed some educational advancement.

A new bout of legislation commenced with the laws of 1763. The compulsory-
attendance provisions of earlier legislation were reasserted, and the country schools
were placed fully under the state, with the clergy supervising and inspecting. All
instruction, hours, curricula, schedules, and texts were regulated by law.

The legislation "was a model for its age," but it was irregularly enforced.
Communities were faced with heavy financial burdens, and the state could give no
aid. The lack of teachers, low salaries, and the opposition of the nobility also
hindered enforcement. Regulations that followed proved no more effective, whether
they provided for evangelical Protestant or Catholic territories. "The prejudice of
the people against the methods used and the textbooks adopted, the poverty of the
parents, poor salaries, the opposition of the lower classes to all education, and illy
prepared teachers were the causes of the small success which [these regulations]
attained."[39] This situation continued until the end of the century.

Circumstances elsewhere in German regions were little different. The eighteenth
century saw similar reforms attempted under enlightened absolutism and statesmen
in Austria and the state of Baden, for example.

In Austria, Maria Theresa and Joseph II saw education as an agency for producing
useful and obedient subjects, and they considered it a concern of the state. The
*Allegemeine Schulordnung* of 1774 centralized the existing educational facilities

**Figure 6.1.** Development of the Prussian *Volksschule*

| | MORNING | | | | AFTERNOON | |
| --- | --- | --- | --- | --- | --- | --- |
| | 8:00–8:30 | 8:30–9:00 | 9:00–10:00 | 10:00–11:00 | 1:00–2:00 | 2:00–3:00 |
| Teacher of the Lowest Class | Prayer. Singing. Roll Call. Reading aloud of the catechism assigned for learning | Learning the letters by use of charts | Spelling and Reading | Arithmetic | Prayer. Roll Call. Learning of the letters. Spelling and Reading | Writing |
| Teacher of the Middle Class | As above | Reading of French Words | German Reading | Arithmetic | Prayer. Roll Call. Orthography and Reading | Writing. Twice a week, $\frac{1}{4}$ hour dictation and $\frac{3}{4}$ hour correction. Teacher sets the copy |
| Teacher of the Highest Class | Prayer. Roll Call. Rules of German Language from Michaelmas to Easter. Reads aloud short stories or fables from a good book. Pupils tell what they have been told, in order to learn to express themselves correctly. They write at home what they have heard at school, and bring it to school next day. Teacher corrects the errors. From Easter to Michaelmas he drills them in essay and letter writing. | | Beginning Latin for boys going to higher schools | Music | Prayer. Roll Call. History. Use of Dictionary | French and also knowledge of things (*Realien*) which add to the happiness of human society. |

Catechism two times a week.

Source: Thomas Alexander, *The Prussian Elementary Schools* (New York: Macmillan, 1918), p. 15

into a national system. Elementary schools were to be supported by local funds, or subsidized by the state, if necessary.[40] Schooling was to be a pleasant experience for the pupils; they were to be instructed by competent, trained teachers, and Jews and Protestants were to be included. However, the regulations proved unenforceable, and the Austrian educational scene remained relatively unchanged.

M. J. Maynes's superbly detailed local studies provide an in-depth look at educational development in the region of Baden. As elsewhere, Baden's elite were attuned to the rhythms of Enlightenment pedagogical programs.[41] Public elementary schools were formally an arm of the state but were administered in practice by the church. The curriculum centered on memorization of the Lutheran catechism and learning the multiplication table. Reading, writing, and arithmetic were the main subjects. Reform efforts stressed an increased secularization while emphasizing the necessity of moral as well as practical training.

In theory, attendance was compulsory for all children under the age of fourteen. Enrollments ranged from 70 to 90 percent of school-age children, a high rate for the period. However, despite the heavily religious content of schooling, the high enrollment rate was not a result of Protestant religiosity; in fact, enrollment was quite high in the Catholic communities in Baden. The reasons lay more in regional factors.

A major factor contributing to the high attendance rate in Baden was the communal pattern of school finance and support, which enabled virtually every community to have some kind of elementary facility. In communal ownership of property and maintenance of communal resources lay the power to provide income for teachers in even the smallest communities. A relatively small portion of teachers' incomes came from cash, salaries, and fees; most remuneration was provided in land or in kind—wheat, logs, bread, meat, wine, tools, etc. Schooling was therefore much more affordable for families in Baden.

Ironically, this kind of "archaic" local base was precisely what enlightened schoolmen sought to change, and in time succeeded in abolishing with their expanding centralization and state maintenance of the educational system. Teachers, however, found the Badenese structure of rewards to their liking, and they were not sympathetic to reformers who sought to centralize and "professionalize" their work by putting it on a regular salary basis.[42]

It is remarkable how little the talk and legislation of the eighteenth century affected these traditional arrangements. Poverty, agricultural dispersion in settlement, and overcrowding were obstacles for the reformers in Baden as elsewhere. The larger problem of teachers and teaching was beginning to be tackled by the end of the century through state licensing and normal schools.[43]

Classes tended to be immense (in Mannheim in 1755, for example, there were two teachers for over 400 Catholic elementary school children), making teaching and learning difficult; even some rural areas reported overcrowding. Reorganization and grading by age levels slowly reduced the extent of this problem.

Literacy levels apparently were high in Baden—80 to 90 percent for men, perhaps 40 to 45 percent for women. Literacy skills had penetrated far down the social structure by the end of the eighteenth century. The informal opportunities available for learning to read and practicing one's skills contributed to the high rates of literacy. On winter evenings and Sundays, family members took turns reading the

Bible aloud. Children learned to read outside the schoolroom—from families, friends, and neighbors.

As earlier, the decision to educate a child was made in the context of the family economy. Children were key contributors to family subsistence, and to many families, schooling represented a luxury that could not be afforded. However, families also calculated the perceived benefits from sending their children to school—for example, the acquisition of job skills and religious values, and the school's child-care functions. Legal compulsion also had its impact.

Work was a regular, expected aspect of children's lives in this period. Rural children tended flocks, cultivated crops, and worked in the fields, and girls worked in and around the house. That lead to "truancy" and highly seasonal levels of attendance, and to seasons for schooling and seasons for working. School central-izers and bureaucrats were slower to recognize and adjust to these patterns than were local teachers, who did not even attempt to hold classes during summer or harvest time. Work needs held higher familial priorities than compulsory-attendance laws.

City and town children, as well, often attended school irregularly. Although seasonal demands on them were lower, odd jobs, apprenticeships, and housework competed with school. In both urban and rural areas, a father's sickness or death could remove a child from school at once. Wars, harvest failures, changing eco-nomic conditions, and subsistence crises all affected educational opportunities. The structure of school finance in Baden reduced the impact of some of these conditions. Schooling had its purposes for families of the popular classes, but their actions also reveal that they did not regard it as preparation for work or life for most children.

Interest was great in enlightened school reform in the German lands, but there was relatively little change in the actual conditions of schooling. On the other hand, many states had high levels of school attendance and high levels of literacy. That should be seen as growth, but not as a "take-off." These levels are best understood in the historical context of continuities of pressures toward schooling and literacy as part of the post-Reformation tradition, a tradition to which eighteenth-century activities added, with the shift from a stricter religious morality to a more civic morality—a shift that should be seen as relative, not absolute.[44]

Firmer confirmation comes from a statistical examination of signature literacy in the largely *Catholic* Mittelrhein region in the late eighteenth century. Of persons marrying in the region during the second half of the century, over 80 percent of men and perhaps nearly two-thirds of women were able to sign their names on the registers. Literacy ability was stratified by social class and rank. Two–thirds of laborers signed, compared to 92 percent of artisans and shopkeepers, 92 percent of civil servants, and 100 percent of patricians, among men. Even for the lower-ranking, these are impressively high rates of literacy.

Although literacy rates were somewhat higher in cities than in the countryside, rural-born immigrants were slightly more often able to sign their marriage registers. The rural-born immigrant to Koblenz was more often literate, among men as well as women, than the urban-born migrant. Immigration, as elsewhere, was selective of literates. Native-born urban women had, compared to males, a greater chance of gaining literacy than had their migrating sisters.[45]

One result of the relatively high levels of popular literacy in eighteenth-century German areas is the apparent participation of some common people in the growth of literature that took place in the second half of the century. Albert Ward notes the extensive sales of calendars and similar publications written for peasants and artisans. Even poverty-stricken village taverns subscribed to newspapers for their customers. There were also early forms of best sellers.[46]

Not all persons could afford to purchase such materials, nor could they read them. They did learn their contents from informal agencies and oral means. Literacy's influence was still shaped by social intercourse. More people were, in one way or another, participating in the publication increase of the period. Traveling booksellers helped their access to the new literature and to popular older forms, such as chap-books—more popular forms of literature to the masses than the newer, middle-class novels. In either form, this use of literacy was hardly enlightened.[47]

## B. Italy

The Counter Reformation in Italy represented the triumph of ecclesiastical monopoly over education. With the sixteenth-century decline of the communes and their humanistic tradition of civic schooling came a decline in the substantial levels of popular schooling and literacy that had been achieved in some of the city-states. Counter Reformation forms of schooling tended to be narrower in their popular base than the municipal school foundations. Literacy, by all counts, declined over the sixteenth and seventeenth centuries.

From the civic model, culture shifted to that of the church and the aristocracy. Revealingly, by the beginning of the eighteenth century, "public education" usually meant that offered by the Jesuit colleges, in contrast to "private education," which was acquired from tutors in aristocratic families. The middle levels of society were less able to shape schooling in Italy than elsewhere in the West. Nevertheless, the eighteenth century was a period in which the educational ideals of the Enlightenment aroused interest and stimulated reformers.

The state of Piedmont, ruled by the house of Savoy, was the first to be concerned with educational reform. From the end of the seventeenth century, the state was undergoing a process of change, which was in many respects an economic recovery from the long crisis of disorganization and downturn. Recovery stimulated the activities of business, artisanal, and professional groups, who turned to the state in opposition to the roles of church and aristocracy.

An important development was Piedmont's transformation from a duchy to a monarchy, which recognized the need to build a modern system, enliven the bureaucracy, and recruit a new kind of official. Educational policy was only one part of a more general plan for economic and social reorganization of the state. In opposition to the aristocracy, the king organized a class of lawyers and bureaucrats, loyal to his state and responsible for reforms. Predictably, his actions led to conflict with the church. Policies were linked to educational activities at primarily the secondary and university levels. Reform was from the top down; only slowly did concern with more broadly based, elementary schooling develop.

In the 1730s, legislative attention turned to creating a network of secondary schools to replace the traditional, mostly Jesuit, religious schools. The middle class was the target, with a new model for developing a uniform culture distinct from the religious. Classical schooling was the goal. Some progress was made in terms of literacy levels, but success was limited. However, the Piedmont efforts were the first in Italy to link education to policies of more general reforms.

In other Italian states, reforms were generally even more restricted, aimed overwhelmingly at the top of the educational and social heirarchy. The creation of a civil class of professionals and officials, with their own, more secular culture, remained the goal. The university was the principal target. None of these efforts went as far as the Piedmont reforms; in no case does literacy seem to have been of much interest.

Educational reforms took on new significance in the 1760s, when measures were introduced in almost all of the Italian states. Public opinion was shifting toward an awareness of the importance of study, and of the inadequacies of the church and family as educators. Education was increasingly viewed as the right, indeed the duty, of the state. Enlightenment ideals were becoming more popular throughout Europe. Interest in education grew quickly, but in Italy, most attention was directed to reforming the universities and training professionals and officials.

In the 1760s, the expulsion of the Jesuits added other problems to the educational agenda. The need to replace Jesuit control and institutions was general in Catholic Europe. This problem involved primarily secondary education. Interest in popular schooling was only beginning; vocational and technical schooling aroused more interest in the context of economic growth and urban development. Technical education tended to be aimed at the lower and middle bourgeoisie. That, in turn, stimulated social differentiation and class formation. New elementary schools began to contribute to this process, especially in Lombardy. Economic development was a primary stimulus to this sort of schooling.

Attitudes toward the masses were little different from those elsewhere on the Continent, but the pendulum was swinging toward an awareness of the necessity for and potential benefits of their schooling. Many economic arguments and even more publications were directed toward the cause of educating the peasantry. Schemes for agrarian academies and vocational schooling proliferated. Yet little was accomplished; aristocratic resistance, paternalism, and the lack of political prestige all meant that mass education was given little attention and that the university and schools for bureaucratic and army officers were far more important concerns. Attempts to delegate reform to the parish priests failed; by the end of the 1770s, the general failure of popular reform was clear.

In Lombardy, a new initiative finally was directed to educating the masses, in the interest of the civil and economic condition of the state. The duty of the government was recognized, and led in Milan to the founding of the first elementary schools. Public opinion was divided; many feared agitation from an educated peasantry and lower class. "These fears fed contradictory attitudes, so that many reformers would support the establishment of strictly vocational schools for the masses where social differences would be maintained and where they would learn to accept their own fate." With universities and secondary schools fairly well reformed by the end of the seventies, problems of elementary education were at least confronted. The reform of the masses, through the school, was a new target.

The first concrete development took place in the cities. In Milan, Florence, and Naples, schooling expanded as an extension of the principles of enlightened despotism. The need to support economic growth, and especially to discipline and control the masses, to guarantee social peace and integration into society and state, led to public initiatives in the secular control of elementary education. Religious orders were to continue as teachers, but under the careful eye of the political state. The cooperation of the clergy was required, as the effort failed miserably in Naples under the conservative resistance of the church hierarchy. Where religious groups were more favorable, in Milan and Tuscany, education was better able to expand and promote civic as well as religious virtues. State intervention was hardly a simple step forward. Among other complications, there was virtually no preexisting foundation on which to build a school system.

Thus, in Torino (excluding the capital) in 1710, 94 percent of brides and 81 percent of grooms were illiterate (of the 50 percent marrying who signed dowries, an upward bias). With expansion of primary schooling, the comparison with 1790 shows illiteracy at 70 percent and 35 percent respectively. Real progress was made, but literacy remained restricted and highly stratified. Torino is probably not a representative case.

Without public political action, elementary schooling stagnated, and was typically only a preparatory phase for advanced training. The vernacular usually was neglected. Charity schooling under the church was virtually the only other primary agency; its program was not dedicated toward intellectual training. Very few town schools existed; the peasants and the poor saw little need for schooling their young. "Indifferent to the incentive of social advancement through education—a possibility too remote to consider seriously—parents tended to use their children as a workforce that became indispensable in the periods of intense farm activity."

Even in this comparative "hot bed" of educational development and interest in Lombardy, more than twenty years were required to establish a network of elementary schools. Financial costs, lack of teachers, and the role of the church all slowed progress. Nor were the peasants and the poor always able to participate. In other states, progress was even slower. The available data on enrollments and literacy rates are far too limited to evaluate the reforms, but progress was made in at least a few areas. On the whole however, the limits are more impressive. The movement coincided with the onset of the French revolution, and ended in the reactionary change in the monarchy.[48]

### A Note on Spain

Data on Spanish literacy from the Tribunals of the Inquisition in Toledo, which range into the eighteenth and early nineteenth centuries, show literacy to have increased from slightly less than 50 percent (in an upwardly biased population) in the sixteenth century, to just above that point in the first half of the seventeenth, to 55 percent in the second half; but it made major strides in the eighteenth century. During the first half of that century, 66 percent of those for whom information is available were able to sign, and in the period from 1751 to 1817, about 76 percent of this population signed: a perhaps distorted, but nonetheless high, rate.

As expected in such a traditional, orthodox Catholic land, men dominated among those increasingly exhibiting basic literacy. From the sixteenth century to the end of the time series, male literacy moved from 46 percent to 92 percent among this relatively elite group, whereas women's literacy gained from 4 to 14 percent. Both city and country dwellers shared in the overall rise in levels of literacy, with urban areas starting and finishing higher. City women outgained their country sisters.[49] Given the paucity of information on the popular and most populous classes and our large-scale ignorance about Spanish educational trends, conclusions are now impossible to contemplate.

## C. France

France was undeniably the center of the Enlightenment. Proposals and discussions about schooling, reform, and the relationship of education to social, economic, and political development were commonplace there during the second half of the eighteenth century. The quantity and quality of educational thought in France were the highest in the West. Eighteenth-century France is also the best-studied area with respect to literacy and schooling. The many available studies allow us to trace changes and continuities in literacy levels and differentials over the course of the eighteenth century.

Literacy levels in France nearly doubled between 1686 and 1790, but this growth took place in a context that was predominantly traditional; that is, the extent of opportunities expanded within structures (social, economic, developmental, sexual, and regional) that changed much less.[50] Continuities shaped the changes that occurred during the last century of the Ancien Regime. The social structure of literacy, consequently, was relatively stable; the potentials for great change emanating from a large-scale increase in the numbers of persons able to read or write were limited. The expansion of the marketplace was one dynamic force; the availability of local "petites écoles," clerically and municipally provided, was another.

The century preceding the French Revolution saw no special changes in the "system" of education in France; reformers' proposals typically came to little. Educational facilities, especially at the elementary levels, overwhelmingly were localized institutions. They existed because of local provision, support, and interest. Their history during a period in which more and more French men and women were acquiring letters cannot be understood in terms of enlightened philosophers' statements, pleas, or hopes, or in terms of explicit social or economic policies. Changes in local and family economies and in school opportunities underlay trends in literacy rates more than any other factors.

Existing interpretations of eighteenth-century French literacy tend to divide into opposing views. On one hand, those who concentrate on the evidence of literacy's growth, especially in the northern areas and the southwest, where the movement exceeded the average and often included women and the upper strata of the peasantry and workers, tend to stress the advancement of such developments. The boundaries of the past and constricting traditions (read: ignorance) were being broken. Modernity and the forces of progressive social change were moving apace. Cultural revolutions have been proposed.[51]

On the other hand, some interpreters see much less change and development. They emphasize the geographic stratification within which literacy's changes occurred and the persisting restrictiveness by class, gender, and region. Looking upon the comparatively lesser development in the sphere of educational institutions, the dominance of tradition (read again: ignorance) and immobility is seen as the central point.[52]

Before the intricacies of eighteenth-century French literacy and its meanings are explored, the situation should be outlined. On the national level, according to the seminal survey of the late-nineteenth-century educational historian Louis Maggiolo, popular literacy increased from 21 percent to 37 percent of brides and grooms marrying and documented in the parish registers in the two periods 1686–1690 and 1786–1790—for men, from 29 percent to 47 percent; for women, from 14 to 27 percent.

These data are averages, and they camouflage an initial regional disparity that persisted throughout the period. That is the geographical boundary that roughly distinguished a northern and a southern France: along a line that might be drawn from the bay at Mont-Saint-Michel (St. Malo) to the lake at Geneva. This line, although not a totally accurate demarcation, separated a "literate" from an "illiterate" France, or, more properly, regions of higher-than-average literacy rates from those of lower-than-average rates.

Thus, in the data drawn from 1686–1690, north of the line, almost every province and department had a literacy rate of at least 20 percent, according to the Maggiolo survey.[53] (For exact figures and maps, see Furet and Ozouf, *Lire et écrire*.) South of the line, the provinces and departments generally fell below 20 percent. A century later, the line remained clearly present. North of it, all departments had rates in excess of 25 percent able to sign. All but one stood above 30 percent, and eighteen of the twenty-six departments exhibited literacy rates in excess of 50 percent. To the south, only three surpassed 40 percent. One hundred years did not, however, see a static persistence of the St. Malo-Geneva line.

The averages also disguise sexual imbalances. In 1686–1690, *men's* rates in almost all the northern departments stood above the 30 percent level. South of the line, to the contrary, men in only three departments passed that point. *Women's* rates ranged from a high of 20–29 percent in the south to 33 percent in the north. A hundred years later, in the north men in virtually all the departments passed the mean; in eleven, proportions signing surpassed 70 percent. That is a remarkable achievement. In the Midi, below the line, five passed 50 percent; the rest were well below. *Women's* signature levels generally ranked well (above 50 percent) above the line, but the Nord and six eastern departments had rates closer to those below than the others above. The pattern of relatively sharp differentiation along this line was beginning to break down; in time it would disappear.

In the south, female literacy rates in most departments were below 20 percent. Thus, change in effect came more rapidly for men than for women. Variation is increasingly found along the line that distinguished a France of fair levels of bridal literacy from a France of much lower achievement. The line tended to distinguish regions of greater socioeconomic development and nonisolated contact and communications. That is not exceptional. More interesting were the variations within those patterns. The latter complicate the making and documenting of linear relationships about the extent of literacy.

The patterns that lie beneath these national averages are more important than the actual numbers. The effects of socioeconomic patterns, gender, and geography were clearly at work. The existence of a fairly distinctive north-and-south pattern points to real cultural divergence, linguistically as well as socially. No simple or mono-causal explanation will suffice, however. School opportunities, institutional development, climate, advance of the market, commercialization of agriculture, protoindustrialization, linguistic factors, transportation and communication, religion, and social structure all underlay the patterns only now coming into focus.[54]

These literacy data suffer from a relatively static viewpoint.[55] The next step is to consider rates of change and their variations. A period-centered review represents a baseline and establishes the facts of the St. Malo-Geneva line between "two Frances" according to rates of literacy. That says nothing of the dynamics. What is interesting is the pace of change (or lack thereof) within regions and departments.

A number of departments south of the line began to "catch up" in rates of *male* literacy during the eighteenth century. Of the nineteen departments that doubled their proportions able to sign between the end of the seventeenth and the end of the eighteenth century, twelve—almost two-thirds—were below the line. For men, whose rates of literacy are typically more sensitive to forces of change than women's, the lines of literacy were moving in the eighteenth century.

During the eighteenth century, the *rate* of *women's* literacy advanced more quickly than that of men. That may be seen from the national totals, too, for women virtually doubled their score, from 14 to 27 percent, whereas men increased by 38 percent. That was not a universal phenomenon: in thirty-two departments, rates of growth for men exceeded those for women. The geography of relative gender-related change is a revealing one: in a general way, growth in female literacy is particularly clear in the departments that led in absolute and relative levels of male literacy. No simple or direct explanation for this pattern has been found, but more than a catch-up or coattails effect must have been at work.

Regional levels of literacy in one period are not necessarily a sure guide to levels in the next. Several important departments whose rank and percentage able to sign were both low in the late eighteenth century rose quickly. But overall, for the eighteenth century, the strongest growth places for men and women were located north of the St. Malo-Geneva line. By the end of this period, the line was beginning to blur, and a newer east-west cleavage was appearing. The low-literacy areas were, roughly, circumscribed in a triangle whose base was the Atlantic Coast, from Brittany to Landes, and whose apex was in the heart of the Massif Central.

A reconstruction of French marriage register signatures from 1740 through the end of the century by Jacques Houdaille and the I.N.E.D. in Paris parallels and refines Maggiolo's data. It reveals several striking patterns. First, from 1740 to 1799, it shows growth in male literacy from 40 to 49 percent: a 25 percent increase. That implies, by extrapolation outside the series, that the pace of change in the earlier period had been greater. The rate of change was irregular: 40 percent in 1740–49, 39 percent in 1750–59, 44 percent in 1760–69, 45 percent in 1770–79, 46 percent in 1780–89, and 49 percent in the final decade. Not surprisingly, the years prior to the revolution saw the most change. Second, women's literacy, expectedly, grew somewhat more: from 19 to 30 percent, and somewhat more

## TABLE 6.1
## Proportion of Signatures at First Marriage (Percentages)

| Date of Marriage | Regions Rural France | | | | | | | | | | Rural Population | | Urban Population | | All France weighted |
|---|---|---|---|---|---|---|---|---|---|---|---|---|---|---|---|
| | 1 | 2 | 3 | 4 | 5 | 6 | 7 | 8 | 9 | 10 | Non-weighted | Weighted | Non-weighted | Weighted | |
| **Men** | | | | | | | | | | | | | | | |
| 1740–1749 | 16 | 53 | 65 | 56 | 63 | 31 | 23 | 10 | 19 | 15 | 35 | 36 | 60 | 61 | 40 |
| 1750–1759 | 16 | 54 | 54 | 52 | 67 | 32 | 25 | 14 | 16 | 12 | 34 | 35 | 58 | 58 | 39 |
| 1760–1769 | 16 | 60 | 61 | 63 | 74 | 40 | 27 | 13 | 14 | 18 | 40 | 40 | 67 | 67 | 44 |
| 1770–1779 | 20 | 63 | 61 | 65 | 80 | 36 | 28 | 15 | 18 | 19 | 41 | 42 | 65 | 65 | 45 |
| 1780–1789 | 20 | 62 | 68 | 64 | 83 | 42 | 27 | 16 | 17 | 18 | 42 | 42 | 65 | 65 | 46 |
| 1790–1799 | 23 | 70 | 59 | 67 | 84 | 42 | 40 | 16 | 20 | 17 | 44 | 44 | 73 | 74 | 49 |
| 1800–1809 | 20 | 67 | 69 | 63 | 91 | 45 | 37 | 22 | 29 | 16 | 46 | 46 | 72 | 73 | 50 |
| 1810–1819 | 26 | 69 | 66 | 67 | 89 | 55 | 39 | 26 | 32 | 24 | 50 | 50 | 69 | 69 | 53 |
| 1820–1829 | 20 | 69 | 61 | 69 | 92 | 54 | 39 | 29 | 34 | 24 | 50 | 50 | 69 | 69 | 53 |
| **Women** | | | | | | | | | | | | | | | |
| 1740–1749 | 8 | 25 | 21 | 21 | 29 | 13 | 6 | 4 | 10 | 3 | 13 | 15 | 40 | 41 | 19 |
| 1750–1759 | 8 | 28 | 22 | 20 | 31 | 16 | 6 | 8 | 3 | 6 | 15 | 16 | 40 | 40 | 20 |
| 1760–1769 | 8 | 35 | 37 | 23 | 33 | 16 | 5 | 5 | 6 | 4 | 18 | 18 | 47 | 47 | 23 |
| 1770–1779 | 8 | 39 | 33 | 26 | 38 | 15 | 8 | 8 | 2 | 11 | 19 | 20 | 44 | 44 | 23 |
| 1780–1789 | 8 | 40 | 41 | 31 | 44 | 20 | 7 | 5 | 4 | 5 | 21 | 21 | 44 | 43 | 25 |
| 1790–1799 | 12 | 51 | 41 | 38 | 55 | 21 | 11 | 7 | 5 | 6 | 25 | 25 | 54 | 54 | 30 |
| 1800–1809 | 10 | 54 | 45 | 41 | 54 | 22 | 11 | 9 | 5 | 7 | 26 | 26 | 51 | 51 | 29 |
| 1810–1819 | 11 | 56 | 43 | 46 | 66 | 27 | 14 | 9 | 5 | 10 | 29 | 29 | 56 | 58 | 33 |
| 1820–1829 | 12 | 58 | 52 | 45 | 67 | 28 | 11 | 15 | 5 | 10 | 31 | 31 | 48 | 47 | 33 |

N.B. For regions, see Figure 6.2; for weighting, see original article.
Source: Jacques Houdaille, "Les signatures au mariage de 1740 à 1829," *Population* (1977). p. 68.

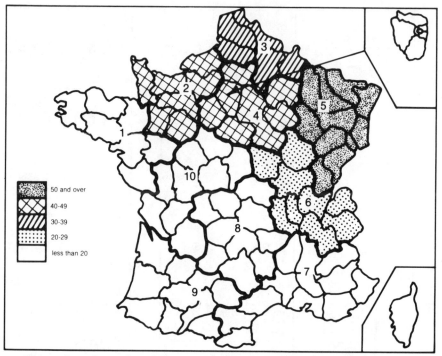

**Figure 6.2.** Proportion of Signatures on Marriage Registers (Men and Women), 1740–1789
*Source*: Houdaille, "Les signatures," p. 69.

evenly. The decadal rates from 1740–49 to 1790–99 were 19, 20, 23, 23, 25, and 30 percent, although the size of the increase during the final decade may be an artifact of earlier changes in literacy. These indications of literacy at time of marriage must be corrected for birth cohorts.

The pace of change outlined here camouflages tremendous variations. Two sources are especially important: regional and urban-rural. As table 6.1 shows, urban rates were always well in excess of rural; that is not surprising. Schools clustered with population concentration, and wealth and commercial development were usually conducive to literacy's growth. The deleterious impacts of industrialization on urban populations largely awaited the future. Houdaille's evidence also suggests that urban residence was a greater boost for women learning to read and write than for men. The absolute and the relative urban differentials are consistently greater for women as compared to men.

The second variation is regional. Captured nicely in the accompanying map, departmental patterns can be viewed with special clarity in this illustration. The northeast of France, from the Meuse to the Jura, stood first for both men and women. It was followed by the north central and the northwest, along the St. Malo-Geneva line, and paralleled the course of contemporary economic development, agricultural change, and, more or less, the presence of schools. The ranking of regions according to marital literacy barely changed during the century. The general impression is of some progress in proportions of the population able to read and write *within* a context of stability. Royal dictums of 1695, 1698, and 1774 ordering rural communities to tax themselves to pay for schools and schoolmasters were not honored equally.

Attitudes toward the value of schooling varied, as did the availability of resources to expend. Where facilities for schooling did exist, opportunities for boys and girls clearly differed. On the whole, Protestant and urban areas provided greater opportunities; higher rates of literacy tended to follow. In cities, not only did rates of literacy stand above those in the countryside, but female rates compared far more favorably to male. Thus, in rural France in mid-century, about 2.7 men could sign for every woman who could; in urban centers, the difference was only 1.5 to 1. The countryside did not catch up until the educational expansion and state action of the nineteenth century.

This sense of development can be refined if the data are reaggregated by generations or birth cohorts. The most significant finding relates to age at marriage. As table 6.2 and figure 6.3 show, women marrying at age 20–24 were more likely to be literate than those aged 25–29. Conversely, men aged 25–29 were almost always more likely to be literate than those aged 20–24. The pattern strongly suggests a relation between social factors conducive to learning literacy and those surrounding the time of marriage. Women who had greater advantages that resulted in their acquiring literacy were more likely to marry younger. For men, the relationship is reversed: advantaged men tended to marry somewhat later. Class and status influenced both timing of marriage and access to literacy during the second half of the eighteenth century. The relationships are especially significant for urban areas, where mediating circumstances of land tenure, inheritance customs, and the like had a lesser impact.

Generational analysis also permits a look at the impact of the French Revolution on rural literacy. It is likely that boys born around 1777, who were adolescents during the early nineties, under the Reign of Terror, were somewhat more likely to be illiterate than others. Opportunities for schooling were disrupted. Girls were less likely to be affected.[56] The impact of the Revolution, it seems, was not great, at least insofar as literacy levels and literacy transmission at the time were concerned.

All the evidence from Maggiolo to the present reinforces the view (albeit with some exceptions) of "une France Double." Usually this phrase refers to a geographic division, the Maggiolo or St. Malo-Geneva line, which all studies end in accepting to a greater or lesser extent. That is true, and important. Yet, it tends to be reified. Writers speak of two Frances, of two civilizations, written and oral. The land north of the line becomes a literate, advanced, schooled area; south of the line, an illiterate and oral France, retarded and ignorant. Rates of literacy do not lend themselves to national territorial anthropomorphism in this way. Understanding the meaning of literacy in the preindustrial, predominantly agrarian, early modern West does not support such a distorting aura. We know that a rate of literacy by itself does not endow a region or its people with one identifying or transcending characteristic. A few readers were always able to enlighten a far greater number; daily communications in such societies depended more on oral patterns regardless of the level of popular literacy.[57]

With this important qualification in mind, let us summarize the overarching con-

TABLE 6.2

**Signatures of Spouses by Generation for Persons Married at 20–24 Years
(Marriages, 1780–1829)**

| Generations | 20–24 Years | | | 25–29 Years | | |
|---|---|---|---|---|---|---|
| | Rural France | Urban France | France | Rural France | Urban France | France |
| Men | | | | | | |
| before 1760 | 55 ⎫ | | 57 | 48 ⎫ | | 54 |
| 1760–1764 | 50 ⎬ 58 | | 51 | 58 ⎬ 75 | | 58 |
| 1765–1769 | 53 ⎭ | | 53 | 46 ⎭ | | 51 |
| 1770–1774 | 49 | 83 | 53 | 52 | 73 | 55 |
| 1775–1779 | 43 | 70 | 49 | 46 | 75 | 50 |
| 1780–1784 | 50 | 59 | 53 | 46 | 70 | 49 |
| 1785–1789 | 50 | 60 | 51 | 53 | 63 | 55 |
| 1790–1794 | 51 | 78 | 51 | 53 | 65 | 55 |
| 1795–1799 | 50 | 70 | 54 | 52 | 75 | 55 |
| 1800–1804 | 46 | 52 | 49 | 54 | 55 | 54 |
| 1805–1809 | 49 | | 49 | | | 34 |
| Total | 49 | 68 | 51 | 50 | 70 | 53 |
| Women | | | | | | |
| before 1760 | 29 ⎫ | | 34 | 27 ⎫ | | 28 |
| 1760–1764 | 31 ⎬ 50 | | 34 | 29 ⎬ 46 | | 34 |
| 1765–1769 | 36 ⎭ | | 37 | 26 ⎭ | | 29 |
| 1770–1774 | 27 | 64 | 32 | 27 | 44 | 29 |
| 1775–1779 | 26 | 68 | 31 | 27 | 41 | 29 |
| 1780–1784 | 25 | 59 | 29 | 26 | 43 | 28 |
| 1785–1789 | 26 | 55 | 30 | 30 | 50 | 33 |
| 1790–1794 | 32 | 66 | 37 | 30 | 44 | 32 |
| 1795–1799 | 35 | 59 | 38 | 31 | 52 | 34 |
| 1800–1804 | 32 | 54 | 35 | 31 | 55 | 33 |
| 1805–1809 | 43 | 35 | | | | |
| Total | 30 | 57 | 33.5 | 28 | 46 | 31 |

Source: Houdaille, "Les signatures," p. 77.

tours of eighteenth-century French literacy that we have now begun to unravel. First is the St. Malo-Geneva line. Although it is easy to distort its meaning, it remains a significant sign of the uneven course of French social, economic, and educational development. With some variation, it remained consistent throughout the period. Second is the fate of female literacy. Lower than that of males throughout the century, it was somewhat more susceptible to change. Women's rates were strongest in the northern departments in which men's rates were high. Elsewhere, either rates paralleled each other's course or women occasionally gained relative to men. The north saw the greatest development. In terms of the pace of change, the first half

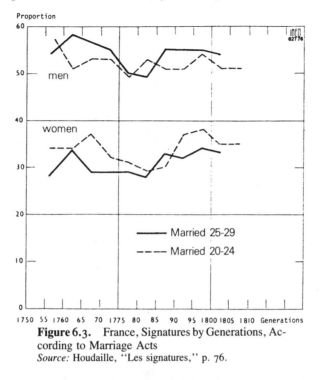

**Figure 6.3.**   France, Signatures by Generations, According to Marriage Acts
*Source:* Houdaille, "Les signatures," p. 76.

of the century seemed to have seen more positive movement than the second. This spurt followed, perhaps, a seventeenth-century increase that died by the first years of the eighteenth. After mid-century, growth ceased or at least diminished again, and perhaps rose after the 1770s. Provence, for example, moved in this way.[58]

Cities and towns were generally more highly literate than the countryside (see table 6.3). Places with very high rates of literacy by the end of the seventeenth century, however, such as Reims and Caen, seem to have increased less rapidly in the next century than other towns. Although rates were nowhere near universality, nor had distinctions of class, status, or wealth been erased, something of a threshold effect is likely. The will and the resources of the period, regardless of the growing sentiments in favor of mass education and public provision, were apparently unequal to the task of further increases. In other cases, such as Angers and Rennes, virtually no increase in literacy levels took place in a century. At the same time, their rural environs' rates were elevated. Here a special case of this pattern is illustrated, as is the diversity of patterns. All was not progress and light.

Other cities, such as Aix-en-Provence, were able to increase their proportions literate by important amounts at the very same moment. Although it does not hold for all regions, Michel Vovelle discovered a population size-literacy gradient for Provence. The largest cities, Marseille, Aix, and Avignon, achieved rates of male literacy close to 50 percent by the end of the Ancien Regime; the smaller cities and towns of approximately 5,000 inhabitants saw male literacy rise to about 30 to 40 percent (for women between 10 and 20 percent); and the places of less than 1,000 residents had lower rates, with men in the range of 15 to 30 percent. That was

## TABLE 6.3
## Percentages Literate (Able to Sign) by Place

| City | Source | Date | Percentage signatures: men | Percentage departmental study of Maggiolo | Percentage signatures: women | Percentage departmental study of Maggiolo |
|---|---|---|---|---|---|---|
| End of 17th Century | | | | | | |
| Reims (Marne) | marriage acts in parish registers | 1668–1699 | 65 | 61 | 42 | 25 |
| Honfleur (Seine-Mme) | " | 1690–1699 | 57 | 39 | 28 | 17 |
| Angers (Maine-et-Loire) | " | 1697–1698 | 53 | 18 | 43 | 11 |
| Rennes (Ille-et-Vilaine) | " | 1697–1698 | 46 | 21 | 32 | 14 |
| Rouen (Seine-Maritime) | " | 1697–1698 | 57 | 39 | 38 | 17 |
| Aix-en-Provence | " | end of 17th century | 34 | 17 | 13 | 4 |
| End of 18th Century | | | | | | |
| Reims (Marne) | " | 1750–1774 | 73 | 80 | 54 | 47 |
| Saint-Malo (I.-et-V.) | " | 1750–1790 | 74 | 28 | 67 | 15 |
| Caen (Calvados) | " | 1780–1789 | 86 | 82 | 73 | 63 |
| Honfleur (Seine-Mme) | " | 1780–1789 | 77 | 64 | 63 | 40 |
| Angers (Maine-et-Loire) | " | 1787–1788 | 52 | 18 | 42 | 12 |
| Aix-en-Provence (B.-du-R.) | " | end of 18th century | 46 | 30 | 27 | 10 |
| Lyon | marriage contracts | 1786–1789 | 64 | 40 | 39 | 21 |
| Rennes paroisse St.-Etienne | marriage acts | 1786–1790 | 52 | 28 | 39 | 15 |

Source: Roger Chartier, M-M Compère, and Dominique Juliá, *L'Education en France du XVIe au XVIIIe siècle* (Paris: Société d'Edition d'Enseignement Supérieur, 1976), p.93.

much closer to the rural rates. Economic development and social structure figure prominently in this hierarchy of places.

Urban residence also had an impact on the sexual balance in rates of literacy. Male-female differences tended to diminish in cities and towns in comparison to villages and rural environments. The percentage of women literate was higher in cities and towns at the end of both the seventeenth and the eighteenth centuries. Within cities, some homogenization of spousal literacy was progressing by the end of the Ancien Regime. Factors of class and wealth held firm.

One special factor could reverse this pattern of urban literacy development, beyond those of the regional and intracity differences. That is the impact of (early) industrialization. The demand for juvenile labor that early factories made, in contexts in which families often desperately required the fullest contribution that each member could bring, competed against the schooling of the young. The surge in population, from immigration and the birthrate, also strained local educational facilities. This type of development reduced opportunities for the education of youth of both sexes.[59]

From these patterns, it seems to follow that a literacy differential would distinguish the abilities of natives from those of immigrants. The advantage would be expected to fall in favor of the native-born town or city dweller. For example, in Bordeaux between 1771 and 1781, native men's literacy rates were fifteen percentage points higher than immigrants' (64 to 49 percent); native women's rates were twenty percentage points higher (43 to 23 percent). In Lyon, Maurice Garden's research reveals a more complex reality. He found that the greater the opportunities for work in a field, the lower the rate of immigrant literacy. Occupational attraction drew in workers in this manner. On the other hand, in a given profession or work area, the natives in the city always had higher rates of literacy than immigrants. As silk work, for example, opened up for women workers during the eighteenth century, rates of literacy among them fell: 43 percent in 1728–30, 41 percent in 1749–51, and 38 percent in 1786–88.[60]

Nevertheless, the native-born advantage was *not* a national urban constant. In Provence, according to Vovelle's studies, and in Caen, according to J. C. Perrot, immigrants had higher levels of literacy than native residents. In the former case, artisans coming to the city were mobile and "enlightened." Immigration apparently was selective of literate persons. In the Normandy example, culturally selective migration seems to have taken place, among men, at least. This pattern is virtually universal among long-distance migrants.[61]

Above all other factors in shaping the patterns of literacy was social rank, or class position, a recurring element of continuity. Bonnin reports (see table 6.4) that all the nobles and bourgeois in Dauphiné were literate during the seventeenth and early eighteenth centuries. For merchants, literacy was more common than not, but much less frequent than for the two higher ranks. In contrast, artisans' literacy was much lower, varying in accord with local economies and pace of development.[62]

As a rule, those at the top of the social order were able to read and write; their positions required it. Literacy as a sign of status and power was an important badge in the world of the Ancien Regime. Women's illiteracy remained virtually universal. For peasants, too, illiteracy was the norm; however, among "mènagers," those

## TÁBLE 6.4
## Literacy in Dauphiné, 18th century

| | | | NOBLES | BOURGEOIS | MERCHANTS | ARTISTS | PEASANTS |
|---|---|---|---|---|---|---|---|
| VILLARD-DE-LANS | approx. 1630 | M | 4 in 5 | 90% | 75% | 8% | 11% |
| | | F | — | 0 | 0 | 0 | 0 |
| | approx. 1670–1680 | M | — | 100% | 80% | 35% | 14% |
| | | F | — | — | 0 | 0 | 0 |
| | approx. 1730 | M | 100% | 100% | 70% | 20% | 11% |
| | | F | — | 100% | 65% | — | 0 |
| THEYS | approx. 1630 | M | 100% | 100% | 50% | 12% | 8% |
| | | F | 100% | 100% | — | 0 | 0 |
| | approx. 1670–1680 | M | 100% | 100% | 66% | 20% | 12% |
| | | F | 100% | 100% | — | 0 | 0 |
| | approx. 1730 | M | 100% | 100% | 53% | 30% | 11% |
| | | F | 100% | 100% | — | 0 | 0 |
| SAINT-JEAN D'HERANS | approx. 1630 | M | 95% | 95% | — | 70% | 38% |
| | | F | 50% | 85% | — | 0 | 10% |
| | approx. 1670–1680 | M | 100% | 100% | 85% | 65% | 44% |
| | | F | 100% | 50% | — | — | 0 |
| SAINT-MICHEL DE SAINT-GEOIRS | approx. 1630 | M | — | 75% | 20% | — | 0 |
| | | F | — | — | — | — | 0 |
| | approx. 1655 | M | — | 100% | 0 | 30% | 21% |
| | | F | — | 0 | — | 0 | 0 |
| | approx. 1690 | M | 100% | 100% | 45% | 67% | 7% |
| | | F | 100% | 100% | 0 | 0 | 0 |
| | approx. 1730 | M | 100% | 100% | 60% | 67% | 13% |
| | | F | 100% | 100% | — | 0 | 0 |
| SAINT-ISMIER | approx. 1620 | M | 80% | 90% | 50% | 7% | 1% |
| | | F | — | 0 | — | — | 0 |
| | approx. 1690 | M | 100% | 100% | 60% | 55% | 30% |
| | | F | — | 100% | 0% | — | 0 |

Source: Bernard Bonnin. "L'éducation dans les classes populaires rurales au XVIIIe Siècle," *Revue de Marseille*, Supplement to Vol. 88 (1972) p.65.

## TABLE 6.5
### Literacy in Lyon

|  |  | 1728–30 % | 1749–51 % | 1786–88 % | Entire 18th Century % |
|---|---|---|---|---|---|
| Day-Laborers | M | 20 | 21 | 37 | 27 |
|  | F | 11 | 7 | 19 | 13 |
| Harvest workers | M | 27 | 23 | 31 | 27 |
|  | F | 17 | 18 | 18 | 18 |
| Gardeners | M | 20 | 32 | 41 | 33 |
|  | F | 11 | 18 | 19 | 16 |
| Domestics | M | 51 | 56 | 64 | 58 |
|  | F | 26 | 37 | 35 | 33 |
| Silk Workers | M | 71 | 72 | 74 | 73 |
|  | F | 43 | 41 | 38 | 40 |
| Hat Workers | M | 32 | 43 | 50 | 44 |
|  | F | 15 | 20 | 25 | 21 |
| Bakers | M | 65 | 72 | 75 | 71 |
|  | F | 62 | 61 | 76 | 68 |
| Shoemakers | M | 64 | 68 | 70 | 68 |
|  | F | 31 | 28 | 29 | 29 |
| Joiners | M | 48 | 70 | 77 | 70 |
| Carpenters | M | 48 | 45 | 53 | 49 |
| Masons | M | 25 | 34 | 28 | 29 |

Source: Chartier et al., *L'éducation*, p. 102.

who possessed seven to fifteen hectares (a peasant "aristocracy"), both male and female rates were higher and rose during the century, even in the Midi.

In the north of France, the social relations of literacy were parallel, but the hierarchy was elevated. Regardless of the facts of change, a firm distinction remained between the well-to-do (master artisans and clerks) and manual workers, and between the men and the women of the two classes. Men, even among the low-ranking hand workers, gained steadily in proportions literate throughout the century, although they never rivaled the class above them. Their wives, however, did not have equivalent rates, as the well-to-do did, but stood much closer to illiteracy.

For an overview of the literacy of the urban class and occupational hierarchy, Garden's Lyonnaise data are superb. At the beginning of the century, the largest groups of male wage workers had a literacy rate at the threshold of 35 percent. From 1730 to the eve of the revolution, progress was generally mediocre, and the distance separating male from female rates declined. In these rates is also seen the trade and manual hierarchy of skill and rewards. In Marseille, the pattern was somewhat different. Male workers' literacy rates increased significantly, from 28 percent in 1710 to 85 percent on the eve of the revolution. Yet, women's literacy stagnated at the low level of 15 percent. Differential migration streams, responding to different occupational attractions, account for the revealing differences.

Among other occupations, the spread of functional necessity can be observed. Shopkeepers and artisans more than ever before began to find literacy useful for their work. The progress of the marketplace and capitalist exchange, with its emphasis on the keeping of accounts, underlay this epochal transition toward a more popular basis for literacy. Among servants, sexually based bifurcation points to another transition, the feminization of the domestic labor force, and the emergence of employers' worries about the errant employment of servants' reading abilities for prying into matters not considered a part of their sphere.

Occupations with the highest levels of literacy—from silk workers to bakers, shoemakers, and woodworkers—were also, on one hand, those with the greatest need for reading and writing and, on the other hand, those ranking well within the orders of the manual workers of the cities. Literacy also came to play a part in craft traditions. At the same time, members of this group of workers with a 75 percent rate of literacy seldom owned books. Literacy, required by one's work, was not necessarily put to use in other ways.

Within a trade or occupation, wealth was a force that related directly to one's ability to read or write. Class, occupation, and rewards ruled the social structure of literacy. As rates increased during this period, the entire social structure of literacy was elevated. The point at which such factors no longer strongly determined the distribution of reading and writing in society lay well in the future—in the next century, in fact.

Wealth also played a decisive influence in the distribution of female literacy. Among the daughters of Lyonnaise silk workers, for example, a clear relationship joined proportions able to sign their name with father's wealth: 36 percent of the daughters of those with less than 500 livres signed, compared to 87 percent of the daughters of those with more than 1,000 livres. The contribution of wealth to the literacy of sons was much less (73 percent and 95 percent respectively), pointing once more to the disparity in opportunities for and attitudes toward learning for the two sexes.

Religion is an often mentioned but much less studied issue in the determination of literacy and schooling. In the lexicon of (Protestant) historians of education, the relationship is simple and direct. Protestantism, it is said, was a force highly conducive to the development of schooling; Catholicism was not. While this formulation is substantially correct, it is a distorting, if not demeaning, equation. Even in sixteenth-century France, the time of the Reformation, a study of Huguenots in Montpellier showed that occupation contributed strongly to the distribution of literacy. Three-fourths of laborers between 1574–76 were illiterate; two-thirds of artisans were not. The impact of the Reformation's educational thrust was hardly universal. That was not sufficient to establish a Protestant-Catholic dichotomy as strong as the usual accounts might suggest. The peasant masses were barely touched.

A century later, in seventeenth-century Dauphiné, Bonnin found clearer indications of Protestant advancement. Comparing two communities, one reformed and the other Catholic, he discovered substantial impact for both artisans and peasants early in the century and a persisting impact of peasants at the end of the period. In the Protestant village, both classes ranked impressively in their rates literate. The Protestant dynamic was not effective at eliminating the impact of class and occupational factors, which persisted powerfully. By the end of the seventeenth century, however, it proved possible for the literacy of Catholic artisans to rise enough to compare favorably to that of Protestants.

In eighteenth-century Provence, Vovelle found Protestant communities well in advance of Catholic ones in their rates of literacy. Protestants' rates rose throughout the century, while in the rest of the region, stagnation ruled from 1720 to 1760. More intriguing, he found that Catholic communities in contact with Protestant villages had much higher rates of literacy than isolated and homogeneous settlements. Not only are more studies of religious differences required, but many interpretive problems may be seen. There is no doubt that more than religion influenced literacy levels. In an enormously important sense, literacy was, in a region Catholic or Protestant, religious. The primary purpose of disseminating literacy to the people was the cause of morality, a religious factor.[63]

With this overview in hand, we turn to examples of in-depth regional and local developments. In this way, we flesh out the skeletal overview and locate the dynamic interaction beneath these patterns. Mary Jo Maynes studied the region of the Vaucluse in southeastern France. The study area, the arrondissements of Avignon and Apt, stood on the geographic and cultural northern boundary of Provence. Geography played a major role in determining trade, migration, and communication patterns. Settlement was relatively urban, with overgrown villages or small towns the most typical (500–2,000 in population). Small cities (2,000–10,000) were also common. The form of urban life was an old one; new urbanization was not developing rapidly. Agriculture was the dominant employer, although industrialization was beginning in the form of a rural textile industry.

The region was mixed in religious adherence. Vaucluse's southeastern mountains had long sheltered Protestant dissidents, but Catholics were numerically preponderant. Maynes found "no simple relationship between religion and educational attainment." At best a "possible, if weak, relationship" is illuminated. Her data also suggest a greater divergence in favor of Protestants before 1780. Religious factors were perhaps more influential in determining literacy levels in the eighteenth century, before much state activity. The relationship, however, was not strong, and it diminished with time, disappearing by the mid-nineteenth century.

The variations were greater by gender than by religion. In 1760, the earliest point of observation, both Protestant and Catholic males had rates of literacy of 40 percent; women's levels were in the low 20 percents for Protestants and the mid-teens for Catholics. (See the graphs for comparisons over time and across communities of different sizes.) No significant relationship tied religious adherence to literacy or schooling. The weak relationships were in the expected direction, but other factors were more vital. Not an independent factor, religion varied in its role and power in differing political and socioeconomic circumstances.

As elsewhere, schools were principally local institutions in the eighteenth century.

**Figure 6.4.**

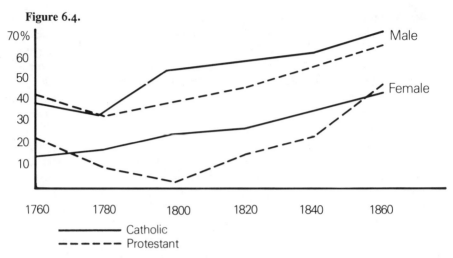

A. Literacy in Vaucluse in Protestant and Catholic *Communes*

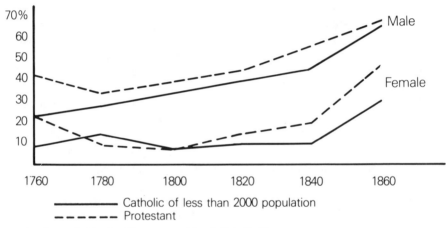

B. Literacy in Vaucluse Protestant and Small Catholic *Communes*
*Source:* M. J. Maynes, "Schooling the Masses: A Comparative Social History of Education in France and Germany," Ph.D. diss., University of Michigan, 1977, p. 39.

They were not rare institutions; literacy, correspondingly, need not have remained low or stagnant. In southeastern France, communities with 700 or more inhabitants were more likely to have a publicly supported school. In the Vaucluse, of fourteen places for which Ancien Regime village budgets survived, twelve included provision for school support. The exceptions were tiny places.

The schools usually were religious in origin and curriculum, but the secular community had much of the responsibility for their financial establishment and administration, for selecting and paying teachers, and for establishing curricula and tuition. Teachers were often lay persons, though in Catholic urban areas, religious orders were important sources of personnel. Annual visitations by local bishops were mandated but were often neglected. Especially in comparison with the post-reform mid-nineteenth century, communities had great autonomy in their educational decisions. Centralization progressed slowly; the traditional organization of clerical control paved its way. Administrative neglect was the French norm, as the state largely ignored educational institutions.

Such arrangements could not meet all needs. Some communities fared better than others. For example, largely dispersed agricultural populations obstructed access to school; some communities were too poor and too small to afford a teacher. Pooling resources from several nearby villages or hamlets was prevented by problems of locational choice for the school. Even in a larger commune, dispersed settlement raised problems of access and attendance. Conversely, growing, overpopulated towns sometimes overran the capacities of their elementary schools. These targets of reformers were common obstructions to schooling and a wider dissemination of literacy.

So were the teachers. Certification was largely a local decision. Eighteenth-century provincial instructors were often indistinguishable from the social classes they served. Like seasonal migrants, they moved from place to place according to opportunity and demand. Often they instructed part-time; only large cities and towns employed year-round teachers. Thus, they needed to supplement their salaries with other kinds of work. Yet, it is revealing that a shortage of teachers was not a special problem.

It is clear that little pedagogical expertise was expected. State licensing started late in France. In the Vaucluse, local communities retained much of their traditional responsibility for schools and teachers well into the next century. Books and buildings were frequently inappropriate or inadequate. Religious materials typically were the first reading materials, especially in the schools of the poor. Catechisms were common fare.

The real foundation of the local school was financial. The Ancien Regime arrangements were simple. The commune was the sole locus for funding, as municipal councils allocated fixed annual salaries from public revenues. Payment was wholly in cash wages. The tax base of the community and the wage level of the teacher were reciprocally related.

Some communities found it difficult to raise the cash salaries. Salaries were lower in the villages, and per capita assessments fell more heavily on smaller communities. Small communities were further disadvantaged because they had fewer school-age children, making it less likely that a teacher would be able to supplement the salary with fees. They were therefore unable to amass sufficient funds to attract a school teacher, and when they did, they had to pay more dearly. Larger towns, by comparison, could afford the services of free teaching orders. Religious schools for girls were also maintained in several towns, where pious endowments from the wealthy helped to meet costs.

In the Vaucluse, fees were of necessity higher in rural areas. Not only were rural families less likely to have cash reserves for schooling, but the higher the level of fees, the lower the level of attendance. "Ironically, it was the advanced monetization of schooling finance in Vaucluse, related no doubt to the level of commercialization of other types of village exchange, that made support of schools relatively more difficult.'' Lack of communal property led to dependence on regressive taxation. School reformers' and philosophes' complaints about the popular classes' neglect of education take on a different light in this context. Schooling remained voluntary, and only in the very largest towns did religious orders attempt to bring the school to the urban poor, in efforts to incorporate them into the moral and social order.

Most communities supported some kind of primary educational institution during the century. Circa 1800, about 4 percent of the population was enrolled. Girls attended much less often than boys, especially in smaller communities. Estimations based on projections of ''school-age populations'' also point to disparities, although school enrollment levels increased with community size. Perhaps 16 percent of those of school age were enrolled in places with under 500 inhabitants, 22 percent in those in the 500–2,000 range, 18 percent in the 2,000–10,000 range, and 29 percent in places over 10,000 population. Even if far fewer girls than boys were enrolled, at best only a minority of boys were enrolled for any stage of their childhood.

Most youngsters spent only a short time in the schools, and attendance was erratic and irregular. It was highly seasonal, especially in rural areas. Some communities did not even hold schools, or hire teachers, for the summer season. Truancy was also quite common. Classes were very large; schools were overcrowded even in some of the rural areas. Throughout the eighteenth century, most teachers taught classes of all ages, experiences, and skill levels in one room. In the cities, though, wealthier parents could send their sons to publicly supported elementary preparatory classes at local colleges. Reading instruction began with the alphabet and progressed to the pronunciation of syllables, and then to whole words. Emphasis was on memory, not comprehension. School conditions were decidedly *not* conducive to effective learning.

Literacy in the Vaucluse was not assumed for the average citizen. Even persons of sufficient status to be elected to rural town councils were illiterate. Limited evidence shows a regional pattern of wide gender difference, though rates for both sexes were low and may have dropped slightly in the last decades of the Ancien Regime. Male rates began to climb on the eve of the revolution; a slower female increase began around 1800. Literacy in the Vaucluse, as in most of the Midi, was low by contemporary French standards, although it was increasing from the end of the Ancien Regime. Literacy levels mirrored school attendance, although they seem a bit above what school enrollment data would predict. Not all literacy learning took place in school, as children could learn from family, neighbors, and friends. Group Bible reading was one source of informal learning. Of course, a short stay in the school was no guarantee of useful literacy. School attendance may have been more important for female literacy learning than for male. Girls apparently had fewer alternative means of acquiring education. Growing up was not yet institutionalized.

Compulsory school legislation was not enacted in France until the last quarter of the nineteenth century. The family and its needs long remained the major factors in determining schooling opportunities. For some families, schooling of any kind could not be afforded. The loss of the child's earning power or physical assistance was a question that had to be answered before the direct costs of fees, books,

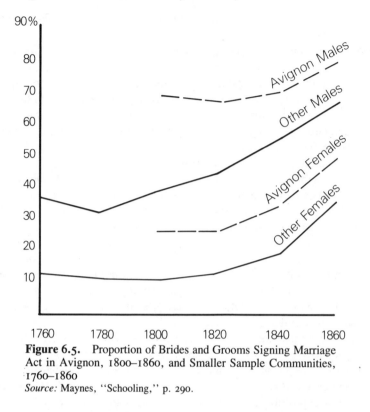

**Figure 6.5.**   Proportion of Brides and Grooms Signing Marriage
Act in Avignon, 1800–1860, and Smaller Sample Communities,
1760–1860
*Source:* Maynes, ''Schooling,'' p. 290.

supplies, and clothing could be considered. The direct and indirect rewards accruing
from literacy represented high costs to be balanced. Combining seasonal labor with
seasonal schooling was not an unreasonable communal and parental response to a
difficult situation.

The relatively high direct cost of maintaining a local school under the Vauclusan
political economy only exacerbated familial difficulties in putting, and keeping,
children in school. Widows and other single, female-headed households faced the
worst complications, but they were far from alone. One result was that children
too young or otherwise unable to work were likely to be sent to school. They were
a liability, since their care obstructed parents and older children in their work. That
could lead to overcrowded classrooms of children too young to sit quietly through
the long school day. Special infant schools developed slowly, though private dame
schools grew up in some cities.

For common folk, one should be hesitant about *assuming* that children were sent
to the schools in planning for social mobility and upward progression into middle-
class and white-collar careers. These were the assumptions of middle-class reformers
(and more recent sociologists and historians), not of the working class, the peasants,
and the poor. For the early modern period, access to a particular occupation had
little to do with the skills gained in schooling. It followed more from familial needs,
aspirations, and ability to invest in training. Schooling made sense only for those
seeking careers that required specific educational qualifications. ''This doesn't imply

that peasants had no use for schooling, but the vocational value they attributed to it must have been minimal.''

Among agricultural residents, the landed had a greater stake in schooling than the landless. Literacy levels began to rise among landholding peasants in southeastern France in the final quarter of the century, and increased more rapidly after the turn of the century. As studies of Provence suggest, schooling in literacy came to be seen as useful for sons; with change in the size and scale of the market and the commercialization of agriculture, they found reading, writing, and ciphering of some value in farm management.

At the same time, peasants in the neighboring Vaucluse were little interested in the niceties of grammar. Arithmetic was valued more highly than the complexities of an advanced literacy. Among the propertyless and the poorer agricultural workers, literacy remained low. Only certain sectors of the population, particularly those with interests to protect and manage, were by the end of the century learning to value its advantages (primarily through seasonal school attendance). Peasant appreciation of literacy was limited largely to male literacy. Sexual discrimination remained strong. Literacy rates remained low, and not only were fewer girls enrolled, but their schooling was also more restricted. Vauclusan schools for girls taught reading and writing but not grammar: '' 'studies which . . . serve no purpose but to make their children waste their time.' ''

For children of parents with property who would not themselves inherit, some sort of specialized vocational preparation was part of their adolescence—apprenticeship in a home or shop for those destined for artisanal or small commercial work, secondary schooling for those following a professional or administrative career. Familial position dictated, in either case, career and schooling decisions. Others drifted into unskilled or semiskilled employment. Neither schooling nor literacy was often a route to new occupational or social places. Apprenticeship was an expensive proposition, well beyond the reach of many families. Not only was a son's contribution to the family economy lost for two to five years, but a lump-sum payment was also generally required. Apprenticeship could also conflict with schooling; life cycle times overlapped, and goals differed. Still, literacy was important for those attending evening and adult classes in the Vaucluse, and artisans valued it. It did not, however, substitute for on the-job-training. Artisanal status was not gained through schooling, although literacy helped to confirm it and to distinguish the skilled person from his lesser and unlettered fellows. With some basis in functional needs, literacy tended to become a badge of skilled workers.

For professional and other ''white-collar'' work, schooling was required. Recruitment into these occupations worked in ways that made schooling a less than determining factor. The cost for the requisite education was too high for virtually all but the most well-to-do families. The church was one route for ''sponsored mobility'' of the talented from below, but never for many. Only later would mobility via schooling make a significant difference for more than the very few. Social class long remained the major determinant of secondary schooling. Costs were too high, payoffs too uncertain. Career paths tended to follow all too faithfully one's origins. Opportunities for the sons of the poor may have been greater in the colleges of the towns in the sixteenth and seventeenth centuries than in the eighteenth. Poverty

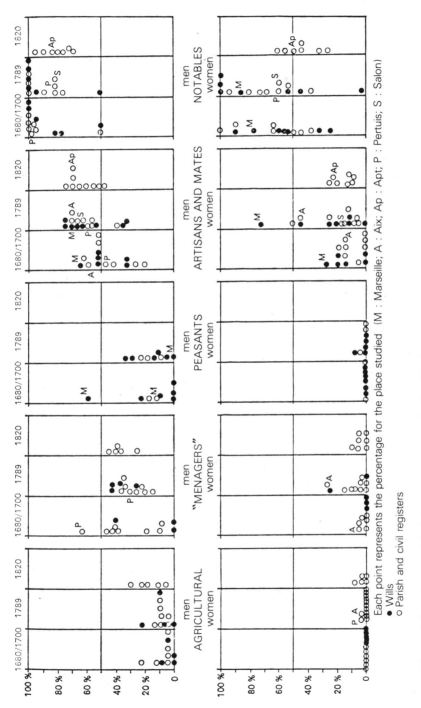

**Figure 6.6.** Literacy of Social Groups, Provence in the 18th Century
*Source:* Michel Vovell, "Y-a-t-il une révolution culturelle au XVIIIe siècle?" *Revue d'histoire moderne et contemporaine* 22 (1975), p. 107.

Each point represents the percentage for the place studied (M : Marseille; A : Aix; Ap : Apt; P : Pertuis; S : Salon)

● Wills
○ Parish and civil registers

was not a complete barrier, but lower-class origins effectively excluded most youths from postelementary schooling, and more than a few from even the achievement of literacy.[64]

In his research on neighboring Provence, Michel Vovelle asked the fascinating question: "Was there a cultural revolution in the eighteenth century?" This issue cuts to the core of much thinking about literacy. That his answer is negative is highly significant. The region south of the Maggiolo line was not high in levels of literacy. Yet, the departments within it saw as much variation as homogeneity.

Vovelle confirms the general contours of Maggiolo's findings. Variation, internal differentiation, and unevenness of change were the basic lesson of the Provencal experience in this period. Size of place, geographic location, occupational position, and class structure were the principal demarcations among the determinants of literacy.

Vovelle points to a "model of Provence" that relates to population concentration. The largest places had the highest rates of literacy. But the gradient of literacy by population size, when portrayed geographically, as figure 6.7 illustrates, is especially impressive. Male literacy, outside the larger centers, was much more sensitive to the dynamics of population size and commercial development than female rates. That held within occupations and classes, as well. The relationships, however, were somewhat stronger and clearer at the beginning of the period than at the end; the transformation away from the traditional social structure of literacy had begun.

Underlying this pattern, as figure 6.8 illustrates, was an extraordinary variation in local rates of change within the region. Simple generalizations are precluded by such diversity. Among the cities, Marseille, for example, increased its rate literate after the 1740s; Aix rose early, then fell, with male proportions increasing again at the end of the Ancien Regime; Avignon showed a ragged road toward progress punctuated by regular declines. Among other, smaller places, even greater diversity is found.

Social and sexual variations, regular stratification by rank and gender, are also present. The notables achieved nearly complete literacy by the beginning of the period and maintained it. Their spouses, while not at the same level, stood highest among women in the region. Even among this group, place of residence had a greater impact on women's literacy than on men's. Commercial development, and with it the need for functional literacy, brought artisans and storekeepers in most of Provence (but not always their wives) to higher rates of reading and writing. The effects of place and size are still present, particularly among women. This "middle" group, nonetheless, stood clearly between the notables and the peasants.

Among peasants, the situation differed. They encompassed 70-80 percent of the inhabitants of the countryside, almost 50 percent in middle-sized towns, and even a quarter of the population in an urban center such as Marseille or Aix. To them we add the *travailleures de terre*, whose illiteracy was equally high. Here was the primary influence on the regional outline. And here one finds the development of literacy, with the encroachment of the marketplace and the commercialization of agriculture, among those who possessed land (the ménager with seven to fifteen hectares). Among the lowest, the travailleurs, illiteracy was total; neither opportunity nor daily requirements were present to push them toward acquiring reading

**Figure 6.7.**

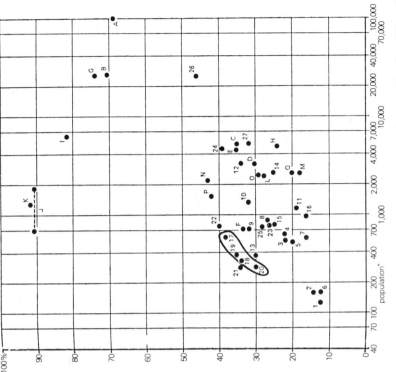

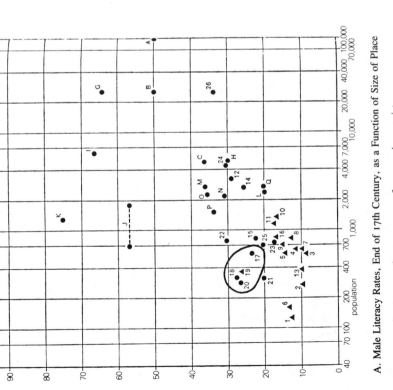

A. Male Literacy Rates, End of 17th Century, as a Function of Size of Place

Place identified by a number: percentage from marriage registers
Place identified by a letter: percentage from wills
Place identified by a triangle: lack of a school in Diocese of Aix in 1730
Groups circled: places reformed from Pays d'Aigues

I. St. Antonin. 2. St. Marc. 3. Le Tholonet. 4. Puyloubier. 5. Vauvenargues. 6. St. Canadet. 7. Venelles. 8. Meyrargues. 9. Peyrolles. 10. Jouques. 11. Le Puy Ste.

B. Male Literacy Rates at the End of the Ancien Régime, as a Function of Size of Place

Rep. 12. Pertuis. 13. La Bastidonne. 14. La Tour d'Aigues. 15. Anjouis. 16. Beaumont. 17. Cabrières. 18. La Motte. 19. Peypin. 20. St. Martin de la B. 21. Vitrolles. 22. La Bastide de J. 23. Grambois. 24. Manosque. 25. Ste. Tulle. 26. Aix. 27. Salon. A. Marseille. B. Avignon. C. Salon. D. Pertuis. E. Manosque. F. Manosque-Campagne. G. Aix. H. Orange. I. Barcelonnette-Campagne. K. Vallouise. L. Eguilles près Aix. M. Cotignac. N. Pignans. O. Cucuron. P. Courmarin. Q. La Tour d'Aigues.
*Source:* Vovelle, "Y-a-t-il," pp. 102–103.

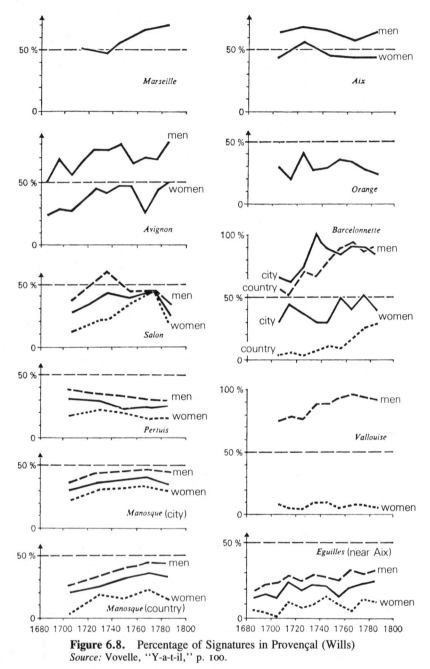

**Figure 6.8.** Percentage of Signatures in Provençal (Wills)
*Source:* Vovelle, "Y-a-t-il," p. 100.

and writing. Social development and economic change worked to divide the social structure; the development of a more rigid class structure was paralleled and reinforced by the manner in which literacy spread. Women remained largely outside the mechanisms that brought literacy to this element of the rural social order.

In a general way, the development of facilities for schooling underlay and paralleled the course of literacy throughout the period. However, the fit was not always close. In some places, such as Basse-Provence, illiteracy was accompanied by a reasonable presence of schools and teachers; in Haute-Provence, intriguingly, the opposite configuration is found. There the highest male literacy rates were in mountainous areas in which school facilities were scarce; the more urbanized plain, with many more schools, had lower rates. This result was not typical.

Alternative learning situations, such as the practice of reading and teaching reading during gatherings on long winter evenings (*veillées*), were common in isolated mountain hamlets. Moreover, young men were motivated to learn to read because of their seasonal migrations; they went down to the valleys to teach during the off-season. Presence of a school and results in literacy were less than two sides of one coin. Intervening variables—other opportunities for learning to read or obstacles to attendance—were obviously important. Further, 1,500 inhabitants was the "threshold" point at which schools became more likely than not. This factor limited opportunities for youngsters, only a few of whom would be able to avail themselves of other options for learning. Nor is it surprising that schools for girls were much less common than those for their brothers.

To the social and cultural factors discussed so far, we add the role of language. In southern France, and clearly in Provence and the Vaucluse, regional dialects, or patois, were commonplace. Knowledge of the French language, together with or in place of the regional tongue, was the exception, not the rule. As an obstacle to the spread of literacy, local languages were important. Vovelle finds that areas in which popular literacy spread were places where French also was diffused. Language was important, and its role reinforced other social distinctions and cleavages. Literacy could often serve that purpose.

Given the foregoing, the answer to Vovelle's original question is of special interest. How did the varied and contradictory developments of late Ancien Regime literacy relate to this issue? The author notes that the restricted state of literacy among rural residents was *not* a total roadblock to rural economic development, in Basse-Provence, for example. Neither agricultural highs nor lows seemed to relate directly to the course of literacy from the late seventeenth through the eighteenth centuries. But even more important, the structures of both literacy and schooling reflected more than anything else the ongoing social structure. Paradoxes and contradictions abound. The contradictions of social development, and the variable relations of literacy to it, underlay the crucial relationships. Literacy often spread with economic and social development, but more often than not its impact was reinforcing, rather than transforming. In the end, Vovelle arrives at the answer "no" to his initial query.[65]

One major obstacle to more informed understanding is the twin pattern of literacy rates within the kingdom. On one hand, there is the traditional interpretive dominance of the St. Malo-Geneva line. Its striking visibility seems to have kept researchers from exploring beneath it for a deeper understanding of literacy in society and culture. On the other hand, the mixed quality of the geographic distribution of literacy rates, amounting almost to a "crazy-quilt" pattern within and beyond the line, complicates generalization. Underlying relationships and rhythms, connecting the rate of literacy with class and occupation, town and country, sex, the family, and geography, are nonetheless important.

In a general way, literacy tended to increase—although not automatically or linearly—with the development of school facilities. Literacy rates moved in conjunction with changes in society and economy. Rich agricultural lands and not-too-dispersed settlements, especially in places where cottage industry and textile manufactures did not develop, tended to provide favorable conditions for the widening dispersion of literacy. Opposing economic and social conditions proved, in most cases, less favorable to literacy's spread. Yet, the literature is filled with contradictions to what otherwise appears as a rule of thumb connecting literacy with rates of development and change. The case of the isolated mountain villages in Hautes-Alpes is only the most renowned; forest communities in the diocese of Reims also suggest persons learning to read and write—through schools or more informally—because of desires to prepare themselves for work or migration, or because of other perceived needs, not the least of which were religious.[66] The detrimental impact of industry, rural or urban, marks another.

Perhaps the major contradiction from the unevenness of school and social development, on one hand, and literacy development, on the other, is geographical. Every local and regional study tells a tale of internal differentiation. Even within areas the size of a diocese, there were real disparities. That reinforces the view that despite the increase of literacy rates nationally, limitations of a fundamentally premodern pattern of development and change were seldom passed. Only the most "advanced" places, largely but not exclusively cities and towns, reached the point at which traditional obstacles began to be relegated to the "past."

The major distinctions related to town versus countryside; gender; the course of commercial capitalism and the penetration of the marketplace; the functional demands of work; openness of community and proximity to communications routes; size of peasant cultivators' holdings; and the deep divisions of class and social stratification. Despite the increases in rates of literacy and, in many places, availability of schooling, real distinctions between the distinct orders remained. Even with basic literacy, the role of fundamental social divisions was maintained. The available evidence on school participation shows the same patterns. The social structure was capable of adjusting itself to real, and in some ways significant, growth in literacy. There were limits to the social progress of literacy's advance in this period, which maintained the bounds of social tradition, continuities, and restrictedness.[67]

Enlightened attitudes led to interesting efforts to translate ideas into policies and educational realities aimed at the popular classes. Some included girls. "These schools were intended, on the one hand, to be of economic utility and, on the other, to foster social order." They also tended to have little organizational development and budgetary requirement. Regardless of intent, these experiments did not succeed in attaining their stated enlightened ends. Rife with normative assumptions about the course of economic development (rooted in the land), the causes of poverty and mendicity, and the stability of the social order, such institutions rarely touched the classes that their promoters and sponsors claimed to influence. Although their curricula often were dominated by moralism and principles of social order, the masses

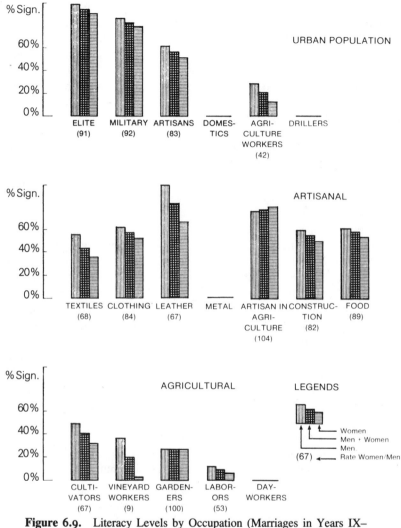

**Figure 6.9.** Literacy Levels by Occupation (Marriages in Years IX–XII)

*Source:* Jean Vassort, "L'enseignement primaire en Véndômis à l'époque révolutionnaire," *Revue d'histoire moderne et contemporaine* 25 (1978), p. 633.

were not found within their student ranks, and some schools were surprisingly secular. The schools were not unimportant, but they contributed little to the enlightened goals of spreading literacy and uplifting the "ignorant masses" of the land.[68]

It is crucial to remember that the purposes of schooling were moral and conservative as well as intellectual. Given the typically poor and often overcrowded classroom conditions, the underqualifications and underpayment of teachers, the overwhelmingly traditional pedagogical orientation of reading instruction, and the predominant use of catechetical materials for reading, we cannot assume that many pupils, especially those from the lower classes, took particularly useful literacy skills from their encounters with the schools. The opposite is a more reasonable assumption. Virtually all accounts and studies of schooling point, on one hand, to problem-laden and impoverished school conditions, and, on the other, to the moral and religious imperative in the lessons of the schoolroom. Even the reformers and philosophers who sought to change the bases of schooling during the second half of the century wished to preserve a moral, if not a sectarian, primacy in the class-room.[69]

Books increasingly permeated the social and cultural world of late Ancien Regime France. Studies document that a real increase in production of virtually all kinds of literary materials paralleled the rise in literacy, and that book distribution also paralleled the outlines of the St. Malo-Geneva line. There was still a large amount of religious literature, but there were also a great deal of history and literature and an increase in science. Professional groups, such as lawyers, tended to own literature relating to their profession. This material did not speak to, and did not find its way to, workers, peasants, most artisans, or the countryside. Darnton notes, "Perhaps it is impossible to generalize about the overall literary culture of eighteenth-century France because there might not have been any such thing. In a country where something like 9,600,000 people had enough instruction by the 1780s to sign their names, there could have been several reading publics and several cultures."[70] Although it remains problematic and requires further substantiation, the trend of the evidence gathered indicates a greater weight of tradition, "inertia," than change or modernity in the distribution of public materials.

Some literary materials were penetrating the countryside. Crude blue paper-covered books called *bibliothèque bleue* were hawked throughout the countryside by peddlers and colporteurs.[71] Accessible and affordable, this literature was the kind available to the literate among the masses. Hardly an example of modern literature prepared for study in private, it was overwhelmingly traditional fare, written to be read aloud by one reader to others. In all respects, it was a form of literature for the masses, and in some ways of the masses, distinct from traditional educated or classical literature and newer forms of the eighteenth century.

> The favourite stories are those which come from the old oral literary tradition and they are enhanced by reading; . . . the well-known themes reinforce the prestige of the written word . . . that just at the time when print was making its way into the lower ranks of society, the standard, traditional stories began to lose face among the literate [i.e., well-educated]—they became *démodé*. The split between sophisticated and unsophisticated reading public was beginning.

Illustrations added to their appeal. Content was simple—almost a continuation of speech: printed conversations, edifying or amusing; sermons; songs.

Only well into the eighteenth century, with almanacs, was more utilitarian content and news carried by the colporteurs of popular literary culture. That was a new development, for "traditional" printing had favored the educated classes, and excluded those outside the channels of classical education. "In cities and towns the ordinary citizen was closer to the privileged classes and so was able to read and speak the common language of inherited culture more readily for himself, . . . he could more or less keep up with the progress of ideas, whereas in the country there were many obstructive factors. . . ." Print nevertheless was penetrating the country-

TABLE 6.6
**Subjects of the *bibliothèque bleue***

|  | Morin's Catalogue[1] | Garnier's Inventory 1789[2] |
|---|---|---|
| *RELIGION* | | |
| Bible stories and Scriptures[3] | 4.9% (68) | 12.5% (55671) |
| Lives of saints[4] | 4.9% (69) | 8.3% (36707) |
| Songs and carols | 11.6% (161) | 9.2% (40746) |
| Religious tracts | 6.7% (93) | 12.7% (56543) |
| Total | 28.1% (391) | 42.7% (189672) |
| *IMAGINATIVE LITERATURE* | | |
| Fairy stories | 5.5% (76) | 6.5% (28788) |
| Tales of chivalry | 12.7% (177) | 8 % (35314) |
| Novels and stories[5] | 13.2% (184) | 8.8% (39200) |
| Burlesque | 1.7% (24) | 2.9% (12839) |
| Plays | 5.3% (74) | 2.2% (9693) |
| Songs | 2.9% (40) | 0.4% (1775) |
| Total | 41.4% (575) | 28.8% (127609) |
| *INFORMATION AND EDUCATIONAL* | | |
| ABCs and spelling books | 1.4% (19) | 3.8% (16795) |
| Etiquette | 1.8% (25) | 0.03% (120) |
| Arithmetic | 1.2% (17) | 1 % (4499) |
| Letter writing, conversation manuals | 3.5% (49) | 4.2% (17821) |
| Morals, satires on the sexes, etc. | 5.2% (73) | 3.9% (17258) |
| Newssheets, satirical pieces, politics[6] | 5.8% (80) | 5.8% (25905) |
| Predictions, magic recipes | 5.3% (75) | 3.6% (15850) |
| How-to-do-it books | 3.1% (42) | 2.9% (13011) |
| History, travels | 0.9% (13) | 1.6% (7069) |
| Total | 28.3% (393) | 26.9% (118328) |
| Other material | 2.2% (30) | 1.7% (8000) |
| Grand Total | 100% (1389) | 100% (443609) |

NB. Figures in brackets (column 1) are the actual editions listed by Morin; in column 2 they represent the actual copies in Garnier's stock, including the reams of paper based on a calculation of 48 pages = 1 book.

1. Included in the total are all the editions mentioned by M. A. Morin which certainly existed (editions included in the catalogues of booksellers selling Bibliothèque Bleue stocks).
2. The figures are calculated on the basis of 48 8vo pages per booklet.
3. One third of the copies listed in 1789 were Psalters.
4. Besides these many hymns and dramatic pieces were in honour of saints.
5. Tabarinades are included.
6. Sketches satirising the professions are included.

Source: H-J Martin, "The Bibliothèque Bleue," *Publishing History* 3 (1978) pp. 79–80.

side, enlarging its markets, and offering a print culture based on peasants' capacity and mentality.

This popular literature was diverse. It tended to emphasize sentiment and to personalize goodness. Much religious material was included. It integrated elementary instruction with morality and was employed in adults' books, even when their purpose was secular. In time, this literature expanded to include social behavior, sometimes with jests about female malice, handbooks on behavior with the opposite sex, and advice on courting, all reaffirming the traditional concepts of marriage and male superiority. Elementary scientific and how-to manuals also existed in number. Literature existed on a wide range of subjects, from herbal remedies to more modern advice on medicine, treatments, and procedures. Almanacs were full of practical information.

Pasttime reading for recreational or leisure pursuits was also common. Old romances were favorites, as were legendary tales of French history and fables. One can envision a collective audience at work in the evening, enthralled by this sort of material being read aloud by one of their more articulate and literate members. Coarser humor, farces, and buffoonery also were popular with rustic audiences. Such literary fare had strong continuities with traditional forms of oral culture and performances.[72]

Some popular literature, such as the repertoire of storytellers in Champagne and Normandy, differed in being designed for individual reading, rather than for listening. Edited, simplified versions were needed for reading aloud. Language differences must have eliminated readers from contact with popular literature. Vocabulary represented an obstacle for country people more skilled in local patois than in French. Many of the texts were more suited to local farmers and landowners than to the peasantry who listened to readings. Employers may have read to their employees, adding additional elements of cultural reinforcement and selectivity to those in the literature. Shepherds' calendars were probably more likely to be read *to* the shepherds than *by* them. Other materials, almanacs, for example, were either wrong or irrelevant.[73]

This kind of reading was not a cultural or intellectual experience suited to broadening opportunities, raising horizons, or inducing personal change. Average readers may have had difficulties in dealing with this literature. Much of it may have been aimed at the level of an intelligent artisan. Courtesy books, with hints on social behavior, had some appeal to ambitious youths and lesser gentry, but not to the peasant or working-class groups.[74]

### D. Low Countries

Knowledge of the course of literacy in the Low Countries during the eighteenth century is limited. During this time, the Netherlands region included both the modern nation of the Netherlands in the north and what in the early nineteenth century became Belgium in the south. Protestant Holland, the Dutch provinces, had in the seventeenth and eighteenth centuries a rate of bridal literacy above that in the southern places. Religious motives stimulated a fuller development of educational facilities and an initiative often lacking in the south. In the common Western Eu-

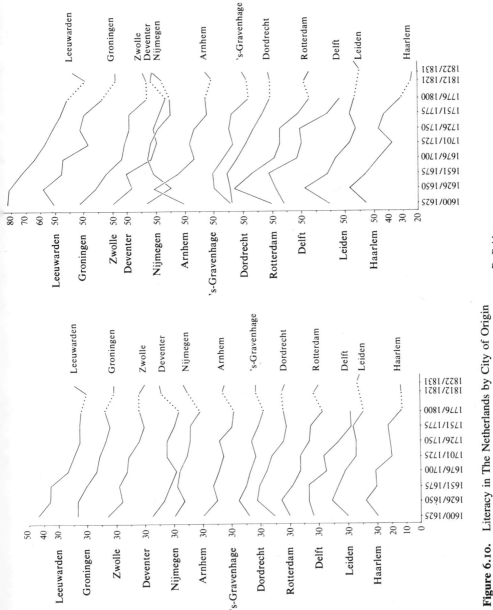

**Figure 6.10.** Literacy in The Netherlands by City of Origin

A. Bridegrooms
B. Brides

*Source*: A. M. Van de Woude, ''Der alfabetisering,'' in *Algemene Geschiedenis der Nederlunder* 7 (1980), p. 262.

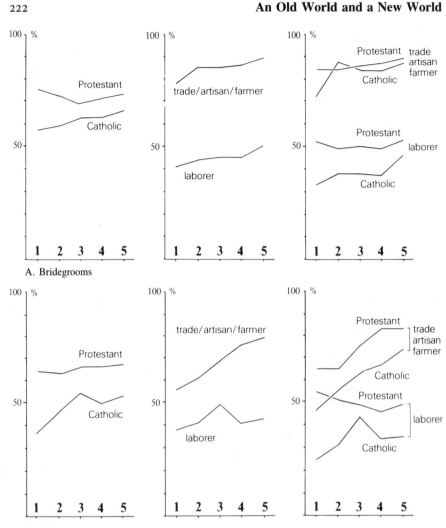

A. Bridegrooms

B. Brides

**Figure 6.11.** Literacy by Occupation and Religion, Utrecht, Rural Region, 1811–1820
Horizontal scales refer to date of birth: 1. before 1781; 2. 1781–85; 3. 1786–90; 4. 1791–95; 5. 1795–1800.
*Source:* Van de Woude, "Der alfabetisering," p. 263

ropean pattern, commercial and industrial developments (with their functional needs and dynamic imperatives), legacies of earlier traditions of literacy, state support, and religious motives combined in this process of geographical differentiation, largely along religious lines. Urban and rural differences were also present. The tables and graphs show the results and their trends over the period.

More than religion was at work. In both areas, the social structures and courses of literacy also were influenced strongly by class and occupation, wealth, place of residence, and sex. Within Belgium, for example, internal difference by geography

TABLE 6.7
**Illiteracy: Percentage Not Signing, Fathers and Godparents, Rural Belgium: 1778–1792**

|  | Men | Women |
|---|---|---|
| Namen | 30 | 60 |
| Henegouwen | 41 | 63 |
| Waals Brabant | 47 | 60 |
| Waals Luxemburg | 27 | 68 |
| Vlaanderen | 44 | 75 |
| Vlaams Brabant | 38 | 61 |
| Limburg | 52 | 72 |
| Duits Luxemburg | 39 | 88 |
| Total | 40 | 67 |

Source: Van de Woude, "Der alfabetisering," p. 260.

TABLE 6.8
**Illiteracy, Amsterdam, Bridegrooms and Brides**

|  | Percentage not signing | | Average percentage per half-century | | Percentage by religion in 1780 | | |
|---|---|---|---|---|---|---|---|
|  | Bridegrooms | Brides | Bridegrooms | Brides |  | Bridegrooms | Brides |
| 1630 | 43 | 68 | 30 | 18 | Calvinist | 13 | 31 |
| 1680 | 30 | 56 | 20 | 12 | Lutheran | 14 | 35 |
| 1729/30 | 24 | 49 | 37½ | 26½ | Roman Cath. | 21 | 47 |
| 1780 | 15 | 36 |  |  | Jewish | 16 | 69 |

Source: Van de Woude, "Der alfabetisering," p. 261.

and ethnicity (Flemish and Walloon) was striking, as eighteenth-century configurations owed at least as much to the past as to present forces. Class, economic development, and geographic origins may have been more powerful influences than religion. In both regions the period was one of progress within a persisting social context, however.[75]

### E. Scandinavia and Iceland

Eighteenth-century Sweden presents a tale of continuity in literacy and schooling.

The widely travelled Joseph Acerbi, who visited Sweden in 1798–1799, asserted: "There is, perhaps, no country in Europe where instruction is so universally diffused among the very lowest of the people as in Sweden, except Iceland, Scotland, and the small republic of Geneva. All the people in towns, villages, and hamlets, without exception, are taught to read. . . . There is certainly no country in the world in which greater provision has been made, and more pains taken for the advancement and diffusion of knowledge among all classes of society, than in Sweden. . . ."

Sweden was relatively well advanced educationally before the eighteenth century began. Probably for this reason, it remained fairly advanced by European standards and provided adequately for the society's educational needs.[76] Despite debate, discussion, and proposals for reform, and some influence of Enlightenment thought, home-based instruction in literacy for primarily religious purposes held sway. Not only did it continue to dominate Swedish schooling, it also continued to produce perhaps the highest rates of literacy in the West. During the eighteenth century, regions not encompassed in the seventeenth-century campaigns were brought into the folds of literacy. As previously, reading was learned nearly universally, whereas writing remained rare. In 1723, the process begun in the seventeenth century was affirmed in a famous royal decree. The document has often been considered as binding for demands of general literacy among the Swedish population. Continuity underlay the history of literacy in Sweden.[77]

Compared with developments of the past century, the eighteenth century was not a time of special events or comparable change. Ideas and proposals there were, but little innovation occurred. In large part, the advanced state of schooling—*without* many schools or institutions—explains this lack of development. There is no evidence that the level of popular education was inappropriate for the demands placed upon it. Given the relative poverty and underdevelopment of the country and its recent decline as a Western power, there were few resources for the creation of schools. Some retrogression from the heights of the previous century is possible, especially as a result of the great northern wars, but the spread of pietism spurred attention to education. The pietists stressed independent devotional reading; the clerical estate responded with an educational thrust to meet this threat to Lutheran orthodoxy's hegemony. Not only did the 1723 decree follow in this wake, but in 1726 the Conventicle Act was passed, forbidding lay religious practice and extending the system of annual pastoral visits to examine literacy, as well as approved religious training to the entire kingdom.

The remainder of the eighteenth century was marked by proposals for further institutionalized development of schools. Few were successful, however. Whether the achievement was less than that elsewhere in Europe is impossible to say at present. For example, the cathedral chapter at Lund, in 1742, outlined a comprehensive plan for schools in that diocese. That brought no action from the government. In the 1760s pastor Severin Schlüter worked out a proposal for a "school and a schoolhouse in every parish." It generated interest in rural education and led to the collection of information on facilities, but only stimulated some other pastors to persuade parishioners to establish schools.

Numerous lay persons were also interested in education. After mid-century, with the influence of the French Physiocrats, many discussed reform for economic development, both rural and industrial. The underlying thrust, typically, was for character and citizenship training for the cause of development, rather than vocationalism or utilitarianism. Interest in mass schooling and in the education of girls accompanied these discussions. Moral and material goals joined, from secular reformers and clerical interests, to support educational action, especially in the context of growing poverty and presumed immorality in the face of economic dislocations in the 1760s.

Political and ideological cleavages also obstructed reform. The nobility and its dominant "Hat" party opposed educational innovation. "Their fear of 'low-born clerks' as instruments of royal despotism went back at least to the sixteenth century while already by 1650 there was apprehension that the new *gymnasia* were producing a socially dangerous intellectual proletariat." As elsewhere, conservatives argued that education was not required by the common people, nor was it socially desirable—it would only make them unfit for manual work and discontented with their positions. This fear, stimulating opposition to educational reform and expansion, was directed toward the middle class, the peasantry, and the working class.

At the same time, there was a definite, if small, expansion of schools. A survey by the state council in 1768 reported 165 "fixed" rural schools, very unevenly distributed throughout the country (not counting Stockholm or the isle of Gotland, where there were parish and endowed schools). There were also nearly 100 moving schools, in which traveling schoolmasters spent short periods on each farm and in each hamlet within a district. Town schools existed, but few of these were "popular"; few had high enrollments or included peasants' children. The total reported was in the hundreds, out of 2,216 parishes; instruction consisted mainly of religious training with some reading, and occasionally writing and arithmetic. The Swedish government did little to change the traditional configuration of literacy transmission. Clerical and private activities were stronger. The Enlightenment's impact fell on them. Charity schools, in fact, were founded in several towns by a *Societas profide*.

Such efforts broadened the base of elementary education "quietly, in piecemeal, uncoordinated fashion, mainly through local initiative, and with rapidly increasing momentum toward the end of the period." By 1802, 240 fixed schools were reported, not including Stockholm or Gotland, with additional moving schools and at least 27 urban schools in fifteen towns principally concerned with primary schooling. In 1768, about 10 percent of parishes had some form of school; by 1802 this figure had risen to about 15–20 percent (and to 45 percent in 1814). Tremendous regional variations are obscured in this total. In sparsely settled north Härnösand, for example, there were very few facilities; in densely populated Lund and Gotland, most parishes had schools.

The nature and quality of instruction also varied. In the 1814 survey's evaluation of the eleven dioceses, two were considered "good," one "fair," five "bad," and three "miserable." More facilities and higher attendance, as well as quality of instruction, were found in the richer agricultural areas, mainly in the south. One cannot conclude that the school as a mass institution had arrived. Through the eighteenth century, "the literacy of the common man [and woman] was rather an aspect of practical pastoral work than of education in the formal sense."

The peasantry showed no great demand for formal parish schools. With their standing obligations to the Crown, to the church, and often to landlords, frequent crop failures, and susceptibility to economic fluctuations, additional schooling for which they would have to pay was an unlikely priority. Even when parish councils chose to establish schools, they often refused to implement them. Given the exceptionally wide distribution of literacy in which the peasantry shared, it would be foolish to consider them hostile to literacy and learning per se. Rather, in the conditions of their lives, this amount of schooling and skill was what they found

TABLE 6.9

**Reading ability in Tuna 1691, in Möklinta in 1705, and in Skellefteå in 1724
related to year of birth. Percentage figures. (N = 385, 1410, and 1489 resp.)
Source: Church Examination Registers**

| Year of birth | Reading ability | | |
|---|---|---|---|
| | Tuna 1691 | Möklinta 1705 | Skellefteå 1724 |
| | % | % | % |
| –1619 | — | 21 | — |
| 1620–1629 | 48 | 27 | — |
| 1630–1639 | 54 | 36 | — |
| 1640–1649 | 60 | 53 | 48 |
| 1650–1659 | 79 | 61 | 58 |
| 1660–1669 | 81 | 65 | 69 |
| 1670–1679 | 90 | 80 | 79 |
| 1680–1689 | 83 | 89 | 86 |
| 1690–1699 | — | 89 | 92 |
| 1700–1710 | — | — | 97 |

Source: Johansson, *History*, p.35.

sufficient. "That instruction in such cases might be less than perfect, especially when it comes to reading, is something that has to be accepted, especially since it makes little difference whether a manservant or maid spells badly. . . . Therefore I do not see why special pedagogues should be considered, who would only impose new burdens and difficulties upon the parishes."[78]

The research of Egil Johansson allows us to follow the progress of the literacy campaign into the eighteenth century (see the accompanying tables and figures). These data show the dynamics of literacy's penetration into the communities. The major factors remained the time and the age of the residents. Age and gender differences passed in time; earlier differences among social groups, rural and urban society, and regions also became less evident. Johansson notes, "The characteristic features of reading ability in the West will thus disappear. This reading ability used to be very low and was largely preserved by the immediate economic and social needs of the community."

In the table and figures, the process is vividly illustrated. In Skelleteå in 1724, for example, only 48 percent of those born in the 1640s and in their late seventies or eighties at the time of examination, but over 90 percent of the thirty-year-olds and almost all of those between fourteen and twenty–four, were recorded *as able to read*. The graphic figures clearly show the continuous growth of literacy from the seventeenth into the eighteenth century. Skanör is perhaps the best example. We see not only the growth to near-universality, but also women catching up to and then surpassing the rates of men. The Visby and Vasteras material adds to these conclusions.[79]

The Swedish church catchetical examination registers, in most cases, provide no information on writing skills. An important exception is the diocese of Lund, where the struggle for national reconstruction overlapped with a campaign for popular

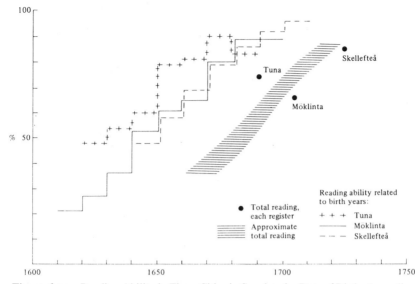

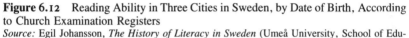

**Figure 6.12**   Reading Ability in Three Cities in Sweden, by Date of Birth, According to Church Examination Registers
*Source:* Egil Johansson, *The History of Literacy in Sweden* (Umeå University, School of Education), p. 37.

instruction. The accompanying figure gives an example from the deanery of Skytt in the far south of the region. The curve for reading shows progress as steady and regular; the difference between town and country is reduced. Writing was included at first in these efforts, and in the towns an initial increase of 15–20 percent was made early. That quickly came to a standstill, but the difference in writers between town and country remained. That shows, on one hand, how instruction outside and beyond the household model was required for writing skills to be disseminated; reading instruction did not require this formal supplement. On the other hand, instruction in writing progressed further in towns. That related to the greater functional utility of writing literacy in town activities. It was, the Skanör data also suggest, a skill concentrated among men. Writing, but not reading, literacy was the Swedish equivalent of the urban-rural and male-female distinctions found elsewhere in the West.

An interesting note on the history of literacy comes from Iceland. The path of literacy for Icelanders was much like that for the Swedes; by the eighteenth century they achieved near-universal rates. In this attainment they were rivaled only by the Swedes. A recent student of this small island writes, "Of the eleven centuries of settlement in Iceland, none was so filled with misery as the eighteenth. . . . Yet it was in this century that universal [reading] literacy was achieved. . . ."

This achievement came in a special context. Since the twelfth century, writers and poets had recorded the history of Iceland, and had given the people a national and historical consciousness rare, and probably unique, in the West. "Indeed, the very survival of this isolated people during the misery of the five centuries ca.

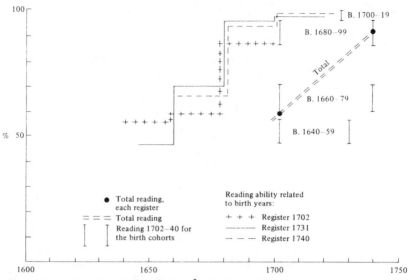

**Figure 6.13.**  Reading Ability in Skanör, by Date of Birth, According to Catechism Registers
*Source:* Johansson, *History of Literacy*, p. 37.

1300–1800 has sometimes been attributed to the sustenance provided by their history, poetry, and literature.'' By the eighteenth century, a large minority of the population could read, apparently, and it is claimed that such had been more or less the case since perhaps the end of the twelfth. A 1925 study discovered that by the mid-eighteenth century, however, less than half of the Icelanders were literate. While behind the Swedes, and perhaps some of the German states, that was not a poor showing. The eighteenth century saw major changes.

The source of the Icelandic literacy campaign was religious reform: Lutheranism. As early as 1634, King Christian IV wrote to all bishops, pastors, and church people, asking them to insure that all children were instructed in the teachings of Luther. Pastors were to visit homes to supervise the process. In 1736, confirmation with compulsory religious education became mandatory throughout the Danish realm, including Iceland, but neither of these directives required reading, nor did they assume it. A clerical traveler named Harboe in the early 1740s found many young people lacking in reading ability and religious knowledge. This visit stimulated legislation that promoted the role of the clergy and the family in teaching the young to read. Something like the Swedish pattern was initiated. In 1744, religious training was required for all youth; two years later pastors were directed to visit all homes regularly to see that this education was carried out. The law also ordered illiterate parents to engage another person to teach their children to read, if they had the means to do so. Similar legislation had been announced a century before, but it had not been enforced.

Formal schooling was never a large part of the transition to full literacy in Iceland. The island's first primary school was not established until 1745; schools were very slow to spread. As late as 1903, less than half of children seven to fourteen were

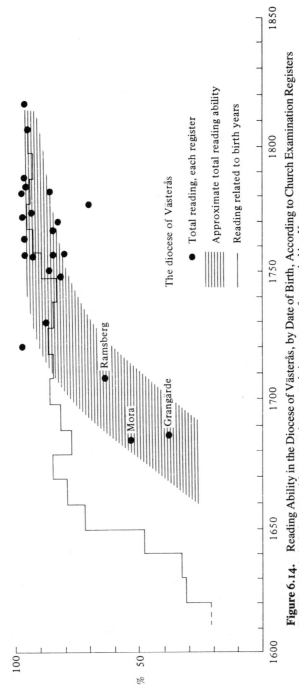

**Figure 6.14.** Reading Ability in the Diocese of Västerås, by Date of Birth, According to Church Examination Registers
Random sample includes 15 parishes, 23 registers, population 15 years of age and older; N = 4371.
*Source:* Johansson, *History of Literacy*, p. 179.

enrolled. Low population densities and isolated farmsteads obstructed attendance, but the tradition of learning to read at home under clerical supervision continued. No nineteenth-century shift to formal schooling took place. Given the right circumstances, formal provision by the state is not required for universal acquisition of literacy. Functional necessity could not have been much of a driving force in this case.

In 1925, an Icelandic librarian, Hallgrímur Hallgrimsson, researched parish records for twenty-seven areas, verifying the achievement of near-universal literacy during the years 1780–1790. These registers were based on the home visits of the clergy and represented data on all residents. After studying parishes in the northern diocese of Holar, Hallgrímur, stated " 'Saying that all who are over 12 can read is to say that nearly all can read. Those who cannot read are, for the most part, old people who were adults at the time Harboe's proposals were made.' " A survey of the records of an additional fifty-seven parishes in the southern diocese showed the same pattern: in the fifty years from 1740 to 1790, the percentage of the population twelve years and older who could read increased from "nearly half" to "probably all of 90 percent."

Icelanders also owned books. Hallgrímur examined the records of 1,000 homes and found only 7, all of them homes of illiterate persons, without books. Most had religious literature. Over 900 persons owned Jón Vidalín's *Postilla*, a book of sermons; Pétursson's *Passíusálmar* (*Passion Hymns*), a book of prayers, was even more common. Icelanders joined the Swedes as the most literate population in the West at the end of the eighteenth century.[80]

## F. British Isles

As elsewhere in Europe, literacy in England increased during the eighteenth century. The relationships between literacy and social change, on one hand, and school development, on the other, were neither linear nor direct. Commercial development, which had helped to propel English literacy to relatively high levels on the eve of the early modern era, continued its push. At the same time, factors of a more personal and less materialistic nature attracted people to the skills of reading and writing.[81]

A principal development was the deepening of class and cultural distinctions and divisions. The "birth of a consumer society" in eighteenth-century England, with its new attitudes toward children and the development of a reading public, was a related conjuncture largely among the middle class. Literacy at this level was virtually universal—without a system of schools or public support. A middle-class culture emerged, related to the consumption of, among other items, the press and printed matter, as a mark of status as well as utility. The working class, however, was not fully a part of this epochal growth. More among its ranks were now literate, and rates were increasing. Yet, its experience was much less than—and often separate from—that of the class above.[82]

Enlightenment sentiments underlay some of these developments, but on the whole they had much less force than elsewhere. Little organized support of state-supported, public, free, and universal schooling developed in England. Some thinkers opposed any increase in the schooling of the poor or the lower class; some worried about any education at all for them.[83] Given the context, the unevenness of literacy's growth is not surprising.

As earlier, literacy in the eighteenth century fluctuated irregularly. Evidence from signatures for the 1720s shows no consistent pattern of growth. The period from circa 1660 to 1680 appears as one of improving rates of literacy, whereas the following, circa 1690 to 1710, was a time of setbacks.

Despite educational rhetoric to the contrary, progressively fewer schools were endowed in this period, and the rural teaching force was declining. There is reason to believe that many village schools stopped teaching. An effort was made to revitalize popular education through charity schools, primarily intended to socialize the poor, to produce "honest and industrious servants." They also helped to spread literacy. The small improvement among tradesmen in the 1695–1704 school generation may have resulted from them, but it was not sustained.[84]

Throughout the century, clergy and professional men were all literate. The experience of other social groups was parallel. Increases during the last third of the seventeenth century ended before the eighteenth. For the first three-quarters of that century, no significant increase took place among artisans and tradesmen, who perhaps had reached their maximum literacy for the period at its onset. Laborers' and servants' rates were also stable for the first fifty years (in the mid-40 percent range), after which they plummeted sharply before rising anew in the last quarter. The rate for both yeomen and husbandmen declined slightly during the first half of the century. "The failure of the rate to increase in the early eighteenth century supports recent suggestions that outside London the much-touted Charity School movement had little or no practical effect." The fall between 1750 and 1775 may be linked to a population's outgrowing the existing educational facilities, whereas the recovery may be explained by an increase in dame schools and Sunday schools.[85]

In these cases, the last decades of the eighteenth century seem to have seen renewed growth in literacy and schooling. The data also suggest a distinct lack of increase in literacy rates among the far largest groups in the population for most of the century. Whatever other development occurred—schools, the press, reading habits, or the like—presumably took place within this context of little growth.

Evidence for the distribution of literacy is superior for the second half of the eighteenth century. Lord Hardwicke's Marriage Act, effective in 1754, required a marriage register to be signed by all brides and grooms and kept by the Church of England. The data contained in the registers relate to the 90 percent of the population ever marrying, indicating their ability to sign typically when in their mid-twenties— about twelve to fifteen years following their probable time of learning to read and write.

Roger Schofield's research using these registers indicates that just under 40 percent of all women marrying were able to sign their names in the mid-eighteenth century, with slow and ragged improvement through the remainder of the century. He suggests that the improvement may be associated with the development of Sunday school education. Male literacy, on the other hand, remained more or less stable, at about 60 percent, until 1795. The ratio of male to female literacy was 3:2, a common differential. For both men and women, stability was the common

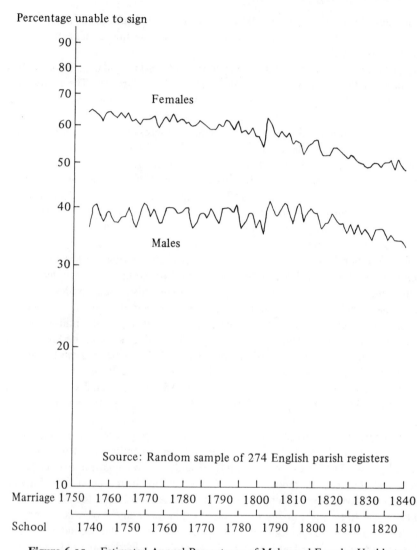

Percentage unable to sign

**Figure 6.15.**  Estimated Annual Percentages of Males and Females Unable to Sign at Marriage, England, 1754–1840
*Source:* Roger Schofield, "Dimensions of Literacy, 1750–1850," *Explorations in Economic History* 10 (1973), p. 445.

experience for the second half of the eighteenth century. The century apparently saw first a period of decline, then a long period of stability with some improvement toward the end.

These figures conceal huge variations. In the years 1754 to 1779, the national male literacy rate was just over 60 percent, while rates in individual parishes ranged from 97 percent in St. Botolph by Billingsgate in London to 17 percent in Hopton by Lowestoft in Suffolk! With parishes weighted by their size, the male average was closer to 54 percent literate.

Percentage unable to sign

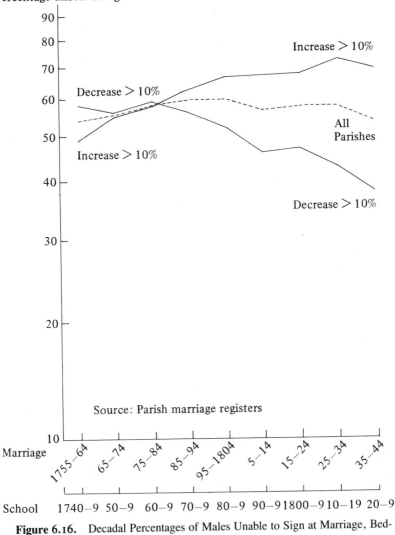

**Figure 6.16.** Decadal Percentages of Males Unable to Sign at Marriage, Bedfordshire
Parishes distinguished in which percentages increased and decreased by more than 10%.
*Source:* Schofield, "Dimensions," p. 448.

Despite these variations, broad regional patterns are apparent. The two London parishes were distinguished by their high literacy. Conversely, parishes with relatively high illiteracy (greater than 50 percent) tended to lie on a wide belt running south and west from East Anglia, through Bedfordshire, Hertsfordshire, North Buckinghamshire, South Oxfordshire, and West Berkshire, and broadening to include Wiltshire, South Gloucestershire, and most of Somerset and Dorset. A narrow wing made an arc across central Northamptonshire, north Warwickshire, South Staffordshire, and South Salop, and ended in southwest Herefs. Low levels of literacy

TABLE 6.10
Illiteracy by Occupational Group, 1754–1784

|  | 1754–1784 | | 1785–1814 | | 1815–1844 | |
|---|---|---|---|---|---|---|
|  | No. | % | No. | % | No. | % |
| Gentry and Professional | 68 | 0 | 170 | 1 | 204 | 3 |
| Officials, etc. | 20 | 0 | 43 | 5 | 94 | 2 |
| Retail | 19 | 5 | 94 | 10 | 150 | 5 |
| Wood | 137 | 16 | 361 | 17 | 448 | 11 |
| Estate | 29 | 17 | 66 | 18 | 87 | 30 |
| Yeomen and Farmers | 97 | 19 | 262 | 18 | 315 | 17 |
| Food and Drink | 57 | 19 | 189 | 18 | 277 | 18 |
| Textile | 41 | 20 | 83 | 39 | 38 | 16 |
| Metal | 60 | 22 | 170 | 29 | 301 | 19 |
| Leather | 78 | 23 | 232 | 30 | 320 | 22 |
| Miscellaneous | 81 | 30 | 129 | 32 | 130 | 25 |
| Transport | 154 | 31 | 462 | 38 | 549 | 30 |
| Clothing | 63 | 35 | 112 | 21 | 135 | 14 |
| Armed forces (non-officer) | 180 | 41 | 773 | 51 | 122 | 32 |
| Husbandmen | 666 | 46 | 560 | 56 | 123 | 52 |
| Construction and Mining | 146 | 51 | 352 | 47 | 499 | 38 |
| Laborers and Servants | 192 | 59 | 596 | 65 | 1,632 | 66 |
| Unknown | 37 | 24 | 130 | 25 | 19 | 26 |
| ALL | 2,126 | 36 | 4,784 | 39 | 5,443 | 35 |

Source: Roger S. Schofield, "Some Dimensions of Illiteracy, 1750–1850," *Explorations in Economic History* 10 (1973), p. 450.

in Norfolk, Suffolk, and to a lesser extent Essex were marked for a large number of parishes with rates below 40 percent. Places with relatively high rates (greater than 70 percent) were found all over the country, but were more common in Middlesex and northern Surrey, the far southwest, northeast Midlands, East Yorkshire, and the northwest. Underlying the picture of stability during the second half of the century is the fact that literacy levels rose in about half the parishes surveyed and fell in the others. Great variability and some volatility are masked by the aggregates; the number of places experiencing great changes, however, were few and small enough that the arrival or departure of a teacher might explain them.

During this half-century, *illiteracy* tended to increase in parishes within a belt southwest from mid-Anglia, through Somerset and North Devon to Cornwall, and in detached pockets such as Sussex, East Suffolk, northeast Norfolk, part of Lincolnshire, the South Pennines, and the Welsh border. In most other parishes, *literacy* tended to increase. Particularly striking (10 percent or more) improvements occurred in the north and east, within an area running from the Scottish border through Yorkshire and the East Midlands to Norfolk, and in odd clusters elsewhere. By the end of the century, the northern and northeastern parts of England were developing distinctively higher rates of literacy, and the mid-century backwardness of northern

East Anglia was disappearing. Despite these broad trends, the variations are at least as important, and perhaps more striking.

Schofield explored the dynamics of literacy in Bedfordshire, the English county with the lowest rate of male literacy in 1835. A full enumeration was made of all the marriages registered in every parish for the period of study, revealing an incredibly varied array of parishes with different combinations of high and low male and female illiteracy, and of increase and decline in illiteracy rates. The literacy rate for men fell in each decade during the second half of the century, from 46 to 40 percent, before improving in the nineteenth century. Only in the decade 1835–1844 was the original position regained. The women's rate was lower throughout the period. Beginning at 28 percent in 1754, it fell during the rest of the century, although somewhat less than the men's rate in the late century. The women's rate improved earlier and more substantially in the next century.

Not all parishes shared this experience equally. In terms of male literacy, there were two extremes: fourteen parishes in which literacy rates increased by more than 10 percent, and twenty-four in which they decreased by more than 10 percent. The divergence was particularly marked after the decade 1775–1784, which seems to be a turning point. In general, trends in female literacy rates paralleled the male rates, although there were parishes in which large declines in male literacy corresponded to rising female levels.

There was little difference in the geographic location of the parishes with such divergent experiences; their rates of population growth and per capita spending on poor relief in the 1780s were also similar. Some of the other differences were weak. Overall, parishes in which illiteracy *declined* by more than 10 percent were more likely to have had a day school, but not a Sunday school; wider dispersion of land ownership; a higher percentage of inhabitants in nonagricultural occupations; and lesser per capita expenditure on poor relief in the 1830s than those in which illiteracy increased. Parishes experiencing marked increases in illiteracy tended to be predominantly agricultural, with little schooling available, and a high per capita expense for poor relief. Social and economic factors clearly interacted in influencing the course of literacy. The presence of schools was one variable important to, but not required for, improvement; also valuable were opportunities outside of agriculture, possibilities for landholding, and a low number of paupers.

A related factor was the marketplace. Literacy was required for greater involvement in commercialized agriculture and the cash nexus of exchange. The spread of capitalism pushed more persons toward functional literacy skills. That is also revealed in the persisting relationship of literacy to occupations within the country. (See table 6.10: twenty-three parishes included occupational information.)

Gentlemen and professional men were all literate—their elite subculture and economic needs presupposed it—followed closely by officials and retail tradesmen. Next came a variety of trades and crafts, ranging in descending order from skilled and clean trades (woodworking, food and drink) to less skilled, heavy, and outdoor work, such as construction and mining. For some, work mandated literacy; for others, it did not. An agricultural hierarchy was also present. Yeomen, farmers, and specialist agricultural crafts (estate) ranked with the leading craft groups, whereas husbandmen were found near the bottom of the range, along with construction and mining workers. Laborers and servants stood last. Literacy had a different practical value to these occupational groups; resources to expend on schooling also differed. We also note the signs of potential cultural differences within the lines of classes then in the process of formation.

The general stability, or lack of improvement, over a period typically considered important for education and social and economic development is a major statement. Those at the top experienced the least change in their rates. Only artisans in the clothing trades showed major improvement. Those employed in less literate trades, along with husbandmen and laborers, declined in literacy. Textile workers suffered most severely; that was the early impact of the factory and mechanization.

Just as the course of literacy was tied to the path and pace of social and economic development, it was tied to the unevenness and contradictions of that development. These facts conditioned, indeed restricted, progress in English literacy. Widespread and slowly increasing literacy must be grasped in this context. The "English experience in the century from 1750 to 1850 may perhaps be taken to cast some doubt on the utility of positing universal relationships between literacy and economic growth."[86]

David Levine, in his study of the Leicestershire village of Shepshed in the second half of the century, investigated whether "one of the cornerstones of the 'modern' world, literacy . . . was regarded by the masses . . . as a valuable skill which should have been and was a prized cultural possession transmitted within families and across generations." He answers negatively. Literacy appeared to be distributed randomly in families, and was not strongly affected by parents' literacy or birth order; opportunities for girls, as elsewhere, were constantly unequal. Such evidence casts doubts upon recent views that a model of "working-class demand" *best* explains presumed rates of schooling and literacy by the lower orders in the period.[87]

From evidence on the distribution of literacy by class in eighteenth-century England, a major distinction appears between the upper and lower levels of the working class. In areas of both high and low general literacy, laborers and servants tended to remain illiterate. On the other hand, artisans stood above 50 percent. For the one group and not the other, personal ability to confront the printed or written word was becoming relatively common. This difference reflects a process of class formation, and proletarianization, during the period.[88] Access to literacy, and its use, separated the experiences of different persons and groups within the population. The working class had no single or homogeneous experience. Literate culture was spreading, continuing a process of diffusion begun in the preceding century and a half.

No one factor can account for the increasing incidence of literacy and the development of a literate culture. Few persons had an irresistible economic need for literacy, although material position and occupation did relate to the likelihood of being literate or illiterate. Although more people were finding some degree of literacy useful for participation in a market and capitalist economy based increasingly in written documents and communications, most work in eighteenth- and even nineteenth-century society could be mastered by illiterates. Many preindustrial artisans functioned without literacy skills. Economic relations were only one force leading men and women toward literacy.

For many persons, learning literacy was not a formal, distinct, or institutionalized activity. It was not necessarily an event of childhood or youth. "Smatterings of these skills might be acquired as the opportunity and the necessity arose so that the process was organically related to the rest of life." Religious edification and leisure also provided motives for learning. These were choices, not requirements; the principle was voluntaristic, not compulsory. The greatest number of examples in favor of this perspective are shopkeepers and artisans, not husbandmen, laborers, or servants. The reach of the printed culture was uneven. Many others, who could not read or write, listened. Literacy was, directly and indirectly, becoming a feature of the popular, as well as the middling and elite, cultures.

Religion was one reason. The desire for direct personal access to the Scriptures drew people toward reading. The Bible was widely circulated by the eighteenth century, and prices were relatively low. There were also countless catechisms, sermons, tracts, and other devotional works.

The printed word was increasingly present in the rural world. Huge numbers of almanacs were printed and circulated. Treatises and articles on farming techniques, technology, and farming news stories abounded. Such information spread more widely through discussion.

Politics also turned increasingly to print. The poor, often unable to read or write for themselves, were ensnared in a system rooted in writing. Political broadsheets were part of public political life. Petitions, warnings, handbills, and other communications, on the side of the people and on the part of the authorities, were written or printed. Regardless of individual abilities, "the printed word formed the bond of political communication between disparate segments of the population. . . . Writing, in other words, was symbolically as well as substantially part of popular protest."[89] The uses of literacy were important in both senses; they bound together literates and illiterates. Much political literature was part of the literature of the streets, pubs, and ports of call. E. P. Thompson has written that no simple distinction can be made between literate and illiterate in the eighteenth century:

> The illiterate hear the products of literacy read aloud in taverns and they may accept from the literate culture some categories, while many of the literate employ their very limited literate skills only instrumentally (writing invoices, keeping accounts) while their "wisdom" and customs are still transmitted within a pre-literate oral culture.

According to Thompson, a culture of the working class was being created in the eighteenth century. People were legitimizing their behavior in terms of customary usage and tradition:

> Traditions are perpetuated largely through oral transmission, with its repertoire of anecdote and of narrative example; where oral tradition is supplemented by growing literacy, the most widely circulated projects (chapbooks, almanacs, broadsides, "last dying speeches" and anecdotal accounts of crime) tend to be subdued to the expectations of oral culture rather than challenging it with alternatives.[90]

The medium of oral discourse mediated the penetration of the contribution of print, just as print influenced the culture of the people. Print did serve functions of hegemony, but it was not an all-determining or -encompassing force.

There were other ways in which the written word was felt. Ballads and tales of folk culture were printed and sold; oral tradition became a part of the written record and was transmitted in this manner as well as orally. The eighteenth century also saw a large market in cheap literature such as chapbooks. These were products for the people: inexpensive, peddled throughout the land, and related to the events and textures of daily lives.

The rates of literacy derive from a confluence of different motivations and causes and material circumstances and opportunity structures. In part, "people learned to read and write . . . because these skills allowed participation in a whole range of religious, economic, political, and cultural activities which would otherwise have been far less accessible."[91] To go much further is more problematic. By the end of the eighteenth century, after the eve of industrial revolution, a majority of the adults in England probably were unable to sign their names and had little literacy ability, as a result of limited progress in popular education and literacy levels and the persisting facts of class, gender, and regional stratification. The demand for literacy that propelled some had little meaning for others.

In the late seventeenth century, a new social attitude toward children emerged among the middle class—a more child-centered, softened set of ideas and expectations. Formal schooling grew in importance. A useful literacy, to be used intellectually, recreationally, and functionally, was emphasized; schools attempted to broaden their curriculum to meet these needs. Morality was still stressed in education, but it was now a social morality. The primary aim of middle-class schooling was to prepare the child for gainful employment.[92]

Schools were one key element in the new marketplace for children's consumption. Spanning most of the century, a steady growth in educational facilities—especially for the commercial middle classes, and probably for some artisans and lesser tradesmen—took place. Richard S. Thompson argues that by 1800, there were about 20,000 schools in England offering some form of elementary instruction, related to an expansion in the study and teaching of English. He points to the publication of numerous editions of English grammars and dictionaries in the second half of the century: an important link between expanding education and class concerns about the conditions of literacy. Concern with the English language reinforced the emergence of middle-class culture and the central place—both utilitarian and symbolic—of literacy.[93]

The "greatest surge" in education occurred among small private schools and academies, most of which offered a more modern and socially oriented education. They varied in quality, curriculum, and cost, but they were ubiquitous in towns and villages. There is evidence of lively competition among them; many masters were entrepreneurial and struggled to gain a share of the market. With some choice available, parents had to be attracted to a school for their own children.

The general expansion benefited most the middle and lower middle classes. Their economic and cultural needs, as well as their social aspirations, demanded it more. The lower middle class may have spent more on their children's education than ever before. "Children had become counters in the parent's social aspirations; their son's or daughters's education reflected status."[94]

The working class and the poor remained largely outside these changes. They gained more from dame schools and less formal means of learning to read and write. Perhaps up to 30 percent of the lower-class youngsters learned their letters in the charity schools, which, although their educational significance has been reduced by recent research, made an important contribution to the schooling available to these youths. Their development was sufficient to attract the attention of those who found reason to campaign against *any* provision of schooling and literacy for the lower ranks.

Bernard Mandeville was the most prominent eighteenth-century critic of charity schooling; his not uncommon opinion was that any such training not only was unnecessary for both the children and their society but also would unsuit them for their future stations in life. In his well-known "Essay on Charity and Charity-Schools," Mandeville argued that such schooling is the result of pity, rather than charity, which he regarded as a poor motive. Mandeville felt that large numbers of ignorant persons were needed to labor for the advancement of the nation. Throughout the century, other voices joined his. Schools that allowed a sizable number of the working class to gain some degree of literacy continued to exist, however.

The charity schools were largely an urban phenomenon. Financed by charitable contributions, they provided elementary schooling with religious and moral ends weighed above any intellectual consequences. Their motives were to control and prepare the poor for socially safe lives of labor. Learning to read the Bible and catechism, it was hoped, would lead to the development of a God-fearing, moral, and subservient working class. Sometimes writing and counting were also taught. Religious and moral schooling, *not* a useful literacy, was the priority. It is fair to ask about the quality and utility of the skills that pupils took from such schooling. For some poor children sent to industrial schools, literacy was even less a part of their training.[95]

Probably most working-class and poor readers gained their literacy in private fee-paying schools. Children of artisans and smaller tradespeople undoubtedly availed themselves of these facilities, with educational investment, for economic, cultural, political, and religious reasons, increasing among them, just as it was among the lower middle class. Their education was rarely extensive. Schoolmasters, typically unlicensed and untrained, often taught because they were unable to secure other employment. Not only are the quantity of training and its costs to families whose existence could be quite fragile uncertain, but its quality was undoubtedly as varied.[96]

The testimony of books and reading points to a substantial degree of literacy in England and Scotland. Among the middle class, literacy was virtually universal. Women participated to a large, if not equal, extent. Earlier developments in educational provision, commercial use of the skills, religious requirements, and cultural usage cohered by the eighteenth century. The history of publications and of reading deepens this sense. On the whole, this development differed from that of the working class, although without a strict and impenetrable cultural separation or separatism.

Members of the working class turned to literary fare of a different sort from that of the middle class, and probably less often; they had less money and leisure time to spend. Their lives were not as influenced by print, nor were they beginning to identify themselves by literacy and literature as was the middle class. In these forms of class differences we find elements of the larger process of class and cultural differentiation that accompanied the social and economic transformation of English society.

J. H. Plumb terms the developments of the eighteenth century a "cultural revolution": "that process by which literature and the arts have ceased to be the preoccupation of small, specialised elites and have become available for the mass of society to enjoy. . . . From the late seventeenth century a mass culture, belonging essentially to the middle class, developed. . . ." Leisure and culture became profitable; that was one aspect of eighteenth-century economic growth.

Daily public newspapers, periodicals, novels, and libraries originated in this period and contributed to the spread of literacy. Reading aloud was popular, so their contents reached nonreaders.[97] Changes in literacy rates may not have been the major determinant of changes in reading habits; other cultural, technological, economic, and political changes led to new elements of a middle-class culture, revealed increasingly in the valuation of printed materials and reading.

Access to printed materials improved with the establishment of circulating libraries and book clubs. The signs (but not necessarily the fact: some book clubs served merely decorative purposes) of reading were becoming a badge of middle-class status. The easier availability of these materials contributed to this new dimension of class culture. The presence of literature was assumed to mark off one class from another and to imbue that class with humanity and civility.[98]

The lower middle class shared in these new developments of literary culture. The kinds of literary fare, their lowering costs, and the terms of circulation and indirect access found men and women of the lower middle class eager to participate "in the growing affluence of England through self-improvement. They lusted for education: for themselves, for their children." Their participation was more fragile, as was their education. Nevertheless, they joined in this cultural phenomenon, which related directly to the use of their literacy—a skill perhaps novel to them. Their participation helped to fuel the consumerism that culture was becoming and to build an industry out of leisure pursuits and reading materials. Functionalism was only one part of middle-class use of literacy. A movement for the transformation of leisure activities from the active toward the more passive—such as reading represented—was just beginning. It was an element of the increasing distinction of middle-class from working-class culture and of efforts to remake lower-class culture and social life.[99]

In the eighteenth century, a distinctive body of children's literature began to develop: amusing while edifying, with larger, more attractive type and simple, concrete language. Some volumes were instructional; others were more literary and entertaining.[100] A proper middle-class message of morality, human shortcomings, charity, and benevolence permeated the books. If youthful literacy was to be practiced, it was to be done on properly instructive fare. That was hardly suited to an upper or a lower class.

The working class's experience with literacy and print was changing. It differed from the middle class in its cultural uses of reading and writing, as the period was one in which working-class culture was developing in a distinctive manner. Print was a part of this culture, directly for readers and indirectly for many others who listened. Within the working class, levels of literacy differed sharply. Religious fare, tracts, broadsides, handbills, ballads, and especially the ubiquitous chapbooks were available, and apparently utilized—and read to the nonliterate.[101] Some among the working class even owned books.

"Something more than the ability to read or to sign the name was necessary in order to permit a man or a woman to play a part in social, political, or intellectual life, perhaps a great deal more, even in the 17th or 18th centuries," writes Peter Laslett. Familiarity with the written and printed word is needed to develop fuller literacy of this kind. That points to the importance of asking *who* was reading and *what* that material was. One rare source is the lists of subscribers included in some books published in the eighteenth century, which sometimes specify the occupations of each subscriber. Laslett found two religious books whose lists of subscribers reveal some interesting information.

None of the women in the lists was given an occupation. By far the most common title among the men was weaver. The wide distribution of occupations and the number of working-class persons are remarkable (see table 6.11). Working-class subscribers, mainly skilled, far outnumbered the others. The number of parsons and merchants was small; few "with any pretense to gentility" were listed. That says something about the character of the volumes' appeal, while it confirms less direct evidence that some persons among the working class were reading, and securing, literature. The almost complete absence of the poor and unskilled is noteworthy, if not surprising.[102]

It is fair to assume that most persons whose names are found on subscription lists were sufficiently literate to read the material; however, some may have obtained the books to show off, or to venerate for religious reasons. They might have been symbolically important objects, of no less significance to their owners if they were not or could not be read. Anecdotal evidence suggests that some illiterate working-class radicals bought and prized the works of Tom Paine, just as earlier and later illiterates sacrificed to purchase Bibles, which they displayed in their homes. The value of books was undoubtedly growing, and some persons unable to read or read well were acquiring them.

Popular literature was coming into its own during the eighteenth century. The Society for Promoting Christian Knowledge, also an agent of the charity school movement, initiated a program of tract publication early in the century. Attempting to reach a wide section of the working class, its publications were addressed to those who it felt were in need of spiritual nourishment and moral reform and among whom it expected to find readers. Never before had anyone consciously attempted to reach a wide section of the poorer classes with printed pious exhortation. Thousands of tracts, pamphlets, papers, and Bibles were issued in this and the next century. There were working-class and lower-middle-class persons able to read this literature (and others to listen to its reading); the degree to which it was perused and believed remains open to question.

Print had an important place in the emerging struggle for social control and cultural hegemony. At the beginning of the eighteenth century, there was a lively popular literature in the form of printed ballads, broadsheets, and chapbooks. The SPCK and like organizations were thoroughly disapproving. They sought to replace its popularity with their own print. "Throw away all fond and amorous Romances,

TABLE 6.11
**Distribution of Occupations among Book Subscribers**

| Occupation | Number of Subscribers | |
|---|---|---|
| | 1757 List | 1759 List |
| Minister of the Gospel | 24 | |
| Minister | | 7 |
| Preacher of the Gospel | 4 | 4 |
| Schoolmaster | 8 | 3 |
| Schoolmaster and Merchant | | 1 |
| Teacher | 1 | |
| Writing Master | | 1 |
| Writer | | 1 |
| Justice of the Peace | | 1 |
| Advocate | 1 | |
| Baillie | 2 | 1 |
| Clerk | 1 | |
| Officer of Excise | 6 | |
| Collector of Excise | 1 | |
| Factor | 2 | |
| Overseer | 1 | |
| Student at Divinity | 7 | |
| Servant to the Univ. Glasgow | | 1 |
| Operator to the Chymistry Class Univ. Glasgow | | 1 |
| Reader | 1 | |
| Bookseller | 1 | 1 |
| Bookbinder | 2 | 1 |
| Printer | 3 | 3 |
| Merchant | 31 | 19 |
| Merchant and Overseer | 1 | |
| Merchant Weaver | | 2 |
| Chapman | | 1 |
| Travelling Chapman | | 8 |
| Farmer | 24 | 41 |
| Gardener | 8 | 2 |
| Deacon of the Gardeners in Glas. | | 1 |
| Portioner | 2 | 3 |
| Tenant | | 1 |
| Land Labourer | | 1 |
| Maltman | 11 | 7 |
| Maltman and Distiller | 1 | |
| Brewer | 1 | 3 |
| Vintner | 1 | |
| Mealman | 1 | |
| Miller | 1 | 3 |
| Baker | 1 | 5 |
| Flesher | | 2 |
| Soapboiler | 1 | 1 |

*Continued on next page*

## TABLE 6.11—*Continued*

| Occupation | Number of Subscribers | |
|---|---|---|
| | 1757 List | 1759 List |
| Coalier | 2 | |
| Collier | | 1 |
| Coalgrive | | 1 |
| Coalheaver | 2 | |
| Hillman | 1 | |
| Tanner | 1 | |
| Shoemaker | 8 | 34 |
| Cordener | | 1 |
| Currier | | 1 |
| Weaver | 120 | 242 |
| Weavers, Present Deacon of N. Quarter Journeymen, Glasgow | | 1 |
| Weavers, Deacon of Red Club, Glasgow | | 1 |
| Journiman Weavers, Late Collector | | 1 |
| Journiman Weavers, Deacon of | | 1 |
| Inkleweaver | | 2 |
| Foreman to the Inkle Factory, Glas. | | 1 |
| Woolcomber | 1 | 1 |
| Bleacher | 2 | 1 |
| Dyer | 1 | 1 |
| Flaxdresser | | 2 |
| Treed Twiner | | 1 |
| Linen Manufacturer | 1 | |
| Stocking Maker | 1 | 4 |
| Taylor | 8 | 23 |
| Hatter (Hatmaker) | 5 | 3 |
| Combmaker | | 1 |
| Cooper | 3 | 6 |
| Glazier | | 1 |
| Mason | 3 | 2 |
| Smith | 6 | 14 |
| Blacksmith | 1 | |
| Hammerman | 2 | 2 |
| Present Deacon of the Hammermen | | 1 |
| Wright | 3 | 17 |
| Late Deacon of the Wrights | | 1 |
| Squarewright | 1 | |
| Turner | | 1 |
| Slater | | 6 |
| Ropemaker | | 3 |
| Watchmaker | 1 | |
| Upholsterer | 1 | |
| Tobaccospinner | 1 | |
| Fitter | | 1 |
| Dytter (?) | | 1 |

*Continued on next page*

TABLE 6.11—*Continued*

| Occupation | Number of Subscribers | |
| --- | --- | --- |
| | 1757 List | 1759 List |
| Innkeeper | 4 | 9 |
| Barber | 1 | 10 |
| Cook | | 1 |
| Sailor | | 4 |
| Servant | 3 | 5 |
| Carrier | 1 | |
| Workman | | 1 |
| Customer | 1 | |
| Indweller—men | 1 | 23 |
| Indweller—women | 2 | 3 |
| *No Occupation* | | |
| Esq. | 2 | |
| Mr. (M.A.) | | 1 |
| Mr. | 5 | |
| Males | 66 | 35 |
| Females | 12 | 8 |
| Total | 398 | 606 |

Source: Peter Laslett, "Scottish Weavers, Cobblers, and Miners Who Bought Books in the 1750s," *Local Population Studies*, 3 (1969) pp. 12–14.

and fabulous histories of Giants, the bombast Achievements of Knight Errantry, and the like . . . " was the opinion of an anonymous author of *The History of Genesis*, who deplored these "vain Books, profane Ballads." The SPCK saw that a "great Variety of plain and useful Discourses have been distributed among the meaner Sort for their more easy Improvement."

There were also traditional broadsheets, flysheets, tradesmen's announcements in larger towns, a fashion for epitaphs in verse on tombstones, engravings on posy rings, sundial mottoes, and wrapping papers. The distinction between oral and written tradition and transmission of much of this content was blurred. The oral tradition was a dominant source for much popular printed literature. After the diffusion of printing, the question of sources and origins became more and more confused, as one element blended into the other. Illustrations accompanied much of this material. Evidence of this print does not, in itself, either prove or disprove popular abilities to read it; it helps to establish a context in which daily life was spent. That context was surely influenced, but not determined, by the presence of considerable print.

Chapbooks were the most common kind of mass literature. Small, paper-covered books, they were peddled widely. There seems little doubt about their central place to working-class readers and listeners. The limited analysis of their content suggests that their origins lay in medieval romances and oral traditions.[103] Chapbooks were small in size, short in length, and simple in language. These qualities related directly to their popularity, as did their low cost and content closely allied to popular traditions and currency of life. Familiarity with the story line, from oral telling or reading, added to the audience (and market). Some chapbooks were essentially collections of popular ballads and songs. Rudimentary readers found this fare more closely within their abilities and interests than the tracts of the SPCK. The common inclusion of woodcut illustrations added to the visual appeal.

In contrast to the ballads, whose principal appeal was topicality and currency, chapbooks tended to have a longer life and a longer time of attraction to readers and purchasers. They may have lasted longer physically. If print was expanding, the appeal of an affordable book may have been growing, in comparison with the less personal and more ephemeral broadside. Growth in a cheap, mass form of literature probably corresponded to the greater development of the habit of recreational reading among the literate working class, the emergence of working-class culture, and the growth of literacy (perhaps consolidation, more than growth, considering the literacy rates) among the upper strata of the working class. The apparent popularity of this use of literacy, in the face of strident promotion of tract literature, underscores the cultural process. This literature was neither the kind likely to find approval among promoters of religious and moral fare and charity schools, nor reading material likely to promote habits of diligence, industry, thrift, and respect for one's betters in a divinely ordained, hierarchical, and stable social structure.[104]

Newspapers and pamphlets, and probably flysheets, as well, were taking the place of ballads for urban artisans and the middle class seeking access to and participation in power and influence on their governors. Political pamphlets became popular during the second half of the century. While not often written in a style accessible to relatively untutored readers, pamphlets and newspapers were popular at taverns, ports of call, and coffee houses, and perhaps at workplaces. Printing was seized by both government and its opposition. This use of print, directly and indirectly, was a more novel form of political socialization, one whose significance would be felt later. Political printing differed from chapbooks and traditional ballads: it appealed to a narrower audience, more urban and more politically aware.[105]

The facts of daily, productive, material life, as well as habits and traditions, distinguished the lives of the working class from those of the middle class. Both classes were in the process of their modern emergence; that complicates matters but perhaps better illustrates the role of literacy in the social transformation. The middle class was well on the way to its major identification with literacy and education. That process was boosted by (and reciprocally served to stimulate) publishing efforts in the eighteenth century. Material conditions were improving, and with them came an expansion of leisure time; a greater functional and occupational need for literacy and schooling also corresponded to a growing positive cultural evaluation of literacy and print.

For the working class, there are similarities as well as the critical differences. The latter, I think, are more significant for the future of English society. Working-class life limited access to literacy and its uses for many. Poverty, lack of time, poor conditions in which to read, inaccessibility of much reading material, lack of skills of a high quality, and demands of work and subsistence mitigated against literacy's playing a more parallel role. Within these differences, and undoubtedly others of taste, preference, and choice, reading grew among many working-class persons. While literacy slowly and unevenly penetrated the working class, it often was applied to different materials. In a general sense, the functional economic and religious employments of literacy could be termed similar to those of the middle class, but to make this assertion risks substituting function for substance. Working-class labor, skilled or unskilled, was by definition different from middle-class work; the place of literacy not only was less, but the uses varied. Much less writing and record keeping, much less correspondence, and the like distinguished workers from clerks, managers, storekeepers, and professionals. Religious practices differed, too.

Reading was increasingly, for the middle class and above, associated with leisure time. It was becoming a cardinal virtue, a "wise" and "proper" use of time. For the working class, popular recreations were different; they involved active forms of expression and play: bull baiting and cock fighting, football and wrestling, cudgeling and cricket, and holiday festivals, fairs, and seasonal rituals. These activities were indistinct from the seasons and rhythms of workers' lives. They were part of the texture of working-class life in a way that reading simply could not be.[106]

Laboring-class play was fundamentally rooted in the physical world and social relationships of the class. It did not require special equipment or separate "leisure" time. Reading could not become an activity with the significance that recreation had until recreation was transformed from the collective and active to the more individual or private and passive. That is not to say that members of the working class were not reading, or that reading was not a collective activity for such persons. Traditions did not support "leisure" reading as they began to among their so-called "betters" by the eighteenth century. Just as much of the material read differed, the time for reading and its cultural role and value varied. Literacy and its uses were becoming one sign of the emerging transformation of the social structure and the development of modern social classes.[107]

For all its prestige as a bastion of special interest in support of popular schooling, a land of enlightenment, and a place of exceptionally high rates of literacy, surprisingly little research has been conducted on literacy and schooling in *Scotland*. From the scant evidence, many researchers place eighteenth-century Scotland among the literacy leaders of the late preindustrial Western world. If that is the case, it is said, it was not because of their state of economic or urban development or the condition of their formal educational systems, but rather because of their adherence to a *reforming Protestantism*. In the wake of the Calvinist Reformation, a national system of compulsory schools was established in the seventeenth century. Adult male literacy may have risen from about 33 percent in 1675 to the 90 percent range by the end of the eighteenth century. Yet Houston reveals the limits of this system and the myths it engendered. The dynamics were in fact closer to those elsewhere.[108]

Local parish schools, under the state but supervised by the clergy, were to insure basic tutelage in the rudiments of education and, especially, the elements of religious instruction. Higher schools were established in larger towns and cities. Masters were to be highly trained. Such an ambitious program of moral and reading instruction did not succeed quickly or completely. Even by the end of the eighteenth century, the population of certain parts of Scotland remained more often illiterate than literate. These tended to be in the most remote, least dense, and Gaelic-speaking parts of the land, such as the Highlands.

Most evidence supports the view of a widely diffused pattern of schooling and a moderate rate of literacy. The minister of Bathgate, West Lothian, for example, commented that "labourers have often paid for teaching their sons to read, write and sometimes arithmetic, and their daughters to sew and write." James Scotland points to the number of endowments used for schoolhouses, teachers, and education for the poor; the interest of philanthropists; and the establishment of libraries. Support for schooling the poor in towns was sometimes available, and Scotland had a charity school movement. There is other evidence that parents were willing to support basic instruction in reading, writing, and some arithmetic for their children, but not often more; they showed "little desire for the learned languages. . . ."[109]

Charity school promoters tended to agree with such sentiments. John McFarlan, writing in 1782, reminded his readers that at the beginning of the century, "some of the most judicious, and even pious men, were of the opinion, that, to give poor children a liberal education out of charitable funds, was neither conducive to the interests of the state, nor in general to their own happiness in common life." Schooling had its dangers, McFarlan stressed, although he indicated that instruction in reading was widespread. It must not, he warned, disrupt the necessary ranks of society, or remove needed labor power; people were required to do the drudgery. "As nothing but early habit can render it tolerable, therefore, to give to the meanest of the people an education beyond that station which Providence has assigned them, is doing them a real injury." In making his case for limited education, the Reverend McFarlan did not wish *no* education for the poor and laborers' children; total ignorance apparently represented a greater danger than the basics.[110]

A special, if not unusual, problem for the spread of literacy was the language question. English came slowly to dominate the land. The preamble to the Scottish educational law stated that "the youth should be trained up in civility, godliness, knowledge and learning, and that the common English tongue should universally replace the Irish [*sic*] language as one of the principal causes for the continuance of barbarity and incivility amongst the inhabitants of the highlands and islands." The link between illiteracy and residence on the islands and Highlands had, among its causes, a language "problem."

Educational legislation had little impact on these regions. Local heritors responsible for instituting and overseeing parish schools ignored the laws, and others able to afford it either sent their children to schools elsewhere or employed tutors. For the poor, no such alternatives were available. "Their children were 'void of religion and education'; for them the legal means had failed and it was left to voluntary efforts to do in the eighteenth century what the law had failed to accomplish." Voluntarism appeared in the form of the Society for the Propagation of Christian Knowledge and the Society for the Reformation of Manners.[111]

Any effort to bring schooling to the Highlands and islands had to confront the issue of language first. The native tongue was not English. The Church of Scotland took care in supplying vernacular preachers for its Gaelic congregations. Irish scriptures were perhaps not the best foundation for Scottish Gaelic literacy, but lacking a proper vernacular translation, they were seen as the best text available. Given the church's and many reformers' views of the Irish, Catholicism, the popish threat, and the barbarity of the Highlanders, a lengthy struggle for the circulation and instructional use of the Irish Bible met with failure.

"All means of wiping out 'Irish' " were sought; the language of literacy instruction and religious observation was viewed as one key means. It was neither the first nor the last time that literacy provision was linked to national colonization, to efforts to replace an alien and threatening culture with an approved one through instruction in literacy. All arguments in support of the importance of a Gaelic literacy or some form of bilingualism met with disfavor from voluntary societies, church, and state. All attempts to bind literacy to the mother tongue in the Highlands ended in failure. The results are hardly unique: "This alienation of language from literacy was a major disaster for Gaelic and was the root of the language problem which dogged highland education thereafter."[112]

As some sensitive contemporaries predicted, poverty prevented Gaelic children from attending school long enough to learn English reading. As a result, their abilities to read and understand were often minimal. Neither charity schools nor voluntary action was sufficient to succeed with such policies. Just as high rates of literacy did not lead to economic development and an end to poverty, they did not eradicate social problems.

Despite the attention accorded the history of education and *il*literacy in *Ireland* in the nineteenth century, little is known about literacy levels and their determinants in the preceding century. What is known comes mainly from the history of English government policies, aimed directly at suppressing, indeed outlawing, native (Roman Catholic) educational efforts (Act of 1709), on one hand, and at Anglicizing the population through educational enterprises, on the other; and from the English-based view of the native Irish as barbaric, superstitious, uncivilized, popish, and therefore illiterate. These are not the best indicators of the state of literacy or schooling. Laws are not always enforceable; there were indigenous educational energies, seen best in the famed (and probably romanticized) hedge schools, relatively informal fee schools that ranged from instruction in reading to Latin and the classics. They indicate popular interest in schooling.

A wide range of Protestant and charity schools was established in an effort to remake the Irish people into English, but their efficacy may be doubted. The eighteenth-century Irish were not barbaric and uncivilized, nor were they all illiterate. Yet, when we project backward from the first systematic evidence of the 1841 census's literacy rate of less than 50 percent, the historical results of Irish poverty and British policy are seen in the lowest literacy levels in the so-called United Kingdom. Ireland provides a vivid example of the intended uses of instruction rooted in literacy to remold a people: in language, culture, morality, and religious beliefs. Here, in the education and cultural wing of English colonization, it seems to have been no more successful than elsewhere.[113]

## G. North America

In the "new world," the level and social distribution of literacy were not static during the eighteenth century. Regional differences, as well as social divisions, had not been erased. New England again led the way. The male literacy level there rose slowly to 70 percent by 1710, and by 1760 it had leapt to 85 percent. By the end of the century, it was almost 90 percent (see figures in chapter 5). Even with comparatively impressive literacy levels and a cultural impetus toward schooling, the data suggest that many New Englanders in the eighteenth century still were ''closer than we have imagined to the credulous word-of-mouth world of the peasant, closer to its dependency on tradition and on the informed few.''

Increasing opportunities for schooling, due in part to educational development in tandem with social development (greater population density and town size), on one hand, and greater need for literacy, due to increasing commercialization of society, on the other, were propelling factors in the rise of literacy. The increase was not uniform throughout the century; the basic rate of change virtually doubled after 1710. The rise was fairly uniform geographically. ''This uniformity argues that the rise in male literacy was a single event embracing all of New England.'' Progress toward universal levels was mainly a movement of less literate groups and less literate regions. In the wake, the relationship between literacy and social status was all but erased, but not differences in status and wealth, which were increasing during this period.

Spatially, the approach of universal male literacy resulted from changes in rural literacy levels. Three-fourths of Bostonians were literate from the mid-seventeenth century; merchants, gentry, and professionals were virtually all literate from the onset of settlement. The rise in male literacy was concentrated among rural farmers, artisans, and laborers, who constituted three-quarters of the population but whose initial rates of literacy barely exceeded 50 percent.

The rate for farmers nearly doubled, from 45 percent in 1660 to 80 percent in 1760, changing more rapidly than that of the society as a whole. By the end of the century, it neared the 85 percent mark, as with rural artisans and laborers. More than rising wealth was at work. Old associations ended; regional and urban-rural distinctions were reduced with literacy nearing universality.

Simultaneously, distinctions in wealth and occupational status no longer were associated with substantial differences in literacy. Men of all ranks and status were becoming literate, although literacy still maintained some association with social status and wealth. Yet, near-universal literacy levels had remarkably little impact on the distribution of occupation and wealth in the society. As literacy increasingly infrequently differentiated men, wealth and occupation continued to do so strongly.

This progress was not the result of rising wealth or changing occupational structures. Some forces not directly dependent on wealth had an impact on virtually all areas within New England, it seems. Education became widely available, and many more took advantage of this accessibility. But increasing literacy did not necessarily involve expectations of social opportunity. The increase was not a result of improving social conditions, nor did it lead to improved economic or social prospects for those now acquiring the skills.

For the shrinking numbers of illiterates, traditional associations between wealth, occupation, and literacy were undisturbed. Although only a few occupations absolutely required literacy, illiterates were obstructed from certain endeavors. Their wealth was also limited, to perhaps one-half that of literate persons. ''The result was that illiterates were so concentrated among laborers and among men worth less than £100 that membership in these groups still carried a high possibility of illiteracy."[114] Illiteracy derived from and reinforced unequal and disadvantaged places in the social structure. Factors that served to move society toward high levels of male literacy did not involve changes in the structure of that society, expectations of facts of opportunity, and universal impact. Within these conditions, the distribution of literacy was transformed.

Women's literacy levels also were altered. Whereas only one-third of the women who died leaving a will before 1670 were able to sign their names, nearly 45 percent of those dying after that date did so. There was less improvement after that point; only in Boston did women's literacy levels continue to increase during the century. There, too, a large male-female gap was present, though women passed the 50 percent mark.[115] One reason for the stagnation may have been educational. In the eighteenth century, some attention was directed to the schooling of girls, but mainly for the provision of low-level skills. Female education continued to lag behind that of males.

For women born in the eighteenth century, wealth became an important determinant of literacy. The fathers of literate daughters were clearly wealthier than those of illiterates. Church membership now made little difference. There is also reason to believe that paternal illiteracy was an obstacle to female schooling, whereas maternal literacy was a benefit. "Location was still a crucial variable, though even those areas most distant from town increased in the likelihood of producing literate women."[116]

The history of literacy is best understood in the context of English traditions and their interplay with social development in the colonies. In early New England, the population was not concentrated sufficiently for school laws to have much impact. Protestant religiosity, on one hand, and demands of social development and commercialization, on the other, propelled literacy during the eighteenth century in a way that was not possible in the first century of settlement. A traditional orientation held, even as the traditional English social structure was modified. The original compulsory-schooling laws derived from a traditional Puritan motivation, but alone they were unable to have much impact. The rise came only after increased concentration of population made schooling much more possible, and other forces added their push.

It is important to note that no other eighteenth-century society surpassed 75 percent male literacy without either compulsory schooling or support of schools, or both. There is no need to discount the contribution of home education or informal channels of learning, but the schools played a major part in the evolution of colonial New English literacy; public action was a basic component wherever rises in high levels took place. And, it was schools that discriminated against women.

As the proportion of New England's population living in towns larger than several hundred persons grew more rapidly after 1710, so did literacy levels. A relatively low threshold apparently was required for school laws to operate successfully and for literacy levels to rise among men. That was perhaps also sufficient for market forces to begin to influence decisions about schooling, adding their force to the persisting traditional impulse. Very high levels of population, as found in Boston, may have proved counterproductive. Literacy levels there may have fallen by the end of the century with the presence of a growing class of poor and illiterate laborers.

In larger towns, the movement of people to new sections or districts away from town centers led to adoption of the "moving school," which rotated among the districts. This innovation became part of town life during the eighteenth century. "There is reason to believe that it brought basic education to the man on the land with greater immediacy than ever before. In the process it enhanced men's awareness of the need for schooling." It also added to tax bases to fund the school. In all, social development made schooling available to many more men; it also increased the chances for proximity to other, informal agencies of elementary schooling, just as it probably stimulated demands for literacy.

In the other colonies, such as Pennsylvania and Virginia, the level of male literacy grew to about two-thirds by the early eighteenth century. How did these other areas, which lacked the Protestant impulse toward literacy and lagged in social development, keep up with New England? In the first place, New England's educational impulse was not well translated into action before the eighteenth century. In the second, the stream of transatlantic migration, which continued into the other colonies later than to New England, included an ever-higher proportion of literates. Dutch men, for example, coming into New York in the mid-seventeenth century had a signature rate of about 75 percent, whereas men arriving at the turn of the eighteenth century averaged over 85 percent. In Pennsylvania, German men coming in the 1720s had a 73 percent rate, compared to a level of almost 80 percent of those arriving later. In Virginia, later migrants also tended to be literate more often. Long-distance migration continued to be selective of literate persons, and the literacy of migrants seems to have increased with time. One result was a relatively similar rate of male literacy throughout early eighteenth-century America.

This moderate advance did not require changes in the social structure or correlates of literacy. Traditional forces and dynamics remained intact. As in New England, in Pennsylvania and Virginia, literacy remained closely tied to wealth and occupation. The rich were almost all literate, but only one-half of farmers and one-third of the poor reached that level. Status was likely reinforced by this association with literacy. Literacy did not seem to cause attitudinal changes.

As the eighteenth century progressed, literacy levels in Pennsylvania and Virginia remained at the two-thirds rate at the same time that New English conditions approached universality. Among the New English, the association of literacy with occupation and wealth was radically reduced. In Virginia, it was not. Toward the end of the century, up to one-half of middling and lower-class men in Virginia were still illiterate. The forces propelling literacy upwards in New England were missing in the other colonies. The result was that by the 1790s, not one county among those studied in Pennsylvania or Virginia had passed the point of 75 percent male literacy, which even New Hampshire had reached long before.[117] Neither intense Protestantism nor school laws, or, perhaps, commercial and market forces, were operating.

A number of historians have associated modernizing kinds of changes with the social and political development of colonial America: educational trends and expectations of individualism, optimism, and enterprise, and a "liberating literacy" that supposedly contributed to the development of a uniquely American culture and political sensitivity. However, an examination of charitable giving as a measure of modernization of attitudes showed that charitable concern declined from the mid-seventeenth to the end of the eighteenth centuries, among literates and illiterates alike. Literates demonstrated the same traditional attitudes as illiterates; their attitudes were not becoming any more "modern" with time.

In sharp contrast to the idea of mass literacy as being "modernizing" and "liberating" is the view of it as limiting and restricting. "If the eighteenth century saw a spread of basic literacy without much improvement in its quality, men may have been further than ever from the skills needed to function independently," and they may have been frustrated by an inability to comprehend a changing world.[118] In this respect, New England farmers would have been little advantaged by their literacy compared to their peers in other colonies.

Despite New England's achievement of near-universal male literacy before the end of the eighteenth century, not much should be assumed about the differences between the American colonies and the mother country. In England, male literacy stood at about 60 percent during the eighteenth century, a time of gradual increase at best. That is not so different from colonial levels, once the evidence is adjusted for age and source biases. Colonial Americans, especially in New England, had a small advantage. In most of America, literacy remained firmly linked to occupational structure and wealth distribution; the rich and the well-to-do, along with those involved with commerce and the market, were typically literate, and the poor were most often illiterate.[119] Only New England seems to have diverged. More detailed analysis may show the often asserted American advantages in literacy and schooling to be even less distinctive.[120] If slaves and Indians are added, American levels may have been somewhat lower than English. Similarities and the persistence of traditional relationships are impressive.

A strong place for the oral, as well as the printed, must be accorded to the culture of eighteenth-century America. Good teachers were not plentiful, and printed texts probably were important instructors, but in both formal schooling and more individualized confrontations with printed materials, traditional means of learning, with their stress on memorization, remained strong. Tension—indeed, cultural contradiction—was present with concomitant increases in literacy, print, and formal education, and the means of print dissemination. The oral culture, and oral means of communication, did not disappear in this process. That is especially significant in recognizing the crucial role of personal oral discourse and communication in the maintenance of society, the Great Awakening, and the mobilization of the population at the onset of the American Revolution.[121]

For example, although laws were written, and lawyers and justices of the peace were participants in a literate culture of long standing, the way in which the law functioned was beyond the limits of the literate. The oral popularized, diffused, mediated, and authorized a key message, which endowed the society with much of its coherence and integration. "In a semiliterate society, it was not in printed opinions of authors, but in ritual actions, in face-to-face familiar meetings in the courthouse, that the reality of law unfolded in a formal setting modulated by routine and repetition." The power and force of personal contact and customary circumstances gave the legal message a basis that printing could not. In a society in which not all persons were literate and in which reading was not a common practice, other means of communication and reinforcement (i.e., practical demonstrations of power and content) were required.[122]

The religious revival known as the Great Awakening also showed the persisting role of the oral in eighteenth-century colonial culture, as well as some of the interactions connecting oral and print modes of transmission. Before this period of revivalism, the dominant style of religious discourse was conservative, orderly, and hierarchical; people identified themselves and related to others according to their rank or standing in the community. Ministers, ordained with special authority, preached in a formal, rational manner. The revivalist preachers, however, attempted to speak directly to the people, using everyday language. The impact of the Great Awakening may well have been to renew the power of speech—in freeing it from conventions and returning public speaking to everyday rhetoric.

"The revivalists' repudiation of polite style and their preference for extemporaneous mass address cut to the very core of colonial culture by attacking the habit of deference to the written word and to the gentlemen who mastered it." Linguistic divisions, as well as uses of literacy, increasingly distinguished the elite from the masses, the "literate" from the popular. Among the elite, a shift toward print and polite style was seen in the appeal of rational religion. The common people, with basic literacy at best, were more and more excluded. Social values were attached to elite print culture. "Power became so closely tied to print that advanced literacy and a classical education were virtually prerequisite to authority. . . ." The elite culture of print and writing was not the culture of the great majority of the population, regardless of their literacy; for them the oral medium remained more common.

Political literature provides yet another example. The style and form of most political writing likely excluded many readers from it. That which gained a wide audience eschewed classical rhetoric and opted, perhaps consciously, for a more popular and commonplace style. Thomas Paine's *Common Sense* is perhaps the best example. Not only were the more popular pamphlets of the revolutionary period more accessible to the skill of a reader with a limited education, they also drew on the Bible for references and imagery, not classical literature or constitutional theory, and sometimes were written to be heard as well as to be read.[123] It was a communications process that linked popular culture, of speech and print, to new ideas that may have brought many people to new ideas and sentiments—to a revolutionary mobilization. To move the people, to gain their support even gradually, the message had to be (re)connected with the oral and with the language of the people.

Rhys Isaac's study of Virginia's evangelical culture offers an analysis of the common people's means of communication and its place in their culture. Isaac stresses face-to-face interaction and oral channels as crucial social dynamics. "Even the fully literate elite would be socialized and attuned to the predominantly oral-aural medium of the society in which they lived."

To Isaac, the Baptist evangelical revolt represented a direct challenge to traditional gentry-dominated society. It proclaimed an alternative way of life with a different system of values. An intense religious conversion was central to the evangelical experience. Literacy contributed little; preaching—oral discourse—was central: *hearing* the preacher's words shaped candidates' experiences, and conversion was reinforced by "hearing the experience" in class or church meetings. "Through extempore preaching in search of 'liberty' the oral culture of the people was surfacing in a form of rebellion against the dominance of the literacy culture of the gentry."

Isaac's studies also reveal how written information was transmitted by means other than the direct, individual encounter with the page. In addressing the people, the gentry communicated through Biblical, rather than classical, imagery—through language and imagery that touched the people's lives. Oath taking and the routine reading aloud of courthouse proceedings underscore the persisting role of the oral culture.[124]

News and opinion about politics, the breakdown of imperial relations, and the early events of the Revolution depended only in small part on literate transmission. Newspapers gave little attention to these events. They authenticated reports that spread by word of mouth, instead of carrying full reports. Newspapers, moreover, were not directed to the general population; their fine print, long reports from European courts, and polemics in learned style were ill suited to a popular audience. "Persons of this rank were expected to receive the more important messages contained in the fine print through reading aloud and through conversations at courthouses, ordinaries, and other places of assembly as news became part of the common stock of knowledge, opinion, and feeling." Here was a link between the literate and the oral modes; in this way the classes and cultures met and exchanged, and news was circulated widely.[125]

Only a minority of eighteenth-century colonial Americans subscribed to and participated in a fully literate culture. Theirs was neither a nonliterate nor an illiterate world. Books were too common for that; reading and writing did have a broad utility. But they were one agency among others in the texture of social, economic, cultural, and political life.[126]

Books and schools became more and more frequent, and were regular aspects of the colonial scene, during the eighteenth century. Literacy was increasingly useful for functional dealings in commerce and the marketplace; political events and controversies of the second half of the century did put important demands on many (if not most) persons' literacy skills. Print was not only more common but also more important. It played its role in the larger communicative context. An indigenous printing industry was forming.

The shift to a dominance of formal agencies for education was largely a nineteenth-century phenomenon.[127] School development took place, irregularly and unevenly throughout the colonies, but the Enlightenment (or perhaps, in the American setting, Jeffersonian) program for more formal, public, and universalistic schooling was nowhere achieved during the colonial era. The Enlightenment had a strong impact on American thought, especially on social, political, and philosophical goals and on higher education. But as far as elementary training was concerned, conservative goals tended to dominate.[128] Reading often was taught in the home, from hornbooks, spellers, catechisms, primers, and Bibles. The young learned largely through imitation and only partly from explanation. Within households, it is possible that much reading was done aloud. These patterns persisted as colonial society developed and more institutions were established. No epochal shift from family to institutions took place in the eighteenth century. Schools and churches, primarily, but also other institutions, from coffee houses to clubs, voluntary societies, libraries, and the like, made their contribution supplementary to that of the family. For those without family, eleemosynary organizations and institutions made some small contribution; most such children were poor and had little access to literacy and its uses. In all, a wide variety of educational agencies and institutions grew up in the eighteenth century. Blacks and Indians were largely outside these structures.

Although educational development and literacy trends should not be equated in lock-step manner, both moved unevenly in the same direction. It seems that areas with high literacy rates housed the largest numbers of schools and the greatest extent of public support. The relationship was only partially direct, only partially causal. New England led, as it did in the supply of books and printers, with the Middle Atlantic colonies and the South following. In the latter regions, which held most of the population, there was less public support, more private initiative, and a lesser extent of development. The penetration of literacy and literate culture was less than in the North. Throughout the colonies, the arrival of a fully literate culture and economy was less than complete at the time of the American Revolution. Religious and moral imperatives remained a dominant motive in the development of primary schooling and the transmission of literacy. Utility was secondary.

The developing print culture of the colonies evolved considerably from its rather sparse beginnings in the seventeenth century.

> By 1762 each of the thirteen colonies could boast at least one press, and the country as a whole around forty, with the result that there was a vast upsurge in the number of newspapers, almanacs, magazines, textbooks, manuals, sermons, legal codes, and pamphlets of every sort and variety available to the literate public.[129]

Whereas much of this literature could be deemed educational, reading it need not have brought that consequence. The chances for the reverse were perhaps no less.

The distribution by classes of literature is revealing. The dominance of traditional forms of print is striking. Theological and religious books had a strong plurality; the law (statutes, proceedings, and the like) and official publications also ranked high. Literature, often moralistic, followed.[130] With time, more innovative and sometimes enlightened kinds of literature began to appear, but among native imprints neither practical or utilitarian nor innovative and modern books had a strong presence. The evidence of elites' libraries, voluntary society collections, and the like should be seen as less revealing of popular tastes and habits than these types of reading.

Book possession became much more common in the eighteenth century, and related to household wealth. Religious literature was by far the most common reading fare. Whereas there is ample evidence of a wide variety of books in the eighteenth-century colonies, there is good reason to place that information in the limiting context of the dominance of more traditional fare and traditional uses of literacy in a culture only partially literate. Growth of bookshops, newspaper advertisements for books, novel reading, and subscription and even public libraries are important signs of a literate and reading public and of cultural development. Let us recognize them while we keep them in their cultural bounds.[131]

The development of colonial newspapers was impressive.[132] These were weekly publications, consisting of a small amount of local news, advertising, and a considerable amount of information on happenings abroad and, increasingly, in other colonies. Numbers and circulation grew in the middle decades, with improvements in transportation and the growth of commerce. Aside from local news, information was not exactly timely. But, except in times of political crises, such material was not really the stuff of the colonial press. More important were trade cards that stood as advertisements and the communications or letters, often signed with pseudonymns.

The periodical press did have a political role, and it surely influenced opinion and carried news outside the centers of its concentration. "Every paper had its distinct political reason for existence. . . . "[133] Some caution must be expressed regarding the impression made on men's and women's minds by these newspapers. For many readers, the style and language of newspapers and pamphlets were hardly easy; their messages required other means for wider circulation, translation, and broadcast.

Other printed items were more popular and widely diffused than books or newspapers. Perhaps the best example is the almanac, for which no advanced degree of literacy was typically required. Its printing began quite early in the seventeenth century. The redoubtable Benjamin Franklin felt that it should serve as "a proper vehicle for conveying instruction among the common people." This practical information (regardless of accuracy) was considered important; almanacs were seen as a normal part of the household's equipage. Virtually all presses published them. The Ames almanacs, for instance, circulated on an average of 60,000 a year from 1725 to 1764. With time, their contents tended to be popularized. They included materials ranging from English poetry and prose to essays on scientific topics, political polemic, and practical advice; from medical remedies and household management to general perspectives on the conduct of life.[134]

Eighteenth-century readers had a great variety of materials on which to exercise their growing literacy. All forms of print were expanding, and their culture was progressing toward a more significant role for print. In this situation we find some elements of modernity, and that is one important part of the story of the eighteenth century: in North America and in much of the European West.[135] There can be no doubt of literacy's significance. Demands for it surely expanded under the combined pressures of market expansion and commercialization, complex and intertwined social changes, and political polemics during the eighteenth century. Literacy was a basis, a low foundation, for expansion and perhaps even liberation, for some persons before the Revolution. It allowed a more complete and comprehending involvement with literary culture and political developments, if additional training or self-education was available and exercised.[136]

On the other hand, there were undoubtedly people with some level of schooling and some ability to read and write whose literacy was not up to the demands that social and political pressures placed upon them. These were persons confused, bewildered, and uncomprehending of the changes that challenged their world and their understanding of it. For them, possession of literacy was not sufficient to be comfortable, let alone liberated.

The literacy to which most men, and more women, had access was most likely a limited literacy, but it need not be especially limiting in daily life, even if it was insufficient for higher-level needs and demands. There were regular means of communication to supplement literate channels and bring access to news, information, opinion, and the like to both the illiterate and many literates outside the elite, literate culture. With the development of society, the increasing density of settlement, and the rising importance of urban society, greater access to the substance of print media by nonliterate means served to moderate the demands on literacy that those same forces could make.[137] Literacy was one part of a larger process: of learning, living, and communicating. The eighteenth century began to change our ideas about that relationship, but did not change the relationship as much.

The essential traditionalism or "premodernity" of the colonial world and, with it, much of the West is inescapable. That was contradicted by new uses of literacy that enlightened minorities were beginning to make; it also was contradicted by new ideas and patterns of thought about the uses of literacy and education in shaping *all* persons within formal institutions under state supervision and control. Both looked to the future.[138]

A great many colonists moved slowly toward political mobilization and participation in a war for home rule from motivations at least as traditional and backward-looking as the reverse.[139] "Modern," modernized, and liberated persons were still few. Demand for a return to a simple life was strong. Literacy, as a modernizing, expansive, or liberating force, contributed little to these processes of human action and human response.[140]

Literacy had grown among the population mainly for traditional reasons and for functional economic demands. That did remarkably little to alter human consciousness and attitudes or the shape of society. This course of development, on the eve of American nationhood, as elsewhere in the West, was indeed contradictory. It was a balance of continuity and change, of literacy's potentials and its realities. That is central to the Western experience of literacy at the time of the Enlightenment, the age of revolutions, the eve of the Industrial Revolution, and the onset of the modern era.

# PART FOUR

# Toward the Present and the Future

Canadian school children in class, late 19th century. *Courtesy of National Photography Collection, Public Archives of Canada.*

CHAPTER SEVEN

🌿

# The Nineteenth-Century Origins
# of Our Times

The fact of schooling is clearly associated with the nineteenth century, and specifically the French Revolution. The eighteenth century, for all its enlightenment rhetoric about education for the lower orders, and even some decrees in Prussia about compulsory schooling for the peasants, was concerned more with wresting from the church the principle of state control over education than with actually providing it.

—KARL A. SCHLEUNES, "The French Revolution and the Schooling of European Society"

THE NINETEENTH CENTURY SAW A REALIZATION of many of the hopes of the eighteenth-century Enlightenments, in the context of societal transformations that moved a largely preindustrial, "premodern," and agrarian transatlantic world into one much more like the contemporary landscapes. It was a key century for literacy—its diffusion reached new heights; its legacies and traditions interacted complexly with the newer processes of change. A set of interrelated developments of the greatest moment was taking place: the origins of our times.[1]

Relatively new forces joined the stage in the nineteenth century, interacting with familiar ones to form new configurations. The relationships between literacy and industrialization, urbanization, commercial development, migration, political developments, centralization and institutionalization, technological advances, population changes, and related aspects of social change often have been regarded as linear, but they are much more complicated, often contradictory, and require more sustained attention and more subtle understanding than previously permitted.

The received wisdom sees the period as one of institutional, public educational reform and growth. The major social transformations are seen as forces promoting the development of schools, at least in the long run. With that development came the growth of schooling and the renewed spread of literacy. Whereas interpreters differ as to whether the stimulus for educational expansion came mainly from above or below, or whether its motives were benevolent or more coercive, they tend to concur on the results seen in various indicators of growth: school enrollments, attendance, buildings, resources expended, teachers recruited and trained, institutional systemic evolution, centralization and bureaucratization, and literacy rates.[2]

Even if potentially disruptive at first, the course of urban and economic development and the increased role of the state are viewed as contributors to literacy and schooling's progress. Literacy and schooling are much more closely allied, and posited to be more often related casually, than in previous eras. The relative novelty of literacy's advancement in the imputedly more "modern" regions of the West is commonly stressed. And, naturally, changes in technology that underlay a rapid growth in the volume, distribution, and differentiation of printed materials are subordinated, interpretatively, to asserted sources of demand from "new reading publics" that serve to propel supply in direct response. Some hold these developments to be positive, liberating, and democratic; others find in them sources of cultural division and decline. When the simplicity of largely linear explanation is punctured by evidence and conceptually grounded analysis, normative accounts fail swiftly.

Opinions vary on the motivations for expanding schooling and for the popular reactions to these opportunities. One view attributes this expansion to the efforts at "enlightenment" of benevolent sponsors who were working for the good of the people and society, despite the opposition of traditional elites and political leaders who saw no need for popular schooling, and despite the perceived ignorance and materialistic self-interest of the masses. Other historians see the working class itself as the activating force, as using the expansion of schools to advance its own interests and place within society. A third view stresses the role of the state in developing school systems in order to further political, social, and economic ends—for example, to instill in the masses proper values and attitudes and to develop needed work skills. Each of these approaches is at base a model of linear, progressive, or evolutionary change. The circularity of such normative interpretations cries out for new perspectives and new approaches.

To a post-Enlightenment, nineteenth-century West, education stood out as a god and an engine of progress. Faith in its beneficial results, for states, societies, and individuals, was one of the premier tenets of the world view that emerged in the era. The diverse efforts to promote the ideals and the variety of means to fulfill them led to the founding of mass institutions on an unprecedented scale. The school itself took on a new form and meaning in this context, and with it, literacy acquired a new significance. That was one monumental nineteenth-century contribution. The meanings and values of literacy—traditional and more novel—were brought together: in thought and theory, and in efforts to realize them in practice.

The meanings of literacy also expanded. It now stood more than ever before as fact *and* symbol. With changes in patterns of work and residence and with the expansion of service and technical work spheres, practical and functional needs for literacy grew. Economic needs for reading and writing reached unprecedented levels. There are good reasons *not* to exaggerate this critical development, or to reify it. Some contemporaries clearly did; more recently commentators and "modernization" theorists have done so. That is an important legacy. The needs and uses for literacy a century and more ago were more subtle, however.

It was during the last century that the individual need for at least basic education became identified as a fundamental prerequisite for advancement or social mobility. For employers, a new emphasis on "educated labor" became a familiar refrain.

Educated labor—that is, properly schooled workers—possessed a number of qualities: punctuality, respect, cleanliness, discipline, subordination, and the like. A
controllable, docile, respectful work force, willing and able to follow orders, was
one of the chief needs of commercial and industrial enterprises during a century of
economic transformation. Literacy's place was not always as a skill or technology
in such formulations. It was the best medium for tutelage in values and morality,
it was discovered during the first half of the nineteenth century. As societies changed
under the massive structural transformations that moved the West, new and different
forms of social cohesion and individual training were desperately required. In the
search for the solutions to this kind of social problem, the power of formal, large-
scale institutions was discovered.[3]

## 1. The Setting

The first few decades of the century saw the passing of most Western opposition
to schooling the masses. That does not signify that mass schooling followed logically
in its wake, as the histories of Spain, Portugal, and Italy, for example, demonstrate.
Although that opposition differed from place to place, the educational solutions
reached were often surprisingly similar in goals and content, if not always in timing,
extent, legislation, and structure. Changes in social context—at vastly different
rates—involving the transformation of economic and social relations joined with
the newer modes of social response to promote new goals for education, including
a new place for literacy. Disappearing were traditional elite attitudes that had stressed
fears of an educated and literate laboring and working class, discontented with its
traditional position of deference. Instead, it came to be accepted that the masses
should be schooled *properly*.[4]

The emergent consensus stressed schooling for social stability and the assertion
of appropriate hegemonic functions. This view emphasized aggregate social goals—
the reduction of crime and disorder, increased economic productivity, and, first and
foremost, the inculcation of morality—rather than the more individualistic end of
intellectual development and personal advancement. Dominating the rhetoric promoting systems of mass schooling, these goals represented primary motives for
*controlled* training in literacy. Literacy alone, however—that is, isolated from its
moral basis—was feared as potentially subversive. The literacy of properly
schooled, morally restrained men and women represented the object of the school
promoters.[5]

Emphasis on the controlled provision and use of literacy was not new to the
nineteenth century. There had been previous similar efforts, by religious groups
who agreed on the need to morally uplift the poor and working classes and competed
for their souls. Religion, especially a reforming Protestantism, was a major dynamic
force in those few societies that achieved near-universal adult literacy before the
nineteenth century. Reading the Bible was the vehicle for this impulse; religious
indoctrination derived from the moral message of this print. This action was not
so much intellectual or liberating as it was ritualistic and conservative. The level
of literacy, moreover, need not have been high: a proper or deep understanding of

the words was not essential. Literacy, however nominal, signified in theory the observance of an ordained and approved social code. Neither the Enlightenment nor "secularization" in the nineteenth century erased that aim.

By mid-century, diverse educational promoters and religious groups agreed in their motives for literacy training; their goals were institutionalized in developing systems for mass education, regardless of sponsorship. Schoolmen, while proclaiming increasingly that education should be nonsectarian, continued to stress Christian ethics and moral training.[6]

The moral bases of literacy accompanied the shift from a *moral* economy to a *political* economy in Western Europe and North America from the late eighteenth through the nineteenth centuries. It developed in response to sweeping societal transformations and efforts to comprehend and interpret those changes. Literacy was expected to contribute vitally to reordering and reintegrating the "new" society of the nineteenth century; it represented one central instrument and vehicle in the efforts to secure social, cultural, economic, and political cohesion in the political economy of the expanding and consolidating capitalistic order. Popular behavior and presumed needs for social learning attracted the attention of many concerned individuals, including those dedicated to the reform of society and the reformation of the masses constituting that society. In many activities that sought to reestablish integration and recreate social order, they developed a conception of literacy rooted in morality and of literacy as an instrument of social stability in a time of change, facilitating both progress and development without (or with a diminished) threat of disorder.

Formal education, through the structured provision of literacy, was intended to elevate and assimilate the population to insure peace, prosperity, and social cohesion. An efficient and necessary substitute for deference, education would produce discipline and aid in the inculcation of the values thought required for commercial, urban, and industrial society.[7]

Changing modes for training in social morality and restraint, and with them a new role for education, were responses to complex social and economic changes rooted in the transition to a mercantile and, later, an industrial capitalist order.[8] Institutions formed one response to new requirements and demands: to meet perceived threats of crime, disorder, and poverty; counteract cultural diversity; prepare and discipline a work force; and replace traditional popular culture with new values and habits. These problems interacted to heighten the need for action and to hasten the pace of institutional response.

Culturally, customary routines and rhythms had to be replaced by the punctuality, regularity, docility, and orderliness required by the new society. Socially, the place of traditional expectations of inheritance of position was preempted by a promise often implicit in education: the triumph of achievement over ascription, or at least the need for individual attainment. Despite this new ideal, specific occupational skills and cognitive traits remained less critical than character, behavior, habits, or attitudes in moral economic formulations. Literacy's role in this process was complex, for the way in which it was to be acquired and the setting for instruction were obviously crucial. Both pedagogical method and institutional structure were elements in the inculcation of morality, in education's struggle to create proper restraint and modes of conduct. These processes, and literacy's place within them, were those of control and hegemony, as social relations and work patterns were reformed in accord with other transformations.[9]

The largest goal of schooling and controlled provision of literacy was the process of recreating cultural hegemony. Hegemony is the result of a complex and subtle process, conscious and unconscious, of control, in which the predominance of one class is established over others, by consent rather than by force. In this formulation, it is achieved by the institutions of civil society.[10] That is precisely what most promoters of education sought to accomplish. It lay at the heart of their efforts to reform and systemize schooling to embrace all the children in controlled instruction. The development of hegemony, they learned, depended on a "level of homogeneity, self-consciousness, and organisation" reached by a social class. Neither narrowly economic nor crudely imposed or conspiratorial, their actions derived from a recognition of the needs of society and the oneness of social interests. The task was to achieve that; the school and literacy were the instruments—through disseminating the message of the moral economy—for stability and cohesion.

The attributes that educational promoters attempted to instill in their pupils, particularly the children of the poor and the laborers, constitute what I call the moral bases of literacy—the major purpose of public primary education. These values, central to nineteenth-century educators and to the society for which schooling was to prepare men and women, reveal the perceived connections between the school, the society, and the economy. Morality underlay social relations, social order, economic productivity, and the development of hegemony. The inculcation of values, habits, or attitudes to transform the masses, not skills, was the task of schooling. Literacy properly served as the tool for this training in a close and reinforcing relationship with morality. That was a source of cohesion and order, and the defense of progress in a developing and modernizing capitalist society.

Schooling and the transmission of literacy, in its institutional role, held out an obvious appeal to many. Virtually all nations in the West attempted to respond to the appeal, some much more successfully than others. A traditional force in society, albeit restricted, education could be remolded and redirected—and greatly expanded—to serve its new social roles, not the least of which was the resurrection of restraint and control in times of rapid and disruptive social change: for stability and cohesion, and now for progress. The language of morality reveals a continuity of concern for hegemony and control—in new forms and for new goals—and an emphasis in social thought and perception on the moral failings of individuals and classes as sources of society's severe problems. Despite resistance and conflict, efforts to reimpose control were established, and in some places succeeded in embracing the great mass of children and in providing them with some measure of schooling. Literacy had important functions to serve. For other persons and in other places, responses and uses differed—sometimes greatly.

This book emphasizes what might be termed the "negative" side of literacy, but there was also the "positive," or liberal, side. There is no doubt that literacy had great importance to diverse individuals and groups in virtually all of Western Europe and North America. It contributed to progress in occupation and wealth, cultural participation and acquisition of knowledge and information, struggles for organization and power, abilities and skills, and consequent senses of self- and social worth. Similarly, but not always directly, literacy had a place in the processes that have come to be called "modernization": social, political, and economic development.

Literacy's roles and meaning were complex, but a balance needs to be drawn. What is required is the continued application of the concept of social and cultural *contradictions*. Contradictions should be expected as key aspects of social development whose understanding demands a sensitivity to their presence and their role in the developing social relationships that make up the essence of history and sociology.

The relationship of literacy to the course of development in the nineteenth century resulted in a heightened and more intense pattern of contradictions. We may merely reiterate the role of post-Enlightenment ideologies and clusters of social thought and theory in providing the grounding for most of our current notions about literacy, and stress that many, though not all, of the facts of development contradict those assumptions and theories. A central point of this book, which is also the clearest lesson of the nineteenth century as the "origins of our own times," constitutes much of what I deem a "literacy myth." We are aware of the powerful legacy it holds. Literacy, to be comprehended fully, must be taken as fact and symbol, as well as myth.

## 2. Literacy's Paths and Patterns

### A. France

By the end of the nineteenth century, illiteracy in France had almost been erased.[11] Whereas in 1854, according to parish marriage registers, 31 percent of grooms were illiterate, in 1900 only 5 percent were unable to sign.[12] The decline in illiteracy was consistent, constant, and regular, decreasing commonly at one percentage point per year. Rural areas, as well as urban, were affected (readers may refer to tables and figures in chapter 6).

Women progressed even more strikingly. In 1854, 46 percent of newlywed women were unable to sign; by 1900, only 6 percent could not. Note how favorably their rate compared to men's literacy by the end of the century, in sharp contrast to the late-eighteenth-century differential of 73 to 53 percent illiteracy.[13] Over the entire period, brides' illiteracy plummeted from 73 to 6 percent. Women's progress was also consistent and regular, especially after mid-century, and more so after 1860.[14]

As in the earlier period, geography influenced sexual differences in literacy rates. In 1871–1875, male literacy rates north of the St. Malo-Geneva line were between 80 and 90 percent. Significantly, female progress still tended to follow that of men. More than 70 percent of women who married in the northern region were able to sign. To the south, matters were different. Still, progress was being achieved. In most departments, male signature levels stood above 50 percent. For women, many of the southern departments fared relatively poorly. Development was real, but it was largely within a scaffolding erected in the previous centuries. Continuities, deeply recessed within the soils of culture and society, represented furrows *within* which change was raising the literacy levels of nineteenth-century France.[15]

Analogously, traditional rural and urban distinctions narrowed and blurred, but were not erased. Class and occupational differences in literacy also began to narrow, but within that tendency, they persisted nonetheless firmly. The school came slowly to the poor and working class, more slowly in the countryside and in the south than in the cities and the northern zone. That is neither surprising nor exceptional to France. Although the extent of literacy varied from region to region and state to state within the modernizing West, key traditional social and economic differentials governed growth and change. In much of the West, with the coming of institutionalized provision of literacy, these differentials, or lines of stratification, were transformed and "modernized."[16]

Comparisons department by department show in general that the traditionally "illiterate" departments were "catching up." This process had begun in the eighteenth century; it accelerated after the Revolution, and even more in the nineteenth century.[17] Whereas in the eighteenth century the greatest advance was concentrated largely north of the St. Malo-Geneva line, the following period saw progress more widely distributed, at least for men, in the southern half of France. The period from the end of the eighteenth century, therefore, was one of decisive change, especially with regard to the geographic and sexual stratification of literacy, and with regard to the north-south, St. Malo-Geneva or Maggiolo line.[18] With this change did not come a complete escape from the lines of the past, or an erasure of differences and inequalities. Deeply rooted traditions were not easily removed.

Many historians have emphasized the French Revolution as a positive contributor to the course of literacy. However, literacy was rising before its outbreak in 1789, and continued to do so. The Revolution, virtually all available evidence indicates, did not substitute any elementary institutions or opportunities of consequence for the clerical system that it sought to destroy. Continuity was far more important than changes during or from it. Literacy continued to spread, regardless of changes in control or structure of schools. Jacques Houdaille, in fact, points to a slight decline in literacy as a result of the Revolution's immediate impact.[19]

Although the Revolution did not bring about immediate results in establishing a national system of education, some important abstract principles were formulated, whose role increased with time. Control of education was to pass from church to state. The system was to be coordinated and fulfill national needs, with compulsory elementary education available to all as a fundamental "right." Education was to be "practical and utilitarian and related to the ordinary life of the ordinary citizen," yet it was also to train the reason. French and sciences would be emphasized, with additional instruction in history, geography, and modern languages. There was to be no religious training, but civic duties and rights and loyalty to the government were to be stressed. This imposing agenda could not have been achieved within a short time or during a revolutionary situation. It was, however, an agenda of significance: for the revolutionary moment, but also—and more important—for the remainder of the nineteenth century, and beyond. Something relatively new, and powerful, had been added to the constellation of thought about mass schooling and literacy in society. A basic legacy had been expanded.[20]

Virtually all the available evidence points to the lack of a direct impact from the French Revolution on the course of either schooling or literacy.[21] Plans and legislation were frequent early in the period but were impeded by numerous factors, from social disruptions and financial difficulties to more pressing political issues. The middle class and higher estates remained hesitant about schooling the masses; the church was opposed to state control of schooling; and ongoing social patterns on which school participation of the common people's children depended were disrupted. There was also less interest in elementary than higher education. Popular, especially rural, interest in schooling did not increase, nor did the relevance of schooling to peasant and laboring-class lives. That literacy continued to spread throughout the period is striking.[22]

The Revolution did nothing immediately or directly to transform the elementary school and the processes of the transmission of literacy. Its contribution pointed to the future, to a long, gradual process of transforming structures and sponsorship in French education that required most of the nineteenth century. Whereas literacy grew continuously throughout the period, education was a political, religious, and ideological battleground. Free, compulsory schooling, for both sexes, came only in 1882; literacy did not wait. With great struggle, the educational philosophy of the French Revolution was, more or less, fulfilled.

The revolutionary ideology contributed far more to the wider diffusion of the post-Enlightenment "literacy myth" than to literacy itself. The changes of the period were in the domain of ideas (which became ideology); the continuities were in the sphere of "facts." In terms of ideas, the school became a central image of society's unlimited powers for the happiness of the individual, contrary to the Ancien Regime sense of the limits of the Christian individual. The Revolution infinitely expanded the aims of schooling in comparison to those accorded to it under the church. The school achieved an ideology of its own, reinforcing the importance of literacy and formal schooling for all. The significance was cast in terms of its value to society and state, as well as to the individual. Many of the components of nineteenth-century ideas about literacy crystallized in the revolutionary educational creed; those from the Enlightenment were brought together and given a new vitality. From this time, public provision of basic schooling for all was seen as required for the integration of civil society and the maintenance and continuation of the political state.

During and for some decades after the Revolution, traditional arrangements remained strong. In many places within France, opportunities were not common. Lack of state initiative for public schooling was not the only problem. Shortages of schools, trained teachers, and materials and equipment all obstructed progress. Private and religious institutions fared better than public; yet, they did not transcend the development of the preceding period. Lack of familial resources and more immediate priorities continued to preempt school participation for many children. Seasonal patterns of demand for child labor still had a strong impact. Schooling was not yet free even in the simple sense of tuition fees. Thus, inequalities persisted. Most pronounced were those of class, sex, and region. Such was the context in which rates of literacy rose.

The contradictions and continuities inherent in this process of development are the most powerful elements. Many families in the cities favored the old schools.

That made the continuation and long-term success of the private sector a reality and a block to the acceptance of the republican, public schools. Efforts to "plant" the new schools in central places resulted only in their inaccessibility for many potential pupils. The private instruction offered in the old schools was more flexible, more accessible and localized, much closer to the society it sought to serve. Most families who desired schooling for their youths, consequently, preferred their cultural continuation.[23]

The schools that followed the revolutionary episode were primarily those of the eighteenth century. The church and the teaching corporations were dominant in educational arrangements of the first three decades, at least, of the nineteenth century. The growing demand was one element that stimulated the gradual but continuous rise of literacy that narrowed earlier differentials in its wake. Until the 1830s, what seems most impressive about the role of the state was its indifference, rather than its activism.[24] Elementary schools remained almost untouched, mired in their long-standing problems of finance, accessibility, instructional force, attendance, and the like.

Attempts to centralize schooling were not totally successful. In addition to problems in administration and balancing the interests of church and state, there were also physical, material, and financial obstacles, including the accessibility of schools in dispersed settlements, small population size, geographic barriers, lack of adequate facilities for growing populations, seasonality, and the weather.[25]

Teachers were a major problem. Although plentiful, they were distributed unevenly, and officials were always concerned with their quality. The state attempted to tackle the problem through licensing teachers and establishing training institutions for them. Lack of enforcement power and local and clerical resistance hampered progress.

Officials also confronted the huge task of regulating the *petites écoles*. These private, local institutions, which represented the schools of the masses, competed with the reformed, centralized schools and caused a conflict which long persisted.

State inspectors frequently found deplorable, makeshift classroom conditions, as well as insufficient or inappropriate books and teaching materials. They sought to replace the religiously oriented traditional instruction materials with official readers. This effort met with resistance from religious authorities and some parents.

Finance was a continuing obstacle to centralized schooling. In the early nineteenth century, a local council typically allocated a fixed annual sum from public revenues for schooling, which was also supplemented by monthly payments from children's families. Smaller, poorer communities had difficulty raising money. The quantity and quality of schooling often depended on the availability of local resources.

In the 1830s, the state began subsidizing teachers' salaries in an attempt to upgrade the profession. State central control accompanied this assistance. Some communities resisted, if it meant that local funds were required to meet state grants, but the minimum required to finance a school could now be amassed by many communities previously unable to do so.

The reforming bureaucrats envisioned their national school system as producing citizens who were "self-disciplined, industrious, prudent, . . . ambitious . . . respectful of the national government . . . and possessed of the minimal skills necessary for the fulfillment of military, fiscal, and legal obligations.'' They could not understand the lack of cooperation, indifference, suspicion, and hostility of the masses. They found it hard to accept the fact that not everyone desired the changes they sought or grasped the supreme value of literacy as they did. Especially glaring was the seeming fact that parents did not accept the promise of school for their own and their children's futures.

The people's indifference was a matter not so much of ignorance and a lack of enlightenment as of irrelevance and improbable benefits. Some families who did send their children to school neglected to send them regularly, especially during work seasons, and some communities refused to raise funds or accept state grants. The reformers regarded such action as ignorance, but these communities apparently felt that what facilities they had met local needs, and they saw little need for the reform of *their* school arrangements.

Local elites often resisted schooling the masses, and the opposed paying the costs through taxes. Some local groups and individuals also objected to centralized state schooling on political and religious grounds. They supported other arrangements, from private religious instruction for the poor to clerical schools for the populace. The role of the clergy in elementary education was a battleground throughout the century. Some towns turned from endorsing public schools to the Christian Brothers' schools. Only after the 1830 revolution did the balance shift back toward public school support.

Despite the resistance, the officials and reformers continued their battle to erect a national system of schools. Their concern about the state of popular morality drove them on. They viewed the dangers of city life, factory work, lack of discipline, removal of traditional familial and communal supports, migration, neglect of children, and child labor as threats to the social order. They felt that only by exposing children to ''correct influences'' in the school could the moral shortcomings of subsequent generations improve.[26]

More and more people came to support the schools in this endeavor, and the opposing factions began to come together. Compromise, it was hoped, could settle overt political and religious questions. Here, then, were the uses of universal instruction in literacy, within the proper environment of the public school.

Religious orders contributed to making free instruction available to the poor in towns and cities, using new methods of group instruction and strict discipline, which the public system soon adopted. They concentrated on reading skills for religious life and catechetical learning. During the nineteenth century, the schools of these orders represented an alternative to the secular public schools. Although the state regretted their competition, many accepted their usefulness in bringing moral instruction to those who would otherwise lack it.

Children at work in factories were a new problem, a challenge to the moral order and the responsibility of the state. Policy makers and most officials sought to reduce abuses and maximize opportunities for schooling alongside factory work. Compromise was the game; enforcement was very difficult. Although the effort to get all children into school was hopeless, schools were expanding, duration of schooling was lengthening, and literacy rates were rising, within a reorganization of schooling designed more for sharpening than erasing the lines of social distinction.

As before, girls' schooling lagged behind that of boys. Whereas the central authorities stressed the need for female schools, girls' schooling continued to emphasize preparation for domestic roles. But within new conceptions of the value of schooling, a new place was made for formal training of girls in their future roles. Girls needed moral training, too, and literacy was a useful way to conduct that training. Relatively little development of public opportunities for girls' schooling took place before mid-century; private schools remained the common female route to literacy.

The length of time spent in schools was generally short, and attendance was irregular. Seasonal rhythms, especially in rural areas, disrupted attendance. But the first half of the century saw attendance patterns changing toward regularity.

With increased enrollment and attendance, class size and overcrowding increased. "Graded schools" were one attempt to counter this trend and to make instruction more efficient. That coincided with a trend toward greater social homogeneity. Wealthier families often sent their children to private schools in order to avoid contact with the poor and to obtain a better education than the public schools offered.

Methods may have changed, but subjects remained traditional—reading, writing, and arithmetic. Comprehension received little attention. With largely ungraded classes, high pupil turnover, and irregular attendance, the quality and level of literacy skills could not have been high.[27]

Trends in literacy rates generally paralleled those in school attendance. The epochal process that would come to link formal, national, and systemic institutionalized settings with literacy learning was underway. The closest relationship occurred in communities of between 500 and 2,000 residents, where public schools were available and were the primary means of learning reading and writing.[28] In smaller places, other agencies and informal means were more important. Female literacy was associated more closely with school attendance; girls had fewer alternatives. By 1840, school attendance had become a good predictor of community literacy. Schooling was becoming the normal, expected path to literacy. Financial obstacles continued, but the increased incidence of free schooling helped to raise attendance.

In this period, elementary education did not necessarily lead to higher education or employment opportunities, especially for the popular classes and women. The benefits of literacy were often indirect. Schooling was becoming more acceptable and literacy more appealing; and the savings to families of the school as a "baby-sitter" cannot be discounted.

With the development of commerce and monetization of the economy, more and more peasants and craftspersons found literacy and arithmetic useful. Most trades did not require extensive literacy skills, and apprentices often turned to evening schools and other arrangements to acquire them. Artisans frequently had strong educational traditions and valued literacy, which is reflected in their commonly high literacy rates.[29]

Schooling and literacy were a prerequisite for the professions, administrative work, and commercial and service sector jobs. Schooling was not enough, though; the costs of the required educational investment and of the necessary capital for entry into the career discouraged all but the wealthy. In the growing nineteenth-century bureaucracies, however, there was often a place for the talented sons of poorer families, through state or church sponsorship. This "sponsored mobility" built up hopes, but for most of the century it directly influenced relatively few.

Although some poorer and peasant children were climbing the social ladder, in general the career advantages elementary education bestowed were shrinking:

> [As] all classes were becoming more educated, more literate, the move into schools was for the last to arrive there a defensive one: rather than opening up new opportunities, the early 19th century democratization of primary schooling simply helped to extend to the poor schooling that was already available to the comfortable, schooling that was quickly becoming crucial for the maintenance of even a modest position. . . . Without significant change in the mode of access to higher education, the democratization of primary schooling represented a very limited advantage to the poor.[30]

Whereas the supply of schooling may have changed less than its cost, demand did increase. The rising rates of school attendance and literacy occurred *before* attendance became compulsory in 1882. Educational developments narrowed the long-standing gaps between the rural and the urban and between the sexes at elementary levels. Improved facilities, better access, and subsidies helped to increase the value of the role of literacy and education. Greater demand for schooling in urban places and higher literacy rates reflected the composition of the population as well as the extent of public subsidies and costs of schooling. Commercialization slowly brought people out of agriculture into other sectors of the economy in which need for literacy was greater. At the same time, however, the overall demand, including in the agricultural sectors, was increasing.[31]

Rural women's rates increased in this manner. More was at work than a response to perceived opportunities in industrial settings, which actually placed a low premium on literacy's skill. Migration to cities was selective of literates, and resettlement for illiterates opened some opportunities after childhood for elementary schooling. Still, it seems that change within the agricultural sector was probably more significant than demands for increased schooling incumbent on a shift from agriculture into semiskilled industrial work. At the same time, regional dialects were beginning to disappear. Military service, more standardized schooling, outmigration, and the like played key parts in this cultural transformation.

In all settings, commercial development was a major motor of change. It is more than coincidental that the beginnings of literacy's rise and the commercialization of France began in the second half of the eighteenth century. That development was uneven and irregular, as was literacy's. No mere economic determinism accounts for the former's course, regardless of its central role in shaping lives, life chances, and perceptions of needs.

Falling mortality levels may have influenced parents in their decisions about using familial resources to "purchase" schooling and literacy. With declining child mortality came smaller families, which also could have contributed to increased willingness to spend for schooling.

While not an independent factor, the rising probability that children would survive to adulthood may have contributed to rising concern about them and efforts to increase their schooling and literacy.[32] Regardless of demography's role, there is

no doubt that childhood was being permanently transformed by a process of institutionalization, which transmitted literacy. Childhood was being marked as never
before as the period for learning one's letters.

Although historians have tended to associate literacy positively with industrialization and urban development, such a relationship is neither necessary nor universal. A traditional form of urban life, based around an artisanal and commercial
structure, is generally associated with and dependent upon literacy. However, a
"modern," industrial form of urban life may tend even to depress literacy rates—
at least in its early phases.[33] The French department of the Nord, an area of "modern" industrialization, provides a useful case study.

From the late eighteenth century through the first several decades of the nineteenth, literacy rates in the Nord were at the national level for women and above
it for men. However, after 1840, at a time when literacy was increasing nationally,
the department began to fall behind. The highest levels were found in largely
agricultural districts with traditional towns, followed by areas with rural textile
industry and then the most industrialized districts. Progress was apparent only in
places least affected by new industries.

The lowest literacy levels occurred in recently urbanized areas with "reservoirs
of unskilled labour drawn into them by . . . the newly established textile industries." Whereas older, established commercial centers had a positive impact through
their cultural and educational influence and occupational demands, in newer industrial places the pressures of life and work acted against demands for education
from above for moral and civil training and from below for advancement. The
impact of urban industrialization on increasing population density was detrimental
to chances for schooling and the acquisition of literacy. Immigration from surrounding areas, the demands of families for children's economic contributions,
poverty, and severe strains on facilities combined in this depressing result.

The availability of schooling had no direct association with literacy levels. In
1804, for example, the district with the largest concentration of schools ranked
lowest in male literacy rates. "In the different regions subject to the initial impact
of massive industrialization . . . the school system proved inadequate and insufficient, even detrimental for the development of literacy." Times of initial and
large-scale development of industry and of urban industrialization were not conducive to the spread of literacy. The impact was felt on the workers, available
schools, and other social facilities. With time and the onset of more favorable
socioeconomic conditions, however, negative impacts could be overturned.[34]

Eugen Weber asserts a special educational importance for the last three decades
of the nineteenth century. Although schools and literacy were widespread before
the educational legislation of the Third Republic, the new laws seemed to be particularly effective. To Weber, it was not free, compulsory education but the new
access to teachers, facilities, and roads "that above all made school meaningful
and profitable, once what the school offered made sense in terms of altered values
and perceptions." He claims a sweeping transformation by the end of the century.
"It was only when what the schools taught made sense that they became important
to those they had to teach." People went to school not because it was offered or
imposed but because it was useful.

Despite the odds *against* learning—with rote learning, an emphasis on traditional moral and religious training, and a neglect of writing—literacy levels advanced regularly through the century. The "alphabétisation" of the French was taking place, making gradual inroads on the traditional distinctions between males and females, regions, city and countryside, and social classes. However, the literacy skills commonly obtained could not have been of a high level.

The highest levels of illiteracy persisted in rural departments. Schools remained irrelevant to many peasants, whose lives were ordered around a family economy to which *all* members contributed. Brief periods of attendance could not have transmitted a high quality of literacy, but such schooling helped to push literacy rates upward.

Country schools provided little stimulation for learning. Wealthier parents avoided them and sent their children to private schools. "The children of the poor had access to poorer schools, less time to attend them, and far less reason to make the most of such opportunity. . . ." In some areas, landowners pressed tenants and workers to keep their children out of school so that the future work force would not be subverted by contact with learning.

Many peasant families were also deterred by lack of access—long distances from the school and poor roads; illiteracy and low educational development usually persisted in widely dispersed areas. However, poverty and indifference were more important factors. Poor, isolated departments had low attendance and low literacy. The irregular attendance of those children who did enroll was also detrimental to effective learning. In rural areas, most children attended only in winter, when there was no work. Many such scholars probably forgot what they had learned in the preceding term.

Regional differences and inequalities were narrowing slowly. The law of 1881 provided for free schooling, but progress toward it was uneven. Many local notables were reluctant to subsidize schools that their own children neither needed nor would attend and that might prepare competitors for their sons. Social distinctions between poor, non-fee-paying pupils and paying pupils resulted in discrimination and abuse. Such a free education might not induce a desire to learn in a stigmatized youngster. Families could not always spare their children for even free schooling, and some could not afford the needed books, materials, or clothing.[35]

There was an increasing popular demand for literacy and schooling throughout the century. The popular classes began to accept the value of schooling not because it was made compulsory and free but because it became "the thing to do." They also began to comprehend the usefulness of instruction. There were high rates of literacy before mass opportunities for schooling; functionality, social pressures, and cultural promotion influenced decisions about the usefulness of literacy and elementary schooling, and these decisions were made more slowly in the countryside and among the poor.[36]

Literacy's large-scale failure to transform the social structure contributed to persisting indifference toward education. The urban poor had some use for literacy and hope of improving their own or their children's position with that learning, but literacy skills were little needed or profitable in the countryside. School learning often was seen as an irrelevant luxury.

There were some experiences that led people to consider literacy useful. Migration

was one. In many instances, migrants and their children grasped the value of schooling and its utility in new, larger, more complex urban settings. Illiteracy and,
especially, poverty were important determinants of migration. Migrants probably
found reading, writing, and arithmetic more likely to be useful in their work and
for maintaining contacts by mail. Even if their abilities seem unimpressive in comparison with the achievements of the native-born, migrants often exhibited a higher
rate of literacy than the population of the areas from which they originated. How
they fared in the cities, however, depended on qualities beyond literacy.

In a study of nineteenth-century Marseille, William Sewell, Jr. surprisingly discovered that sons of peasants (immigrants) moved into nonmanual occupations
considerably more often than sons of workers. The peasants' sons had a lower rate
of literacy (67 percent) than the workers' sons (70 percent), so other factors were
obviously at work.

Sewell posited that the apparently paradoxical success of the peasants' sons lay
in reasons beyond achieved characteristics such as literacy or competitive advantages
in the labor market. He looked to values for the answer: many workers chose to
remain in their traditional working-class world; they identified with their class,
occupations, community, traditions, rituals, and sanctions. Peasants' sons had no
reason for such a preference; in addition, the peasants' uprooting may have made
them more responsive to opportunities. Since workers' sons who migrated to Marseille also had a higher rate of entry into nonmanual occupations, migration likely
helps to explain these achievements. Literacy did not play an independent, determinative role.[37]

In anticipated benefits and striving to better prepare themselves, migrants had an
impetus for acquiring literacy. That held even more true for their children. Perceptions, school promotion, and concrete needs and benefits combined into a new,
strong stimulus toward acquiring literacy. In a number of areas, literacy rates were
highest where there were many migrants.[38]

The army was another experience that influenced the course of literacy. Throughout the nineteenth century, conscripts tended to exhibit higher levels of literacy than
others. Of course, their age and youth made their status a reflection of recent progress
in the dissemination of literacy, the expansion of the school system, and changing
attitudes about needs for these skills. The law of 1872, which gave advantages to
men who could read and write and threatened illiterate conscripts with an additional
year of service, was a direct motivation for the acquisition of literacy. School
authorities used the law to persuade parents to send their children to school.

Military service itself was seen as a school. By the Third Republic, universal
service was favored by many, partly because they saw it as a means for making
instruction more common. The French defeat at the hands of the compulsorily
educated and nearly universally literate Prussians was not only a national shame
but a boon to education and military training. The conscription law of 1818 tied
promotion to literacy and led to the establishment of regimental schools, which
taught not only literacy but also the French language for recruits who understood
only their regional patois. The army also taught the value of cleanliness, discipline,
and obedience. In the end, many peasant recruits became migrants, unwilling to
return to their places of origin after the lessons learned in the service.[39]

A third factor leading to literacy was the growing number of public and private service employees, who were required to have a certificate of elementary studies. One example of this phenomenon, which increased in the later decades of the century, is the small school of Mazières, publicized by Roger Thabault. There was an increased amount of occupational mobility from the lower levels of society through literacy and elementary education by the last three decades of the century. More persons of different classes perceived new opportunities. However, studies confirm the persistence of the strong, often determining role of social origins and the key place of the school in the intergenerational reproduction of the social class order.

Nevertheless, high school attendance rates in areas that long had had high rates of illiteracy, as well as the literacy rates themselves, indicate the increased recognition of new possibilities and the school as a link to them. The hopes for migration to a city, a nonmanual or nonfarm job, better living conditions, and greater material benefits were major aspects of the seeking of new opportunities through schooling. Others included the functionality of reading and writing and the desire to improve one's position.[40]

The schools sought to do more than encourage mobility and assist in its achievement. They struggled to " 'modify the habits of bodily hygiene and cleanliness, social and domestic manners, and the way of looking at things and judging them.' " The school was to reform the people most in need of reformation, such as rural peasants, as well as the urban working class. That was the expected, long-sought-after end of schooling: the product of properly controlled training in literacy. Instruction stressed personal conduct, attributes, character, habits, and attitudes. Cleanliness, labor, justice, knowledge, and the school itself were taught as duties and a secular morality.

The "greatest function" of the modern school was to teach "a new patriotism beyond the limits naturally acknowledged by its charges." The school was first a socializing agent. The message was communicated most effectively together with reading and writing. The school's task included not only national and patriotic sentiments but establishing unity in a nation long divided by region, culture, language, and persisting social divisions of class and wealth. Learning to read and write involved the constant repetition of the civic and national catechism, in which the child was imbued with all the duties expected of him: from defending the state to paying taxes, working, and obeying laws. In republican France, especially after 1871, national defense ranked among the highest duties for the young to assimilate. Instruction in the history and geography of France got a major boost in the 1870s—subjects of the utmost importance to which literacy was applied.[41]

To a considerable extent, the campaign for "alphabétisation" and schooling succeeded by the early years of the twentieth century. Success was not unambiguous, however. For many children, the literacy and language that the schools taught was not their native tongue. What was dispensed and required was an alien, artificial language; that was true also for French-speakers. French language and literacy were taught "largely through the discipline of dictations." As one result, many pupils learned to speak freely in French, but had trouble writing. Imitation was common as the result of rote learning of written expression. As Weber remarks, "Education created stupidity by setting up standards of communication that many found difficult to attain." Schooling and learning by rote were divorced from assimilation, which retarded the schools' progress. Words also were divorced from reality. Children were able to spell, but the syllables held no meaning for them. They read but did not understand. Many had difficulty identifying words learned in French with objects around them. In this context, literacy levels reached new heights, and linguistic unity was being created.

The process of literacy's transmission sometimes exacerbated generational tensions. In many families, illiterate adults had to depend on children to conduct tasks that were becoming more important, from accounting to correspondence and reading documents and newspaper items. With information and shifting values came new gaps between generations. Literacy and its dissemination also accentuated other tensions. For example, manual labor was devalued, or, rather, aversion to it was heightened by the teachings of the school.[42] Scholastic values posed problems for the labor force, for one's own expectations, and for the larger culture. For how many youths were expectations and ambitions created that society and economy could not meet?

Historians often have considered literacy and communications to be a stimulus to politicization and social mobilization.[43] However, Tony Judt, in an interesting study of Provence, found "absolutely no correlation." Politics and new ideas came to rural areas in ways that reached literates and illiterates alike. Oral transmission was the key. Public, social reading of newspapers by literates enabled anyone to be conversant in politics.

By the end of the century, the role of literate artisans was changing. Except in the most economically backward or isolated communities, the peasants did not seem to need their leadership—"in part because it was no longer readily available." That does not mean that artisans were not among the politically active radicals or among those reading to circles. With advantages and status, they had much to contribute. Literacy could bring them prominence, but not control. Peasants were therefore not disadvantaged; illiteracy neither kept them from political movements nor placed them under the dominations of artisans. A few literates played a key role in this context, but it was shaped by the environment and the collectivity.[44]

In French history, the negative impact of regional languages has been a persistent theme. Regions in which the native tongue was other than French were places in which the spread of literacy was retarded in the eighteenth and nineteenth centuries. In 1789, six million people in France relied on foreign languages and dialects: Flemish, Celtic, Basque, German, and thirty patois. At the time of the Revolution, systematic language intervention was attempted to deal with the problem of communication with non-French-speaking citizens. At first decrees were translated into the major dialects to make them more accessible to the people. After 1792, however, came a time of "linguistic terrorism." This new movement, rooted in the politics, ideologies, and class conflicts of the major factions, attacked dialects in an attempt to establish "one people, one nation, one language."

From 1790 to 1794, proposals for grammatical and orthographic reform abounded. Idioms and dialects were considered unrepublican and reactionary. Yet, the evidence does not support an equation of patois with counterrevolution; conterrevolutionaries tended to reside in more modern, French-speaking areas. Linguistic purges, therefore, could not resolve political problems.

Language was becoming more an ideological question than a matter of utility. The shift from linguistic tolerance to denunciation of patois as an enemy of equality took place along with terror against other supposed enemies. This spirit held through the Directory. Its ideological radicalism was diluted among the poor, however. Efforts to establish a system of primary education with French-speaking teachers were abandoned, and patois was left to its own fate. Reform from the top replaced more thoroughgoing efforts.

Success did not come even among the bourgeoisie or in Paris. The final unraveling of the linguistic and grammatical reform occurred with the rise of Napoleon. Latin was reinforced, although it remained "a weapon turned against the lower class." The masses were to be neutralized, and patois was not tolerated. "French might yield to Latin, but not to any other tongue."

Despite the failed attempts at reform and the occasionally counterproductive efforts, by 1815 French was spoken much more widely than before the Revolution. Processes *beyond* legislation and political debate were more powerful. National dislocation forced the language upon draftees, newly elected officials, refugees, prisoners, and others, "but many more people . . . learned to speak French because they wanted to. . . ."

With the spirit of national linguistic development and increased intolerance of dialect, class differences in language and literacy were reinforced—new divisions developed that persisted despite the slowly, if widely, diffusing popular literacy and acceptance of the French language. On the eve of the nineteenth century, the elements of new differentials that maintained cultural and social stratification emerged even as elements of the need for universal literacy and language were propelled.[45]

Despite the state and school policy of Francification, patois persisted. The problem was that for children in a number of places, French was not the language they brought to school. Learning problems, especially in oral abilities, were a common complaint. The use of patois was forbidden in school, but resistance was common. The environment beyond the classroom reduced the effectiveness of attempted controls; "most children came from patois-speaking families."[46]

Resistance did not prevent linguistic change. The penetration of French was seen as the advance of civilization and progress. Migration, hopes for urban and white-collar work, armed-forces training, and the growing volume of print materials stimulated the increase in French speaking, reading, and writing in the countryside. The use of French came quickly to be a sign of social status. However, the shift away from a deeply imbedded and valued regional tongue was not made easily or without regret and resistance.[47]

Where progress in eliminating illiteracy was slowest, natives did not speak French. Perhaps one-fifth of the population fell into this group in 1863. Teaching children a language that they seldom heard was a complicated challenge. Consequently, instruction had little impact on many; they returned to patois upon leaving school and forgot their French. Factors of environment, motivation, hopes, and perceptions were required for language learning to be more effective and reinforced. Nor were many teachers, especially in poorer, rural areas, well versed in French. Literacy thus acquired, in a "foreign" language, was often *not* of the highest quality.

For the school and the state, the results, although limited, were positive. The symbolism learned at school created a new language, which provided shared points of reference. The schools taught, through literacy, a unifying and integrating idiom that went beyond words. References and identities of nation, state, and authority were learned. The values and morals deemed so crucial were transmitted.

On the other hand, consequences included alienation, intergenerational rifts, and weakening of rural values and communities. The uses of French and patois differed. The latter emphasized the richly particular, the descriptive, and the everyday, while the former was more formal, general, and abstract. The pupils', and older persons', mentalities and ways of thought must have been affected. At best, it took some time before the French learner ceased to think in his or her native language. If one remained in an environment in which oral patois was most common, strains could be severe. Transitions could be hard to make, with pain and social and cultural costs to bear.[48]

Regional languages had many implications for the history of literacy. Contemporary commentators pointed endlessly to the negative roles of patois—a roadblock to progress and to the establishment of civic morality through the schools' transmission of literacy (literacy in French, that is). However, there were areas in which non-French languages dominated, but in which literacy levels did *not* suffer in consequence. Intervening factors of geography, economy, and communications were significant in these places.

The Morbihan area of Brittany is a good example. Depending on one's residence within the region, literacy levels did not always correlate with language. Some Francophone cantons had lower-than-average literacy levels, while some Breton cantons were above average. Among the latter, for instance, were an urban administrative center, a maritime area, and areas adjacent to the "linguistic frontier." Cantons with the highest rates of literacy were mixed linguistically and maritime and contained two principal cities (French was used there more often than in the countryside). Finally, the cantons with the lowest levels of literacy were entirely Breton, situated in the interior of the region, and rural.

Occupations also reveal similar stratification: low-ranking workers in Breton cantons had much lower literacy rates than their French-speaking peers, but the contrast with merchants and artisans was less. Location of residence, status of work, and local economies all cut into a direct literacy-language linkage. Social status and wealth combined with geography to determine linguistic-literacy barriers within Brittany. Similar relations held elsewhere.

During the second half of the century, new dynamics emerged. Literacy rates rose rapidly in the most disadvantaged areas, and even more in the French-speaking regions. The growth in literacy in Breton regions was, relatively, less of an increase, as they shared less in the process of "alphabétisation" than those from French-speaking places. The race they ran, in terms of the acquisition of literacy and the potential advantages perceived, was not so victorious when examined in this way. Such progress, no doubt with great pains for individuals and loss to the traditional culture, left the Breton areas actually further behind than they had been. Differentials were not erased. That is what is often termed a process of "modernization."

The levels of inequality were deep and inescapable in the nineteenth century, despite great progress. The promise of literacy and schooling was not met. The effort to bring the public school to the non-French-speaking was successful in raising the rate of literacy, but in the consequences of schooling, the results were not leveling or equalizing. The democratic promise of the democratic school was not achieved. National integration and cultural-linguistic homogenization had obvious limits.

Poverty, culture and history, and sociopolitical inequalities were closely connected with regional language development and illiteracy. For example, those places where oral culture was strongest tended to lack a strong tradition in the written language. Traditions continued to differ from the developing national culture. Social and cultural needs were met differently. Basque areas are one example. Resistance to centralization and encroachment of the state sometimes resulted in resistance to the school and literacy as aspects of the intended penetration. It was not, however, a resistance to literacy per se. Poverty also frequently obstructed the growth of literacy in such areas. "France pauvre, France orale, France rebelle."[49]

One truism about the more developed areas of the West in the nineteenth century centers on the great expansion of publishing and distribution, sometimes called the era of the popular press or a democratization of literature. This conceptualization misses developments in popular literature and the distribution of cheaper print materials during the preceding two centuries. Nevertheless, it is clear that, owing in part to technological developments in mechanized printing and related advances, popular demand for reading materials, entrepreneurial interests, cultural reforms, and the spread of literacy and schooling, an unprecedented level of publishing took place during this century. Literacy did not *cause* this outpouring; the volume of literature and publishing in any society is a poor guide to levels of literacy. Regardless, mass consumable literature expanded greatly during this period. A "mass" culture, more or less, was born.[50]

As printing entered the industrial age, interest grew in printed information. Class differences in culture furthered the development of literary forms. Commerce and entrepreneurs responded with new forms of production and dissemination, from street literature to serials, newspapers, and new libraries. Part of the story lies in the laws of supply and demand, but cultural and economic forces put new pressures on authors and publishers to locate and develop markets. Some sought only pecuniary success; others to reform the masses. Some sought political influence; others to amuse and titillate. Persisting illiteracy and levels of literacy suited only to unsophisticated reading put limits on the scope of production and sales. Individuals, of course, need not have read alone to secure the benefits of print.

From about the 1820s, attempts were made to print proper reading materials for the masses. "Good books" were Christian, moralizing, and reformist, not the most appealing to many among the popular classes. It seems that they reached mostly the middle class and those who hoped to rise to it. "The poorer inhabitants of urban centers, assuming that they could read, lacked the privacy in which to read a book, the light by which to read it, and most probably the time and energy to attempt it."

Change was slow, and major change took place only after mid-century. That is when "popular libraries" in larger industrial towns competed for the popular interest and mind, and when "savings societies" (e.g., for newspaper subscriptions) are recorded in small provincial towns. School libraries were also growing in number, but they lent few books before the last decades of the century. The impact of print remained restricted and concentrated within cities.

Despite the printing revolution, "novels, children's books, and other 'respectable' works selling at a price equivalent to one or two days' wages were not aimed at the working class, but at the small bourgeoisie." The growth of "taste" in literature was long a middle-class phenomenon. Many indicators point to the increasing demand for literature, but also to class differences in quantity and quality of materials. The few working people who purchased much literature tended to acquire print from street vendors: cheap abridgments of old but popular tales (Robinson Crusoe, Telemachus, Paul and Virginia, Bayard's life, and Aesop's fables). On the whole, however, the urban working class read rather little, concentrating more on the press and even shorter cheap forms of street literature.[51]

An explosion of print may have taken place, but it was restricted in its audience. First, the press and novels were centralized in Paris; circulation was in large part urban, and novels were overwhelmingly bourgeois in appeal and moral bias. Second, prices remained very high through the middle of the century; working people could not afford the newer, expanding classes of print and literature. Any popularization and increasing access brought the press to the lower bourgeousie, now more likely than ever to be literate and wanting to confirm their middle-class status and cultural airs with the level of literature that they assumed was properly stylish, current, and status-conferring, but still "respectable."

Prices were still high for this social group until two innovations in the distribution of literature: *cabinets de lecture* and the serial novel. Rising demand intersected with literary entrepreneurship in shaping the popularity particularly of the romantic novel. Popular fiction and poetry were the rage from the 1820s through the 1840s. The taste for literature among the middle class postdated the two-decade rapid rise and fall of romantic fare. With this influence, the book trade expanded; it began to assume aspects of its modern structure.

The *cabinets* may have been the most important outlets in large cities. In an age in which public libraries were few and books were relatively expensive, they were the reading public's most accessible source. They rented books at low fees, bringing them to many who otherwise could not afford them. Most specialized in one genre of popular fare, maintaining catalogues of their holdings. Supply and demand, in the context of increasing opportunities for schooling and rising rates of literacy, grew in this manner.

Although some among the highest ranks of the working class had their interests whetted and their literacy ability challenged, the middle class supplied most readers, borrowers, and buyers. They had the surplus wealth and the leisure to expend on the new popular literature. Others gained the means and interest more slowly. Popular culture did not mean unified or homogeneous culture, even in the cities. Although long a middle-class phenomenon, reading of this newer and accessible popular fare was condemned as pernicious and immoral. Such censure was not reserved solely for the popular class.[52] Serial novels and the daily press fed on the same demands.

There were radically different rates of literacy within the working class, and its ranks were sharply stratified by status, skill, wealth, residence, income, and traditions. Changing economic conditions and industrial organization presented difficulties for workers in their efforts to maintain or gain their reading and writing skills. Traditions of oral reading continued in the cities as in the countryside. The workplace, cafés, street corners and squares, and the home were all common places for collective readings.

The newspaper was one literate medium seized by working people, especially for political ends. During radical activities in the 1830s and 1840s, for example, many workers' papers were born. Almost all were short-lived, however, in the face of expenses that outran resources, censorship and surveillance, and massive court fines. In addition to political matters, social and moral reforms also were promoted.

Statistics on duration of newspaper publishing and circulation do not support interpretations of major influences on public opinion. Those data must be qualified by the wider circulation, through oral means, that these organs had. These included not only reading circles but also the societies and working-class lending libraries. These papers were the domain principally of the higher-status, skilled, and often literate workers, such as the silk workers of Lyon, who sacrificed to secure literacy for themselves and their children. Workers' papers met real needs by printing lists of current piece rates and reporting which firms were hiring or filing for bankruptcy. They were aspects of working-class life and collective organization, at least among the upper levels. They had an impact on ideology and consciousness, shaping and reflecting attitudes, propagandizing, and informing. That was a function that print could serve far more easily, quickly, and widely than nonprint means.

This impact was not diffused to all workers; it was concentrated, relatively if not absolutely, among certain sectors of the trades and strata of the class. The press's development and utilization took place in periods of need, rising consciousness, and high interest. The significance of print and literacy varied from time to time, place to place, and group to group. Social structure, geography, economy, traditions, patterns of interaction, and many other factors were highly important.

Just as literacy came more slowly to the working class (and even more gradually to the people of the countryside), the habit of reading and the uses of literacy were less established, perhaps less needed, than among the middle classes. Such was especially the case among the unskilled, the semiskilled, and the poor.[53] The dream of a literate, educated popular class was realized slowly. Although it was a dream envisaged in widely different forms by middle-class reformers, the state, many among the religious, and the workers and the people themselves, it is doubtful that many were wholly satisfied. The gains of literacy neither erased the many levels of inequality nor remade the population of France into the form wished by many of the dreamers.

For the countryside and the peasant, colporteurs and peddlers brought almanacs and other fare for perhaps two centuries. Print was not absent, although the volume no doubt depended on the accessibility of an area. Evidence for 1860–61, from a Ministry of Education survey of local reading habits, reported that reading was rare, and novels almost nonexistent. That seems as true for the towns as for the countryside. There was also evidence of "bad" books: "immoral serials," almanacs, songbooks, tales, and the like.

Two patterns—nonexistent or infrequent reading, and "improper" reading—were present. That is what fed new printing and publishing industries and was how many in the populace practiced their new abilities. They seldom read the books in school libraries, except perhaps those meant for children. Neither approved moral fare nor technical, scientific, or agricultural materials were attractive to many. When they read, it was most likely " 'small writings . . . that are the library of the poor and the first books of childhood': almanacs, calendars, yearbooks, chapbooks, collections of tales and stories, songs, prophecies, canticles, ballads, accounts of recent events and judgments of criminal courts, primers and the *Croix de Dieu*." Continuities in supply, as well as taste and demand, linked the growing number of potential readers to the most popular types of literature of the past. Newer were accounts of trials and songs with political overtones, speeches of the Revolution and Republic, and catechisms of the Republic. In this regard, one suspects less division between the town and the countryside than is often presumed.

Itinerant peddlers and colporteurs continued to bring this material to rural areas. Religious items and pictures of all kinds were especially popular. There were also *canards*, small pages that were illustrated and discussed as news items, included useful tips, and provided calendars. Peddlers also carried books of history, practical advice literature, collections of model letters, and "immoral" volumes of stories. Almanacs were the single most significant item—at least in popularity. Bollème concluded that they were *the* reading matter of the poor, those who had little time, and those who read little. In the mid-nineteenth century, it was estimated that "15 million Frenchmen learned the history of their country and its laws, the world's great events, the progress of their sciences, their duties, and their rights only through the almanac."

A gap between the literary fare and its use, between the country and the city, persisted throughout most of the century, narrowing toward its end. Homogenizing tendencies progressed, along with, but more slowly than, literacy levels and schooling. More current news reached the countryside; moral stories and collections arrived with traditional fare in the peddlers' packs. Newspapers replaced the *canards*. The image industry declined as newspapers circulated more widely; pictures and broadsides were becoming hard to find by the end of the century.

Improved communications and transportation were perhaps more important than literacy levels. The press and book trade actively sought new markets in previously "printless" places. Change was very slow, and we must be alert to collective use of both books and newspapers to understand their increasing presence in the countryside. Gradually, the content became accessible to the peasants, who were increasingly likely to have some literacy ability.

We must be cautious in imputing the impact of this complex cultural and political transformation. In general, Weber is probably correct that scales changed, as did awareness levels. A greater extent of common information and perhaps consciousness developed. "As with the schools, as with politics, the press advanced both the process of homogenization and the level of abstract thought. The cultural tradition reflected in the press leaned to generalities, favored national or universal themes over local, specific ones." To presume that that "in due course rubbed on the readers' thinking" and language is perhaps too much. What we see are tendencies of the progress of print and literacy's impacts, rather than personality or mental transformation. The levels of literacy, which were often rather limited, were still enough for the abstraction of information, selectively, from newspapers, for amusement from stories and collections of tales, and, of course, for participation in collective events, though not always for abstract thought. No complete homogenization occurred, even if some differences blurred.[54]

Literacy's potential uses and impacts were many. Demands were various and diffuse. The evidence points to the conservative, continuous, and contradictory impacts of print and changing levels of individual access to it, more often than to radical, linear consequences. Both tendencies were real and present. Neither the proponents of literacy transmission for cultural hegemony and moral reform, nor those of individual and collective action for change were wholly successful. In a supportive, conscious, and integrated communal context, the contribution of the press, working-class libraries, print communications media, and literacy *could* be especially valuable. Literacy also had direct economic, as well as traditional, significance. With such factors combined, literacy and print *could* be powerful tools.

In other contexts, supporting factors were not always so strong. The demand for literacy often had an economic component. In accounting for the "alphabétisation" of France, Jacques Ozouf is right to insist on the demand side; that is a needed correction to the usual concentration on supply of schools. Both sides of the equation were required for literacy to develop. But we cannot remove the impact of the school. Both it and literacy were required for the path that development took.

Demand cut both ways, and its boundaries could often be narrowly inscribed by functional, economistic considerations. Demand came from above and below, and was increasingly met in the institution of the school. That was a process of development that occupied much of the century, with earlier demands being met by informal, clandestine, clerical, private, and state-public schooling. Social institutions sought to mediate social changes and perceptions that led to growing interest in the acquisition of literacy and the social order itself. The needs for order and control, the reestablishment and maintenance of cultural hegemony, played an obvious role. To them are added the needs of employers for disciplined industrial workers and literate service employees. Popular demands, if not wholly congruent, overlapped with these forces.

Opposition was also present. Many feared the consequences of an educated lower class and peasantry. They eventually were proved incorrect in many of their fears. The causal attributions of rising literacy to the revolutions of 1830 and 1848, which brought outpourings of anti- as well as popular educational statements, are too weak to be accepted. Clericals and notables who struggled against the growth of literacy and schooling lost their battle. Increasingly, however, they turned to conservative uses of controlled learning; in this regard they cannot be said to have been wholly defeated, even if the state system emerged as most dominant.

The legacy of the Revolution was successively achieved, on one hand, in the progress of schooling, and, on the other, in the "alphabétisation" of *les Français*. But its spirit—the aspect of its thrust that centered on free-thinking, liberal, independent citizens trained up in preparation for worthwhile contributions to society—was not as well satisfied. That power was not within the realm of elementary instruction in reading and writing and in the institutions that disseminated it, public or otherwise. Nor did the builders of the system fully desire that end. Certainly most of the competition did not seek to provide a "liberating literacy."

The floor of the social pyramid was raised, but many revealing differentials continued or were added. Discrimination against female education, for example, was not canceled in the fact of the impressive increases in women's literacy and school attendance. School attendance did not transform young women's expectations of the benefits of work, or reshape their occupational opportunities. The principal social groups saw some narrowing of traditional differentials in literacy levels. With the hierarchical expansion of educational systems and more complete class-cultural formations came new means of maintaining differentials and stratification. High rates of popular literacy, by the end of the century, did not threaten the social structure or its social divisions.

Although literacy levels rose throughout France, and many differences were narrowed or blurred, important geographic differentials also persisted. Deep continuities within the social structure played an important part in the processes of change and the new opportunities that arose with rising literacy. Family strategies for survival and family economies that determined schooling chances were not reduced by the commercial and industrial, agrarian and urban transformations of the society. At the century's end, schooling of children remained an option secondary to more pressing material needs, regardless of the inherent value that literacy and education were assuming. Literacy was *not* a skill that many children acquired easily or without familial sacrifice. That so many more were gaining some exposure to the schools for at least a short time attests to the power of its presumed value and popular acceptance. Its contribution to the lives of men and women remains a critical question, rather than a logical conclusion. Urban *and* industrial development in time raised standards of living and made schooling more accessible, but sometimes had negative consequences on life and literacy.

In evaluating popular demand, these considerations need to be taken into account. There can be no doubt that real demand from the working class was expressed and that even in the most isolated peasant areas, indifference was passing by the end of the era. A number of elements are suggested by the phrase "popular demand," not all new. There is, for example, the level of dignity, pride, and respect of the literate person. That was perhaps first an urban sentiment that spread slowly but widely. Related are issues of perceptions of the economic need for, or at least usefulness of literacy. Its value was perceived by many, and also promoted. Related were hopes for the children: first, but not exclusively, sons. Their betterment was sought by more and more parents.

Plans to migrate to places in which greater opportunities were expected to relate to literacy increased. Literacy was useful in the search for urban adaptation, migration, work, social mobility, and rewards. But equally, it was neither an absolute requirement *nor* a guarantee of success. It probably also related to frustration and alienation. Nevertheless, the social and economic realities of change combined, differentially and irregularly, with changing perceptions of the necessity and utility of literacy. This conjuncture bore fruit in popular, growing demands, which in turn resulted in increasing rates of literacy. Cultural and class dimensions also promoted rising interest in literacy from below.

Neither forces from above, of conservatives or liberals, nor those from below alone determined the path of French literacy. Continuities, especially the long-term continuation of growth, were important. No school system or enormous state contribution was required for literacy to rise—within certain class, regional, and sexual limits. In the nineteenth century, however, much changed. Social, political, economic, and ideological changes put the importance of a literate population in a startlingly new light. New mechanisms for social learning, as well as skill learning, were required. New levels of popular demand arose in the same context as that which sought to control the process and results of learning: the uses of literacy. The results were less than a consensus on schooling and literacy, although the consequences tended more to the needs of the society and the economy than to the individual or the "people." That the bottom line must remain ambiguous and contradictory to its latter-day interpreters should not be surprising.[55]

## B. Germany

The German lands were not a unified national state until the late nineteenth century. Different states and principalities had different traditions, as well as different governing structures and policies. These resulted in different courses for literacy. Virtually everywhere, Enlightenment ideas intersected with perceptions of social change and development to give a new level of interest to literacy and schooling. Both elements came increasingly to be viewed as parts of the same parcel, dedicated to the same social, cultural, political, and economic ends. A conceptualization that binds the two too tightly risks distortion, especially if one attempts to deduce levels and trends in literacy solely from educational policy and schooling legislation. The fit grew tighter in many areas, but was itself a result of historical developments.

TABLE 7.1

**Illiteracy (neither reading nor writing) in Population Aged 10 Years and More in the Kingdom of Prussia in 1871**

| Province | M | (percentages) | F |
|---|---|---|---|
| Prussia | 27 | | 34 |
| Brandenburg (including Berlin) | 3 | | 8 |
| Pomerania | 8 | | 15 |
| Posnania | 32 | | 41 |
| Silesia | 11 | | 17 |
| Saxony | 2 | | 5 |
| Schleswig-Holstein | 3 | | 5 |
| Hanover | 4 | | 8 |
| Westphalia | 4 | | 7 |
| Hessen-Nassau | 2 | | 5 |
| Rhineland | 5 | | 10 |
| The whole kingdom | 10 | | 15 |

Source: Carlo Cipolla, *Literacy and Development in the West,* (Hardmonsworth: Penguin, 1969), p. 85.

Variation was striking throughout the territories. In the unified Kingdom of Prussia in 1871, the rate of literacy of those aged ten or over was high, at 85–90 percent. This level placed Germany, or more specifically Prussia, among the most literate places within Europe. But beneath an accomplishment that brought much praise and competition was a more variegated and less consistently high rate of success. The relatively high rates of *illiteracy* in Prussia proper and Posen reflect the population of destitute Polish peasants and the traditional antieducational stance of eastern Prussian landed noblemen.

Geographic and class variations were not new to the second half of the century. Nor were they erased during literacy's march toward universality. Almost everywhere during the "literacy transition," traditional social differentials tended to be maintained or, in time, replaced by new class and cultural divisions. Despite its potential, literacy seldom served as a leveling factor. These data also highlight the sexual differential common to literacy's history. The ratio of female to male illiteracy typically was about 3:2–2:1; the German case, with long traditions of literacy and schooling, was no exception.

Another persisting gap appears in the religious adherence of the population. For 1871, the census revealed the following rates of illiteracy for Prussia:

| Religion | M (percentage) | F |
|---|---|---|
| Protestants | 7 | 11 |
| Catholics | 15 | 22 |
| Dissidents | 5 | 9 |
| Jews | 7 | 13 |

But this extent of illiteracy for German Catholics (including many Poles) was comparatively low for Europe. Religion was not the sole factor that determined literacy's diffusion. In comparison with the Prussian Catholic rate, Catholic adult literacy in Ireland was about 40 percent, and in Italy about 69 percent. On the one hand, there is the expected association of literacy with centuries of Protestant tradition; but on the other, there is no universal pattern for Catholicism. When the net is broadened to include England and the southern United States, a Protestant-literacy connection breaks down in the face of more important mediating factors. Virtually all non-homogeneous national areas camouflage sharp internal variations within their aggregate rates.[56]

Continuities shaped the developments of the period. Given the heritage and the new commitment to compulsory institutional systems of mass schooling, it is not surprising that no more than 10 percent of Prussian military recruits could not write around 1840, or 5 percent in 1851; that only 5 percent of grooms and brides could not sign in 1881–1882; or that laws were relatively hard to evade.

The dynamics of German literacy development are cloudy. The outlines of the institutional structures and the history of legislation are well known, but they do not tell the whole story. The state of Baden provides a useful case study. It was an area with a pervasive history of official commitment to the written word. By the mid-nineteenth century, most of Baden's population could read and write; universal literacy was achieved by the third quarter of the century. The progress of schooling was nearly equivalent with that of literacy.

The Badenese case shows that these phenomena cannot be explained satisfactorily by administrative and legal history alone. Models of school systematization neither as political and economic modernization nor as liberal encouragement to advancement through education account for its history. Rather, Baden reveals the vital role of the dialectic between popular demands and needs and state-bureaucratic policy enactment and the shaping factors of context. Different interests intersected in determining the course of literacy and schooling, from elites and officials to families and individuals. The path of social development and economic transformation shaped, but did not universally determine, patterns of literacy and schooling.

Baden's history also illustrates the fallacy of explanation by religious adherence. A confessionally mixed area, about two-thirds of its population was Catholic; religious affiliation varied regionally. Despite the global tendencies to relate religion to literacy, at the community level no simple relationship is found. Any such differentiation seems to have disappeared before the end of the eighteenth century "in the face of stricter enforcement of school attendance and tremendous advances in literacy."

Although the seeds of systematic popular school development should be located in the eighteenth century, the struggle to erect integrated, hierarchical systems belongs to the nineteenth. Neither literacy nor local school opportunities awaited that time; real development on both accounts took place before the chronological divide of "modernity." With the nineteenth century came a more active effort at central state coordination, intervention into the local communities, and attempts to develop specialized, professional corps of teachers. Local context shaped alternatives and actions.

In Baden, schools were common even before the reform movement. Pre-nineteenth-century schools were usually religious, with teachers subject to the supervision of local pastors. The community's responsibility was expressed in finance and administration, selection of teachers, and setting of curriculum and tuition fees. A large degree of local initiative and authority was realized, despite the formal power of the churches. Limiting the extent of local autonomy was one major change of the nineteenth-century reforms.

Centralized state school systems were relatively easy to establish in the German lands, where there were existing church schools and early compromise between state and church. Early-nineteenth-century consolidation, as part of the reorganization of the Badenese state under Napoleon, put church direction under a government ministry with special sections for each faith. An active role for church bureaucracies in school administration "was more or less taken for granted." That persisted until the 1860s, despite local and governmental controversies.

Badenese educational officials faced a number of obstacles, despite the relatively advanced conditions. Most severe were those of small and isolated communities, where distance from schools, weather, and poor transportation limited attendance. In contrast, in growing urban areas, teaching was hindered by crowded and unsettled classroom conditions. Urban migration also made it difficult to keep children in schools.

Teachers were the first area of attention. Given their low social status, work history, poor pay, and lack of training, that was a huge undertaking. Reformers expressed continued concern with the quality of teachers and their instruction. The evidence also suggests problems with the quality of the literacy skills they imparted. Officials were equally dissatisfied with their immorality and poor character; complaints of drunkenness, brutality, and negligence persisted. Censure of insubordination multiplied when newly organized progressive teachers began to demand a separation between pedagogical and religious duties. Private school teachers were also seen as a threat as they competed for pupils. The solution was training institutes and tightening of licensing guidelines. By the 1820s, hiring had become a bureaucratic routine.

Although Baden was well supplied with permanent facilities, their quality varied. Another problem was the lack of appropriate material for classroom use, especially with the shift to simultaneous instruction and other "modern" pedagogical emphases. Standardized readers, officials urged, must replace the varied materials in use. ABC books and elementary readers were made available, although the Bible long dominated. Progressive, graded texts became more common by the 1840s, especially in the larger communities, where age and ability grading was more practicable.

In many places, the most basic obstacles to school reform were financial. Although local resources varied, and smaller communities were less able to supply competitive salaries and decent facilities, nearly all communities in Baden were able to provide some schooling. A large variety of resources were drawn upon. Teachers, consequently, received income in cash and kind. A far more extensive network of schooling opportunities and higher rates of literacy were thus possible.

With reform came a movement to convert payments to cash. Parents and communities often had difficulty raising cash substitutes; traditional arrangements persisted, especially in the smallest communities. Even with professional organization and reform of payments, teachers were unwilling to commit themselves wholly to cash, although they sought to abolish the more archaic and demeaning (to them) forms of payment, which had made widespread schooling possible in even the smallest places. Teachers' struggles for better wages and recognition of their new status advanced slowly during the first half of the century.

The state officials had well-defined notions about the expected results of mass training. More conservative elites and ruling parties did not accept all of their liberal, modernizing goals and plans. Nevertheless, school promoters held that for a strong and prosperous nation, the people should be united in language, disciplined, industrious, prudent, respectful of law and government, properly (but not excessively) religious, and capable of the minimal skills required for military, fiscal, and legal duties. The ability to respond to social and economic changes, and to some degree to seize new opportunities, was also among the ideals. These were to be the products of a common, universal educational experience, as traditional fears of educating the peasantry and lower class were replaced with new convictions of the necessity of schooling all the people.

One important conviction shared by observers, elites, and officials was that the condition of popular morality was in danger, and especially susceptible to corruption in the face of social change. Once all the children were within the confines of classrooms and trained properly, it was believed, the future would be guaranteed. The twin battles were to reform the school to make its work effective and efficient and to capture the children within it, to train them in literacy and social morality. Traditional religious concerns were redefined with state intervention; secularized morality tied firmly to the transmission of literacy was trumpeted as the goal.

Special schools were created for those who, it was feared, could not be herded into the public schools. Charity and poor schools were one approach; infant schools were another, to prepare children for learning in a way that their homes were considered unable to do. Segregation of children was expected to stimulate other parents to send their youngsters to the public institutions, now untainted by corrupt youths. For children in factories, work was supposed to be combined with a reduced, but still daily, dose of schooling. Industrial schools also were initiated. Many special schools had their hours determined by the schedules of the families whom they expected to serve.

The results of systematic school development were many. Higher rates of enrollment, attendance, and literacy were achieved. A highly rationalized, and relatively efficient, institutional network was erected. A class-oriented structure of elementary education was articulated. The system was built on the assumption that different classes had different values for schooling and different demands on their children's time. Opportunities and structures for schooling varied accordingly, as long as every child was schooled. "It was, ironically, the more explicit recognition of social class distinctions built into the Badenese school system, and the institutional variability which followed, that allowed the obligation of universal school attendance to be enforced in what was obviously a highly stratified society."[57]

The data show that Baden was well supplied with schools and that per capita enrollments were high. Enrollments in even small communities approached 15 percent of the total population and remained there during the early nineteenth century. Larger places had somewhat lower enrollments, but overall the level was approximately 10 percent. The ratio of girls to boys was apparently low at the end of the eighteenth century but increased throughout the nineteenth century. Discrimination by sex virtually disappeared at the primary-school level by mid-century, early for such "equality" in Europe.

The records in Baden allow a finer focus on levels of attendance. By the late eighteenth century, the concept of a "school-age population" was established legally; laws marked the years of schooling as six or seven until about thirteen or fourteen. Reconstructed estimates of attendance levels indicate that attendance was increasing and that Baden's levels were high. Urban areas, Mannheim and Heidelberg, increased strikingly; across the sample, enrollments in excess of 80 percent were common and approached 100 percent of school-age children by mid-century. The urban increase perhaps derived from the more rigorous enforcement of attendance regulations in the early nineteenth century.

Although enforcement of mandatory attendance laws kept more pupils in school for the legal minimum of seven or eight years by the middle of the century, a significant number left before the legal age of thirteen or fourteen. Attendance was often irregular. Especially in rural communities, patterns were highly seasonal, and in some places, no classes were held during periods of intense agricultural labor, despite laws to the contrary. Truancy rates were high during the early part of the century, although they began to decline. That had an impact on the quality of the learning process, and reflected familial decisions about the value of schooling.

Within schools, classes often were very large. Teachers complained that over-crowding made effective instruction difficult. Even in rural areas, class sizes ranged over 100, as facilities and staff failed to keep up with the growing population and efforts to enforce the school laws. This aspect of educational expansion could not but complicate learning, despite the measures initiated to ameliorate conditions. In the spirit of "modern reform," some communities attempted to standardize school populations. Some banned the youngest children from classrooms; others established split shifts or reorganized classes to provide more time for older students or to promote more efficient teaching. Age and ability grouping was established when and where the facilities and the number of teachers permitted.

The movement toward homogenization in classrooms by age and ability, fittingly, was matched by a simultaneous trend toward social homogenization. "The schools, particularly in cities which could afford many teachers, were becoming specialized and children were increasingly likely to meet only their social equals in the class-room." Class size, range of subjects, facilities, and, no doubt, quality of instruction and learning all were reflected in these class differentials. A new level of concern about discipline accompanied pedagogical reforms. Instruction included a large amount of memorization and repetition, especially of the Bible, the catechism, and related fare—frequently as part of the regular tutelage in reading and writing.

The question of the quality of literacy obtained from the available agencies of primary schooling, or from more informal means, is difficult to resolve. Indicators suggest that for many children, high-level skills were not a likely outcome. Those who reached the upper grades probably possessed at least minimal literacy skills, but only a minority of pupils reached that level.

By the first half of the nineteenth century, literacy in German areas, where it long had been a goal, was assumed by many to be a prerequisite for civilization itself. Most citizens, and certainly all school persons, assumed literacy to be a normal accomplishment of the citizenry. Its absence was a sign of deviance and a threat to the community and its progress. This consensus had advanced farther and deeper than in some other parts of Europe, reflecting traditions and continuities as well as contemporary realities. Relatively high rates were found before the nine-teenth century, and by that century they were high even among the poor, the unskilled, and prison inmates.

Literacy rates paralleled trends in school enrollments. A simple causal relationship did not always join the two. Informal, communal means of learning to read and sometimes to write persisted through the period of institutionalization, although the school, under state bureaucratic direction, was gaining a near-monopoly over the transmission of literacy—changing the experience of growing up in the process. One key consequence is that high levels of school attendance and literacy had a limited impact on career and occupational determinants. "Since educational ac-complishments are potentially determinant of career choice only where there are broad differences in these accomplishments among individuals, the virtually uni-versal school enrollment pattern in Baden must have made the independent value of primary school minimal. . . ."[58]

Postprimary schooling made a greater impact. Opportunities beyond the elementary level expanded with the elaboration of a hierarchical education system. Patterns of attendance reveal some increasing artisanal interest in vocational training, but evidence is mixed. Educational alternatives to apprenticeship were often unpopular and met with limited response. The context was one in which sons of German manual workers perceived the notion of mobility "through a prism of limited opportunity, modest expectations, and in some cases very great fears. Their main concern was probably security. . . ."[59] The context was one in which primary schooling and literacy were perceived as prerequisites to economic security.

The upsurge in primary, and other, school enrollments was not matched by rising enrollments or changing class composition in more traditional institutions of higher education. Newer such institutions, however, apparently made room for the sons of at least skilled craftsmen and shopkeepers. Education could be rewarding for those in more traditionally educated classes and within the middle ranks. The children of other workers had more restricted options for advancing beyond the initial, literacy-transmitting levels. "Despite administrative fears the most popular secondary courses were those new ones tailored to the concrete needs of particular local social classes—to commercial and shopowning craftsmen." As this kind of schooling developed, parents began to use it; but secondary education remained the prerogative of the comfortable minority.

In Baden, the local political economy of schooling placed a lesser burden on individual families. The costs for poorer agricultural or industrial families should not be minimized, however; educational decisions remained aspects of the family economy. Although rates of enrollment and levels of literacy indicate a major difference from other places, children's economic contributions were valuable. Seasonal demand for labor is one instance; the factory school was one reform measure to reduce the impact of negative consequences for school opportunities. Schooling patterns reflected needs and demands for children's labor.

Although there were generally fewer opportunities for young girls to contribute economically to their families' well-being, and thus a lower opportunity cost, that did not result in their higher attendance. Traditional attitudes reinforced the belief that schooling was less important for girls, and often led to lower attendance. In Baden, that was less of a problem, as girls attended almost as often as boys. That their earning potentials did not offset the fines increasingly assessed for nonattendance made it less costly to send them to school. Such was not always the case with their brothers. Traditions that stressed women's needs (religious, maternal, domestic) for literacy also intervened.

In Baden, the *Konfirmation* ceremony often marked the end of schooling and the onset of economic life. For families who had some choice, that was when a decision about further education was made. For most children, the brief period of elementary education ended. Even with rising rates of attendance and literacy, school and work continued to be options that parents with employable youths chose with regard to familial needs and opportunities for labor. As long as there was work for children, schooling suffered. The stratification of attendance underscores the inequality that persisted beneath the surface of near-universal schooling and literacy.

Parents probably did not see the elementary schools as major preparation for new careers or mobility. Basic literacy skills, increasingly perceived as needed for economic survival, were not absolute requirements for work or life. For specialized artisans or industrial training, apprenticeship long remained the norm. Preparation for most sectors of nonmanual work—the professions, administration, commerce, and service—was related to formal school training, but recruitment into these positions made schooling largely insignificant as an independent factor. Either costs for schooling were too high or the requisite capital for entry was unavailable, for all but the well-placed and advantaged. In bureaucracy, however, "schooling, and schooling alone, could sometimes qualify a few exceptional individuals for positions commanding a certain income and prestige. The talented younger son of even a poor peasant, artisan or veteran" could be encouraged and sponsored in his mobility.

Just as access to primary education was becoming universal, schooling and literacy almost an average achievement, and consensus widespread on their value, their relative career advantages probably were narrowing. Ironically, access to instruction and an environment that facilitated the acquisition of virtually universal literacy took place early where education was administered by bureaucracies created by an absolutist state. The achievement was much greater than in neighboring France, with greater local autonomy and greater potential for democratization. "Because state and church authorities had decided that universal education was critical to their ends, and because the resources necessary to implement it were at hand, mass schooling became a reality. The population, by no means necessarily opposed to the idea, nonetheless complied without being consulted."[60] Compulsion and centralization without the consent of the people, that is, a demand for schooling, would have proved insufficient. Just as there was no one route to literacy, there was no one outcome. The German example, in its changes and continuities, its similarities to and differences from the rest of the West, is significant and revealing as one path.[61]

Educational development has been regarded by most historians, and economists, as one of the basic prerequisites of Germany's economic revolution. What was the role of elementary literacy training in the mobilization and preparation of human labor power? Peter Lundgreen notes the many links between education and the economy, but in his research on the subject he found that very little (only about 2 percent) of Germany's impressive economic growth can be attributed to the growth of education: "The quality of labor, if measured solely by years of school embodied, did not increase very much over time and thus cannot have contributed significantly to economic growth."

Moreover, the lack of a high rate of educational contribution to economic growth occurred not only in a context of initially high levels of literacy and primary schooling, but also in a context of rising educational expenditures. The cost of investment in education grew to high levels, whereas the returns were neither high nor changing in terms of measurable output.

The important connection between education and economic development in nineteenth-century Germany lay more in the fact that mass literacy and schooling preceded large-scale industrialization and economic growth, and in the availability of a population trained in the largely noncognitive characteristics required for productive labor: discipline, orderliness, cleanliness, respect for authority, punctuality, responsibility, respect for social order, religion, and the state, and the like. Special job skills usually were gained in on-the-job training, rather than in formal schooling.

According to Lundgreen's research, only at the level of more highly skilled technicians, schooled beyond elementary and literacy education, were educational formation and the utilization of manpower directly related to industrial progress. "As to unskilled labor, including women and children, a minimum standard of literacy and such qualities as discipline, obedience, punctuality, and honesty are demanded. This kind of work ethos for industry can be inculcated by education, and Prussia early achieved a high standard in this respect." Literacy, if provided to virtually all persons in proper settings, had a basic significance to the society and the economy. The achievement of mass literacy, on the other hand, did not help the working class escape the insecurities of their economic lives or rise in occupations or status.[62]

Until about 1870, few among the German masses owned many (or any) books. The literary tastes of the lower class were conservative, with a predominance of religious material; calendars, news flyers, and practical guidebooks were the main secular fare. There was little reading for entertainment purposes; contact with stories and tales came largely through the oral tradition of sagas, legends, and fairy tales.

Despite the high rates of literacy, education, printing, prosperity, and the progress of urbanization, many people were not making much use of their literacy. With the abolition of guild-based entry requirements for trades and occupations in the late 1860s and 1870s, new opportunities for speculative publishers were created, and attempts were made to expand the market. The colporteur novels were the most successful experiment. Works of fiction issued in installments, they were sold cheaply door to door, and in style and content were aimed at the lower class. The volumes of sales in this market grew sevenfold from 1870 to the early 1880s.

The colporteur novel was supplanted by the mid-1890s by newly developing mass-oriented newspapers and magazines and series of book-length stories. The books were too long and boring, and the people learned that they could get the same impact from the cheaper, better illustrated, and shorter literary forms. "The 'colporteur novel' initiated an increase in the consumption of reading matter by the lower classes which did not abate, but rather continued to increase for decades afterwards."[63]

Some among the urban working class joined workers' libraries in the last part of the century and the pre-World War I years. Such libraries were large and included a variety of ideological, political, scientific, philosophic, self-improvement, and other fare. However, reports show a steady increase in the amount of literary fiction being borrowed, as demand for social-science and party literature dwindled. Despite their activism, the literacy of the working class seems to have been directed toward other kinds of literature.[64]

Hans-Josef Steinberg concludes that most socialist workers were "absolutely alien to socialist theory and had little interest in theoretical party literature." The literacy skills of the members of this class probably had a great bearing on their preference for literature over science. As there were limits to popular levels of ability of the literacy transmitted in the schools, there were also limits on the literacy that was in use.[65]

In nineteenth-century Germany, the legacies of the eighteenth century and the Reformation came to roost. The role of the state, and before the 1860s and 1870s the church, was considerable in the process of erecting a mass, compulsory, hierarchical system of schools, which elevated traditionally high levels of schooling and literacy. Formal schooling for the masses took the form of what historians have called a "Prussian" path. It was not, however, a complete imposition from above or outside the structures of daily life or local communities. Nor was it a simple process that can be explained by appeals to modernization theory, or to an amalgamation of modernization, social control, and integration perspectives. Those elements were present, but the process of social development in its relationship to literacy's contours transcends such labels.

Despite elite conservative opposition, a consensus about the need and the institutional mechanism for the controlled transmission of literacy and morality to the masses ruled the day. The development of universal literacy through mass schooling was clearly associated with the social and economic transformation of the German regions—as cause and effect, but not as an independent factor. At the same time, it was equally central to the many programs that sought the integration or reintegration of society. Although the uses of literacy were sometimes (and importantly) otherwise, the thrust of development and the dominant functions of literacy fell in the direction of social order and economic progress, not individual advancement. This fact underlay the social mythology that developed around the schools—and was extremely influential.

From opposition to mass schooling in the late eighteenth and early nineteenth centuries came a central respect for school policy as a priority in the struggle against revolution in the late 1840s and 1850s and the national power thereafter. That is not surprising. That an authoritarian nondemocratic state introduced a modern, potentially revolutionary elementary school system is no paradox. "It was a state that attempted to keep such schools under firm control, sought to permeate them with authority and obedience as primary values, and wished to carry out sectional modernization without endangering its conservative structure. . . ."[66] Here was one of the contradictions that give substance to literacy's history. Social transformation, and the response to it, required as much. Here lay Germany's achievement, and an attraction to its imitators and students.

## C. Austria, Italy, and Spain

The high levels of literacy achieved in many of the German states proved rarer in the lands to the south. In 1900, *Austria* presented a crazy-quilt pattern of literacy levels. Although its overall rate of change was not *un*impressive, it did not rank high. Neither the eighteenth-century explosion of interest in education nor the responses to nineteenth-century social and economic transformations were enough to transform the nation and its territories into a land of high literacy. In 1900, the adult illiteracy rate (ten years old and above) was 23 percent: 21 percent of men and 25 percent of women could neither read nor write. That placed the Austrian region in the middle range of European national literacy levels.

As the tables suggest, that 23 percent "moderate" level hides a great deal.

TABLE 7.2

**Illiteracy in the Adult Population of the Austrian Empire,
1900: Administrative Districts**

| District | M | Neither read nor write<br>F<br>(percentage) | MF |
|---|---|---|---|
| Lower Austria | 3 | 5 | 4 |
| Upper Austria | 2 | 3 | 3 |
| Salzburg | 5 | 5 | 5 |
| Styria | 12 | 15 | 13 |
| Carinthia | 18 | 23 | 21 |
| Carniola | 21 | 20 | 21 |
| Trieste | 11 | 18 | 14 |
| Gorizia e Gradisca | 23 | 29 | 26 |
| Istria | 48 | 59 | 54 |
| Tyrol | 3 | 4 | 3 |
| Vorarlberg | 1 | 1 | 1 |
| Bohemia | 2 | 4 | 3 |
| Moravia | 3 | 5 | 4 |
| Silesia | 6 | 6 | 6 |
| Galicia | 52 | 60 | 56 |
| Bukovina | 61 | 71 | 66 |
| Dalmatia | 65 | 82 | 73 |
| Total | 21 | 25 | 23 |

Source: Cipolla, *Literacy*, p. 16.

Geographic and ethnic-linguistic variations are clearly keys to underlying processes of social and economic development, opportunity and inequality, discrimination, poverty, and traditions of literacy. The differentials are not primarily religious, or Protestant-Catholic; the areas of Austrian origins and Germanic language exhibit rates of literacy that compare favorably with those of any other place within the West. These were more developed, urbanized, and schooled areas. In the heartlands of the empire, at least, Maria Theresa's legacies bore results.

Despite the persisting illiteracy, there was some progress, especially during the second half of the century. Some advance occurred in Austria itself, Bohemia, Moravia, and Silesia during the first half of the century. Not all of the development occurred in the more economically advanced regions; high rates are found in the mountainous regions of the Tyrol and Vorarlberg, for example. These conditions are reminiscent of those found in Alpine villages in France, which sustained high levels of literacy without schools and other indicators of social development. In general, however, educational development and trends in literacy were becoming much more closely associated during the nineteenth century.

TABLE 7.3
**Illiteracy in Adult Population of the Austrian Empire,**
**1900: Linguistic Groups**

| Linguistic Group | Population over 10 years of age | | | Neither read nor write | | |
|---|---|---|---|---|---|---|
| | MF | (x000) | M | M | F | MF |
| German | 7,017 | | 3,413 | 5 | 6 | 6 |
| Bohemian Moravian Slovak | 4,377 | | 2,100 | 2 | 4 | 3 |
| Polish | 2,962 | | 1,426 | 45 | 42 | 40 |
| Ruthenian | 2,358 | | 1,184 | 71 | 84 | 77 |
| Slovenian | 877 | | 423 | 22 | 24 | 23 |
| Serbo-Croatian | 506 | | 255 | 67 | 83 | 75 |
| Italian | 548 | | 264 | 14 | 17 | 16 |
| Rumanian | 160 | | 81 | 71 | 80 | 75 |
| Magyar | 6 | | 3 | 50 | 63 | 56 |
| Other minorities | 52 | | 39 | 19 | 26 | 21 |
| Aliens | 418 | | 225 | 11 | 10 | 11 |
| Total | 19,281 | | 9,413 | 21 | 25 | 23 |

Source: Cipolla, *Literacy*, p. 17.

Two indexes illustrate the progress of literacy within the larger Austrian Empire. The first derives from 1890 census information presented for the empire, the Austrian region, and Bohemia, Moravia, and Silesia. To them we add army conscription data—in 1867, 66 percent of recruits were recorded as illiterate; by 1894, the percentage had plummeted to 22 percent. The decline was steady: 49 percent in 1870, 39 percent in 1880, and 22 percent in 1890. Particularly rapid change took place in the later 1860s and the 1880s.

Contrasts between the Austrian and Bohemian, Moravian, and Silesian regions, and most of the rest of the empire, are especially clear. Regional (and linguistic-ethnic) differentials appear as long-standing, spanning at least the nineteenth century. Nineteenth-century advances in proportions of both sexes literate, significant for all regions, sharpened the distinctions between the empire and the areas more favored in literacy. The advantage held by men in Bohemia, Moravia, and Silesia over the Austrians was also lost. These data suggest that some periods were more important for the growth of literacy than others.[67] Extrapolating backwards, to postulate both birth decades and probable periods of schooling or literacy training (largely by the age of fifteen), the second and third decades of the century appear to have been significant for a widening of educational opportunities. That was a time of interest in the education of the masses, but also a time in which a conservative leadership held sway.

TABLE 7.4

**Illiteracy by Age Groups, Austrian Empire, 1890**

| Ages | (percentages) Austrian Empire | | Austrian Region | | Bohemia, Moravia, Silesia | |
|---|---|---|---|---|---|---|
| | M | F | M | F | M | F |
| 11–20 | 22 | 26 | 4 | 4 | 2 | 2 |
| 21–30 | 26 | 29 | 6 | 7 | 3 | 4 |
| 31–40 | 27 | 30 | 8 | 10 | 4 | 5 |
| 41–50 | 29 | 32 | 11 | 14 | 4 | 7 |
| 51–60 | 32 | 36 | 15 | 20 | 6 | 10 |
| 61–70 | 32 | 36 | 18 | 24 | 7 | 15 |
| 71–80 | 31 | 37 | 22 | 28 | 10 | 22 |
| 81–90 | 32 | 41 | 27 | 36 | 13 | 28 |
| 90 and more | 53 | 56 | 46 | 49 | 35 | 46 |

Source: Cipolla, *Literacy*, p. 93.

*Italy* exhibits similarities, as well as more dominant differences. Literacy rates there were among the lowest in the West. Data and interpretation are both problems, given the paucity of information and the political confusion before, and even after, unification in the 1870s. National-level census scores for the population six years and older indicate that 62 percent of the population was unable to read and write: 55 percent of men and 69 percent of women. Only Spain's illiteracy rates were higher, at 72 percent in 1877 (63 percent of males; 81 percent of females). Both states exhibit a higher-than-usual male-female differential, which reflects the lower opportunities available to women in places where "traditional" attitudes remained strong and where educational development was especially uneven and slow. In both places, poverty and lack of development underlay the low levels of literacy. Various combinations of social, cultural, and economic factors combined to prevent either mass demand for schooling and literacy and/or the erection of systematic opportunities.

Tremendous regional variations lay behind the totals. There was a sharp distinction between northern and southern Italy. This pattern was not novel to the nineteenth century, but was present at least as early as the Middle Ages. The differences are even clearer when grouped. In 1871, around the national rate of 69 percent, were northern Italy with 54 percent illteracy; central Italy with 75 percent; southern Italy with 84 percent; and the islands with 86 percent. As table 7.5 shows, the steep regional differences, which paralleled patterns of social and economic development and the geography of poverty, were maintained into the twentieth century. Italian illiteracy was beginning to decline during the second half of the nineteenth century. Yet, regional stratification represented steep ridges that ordered that advance. In the most illiterate regions of the south, rates of illiteracy fell significantly, twenty to thirty percentage points, from 1871 to 1911. At the same time, illiteracy declined by the same absolute margin in the more developed north. Not only was regional superiority maintained, but the "problem" of illiteracy became relatively much smaller in the north.

TABLE 7.5
**Illiteracy in the Italian adult population (6 years of age and above) by Regions**

| | Percentages | | | | | | | | | | | |
| | 1871 | | | 1881 | | | 1901 | | | 1911 | | |
| | M | F | MF | M | F | MF | M | F | MF | M | F | MF |
|---|---|---|---|---|---|---|---|---|---|---|---|---|
| Piedmont | 34 | 51 | 42 | 25 | 40 | 32 | 14 | 21 | 18 | 9 | 13 | 11 |
| Liguria | 49 | 64 | 56 | 37 | 52 | 44 | 22 | 31 | 26 | 14 | 20 | 17 |
| Lombardy | 41 | 50 | 45 | 33 | 41 | 37 | 20 | 23 | 22 | 13 | 14 | 13 |
| Veneto | 54 | 76 | 65 | 43 | 65 | 54 | 28 | 43 | 35 | 20 | 29 | 25 |
| Emilia | 67 | 77 | 72 | 58 | 69 | 64 | 42 | 51 | 46 | 30 | 36 | 33 |
| Tuscany | 62 | 75 | 68 | 55 | 69 | 62 | 42 | 54 | 48 | 32 | 42 | 37 |
| Marches | 73 | 85 | 79 | 66 | 81 | 74 | 54 | 70 | 62 | 42 | 59 | 51 |
| Umbria | 74 | 86 | 80 | 66 | 82 | 74 | 52 | 69 | 60 | 41 | 57 | 49 |
| Lazio | 62 | 74 | 68 | 52 | 66 | 58 | 38 | 51 | 44 | 27 | 39 | 33 |
| Abruzzi | 76 | 93 | 85 | 70 | 90 | 81 | 58 | 80 | 70 | 46 | 67 | 58 |
| Campania | 73 | 87 | 80 | 67 | 83 | 75 | 57 | 73 | 65 | 46 | 61 | 54 |
| Apulia | 79 | 90 | 84 | 74 | 86 | 80 | 64 | 75 | 69 | 54 | 65 | 59 |
| Basilicata | 81 | 95 | 88 | 77 | 93 | 85 | 66 | 83 | 75 | 56 | 73 | 65 |
| Calabria | 79 | 95 | 87 | 76 | 93 | 85 | 69 | 87 | 79 | 59 | 78 | 70 |
| Sicily | 79 | 91 | 85 | 75 | 88 | 81 | 65 | 77 | 71 | 53 | 63 | 58 |
| Sardinia | 81 | 92 | 86 | 73 | 87 | 80 | 61 | 76 | 68 | 52 | 64 | 58 |

Source: Cipolla, *Literacy*, p. 19.

Poverty, lack of educational facilities, higher priorities for survival than literacy among families, agrarian seasonal cycles, and the like obstructed the progress of literacy throughout the Italian peninsula, but were far more severe in the south, where conservative elites also stood in the path of educational development. On one hand, the conditions of life mitigated against opportunities and motivations for acquiring literacy. On the other hand, school development was retarded. Nowhere were complications lacking. For example, in 1829 in Naples, of 2,000 girls attending twenty-three girls' schools, only one-fifth learned to read. Effective learning of high-quality skills was difficult in even the more advantaged areas.

The massive illiteracy and regional inequalities within Italy are only part of the entire story. National, if regionally stratified, progress after the middle of the century was impressive. During the half-century from 1877–78 to 1925, the illiteracy rate of bridegrooms fell from 50 to 10 percent, with the rate of advance quickening toward the end of the period. Cohort data from national censuses also capture the irregular but strengthening path of this progress. In 1881, 51 and 57 percent of eleven- to twenty-year-old males and females respectively were illiterate, as were 47 and 63 percent of those aged twenty-one to thirty. Opportunities for women were beginning to expand. In contrast, in the same census year, 59 and 80 percent of those aged fifty-one to sixty, and 61 and 82 percent of those aged sixty-one to seventy, were unable to read. The overall course is even clearer in the data in table 7.6.

TABLE 7.6
**Illiteracy by Cohorts of People at Census Years in Italy**

| Cohorts of people born in the years indicated below | Percentage of illiterates in | | | | | | | | | |
|---|---|---|---|---|---|---|---|---|---|---|
| | 1871 | | 1881 | | 1901 | | 1911 | | 1921 | |
| | M | F | M | F | M | F | M | F | M | F |
| 1817–26 | 61 | 80 | 60 | 82 | 62 | 80 | 62 | 76 | — | — |
| 1827–36 | 60 | 78 | 58 | 78 | 59 | 78 | 58 | 75 | 54 | 65 |
| 1837–46 | 58 | 74 | 54 | 74 | 54 | 74 | 52 | 70 | 49 | 62 |
| 1847–56 | 58 | 69 | 49 | 68 | 47 | 68 | 45 | 64 | 42 | 56 |
| 1857–66 | 66 | 72 | 49 | 60 | 40 | 59 | 37 | 55 | 35 | 47 |
| 1867–76 | | | 63 | 61 | 36 | 49 | 31 | 45 | 29 | 38 |
| 1877–86 | | | | | 35 | 41 | 26 | 36 | 22 | 30 |
| 1887–96 | | | | | 49 | 39 | 25 | 30 | 18 | 24 |
| 1897–1906 | | | | | | | 31 | 29 | 16 | 19 |
| 1907–16 | | | | | | | | | 25 | 26 |

Source: Cipolla, *Literacy*, p. 94.

TABLE 7.7
**Adult Illiteracy According to the Census, Italy**
**(percentages illiterate of those aged six and over)**

| | M | F | MF |
|---|---|---|---|
| 1871 | 62 | 76 | 69 |
| 1881 | 55 | 69 | 62 |
| 1901 | 42 | 54 | 48 |
| 1911 | 33 | 42 | 38 |

Source: Cipolla, *Literacy*, p. 127.

Illiteracy among Italians fell from abysmally high levels to moderately high ranges by the end of the first quarter of the twentieth century. Among military recruits, illiteracy declined from 59 percent in 1870 to 10 percent in 1913, with progress quickest after the turn of the century. Among bridegrooms, the decline was from 60 percent unable to sign in 1867 to 34 percent in 1890; among brides, from 79 to 48 percent.

Rigid class, sex, and geographic differentials ordered the decline, and even at the end of these years, illiteracy continued to plague Italians and to place the nation low in comparison to the rest of the West. Only Spain and Portugal had higher rates of illiteracy. Illiteracy was generally lower in urban areas, and the rank order among major cities also reflected their geographic location. Naples, in the south, was clearly in a class by itself.[68]

Recent research by Rudolph Bell provides a local context for these rates and their change. Bell examined four distinct socioeconomic settings: the mountain village of Albareto in Parma; the town of Castel San Giorgio on the plain in Salerno; the

TABLE 7.8
**Illiteracy in Italian Cities, 1901: Percentages of
Those Aged Six and Over**

| City | Population | | Illiteracy | | |
|------|------------|------|------|------|------|
|      | MF         | M    | M    | F    | MF   |
|      | (in thousands) | |   |      |      |
| Turin | 305 | 147 | 6 | 11 | 8 |
| Milan | 442 | 219 | 9 | 12 | 10 |
| Florence | 186 | 88 | 15 | 23 | 20 |
| Rome | 411 | 214 | 17 | 27 | 22 |
| Naples | 493 | 239 | 38 | 48 | 43 |

Source: Cipolla, *Literacy*, p. 129.

mountain town of Rogliano in Calabria in the south; and the plateau village of Nissoria in Sicily. He found distinct configurations of literacy and communications networks distinguishing the four rural settings. Location, traditions, physical nature of the settlement, local elites, nature of the economy, and degree of commercialization interacted to form patterns of communications. No one factor appeared determinant. Rates of literacy varied, too.

There were important common patterns and processes of communication. First was the church. Its communication was basic to the structure and texture of life; literacy was largely irrelevant. The church established and marked with rituals the major turning points in the lives of the individual and the village as a whole. "The language of these ceremonies was unintelligible, but their physical and visual symbols invoked for rural folk a sense of community that extended both horizontally to all other 'Christians' and vertically to their ancestors." Seasonal changes, feasting and fasting times, and jubilees and centennials were organized for the village. The local priest usually served as a major vehicle for communication into and out of the locality: for emigration permits, news of a relative, or delivery of messages.

The army was the second major means of communication. As the data on recruits' literacy attest, the army was to many rural youths a school, as well as a broader-based educational experience. One town reported, " 'The peasant leaves as a boor, violent and uncultured; he returns educated, civilized, respectful, and obedient, and he knows how to read and write.' " Although that was not always the case, the moral bases of literacy were reflected in such sentiments. Italian institutionalizers and educators shared this goal.

A third avenue of communications was also sometimes related to literacy: physical artifacts. "Coins, postal stamps, legal seals, paper currency, and posters legal or otherwise generally circulated at a slower pace than orally and personally conveyed news, but what they lacked in speech was more than counterbalanced by their authoritativeness." Not distinct from the strong, traditional oral culture, these channels based in print were short, directly to the point, accessible to those marginally skilled in literacy, and transmitted to those who were not.

These important means of communication drew on oral channels and shaped, directly and indirectly, the coming of wider distribution of literacy itself. By the late nineteenth century and the first decades of the twentieth, literacy was penetrating the villages. Its progress was irregular, and regional stratification remained distinct. The process took longer than in most other areas of the West. Geography, culture, and language were only some of the barriers to the "penetration" of urban culture into the rural countryside. Penetration came with the movement of trade and commerce, the capitalization of agriculture, the monetization of the exchange economy, and worker migration. These were related almost everywhere to the diffusion of literacy, but they often preceded the process of a population's becoming literate. Over one hundred years were required for "modern" development of literacy, which is not yet complete.

In Bell's four settings, nineteenth-century census data reveal "a truly dismal portrait." Peasants were the victims of elite power holders, especially landowners who feared that social unrest would follow directly upon mass educational opportunities. The conservative elites were among the slowest in the West to grasp the training and ordering potentials of systematically controlled instruction in literacy and morality. They rejected legislation that sought to promote national schooling.

Some historians, such as John Briggs, suggest that when Italian peasants, *contradini*, gained an opportunity to learn, they seized it with enthusiasm. In some cases that was true, but circumstances typically restricted peasant opportunities. Long-standing illiteracy should *not* be taken as evidence of peasants' contentment or used to stereotype them disparagingly, of course. What needs study is the relationship of opportunities to life chances and the perceptions of the relevance for literacy in diverse localities. For the moment, until in-depth studies are completed, "the facts remain that most *contradini* could not read or write; that educational opportunities spread far more rapidly in urban areas and in the north, thereby exacerbating the dualism of Italy's economy; and that rural women suffered particular disadvantage."

Bell's case studies reinforce the conclusions of the national-level data. His southernmost example, Nissoria, shows the lack of educational development in the south. In 1881, few attended school; there was really no proper school, and local teachers were underpaid. Abandoned rural structures were used as schoolhouses. Children of the peasantry do not seem to have attended. In towns such as Rogliano as late as 1906, more than one-third of those legally required to attend school did not. Even the requirements of military conscription left most rural Italian males illiterate. That was the setting that endowed the priests and other individuals with a special provenance, promoting the influence of intermediate power brokers, who read and wrote for a fee or favor. With long-distance—including overseas—migration, padrone power over illiterate peasants increased.[69] Literacy may not have resulted in special opportunities; its absence, however, increased the relative dependence of persons already dependent.

## D. Switzerland, the Low Countries, Sweden, and Iceland

*Switzerland* long stood among those European countries with a high rate of literacy. Over 70 percent of the Swiss were able to read by the mid-nineteenth century. When data on military recruits' literacy become available in 1879, only 6 percent were scored as illiterate. This proportion dropped to 2–3 percent by 1890 and to 1 percent by the turn of the century.

Switzerland was among the first states in Europe to establish a system of free, compulsory primary schools. By 1830, public schools were introduced into the countryside; in 1848, the constitution proclaimed the principle of mandatory primary schooling, while leaving to the cantons responsibility for determining ages for legal school leaving. This law was supported by other legislation.

From 1875 to 1913, the Swiss examined their draftees rigorously. Not only was their ability to read and write tested, but they also were examined in composition, arithmetic, the constitution, history, and geography. The results underline the fact of virtually universal literacy (although the quality of that literacy varied widely). They also show areas of high literacy to be Protestant regions and urban centers with high levels of income and a concentration of professionals. Although places of low altitude tended to be regions of high literacy, the correlation was weak. Alpine people were not disadvantaged in opportunities for literacy learning.

Illiteracy was rare and elementary instruction compulsory, but few students went beyond the primary level. Postprimary schooling continued to be the prerogative of the elite and was concentrated in the cities. Administrative and commercial cities had the most schooled populations. This form of educational stratification become more important as virtually all persons were acquiring basic literacy. Correlations of literacy with religion diminished as the century progressed; Protestant-Catholic differences were passing at the elementary levels, although German Catholicism appeared to be less negatively associated with literacy than French Catholicism.[70]

The Swiss transition to near-universal levels of literacy was rapid and even. Regional distinctions were not erased completely, but literacy was becoming a normal condition for men and women of all classes and wealth levels. The few illiterates belonged to the lowest class: servants and laborers. However, the consequences of this Swiss development did *not* remake the social or cultural fabric of the society. Literacy's consequences are seldom massive or direct, even in such a quick achievement of high rates of literacy.[71]

The few studies of Dutch literacy have placed *the Netherlands*, or Holland, among the nations with high adult literacy by the nineteenth century. This opinion draws upon the impressive legacies of traditionally high rates in the area and the formal motivation to develop a modern school system in the first half of the century. None of the available evidence contradicts that picture. It does, however, reveal Dutch literacy development to be more interesting and variegated.

Before the nineteenth century, and continuing into that period, Holland replicated the north-south differentials in literacy achievement found also in France, Italy, and to some extent the German lands. The region of southern Netherlands, which became Belgium upon independence, lagged behind the north. The difference was based on wealth, social and economic development, school development, and religion.[72] The extent of Dutch literacy is symbolized by the 70 percent rate of signing among Amsterdam bridegrooms as early as 1680, which rose to 76 percent in 1729–30 and 85 percent in 1780. Women's rates there were well behind the men's, although they rose before the nineteenth century: 44 percent in 1680, 51 percent

TABLE 7.9
**Illiteracy: Percentage Not Signing, Bridegrooms and Brides,
Netherlands Provinces, 1813–1819**

| Bridegrooms Rank-Province | | | Brides Rank-Province | | |
|---|---|---|---|---|---|
| no. | | % | no. | | % |
| 1 | Groningen | 13.5 | 1 | Drenthe | 24,6 |
| 2 | Drenthe | 14.1 | 2 | Groningen | 27,3 |
| 3 | Friesland | 15.8 | 3 | Friesland | 30,3 |
| 4 | Noord-Holland* | 17.8 | 4 | Noord-Holland* | 33,0 |
| 5 | Zeeland | 21.1 | 5 | Overijssel | 39,3 |
| 6 | Zuid-Holland | 27.1 | 6 | Utrecht | 41,2 |
| 7 | Overijssel | 27.1 | 7 | Zeeland | 41,4 |
| 8 | Gelderland | 27.8 | 8 | Zuid-Holland | 42,9 |
| 9 | Utrecht | 28.8 | 9 | Gelderland | 45,9 |
| 10 | Limburg | 34.0 | 10 | Noord-Brabant | 51,3 |
| 11 | Noord-Brabant | 34.3 | 11 | Limburg | 57,6 |
| | Nederland | 24.6 | | Nederland | 40,4 |

*Except Amsterdam

Source: A. M. Van de Woude, "Der alfabetisering," in *Algemene Geschiedenis der Nederlunden* 7 (1980), p. 260.

in 1729–30, and 64 percent in 1780. In the south, rates were lower; Belgian recruits' literacy rates were 49 percent in 1844 and 56 percent in 1850, compared to 74 percent for Dutch recruits in 1846–49.

Dutch patterns were far from homogeneous. Deep social, geographic, cultural, sexual, and economic differentiation underlay the overall attainment. Within rural Netherlands, bridegrooms' literacy in 1813–19 ranged from a high of 86.5 percent in the province of Groningen to a low of 65.7 percent in Noord-Brabant. The average for the Netherlands was 75.4 percent. Among brides, whose average rate was 59.4 percent, levels ranged from 75.4 percent in Drenthe to 42.2 percent in Limburg province. Although the rank order of male and female literacy rates by province was not exactly the same, the parallels are impressive. Male and female levels were associated on the regional level in rural Netherlands, despite the constant male advantage. These differences are significant, but they are hardly as large as those in places where the average achievement was much lower. That was part of the process of the growth of literacy in the Netherlands.

Regional and sexual differences were not the only regular socioeconomic factors that ruled Dutch literacy development. Data from rural Utrecht for the early nineteenth century show the effects of religion, occupation, and the interaction of cultural and economic factors. Protestants had high levels of literacy among both bridegrooms and brides. Class, or occupational status, was a more important influence. The literacy level of tradesmen, craftsmen, and farmers was 40 percent higher than that of laborers. Although both rates were rising, the gap was not closing by the

TABLE 7.10
**Illiteracy, Low Countries**

Table A. Percentage Not Signing, Bridegrooms and Brides, 1840–1849

| City | Bride-grooms | Brides |
|------|------|------|
| Rotterdam | 8 | 24 |
| 's-Gravenhage | 8 | 25 |
| Dordrecht | 11 | 30 |
| Gouda | 29 | 53 |
| Leiden | 23 | 43 |
| Haarlem | 9 | 23 |
| Leeuwarden | 11 | 25 |
| Maastricht | 23 | 46 |
| Roermond | 23 | 45 |
| Venlo | 19 | 49 |
| Arnhem | 11 | 31 |
| Groningen | 7 | 20 |
| Zwolle | 9 | 23 |
| Deventer | 8 | 27 |
| Utrecht | 19 | 36 |
| Amersfoort | 30 | 49 |
| Enkhuizen | 9 | 15 |
| Schiedam | 8 | 28 |
| Middelburg | 9 | 25 |
| Vlissingen | 11 | 40 |
| Breda | 28 | 49 |
| Nijmegen | 15 | 45 |

Table B. Percentage Not Signing, Bridegrooms in Belgium

| City | 1810–1815 | 1820–1830 | 1840–1850 |
|------|------|------|------|
| Aalst | 43 | 55 | — |
| Brugge | 52 | 60 | 51 |
| Brussel | — | — | 43 |
| Charleroi | 38 | 42 | — |
| Hasselt | 50 | 52 | — |
| Leuven | 43 | 40 | 27 |
| Tienen | 52 | 53 | 56 |
| Turnhout | — | 58 | 34 |

Table C. Percentage Not Signing, Brides in Belgium

| City | 1810–1815 | 1820–1830 | 1840–1850 |
|------|------|------|------|
| Aalst | 47 | 58 | — |
| Brugge | 59 | 65 | 71 |
| Brussel | — | — | 49 |
| Charleroi | 51 | 58 | — |
| Hasselt | 67 | 58 | — |
| Leuven | 45 | 47 | 47 |
| Tienen | 40 | 52 | 53 |
| Turnhout | — | 67 | 65 |

Source: A. M. Van de Woude, "Der alfabetisering," in *Algemene Geschiedenis der Nederlunden* 7 (1980), p. 259.

early years of the century. The much smaller, 10 to 20 percent, Protestant advantage over Catholics pales in comparison. Table 7.9 shows these patterns, and the greater role of class and wealth than religion when both factors are plotted together.[73] These were persisting divisions that ordered the growth of literacy and continued in the form of new levels of education once near-universal literacy was reached shortly after mid-century (see also figure 6.11).

In Belgium in the mid–1840s, 50 percent of recruits were illiterate; that fell to 20 percent by 1880–81, and to 10 percent illiteracy only in 1904. The national adult literacy rate of about 50 percent circa mid-century placed Belgium within the middle ranges of European levels. Evidence from censuses tells the same story, and also points to the narrowing of sexual differences. Cohort data from the 1880 census reaffirm the slow, relatively even nature of literacy's growth and point to an acceleration of progress after mid-century. That was a time of educational development.[74]

TABLE 7.11
**Adult Illiteracy in Belgium, Census Data,
Those Aged 10 and Above
(Percentages)**

|      | M  | F  | MF |
|------|----|----|----|
| 1880 | 27 | 34 | 31 |
| 1890 | 23 | 28 | 26 |
| 1900 | 17 | 21 | 19 |

Source: Cipolla, *Literacy*, p. 127.

TABLE 7.12
**Literacy in Belgium, Census Data,
Percentages, "Population Totale"**

|    | 1866 | 1880 | 1890 | 1900 |
|----|------|------|------|------|
| M  | 50   | 60   | 64   | 69   |
| F  | 44   | 55   | 60   | 67   |
| MF | 47   | 60   | 62   | 68   |

Source: Joseph Ruwet and Yves Wellemans, *L'Analphabétisme en Belgique* (Louvain: Bibliotèque de l'Université Louvain, 1978), pp. 15.

TABLE 7.13
**Rate of Literacy by "Cohortes Scolaire," Belgium,
1780–1859, Percentages**

| Cohortes scolaire | M  | F  |
|-------------------|----|----|
| 1780–1789         | 57 | 47 |
| 1790–1799         | 52 | 49 |
| 1800–1809         | 52 | 43 |
| 1810–1819         | 50 | 45 |
| 1820–1829         | 51 | 46 |
| 1830–1839         | 56 | 43 |
| 1840–1849         | 61 | 46 |
| 1850–1859         | 63 | 56 |

Ibid., p.18

The lack of educational expansion and political independence placed constraints on literacy levels. Religious, ethnic, and linguistic conflicts also contributed to the relative lack of advancement and of a foundation for school development with more systematic transition of literacy skills. That is one reason why *il*literacy increased during the first third of the nineteenth century in the towns of Belgium (see table 7.14). Regional variation and, especially, sharp sexual differentiation were central to the distribution of literacy. The lack of common agencies for the dissemination

TABLE 7.14

**Illiteracy by Age Group, Belgium, 1880 (Percentages)**

|  | 11–20 | 21–30 | 31–40 | 41–50 | 51–60 | 61–70 | 71–80 | 81–90 | 90 and over |
|---|---|---|---|---|---|---|---|---|---|
| Male | 19 | 20 | 25 | 32 | 39 | 42 | 47 | 50 | 52 |
| Female | 20 | 24 | 33 | 41 | 48 | 55 | 62 | 66 | 69 |

Source: Cipolla, *Literacy*, p. 93.

of reading and writing was shared widely throughout the country, reducing geographic variation.

Virtually all research on literacy in nineteenth-century (and eighteenth-century) Belgium has centered on urban places.[75] Studies of seven cities, summarized by Yves Wellemans, reveal a remarkable pattern from the late eighteenth century through the mid-nineteenth. In four of the towns, Bruges, Alost, Turnhout, and Anderlecht, *il*literacy increased, while in the other three, Louvain, Charleroi, and Tirelemont, it became less widespread. On average, about one-half of men were illiterate, compared to about 60 percent of women. Literacy levels and school development were growing increasingly interrelated over the course of the century; parishes with the highest proportion of children in school had the lowest illiteracy rates.

Marriage patterns indicate that two-thirds of literate men married literate women, and 80 percent of illiterate men married illiterate women. Rather than literacy's being a strong influence on marriage, that was yet another reflection of intraclass, endogamous marital and association patterns. Inequality and social stratification reinforced, and were reinforced by, literacy and illiteracy. In Belgian towns and cities, 60 percent of sons and 75 percent of daughters of illiterate parents were illiterate themselves. Familial circumstances pressed hard against the next generation's opportunities. A strong force, it was not automatic, as literacy levels rose in nineteenth-century Belgium.[76]

Of the seven towns that have been studied in detail, illiteracy in four rose during the first thirty or forty years of the century, not beginning a steady decline until the 1840s and 1850s. That raises questions about the impact of the 1843 national school legislation. Three other towns did not share this decline after the Revolution and the end of the Ancien Regime, a period when the region was controlled politically by first Napoleon and then Holland. In Louvain, Charleroi, and Tirelemont, rates of male and female literacy declined from the first decade of the century. Regardless of the level at which they began the century, their literacy levels stood above those in the other towns. Charleroi and Tirelemont had a wider distribution of literacy at the beginning of the century, which they maintained.

Analyses of trends over time are preliminary and somewhat superficial. The last decades of the Ancien Regime were *not* the most destructive to schooling or literacy, as some earlier students had surmised. Belgium was governed by the Austrian Empire under Maria Theresa, and the towns benefited from the presence of a number of "écoles triviales." During the subsequent French and Dutch regimes, in most places there was little educational progress. On the whole, steady advancement in literacy and school awaited the educational imperatives that came with national independence in 1830 and the school laws of 1843, which represented a compromise between the contending forces of liberal reform and clerical control of schools. Compromise, in the form of the "loi organique" of 1843, continued until the 1870s and permitted a widening distribution of literacy within the towns and cities, as well as in the more developed parts of the countryside. In several of the cities, only after the 1830s were 1780s levels regained by men. Only slowly during the middle period of the century did female rates of literacy, based on increased schooling opportunities, begin to approach those of the men.

In the Belgian towns, occupational class (and less directly wealth) was clearly related to literacy. Tradesmen and workers, constituting a majority of the working populations, were the least often literate. For these persons, skill and status apparently did not depend upon the acquisition of literacy. In all groups, however, literacy levels rose, especially after independence from the Dutch; yet, group differences barely narrowed. In Belgium, literacy long remained a symbol *and* a fact of social inequality and the stratification of town society.[77]

Belgium included two major cultural groups, the French-speaking and dominant Walloons and the Flemish. Illiteracy in the 1860s was four times higher among Flemish-speaking males than among the French-speaking. Among women, the difference was almost five times.[78] National census data indicate that literacy levels in Flanders were ten to fifteen percentage points lower than in Wallonia. The problem of regionalism interacted with nationalism, ethnicity, and language to yield a literacy differential that bifurcated Belgian society. The issue was more than one of Flemish unilingualism, but a deeper division within the nation. In 1880, adult literacy rates exceeded 80 percent (15 to 55-year-olds who could read and write) in only two arrondissements in Flanders; both were rural. That contrasts with ten in Wallonian Belgium. It is possible that domestically based protoindustrialization, with a heavy use of child labor, also underlay Flemish patterns.

By the late nineteenth century, a negative relationship between the level of adult literacy and the levels of urbanization and industrialization spanned both Flanders and Wallonia. Industrialization in Belgium, if late, did not put a primacy on high rates of literacy among the work force, although it may have been based in part on schools' elementary instruction of a sizable proportion of the work force. Economic development—in the form of urban industrialization and rapid change—was *not* favorable to high rates of literacy.

Belgium had a dual school system, with one section controlled by the Catholic church and the other by state or communal authorities. Before 1900, many villages had only a Catholic parish school, which precipitated a "school war" in areas where non-Catholics and liberals wished to create alternatives. The large-scale eradication of popular literacy by the early twentieth century was a result primarily of the efforts of the church, especially in rural and semirural areas, where it held a monopoly. That lent to literacy's transmission a strong moral cast, and helps to explain the correlations: "It seems that the eradication of illiteracy through the development of primary-school education contributed more to the continuity of the existing moral norms than to their change. As a result, the degree of literacy in Belgium could be a better indicator of traditionalism than of modernization."[79]

During the nineteenth century, *Sweden* continued as one of the most literate nations in the West. Basic changes, however, occurred in the mechanisms for disseminating mass literacy and the form of that literacy. Adult literacy levels remained impressively high, at over 90 percent. The frequency of illiteracy among military recruits in 1891 was a meager nine per thousand conscripts. That truly high rates of literacy persisted in Sweden cannot be doubted. It no longer held the unique place that it had in earlier centuries, but it remained among the leaders.[80]

During the nineteenth century, transmission of literacy shifted from the traditional agencies of home and church to formal, institutional means of systematic public schooling. The dimensions of literacy were also broadened beyond a narrow focus of catechism and religious doctrine. Although the movement to replace the traditional processes of learning was symbolized and codified in the famous elementary school law of 1842, which established a common school, precedents had developed over the past three-quarters of a century. The principles of the Enlightenment, the efforts of philanthropic reformers and Pietists, popular demands for schooling, government and official interests in uniform popular schooling for civic training and national preparation, and generalized beliefs that the course of social and economic change required a new approach to popular socialization cohered in the legislation of the 1840s and 1850s. Economic conditions allowed state action that had been less fiscally feasible in preceding decades. External developments interacted with internal interests, as Swedish educational development was part of a broader Western search for means of promoting development, order, and progress.

In the early 1840s, a law was promulgated establishing a national elementary school system rooted in the parish. A measure of communal or parochial authority was retained, leading to some unevenness of support and distribution in the first years. Many new schools were founded, and between 1847 and 1859 the number of children receiving no schooling fell from 22,606 to 7,372.[81]

The expansion of elementary education at first neglected basic literacy instruction. As over a century earlier, in the School Statute of 1724, which created the "trivial school," the entrance requirements in the 1842 common school law required some reading ability for admission, taking for granted initial instruction in the home. Not until the establishment of the "junior school" in 1858 was beginning reading instruction placed on the schools' schedules. Traditional patterns were not abolished. Not only were they respected, they also were depended upon. The earlier processes of learning literacy thus helped to shape the introduction of common schooling.

In the mid-nineteenth century, a major transition distinguished two eras in Swedish educational history. With the emergence of institutionalized mass schooling, the church was relieved of much of its responsibility. The transition was complicated and lengthy, as the traditional pattern long remained. The common school lacked a foundation in many parts of Sweden; many persons desired continued operation of both systems. The school was required as a " 'school for the poor' for pupils with deficient home instruction" and as a " 'school for citizens' for most pupils." Literacy transmission was retained, and gradually transferred from the home to the elementary school. A more efficient, uniform, and controlled process of learning

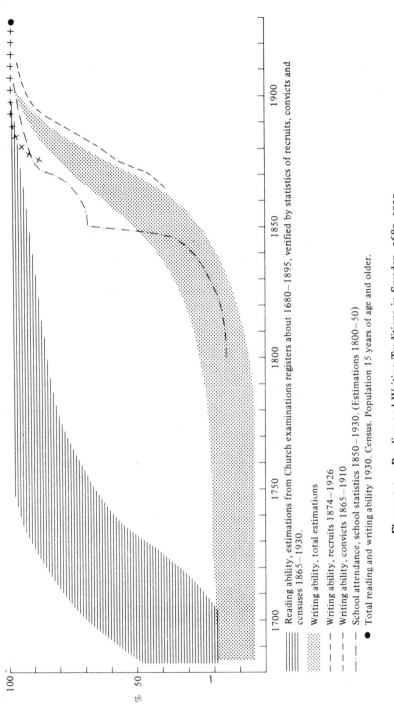

**Figure 7.1.** Reading and Writing Traditions in Sweden, 1680–1930
*Source*: Johansson, *History of Literacy*, p. 64.

Reading ability, estimations from Church examinations registers about 1680–1895, verified by statistics of recruits, convicts and censuses 1865–1930.

Writing ability, total estimations

Writing ability, recruits 1874–1926

Writing ability, convicts 1865–1910

School attendance, school statistics 1850–1930. (Estimations 1800–50)

● Total reading and writing ability 1930. Census. Population 15 years of age and older.

values, attitudes, social morality, and skills gave the formal institution of the common school a new importance.

Literacy levels remained high, and with the shift to the school came the emergence of writing as a core ingredient in literacy. The histories of most other places show a much closer relationship between reading and writing in the nineteenth-century movement toward mass literacy. The Swedish writing campaign was rapid, as was the reading campaign of the earlier centuries.[82]

Although Sweden had a long tradition of popular literacy, its quality diverged greatly from its quantity. According to the results of reading and comprehension tests, good reading ability did not relate strongly to the ability to understand. Popular skills tested well in assessments of oral reading and in memorization. They were, however, much less useful when it came to comprehension. A gap of this nature distinguishes the levels of literacy produced by school (and mass home-church) learning from the qualitative utility of those skills. A gap between quantity and quality may be a long-term aspect of the development of mass literacy, which suggests great caution in the interpretation of literacy rates.[83]

Even near-universal Swedish literacy was stratified. Table 7.15 indicates that social structure and geography both influenced the extent of learning. Not surprisingly, members of high-ranking and wealthy families scored highest on reading tests; farmers, craftsmen, workers, and servants scored low. Class and occupation affected enrollment, as well, as the children from higher-ranking families attended most often.

TABLE 7.15

**Grades in reading for 1862, distributed on the basis of occupational categories and the number of tax-payers per household. Number = 1,493**

|  | Total Absolute Figures | Highest Grade Grade in Reading % |
|---|---|---|
| Public Officials, etc. | (115) | 80.9 |
| Freeholders (Peasant Proprietors) | (683) | 31.3 |
| Rural Farmers, Settlers | (149) | 16.1 |
| Craftsmen, Soldiers, Crofters | (126) | 14.3 |
| Workers, Lumberman, etc. | (191) | 16.8 |
| Dependent Tenants, Cottars | (100) | 19.0 |
| Servants | (129) | 13.2 |
| Number of capitation tax per household 6 or more | (103) | 55.3 |
| 4–5 | (244) | 45.5 |
| 3 | (217) | 31.8 |
| 2 | (455) | 18.7 |
| 1 | (155) | 23.9 |
| 0 | (319) | 18.2 |

Source: Egil Johansson, "Literacy Studies in Sweden: Some Examples," *Literacy and Society*, ed. Egil Johansson (Umeå, 1973), p. 58.

TABLE 7.16
**Children of school age in Bygdeå's southern school district
for the period 1847–1862. Number = 777**

| Occupational | Distance from home village to school | | | | | |
| | Within ca 5 km | | More than ca 5 km | | Total | |
| | Total Abs. Fig. | School Children % | Total Abs. Fig. | School Children % | Abs. Fig. | School Children % |
| --- | --- | --- | --- | --- | --- | --- |
| Public Officials, etc. | (38) | 73,7 | (45) | 40,0 | (83) | 55,5 |
| Farmers, Settlers | (167) | 44,3 | (313) | 5,7 | (480) | 19,3 |
| Craftsmen, Soldiers, Crofters | (43) | 44,2 | (24) | 4,2 | (67) | 29,8 |
| Workers, Dependent Tenants, Lodgers, etc. | (70) | 24,3 | (77) | 16,9 | (147) | 20,4 |
| Total | (318) | 43,5 | (459) | 10,9 | (777) | 24,2 |

Source: Ibid., p.61.

Children of workers and other low-ranking families who lacked opportunities for home instruction often came to school even if they had to cover a distance that might be prohibitive for other children. Benefits from schooling were unequal; yet, the school did serve the poor who lacked means of learning at home. Social recruitment and some opportunities for the poor were key elements in the transition from home to school education. Maintaining its impressively high rate of literacy, that was the way in which Sweden shifted to formal, institutionalized schooling along with much of the rest of the West.[84]

The exceptional Swedish data shed light on the relationship between literacy (or education) and migration. Normative considerations of the contribution of literacy to the decision and propensity to move are contradictory. On one hand, theories and images stress the rootless, almost aimless poor and illiterate moving often, in search of jobs, opportunities, and security. On the other hand, different conceptions and another body of social and psychological imagery depict the illiterate as incapable of moving, not only without the resources and information necessary for migration but also trapped in a paralyzing "culture of poverty." The expectations for literate persons are somewhat simpler. Given the benefits of their training and skill, no such contradictory assumptions govern theoretical premises regarding their propensities and abilities to move. The expectation is that literate persons are more able to respond to information and opportunities, and to migrate when their situations lead them to evaluate that as a reasonable course of action.

Studies of Swedish parochial records, which include information on migration, point directly toward a conclusion that migration is a selective process, and that literacy is one of the basic elements in that selectivity. It appears that those with high levels of literacy (as illustrated by their reading scores) *and* those with low levels were likely to move. Whereas some persons may have been advantaged by

E) Learn only the Minimum

Occupation Total

| Publ Off | (18) | 61.3% |
|---|---|---|
| Farmers | (87) | 33.3% |
| Others | (41) | 22.0% |
| Total | (146) | 33.6% |

C) Including School Attendance

Occupation Total

| Publ Off | (44) | 84.3% |
|---|---|---|
| Farmers | (91) | 36.4% |
| Others | (45) | 24.4% |
| Total | (180) | 45.0% |

A) All School Age Children

Occupation Total

| Public Officials | (78) | 83.1% |
|---|---|---|
| Farmers | (469) | 36.6% |
| Others | (201) | 32.9% |
| Total | (748) | 40.5% |

B) Only Home Instruction

Occupation Total

| Publ Off | (34) | 82.3% |
|---|---|---|
| Farmers | (378) | 36.7% |
| Others | (156) | 35.3% |
| Total | (568) | 39.1% |

D) Learn over the Minimum

Occupation Total

| Publ Off | (26) | 100.0% |
|---|---|---|
| Farmers | ( 4) | (4) |
| Others | ( 4) | (2) |
| Total | (34) | 94.1% |

**Figure 7.2.**  Grades in reading for all children of school age in Bygdeå's southern school district during the years 1847–62. Proportion of highest grade in percent. *Source*: Johansson, "Some Examples," p. 63.

literacy ability, others were not trapped or paralyzed by virtue of their lack or low level of literacy. Comparative data affirm the generality of the Swedish findings.[85]

The inhabitants of *Iceland* maintained their virtually universal levels of literacy through the nineteenth century. The effective transmission of reading also continued, apparently, *without* extensive development of schools. As late as 1903, only 5,416 of the 12,030 children aged seven to fourteen were enrolled in school. Richard F. Tomasson suggests that the "great distance in Iceland between isolated farms had made the establishment of schools for rural children a great problem, but the tradition of learning to read at home with supervision from the clergy has continued into the present century." In contrast to Swedes, Icelanders apparently did not face either the demands for such a change or the sociopolitical or socioeconomic transformation perceived as necessitating institutionalization. In this respect, Iceland is unique. The small size of the country and the relative equality noted by nineteenth-century travelers perhaps were underlying factors. Both tradition and the lack of large-scale industrial, commercial, and urban transformations made continuity possible.

Travelers in the nineteenth century were much impressed with Icelanders' literacy levels. Reading was seemingly a common habit. Comments on family reading circles and the reading practices of the young were frequent. It was not unusual for such observers to ascribe some responsibility to the climate, perhaps not wholly unfairly! The legacies of Icelandic literacy and the traditions of its frequent use continued from the past.[86] That was another path to literacy.

## E. England and Ireland

The English experience in literacy was neither unique nor typical during this period. England lost its earlier rank; it was not among the leaders in building a state system of primary schools. There was conflict between church, sect, and state over the control and support of elementary education. Despite the lack of a uniform system, schools were expanding and increasingly transmitting literacy. Goals developed in support of mass literacy dispensed through social institutions created largely for that purpose. The effort to provide literacy to a growing population derived from the need for social order and morality in a time of unprecedented social and economic transformation. Education was a Victorian obsession.[87]

According to Schofield, who studied signatures and marks in marriage registers for the period, "the achievement of the second half of the nineteenth century is remarkable." The percentage of men unable to sign fell from over 30 percent in 1850 to 1 percent in 1913; the percentage of women unable to sign declined from just over 45 percent in 1850 to 1 percent in 1913. The most rapid improvement was among those marrying after about 1885, or leaving school after about 1870 (see figure 7.3; see also figure 6.15).

Trends early in the period are more difficult to discern. Most of the information available derives from samples of selected communities. Many are unrepresentative of larger patterns or are based on skewed sources, such as wills. Schofield has prepared a reliable random sample of 274 parishes for the pre-1839 period. It shows the proportion of women not able to sign at just over 60 percent in the mid-eighteenth century, rising slowly to almost 50 percent by 1840. Improvement after 1800 was somewhat quicker. The increase in women's literacy may be associated with developments in Sunday school education. Male illiteracy remained fairly stable for fifty years. Almost 40 percent of men were unable to sign until around 1795. This percentage fell around 1800, rose around 1805, then fell again, at a rate similar to that of women, to 33 percent in 1840. The turning point probably was between 1805 and 1815. "If we assume that entry into the labor force may be taken to be the age of leaving school, then some point in the 1790s marks the date around which the literacy of entrants to the labor force may first be said to be increasing since 1740."

Such aggregates conceal important variations. Geographic location, opportunities for schooling, concentration of land ownership, dispersion of settlement, wealth and occupational distribution, and employment structures all influenced literacy levels, as well as literacy's relationships to social, economic, cultural, and political development.

In a context in which the overall rate of change was slow between the mid-eighteenth and mid-nineteenth centuries, expectations about transformations in the occupational structure of literacy or the contribution of rising literacy to economic change should be cautious. There was a distinct occupational hierarchy of literacy, and it was "one of the most consistent features of illiteracy in the past." Until the mid-nineteenth century, traditional hierarchies persisted, and in some places of heavy industrial development, rates fell before they rose to near-universality by the end of the century. The expansion that did occur, such as the shift in women's

Percentage unable to sign

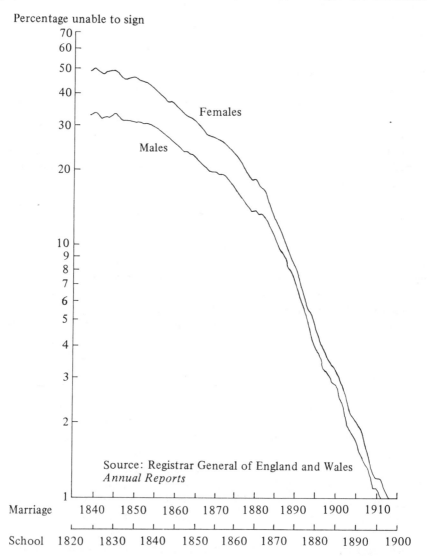

**Figure 7.3.**   Annual Percentage of Males and Females Unable to Sign at Marriage, England and Wales, 1839–1912.
*Source:* Schofield, ''Dimensions,'' p. 442.

literacy from 36 percent in 1750 to 50 percent in 1850, suggests that persisting
social stratification ruled. Tradition, as much as change, governed the transition to
higher levels of literacy.

Even in this context, literacy was fairly widespread; illiterates probably had access
to readers who could share that literacy with them. If English society comprised
more than one homogeneous culture, the extent of literacy was not the major cause.
Practical economic skills were learned distinctly from literacy, and presumably were
more important.[88]

The usefulness of and necessity for a literate population became increasingly valued in the nineteenth century. English elites were *not* among the leaders in the push for literacy. As one consequence, the concept of ''public'' and ''popular'' schooling took on a peculiar meaning. One reason was that acceptance of the need for mass schooling for social stability, and subsequently social progress, was a minority view at the beginning of the century, prevailing only against strong aristocratic opposition. There was an emphasis on ''collective goals—such as the reduction of crime and disruption, and to some extent, increased economic productivity—rather than individualistic goals—such as intellectual growth or personal advancement . . . education for social stability. . . .'' The schooling of the masses was consonant with English liberalism, even though it was interventionist. England was not alone in overcoming ''conservative'' opposition to organized schooling in this period.

A lively debate over mass schooling took place. The conservative opponents adhered to the views of Mandeville and Jenyns, who attacked charity schools, feared an educated lower class, and desired an ignorant work force. The reformers, proponents of mass schooling for stability, followed more from those clergy who sought to expand charitable opportunities for schooling. In the context of the French and American revolutions, internal tumult of urban growth and industrialism, and the aftermath of the Napoleonic Wars, the debate intensified from about 1790 through 1820. The reformers emerged dominant, but their ideological success was not immediate; mass institutionalization took time.

At the same time, as a consequence of dissenters' educational actions, fears of political radicalism, and widespread opposition to change in the social structure, opponents also grew stronger. This opposition stressed two basic arguments: education would unfit the lower classes for their occupational role, and would subvert authority by spreading ''seditious and atheistic ideas.'' Education, in this view, was associated with mobility and disorder.

Reformers insisted that ''moral training, including rudimentary reading, would make men content with their lot, not ambitious, and that education would increase social stability, not disruption.'' The social transformation required a replacement for traditional ranks and deference; schooling, with literacy the vehicle for its moral bases, was to be the new social cement. In part, reformers prevailed by arguing that their program would serve conservatives' own goals: stability, discipline, and deference. An emphasis on social morality formed the core of the emerging consensus.[89]

Mass schooling carried the potential for other uses of the skills and for individual and class advancement. This consequence was feared by its opponents and was not accepted by many advocates of popular schooling. Some, influenced by the Enlightenment and other contemporary sentiments, were more tolerant. They felt that *some* mobility, for example, was a good thing; it could bind its products firmly to the social order. Regardless of divisions on this point, what came to dominate was a deep faith in the shaping power of properly supervised, carefully controlled, institutionalized schooling.

Many supporters of mass schooling believed that education would reduce the burgeoning birthrate among the lower classes. ''The fertility effect was supposed to arise in two forms: either as a simple correlation of education and infertility, or in the Malthusian guise as a means of leading the poor to an appreciation of the means of their own salvation.''[90] Here were the moral bases of education in action. Malthus was one of the many who promoted restraint through expanded provision of literacy and schooling. About the precise ways in which this impact was to take place, the advocates were less clear.

Education also took its place in theories of political economy. The potential contributions from education to preventing the degradation of laborers, to morality, and to social order, respect, and obedience were powerful influences on later generations of economists, reformers, and policy makers. Adam Smith wrote, and his followers accepted: ''An instructed and intelligent people besides, are always more decent and orderly than an ignorant and stupid one. They feel themselves, each individually more respectable, and more likely to obtain the respect of their lawful superiors.'' The neglect of discussions about the formation through schooling of ''productive skills'' is not as much as a failure of the early classical political economists as a reflection of the place of education. Productive skills were more general attributes of the school's training than any specific job skills. A narrowly conceived vocationalism was not part of the promotion of mass schooling.[91]

What was newly developing in the context of economic development and socioeconomic change was the desire ''to get all working-class children into a school for some part of their lives.'' A plethora of elementary institutions emerged during the first half of the century. For the first time in English history, reformers, educators, the clergy, and more elites and entrepreneurs sought a comprehensive approach to popular education and socialization. In part, it was also a response to working-class demand from below. As David Vincent has shown, literacy and the struggle for ''knowledge'' and ''freedom'' through it were an important emphasis in the forming working-class culture increasingly penetrated by print.

The quality of instruction and learning was often low, but this approach to schooling was less alien, less paternalistic, and less controlled by other class interests. Its relationship to the new schooling developments that sought to embrace the masses and train them up in social morality and literacy remains one of the most important problems in the history of literacy and schooling. In contrast, the emerging approach to education was sponsored and provided by *others*, ''public'' and ''popular'' in a new sense.

Value and attitude formation took precedence over cognitive training. Pedagogy and curriculum reinforced the moral message; literacy contributed, as schools sought to establish a new hegemony and to replace traditional working-class culture with a new moral order. The economy, the society, and the nation were all to benefit. Many among the working class were less than accepting; the impact of schools on the population was nonetheless considerable.[92]

The expansion of schooling, from upper- and middle-class efforts to instill a new attitudinal and behavioral code among the lower class to local working-class self-efforts, points to changing perceptions of the value of literacy and schooling. This development must be understood alongside the likelihood that literacy's relationship to work and economic development was not strong. The cultural imperative blended in different ways for different persons and groups, and included religious, political, leisure, and economic motives. What is clear, however, is the emergence of *new* levels of demand for literacy, which did not always match supply.

The nature of the working class, its margins and insecurities, complicated and mitigated these urges. John Hurt's portrait of 1865–1914 illustrates the conditions of life and survival that reduced the impact of whatever demand existed and lessened the effect of changing school opportunities. These factors ensured the perpetuation of a gap between the growing numbers of literates and their qualitative abilities to use the skill. Changing patterns of popular recreation and their relationship to print reinforce the point. Cultural divisions, relating to literacy, came to distinguish elements within the working class, as well as between it and other classes.[93]

The complexities and contradictions inherent in literacy's history did not end with nineteenth-century transformations. The development of the moral bases of literacy and schooling, by reformers' promotions and by some working-class agencies, was shaped by this context. Working-class demand *and* intervention from "above," and their consequences for literacy, can also be seen in this context. The cultural hegemony of public (in the sense of control and payment) education thus developed.

Thomas Laqueur emphasizes the influences of working-class parents in securing private schooling for their youngsters. Parents could be selective of the agency to which they turned for their children's elementary schooling, and they were sometimes not only suspicious of alien institutions but also discriminating in their choices. Private, local schools were more like parts of the community. Some persons undoubtedly acquired basic literacy in such agencies; a few gained theirs *without* formal learning.

Sunday schools are a case in point. They were supplements to or substitutes for other schooling, and played an important role in disseminating reading skills. The level and quality of the skills imparted from their once-a-week instruction is doubtful. Their contribution to the maintenance of literacy rates during the most disruptive periods of social and economic transformation and to the post-1840 increase (and perhaps the earlier gains of women) is more likely. At their core, they were religious and moral institutions. Schools for the working classes, their curriculum was similar to that of the day schools: reading, writing, and arithmetic. They also promoted cleanliness, orderliness, punctuality, discipline, and regularity. As in other schools, the learning of literacy was not a neutral training; in instruction both religious and secular, the moral bases came to the fore.[94]

The relationships between literacy and economic development represent a central problem. Numerous researchers have considered literacy to be essential to economic development, and there is an increasing tendency among economists and governments to "justify" investment in education in economic terms (as "human capital").[95] However, from the time of the industrial revolution, evidence suggests that facilities may have been broken down in the wave of population growth that preceded and accompanied industrialism, that industrialization itself put no primacy on skill acquisition, and that the process of development, at least for the initial decades, was more disruptive to education than promotive.[96] Schofield muses, "Insofar as economic growth resulted from the increased productivity brought about by the shift from domestic to factory production, literacy and education were also probably largely irrelevant for many of the new industrial occupations recruited a mainly illiterate work force. . . ." He speculates that "the usual causal relations between literacy and economic growth might probably be reversed," and that the decrease in illiteracy in nineteenth-century England may be more a cultural change caused by economic growth than the cause of growth.[97]

An intriguing argument in support of the connection between literacy and economic development concerns the transmission of "know-how" and intellectual skills. "Arrangements for the shaping of men to participate in change include schooling but go beyond it; they include diverse sorts of learning at work and the diffusion of know-how by migration."[98] This factor certainly contributes to economic change; but it relates not to literacy but to innovations and entrepreneurial risk-taking by special individuals or small groups. Their seminal contributions were other than those deriving from basic reading and writing, and in numerous cases diverged from education. Recent writings on innovation and technological insight in the past, in fact, suggest that visual, nonliterate skills were relevant to this kind of contribution.

The lines of recent research and writing have contradicted the dominant assumption that education is at once central to the process of industrialization and logically must precede "take-off into sustained growth."[99] Productivity and wealth do not necessarily follow from mass literacy, as the histories of Sweden and Scotland firmly demonstrate. C. Arnold Anderson and Mary Jean Bowman have defined a "threshold of economic development" as 40 percent adult literacy or primary enrollment; however, England almost certainly had reached that level by ca. 1750, *before* the onset of industrialization. That fact becomes less interesting and less revealing when we consider that England no longer led among the nations of the West and that a fair number of other regions surpassed it but did not then "take off."

Urban surveys and regional studies contradict the assumed linear relationships between levels of urbanization and industrialization and levels of literacy. W. B. Stephens shows that as literacy levels varied widely, so did towns and their activities. The evidence includes examples of improvement and of decline. A basic pattern, however, is suggested, in which "literacy levels were manifestly related to some extent to the economic function of the town. Towns which experienced an expansion of industry seem also to have suffered a decline in literacy levels at various times. . . ." The effects of rural as well as urban population increase that seem to have preceded massive industrialization, rural protoindustrialization, urban economic expansion, labor-force migrations, and the like were elements of the process. Since the timing and impact of these transformations differed locally and regionally, it is not surprising that the consequences for literacy and schooling did, too.

Dozens of local studies point to the role of population change; some to factory capitalism; some to other factors in terms of literacy trends. No one factor can be accorded unique status. The timing sometimes followed national patterns of economic change; at other places, it preceded, as in the example of Lancashire, where literacy declined under the press of population *before* the spread of the factory. Local factors and human responses combined in determining the connections between change in literacy and socioeconomic and demographic transformations. In important cases, school facilities were insufficient or child labor too common. In textile towns, "the shift from domestic to factory production may have further affected the opportunities for education by depressing the standard of living of the handloom weavers who could no longer afford money to educate their children and needed their help or wages." More generally, in early industrialization, opportunities to advance were not necessarily connected to schooling. Thus, investment in education held less attraction.

The decline in literacy during the later eighteenth and early nineteenth centuries was neither an exclusively urban nor an exclusively industrial phenomenon. Some nonindustrial market towns also experienced a decline, although that was a rarer consequence. In nonindustrial centers where literacy increased, occupations associated with the growth of trade encouraged its acquisition. Market towns frequently were ancient boroughs, places where schools traditionally existed and educational standards were higher, and where population growth was not sufficiently rapid to cause dislocation. Some nonindustrial urban places, such as York, also saw a negative impact of growth and immigration on literacy rates.

No formula will account for this variety. What is clear is that such massive changes as English society was undergoing in this period were not conducive to major educational expansion, and that the changes themselves were not propelled by rising levels of schooling for most of the populace.[100]

The data, although incomplete and imperfect, do not contradict the perspective of an initially depressing and subsequently negative impact of development upon literacy. The stagnation and decline in literacy did *not* impede economic growth. The nature of this classic industrialization made very low demands on literate workers and the educational system. That the upsurge in interest in schooling for the masses largely followed trends in the economy supports the argument. Changes in patterns of working-class demand for schooling can also be interpreted in this light. In contradiction to arguments for the productive value of educated and literate labor's skills, early industrialization often disrupted education. The demand for child labor reduced chances for lower-class children to attend school. The few factory schools were ineffectual and irregularly attended. Secondary education was rare for children of the working class.[101]

David Levine's study of Shepshed reveals the impact of rural industrialization, or protoindustrialization. He stresses, on one hand, the constraints that families faced in securing schooling for their children regardless of "popular demand." On the other hand, he documents the realities of the impact of social changes on familial life and, especially, on literacy. Parish marriage registers show that from 1825 to 1844, 41.4 percent and 68.6 percent of men and women respectively were unable to sign. That represented virtually no change from the rates over the period 1754 to 1824, although short-term fluctuations, with changes in male and female rates largely independent of one another, were common. Shepshed's literacy levels were neither stable nor consonant with national patterns. For men, an increase in literacy after the end of the Napoleonic Wars was followed by a fall to earlier levels. Rural industrialization in this area did not raise literacy rates.

Occupationally, framework knitters fared worst in terms of illiteracy, closely followed by agricultural laborers. Almost two-thirds of them could not sign; in contrast, almost all artisans, tradesmen, and farmers could. The acquisition and intergenerational transmissions of literacy skills within families occurred almost at random; birth order and family size, for example, were not important determinants of opportunities to secure literacy during rapid economic and demographic change. Literacy was stratified between males and females and between the children of literate and illiterate parents (the latter stratification was a function of class and wealth, as well as of needs and perceptions of utility in the context of opportunities for one's children), but "among the villagers of Shepshed it does not seem that literacy was inordinately prized." "Not all artisans or tradespeople, let alone proto-industrial workers, could arrange that all their children learned to read and later to write. . . . perhaps, the voices that made the most noise, that were most insistent, have captured the historian's attention."

In the context of rural industrialization, Levine asks whether illiterates were different in their behavior from literates. Normative wisdom stresses that the literate are more rational and calculating in their approach to family formation, reproductive strategies, and child care; however, the empirical evidence is mixed.

The illiterate, after 1825, married earlier than the literate; that was especially true for illiterate women. Earlier marriage typically is considered a correlate and cause of higher fertility and the opposite of a strategy aimed at limiting births. The data, however, show that *literate* couples had the highest levels of fertility, and illiterates the lowest. Literate women perhaps compensated for later marriage with higher fertility. Mixed marriages, of one literate and one illiterate spouse, had highest levels of fertility. Non-industrially employed couples in which both partners were literate also had high levels. Early marriage and high levels of infant mortality among the illiterate were not accompanied by higher rates of reproduction. The normative wisdom of modernization and demographic transition theories is strikingly contradicted by these responses.

Variations in group fertility attest to a lack of homogeneity in demographic behavior or in responses to changing conditions. They also suggest that illiteracy did not contribute to careless, prodigious childbearing. "Literacy and 'rationality' were not synonymous and contemporary social reformers—and later historians of family life in England—were quite wrong in attributing this section of the working class with profligate and unthinking attitudes towards their domestic responsibilities." Such findings argue against the "modernization theory which posits that the illiterate were somehow not fully rational in their family lives. . . . that functional literacy was not a significant indicator of differentiation among the popular classes. . . . possession of literacy seems to have been a relatively unimpressive signifier of special status."

That demand for literacy neither increased during industrialization (at least as signified by rising rates of literacy) nor was maintained among families of literate parents reinforces the impression that the English industrial revolution was not fueled by growing literacy and did not stimulate education in its wake. Regardless of individuals' and families' perceptions of the worth of literacy, the circumstances of their lives saw no overturning of a "traditional" social structure of literacy and illiteracy. Although the children of literates were more often literate themselves, that advantage could not always be maintained; other aspects of life and familial economic strategies were more important.[102]

Lancashire was in many respects the "heartland" of the first industrial revolution. Its experience during the second half of the eighteenth and the early nineteenth centuries additionally confirms the lack of a direct connection between literacy and early industrial development and the negative impact of early development on schooling opportunities.

It appears that there was a decline in literacy in the region, which preceded the emergence of industrial transformation but was followed by a later increase. The decline seems not to have impeded the "upsurge of economic growth because the nature of the industrialization was such as to make very low literacy demands on the educational system," and presumably on literacy skills of the work force. Improvement in the first half of the eighteenth century was followed by a downturn in schooling opportunities and rates of literacy during the second half. Population growth, from rising birth rates and in-migration, initiated the decline before much industrial change. The sharpest declines in literacy came later in the century, especially under conditions of deteriorating wages, needs and opportunities for child labor, and insufficient supply of educational agencies.

Factory work reduced opportunities for schooling. With employment of children, it offered a full-time alternative to day schooling; with its impact on workers' skills and earnings, it heightened families' needs for their children's economic contribution. Industrialization also stimulated changes in lifestyles and modes of behavior that did not support regular school attendance. "The effect of all these changes caused by the new industrialization was to make it even less likely than before that a child of the lower classes would be able to receive such an efficient full-time day education as to make it permanently literate."

Literacy levels in industrializing parishes exhibited an irregular decline from the mid-eighteenth century into the early nineteenth. There was, however, a marked improvement by the mid-nineteenth century. Women's literacy suffered more than men's; urban manufacturing areas in the south of the county were harder hit than many rural areas. The process was apparently not fully reversed until the late 1820s and 1830s, pointing to a renewed schooling effort from the 1810s and a one- to two-decade gap between the fuller impacts of industrialization and recovery. A variety of "public" and private educational institutions were founded; their impact on literacy was not immediate.

Each aspect of the complicated relationship of industrialization to literacy and schooling remains open to discussion. "The assumption that a literate labour force was relevant for the economy as a whole at this time is open to question in light of the available evidence." It may be the case that the greater the extent of industrialization, the greater the impact on education. Yet, it does not appear that industrial setbacks derived from educational problems. Certain positions in the factory work force required literate labor; for them, supply was sufficient.

Evidence on literacy by occupations is revealing. Almost all of those in the spinning and weaving trades were illiterate; their rate was also below the county average of 36 percent for the period 1813–1839. That contrasted markedly with clothing and wood- and metalworking crafts, which demanded a higher level. "One thus finds the interesting situation of an emerging economy creating a whole range of *new* occupations which required even *less* literacy and education than the old ones." Declining skill levels were often mirrored in declining literacy rates within occupations. Learning new industrial jobs did *not* depend on using one's literacy; as Michael Sanderson put it, "Knack was more important than literature-based learning." That is not to suggest that literacy had *no* place in development. A few persons, in crucial positions, had to be literate; most did not. In fact, employers may not even have valued literate labor.

Sanderson also inquires into the relationship between literacy and intergenerational occupational mobility. He postulates that during the period of declining literacy levels, those with the skill would be advantaged, but after the mid-1820s, when literacy was increasing, its possession would represent less of an advantage. He finds, in evidence from marriage certificates, "that by the 1830s there was not a high degree of social mobility in Lancashire." There is no preindustrial bench mark with which to compare this conclusion, although there are indications that some mobility resulted from elementary schooling in a nonindustrial setting within Lancaster and that the educated were not entering the developing textile industry. The textile industry "did not need boys educated to this level and it did not attract them; it was not a factor which added to social mobility." In this example, sons of the low-ranking became less often low-ranking themselves. Laborers' sons improved upon their fathers' positions after charity-school education.

Regardless of the extent of mobility earlier, patterns were different from the late 1830s. Chances for mobility through elementary schooling may have declined; regardless, chances for upward mobility through literacy later were not impressive. Of 219 sons of laborers, 106 became laborers, including 39 who were literate. Twelve, of whom 3 were literate, fell into lower groups. The remainder, who were primarily literate, moved into 43 other occupations, of which the highest-ranking was bookkeeper. That was not a major shift upward, even for the literate. Sanderson then compares his earlier analysis with results from the 1830s. Although he may exaggerate the extent of mobility earlier, he concludes that "in an eighteenth-century commercial society unaffected by the development of the cotton factory industry, the possibility of social mobility for the educated son of a labourer was vastly greater than in the 1830s in a society considerably affected by such industrialization. . . ."[103]

Sanderson's interpretation does not apply, as he notes, to later experiences of industrialization in which the relationship of literacy to timing of development differs. The "second industrial revolution" of the second half of the nineteenth century was different. It followed, rather than led, rising rates of literacy and school expansion. Less labor-intensive, it placed a greater primacy on technological skills and postprimary forms of education related to those skills. It also drew, along with the rest of the economy, upon bureaucratic and administrative employees, who required a standard training in literacy. The place of literacy, while more central, can also be exaggerated in that case.

Nevertheless, places that industrialized later than England typically drew upon more educated, more literate labor forces. A "fit" developed that, while not wholly absent from the English experience, reflects back upon it in important ways. Industrialization, if not "nourished" by or especially "nourishing" for literacy, did relate to it. That school development and rising literacy were not far removed chronologically from one another is revealing. The impetus to reform schooling and expand it to embrace all the children was shaped not only by fears of working-class radicalism or revolt, but also by concerns about the supply and quality of workers for a transforming economy. A connection was developing between the school and the economy.

If not education as preparation for productive, skilled labor, what, then, was the relationship? Recent historians have shown that the laboring population had to be trained for factory work and taught industrial habits, rules, and rhythms. Traditional social habits and customs did not fit the new requirements of industrial life; they had to be replaced with new, "modern" forms of behavior. Although literacy was seldom central in the creation of an industrial work force, its potential for assimilation was soon recognized. The impact of early industrialization on schooling, as well as community stability and family life, stimulated new, more systematic efforts for mass schooling.[104]

Schooling, systematic and controlled training in literacy and morality at the elementary and popular level, had little to do with specific job skills or work preparation. Those were acquired in the family, in the neighborhood, and, increasingly, on the job. The newer schools were created for children whose likely destination was not technically skilled work. However, it was not necessarily the better, more highly skilled workers but the stable ones who were worth more to the manufacturers and other employees. Discipline, and new standards of behavior, were required to produce goods on time. Toward this end—reshaping character, behavior, morality, and culture—factory owners and other capitalists joined with social reformers and school promoters, seeking better approaches to socialization. Increasingly, they turned to public schooling, literacy transmission, and mass institutions.[105]

In the attempt to establish the hegemony of the school and its moral bases, instruction intervened in working-class culture, to limit its reproduction in the interests of social order, properly trained labor, and normatively socialized citizens. From charity and monitorial schools to "reformed," less coercive methods by the 1830s, children were taught the moral bases and, increasingly in such settings, literacy. Kept constantly occupied, their ceaseless activity in the school was structured by rules and discipline, as new forms of behavior and conduct represented the approved standard. The value of formal education was increasingly being recognized. The schools were dealing more effectively and efficiently with a growing population at a time of great change; they also attempted to reform adults through the inculcation of morality and self-restraint in the children. As a result, the process of assimilation was tied closely to the spread of literacy and institutionalized schooling.[106]

Illiteracy came to signify that the training required for civilization and progress remained incomplete. The consequences of persisting illiteracy, the dire threat to society that it represented, were matched only by literacy uncontrolled by morality. Although complete success was impossible, and members of the working class resisted in many forms, the goal became clearer. When reformers wrote of idleness, drunkenness, pauperism, vice, improvidence, crime, and especially ignorance, they spoke to the social "problem" of those untrained and uncontrolled by the instillation of discipline and morality through controlled socialization aided and speeded by literacy. The integrative and hegemonic functions of literacy are clear. On balance, this contribution of literacy was most significant, contemporarily and over the long term.[107]

Literacy was one of the core elements of England's centuries-old radical tradition. It had also, even prior to the eighteenth- and nineteenth-century reinterpretation of its universal utility, become an aspect of artisanal and craft traditions. In the context of a complex interweaving of political, cultural, social, and economic changes, an essentially new element in literacy's history was formed: the association of literacy with radical political activities, as well as with "useful knowledge," one of the many factors in the making of an English working class. As part of anxieties and social tensions, the uses of literacy by radical working men and women were associated with challenges from below and new attempts to reorder and reintegrate a changing society. However, the contribution of literacy was complicated on the one hand by its contradictory impacts and uses and the means of its learning, and on the other hand by limits on its power and its relationship to other, equally and more important parts of the contemporary context.

By the late eighteenth century, working-class radicals had come to associate literacy with social and political goals and with individual self-improvement and respectability. "It was part of the working class's rise to political power and its defense against oppression. . . ." Education had the potential for integration with the dominant value and behavioral code, as well as for independence. However, a division within the working class, as well as between classes, was exacerbated by the new quest for rational forms of recreation and badges of education.[108]

A genuinely radical political culture developed during the late eighteenth and early nineteenth centuries, and literacy was a part of it. Many among the working class were able to read, if not always with the highest levels of understanding. Print and reading were elements of this culture, especially among artisans with long traditions of literacy and key roles in the newer organizations and politics. Reading and striving for education helped the working class to form a political picture of the organization of their society and their experience in it. They valued literacy's contribution to advancement. Its employment in the *context* of their lives, the social and political changes that surrounded them, and their social relationships was important.

Of course, political involvement and discourse were not limited to the literate. In active, intense times of radical engagement, oral means of communication became even more important: from small reading and discussion groups to huge gatherings for orations. In addition, the ability to read or write did not mean a practical or high-level skill useful for political interpretation or analysis. "Ideas and terms were sometimes employed in the early Radical movement which . . . had for ardent followers a fetishistic rather than rational value."[109]

During an extensive campaign of organization and communications, artisan-led radicals seized the press as a major instrument. Societies, institutes, libraries, schools, and newspapers were among the efforts instituted to raise the level of political awareness; permanent news- and reading rooms were established in large centers. Printing and literacy had important uses for information, stimulation, communication, exchange, and mutuality of interest across space. However, the setting that brought individuals together and led to intercourse and interchange, and amplified the printed word for those who could not read, was as significant as literacy and print themselves.

Although schooling developed largely as a hegemonic inculcation of the moral bases of literacy, that result seemed uncertain to many among the middle classes and elites during the first half of the century. Many working-class readers read only handbills, advertisements, or newspapers; some read merely to escape. "As in any class at any time the number of students and eager or even moderately deep thinkers was very small." Oral reading added to the diffusion of print.

On the other hand, the unprecedented extent of print's use among the working class engendered fears among their "betters" of revolution. Responses included overt coercion and attempted reform and expansion, and, increasingly, the development of new publications aimed at the reform, control, and reintegration of the working class. Many of the same assumptions about literacy and the power of print came to be shared by those who sought to develop means of reforming and controlling the working class as by those within the class itself; herein was established a further legacy of literacy.

As efforts to control the acquisition of literacy were relinquished as ineffective, the broader, "reformed" creation of public schools (although not yet centralized or standardized) to embrace all the children of the masses and insure their morally based literacy emerged. A long, difficult process of institutional development and attitudinal and behavioral adjustment began. It was launched at the same time as the impetus to combat seditious working-class literature with other forms of print. Many of the same persons were involved in both.

The schools and reading material aimed at the same ends and the same persons. Organized efforts, as well as individual commercial efforts, were directed toward the reading of the working class, and through it the minds of men, women, and children. Instruction in political economy was central to both campaigns for reading. That is not to say that it was the same political economy that radicals and middle-class reformers (and sometimes reactionaries) had in mind. Education, formal through institutions or informal through reading, was, despite denials by some, a political force. As some among the working class struggled to make themselves and drew on literacy, education, and print in the process, others tried to remake and reform them. They turned to the same means.

In order to reach the working class, prices of the reform literature had to be kept down. Free distribution by the middle and upper classes was one solution. The popular literature of the day—the chapbook, and later popular journals and newspapers—was imitated as a way to attract the interest of the working man. Broadsides, tales, dialogues, parables, and illustrations were also employed.

Among some working-class readers and others who struggled to gain literacy, pursue knowledge under great difficulties, acquire books, and use their knowledge for their own and their class's independence and freedom, an idea of "useful knowledge" developed that overlapped with but also diverged from reforming interests. For them, knowledge could be useful, but not in a practical, daily sense. By contrast, the concern of the middle-class propagandists was more with social and cultural integration, national progress, and economic development than with individual and collective consciousness, awareness, and freedom, despite the elements shared by the two approaches. "Both sides were attempting to define the character of a literate culture which was being constructed on the foundation of one in which literature [and literacy] had played a much smaller part." The efforts of both bolstered the post-Enlightenment "literacy myth."

Although there were problems with the middle-class attempt to reform the working class—in level, style, and understanding, as well as distribution and interest—the effort was not a total failure. Working-class culture was not redrawn in mirror image of that of the middle class, but influence and cultural impact there were. The new literature was not well accepted, however; "the great part of the working classes,

like the great part of any class, were not actively interested in learning; they wanted
to be amused, and were so in one way or another.''[110] That is a critical point, for
the differentiation of the working class included the bifurcation of those employing
literacy for "rational," improving, and recreational reading from those using it for
amusement and entertainment of another kind or not at all. That does not signify
that the moral economy of literacy, and the manner in which they increasingly
gained their reading skills, did not influence them.

From early in the century, charity, monitorial, Sunday, and increasingly "public"
(if often denominationally controlled or oriented) formal institutional settings came
to replace less formal agencies for the transmission of basic literacy. Subsidized
schooling for the working classes expanded greatly. Informal agencies and demand
for literacy were still important, but more children were learning to read and write
because of easier access and more systematic instruction of nearby "public" or
national facilities. Fees were reduced, and provision became more systematic. The
probability of a working-class child's securing some formal schooling increased;
school attendance and literacy acquisition were becoming more often synonymous
experiences with youth.[111]

Approved schoolbooks spread the doctrines of order, harmony, and progress,
ignoring conflict and inequality. The child did not need to be proficiently literate
to comprehend the moral message. Until at least mid-century, before silent reading
was valued as a pedagogical tool, oral reading dominated in the classroom. The
constant repetition surely dented the minds of the young, regardless of their ability
to decipher the written word.

A number of texts were written and distributed after 1830. Before that time,
charity and monitorial schools stressed reading in the catechisms and directly in
the Bible. The new national reading books promoted secular values, but they were
permeated by Christian ethics. Through they might no longer contain Biblical passages or moral tales, their heroes were inevitably good Christians. In their daily
lessons, pupils learned rationales for government, military and police, private property, rich and poor, and the interdependence of the social classes; social mobility
was not advanced. The duties of citizens and the need for obedience, cleanliness,
industriousness, sobriety, honesty, and frugality were brought home to them.
Through drill, repetition, and memorization, youngsters absorbed a code for social
behavior.[112]

The organization of the school also helped to transmit the moral bases. It acts
as a "hidden persuader" that implicitly contributes to learning the rules of personal
action. In their internal organization, schools reflect social relations and ideology
and serve as key agents of transmission, at once legitimizing the social order and
assimilating their charges in it. The noncognitive behavioral and attitudinal prop-
erties of schooling help to link students to the larger social structure, teach them
to "participate in authority relations based on inequalities," "link the family with
the public institutions of adult life," and integrate schooling with work and politics.
In these ways, hegemony is transmitted through the institutions of education.[113]

The skills transmitted by the schools were often low in quality. Children were
influenced by the moral economy of literacy in numerous ways, but despite the
increasing rates of literacy, they *were not learning to read well*, in terms of either
fluency or comprehension. Most popular education was not dedicated to the de-

velopment of high-level, critical literacy abilities. Charity and monitorial school instruction overwhelmingly emphasized memorization and repetition rather than useful skills. A report to the Council of Education in 1851–52 maintained that instruction in reading was such that "the subject-matter of the book becomes practically of little importance," that both teacher and pupil "remain equally ignorant of what it was intended to teach; and it is degrading into a mere implement for the mechanical teaching of reading. . . ." Leaving school by age ten or eleven was common, limiting exposure for many children. Even in the "best schools," fewer than one-third reached the standards.[114]

The problem hinged in part on concentration on oral reading and neglect of attention to meaning. Reading was the most deficient subject, but little proficiency was found in either aspect, as pupils learned by memory and were unable to connect meaning with the sounds of the words. Schoolmen and teachers confused oral skills—fluent, proper-sounding, cadenced, and well-enunciated reading—with the skills of reading for meaning and understanding. Nevertheless, pupils could "often reach a comparatively high position in the school, reading inarticulately, spelling incorrectly, and with the vaguest notions of numeration." To many of the children, the language of books was a foreign language; "the children are baffled, confused, and disheartened, and as a natural consequence, they subside into stolid indifference."[115] That was one result of schooling, even in the places with the highest levels of literacy acquisition.

Such damning reports were instrumental in changing the structure of school support. The immediate impact was the institution of a system of "payment for results" to promote basic skills. Yet, this change brought no reports of progress; skill in reading, even mechanically, remained to many observers at a low level.[116] What verbal fluency there was obscured the absence of comprehension. As a result, there was a new emphasis on interrogation in examinations, to certify the results for which payment was made. Such interrogation "must have bred a deep distaste for the printed word in countless pupils. The child was seldom urged to reflect on the total meaning of a sentence or a paragraph, let alone allowed to take any pleasure in what he read." The schools often had few books on which to practice or to learn to value. Yet, after constant drill, around 90 percent of pupils passed elementary reading tests. They were considered literate, although inspectors realized that as the fluency of their oral utterings of printed words increased, understanding of them often steadily decreased.[117]

Rates of school enrollment and of literacy were both increasing, especially in the second half of the century. However, circumstances of daily life limited opportunities for many children. Needs for a child's contribution to the family economy persisted for many, especially in the countryside, where seasonal routines and work opportunities drew out urban as well as rural children. Expansion and reform took place within the context of traditions and economic constraints, and of perceptions of a limited value of schooling persisting among many families.

For many children, both parental support and individual motivation were absent. At the same time, schooling and literacy had become important for some kinds of work; especially important were low-level, "white collar" jobs, often a result of structural shifts in the economy and occupational hierarchy. Both elements are key aspects of the historical development of literacy to universality in late-nineteenth-century England. On one hand, we underscore the rising fact, and perception, of literacy's practical significance in work and small-scale occupational mobility. On the other hand, we underline the limits of the value and quality of literacy and its relevance to daily life. To the extent that achieving literacy could be liberating and expanding, the facts of life and work for most persons limited its consequences.

Schooling did contribute to mobility for some working-class children, especially those with some parental advantage, and for new kinds of nonmanual work. Mobility directly through literacy was not an experience of the masses. Parents understood that basic elementary learning was required increasingly for their children. The economy, by late in the century, drew upon literacy's skills as never before. However, a limited literacy was all that was required, and that was what the schools were concerned with providing. Literacy did not change society or overturn the social order.[118]

Failure in instruction and learning was not solely the province of the poor or the working class. It also did not signify that the school was not achieving many of its aims: in fostering hegemony and socializing pupils. Training in literacy involved more than understanding all that was read. Its uses included oral training as cultural conditioning; respectability, manners, taste, morality, and speech habits would be inculcated in the process of instruction. As recent social and psychological inquiries suggest, it is precisely the noncognitive functions of schooling that most directly relate to the creation of a work force required by modern capitalism, and a citizenry not disruptive of social order regardless of other social distinctions. Schooling's contribution came in these other kinds of skills.

The relationship of schooling and literacy to specific job skills remains vague. It is not known how much education a carpenter, shoemaker, mechanic, painter, storekeeper, or hotelkeeper actually would need to do his work. He might need arithmetic, but that could be gained without schooling. Examples of self-taught readers or writers are almost legendary, and they are central to many working-class cultural traditions. But the extent to which these skills, the tools based in literacy, were required remains questionable for those not employed in professional or clerical endeavors. Practical job skills were not part of the literacy-centered elementary school curriculum.

There was, of course, a growing demand for literate workers. Virtually all public-service, professional, and clerical workers had to be literate. In other sectors—construction, sales, transportation, and domestic service—literacy could be useful but was not an obvious necessity. Railroad companies, however, required literate workers; that was in part a testament of character, as well as a result of the regular use of printed instructions and timetables. Mining and agriculture demanded far less literacy, although some farmers and mine operators saw some need for it.

In the manufacturing sector, literacy and arithmetic were needed in some jobs, but educated workers were desired mainly for their presumed work habits and such qualities as social discipline, trustworthiness, respect, and conformity. Literacy was more than a skill, it was a sign of training and of schooling in morality and character.[119]

Literacy apparently did raise incomes. Within specific occupations, however, the difference in earnings between literates and illiterates was less than that between literates and illiterates in general. It is impossible to control for local economic conditions or the impact of family and social-class background, but literacy's value appears to have risen with occupational level, and its independent effect on wages seemingly was less than its combined impact with occupational level and background. As the most thorough study concludes, "Although literates appear to have done better on average than illiterates, [analysis] shows that over 60 percent of literate sons of laborers were in the lowest wage class." Literacy by itself typically was insufficient to boost earnings within an occupation or to raise workers' occupational levels. Literates, however, may have had an easier time finding steady work.

Rather than having a universal and direct value, literacy probably was important primarily to the most able, especially those seeking promotion. " 'It would be a great mistake to point out to children instances of persons raised by successful industry, or by remarkable talent, to dignity and wealth, as illustrating what education may do for them. This, with respect to the greatest number who never can so rise, would form in them expectations which must be disappointed,' " wrote one respondent to an educational commission. An Assistant Commissioner on Education added,

> There are no doubt a few occupations, that of an overlooker in a mill, for example, for which writing and arithmetic are indispensible, but the amount required is small, indeed not more than is usually brought away from a National school, or maybe easily acquired afterwards, if the prospect of promotion is held out. *But posts of this description are not the rewards of education as such, but of dexterity, honesty, and industry. . . .*

That did not mean that working people found no value in literacy or did not seek it when they were able. Some hoped for better positions for their children. Others had religious, political, cultural, and other nonfunctional motivations. Many valued literacy regardless of its relationship to work and its rewards.

Labor-market incentives joined with other factors in propelling the growth of literacy. Demand for schooled workers varied across economic sectors and geographic regions. As the labor force became more literate, the direct economic returns for literacy may even have declined. Demand for literate workers undoubtedly reflected perceptions of literacy's value, the rising popular diffusion of literacy, and the beginning of structural changes in the work force. Rising standards of wages and living during the second half of the century make it difficult to determine if economic returns from possession of some elementary schooling were rising or falling.

Between 1841 and 1891, the male labor force was gradually shifting toward the "more literate" sectors of the economy. Women's work was also shifting in that direction, with the expansion of sales, teaching, and, to some extent, domestic service. With respect to women's labor-force participation, David Mitch finds that factors such as husband's income and general demand for female labor were more important than increasing incentives from the labor market for women to become literate. He also discovered that women not in the labor force had about the same literacy rate as those in it.

The issues here are complex: "Although shifts in occupational composition suggest a growing demand for literate workers, those shifts could have been caused by shifts in the supply of literate workers. For most of the compositional shifts . . . , one can point to forces causing them independent of the supply of literate workers.'' Some of the increases in demand for literate workers also followed from shifting technical changes within occupations. With the introduction of more machinery, it became assumed, regardless of accuracy, that laborers operating machines should be able to read. Those who spoke in favor of education and literacy for such workers continued to stress morality and discipline, as well. A shift from a labor-intensive to a more mechanical and capital-intensive approach to productivity commanded a new look at the labor force.

Technical change was *not* raising the value of literacy in all sectors of the economy. Declining skill requirements reduced the primacy on literacy for some; in other areas, such as mining and building, no new technical developments influenced the value of literacy to workers. Counterforces existed. The extent to which new demands for literate workers offset these pressures is unknown.

With mechanization and the reorganization of production, earlier demands for a trained work force did not abate. The factory system demanded coordination among production workers, and increased the demand for orderly work habits. The spread of unions caused some employers to raise their appreciation of the educated workers: educated workers were reported to be less likely to join unions, and in the event of a strike, they were easier to negotiate with. Irony and erroneous perceptions mark the continuities and contradictions in these expectations!

Literacy, finally, may be related to advancement in occupation and wages through migration. It was an asset in migration and its opportunities, especially in longer-distance moves. Increasing opportunities, in part through transport developments, to move in response to trade conditions and demand, were probably associated with literacy, contributing to the expansion of the numbers of the literate.[120]

In sum, economically, a number of factors developed during the nineteenth century to induce more persons to value literacy. These underlay, in part, major shifts in the literacy rates of England, especially after 1840 or so. Economic incentives and work-derived motivations for the acquisition of literacy were important, but the economic was only one factor associated with literacy's history in this key period.

What was the relationship of literacy to life in nineteenth-century England? Despite the oft-cited ''explosion,'' society and culture were not dominated by print; access to information and work did not always demand much literacy. Unskilled or semiskilled labor seldom required reading and writing. Much skilled work consisted of practical knowledge, job experience, and good work sense and abilities; these must not be confused with the potential, but not necessarily required, contributions from literacy. Nonmanual workers often had more need for literacy, for clerical work, book- and record keeping, billing, inventorying, and ordering. Here, too, routines and habits may have played a more common role than advanced literary skills. Although not often required, literacy had important potential uses in gaining further knowledge and enrichment, facilitating access to culture and learning, and influencing social standing, self-esteem, and respectability. These were areas in which illiterates suffered most.

Underlying continuities combined with contradictions to determine the place of literacy. There was a new quality to the volume and distribution of printed materials. The industrial revolution opened new avenues of economic, political, and social action, and perceptions of the nature of literacy and its cultural role shifted greatly.[121] Newer economic requirements were also an influence. The higher population densities in the cities created new opportunities for communication and a demand for mass journalism, especially "street literature": newspapers, sports journals, songbooks, almanacs, political and religious pamphlets, "penny dreadfuls," and small books.[122] New levels of print were all around the people, increasingly as the century progressed. Even with the growth of print and the shift toward a more literate and literacy-related culture and society, literacy was not needed and used equally; its importance varied from class to class. The commonness of the habit of reading at all must be questioned, and it appears that those among the popular classes who did read often were reading neither what middle-class reformers and promoters urged nor what working-class radicals and their traditions promoted. The cheap, popular fare that they preferred contributed nothing to their cultural improvement.[123]

Throughout the society, demands for a higher literacy were seldom made, or required, for work, leisure, or intellectual pursuits. That remained true regardless of changes in the supply of schooling, diffusion of print, or distribution of basic literacy. Contemporary reformers pointed to a central truth. For many in this society, and not merely the working class, the literacy possessed commonly either was used less frequently, for study, work, or recreation, than literature alone suggests, or was exercised on cheaper, popular, and primarily amusing and entertaining forms of print.

The history of the West since about 1800 or 1850 is usually discussed in terms of the rise of mass institutions and mass communications; and the decline of community, the family, interpersonal relations, traditional cultures, and small (primary) groups.[124] Literacy and print are held to be an integral part of these consequences of modernization and their presumed alterations of social and psychological consciousness. New paradigms of culture, thought, and awareness are assumed to replace traditional oral and localized patterns. Logical procedures accompany literacy, it is argued, as a visual, print culture replaces an oral-auditory one; standardization proceeds with alphabetization and literacy. Psychic rootlessness, alienation, and privatized-individualized relations become more likely. The writings from which these speculations derive are fascinating and important; yet they remain largely undocumented, overstated, and exaggerated.[125]

Long-standing continuities in literate and print culture that developed over a period of at least two thousand years cannot be neglected without truncating history and wrenching literacy out of its context. The lack of a long-term view also serves to heighten and exaggerate the degree of change linked to the modern, urban-industrial eras. An epochal, irreversible transition from one condition of society and culture to one vastly different cannot both describe and explain any "great change." The complexities, continuities, and contradictions in the nineteenth-century history of literacy demand greater subtlety and sensitivity.

In the nineteenth century, print media did not achieve cultural dominance. Oral communications, symbols, and visual signs abounded. The oral and the print culture existed side by side, one sometimes supplementing or interacting reciprocally with the other. Pubs, for example, demarcated by their charming but socially significant signs (tools, animals, and trade and ethnic symbols), were social and cultural centers, places of communications, news, debates, and dialogue; they were also places where oral reading took place and newspapers were found. There is little reason to suspect that the daily culture overly emphasized the printed word, or that much literacy was required to learn its ways.

Experience was at least as much the teacher for everyday life as the school. Workplaces, mixed residences, and other institutions, as well as recreational settings such as pubs, provided news and information, supplementing the print on the street and compensating for those who missed it. They also provided contact points, culture, and learning where oral media were important. Print and preaching, orations and the press, song and traditional culture all blended into the changing culture, lifestyles, and political consciousness.[126]

Other information (and much amusement) was gleaned from newspapers, broadsides, or printed notices. The new forms of cheap literature neither required nor expected a high level of comprehension or deep study. Pictures and other symbolic representations frequently added to the appeal and meaning of these forms of print; in this way, the visual sign corresponds to but is not synonymous with the letters of literacy. Both demanded an exercise of the powers of "reading." Politics, religion, leisure, and other forms of cultural expression remained connected to the oral and visual focus, despite the growing encroachment of print.

Styles of social and cultural life reveal the same patterns. Michael Anderson's pioneering analysis of working-class family life in mid-nineteenth-century industrializing Lancashire indicates that work, family, and "critical life situations" were little affected by the concomitant rise of literacy and schooling. The basic means of survival and assistance of families and individuals came from informal, traditional means, not from bureaucratic, institutional settings in which literacy could be more significant.[127]

In other areas of life—culture, leisure, recreation—the use of literacy and print was increasing. It is, nonetheless, important to see the limits on literacy as a direct influence: in its impact and employment. A distinction must be made between different strata of the working class and distinct classes, and between the hegemonic functions of mass literacy and schooling and literacy's roles in daily life. Literate and other patterns intersected in complex ways.

In the course of the many changes that were transforming working-class culture in the nineteenth century, some members of that class, for example, the marginal members of the lower middle ranks, seized elements of middle-class habits of morality and respectability as they were able. They saw their path to occupational mobility, recognition, and security through literacy and education. Their uses of the skills were conservative, as were their political and personal orientations. The quest for mobility and security never led to a link between literacy and radicalism or organization. The quest was predicated upon literacy, and it was undoubtedly a stabilizing factor in the social order. Cultural imitation of the middle class appeared to be the path to individual progress; that led to efforts to distinguish themselves from the working class, in style, conduct, manners, residence, and color of collar.[128]

The lower middle class rushed toward the new "rationalized" recreational opportunities that developed in the second half of the century. Institutions for improvement, lectures, and churches attracted them. At the same time, a privatized home environment and new attractions such as the music hall assumed much of their time. That tension, exacerbated by reformers' cries for respectable and rational use of leisure time, marked their lives, and the place of literacy and reading within them cannot be doubted. Rationalized and respectable behavior meant a new prominence for literacy, but not necessarily its active employment.[129] Literacy took its place as one among other means of approved activities.

Schools often left in their products little taste for further education. The radical belief in the efficacy of education, a form of the "literacy myth," had come to this major contradiction. On one hand, the schools helped to stabilize and shape the evolving culture and left some message on the minds of their pupils, in part through the process by which the potentially radical skills of literacy were transmitted. On the other hand, comments about working-class indifference toward education were heard frequently after the late 1880s.[130]

More reading probably was taking place, but it was not often based on virtue, morality, or knowledge. Street literature, the increasingly illustrated "penny press," cheap and entertaining (but hardly elevating) fiction, sporting news, magazines, and especially newspapers proliferated. Reading shared with indoor games, music, arts and crafts, and handiwork as time and means allowed. The impact of literacy was much more mixed than either working-class radicals or reformers had hoped. The new reading public turned its often imperfect literacy toward neither politics nor self-improvement.[131]

Although they competed with a large range of alternative forms of recreation, many publishers turned toward working-class readers. From penny dreadfuls to illustrated newspapers, genres of print were developed and expanded. Most persons in the working class, and many in other classes, did not read very much, and when they did, it was more often for amusement than for learning or knowledge. Beyond newspaper reading, other kinds of reading remained rare into the twentieth century. The working class grasped the need for elementary literacy. They remained ambivalent about the schools and had little enthusiasm for extending education or improving literacy. The minority, who sought education for political and self-improvement purposes, are enshrined in the annals of labor history and in our popular images of literacy and education. As important as their uses of literacy were, to them and their agenda for the society, they were not representative of the working class.

The hopes of radical political use of literacy and schooling for an organized, educated, independent, and self-conscious working class became a minor if persisting legacy of literacy, embraced by those seeking changes from below in many parts of the world. That has not proved to be a major impact of literacy. Education seldom served to fulfill such hopes; they depended on more than the kind of schooling that was developed for the majority of working-class children and their parents.[132]

For most of the working class, the spread of literacy and institutionalized, public schooling accompanied a process of transformation and stabilization. Too much cannot be claimed for literacy and schooling alone; their role was neither independent nor determinative. Yet, their contribution has perhaps been too often overlooked. The working class was more than ever before concerned to demonstrate self-respect, respectability, stability, cleanliness, tolerance, and orderliness. While not accepting middle-class redefinition, new and "higher standards" of behavior were widely adopted. This trend permeated most aspects of life, and was caused in part by literacy through formal schooling. The class was also becoming more conservative. Political activism, organization, and independence all suffered in consequence. The disintegration of the artisan tradition, based on the active pursuit of improving uses of literacy and education, was an important cause and consequence of this process of transformation.[133]

The "aristocrats of labor," the upper stratum of the working class, were most likely to seek schooling and the moral bases of literacy for themselves and their children. They were also most likely to require literacy for their work, and to follow some elements of artisanal cultural traditions rooted in reading and writing. Of literacy's and schooling's impact on their behavior and attitudes, there is little doubt. The question remains of the degree of influence, the uses of literacy, and the impact on their independence. Although they sought respectability, independence, morality, and distinction from many beneath their social position, artisans and "aristocrats" did not merely mimic those above. Rather, they sought their social and cultural goals overwhelmingly *within* the working class, struggling to separate themselves from both the middle class (whose habits and attitudes they nonetheless resembled, and to some degree adopted) and the poorer, less respectable and conscious workers below them. They rejected patronage, but courted social approval and status confirmation. They sought education for its economic value, but also for its badge of status.

To gain the rewards of respectability, separation without isolation, home ownership, security and status required a commitment to such valued Victorian characteristics as morality, character, industry, sobriety, and thrift. Discipline, decorum, restraint, and proper manners signified to them, however ironically, the marks of the respectability for which they strived. The desire for education was linked to this process. Consequently, basic attitudes, values, and habits were shared by the middle class and labor aristocrats.

Schooling was essential to their maintenance of status and to their children's mobility, even within the working class. The limited historical evidence on the relationship of schooling to mobility suggests that it was largely, if not exclusively, the respectable working class that had any chance to gain. The perception of schooling's import, for work as well as proper attitudes and values (though perhaps modified within the home and family), combined with a longer and regular stay in school, and selection of higher-quality schooling, to give a greater exposure to the moral bases and skills.

The aristocracy of labor must be distinguished from the middle class. That holds true for behavior as well as attitudes, for literacy and education, despite the important commonalities. Their values and their relationship to literacy differed, in efforts to exist and to contend with their experience of the world around them. Despite these crucial differences, the results with regard to literacy and its social functions deviated less.

This element of the working class defined itself less by badges of education, degree of literacy skills, and what was read than middle-class members did. Labor aristocrats in some cases quested after knowledge and were serious students. Some applied it to active organization and political functions, but they were a minority. Many, however, exercised their skills on more popular, entertaining fare. Yet they also valued schooling, sought it for their children, and considered it more instrumental than others within the class. To a significant extent, regardless of the realities or contradictions of their daily use of literacy and its economic value to them, they accepted the ''literacy myth,'' and aided in its promotion and endorsement. They mediated partially the maintenance of hegemony within the social and cultural system.[134]

There were important working-class political and intellectual uses of literacy. The Victorian faith in education and the positive, liberating, and activating roles of literacy led to an education hunger, through formal institutions and self-improving means, that sometimes resulted in criticism of the education provided *for* the working class by others, but sometimes an embrace of available opportunities for learning.[135] The contents of the libraries of the Alliance Cabinet Makers' Association, for example—primarily literary fare, with some self-help books and a slight nod toward science, yet little socialism and no truly revolutionary works—reveal the class-consciousness and political awareness of this working-class group.[136]

The Victorian middle class constituted a major source of reform. They came virtually to wear education and literacy as a badge of status and identification. As education expanded, so did the clerical and professional spheres of work. The middle class dominated in opportunities for postprimary schooling as its members did in literacy-oriented cultural expression and cultural life. They fed that minority of the reading and opinion-seeking public that is termed ''articulate.'' They led in the rising incomes and time for leisure associated with these and related changes. The values of the moral bases of literacy were theirs.

The literacy acquired at school by many middle-class children, however, was often less than perfect. For the majority unable to afford elite, higher-quality private schooling, the educational conditions outlined earlier were shared. Parents who wanted better for their children may have had difficulty finding it. The uses of that literacy were also unclear; the available indicators suggest that even middle-class literacy was neglected, and that it was typically employed in reading for amusement, entertainment, and the like—noninstrumental and often-censured uses of literacy, instead of or in addition to promoted or pragmatic uses.

There were a growing number of alternative forms of leisure. The persistence of family reading suggests continuities in cultural transmission and activities related to the uses of literacy for oral circulation and familial cohesion. With increasing leisure time and rising incomes came the family excursion, the vacation to the seashore, the theater, concerts, lectures, choral societies, gardening, clubs and associations, conspicuous consumption, church and chapel, and, of course, middle-class sports. In the prized, sentimentalized domestic refuge, there were also activities from which to choose: music, toys and games, and crafts and sewing. Some of these activities could be related to uses of literacy, while others provided attractive diversions and competition.[137] Literacy existed in a context of variety and choice.

Middle-class work was essentially literacy-based and -oriented, and reading was more common, economically as well as culturally and intellectually. For women that was particularly true. The proliferation of domestic advice and how-to literature was read and had some influence. Novel reading was also very popular among women, despite the persistent criticism and censure that clerics and recreation reformers addressed to the apparently pervasive habit.

The Victorian sentimental novel, according to Sally Mitchell, "supplied for women of the middle class both a means of filling leisure time and a mode of recreation in the true sense of the word." Popular novels supplied a needed, socially conservative outlet. In other words, the "women's novel provides satisfaction which real life often lacks. It offers vicarious participation, emotional expression, and the feeling of community that arises from a recognition of shared dreams . . . sensibilities about her own character, her virtues, and her moral values are not violated." Popular novels gratified common needs, providing a distance that gave repressed emotions publicly acceptable forms and made them a source of pleasure. This reading may have assisted adaptation to one's life. Hardly liberating or even challenging, the message learned was predominantly socially conservative. This reading had its dangers, too. "It may supply too much catharsis and become a self-indulgent escapism. The happy ending may well be an opiate, the pathetic ending a diffusion of emotion. . . ."[138]

Among the middle as well as the working class, popular uses of literacy fed upon the newer and less expensive popular fare, aiming at pleasure and amusement. Different print appealed to different classes, and different persons within classes. Street literature was perhaps the working-class parallel to the novels of the middle class. It was inexpensive, short, easy to read and understand, appealing, and exciting, as well as socially and politically current. Illiterates heard broadsides and pamphlets read by others and cried out in public; this material was integrated easily into popular traditions and oral culture, without sharp discontinuity. One part of daily street education, for which popular skills were sufficient, it aimed overwhelmingly at noninstrumental aspects of entertainment, amusement, and common culture.[139] The middle-class criticism (an outgrowth of the reforming instinct) directed at this literature and its readers does not detract from its significance as an important employment of imperfect, mass literacy skills.

There was another middle-class reading public, a minority subculture known as the "articulate." For this numerically growing, if perhaps not proportionately enlarging, segment, special genres of print, books and periodicals, were maintained and spread. The new journals and books responded to the expansion of higher learning and knowledge, on one hand, and to the demands of the newly educated (well above literacy) for information on developments in fields from geology, political economy, and Biblical criticism to anthropology and sociology, on the other. Genuine demand for knowing and understanding mixed with that for conversation fodder, currency, and badges of pseudoeducation.[140] In a time of cultural crisis, new forms of print, devoted to giving information, often in condensed or digest form, added the certainty of an authority's opinion, giving breadth as well as depth. Structures of authority and the shaping of opinion, values, and responses were among their functions.

Despite the anxieties of reformers about the perceived threat of morally uncontrolled activities, by the end of the century, recreations and leisure pursuits were common among members of all classes.[141] In many respects, patterns of cultural activity among the middle and working classes were becoming more similar. Class lines were not disappearing, however, and may have hardened. Literacy and print media contributed distinctly to this vital transformation and the birth of modern and consumer culture. Some differences between classes declined, although they were not erased, with the development of universal schooling, literacy, and mass media. Thus, there is no doubt that literacy is important to modern culture, but it is neither dominant nor central in its contribution.[142]

The link between literacy and criminality—"Diminish the ignorance, and you diminish the crime"—was a widely accepted assumption of English school promoters and reformers, and it continues to be so today. The reduction of crime and disorder via controlled schooling and transmission of literacy ranked high among education's presumed socializing functions. Ignorance was considered the first cause of criminality, and schooling was to eradicate ignorance. The extent of literacy marked success, in theory.

Other educationists did not make such a direct connection. They believed that literacy, if unrestrained by morality, could be dangerous. Some schools, it was felt, could stimulate rather than prevent crime, and if schooling prevailed without morality at its core, illiteracy would diminish while crime increased.[143]

Statistics did not decide the issue. In several studies, criminal offenders were found to be only slightly less literate and educated than the population as a whole. The expansion of educational provision did not prevent crime; other factors were obviously at work. The links between poverty, arrest, and punishment, on one hand, and poverty and illiteracy, on the other, bear study. Illiterates were disadvantaged in court, and there were prejudices against them and expectations about their guilt because of their illiteracy. For the nineteenth century, the asserted beneficial role of literacy and education was never proved.[144]

The mysteries of the extent of literacy in *Ireland* end with the availability of national data. The origins of an Irish "literacy transition" are found in the nineteenth century.[145] The 1841 census confirmed the country's massive illiteracy; despite the hedge schools, charity school efforts, and informal means—all of which point to an awakening of educational interest before the nineteenth century—only 27.6 percent of the population in 1841 could read and write, and another 19.8 percent could read only.

Although these aggregates camouflage variations of sex, geography, type of residence, and age, they indicate that this relatively low level placed the Irish *above* the lowest literacy levels in the West. The Irish no longer can be seen as anti-educational. For many, the conditions of their lives restricted opportunities for education and placed no primacy on literacy and schooling. Facilities and opportunities for education developed and penetrated the countryside slowly. These facts combined with socioeconomic realities and traditional attitudes to underlie the statistics of literacy in prefamine Ireland.

The male-female and urban-rural differentials were striking. Schooling was more readily available and the need for literacy greater in towns and cities, for men *and* women. In urban areas, women's rates were much higher than in rural. Town literacy levels were not independent of their regions, however. Regional disparities also reigned supreme. As a map of the 1841 census shows starkly, in large parts of the west, at least three-fourths of the population could neither read nor write. The underlying roles of poverty, landlessness, and related factors emerge.[146] Literacy did spread, and rapidly, but social conditions and levels of living changed much more slowly.

Emigration varied along with the levels of literacy and poverty. The most illiterate and poorest western counties thus sent few permanent migrants before the end of the century. Migration related to literacy, especially in the context of economic development. Such is particularly the case with long-distance, transatlantic emigrants. Factors that triggered migration also stimulated desires and opportunities for literacy. The poorest usually had neither the means nor the information, connections, motivations, or perhaps even self-confidence required for such a major step. Those Irish immigrants who peopled the cities of North America and Australia, regardless of their literacy levels, were not the dregs of their homelands that contemporaries considered them to be. The implications for the social development of the receiving land—and for Ireland—demand reconceptualization.[147]

Its role in the migration process emerges as one of literacy's most direct correlates. With the increase in literacy and the growth of print, the Irish were exposed to news and information about the outside world, and about the possibility of finding a better way of life abroad. Of course, many illiterates also made the long voyage. Their personal connections and places of residence likely compensated for any disadvantage from their lack of literacy. Limited data suggest that such migrants were most likely to come from places of relatively high literacy; information came from their neighbors, peers, and the "environment" more generally. They were possibly more advantaged by their geographic, economic, and cultural locations than were literates in less developed, less well-integrated places, and much better placed than illiterates in those places.[148]

Literacy apparently also influenced distance of migration. Many Irish migrated only as far as Great Britain. Researchers such as Robert Webb have located areas of Irish residence in England with higher rates of illiteracy than those of predominantly native-born districts, and Irish parishes with higher illiteracy rates than mixed areas. Education-society surveys of two London areas in 1837, for example, reported 49 to 55 percent of adults unable to read. Comparison of these rates to those from the 1841 Irish census shows that short-distance migrants had literacy levels at best only marginally above those of people at home; the difference does not compare with that of those who made the lengthier and more arduous journey to North America. These Irish, however, were not marginal, irrational, and disorganized persons.

In three Ontario cities, around mid-century, the Irish contributed the largest number of illiterate adults. However, their rate of adult illiteracy was only 20 percent, much less than comparable levels in Ireland, urban or rural. Not until the late 1870s and 1880s did Irish national literacy levels begin to approximate those of these urban Canadian (largely Catholic) Irish: a gap of as much as thirty or forty years in educational advantages for emigrants. That was as true for Catholics as for Protestants, for females as for males. In literacy, these migrants were special persons, whose experience indicates an important relationship. This selection process resulted in a highly literate immigrant population, even among economically depressed Irish Catholics.[149]

Irish illiteracy declined relatively rapidly after the inception of the national school system.[150] Although it was not the sole agent for transmitting literacy, the system had an important effect on literacy levels. The rate of illiteracy declined steadily, from 53 percent in 1841 to 14 percent in 1901. Rates for those who grew up under the system are lower still. However, poverty, landlessness, social problems, and underdevelopment were hardly reduced by the educational achievement and mass levels of literacy.

Literacy levels rose among all religious groups from 1861 to 1891. Roman Catholic illiteracy declined from 46 percent in 1861 to 16 percent by 1901. That was the largest proportional decrease among the major denominations. However, Catholics had the highest illiteracy in 1861; despite the extent of change, in 1901 the gap between Catholic and Protestant remained substantial. Literacy did not alter the divisions in development, wealth, status, and power in Irish society.

Gender differentials virtually disappeared by the end of the century. The 1841 census reveals the discrimination against women's education in a traditional, Catholic, and underdeveloped society. Although the difference among illiterates was not large, there continued to be a larger gap between those who could read and write, and those who could only read. For all its growth in the extent of literacy, Ireland at the end of the period lagged behind England, Wales, and Scotland, lands with different traditions, social structures, and educational legacies.

These issues are further complicated by the language question. The new national educational system taught literacy in English, not Irish. The existence of a long heritage of rich literary traditions tells little about the state of popular literacy. Ireland's literary traditions may owe more to the strength of its renowned oral culture and Gaelic, a tongue in which the majority of the population may well have *never* been literate. Data from mid-century through its end show popular familiarity with the Irish language. They reveal limits in the diffusion of Irish, and its decline during the second half of the century. Irish, it appears, had ceased to be the national language before mid-century.

Regional variations parallel the paths of literacy and social change. Anglicanization had long been a policy of English and native Protestant schemes for schooling. No institution or system can be held solely responsible for the decline of an indigenous language, of course, and total blame should not be assigned to the national schools. The onset of the reduction in popular familiarity with Irish likely preceded the development of the school system; and earlier programs simply never were able to secure and maintain the students long enough to have any such impact.

The market economy and increasing contact with other regions and peoples accompanied and stimulated the functional need and demand for English-language ability for economic and informational purposes. Donald Akenson notes, "The obvious economic advantages of speaking English and the insistence of the Roman Catholic clergy upon the use of English were largely responsible for the decline of the language." The development of protest by the 1870s is one indication of the costs of monolingual instruction in a society with a heritage of another language. The legacies continue to be felt. The groundwork that remains in the history of Irish literacy must confront the language question and its meaning for mass schooling and literacy. The national system's basic neglect of all subjects relating to Irish culture raises further questions about the content and orientation of the literacy that it helped to spread rapidly, if unevenly and unequally, by the end of the nineteenth century.

Some researchers have found it incongruous that such an economically and socially underdeveloped country achieved a national system of education and high rates of literacy in the nineteenth century. However, Ireland was undergoing a social, economic, and demographic transformation at the time. ''Social problems'' such as glaring overpopulation and the uneven impact of the market and commercialization made many concerned about the state of the masses. At the same time, demand for literacy and schooling, from peasants, working class, and middle class, was increasing in response to social and economic changes. That the development of a system, a political and religious compromise as well as an importation of current Western ideas and ideals about the need for a systematic approach to educational provision, took place is less than startling.

Political, religious and moral, and economic interests were powerful forces in the creation of the system. Popular desires for literacy aided its rapid acceptance. The hegemony of the system, with its thoroughgoing moral bases, rested on this sometime fragile process of acceptance and accommodation. The curriculum was permeated with the moral bases of literacy. As elsewhere, an officially religiously nondenominational approach to mass education did not prevent a fundamentally moral approach to formal socialization and transmission of basic skills. Despite differences, all denominations agreed on the centrality of a moral core. Elementary training, all that virtually all students received, was not directly relevant to the economy. Few received more than a basic acquaintance with literacy or progressed beyond the lowest levels. The curriculum was not a practical one.[151]

The state, the social order, the polity, and the economy benefited from the process as much as, if not more than, the individual. The rub, perhaps, was the more limited uses of a functional literacy (of a restricted quality) in the circumstances of limited Irish development. Many persons took their literacy abilities abroad. At best, the impact on Irish society can be termed ambiguous.

## F. North America

The educational imperative that accompanied nationhood in the early American republic is among the factors typically associated with an asserted American ''uniqueness.''[152] The United States is often said to have been born modern, largely because of the existing base of high literacy. The educational historian Lawrence Cremin has argued for an expanding ''literacy environment'' in the nineteenth century, for ''the opportunity to use literacy for liberation,'' and for the advancement of equality through education. For him, literacy and education led to increasing diversity and choice, and the interaction of the individual with literacy and an expanding environment made possible a change in the quality, usefulness, and quantity of literacy.[153]

However, this transformative influence has not been proven. Literacy had other, nonliberating uses. Its potential for liberation was at best one use among many, and perhaps not the dominant one. Literacy was also used for order, cultural hegemony, work preparation, assimilation and adaptation, and instillation of a pan-Protestant morality; in addition, it contributed to work and wealth. America was not really unique or exceptional. High rates of literacy did not preclude contradictions or inequalities, regardless of rhetoric.

A surge of interest in education followed the advent of nationhood. There was a virtual consensus that education for republican life was among the nation's first requirements.[154] The educational legacy of the late eighteenth century, which congealed in the Enlightenment tradition, comprised the Renaissance ideal of education for developing the scholar-gentleman; the scientific ideal of mastering the environment for human betterment; the ideal of education for moral, ethical, and religious development; and the contemporary ideal of education as a function of and for the state, the training of free citizens for their civic, social, and intellectual duties. The moral and the civic goals were the most important.[155] At this level, agreement was possible among both radicals and conservatives. If people were to improve their society and themselves, they must be educated.

Numerous plans were proposed for state and national educational systems. Although they proved premature (literacy continued to be provided by home, church, and local schools), a postrevolutionary legacy, which sometimes stressed equal, free, public, and uniform schooling, had been planted.[156] A remarkably broad consensus developed by the early nineteenth century about popular education centered on schooling for the goal of transmitting literacy with a common core of morality, patriotism, and knowledge.

In contrast to the English context, there was little opposition to mass schooling for free whites in the United States. The promotion of such schooling for social stability, a minority view in England at the onset of the nineteenth century, was the dominant view in the young republic. Yet, "American urban reformers nonetheless repeated the social justifications for mass education offered by their counterparts." Both emphasized collective goals of education—reduction of crime and disorder and, to a lesser extent, economic productivity—rather than individualistic ends. American reformers eagerly adopted English institutions for educating the poor (Sunday, monitorial, and infant schools). Anglo-American contacts were constant and lively, as "similar institutions mirrored a similar social philosophy."

Conservative opposition was powerful on one issue: the education of slaves. The reform argument concerning schooling for social stability was not accepted by writers on slave education. Early charitable efforts to school slaves for obedience and subordination were actively discouraged, and after 1820, in response to revolts and abolitionist literature, education of slaves was legally prohibited.

The idea of mass education for progress and social stability was quickly accepted. The colonies had a relatively high base of literacy, and a tradition or legacy promoting literacy was more firmly rooted. Literacy on a popular basis was perceived to be conducive to and supportive of a republican revolution; that was taken as part of the new nation's heritage. A further reinforcing factor was that mass schooling was becoming increasingly acculturated with rising levels of immigration.

The use of schools for assimilation and sociocultural cohesion developed rapidly as a social goal in the early nineteenth century.[157] The need for a population trained in literacy controlled by morality was an original goal of the nation. However, many were excluded from the benefits of schooling. In postrevolutionary Philadelphia, for example, the poor began to be viewed as a threat, associated closely with vice and criminality. Reformers initiated educational programs aimed directly at them.

"Optimists" believed in the worthiness of the poor, and urged a secular, free educational system to help the talented to rise, and to enlarge opportunities for political participation. They argued that a proper educational environment could contribute to a more equal society, and that education was an equal right. Their efforts failed.

"Pessimists," the great majority, promoted education for the poor to train them to accept their inferior status—the desire was to control the lower class, not to assist their advancement. They believed that properly religious and moral education could replace vice, idleness, and disorder among the poor with virtue, order, and happiness. Social order and stability, property, and productivity would then benefit.

In response, educational opportunities expanded greatly after 1784, emphasizing religion and morality, including through literacy. A Negro charity school, schools for poor boys, and church and Sunday schools were quickly founded, operated mostly free of charge by voluntary societies. Through them more than 2,000 young persons had received some education by 1800.

Reformers of each stripe supported schooling for social stability. Literacy and its links to morality were emphasized by both sides, regardless of divergences over desired outcomes.[158] Literacy itself, however, did not emerge as the goal of education; herein is one key meaning for its provision in the new nation and for the expected and promoted uses of its skill.

Literacy rates from the late eighteenth century show a lack of consistency. There were sometimes large gaps in literacy between members of different socioeconomic groups; however, a low level or the absence of literacy did not preclude economic or political participation before the nineteenth century. Lee Soltow and Edward Stevens have attempted to shed some light on the confusing rates of literacy in the precensal period (until 1840 and 1850), using such indices as records of American seamen and army enlistment files.

Among their findings was the striking contrast between the literacy levels of whites and nonwhites. The 74 percent illiteracy rate of nonwhite merchant seamen reflected a near-total neglect of schooling. In general, Soltow and Stevens found that the rate of illiteracy declined throughout the period to 7 percent by the end of the nineteenth century. Prior to 1850, nearly 40 percent of army enlistees were illiterate; the school reforms of the 1830s and 1840s had not yet made their impact felt.

Among the enlistees, farmers and laborers, who constituted the largest group, had a higher-than-average rate of illiteracy. Foreign-born enlistees had a higher rate than the native-born until 1850, when their rates became virtually equal. Northerners were considerably more literate on average than Southerners; this gap was rooted in traditions, as well as ongoing social realities. Beginning in the 1830s, however, the South experienced substantial progress. For all enlistees, the rate of illiteracy was halved over the period. The decline affected all occupational groups; however, class differences were *not* erased. Place of birth, ethnicity, place of residence, and occupational level all influenced literacy levels.

By the time of the 1840 census, a strikingly low national level of illiteracy (9 percent) was reported—a probable result of expanding local provision of primary education and the promotion of reading and the press. As the following table shows, regional differences remained; the image of a North-South axis was reinforced.

Percentage Illiterate by States, 1840

| | | | | | | | |
|---|---|---|---|---|---|---|---|
| North Carolina | 28 | Indiana | 15 | New Jersey | 4 |
| Tennessee | 24 | Illinois | 14 | Rhode Island | 3 |
| Arkansas | 22 | Mississippi | 12 | Michigan | 2 |
| Georgia | 20 | Florida | 10 | Vermont | 2 |
| South Carolina | 19 | Maryland | 8 | Maine | 1 |
| Virginia | 19 | Louisiana | 6 | Massachusetts | 1 |
| Delaware | 18 | Iowa | 6 | New Hampshire | .6 |
| Alabama | 18 | Ohio | 6 | Connecticut | .3 |
| Kentucky | 17 | Pennsylvania | 5 | | |
| Missouri | 15 | New York | 4 | | |

States with high levels of illiteracy at the beginning of the century continued to have high rates; school provision and support also varied in this fashion, although the traditional image of an antieducational South should be revised. With regional differences in economics, settlement patterns, and levels of commercialization, differences in needs and demands for literacy provision also varied.

Schooling and literacy levels corresponded strongly by the mid–nineteenth century, especially in the North. In the South, where there were higher illiteracy rates and a limited development of schools because of a lack of traditions, low tax support, sparse population, lack of commercial development, and family patterns, the growth of literacy was a result more of informal schooling and irregular learning, through church, family, friends, coworkers, and printed materials.

In both the North and the South, illiteracy fell more or less regularly as the size of a county's white population increased. In the North, however, a large population (over 10,000) led to a *rise* in illiteracy, reflecting a strain on facilities. Wealth per capita, books per capita, proportions of persons native to a county, and the numbers of schools also related negatively to illiteracy levels, as, not surprisingly, did the extent of commercialization and manufacturing activity. With population growth came institutional development, as well as publishing activity. Northern areas were more favored by such development. The 1840 survey points again to the conclusive link between literacy and social and economic development. In the South, urban residence was especially conducive to literacy; poor, sparsely settled counties where schools were slow to develop had traditions of intergenerational illiteracy.

Between 1850 and 1860, the national rate of adult illiteracy fell to 8.3 percent. Sharp variations by race, geographic region, and sex remained, however. The promotion of literacy and schooling through formal, institutional means was reaching new levels. Reformers showed a new awareness of the connection between illiteracy, poverty, and criminality; the need for a literate, morally schooled population, to protect social order and maintain the fabric of society, led to a new concern with eradicating illiteracy.

The figures from the 1870 census indicate that illiteracy had risen in the preceding decade. However, the apparent increase was likely due to two changes made in collecting and categorizing data, as well as to possible disruptions from the Civil War. The population for whom information on literacy was gathered was expanded to include those aged ten to nineteen, and a distinction was now made between

TABLE 7.17

**Percentage of Persons over Twenty Years of Age Who Could Not
Read or Write, 1850 and 1860**

| | Whites | | | | Free Blacks | | | |
| | Males | | Females | | Males | | Females | |
| Region | 1850 | 1860 | 1850 | 1860 | 1850 | 1860 | 1850 | 1860 |
|---|---|---|---|---|---|---|---|---|
| New England | 3.2 | 3.9 | 3.6 | 5.4 | 14.0 | 10.0 | 13.8 | 9.6 |
| Middle Atlantic | 4.6 | 4.4 | 7.2 | 6.5 | 29.6 | 25.0 | 32.1 | 28.2 |
| North Central | 7.2 | 5.6 | 12.9 | 9.2 | 38.2 | 32.9 | 44.2 | 37.4 |
| South Central | 14.9 | 12.0 | 25.7 | 20.0 | 38.5 | 29.0 | 43.4 | 29.0 |
| South Atlantic | 14.1 | 12.1 | 22.7 | 17.8 | 52.2 | 20.1 | 53.7 | 51.2 |
| Total percentage for five regions | 7.3 | 6.6 | 12.4 | 10.1 | 39.7 | 36.1 | 42.8 | 38.4 |

*Source:* U.S. Census Office, *Eighth Census, 1860* (Washington, D.C., 1864–1866).
Note: national rate of illiteracy, 1840: 8.5%; 1850: 9.7%; 1860: 8.3%; 1870—ten years and over (whites): 11.5%; (blacks) 79.9%. 1850–1860 national: native–born illiterates decrease 1.5%; foreign-born illiterates increase 72.7%.

reading and writing literacy. Twenty-five percent more persons were unable to write than were unable to read, a fact that in itself could account for the difference. The proportions in 1870 unable to read show no decline from the previous census.

In a Soltow and Stevens sample from the 1860 census, improvement in literacy levels is indicated for men in the North, especially in more densely populated areas, but not for those in the South. There was a noticeable decline in illiteracy by age in the North, and a striking farm and nonfarm occupational distinction, with a clear advantage for nonfarm–employed men aged thirty-nine or younger. In their sample from 1870, farmers still had a higher rate of illiteracy than nonfarmers. Nativity and residence cut across this difference; in the North, rates of illiteracy were slightly lower among farmers than among nonfarmers—in part a result of the number and high illiteracy rate of foreign-born in Northern cities. In the South, illiteracy was considerably higher in all categories.

Regions of residence and birth remained major contributors to literacy patterns in 1870. Simple North-South or urban-rural distinctions disguise significant differences in opportunities for schooling, in poverty, in sanctions and pressures for school attendance, and in demands for literacy, as well as in religious, familial, and economic factors.

The 1870 data show that inequality in literacy across the nation had declined since 1840. Literacy levels were still associated with social development. Population density, wealth, and indices of economic development continued to have an inverse influence on illiteracy rates. The relationship between school attendance and literacy was stronger, with the spread of systemized public schooling, especially in the North.[159]

The 1860 and 1870 samples indicate comparatively minor gender differences (2.2 and 1.3 percent respectively) with regard to literacy. There was a greater discrepancy between male and female rates in the South; women had less opportunity in areas where literacy levels were lower and less developed. Women's education was at-

TABLE 7.18
**Illiteracy, Related to Nativity and Residence for Male White Adults
in the United States in 1870 (in percentages)**

|  | All | North | South |
|---|---|---|---|
| All | 8.7 | 6.4 | 15.1 |
|    farmers | 10.1 | 6.0 | 16.2 |
|    nonfarmers | 7.5 | 6.8 | 7.6 |
| Native-born | 8.0 | 4.1 | 17.7 |
|    farmers | 10.2 | 4.7 | 18.2 |
|    nonfarmers | 5.3 | 3.5 | 6.8 |
| Foreign-born | 10.5 | 10.9 | 10.6 |
|    farmers | 9.8 | 10.1 | 11.6 |
|    nonfarmers | 10.8 | 11.2 | 7.8 |

Source: Based on unpublished table prepared by Lee Soltow and Edward Stevens.

TABLE 7.19
**Illiteracy Rates for Free Men 20 and Older in the United States in 1860,
Classified by Age, Occupation, and Residence (in percentages)**

| Age class of adult male | North | | South | |
|---|---|---|---|---|
|  | Farmers | Nonfarmers | Farmers | Nonfarmers |
| 20–29 | 4.3 | 2.0 | 13.1 | 8.5 |
| 30–39 | 4.8 | 2.7 | 10.0 | 8.1 |
| 40 & up | 4.8 | 5.3 | 11.3 | 8.0 |

Source: Unpublished table prepared by Soltow and Stevens.

tracting great interest and attention. Expectations of their proper place, cultural and religious impetuses, the requirements of motherhood and domesticity, and, in some areas, expanding opportunities for work intersected with familial resources and choices and local opportunities. The new culture and ideology stressed education for girls as part of social and cultural preparation.

Younger and native-born women had lower rates of illiteracy. The lowest levels occurred among native-born women in Northern cities, probably because of greater exposure to schools, print, libraries, churches, and the like. By 1890, the literacy rates for males and females under the age of twenty-five were almost identical. Foreign-born women, on the other hand, had considerably lower literacy rates. Traditional familial attitudes, poverty, lack of resources, and higher priorities contributed here.[160]

For many poor, working-class, and often immigrant families, children's schooling had a low priority. Children had a direct economic value to the family; in addition, direct forms of security such as home or property ownership were considered more important—after that goal was achieved, education for children became more often possible. Older children thus had less chance for schooling; primary-school attendance rates increased through the birth order in illiterate-headed families.[161]

TABLE 7.20

**Cumulative Proportions of Illiterates, Classified by Cumulative Proportions of Wealthholders (Nw) for the North and South for Free Adult Males in 1860 and White Adult Males in 1870 (in percentages)**

|  | North | | South | |
|---|---|---|---|---|
| Nw | Free Adult Males, 1860 | White Adult Males, 1870 | Free Adult Males, 1860 | White Adult Males, 1870 |
| .10 | 2.3 | 3.0 | 0.7 | 4.2 |
| .20 | 9.2 | 9.0 | 6.0 | 10.6 |
| .30 | 12.3 | 14.9 | 10.0 | 18.1 |
| .40 | 22.3 | 23.2 | 20.7 | 29.0 |
| .50 | 33.9 | 34.5 | 36.0 | 42.1 |
| .60 | 43.8 | 47.4 | 47.3 | 54.9 |
| .70 | 63.1 | 60.0 | 63.9 | 66.3 |
| 1.00 | 1.00 | 1.00 | 1.00 | 1.00 |
| G | 20.0 | 19.6 | 20.3 | 11.7 |

Source: Lee Soltow and Edward Stevens, *The Rise of Literacy and the Common School* (Chicago: University of Chicago Press, 1981), p. 179.

The contribution of literacy to economic welfare is a major question. It was often claimed that literacy and schooling were required for economic survival, but the data prove otherwise.[162] According to the 1860 and 1870 censuses, illiteracy was a handicap, as were the social characteristics most frequently associated with the lack of education: working-class origins, Irish Catholicism, female gender, older age, etc. There was, in other words, some important support for the "literacy myth." At the same time, however, 36.1 percent of the illiterates were above the median wealth line: an indication of the economic achievements possible to those without the skill and potential advantage that literacy was presumed to signify. Furthermore, economic stratification by literacy did not increase over the decade, and may, in fact, have weakened.

Literacy *was* valuable in the socioeconomic system of the period. Its importance to individuals and to the commercial-industrial economy was increasing. It was becoming more important for individual economic advancement, especially for older men; progress over the economic life cycle became more limited for the illiterate. The economic contribution of literacy to farmers was also increasing. Of course, just as illiteracy did not preclude all economic gain, the achievement of literacy was no guarantee of either mobility or solid well-being.[163] Its contribution to economic prosperity was sometimes limited and often contradictory.

For example, Thomas Dublin's study of the textile industry of Lowell, Massachusetts shows that earnings of literate and illiterate pieceworkers were virtually the same. Dublin concluded that the 17 percent wage differential between native-born and immigrant workers was a result *not* of differences in literacy levels but of ethnic and class discrimination (immigrant newcomers were channeled into low-paying work). Literacy did relate to patterns of job placement; mill managers apparently considered the productivity of literate, educated workers to be higher, and placed them in the most skilled positions. Thus, they earned higher-than-average wages. Formal, controlled training in literacy presumably produced more punctual, orderly, malleable, and obedient workers, and such workers were rewarded by job placement.[164]

Over time, children began to stay in school longer, as both the ability of families to support them and the acceptance of the values of literacy and schooling were increasing. Educational progress, although slow in New England mill towns, was heavily promoted. The working class recognized the contributions of schooling to economic opportunities; education in literacy and morality was also seen as a solution to the social problems associated with urban conditions (vice, immorality, poverty, and the like). Both native and immigrant families, rural as well as urban, accepted this function of the schools. Gradually, more children were instructed in the moral bases of literacy, in the dominant culture's behavioral and attitudinal standards, as immigrant and lower-class children were assimilated to the social order.[165]

Ontario, Canada in the 1860s and 1870s was an overwhelmingly literate society, with a rate of over 90 percent, despite the large foreign-born population and Irish concentration in its cities. In wealth and occupation, there was superficially a significant stratification by illiteracy; the majority of illiterates labored in semi- and unskilled work. However, many illiterates were employed in skilled, artisanal, and higher occupations. Most of the low-status positions were occupied by literates: despite the development of public schooling and the promotion of the literacy myth, these workers had failed to secure its essential benefits. The acquisition of some education was not enough to overcome the dominance of ethnic and class ascription in attaining rank and status in an unequal social structure.

The situation was similar with regard to wealth. Most illiterates were poor, but many achieved at least a moderate economic standing, and the majority of all poor were literate. Illiteracy could be severely disadvantageous occupationally and economically, but literacy proved of remarkably limited value to many workers in their chances for higher status or greater rewards.

Although literacy resulted in very little economic advantage among the skilled and semiskilled, it did have its rewards. It helped in attaining skilled or artisanal work, which fact was significant in the acceptance of the value of schooling by working-class families. Most of literacy's benefits were unclear and limited. The relationship of education to work and earnings was complicated by such factors as ethnicity, class, race, age, and gender. Education alone seldom dramatically altered class or social position in the nineteenth century.

Literacy also helped to bring social and cultural advantages. Access to a rapidly expanding print culture was open to those who could read and write. Education was associated with respectability and advancement; here illiterates surely were disadvantaged. Social and cultural needs for literacy, however, while growing in number and import, continued to compete with the needs of daily life, survival, and popular recreations—for these literacy was not often central.

Although the poor, the immigrant, and the uneducated usually have been associated with a "culture of poverty," and assumed to be disorganized, unstable, irrational, and threatening to the social order, illiterates in the Ontario study proved otherwise. Using their traditions and resources effectively, they strove to protect themselves and their families against the marketplace and poverty—purchasing homes when possible and regulating the size and organization of their families and households.

As in England, literacy was an advantage but not a requirement for life and for learning the ways of society. Oral and visual means of communication were central to daily existence, and experience was a teacher for life and work. Family, religion, the workplace, informal associations, voluntary institutions, schools, and the press were all educational influences. There were many ways to gain skills and information; literacy, while growing in importance, was only one skill among others.[166]

Soltow and Stevens have documented the persistence of educational inequality in the 1860s, despite the expansion of schooling. Up to 20 percent of Civil War soldiers born in Kentucky, Tennessee, and Canada; 15 percent of Irish-born; and 5 to 12 percent of French-born had never been to school. Illiteracy was very low among Scandinavians, Germans, and especially the Scottish-born. Almost half of all Northern soldiers were reported as having *limited* common schooling, including 34 percent from New England, 44 percent from New York, New Jersey, and Pennsylvania, 52 percent from Ohio and Indiana, and 66 percent from Michigan, Wisconsin, and Illinois. The extent of inequality in years of education was large.[167]

Such a limited exposure to schooling probably resulted in low-quality literacy skills. As in Europe, near-universal levels of literacy did not signify a high level of popular abilities.[168] And if, as Soltow and Stevens argue, the system of schooling and enrollment levels declined during the 1860s, the effectiveness of popular education in transmitting literacy skills suffered even further.

As with illiteracy, the strongest differential in school attendance was that between the North and South. Southern efforts to develop common schooling before the Civil War did have an impact, but they were insufficient to match efforts in the North. The regional difference is also reflected in the Northwest's rapid development of schools and achievement of attendance rates almost equal to those in the Northeast. Social and institutional development in the West supported schools and literacy; settlement of persons from Eastern areas with traditions of literacy and schooling interacted with county formation, public school provisions in the Northwest Ordinance, population concentration, and wealth for the promotion of public schooling.[169] Soltow and Stevens also studied the relationship between school enrollment and wealth. They discovered that in the North, enrollment was not a strong function of family wealth among the young, but it was at higher ages (10–14 and 15–19). This influence was felt in both urban and rural areas, although rural children were more likely than urban to attend at older ages. In cities, children of foreign-born parents often were disadvantaged because of discrimination. School attendance was lower for the children of the foreign-born than for those of the native-born. Foreign-born parents had fewer children enrolled in each age group and at each wealth level. As with the native-born, wealth was important in determining children's schooling (and probably occupational attainment).[170]

The curriculum and materials of the schools were permeated with pan-Protestant, American norms, values, and attitudes. The message was moral, civic, and social.[171] Even in rural places, teachers considered the main function of education to be the instillation of restraint; they "tied literacy and morality inextricably together." Without restraint, literacy was seen as dangerous. The fact that crime and

TABLE 7.21
**Enrollment Rates (SCH) of Northern Children Living in Families
in 1860 Related to the Wealth of Their Parents**

| Wealth Class of Parents ($) | SCH by Age of Child | | |
| | 5–9 | 10–14 | 15–19 |
| --- | --- | --- | --- |
| 0–99 | .66 | .65 | .25 |
| 100–999 | .62 | .77 | .43 |
| 1,000–9,999 | .70 | .81 | .56 |
| 10,000 and up | .69 | .88 | .58 |

Source: Ibid., 128.

TABLE 7.22
**Enrollment Rates (SCH) in the North in 1860 by Nativity of Parents**

| Wealth Class of Parents ($) | SCH by Age of Child and Nativity of Parents | | | | | |
| | 5–9 | | 10–14 | | 15–19 | |
| | Native | Foreign | Native | Foreign | Native | Foreign |
| --- | --- | --- | --- | --- | --- | --- |
| 0–99 | .64 | .55 | .71 | .59 | .37 | .10 |
| 100–999 | .66 | .57 | .83 | .68 | .51 | .28 |
| 1,000 and up | .72 | .65 | .84 | .76 | .61 | .41 |

Source: Ibid., p. 130.

immorality could coexist with a high level of literacy led schoolmen and reformers to presume a causal linkage. However, trends in literacy and education were not directly related to those in crime; class and racial relationships, prejudice, poverty, social change, and police and judicial development were more important factors.[172]

Through such teaching, the moral bases of literacy were transmitted, and many young persons were assimilated to the hegemony of the dominant culture.

> For students who learned to read and write in schools, the process of acquiring literacy was not as unequivocally liberating. . . . In both the country and the city, students were required to memorize and declaim, to imitate and reproduce texts, to repeat rather than formulate ideas, to recite rather than criticize a piece. . . . As they learned to read, these urban children were learning to suspend judgment, to obey instantly, to read and write unwittingly, to derive standards of conduct from rules and regulations imposed by teachers. Paradoxically, the opportunity to learn represented an opportunity to engage in a network of restraining regulations and impersonal relationships. . . .[173]

For rural children, distance from the core pan-Protestant morality and training for sociocivic values was less; a different process of socialization was required. Training in literacy advanced the inculcation of morality and values, the process of nation building, and the transmission of the code of conduct for work and social life, and contributed to the moral bases of the emerging "modern" capitalistic order. Assimilation was one aspect of the larger endeavor.

Children of the foreign-born, although their period of public schooling was shorter, were at least partially influenced by this process. The rates of enrollment and attendance of children of the Irish, for example, had shifted by 1870 from relatively low to very high—an indication of the acceptance of schooling, despite the fact that many of their parents remained illiterate.

Among the central points that emerge from the data is the relative decline of ethnicity and lack of wealth as factors determining or perpetuating illiteracy. Despite poverty, familial constraints, and discrimination, the children of the foreign-born were commonly able to acquire some measure of literacy. Most children were enrolled in schools by 1870.

Literacy probably was also losing significance as a factor relating to opportunities and social position. With near-universality of literacy, other means of stratification and social selection came to the fore.[174] Class, ethnicity, gender, age, and race were the central elements in social divisions and opportunities for advancement. Literacy in and of itself was insufficient to erase other elements that shaped the stratification of society and the structures of inequality; it did not prove liberating in that respect.

The triumph of common, public schooling took place *without* that kind of result. In fact, individual advancement was a relatively minor theme in the articulation of the value of schooling; collective and social ends were more important. "It appears unlikely that the common school served as a vehicle for occupational mobility. . . . [It] did not alter patterns of economic inequality, but, rather, tended to perpetuate them."[175] Literacy did pay off to some extent, but it was still possible for illiterates to achieve some economic success in the 1870s. Literacy was not a guarantee of success or even escape from poverty.

Clyde and Sally Griffen's study of Poughkeepsie, New York suggests that high schooling did result in higher occupational status: important evidence for support of the value of education. Few attended high school, however. This level was not proscribed from the immigrant or the poor, but they seldom were able to seek its potential benefits.

The benefits of formal education usually went to those who already had an advantage in occupation or property. It was the "moderately comfortable but not wholly secure" middle class who most valued education for their children, to ensure the maintenance of their children's social position and grant them an opportunity to succeed. In Poughkeepsie, as in many other places, extended opportunities for schooling, to levels where a chance for some payoff was possible, followed from, rather than preceded, success among the parental generation.[176]

The context for the special American emphasis on mass literacy and rush toward institutional schooling is crucial and needs to be addressed directly. Literacy was maintained under conditions of rapid and confusing social and economic changes, differing institutional arrangements, mass immigration, and needs to integrate and assimilate ever–growing numbers of nonnatives into the population. It was not until well into the nineteenth century that the line between public and private schooling was precisely drawn.[177] The Western faith in and commitment to education as a requirement for cohesion, stability, and progress were being translated into practice;

mass public education was created and spread for the systematic and controlled transmission of literacy and the values that accompanied it.[178]

The transformation of society underlay the spread of formal, institutionalized schooling. Central to that change were the development of commercial capitalism, urbanization, industrialization, immigration and migration, the increasing role of the state in social welfare, the acceptance of institutionalization as a solution to social problems, the redefinition of the family, and broadly based middle-class Victorian culture and morality. Educational development was one part of a larger process of change.

As Tyack argues:

> The concept of a competitive capitalist order of a free market and free labor was inextricably bound up with a view of the polity shaped by millenist Protestant thought. And the ideology of public education, in turn, held up that the public school should produce moral, industrious, literate, Christian republicans.[179]

Capitalism had a special relationship to institutional change. Institutions increasingly reflected its drive toward order, discipline, rationality, and specialization, and applied that approach to social problems. The problems of crime and poverty, increasing cultural heterogeneity, and the need to train and discipline the work force related closely to the carefully controlled, institutionalized dissemination of literacy and its moral bases. Such public schooling was considered an appropriate method to establish cultural homogeneity and hegemony.[180]

Public schooling was seen as necessary to help train a work force for the demands of the new economy. Instead of their traditional work routines, rural migrants, urban lower classes, and immigrants faced the starkly different needs of new, larger-scale, mechanized work settings. Habits of regularity, docility, punctuality, orderliness, and respect had to be learned; the demands of production were now set by the clock and an imposed schedule. The attitudinal and behavioral qualities imparted by education were more important than job skills. The best educated were the most profitable and the best paid—but not as a direct result of literacy's cognitive skills. Many school promoters, political leaders, and large employers grasped these relations.[181]

A new, democratic ideal was proclaimed with the rise of mass schooling: through achievement in institutional terms, such as the acquisition of literacy and schooling, individuals would attain the ability to overcome their origins. This ideal became a plank of democratic ideology. However, the link between mobility and literacy and schooling is not clear. Social ascription—in terms of class, ethnicity, gender, and race—has long remained an important characteristic of North American social stratification and its structures of inequality. Literacy did not overturn those relationships.

Virtually all parents came to desire some education for their children. The schools' new demands for punctuality and regularity of attendance were accepted more slowly, and sometimes were resisted. Some immigrant, working-class, and rural parents found the substance of the moral bases of public schooling offensive to their own values and interests. However, conflict was seldom extended or harsh, and the hegemony of the public school triumphed rapidly.

Public schooling was valued differently by different segments of the population.

The middle class rushed their children to school because of fears of falling down the social scale. Artisans responded to the mechanization of crafts and industrialization's degradation of labor; through schooling they sought alternative occupations for their children. For girls, the motivation was often the expanding opportunities available in teaching. The working class associated education with respectability, and some also accepted it as necessary for class organization, power, and advancement. Cultural emphasis combined with commercialization and the market induced farmers. The reasons differed, but the values of schooling were widely embraced. Popular acceptance of public schooling signified the establishment of hegemony, the acceptance of the direction imposed on social life by the dominant group. Legal compulsion was seldom necessary.

In part, public education gained assent because of its close relationship to the dominant ideology of democratic capitalism in nineteenth-century North America. In theory, lack of success or of achievement was a consequence not of inequality or social structure but of insufficient individual ability, energy, or responsibility. The place of literacy and schooling in society paralleled this belief.[182] The transformation of society required an institutional approach to perpetuating and transmitting hegemony. The sociology of education shows how schools, with internal organization and "hidden agendas" as well as actual conduct and curricula reflecting the social ideology, teach the legitimacy of the social order itself.[183] The "literacy myth" was maintained in this way.

In addition to socioeconomic transformations, traditions, the legacies of literacy in North America, and the emergent culture of the dominant population were also crucial to these developments. Protestantism, nationality, and the bourgeois culture shaped responses to material changes. In part, they account for the early rise of high levels of literacy and school attendance and the spread of public education in places less touched by the commercial, industrial, and urban revolution.

In many respects, the North American political economy was a moral polity, requiring great effort and vigilance to educate and reform individuals and save them from political subordination and sloth. Public schooling often took on the image of a moral crusade. That religious persons and societies were actively involved is not contradictory.[184]

Early-nineteenth-century North America witnessed an explosion of print. Competing religious sects, political parties, educational interests, and cultural promoters plumbed the market, seeking sales and influence. Numerous specialized periodicals were created to address particular audiences. Schoolbooks as well as novels, guide and advice literature, and books of opinion dominated the book market; periodicals, especially newspapers and tract and pamphlet literature, were the largest categories of print. To these publications were added the innumerable volumes of "cheap" literature, the most popular fare of all.

Publishing was increasingly becoming concentrated in Eastern cities, and into a small number of large firms. Institutional, transportation, and technological developments all supported print and reading; new presses and other machines and cheaper means of paper and ink manufacture made it possible to mass-produce books. The growth in magazine and newspaper publishing was even larger. This rapid diffusion

## TABLE 7.23
## Newspaper Publication: United States, 1790–1840

| | 1790 | 1800 | 1810 | 1820 | 1830 | 1835 | 1840 | 1840/1790 |
|---|---|---|---|---|---|---|---|---|
| U.S. Population (thousands) | 3,929 | 5,297 | 7,224 | 9,618 | 12,237 | 15,003 | 17,120 | 4.4 |
| Newspapers published | 92 | 235 | 371 | 512 | 861 | 1,258 | 1,404 | 15.3 |
| Newspaper editions per week | 147 | 389 | 549 | 759 | — | — | 2,281 | 15.5 |
| Daily newspapers | 8 | 24 | 26 | 42 | 49 | — | 138 | 17.3 |
| Annual circulation (thousands) | 3,975 | 12–13,000 | 24,577 | 50,000 | 68,118 | 90,361 | 147,500 | 37.1 |
| Annual newspaper copies per capita | 1.0 | 2.4 | 3.4 | 5.2 | 5.6 | 6.0 | 8.6 | 8.6 |

Source: Allan Pred, *Circulation of Information*, p. 21. See his Table 2.1 for his sources and notes.

of print was not a result of major changes in literacy rates; social, cultural, economic, and political factors underlay the trend.[185]

Reading apparently was increasing. Too many developments in types of literature, means of production, cost factors, competition for audiences, and processes of dissemination took place within a relatively short period *not* to have had an impact on cultural and social styles and levels. That does not imply that all were reading or that habits and tastes were becoming homogeneous. Different reading cultures were forming, often in terms of class, region, gender, or even ethnicity. The functions of print were not the same for all readers.

Despite the fact of a population among the most literate in the world, reformers found much to criticize about common reading habits and the commonness of reading as a habit. Many persons were not reading often, and when they did read, their choice frequently was not approved, ''proper'' material. They preferred fiction, cheap books, and street literature. A great many people were reading, but it apparently was not the kind of reading for improvement urged by the promoters of literacy and its moral bases.[186]

In the frontier areas of the old Northwest, reading was not particularly common, but some (primarily wealthier) people did own a small number of books. The usual reading fare was largely traditional. Reading was reinforcing, promoting the moral bases of society and its ideology, rather than ''liberating.'' Religious volumes dominated; schoolbooks, dictionaries, histories and geographies, biographies, and law books also were found. The little visible evidence of literary culture—the possession of classics and books by major English authors—tended to be the preserve of the wealthy.[187]

A study by Joseph Kett of three counties and one thriving commercial city in Virginia sheds light on the differences in book possession between urban and rural places. Book ownership in this area of the country was not uncommon, although it was not as common as among New Englanders in the period. Although a higher proportion of book owners was found in a remote, rural county than in the city, county holdings overall were usually small and confined to religious works. In rural regions, the use of literacy was relatively narrow and traditional. In contrast, urban residents tended to possess more volumes and more secular books, a reflection of differential access and choice, larger and more diverse cultural influences, different levels of wealth, consumption of nonnecessities, access to schools, and wider tastes and awareness. Books owned by city dwellers also had higher assessed values.

In all the Virginia areas studied by Kett, wealth was the greatest determinant of book possession, but in the city, many more persons of modest means also owned books. Occupation was another influence; in all areas, professionals and merchants were more likely to own books than others, and the greater numbers of such persons in the city contributed to the higher level of book possession.[188]

By mid-century, most North Americans were literate, and many of them were readers. Their reading was not always expansive or wide, however; commonly it was narrow, reinforcing, and traditional.[189]

Reading was widely promoted, for differing reasons, and publications and libraries were growing, but many literates still were not reading very much. The relatively infrequent use of literacy was also supported by a common lack of direct need for reading and writing in the work requirements of many persons, as well as by the orality of the culture. Learning took place in many ways.

Many infrequent readers or nonreaders had access to print through hearing oral reading of the contents of written or print media. Reading was still a social activity; "individuals increasingly read silently and in solitude, but it continued to be widely assumed that at some point they would 'set' what they had gleaned from their reading through discussion and mutual inquiry. . . . The written word and the spoken word remained inseparable."[190]

One of the most common and important uses of literacy was in extending the moral bases of society. Much reading was religious and moral in origin, orientation, and content. From the mid-1820s, religious groups published literally millions of copies of books, tracts, periodicals, and newspapers, and developed means of distributing them widely. Such publications were aimed at women, families, and youths; the field of children's publishing, in particular, was revolutionized. These were the common materials that families shared and from which the young sometimes learned their letters or practiced what skills they acquired in school.[191]

Another common and growing use of literacy was the reading of the new cheap newspapers and novels, especially among the urban middle and lower middle classes. This use of literature was not the proper and approved use that so many commentators sought to promote; nor was it usually a self-educating or self-improving application of an individual's literacy abilities. It was an important use of literacy, however.

The highly disapproved-of new popular fiction, cheap street literature, and the popular press did not always run counter to the morally reinforcing role of literacy and print.[192] Novels celebrated the virtues of the dominant morality and culture.[193] Women, especially middle-class women, read avidly, contributing to the emerging culture as they fueled the demand for periodicals and fiction. Such reading was central to their lives; it was a fashion and a use of leisure time. Yet it was also cultural participation and consumption. It was an expression of their own cultural and social condition, and they were shaped by this use of literacy, just as they helped to shape literary production and its economies. The cultural impacts of this reading included socialization, expectations, identification, roles, models of thought and behavior, and escape and fantasy. Contemporaries approved of the reading habit but were at best ambivalent about the reading of popular fiction.

Diverse commentators agreed that reading was an important activity for women: for education, moral improvement, and nurture. Some fiction, however, was considered potentially dangerous, appealing to emotions and sentiments and undercutting morality. Yet both kinds of reading were integrative, satisfying, and psychologically important. Popular fiction, in its potential for salving the strains of women's roles in the culture, may have contributed more directly and satisfyingly to adaptation, adjustment, psychological maintenance, and emotional release—in a safe, nonthreatening way.[194]

Literacy also had a key functional value for more women in this society. The increase in women's work both outside and inside the home was linked to these cultural developments. Functional use was tied to ideological impulses and moral spheres; trends in literacy and schooling reflected that. Literacy, in the process, achieved a new importance for women, and through them for the larger culture.[195] Women's work was celebrated and remunerated, but with lower status and pay than men's work. Literacy was even less a guarantee of fair and commensurate rewards for women than it was for men. Salaries were geared to gender, rather than education or literacy, training, skill, or physical strength.

By mid-century, North American publishing was firmly on course. The reduced costs of many types of print, development of new genres and classes of print, growth of schooling, better distribution, and libraries made reading materials more accessible. However, class, ethnic, racial, and regional disparities in literacy, resources, time, tastes, and interest underlay differences in access to and consumption of print. "Serious" reading continued to be cited as an aspect not often practiced; given the people's interest and skills, it is not surprising that popular fiction and mass periodicals continued to be the preferred fare. At the same time, children's and religious publications were also in demand.[196]

"By the 1830s and 1840s, it was commonplace in the United States for newspapers to assert the people's need for knowledge and special role of the press in serving that need." Knowledge, and the ability to gain it through literacy, was one of the promises of the republic itself and of the schools. Since that time, it has been the newspaper to which most individual (and collective) applications of literacy have been made. Influence and manipulation of opinion underlay their popularity.[197]

As population and territory grew, literacy became more and more essential for its integrating and binding roles: within and across classes, ethnic groups, and other divisions. It could not prevent class, ethnocultural, racial, or gender conflicts, however; the level of integration was not all-pervasive.[198] The power of print was more to shape and reinforce opinions and beliefs already present. Reinforcement by reading was most critical to developing and maintaining the culture of Victorian America.

For most of the working class, time and resources for reading were limited. When they did read, it was usually popular, cheap literature rather than improving, scholarly, literary, and political material. Although literacy was occasionally required for work, useful for mobility, and valuable for organizing along class lines, it was neither essential nor seized regularly for those kinds of purposes.

The working class by and large came to accept the hegemony of the school and gained literacy and its moral bases from that institution. Literacy was neither opposed by nor imposed upon either native- or foreign-born members of the class. Although they typically were not promoters of educational expansion or reform, they were often receptive to opportunities that might benefit their children. Literacy levels and educational enrollments rose throughout the century; efforts became widespread to train up a rising generation in common morality, values, habits, attitudes, and discipline. The lack of class-specific opposition was striking.[199]

The North American working class was not always consistent in its approach to schooling. Poverty, familial survival strategies, and cultural traditions and conflicts often limited opportunities or enthusiasm for education. Some "traditionalists" apparently saw little need for school learning or moral reinforcement. Attendance problems were common. Schools also faced the challenge of new waves of working-class migrants and immigrants.[200] Nevertheless, the working class was responding to the schools and coming to accept their importance. With time, a foundation in perceptions of changing economic and occupational requirements, and the pressures of promotion of the needs for schooling, a limited acceptance of hegemony developed. Literacy and its moral bases were transmitted and were essential elements in the integration of society.

Traditionalists came to accept this position grudgingly. This segment of the working class rejected the "new code" of industrialism and preindustrial values. "They refused to give up their casual attitudes toward work, their pursuit of happiness in gaming and drinking. . . . Traditionalists still deferred to the silk vest. . . ." The schools, through instruction in literacy and inculcation of its moral bases, were a major weapon against their culture and ways.[201] With difficulty and time, the schools began to succeed in securing a fair measure of acceptance and consent from working-class families. The assimilation of the working class was a gradual struggle, central to the making of that class and the society.[202]

The "loyalists" and radicals more quickly embraced the schools. Both elements valued literacy and sought schooling for their children. Both linked, to some degree, literacy and education to respectability, morality, and advancement. But despite their common quest for literacy and morality, their approaches to political economy and public schooling were not the same.[203]

The loyalists usually accepted the ideology and promise of the school. Social integration, acceptance of the dominant culture's emphases, and quests for advancement were responses to their often insecure economic positions. When they considered social issues, they often saw a mutuality of interests between capital and labor and sought to appear respectable and of common culture with the middle class and their employers. Acquisition of literacy was one path toward this end, as were temperance, religious practice, and the like. Loyalists probably perused popular literature and cheap street fare, but their reading habits were marked, at least symbolically, by religion and temperance materials and daily papers. The frequent use of literacy for serious reading probably was not typical, however.

It would be distorting to depict the "radicals" as more highly literate and more instrumentally politically literate than others among the working class. Literacy, reading, and print were important: for learning and teaching, developing a radical republican ideology and theory of labor value, communicating, informing, organizing adherents and followers, and the like. However, literacy was not determinative for them.[204] Oral means of communcation were more important; print and literacy reinforced them, supplemented them, and perhaps changed them, but did not supplant their significance.

The radicals believed firmly in education and improvement. Pressing for constructive use of leisure time, they stressed reading as well as discourse, discussion as well as study. Their ideology grew out of an intellectual heritage, passed on to them orally and by reading radical literature; it also stemmed from material conditions and associated patterns. Much of their education took place in the oral, public settings of lectures, debates, and rallies, as well as in workplaces and other informal gatherings.

The radicals agreed with the loyalists and with the moral bases of literacy in their support of temperance and frugality, respected the canons of propriety in dress, speech, and demeanor, and opposed moral degradation. However, they also criticized capitalist exploitation and economic injustice. Poverty, for example, they viewed as a result of economic decisions and conditions, and as the cause rather than the consequence of individual failures or moral shortcomings. "They accepted a code of morality which they shared with their employers but used in their own class interests."[205]

Although they were supporters of public schooling and eager to gain literacy for themselves and their children, many radicals nevertheless were critical of the schooling offered. They attempted to combine moral reform and an emerging working-class consciousness. They were unable to develop alternative means of mass, basic education or to gain control of the schools, and so they sent their children to the existing public schools. Despite their opposition to some aspects of the moral bases of that schooling, some assimilation no doubt occurred, and some pupils embraced the morality, values, and code of the dominant culture. Lessons first learned *with* literacy were reinforced in the political arena. That mass provision of literacy grew up with and was related to political democracy forms an essential link.[206]

Working-class radicals realized that literacy was a two-edged sword: although it was a useful tool in their ideological and organizational development, it was also a limiting element. Spokesmen of the labor movement trumpeted in support of schooling, accepting some of the schools' hegemony. Workers desired education, but to them it should not be viewed narrowly as job preparation or the making of better workers; they also wanted an intellectual and character-development emphasis. "They must educate themselves to think; they must also learn to think for themselves."

Their proposals for combining work and study differed from the common schools' curriculum. For them, education was a higher ideal and a different goal: it was training for the future man (or woman). Public schooling was "class education," aimed at misdirecting and seducing the future working man. Critics claimed that the system gave the working class a taste for cheap reading and was biased against them and their interests. Instead, the labor press promoted self-education and the frequent use of literacy—for amusement, comfort, consolation, and leisure, as well as for economic and political ends. Reading ("good" reading, of course) and the development of "mental culture" were encouraged, as was the attainment of more useful literacy skills.

With a few exceptions, most among the working class either read very little or tended toward cheap fiction and other popular fare. A high level of literacy and a very high level of publishing did not lead to elevated uses of literacy. Workers seem to have spent little of their income on reading matter. Popular skills likely were inadequate for the heavier demands that reading's promoters placed on them; they were more suitable for gaining some useful information, learning and reinforcing morality and culture, and pursuing entertainment and amusement. For higher learning and serious studying, literacy was often a limited skill on which to build.[207]

The popular skills obtained from schooling in the nineteenth century were often restricted in quality.[208] Schooling itself was one reason; problems of physical conditions, attendance, teacher ability, and instructional method often militated against effective early learning and the development of proficiency in literacy. School facilities were often inadequate. Uncomfortable temperatures, drafts, lack of ventilation, and overcrowding threatened health and led to an aversion to study, contributing to the problems of low attendance and enrollment. Poor instruction also was an impediment.

Despite improving levels of preparation and requirements for certification, many teachers remained poorly qualified, and the better-qualified (but higher-priced) teachers were not always affordable, especially in nonurban areas. There is also the question of *how* the teachers taught, particularly in circumstances that included inadequate conditions, large classes, and irregular attendance. Family mobility and situations demanding periodic removal of youngsters from school to work or assist the household added to an already severe problem.

Reading instruction was the area in which the schools were regarded as most deficient. Children were reading but not understanding what they read. To many teachers, good reading was reading that *sounded good*: enunciation and pronunciation were stressed. Contradictions and differences in style and diction between the language of the home and street and that of school and books were apparently ignored. Comprehension was neglected.

Classroom management frequently was also inadequate. Children sat inactive for most of the day; silence and stillness were required for order to be maintained. Asking questions or speaking was a disruptive activity. The desire for learning and study was crushed from the beginning.

The situation did get better as the century progressed. Larger, more comfortable facilities, with more modern learning equipment, accompanied the expansion and systemization of education, especially in urban areas. Teachers improved in quality and preparation, and new, "soft," pupil-oriented, active pedagogies were promoted. Enrollments rose to near-universality, and pupils were more efficiently classified and graded by age.

Problems persisted, however. Low daily attendance continued; each day, 25 percent or more of the pupils were absent. The amount of time required for learning good reading skills is uncertain, but irregular attendance is an important obstacle to more satisfactory levels of literacy. Pupil-teacher ratios remained high, especially in cities. In addition, female teachers—underpaid and often less qualified than their male counterparts—increasingly taught the youngsters. Group activities, military–like drills, mechanical exercises, and rigid time-tabling became common practice, so that no pupil would be unoccupied or become restless. The classroom setting was not conducive to the acquisition of high-quality skills.

Dissatisfaction among educators with the quality of popular reading skills led to a widespread debate about instructional methods, primarily about whether the alphabet or whole words should be taught first. In addition, the style of reading that usually formed the explicit goal of educators confused oral with cognitive ability.[209]

Detractors of the alphabetic method claimed that with the rote repetition of the letters, the meaning of what was read was neglected. Pupils did not master the sense of their lessons or grasp the ideas or feelings intended by authors. Reading was little more than "a mere utterance of sounds" and "a mere affair of memory." Fluent-sounding reading obscured a lack of comprehension.[210]

Promoters of the "words first" approach argued that being able to combine short, simple, familiar words into sentences would be more pleasing to pupils, and the "form or appearance" of the word would be learned together with its meaning. "Children begin to *talk* with words, and why should they not begin to *read* with words?" The relationship between print and sound, and the connections between sight and speech, as bases for learning to read, were never considered.[211]

Many schoolmen joined in criticisms of the "old method," finding that it produced readers who did not understand what they read. Yet, alphabetic instruction did not disappear swiftly. Some instructors remained convinced of its success, and responded that the new method did not train children to read well. "Primary school teachers . . . testify that when children learned a word in one connection, they are unable to recognize it in another." These masters claimed that the word method confused written and spoken language, to the detriment of reading. To them, the teacher provided the meaning in giving the word and its sound, neither teaching children to read for themselves nor providing a source of motivation.[212]

Regardless of the differences in views, the two sides of the debate joined on one central issue: *children were not learning to read well, with regard to either fluency or comprehension.* Failure to achieve good reading—for meaning—was, at the very least, quite possible regardless of the method adopted and the prevailing style of pedagogy. No doubt pupils learned something that could be called reading, for over 90 percent of them considered themselves able to read. But students continued to leave school early with imperfect and deficient skills.[213]

Taught either the words or the letters first, children learned to reproduce what they saw mechanically, whatever their proficiency in articulation or comprehension. According to Daniel Calhoun, however, they had difficulty in talking about what they read: "Whether a pupil understood all the words he could pronounce was doubtful enough, and whether he understood whole passages and ideas was hardly doubtful. He did not." An inability to read with understanding adversely affected all other attempts at learning, Calhoun reports.[214]

By the 1870s and 1880s, reading instruction centered largely on natural articulation. This emphasis continued until the rise of silent reading in the last decade of the century. Natural, expressive, emotionally committed behavior was elicited from pupils. Good-sounding reading was equated with comprehension. Not only did such instruction err in making that equation, but educators made it even more difficult to judge how well the pupils understood what they articulated.[215]

Failings in instruction did not signify that schools were not achieving many of their aims: in fostering hegemony and socializing pupils. Training in literacy involved more than understanding all that was read. The moral bases could be transmitted and reinforced in a number of ways, symbolically and orally, in conjunction with literacy. Respectability, manners, taste, morality, and speech habits would be inculcated in the process of instruction.[216]

One significant use of literacy training was to homogenize the speech of the pupils. The stress upon proper articulation was an aspect of the socializing function of the school. By proscribing differences in speech under the comprehensive condemnation "school reading," reformers could justifiably move to Americanize or Canadianize the children of the immigrant and the laborer. Schools in nineteenth-century North America were promoting a class society, and one of the ways to ease social tensions was through homogenizing language, erasing some of the visible signs of diversity.[217] In uniting the heterogeneous peoples of new nations and eradicating the *superficial* distinctions that separated classes and cultures, in assimilating the values and manners of one class to those of the others, literacy could be a valuable tool.[218]

The implications for the usefulness of popular literacy are clear: they were limited. More children were exposed to more regular and formal instruction, but learning could also be obtained informally, through daily life, interactions, work, recreation, and institutions, for which literacy was not always central. The apparent increasing emphasis of society and culture on print and reading was sometimes superficial. A literate society statistically, this society was also one in which individuals could read only after a fashion. How well they read and understood must be distinguished from their possession of nominal literacy.

The advantages that imperfect skills brought to literates may also have been limited. Verbal ability could be quite another matter, however, and here schooling had more to contribute. Verbalism, rather than high-quality skills, may have been more attuned to social settings and needs for literacy. Many people saw no need for levels of useful literacy to be high, but those without literacy suffered a disability in verbal skills and skills acquired in formal or institutional settings.[219] Perhaps that was one cause of their restricted occupational distribution and their inability to escape criminal conviction.

Training at home, at work, or on the streets could not prepare illiterates for all exigencies. The importance of literacy in *practice* was limited, paralleling the level of skills, but even the imperfect levels commonly possessed had social uses, not the least of which was the promotion of hegemony. Literacy in this society functioned on several levels, for while the quality of literacy was adequate for many needs, it was inadequate for others, and not necessary for all aspects of life.

The mass illiteracy of black Americans throughout the nineteenth century, and beyond, was rooted in the social, cultural, economic, and institutional structures of North America. However, the extent of their literacy, when legal and de facto obstacles to schooling are considered, is impressive. The black experience reinforces the value placed in literacy, the way in which a group who desired literacy was able to develop means for acquiring it, and the limits to many that the attainment of literacy represented.[220]

To black Americans, literacy and learning represented liberation, or at least an opportunity for it. Although slaves were usually assumed to be illiterate, at least 5 percent of them apparently could read and write: a result of the efforts of some benevolent planters, exceptional efforts at self-education, schooling of youngsters on a few plantations along with white children, and clandestine education in slave quarters and towns. For free blacks, literacy and education were more accessible. Their literacy rates in no region approximated those of whites, but they regularly followed regional distinctions among white populations. In 1850, 39.7 percent of free black men and 42.8 percent of women were unable to read or write, compared to 7.3 and 12.4 percent of white men and women; a decade later, the percentages for blacks were 36.1 and 28.4, compared to 6.6 and 10.1 percent for whites.

Poverty and social and cultural patterns prevented even free blacks from achieving equality in opportunity for or access to schooling or training in literacy. Even where schooling was free and open to blacks, segregation and unequal facilities were often the result.

> Free blacks sought to establish their own churches, schools, and benevolent associations. And, as the number of such agencies increased, white hostility and fear also increased, locking both groups into a cycle of teaching and counterteaching not dissimilar to the one that existed on the plantation. Thus, free blacks, like their enslaved counterparts, though able to travel, hold property, and go to school, were subjected, on one hand, to white efforts to teach inferiority and, on the other hand, to black efforts to teach pride, resistance, and community solidarity.[221]

Rising levels of literacy did not pay off occupationally or economically. However, in the social context of racism and structural inequality, and the cultural domain that stressed black inferiority and deficiency, the extent of the attainment of literacy by free blacks, regardless of personal or institutional means, must be considered an incredible success.

Slaveholders accepted traditional elite conservative fears of the power of literacy. They considered education and literacy unsettling to the bound underclass, believing that it taught them to despise their condition, unsuited them for menial labor, gave them access to seditious literature, and poisoned their minds and morals. A population of literate bondspersons could only be threatening, regardless of literacy's actual potential for overturning Southern society and power relations. Ironically, withholding literacy only added to slaves' desire for it.

Towns and cities provided the most conducive element for attaining literacy and for opportunities for black initiatives. However, a few literate slaves appeared everywhere; "thus the most restricted and isolated plantation slaves normally had contact with some who could transmit information about the wider world. . . ." Some masters, mistresses, and white children instructed favorite slaves, especially house slaves, who were physically and often emotionally closest to their owners. In time, literacy possibly was extended further as those slaves taught others. Self-education was another method of learning.

If literacy was rare among the slave population, a deep value in education was not. The roots of black educational faith and enthusiasm were long in the slave past, and led to risk taking under threat of severe penalty by slaves, and exceptional efforts among freed persons. Penalties for literacy included whipping, loss of fingers, branding, and sale or segregation. Black educational struggles stand among the most impressive and moving chapters in modern history.[222]

A literate slave gained status and importance in the quarters. A source of news and information, forger of passes, and reader of the Scriptures, such a person stood as a symbol of black educability and achievement and a symbol of defiance. The benefits of literacy were more than material, more than narrowly functional. Regardless of the threat that it represented to the slave system, it had a powerful meaning to the slaves themselves.

Literacy played only a small part in plantation routines. The culture was essentially oral and was maintained intergenerationally by oral means. Plantation life itself was an educational experience in the broadest sense: for work, behavior, habits, and attitudes. Instruction by white masters was oral and repetitive, backed up by a system of rewards and punishments set in the reciprocal context of bonded paternalism. That by slaves themselves was more sophisticated, nuanced, and elaborated in the context of Afro-American folk culture. Rooted in community and family, theirs was a culture of song and story into which each generation was assimilated. "Their world remained a world of sound in which words were actions." Even communication between plantations was little dependent on literacy; the "grapevine" operated through individuals' passing news and information orally. That was much safer than writing messages.[223]

After emancipation, literacy became one of the chief symbols of the freed peoples' new status. Literacy and schooling represented great promises of progress, as well as symbols of liberation. "The desire for education everywhere exploded. For the freedmen, as for slaves before them, it represented the Keys of the Kingdom." Young and old alike eagerly crammed the schools. In material terms, blacks may have contributed more to the cause of their own education in the South than did whites.[224]

The hunger for education among blacks was rooted in the hope for and perception of personal and collective freedom and liberation. For many, religious motives were important. They longed to learn to read the Bible; reading lessons were considered a religious exercise in themselves.[225] Other, more material concerns and desires also contributed to the struggle: literacy was perceived as necessary for blacks to compare, and compete, favorably with the rest of society. Blacks, too, embraced the "literacy myth." There is no doubt that literacy could be an advantage for them, but it probably brought fewer benefits to them than it did to other groups in the population.

Blacks left slavery with a legacy of illiteracy on a massive scale. The speed of the transition to literacy in the context of mass poverty and obstructions to educational development was remarkable. At the time of emancipation, perhaps 93 percent of adult blacks were illiterate. That proportion had dropped to 80 percent by 1870; 56 percent by 1890; 44 percent by 1900; 30 percent by 1910; 23 percent by 1920; 16 percent by 1930; 11 percent by 1940; and 10 percent by 1950: eight decades of regular progress, often the result of self-help and blacks' own efforts.

Literacy changed black culture and black consciousness.[226] However, it did not lead to occupational or economic gains. Discrimination against black students, particularly in the South, resulted in unequal education for them; but no level of equality in literacy or education could have overcome such factors as racism, assumptions of inferiority, and structural or institutional inequities. Education conferred greater material benefits upon whites. As levels of literacy among blacks rose, race became more important, and literacy less so, in determining occupational levels. The contradiction between the promise of literacy and its reality was stark. Educational efforts had a dramatic impact on literacy, but they could not influence the place of blacks in the social order.[227]

A lack of literacy often proved a greater disadvantage than its possession was an advantage. Blacks were aware of that and took major steps to eradicate their mass illiteracy.[228] The practical value of education seemed clearest after emancipation, as illiterate black laborers learned from hard experience how whites used literacy against them. To some blacks, that was stimulus enough to send their children to schools, regardless of the direct costs of their absence from work.

The mass movement for schooling was based on faith, sacrifice, and struggle. Not all blacks were able to secure much schooling for themselves or their children, no matter how intense their commitment. Not only were there white resistance and a shortage of teachers, funds, and facilities, but some parents simply could not afford the loss of children's labor. Rates of turnover and irregular attendance were high.

The demand for schools increased so quickly that hiring teachers and finding accommodations for classes were a persistent problem. To attract laborers and entice former slaves to stay, planters sometimes offered facilities for education. Blacks more often demanded schools as a condition of employment. The little tax-supported public education that developed for blacks was often limited and short-lived. As public education grew in the South, it was rooted in segregation and inequality. Most Southern black education was instigated and supported by the freedmen themselves and by white and black teachers who migrated from the North and West.

Many teachers perceived massive cultural and intellectual deficiencies in their charges.

> To make the freedmen ''all that we desire them to be'' was to instruct them not only in the spelling book and the gospel but in every phase of intellectual and personal development—in the virtues of industry, self-reliance, frugality, and sobriety, in family relations and moral responsibility, and, most importantly, in how to conduct themselves as free men and women interacting with those who had only recently held them as slaves.

Duties, relationships, and conduct were as much a part of schooling as were reading and writing lessons. The inculcation of middle-class values was included in the teachers' attack. ''Through appropriate readings, songs, and exercises, positive moral and patriotic images would be implanted in the minds of the pupils.'' The extension of literacy to former slaves was construed in the same manner as the extension of literacy to other ''alien'' people and races. Literacy's functions were collective, stabilizing, and assimilating.

Many Southern whites feared this instruction. Some hoped that proper schooling would instill deference, respect, industriousness, orderliness, and other values to maintain the labor force and social order. Others, however, were more skeptical. Many of these sentiments were rooted in assumptions of black intellectual inferiority and ineducability. In more and more areas, especially after Reconstruction, mounting opposition closed off opportunities.[229]

Substantial educational efforts did take place, but their limits are revealed in the precariousness of many endeavors, the level of hostility, and the trends in illiteracy. Southern whites feared that Northern teachers were teaching racial equality. The distribution of schools was a further problem; the majority were located in towns, not the rural areas where most of the black population resided. The consequence, revealed in illiteracy as well as school attendance data, was the reinforcement of prior differentials within the context of improvement.

Direct federal support was short-lived, effectively ending by 1870. It did contribute to a legacy of public schooling in the South, however, for blacks and whites. Support for an integrated, equal system was slight. By 1872, every Southern state had established a state-financed and state-organized school system with property taxation as the basis for funding. Taxes added to racism as stimuli for white criticism and opposition to public schooling. Numerous persons objected to paying for the education of blacks. Poor whites, fearing economic competition, added their voices and actions to those of the landed class.

White violence further reduced opportunities. Fewer schools and teachers, inferior schooling, higher concentrations of children per school, lower enrollments, unequal expenditures, lower teachers' salaries, and inadequate materials all helped to restrict the educational advancement of blacks. Black enthusiasm was not extinguished, however, and literacy levels rose during the last two decades of the century.[230]

A dramatic example of the disadvantages of illiteracy and the possibilities for blacks without education is found in Edgefield County, South Carolina during Reconstruction. In the struggle for political and economic power "between an oral Afro-American culture and a literate white culture," the whites' superior communication system gave them a distinct organizational advantage. While blacks relied on personal contact for communications, whites were able to "organize, persuade, propagandize, and mobilize their membership through printed media."

However, blacks were capable of organizing and challenging white dominance without literacy—through organizational skills and leadership in religious, military, and political affairs, and through organizations such as the church, schools, and militia. In spite of violence and intimidation, the whites' economic and communications power were not enough to stop black political activity.

The reestablishment of white hegemony by the late 1870s was accomplished without the use of literacy and print as a primary instrument. Land and labor control were central to the struggle; intimidation, fraud, and physical force were more important than leadership and ability to organize among blacks. Rather than being central to this program and its victory, literacy and the media symbolized more the depth of white power and reflected its social base. Even as black illiteracy began to decline, it was impossible for black leaders to encourage militancy or agitate for equality.

Ironically, even contradictorily, it was after the restoration of white hegemony that the development of black community and institutions began. After 1876, the freedmen organized primarily through the churches and schools. They included women and children, and promoted the values of education and literacy. Through their churches and the closely related schools, Edgefield blacks transformed themselves from an oral to a literate culture.[231]

Literacy was directly important in its relationship to migration and physical mobility. In the South, the strong desire of blacks for education for their children (as well as for survival and protection) led many to cities and towns. There they did all in their power to see that schooling was possible: establishing schools, paying for them, building them, and sacrificing to keep their children attending.[232] Literacy often related to longer-distance migration. Postbellum migration of blacks from the South to the North and Midwest was in all likelihood a selective process, and literacy was one element in that selectivity.

Southern blacks who migrated to Boston, for example, as a study by Elizabeth Pleck shows, tended to be "city-bred" and to have above-average literacy. Literacy was both preparation and influence: former slaves from urban areas were better informed about the North than illiterate slaves from rural plantations, partly because of their having had better chances for learning to read. But despite their levels of literacy and preparation, Boston blacks fared poorly economically. No other ethnic or racial group was as concentrated at the bottom of the occupational hierarchy. This situation was not the result of a lack of literacy or schooling; "the one overriding disadvantage blacks faced was the deeply rooted racial prejudice of their fellow Bostonians."[233]

For blacks, the legacies of literacy were often meager in confronting the massive obstacles to advancement and integration. In facing those barriers, rooted in prejudice, discrimination, and racism, black literacy and educational levels did suffer. Nevertheless, the black literacy achievement remains impressive. What is not impressive are the advantages that followed from that level of skills. Although the rewards of their literacy are clearly not those its promoters have imbedded deeply into Western culture and ideology, the case of black Americans is exceptional.

On one level, it has been argued that black inequality of access to and opportunity for schooling is the cause of their lack of social and economic advancement. However, the fact that blacks have been limited in schooling is more an effect than a cause of their position. That so many black parents, and youngsters, too, continue to maintain their faith in education attests to the depth of their commitment to the ideology of improvement and advancement in American society.[234]

The "new immigration" of the late nineteenth and early twentieth centuries raises numerous questions about the roles of literacy and illiteracy. Contrary to the popular view, nearly three-quarters of all immigrants entering the United States between 1899 and 1910 were literate, at least in comparison to their fellow countrymen: opportunities for elementary schooling were expanding in Southern and Eastern Europe at the time, and levels of literacy were an important element in the selectivity of long-distance immigration. The actual extent of literacy (in either native tongues or English) is impressive.[235]

As twentieth-century literacy and school enrollment data show, the new immigrants were willing and able to obtain basic literacy for their children. Economic needs, a desire to maintain cultural identity in the face of alien values and challenges to tradition, acceptance of the dominant society's educational ideology, and group strivings for success combined in the desire to maintain or secure high levels of literacy. That does not signify that all immigrants embraced the ideology of success or assimilation through education or that they shared equally in accepting the importance of education. Many did not consider schooling a high priority or were not able to put plans into practice. In addition, those who did not plan to settle permanently in the New World, and many who found homes in large urban ethnic enclaves, were less often stimulated to acquire literacy in English.[236]

Literacy was often viewed instrumentally, especially at first, and should be understood as part of the strategy of migration, settlement, and adaptation to new environments. It was an undoubted advantage, economically (higher levels of literacy were associated with higher earnings), socially, and culturally. However, it was not a requirement for or a guarantee of success.[237]

Slavic immigrants, rejecting challenges of conformity and Americanization, regarded the purpose of schooling to be conservative and preservative: it was to be

TABLE 7.24
**Characteristics of Adult, Male, Foreign-Born Workers in Mining
and Manufacturing Occupations, 1909**

| Group | Number Reporting Earnings | Ave. Weekly Earnings in Dollars | Percentage Speaking English | Percentage Literate[a] | Percentage Residing in U.S. 5 Years or More |
|---|---|---|---|---|---|
| Armenian | 594 | 9.73 | 54.9 | 92.1 | 54.6 |
| Bohemian, Moravian | 1,353 | 13.07 | 66.0 | 96.8 | 71.2 |
| Bulgarian | 403 | 10.31 | 20.3 | 78.2 | 8.5 |
| Canadian, French | 8,164 | 10.62 | 79.4 | 84.1 | 86.7 |
| Canadian, Other | 1,323 | 14.15 | 100.0 | 99.0 | 90.8 |
| Croatian | 4,890 | 11.37 | 50.9 | 70.7 | 38.9 |
| Danish | 377 | 14.32 | 96.5 | 99.2 | 85.4 |
| Dutch | 1,026 | 12.04 | 86.1 | 97.9 | 81.9 |
| English | 9,408 | 14.13 | 100.0 | 98.9 | 80.6 |
| Finnish | 3,334 | 13.27 | 50.3 | 99.1 | 53.6 |
| Flemish | 125 | 11.07 | 45.6 | 92.1 | 32.9 |
| French | 896 | 12.92 | 68.6 | 94.3 | 70.1 |
| German | 11,380 | 13.63 | 87.5 | 98.0 | 86.4 |
| Greek | 4,154 | 8.41 | 33.5 | 84.2 | 18.0 |
| Hebrew, Russian | 3,177 | 12.71 | 74.7 | 93.3 | 57.1 |
| Hebrew, Other | 1,158 | 14.37 | 79.5 | 92.8 | 73.8 |
| Irish | 7,596 | 13.01 | 100.0 | 96.0 | 90.6 |
| Italian, North | 5,343 | 11.28 | 58.8 | 85.0 | 55.2 |
| Italian, South | 7,821 | 9.61 | 48.7 | 69.3 | 47.8 |
| Lithuanian | 4,661 | 11.03 | 51.3 | 78.5 | 53.8 |
| Macedonian | 479 | 8.95 | 21.1 | 69.4 | 2.0 |
| Magyar | 5,331 | 11.65 | 46.4 | 90.9 | 44.1 |
| Norwegian | 420 | 15.28 | 96.9 | 99.7 | 79.3 |
| Polish | 24,223 | 11.06 | 43.5 | 80.1 | 54.1 |
| Portuguese | 3,125 | 8.10 | 45.2 | 47.8 | 57.5 |
| Roumanian | 1,026 | 10.90 | 33.3 | 83.3 | 12.0 |
| Russian | 3,311 | 11.01 | 43.6 | 74.6 | 38.0 |
| Ruthenian | 385 | 9.92 | 36.8 | 65.9 | 39.6 |
| Scotch | 1,711 | 15.24 | 100.0 | 99.6 | 83.6 |
| Servian | 1,016 | 10.75 | 41.2 | 71.5 | 31.4 |
| Slovak | 10,775 | 11.95 | 55.6 | 84.5 | 60.0 |
| Slovenian | 2,334 | 12.15 | 51.7 | 87.3 | 49.9 |
| Swedish | 3,984 | 15.36 | 94.7 | 99.8 | 87.4 |
| Syrian | 812 | 8.12 | 54.6 | 75.1 | 45.3 |
| Turkish | 240 | 7.65 | 22.5 | 56.5 | 10.0 |

[a] Able to read.

*Source:* Robert Higgs, "Race, Skills, and Earnings: American Immigrants in 1909," *Journal of Economic History*: 31(1971), p. 424.

used to maintain their cultural, linguistic, and religious values. Only a minority of second-generation children spoke in favor of education for social mobility. Schooling was limited for Slavic children, although most attained basic literacy. Work was valued more highly, as an alternative ethic to the "literacy myth" developed. Child labor was emphasized; family survival took first place. When Slavic immigrants did insist on education, ethnic culture and religious vocations were accorded most importance.

Many immigrants were opposed to the materialism of American society and to the place of public schooling in transmitting that attitude. That was one reason for the development of separate, parochial schooling. A distinct morality permeated the Poles' and Slovaks' opposition to the evils of American life; they enunciated their own moral bases of literacy and schooling, a stricter, more explicitly moral and religious ethic. They differed, however, in their perceptions of the kind of education needed. Their conception of the promise of schooling was opposed consciously to the "literacy myth."

School attendance rates reflect this skepticism toward public schooling. A 1911 study found that Poles and Slovaks ranked lowest in attendance among ethnic groups in large urban places. Few children attended beyond the primary years; virtually none went on to high school. Literacy could be attained in this way, but little more.

Slavs did not immediately embrace the idea of advancement through education. On the one hand, unskilled industrial work offered few opportunities for occupational mobility. "Public education simply did not offer skills that were useful to blast furnaces, open hearths, mines, or textile mills."[238] On the other hand, members of this ethnic group were strongly concerned with survival, limited visions of the future, and spiritual, rather than material, aims. Without a stereotypical expectation of mobility into the dominant society, these immigrants were not so disappointed with their lack of schooling or of occupational and economic progress. The adaptive goals of continuing residence, security, and community formation were more important than those offered by the dominant culture's "literacy myth" and ideology of advancement through education.[239]

In addition, it is possible that such immigrants were aware of the contradictions of the "literacy myth": the acquisition of literacy and education has by no means served to guarantee individual or collective advancement, and many have advanced without their benefits.[240] For example, sons of semi- and unskilled Welsh immigrants in Scranton, Pennsylvania at the end of the century had greater opportunities for occupational advancement than sons of similar Irish immigrants, despite having less schooling and going to work earlier. At all ages, Irish sons were more likely to be in school or at home and less likely to be working than the Welsh, and after the age of ten, all of the Welsh were working.[241]

"The socialization of Welsh children included greater exposure to adult occupations, thus giving Welsh boys valuable industrial skills. . . . keeping children home longer . . . appeared to be placing a disadvantage on Irish youth in the competition for economic success in industrial society."[242] Literacy and schooling were of little benefit. Schooling was not the only or necessarily the most appropriate way to prepare youths for their futures.

School attendance rates for all working-class youth in Chicago, for example, regardless of age and ethnic background, rose late in the century. David Hogan has shown that this increase was not a result of popular, shared demand for schooling; "rather, the educational behavior of the American working class can best be explained as part of the general conflict-ridden accommodation process to the structure of social relations in America, particularly to the existence of the wage system."

Different groups within the urban working class made a series of educational accommodations in relationship to their class and socioeconomic positions, in a context in which success was believed to depend on ability to secure and maintain work. Educational choices stemmed from the interaction between wage labor and cultural traditions; acceptance of American educational ideology was secondary. "All immigrant groups developed a positive, instrumental attitude toward education as a means of ensuring the economic welfare of their children." That does not mean that all immigrants viewed education in the same terms—or accepted the ideology of schooling. Groups varied in their responses; attitudes, traditions, and material resources conspired in that result. The need for children's labor was a frequent obstacle to schooling, as was parental skepticism about the value of education.

According to Hogan, an immigrant family cycle developed, linking school attendance, child labor, family income, and home ownership. The goal, which came with adaptation, was home ownership. One way to achieve it was by sending children to work to boost the family's earnings. However, it was becoming increasingly necessary to keep children in school longer in order to increase their value in the labor market. At this point, educational attitudes began to change. Literacy, and extended schooling, were beginning to be perceived as a *requirement*, not a choice or option, for survival. "The exigencies of economic survival in a wage labor society created then a conflict between making a sufficient living in order for their children to go to school and the necessity to go to school in order to make an adequate living."

There was also a basic, deep cultural conflict among immigrant groups about the impact of education on ethnic solidarity and cultural survival. The Slavs and Jews in Chicago were characterized by high rates of child labor and home ownership and low levels of school attendance; these parents believed that early, steady work was the path to survival and security. However, they did see a need for education to maintain ethnic identities and communities against the threat of American society and Americanization. Consequently, they valued literacy highly, but their conception differed from that of the dominant culture and the public schools; their notions included traditional moral bases, native language, sectarian religious education, and ethnic culture, in addition to English. Gradually, however, Slavic children began to stay longer in school. With the rising educational requirements of the labor market, they were learning to secure work and to survive. Extended schooling was an accommodation to their class position, and a major change in educational behavior.[243]

Jews emigrated to North America with a different educational tradition. Yet, in their social relationship to the economics of survival, they, too, were forced to adopt an instrumental approach to education: they viewed it as one key to progress. The desire to preserve their culture overlapped with such economic motives.

Jews were among the most literate of immigrants, but the notion of a cultural linkage is too simplistic. In a study of New York Jews, Selma Berrol noted that the extent to which Eastern European Jews used the public schools varied with their dates of arrival; both educational requirements and opportunities changed during the late nineteenth and early twentieth centuries. Because of familial needs and a lack of school space, many children had only a short stay in school; few gained postprimary education. Schooling may have had less impact on economic mobility than is typically assumed.

Most first-generation Jews were employed in manual work, which did not require much schooling. However, a shift among the second generation from manual labor to better-paid, higher-status occupations was under way. Literacy was a prerequisite for this shift, but prolonged schooling was not. "Educational achievements could not have been the prime cause of status improvements for the first few generations. . . . the community did so well because so many of the newcomers brought skills and experiences which were exactly right for the needs of the city at the time they arrived." Prior skills, urban life, commercial background, and comparably high levels of literacy were more essential at first than much schooling in the new land. Education, as for others, may well have *followed* occupational and economic gains, rather than preceded and caused them. Here is one recent version of the "literacy myth."[244]

Jewish immigrants also experienced cultural conflict and parental dilemmas. The traditional Jewish equation of education with learning, especially in the Talmudic tradition, was not synonymous with literacy learning for work preparation, either in Eastern Europe or in North America. The choice between educational strategies became a painful dilemma for many parents. For this group, more so for the poorer Polish and Russian Jews, schooling was also assessed in terms of the daily struggle for familial subsistence and survival.

In accommodation, Jews developed a more instrumental and pragmatic approach to schooling; but education in their culture, tradition, and heritage was also stressed. "The traditional Jewish emphasis and pride in academic achievement was valued because it contributed to the economic value of the Jews and bound them together as a cohesive cultural and religious group." Many attempts were made to preserve cultural continuity and identity. Yet, Jews tended to assimilate more quickly and in greater numbers than other groups. Education and mobility contributed there. Cultural contradictions and their relationship to schooling generated strains, as the traditional educational imperative, when transformed into education for economic necessity and progress in accommodation with American society and political economy, led to a challenge and some undermining of that culture itself.[245] Progress had its costs.

In their educational strategies, immigrant groups responded differently, and in the process they shaped their own accommodations to the dominant culture. The ideology of education, promoted by the dominant culture and its system of schooling—which expanded rapidly during the period of massive immigration—was perhaps challenged but not contradicted. On the whole, it was elaborated, and with new certification requirements was reinforced. That was a developing legacy of literacy from the nineteenth century.

Immigrants were not often transformed by the passive reception of Americanization without independent desire on their own parts. They were not simply re-shaped by the moral bases of schooling promoted so vigorously by agencies of Americanization, as once was assumed. The "literacy myth" was reshaped by and for these groups, and in time, many more of them came to accept its parameters in elaborated forms of higher schooling. That took time, and was a radically differentiated process among groups and their members.

Americanization activities were a response to the threat that many among the dominant culture saw in the new immigrants. Both illiteracy and literacy in a foreign tongue were feared as fact and symbol of alien individuals and alien cultures that would disrupt North American society. That so much of the response to these late-nineteenth-century immigrants was cast in terms of education, with instruction in literacy and its moral bases at the core, is striking. Even if many immigrants failed to be transformed by such efforts, many were able to acquire some ability to speak the new language, and to read and write it, gaining a practical skill.

Training in literacy and its social, cultural, and economic concomitants was assumed to be the most effective path to the reformation of the immigrants and their children. Assimilation was the goal, and education, in one form or another, was the most common and valued approach. Reformers differed in their assessments of the nature of assimilation, of the extent of pluralism possible and desirable, and of immigrant cultural traditions, but all agreed on the importance of literacy and familiarity with the moral bases of American society.

Many corporations brought language and literacy programs to their immigrant workers. The training in language in Peter Roberts's popular courses, for example, focused on social and civic values and industrial welfare and safety. These lessons were designed to introduce foreign speakers to and instruct them in the English language.[246] In factory and night schools, circumstances militated against the transmission of much of the moral bases, but many immigrants did gain some knowledge of English there.

A greater impact was possible, although not guaranteed, through public schooling for these immigrants' children. For school reformers, getting these children into the classroom was a major strategy; compulsory education was one aid. In the schools, children were to be provided not only with English and literacy in English, but also with an efficient and standard civic morality, as adjustment to cultural and commercial patterns outside the home.[247] Many parents (and children, too) were hostile to such training, and it led in some cases to generational conflict. Some children were affected by the moral bases of schooling, at least to the extent of deviating from traditional ways. No doubt at least some were assimilated to it.

Italians, for example, eschewed Americanization efforts in the schools in many places. The public schools were a social agency outside their culture, community, and control; irregular attendance and early leaving were common patterns for their children. Resistance to state intervention in family affairs, as well as the need for children's labor, underlay their reactions. Their class and cultural morality differed from that of the public schools. Daughters, more than sons, had educational opportunities restricted and sacrificed for familial interests. Family interests and cultural maintenance were better served by financial security and property acquisition than by children's education and leisure. Work for sons and home for daughters were seen as a better path, and a mode of accommodation to the opportunities and the threats of new settings. In time, attitudes and traditions relaxed, but they long continued to shape behavior. Basic skills could also be gained or supplemented through other agencies, such as night schools. Literacy rates did increase, and these immigrants' behavior should not be seen as antieducational.[248]

For many, then, literacy could be gained from limited exposure to schooling, but its concomitants in civic and social morality and the ideology of success through education were often reduced. Literacy and schooling were not always linked to mobility. Jews and some of the smaller Eastern European groups proved partial exceptions, with their greater valuation of schooling, and quests for success through its acquisition.[249] In those cases, emphasis on education in and of itself has been exaggerated and removed from its context of cultural conflict, prior experience with urban, skilled, and commercial environments, and the extent to which promotion of and striving for education followed, rather than preceded, adaptation and some economic success.

Despite the limitations of Americanization, instruction in English-language literacy and school training contributed to a diffuse process of assimilation. Values, attitudes, and behavior were not completely reshaped, but a learning process—of learning to adapt, to deal with a different culture and society, and to mediate its values with one's own traditions—lay at the very center of the immigrant accommodation to North America. In different ways and to varying degrees, new values and goals were being learned. Some of the "literacy myth" persisted and was transmitted to many among the new immigrants.[250]

Toward this progress, schools began to change, too:

> The new schools offered a new education which included a wide variety of courses and activities designed to equip students with knowledge and skills necessary for a variety of roles in an organic urban environment. They stressed efficiency, punctuality, regularity, obedience, order, industry, self-reliance, and resourcefulness, as well as social virtues for the greater good of the community, and sought to develop habits of cleanliness, awareness of health and sanitation rules, and respect for public and private property as agents of civic responsibility.[251]

As with earlier immigrants and the native-born working class, the schools attempted moral training, value inculcation, citizenship instruction, and character formation. The moral economy of literacy continued to underlie the schools' efforts, but for these students a new level of education for work preparation and social domestic training was introduced. The underlying continuities in noncognitive aspects of instruction are as important in these aspects of elementary training as are changes.

The legacies of literacy thus persist. Contradictions and continuities continue to shape attitudes and realities toward reading and writing. Efforts to build a common culture, rooted in the moral bases of literacy, that unified so many efforts at formal and informal instruction in the nineteenth century have weakened and diffused but have persisted in the face of a divided, pluralistic culture.[252]

# EPILOGUE

## 𝔰

# Today and Tomorrow: Revisioning Literacy

What is important to note at this point is that there is no *true* definition of literacy. Rather, each definition must be defined for the purpose to which it is to be put, and its correctness may be judged only in terms of how well it serves that purpose.

—JOHN R. BORMUTH,
"Reading Literacy: Its Definition and Assessment"

The twentieth century has seen new efforts aimed at promoting higher levels of literacy, within both the developed West and the underdeveloped regions of the world. Despite the dramatic increases, however, we are firmly in the midst of a "literacy crisis." It is not the first such perceived crisis; at times of large-scale, rapid change and confusion about the condition of civilization and morality, literacy has seemed to suffer a "decline" almost generationally across the span of recorded history. Given the massive Western emotional, intellectual, and fiscal investment in education, and the many legacies of literacy, disappointment with the products of schooling is not surprising; it is persistent, perhaps unavoidable, and fundamentally historical: one of the central contradictions of the historical course of literacy itself. "Since the initiation of the public school systems . . . national leaders have periodically issued statements of a 'literacy crisis' and have launched reform programs designed to eliminate illiteracy. . . ."[1]

Before the pressing tasks at hand can be confronted, several interrelated issues must be considered: trends in basic literacy levels during the twentieth century; the asserted and presumed impacts and consequences of literacy; the condition of literacy in the West today, and the accuracy of perceptions of a crisis; the changing and persistent uses and meanings of literacy and their place within the larger network of shifting communicative modes; and the legacies of literacy and their intersection in the meeting of literacies "old" and "new." Just as literacy has a long and vital, if neglected, past, which shaped and conditioned its present, it has a future, even if the shape of that future can barely be outlined today.

The very notion of literacy is problematic.[2] Dictionary definitions frequently go beyond the basic ability to read and write, and include such elements as learning, education, instruction, liberal education, literature and literary qualities, polish, and articulateness. These historically based notions, with their core of post-Reformation and post-Enlightenment valuation and endorsement of the provenance of literacy and corresponding censure of illiteracy, blur essential distinctions and inflate the meaning of literacy. An ability to read and write, regardless of level of skills, is linked with such attributes, regardless of the distance that separates them. The literate and the illiterate tend to be diametrically and dichotomously opposed: with respect not only to reading and writing, but also to a range of personal, cultural, and communicative characteristics.

It requires an active exercise of the mind and will to overcome such deeply rooted linguistic and epistemological obstacles. Literacy represents a range of abilities or skills that may or may not lead to a distinctive personal, social-psychological condition or orientation. Its meaning is established only in precise historical contexts; it is not universally given or proscribed. It need not connote dimensions of the liberal, the polished, or the literary, and may not even contrast strongly with illiteracy. Changing terminology will not solve the problem. A more difficult task is called for: a revision and reconceptualization of the ways in which we think about literacy and illiteracy. Literacy must be seen as *symbol* and *symptom* as well as *fact*; that is one consequence of its historical development.

That the decade of the 1970s marked a new period in the history of literacy is not surprising. The passing of numerous movements—in politics, ideology, economics, culture, social thoughts and programs, international affairs, and educational institutions and practice—took its toll on the world we live in and the way we think about it. All of these were connected in some way to perceptions about or uses and meanings of literacy. As in previous ages of transition, literacy is the object of a great deal of attention. Along with the continuities, of course, there are changes: just as the social structures, polities, economic systems, modes of technology and communications, and cultural dimensions today differ from those of the past, so do many of literacy's roles and meanings. What is impressive, nonetheless, is the fact that literacy attracts so much attention today, just as it did in those times. The lessons of this recurrence bear reflection.

## 1. Twentieth-Century Trends in Literacy Levels

A review of census statistics from Europe at the beginning of the twentieth century points to continuities from the mid-nineteenth. Although all countries had progressed, their order by literacy levels had not changed. Levels in Central and Northern Europe were over 95 percent; in Western Europe, over 80 percent; in Austria and Hungary, over 70 percent (a dramatic improvement); in Spain, Italy, and Poland, over 50 percent; and in Portugal and the orthodox Catholic countries, only around 25 percent.[3] With the building of educational systems and the beginning of "modern" economic development, previously disadvantaged regions were joining the mainstream of high levels of literacy. However, neither differences in levels of living, wealth, productivity, and national standing nor internal inequalities by region, age, sex, class, or ethnicity were erased.

By 1950, Southern and Eastern Europe were 80 percent literate, with the exception of Portugal, the Mediterranean Islands, and Albania, where the rate was only about 50 percent.[4] Literacy had continued its long-term impressive increase, and in the process, national gaps in basic levels were decreasing. Nowhere, however, did ever-

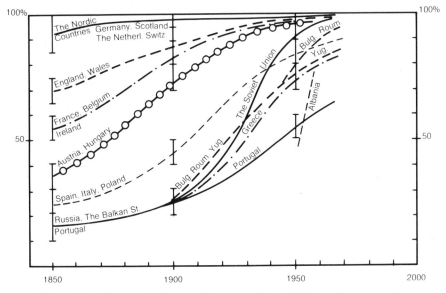

**Figure E.1.** Literacy in Europe, 1850–1970, Compiled from Censuses and Statistics for Recruits, Convicts, and Signatures for Bridal Couples
*Source*: Johansson, *History of Literacy*, p. 72

rising literacy levels result in fundamental changes for nations, societies, or individuals. Poor persons and poor nations largely remained poor, and other gaps—geographic, social, and age- and gender-related—persisted.

The United States, as compared to most of the rest of the West, had existing high levels of literacy. The levels continued to increase over the century, rising from 80 percent in 1870 to 97.1 percent in 1940. By the 1960s, illiteracy had fallen close to the irreducible minimum of the disabled and handicapped. Such aggregates, of course, hide the persisting variations and inequalities by region, ethnicity, sex, age, class, and race.[5] The three most prominent gaps were white-black, native-immigrant, and North-South. Neither literacy by itself nor the agency that transmits it—or the contradictory sentiments that led to the goal of universal literacy through compulsory schooling—was meant to achieve a level of universal opportunity or equality of results.

Occupationally, by mid-century, illiteracy was higher among the unemployed and those not in the labor force than among the employed, and higher among farm and nonagricultural laborers than those in other occupational fields. According to 1959 census statistics, clerical and professional and technical workers were the most literate, followed by managers and proprietors, craftsmen and foremen, service workers, operatives, private household workers, farmers and farm managers, general laborers, and farm laborers and foremen. All occupations had fewer illiterate women workers than men. Hinted directly by the occupational stratification of the nonliterate is the class structure. Income, race, residence, and employment data reinforce the point.[6]

In 1959, blacks continued to have higher illiteracy rates (7.5 percent) than whites (1.6 percent), and the percentage of illiterate black men was higher than that of

TABLE E.1

| Year | All U.S. | Native-born | Foreign-born | All Whites | Blacks | Males | Females |
|------|------|------|------|------|------|------|------|
| | | White | | | Blacks | Males | Females |
| 1870 | 20.0 | — | — | 11.5 | 81.4 | 18.3 | 21.9 |
| 1880 | 17.0 | 8.7 | 11.8 | 9.4 | — | 15.8 | 18.2 |
| 1890 | 13.3 | 6.2 | 13.1 | 7.7 | 57.1 | 12.4 | 14.4 |
| 1900 | 10.7 | 4.6 | 12.9 | 6.2 | 44.5 | 10.1 | 11.2 |
| 1910 | 7.7 | 3.0 | 12.7 | 5.0 | 30.4 | 7.6 | 7.8 |
| 1920 | 6.0 | 2.0 | 13.1 | 4.0 | 22.9 | 6.0 | 5.9 |
| 1930 | 4.3 | 1.5 | 9.9 | — | 17.5 | — | — |
| 1940 | 2.9 | 1.1 | 9.0 | — | 11.5 | — | — |
| 1952 | 2.5 | — | — | 1.8 | 10.2 | — | — |
| 1959 | 2.2 | — | — | 1.6 | 7.5 | — | — |

Source: U.S. Census Bureau

illiterate black women; the discrepancy (9.8 to 5.4) was greater than that between white males and females (1.7 to 1.4). Illiteracy was higher among the rural farm population (4.3) than among the rural nonfarm (2.2) and urban (1.7) populations, and among Southerners (4.3) than among residents of the Northeast (1.5), North Central (1.0), or Western (1.3) regions of the country. Illiteracy tended to decline with higher levels of income.

Data from the 1960s and 1970s show more continuity than change. Progress continues to be contradicted by these persisting and perhaps increasing disparities. Despite the achievement of near-universal levels of basic literacy, a large segment of the American adult population still suffers some disadvantage as a result of limited education. "In this country persons with limited education are often the same persons who suffer from one or more of the other social disadvantages. . . . Inadequate education will probably be only one manifestation of their deprivation."[7] This social, economic, political, and cultural "problem" is a common, regular feature throughout the Western world. It is central to the contradictions that constitute the legacies of literacy.[8]

All results point to one conclusion: the population most affected is the lower class, the poor, blacks, and Hispanics, and the aged. Non- and semiliterates are found in large numbers "wherever there are poor people and wherever there are congregated racial and ethnic minority groups. . . . more . . . in the South than in the North, more in the East than in the West." Those groups who occupy the lowest rungs on the class structure are precisely those who have always done so, despite their undoubted advancement in proportions literate and in years of schooling.[9]

The tendency today, as earlier, is to blame the poverty, underemployment, low positions, and the like of such groups on a lack of literacy and educational achievement. However, blacks, convicts, and Hispanics are not poor, imprisoned, or unemployed solely because of their high likelihood of being illiterate; literacy is much more a result and reflection of other social and economic factors and a symptom

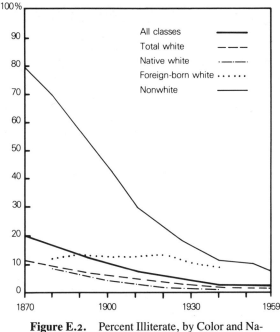

**Figure E.2.** Percent Illiterate, by Color and Nativity, United States, 1870–1959
*Source: Current Population Reports*, Series P-20, No. 99, February 4, 1960.

or symbol of them than it is an independently contributing factor. Being literate provides no solution.

Literacy is important, of course. However, our concern with it "has led us to undervalue other types of skills—those associated with commonsense orientation, those of practical action, those of interpersonal dialogue, . . . those associated with the visual arts. . . ."

> For many families and communities, the major benefits of reading and writing may not include such traditionally assigned rewards as social mobility, job preparation, intellectual creativity, critical reasoning, and public information access. In short, literacy has different meanings for members of different groups, with a variety of acquisitive modes, functions, and uses; these differences have yet to be taken into account by policy makers.[10]

The concept of literacy must be recast. That is one lesson to be learned from the contradictions and "crises" of the present.

On a global level, there is a huge variation in literacy levels among different continents, regions, and states. For the years 1960 and 1970, "world literacy" was estimated at 40 and 34 percent respectively. Incredible progress has been made in such places as North Korea, North Vietnam, Cuba, China, Tanzania, and Nicaragua as a result of well-organized "literacy campaigns." Other areas, such as Africa, remain highly illiterate, although even they have made progress.[11] It would be hard to demonstrate that the degree of literacy improvement was equaled by increases

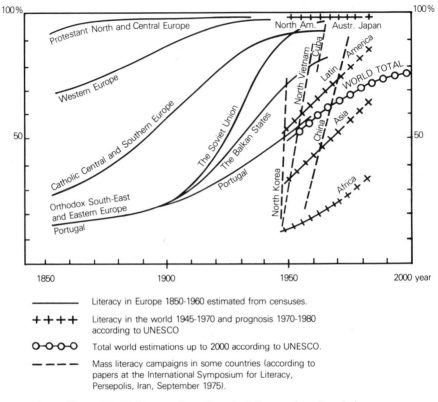

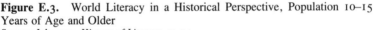

Literacy in Europe 1850-1960 estimated from censuses.

++++ Literacy in the world 1945-1970 and prognosis 1970-1980 according to UNESCO

O-O-O-O Total world estimations up to 2000 according to UNESCO.

- - - - Mass literacy campaigns in some countries (according to papers at the International Symposium for Literacy, Persepolis, Iran, September 1975).

**Figure E.3.** World Literacy in a Historical Perspective, Population 10–15 Years of Age and Older
*Source:* Johanson, *History of Literacy*, p. 74

in indexes of well-being, democracy, and other social changes. Developments in literacy and schooling tend to *follow*, rather than precede or cause, economic and social development. That is not often recognized in most developmental schemes.[12]

Disparities and inequalities—for example, sexual differentials and urban-rural gaps—are great. Not only do nations with highest illiteracy rates tend to have the highest birth rates, but they also tend to have the highest female illiteracy levels. Moreover, regardless of advances in women's "rights," the percentage of illiterate women is increasing steadily. Even as literacy rates increase around the world, absolute numbers of nonliterate persons continue to grow.

Changing age structures of populations have a favorable impact on literacy levels. Even more important have been the imaginative, realistic steps taken by some governments to eradicate illiteracy. Elsewhere, though, no serious efforts have been made. The UN Secretariat blames that failure on the West ("The developed countries have not given the eradication of illiteracy a high priority in their . . . aid programmes"); however, in the 1950s and 1960s, the Western nations did seek to export their own models of universal literacy training. The fact that these efforts proved futile indicates that Western priorities were not the answer for the non-West.

Among the obstacles to the provision of literacy programs, as well as to the

## TABLE E.2
### Adult (15+) Literacy around 1960 and 1970

| Major regions[a] | Around 1960 | | | | Around 1970 | | | |
|---|---|---|---|---|---|---|---|---|
| | Adult population (000) | Literate adults (000) | Illiterate adults (000) | Illiteracy percentage | Adult population (000) | Literate adults (000) | Illiterate adults (000) | Illiteracy percentage |
| World total | 1,869,000 | 1,134,000 | 735,000 | 39.3 | 2,287,000 | 1,504,000 | 783,000 | 34.2 |
| Africa | 153,000 | 29,000 | 124,000 | 81.0 | 194,000 | 51,100 | 143,000 | 73.7 |
| Northern America | 136,000 | 133,000 | 3,300 | 2.4 | 161,000 | 158,000 | 2,500 | 1.5 |
| Latin America | 123,000 | 83,100 | 40,000 | 32.5 | 163,000 | 125,000 | 38,600 | 23.6 |
| Asia | 982,000 | 440,000 | 542,000 | 55.2 | 1,237,000 | 658,000 | 579,000 | 46.8 |
| Europe | 464,000 | 439,000 | 24,500 | 5.3 | 521,000 | 502,000 | 18,700 | 3.6 |
| Oceania | 10,600 | 9,400 | 1,200 | 11.5 | 13,000 | 11,800 | 1,400 | 10.3 |
| (Arab States) | (52,700) | (9,900) | (42,700) | (81.1) | (68,300) | (18,400) | (49,900) | (73.0) |

[a]The world total covers the whole world, including Unesco Member States, non-Member States and non-self-governing territories; Africa covers the entire African continent, including the Arab States of Africa; Northern America includes the United States, Canada, Bermuda, Greenland and St. Pierre and Miquelon; Latin America covers the South American continent, Central America, Mexico and the Carribbean; Asia covers the entire Asian region, including the Arab States of Asia; Europe includes the Union of Soviet Socialist Republics; Oceania covers Australia, New Zealand and the surrounding islands; the Arab States as a separate grouping are presented in parentheses as they are already included partly under Africa and partly under Asia.

*Source:* UNESCO Secretariat, "Literacy in the World since the 1965 Teheran Conference: Shortcomings, Achievements, Tendencies," in *A Turning Point for Literacy* pp. 4, 5, 6, 7, 8, 9, 10, 11, 12, 13.

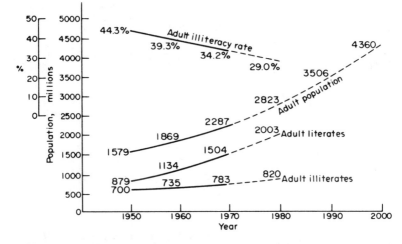

**Figure E.4.** Growth of the World Adult Literate/Illiterate Population and Decrease of Adult Illiteracy Rate
*Source:* UNESCO, *Learning to Be* (Paris, 1972), pp. 298–299.

motivation of learners, have been social, political, and economic inequalities; misdirected education aimed primarily at elites; inappropriate standards for the general population; social and economic situations that do not require literacy; and cultural alienation. Even where programs do exist, they often are hindered by such factors as insufficient resources, unrealistic content, poor communication, a lack of transport, scattered population, language problems, insufficient materials and teachers, and "the 'lack of a literacy environment,' i.e., the social structures and facilities geared to the uses of literacy."[13]

Another very important factor is the conceptualization of literacy. Assumptions about the consequences and transformations expected to result from the achievement of literacy still dominate. According to Johan Galtung, literacy is propagated and utilized to create the illusion of equality. "The literacy is not functional, it is only a statistical artifact for large groups of the populations—in underdeveloped and overdeveloped countries alike. . . ."[14]

Since the 1960s, especially under the influence of the pioneering work of Paolo Freire in Brazil and Geneva, mass literacy campaigns without the erection of formal, public, institutionalized school systems have become increasingly popular. Despite the importance of their goals and approaches, many problems exist. Foremost is the question of the potentially disruptive introduction of literacy into largely nonliterate cultures. Complex interrelations change over time in the relationships between oral and literate cultures, and elites and states sometimes use literacy for domination and control. The penetration of literacy into an overwhelmingly oral, native culture tends to cause massive social, religious, ideological, political, economic, and cultural changes.

Programs such as Freire's, with their locally based, informal instruction in small groups with active roles for learners and relevant, experiential text content, bring about incredible improvement in mass, elementary literacy levels. Their approach has been far more successful than normative, "modern" Western formal institutional schemes. Freire's critique of political oppression and the use of generative literacy learning as a path to political and cultural freedom are attractive to new, typically socialist regimes. Through the achievement of an active, partially self-taught literacy, rooted in dialogue and new visions of the world, men and women presumably are able to transcend the boundaries of their former social, political, and cultural conditions. In Freire's method, learners take a major part in shaping the "curriculum." Literacy materials, not precast and preprinted, emerge from a process of critical dialogue. "Conscientization" is the goal. Literacy is a method, not an end.

Scale, scope, timing, efficiency, and available resources make Freire's approach impractical on a national scale. In the best-known cases of mass campaigns, literacy materials are prewritten and preprinted by "experts" in ministries of education and culture. There are problems with young, inexperienced, speedily trained teachers. Yet, the rate of success in raising basic literacy rates and in spreading elementary reading and writing skills is impressive. Underlying this progress are such factors as exceptional motivations of teachers and learners; national enthusiasm and competition; literacy materials and the planned curriculum; visions of the campaigns as "wars" for progress for the people; and the explicitly ideological and political nature of the movement.

Not all aspects of these campaigns have been positive. It is too early to tell whether skills so learned will be retained and used, or whether they are high-level and critical abilities that can readily be transferred to other materials and contexts. In addition, the results of such politically oriented programs can be contradictory. The officially prescribed content and its links to unifying, integrating, and motivating social goals cannot but have a strong impact on the kind and quality of literacy skills obtained. The skills and the lessons that are learned in the process of their transmission and acquisition do shape and condition the purposes and uses of literacy. The self-activism and full awareness that are anticipated to result from this approach to literacy, and which well transcend the skills of literacy themselves, do not emanate from the learning of literacy shaped by explicit ideology. Literacy is never neutral; in practice—in learning and in use—it is also limited. It is no different in mass "literacy campaigns."

In the Third World today, we see the elements of the "literacy myth" and many other elements of the legacies of literacy.[15] That is not to say that history is repeating itself or that context, processes, or outcomes are the same or predetermined. The point, rather, is to seek the key connections; to link the past with the present, the West with the non-West; to discover the vital roles of contradictions and continuities: as ways to understand, criticize, and formulate new paths to the future.

## 2. Imputed Impacts and Consequences; or, Great and Other Dichotomies Revisited

Frequent assumptions are made about the qualities that are expected to accompany the possession and use of literacy. They exist on many levels, from the individual to the societal, and include the psychological, cognitive, attitudinal, social-relational, behavioral, symbolic, motivational, participatory, and productive. Historians stand beside psychologists, literary scholars, and economists in accepting and perpetuating this causal "syndrome" of literacy's consequences and correlates.

Thus, literate persons, it is asserted, are more empathetic, innovative, achievement-oriented, cosmopolitan, media- and politically aware, identified with a nation, aspiring to schooling, urban in residence, and accepting of technology. Literacy is said to correlate with economic growth and industrialization, wealth and productivity, political stability and participatory democracy, urbanization, consumption, and contraception. Such claims are not well documented; nor are their relationships well specified or conceptualized. Any meaning that they retain has substance and credibility only in precisely delineated contexts.[16]

In the long tradition of Western ideas about literacy, most of this thinking relates to what Jack Goody calls the "Grand Dichotomy," and Ruth Finnegan the "Great Divide."

> When people wish to make a basic comparison between different societies or historical periods, one of the commonly invoked criteria is literacy. In particular those who wish to avoid the connotations of "primitive," "uncivilized," "aboriginal" tend to turn to a description in terms of "non-literate" or "preliterate." . . . One common answer that is often implied is that the presence or absence of literacy is of absolutely crucial signficance for the quality of thought in a given culture.[17]

Literacy is held to be not only important and useful but also an unambiguously positive thing, associated closely with the vital necessities of "modern," "developed" persons and societies. Dichotomization of this type suffers from a lack of grounded, empirical evidence. In addition, scholars, writers, and other constant users of literacy are referred to as examples in support of generalizations. Especially curious is the scholarly reification at the core of such intellectual acts, as men and women of the book project their presumed advantages and disadvantages on others.

G. H. Bantock, for example, in his address "The Implications of Literacy," asserts (repeating Marshall McLuhan) that print's role "introduces subtle modifications into social relationships and the individual consciousness of men." The preliterate world is contrasted starkly with the literate; the "coming of the printed book" "gradually changes" cultural and social relations. Books, thus literacy, cause self-consciousness and social distance; they also reinforce privacy and individualism, inwardness and detachment. Print results in "a certain narrowing of experience," but at the same time it also broadens horizons. Similarly, literacy and print simultaneously increase problems of identity and rootlessness while they aid in their solution.[18]

Bantock's series of antinomies or oppositions—implicit contradictions—may not be erroneous. But he does not embrace their oppositional or contradictory qualities. Rather than grasping that literacy, in a specific context, can contribute to opposing outcomes, or that in different contexts it can work toward a variety of consequences for individuals, societies, cultures, states, and economies, he confuses its relations. Overly simplistic, unmediated, linear relationships are seldom among those that remain after scrutiny and criticism.[19] If the history of literacy comprises contradictions at its core, its consequences are also likely to be contradictory.

Jack Goody has produced some of the most exciting and significant writings in the field. Goody is well aware that literacy does not represent civilization and progress, and that its absence does not indicate barbarity. Much of his writing stresses the accomplishments of non- and preliterate civilizations. However, the claims that he does make for the consequences of literacy are often contradictory, especially in his earlier writings.

Using fifth- and sixth-century Greece as their model, Goody and Ian Watt (his collaborator on the paper "The Consequences of Literacy") claim that the introduction of alphabetic writing into a previously oral culture results in such "cultural innovations" as a shift from mythical to logico-empirical modes of thought; new relationships between words and their referents that are more general and abstract; individual, critical, and rational syntheses; a distinction between myth and history; the spread of criticism and skepticism; and a recognition of the categorical importance of time and space. They assert that there is a "causal connection between writing and logic," and that contemporary civilization results from the "intrinsic differences between non-literate (or proto-literate) and literate societies."

For Goody and Watt, widespread literacy is central to the development of political democracy, and to the concept of a world of knowledge crossing political boundaries and longer-distance administrative controls and cultural traditions. However, at least as important as literacy here are context, parameters, and preconditions, and kinds and qualities of associations. Literacy is best seen as a *dependent* factor, a result itself, and as more an interactive, conditioning, and shaping instrument than a determining one. As to contradictions, Goody and Watt note:

> Yet although the idea of intellectual, and to some extent political, universalism is historically and substantively linked with literate culture, we too easily forget that this brings with it other features which have quite different implications, and which go some way to explain why the long-cherished and theoretically feasible dream of an "educated democracy" and a truly egalitarian society has never been realized in practice.

Neither in Greece nor in the present with virtually universal literacy has this "progress" arrived.

Goody and Watt also claim that with the recording of the cultural tradition came an awareness of "the past as different from the present" and "the inherent inconsistencies in the picture of life as it was inherited by the individual from the cultural tradition in its recorded form." No doubt writing and reading aid this process, but the issue may be more one of record and its extent than one of causality. Goody and Watt are more convincing in pointing to the "bulk" and "depth" of written records, although these, too, are problematic:

> This unlimited proliferation also characterized the written tradition in general: the mere size of the literate repertoire means that the proportion of the whole which any one individual knows must be infinitesimal in comparison with what obtains in oral culture. Literate society, merely by having no system of elimination, no "structural amnesia," prevents the individual from participating fully in the total cultural tradition to anything like the extent possible in non-literate society.

Here one must also recognize the all-too-frequent manipulation, control, rewriting, and destruction of "history" in the form of written records.

With other commentators, these authors stress the "inevitable" and "ever-increasing" cultural lags in literate society. The scope and scale of the literate tradition expand constantly. However, that is a condition more of intellectuals and their peers than of most persons. Most people do not "live" in the broadest traditions and cultural modes, for better or for worse. A far more careful approach is needed to individuals and groups in their cultural and social systems and to the impact of communicative modes.

Goody and Watt are on firmer ground in discussing social stratification. Despite its promise, literacy has served to exacerbate inequalities.[20] The relationship between schooling and success, and the importance of achievement over ascription constitute two of the most profound issues in modern social science and social theory.

With "modernization" and mass education, the school supposedly became the setting for more equal opportunities to advance, as attainment was substituted for social origins.[21] However, recent Western data contradict assumptions or expectations of direct links between school achievement and job, wealth, or status achievement.[22] Social background still plays a significant role; education is important, more so than ever, but it is strongly influenced by social class and other ascriptive factors (race, ethnicity, gender, etc.) in its relationship to mobility and individual advancement. A great deal of movement does take place, but much of education's function is to reproduce intergenerationally the social and class structures and to shape the processes of intergenerational inheritance of wealth and status.[23]

In *Education and Jobs*, Ivar Berg has made some interesting observations. He found no increasing link between education and occupation. Education across the West expanded more rapidly than net changes in skill requirements; the problem thus becomes whether education offers less in rewards than it engenders in expectations. Berg also found self-fulfilling prophecies of the value of education for occupational requirements to be rampant among managers and employers. Not only is there overeducation for job requirements, but there has been little, if any, relationship between changes in educational levels and changes in output per worker. Education may predict initial salary and job title, but not promotion or productivity. In professional and managerial positions, Berg also found, educational achievement was rewarded rather than actual performance.[24]

This situation is not limited to the United States, or even to the West. In a study of 140 nations, Gerald W. Fry found that educational expansion bore little relationship to changing patterns of inequality or economic development. "It appears that greater equality does not result from the expansion of schooling, but rather from fundamental structural changes that reduce dependency on foreign capital." Educational expansions and rising levels of literacy may be relatively independent of many of the forces with which they are normatively linked.[25]

According to the "literacy myth," education is supposed to do many things: stimulate economic development, provide a foundation for democracy, and expose people to common values, institutions, and languages to unite and integrate them. But "despite much higher educational attainment rates today than fifteen or twenty years ago, there is still little democracy [or economic development, or social equality] in Africa, Asia, or Latin America, and the optimism that there ever will be is fading." Education and literacy change, but the presumed consequences do not follow.[26]

A further social tension, according to Goody and Watt, derives from the fact that "even within a literate culture, the oral tradition—the transmission of values and attitudes in face-to-face contact—nevertheless remains the primary mode of cultural orientation, and, to varying degrees, is out of step with the various literate traditions." That is an abstract truism. Different modes of communications—learning broadly defined—mediate one another, and serve as filters, sometimes in conflict but at other times most conjunctively. "Mass media are not the only . . . social influences on the contemporary cultural tradition as a whole."

Goody and Watt do grasp the fact that "the literate mode of communication is such that it does not impose itself as forcefully or as uniformly as is the case with the oral transmission of the oral tradition. . . ."[27] In fact, literate culture can be avoided by many; most people do not read very much. The alienation and individualism, as well as progress and democracy, that are claimed to accompany and perhaps result from the spread of literacy stand out among the contradictions. Literacy can also be as much an integrating as an individualizing force. The hours of daily private study of scholars are not a common experience.[28] Tendencies in one direction or another exist in all literate cultures; where the balance may lie varies with numerous other factors.

By his later writings, Goody realized that the "consequences of literacy" were often other than direct causal results of changes in communicative modes or techniques, often contradictory, and often the consequences of factors other than literacy. However, he still sought grand themes and sweeping statements for the import of literacy's impact: complex bureaucracies depend upon writing; long-distance, center, and periphery communications are advanced; accounting efficiency is improved, as is the organization of trade and agriculture. The emphasis remains, but with a difference in language, a more flexible and less deterministic conceptualization. There is a greater awareness of the restrictions of literacy.[29] The shift relates more closely to the continuities and contradictions central to the history of literacy. By *The Domestication of the Savage Mind*, literacy emerges as an "analytic tool" that *may* lead to other potentials and possibilities. Of course, "the social structure behind the communicative acts is often of prime importance."[30]

In this way literacy can be understood. Dichotomies must be left aside, along with other of literacy's legacies. As Goody notes, the elements of dichotomies are best transformed into variables for study. From this perspective, we can begin to approach the issue of literacy's impacts: on psychology, culture, schooling, and language; economies; and social relations and structures.

One of the dichotomies that need to be transcended is the relationship of literacy to modernization. Such a correlation has not been proved in studies. Alex Inkeles, for example, hypothesized that literacy was central to individual modernity, and conducted a six-nation field study.[31] Education, he wrote, "has often been identified as perhaps the most important of the influences moving men away from traditionalism toward modernity. . . . Our evidence does not challenge this well-established conclusion."

Inkeles's study, however, confused schooling with literacy and skills with attitudes. Education and literacy were not examined with regard to skills or cognitive characteristics. The "modernity" test was a test of attitudes; the "effects of the school . . . reside not mainly in its formal, explicit, self-conscious pedagogic activity, but rather are inherent in the school as an *organization*," which also possesses a hidden curriculum.[32] In the end it was repeated that "a man *can* become very modern without the benefit of education," but that "in large-scale complex societies no attribute of the person predicts his attitudes, values, and behavior more consistently or more powerfully than the amount of schooling he has received." The schooling effect, nevertheless, was to some extent an artifact of the relationship between education and an individual's social characteristics. Inkeles concluded that "how much you benefit from schooling depends on what happens *later* in life."[33] Literacy is lost as a major independent variable.

In another study, literacy was maintained to be "a factor which completely pervades and shapes a man's entire view of the world." However, both positive and negative findings were reported when the attitudes and values associated with literacy were examined, leading Inkeles to conclude that literacy is "limited to those spheres where vicarious and abstract experience is especially meaningful. The more practical part of a man's outlook, however [the concrete social and economic domains], is determined by his actual daily experience in significant roles." The role of literacy may be less than it appears in most formulations of "modernization."

Inkeles's findings reinforce the importance of concrete situations and context,[34] underscoring the limits of literacy by itself. Abstract, universal generalities have little value; literacy is rarely an independent factor. Schooling, or literacy as Inkeles interchanges the terms, may "merely [lay] the ground work which made it possible for later life experience to give concrete content to a more general disposition established in childhood." While it presumes that literacy always results from schooling, this notion does leave open the possibilities of further effects on their absence. And as Charles Tilly put it, this approach applies to "talking modern," or communicative behavior—responses to questions—not to concrete behavior.[35] The results of other studies are no less ambiguous. Nowhere are the massive generalizations of either McLuhan's "Gutenberg Galaxy" or Lerner's "communications theory of modernization" borne out: not, at least, at the level of literacy.[36]

In a study of Colombian peasants, Everett Rogers and William Herzog found that literacy did not always correlate highly or consistently with exposure to media or with reading newspapers or magazines. It is possible, the authors postulate, that "*literates* are not reading to any great extent . . . [or] *illiterates* are using the print media by having family members or friends read to them." They correlate literacy with empathy, innovativeness, achievement motivation, farm size, "cosmopoliteness," and political knowledge; yet, their tests are problematic, and many of the associations are not statistically powerful. The contradictions are reinforced by the finding that opinion and influence are often based in personal dealings with individuals and that opinion leaders are "far from 100 percent literate."[37] The variation among villages proves again that context is central.

J. E. DeYoung and C. L. Hunt's analysis of "communication channels" and literacy in Philippino barrios adds to the perspective. Regardless of literacy, only a minority of barrio residents were regularly exposed to mass media of any kind, and "if the radio, the press, and the movies have an extensive influence, it is by diffusion of their message through personal contact rather than by direct impact."[38] As in the Colombian villages, print materials were scarce. Other individuals were named as best sources of information. Oral communication dominated, although those who read newspapers and magazines more often ranked those organs as their best source of information. Literacy and print, among other mass media, were penetrating the society, and literacy rates were increasing, especially among the young: that was not regularly translated into more reading.

Daniel Lerner accorded a key role for "literacy and initiative" in his study in a Turkish village of his "communications theory of modernization." "It is our hypothesis that the most effective way out of the vicious circle of poverty—the mechanism which can transform the inertial process of immobility—is *literacy*." Lerner attempted to establish the fact that literates possessed greater physical, social, and psychic mobility; however, in his study, literates proved only somewhat more mobile and more empathetic than nonliterates. They did have more "modern" attitudes— they "talked" modern—but that relates to feelings and perceptions, not to behavior.

Literates were more frequently identified with innovators and were more willing to "be first" in their village to try a new way; but given their higher occupational status, greater resources, higher origins, and the like, that is not especially striking or likely a concrete outcome of literacy by itself. Moreover, the differences are not overwhelming: 95 percent of literate men compared to 83 percent of illiterate, and 83 percent of literate women to 69 of illiterate, claimed a willingness to be first.[39] If that is taken as the most important indicator of modernity and tendency to leadership, the illiterates are perhaps more impressive than are those so advantaged by their literacy.

Henry Dobyns's analysis of social change in an Andean village deals with literacy's relationships to economic development and power. With the help of the Cornell Peru Project, the village of Vicos developed material bases of production and a program of schooling. However, "increasing investment in formal education and increasing economic productivity . . . [were] two independent processes that happened to be occurring concurrently without being causally connected." The expansion of schooling "benefited from and was made possible by the economic expansion. . . . [but] did not . . . set in motion the increase in farm productivity." The economic development was based on learning, but not formal literacy-based classroom instruction. In contrast with most formulations of "modern" development that place literacy and schooling at their core and see them as strong causal factors, case studies increasingly point to education's following after economic change.[40]

With the diffusion of literacy in Vicos, power relations changed, and centuries-old age-based hierarchies were reordered in a decade. Literacy, cumulative knowledge, democratic discussion, and decision-making abilities acquired new value. Literacy also came to carry new functional powers, especially in administrative and business affairs. Newly literate schoolboys often were recruited for tasks that now required reading and writing; in this way, the young acquired some of their power, as they also did through teaching opportunities, leading to new power relations and forms of personal interaction. Formal political power, however, awaited their aging. New power also came from the nonliterate skills that artisanal training developed; the rise of classes of "specialists" was not based wholly on classroom training in literacy.

Literacy in time led to many structural and cultural changes in Vicos. Assumptions and attitudes, roles and responsibilities, power and participation, and perhaps even "personality" were changed, especially as young literate men were elected to offices, attained further schooling, traveled, and took part in new kinds of economic dealings. Intriguingly, the young literates were voted off the council as others came to distinguish between writers and literates as scribes or secretaries and as policy makers. Some literacy-related power proved ephemeral. Context, timing, local history and social structure, opportunities, and the like all influenced the ways in which literacy related to change.[41]

Recent studies of learning and culture struggle to break away from the limitations of dichotomizing thinking.[42] Literacy and schooling are beginning to be seen as conceptually distinct; in the most exciting research on this topic, Sylvia Scribner and Michael Cole asked specifically about the nature of literacy and its intellectual effects. They focused on comparisons of unschooled and schooled populations, but also on schooled and unschooled literates.

In the first instance, they found that the unschooled "tended to solve problems singly, each as a new problem, whereas schooled populations tended to treat them as instances of a class of problems that could be solved by a general rule." The conclusion stresses generalized solution processes as a product of schooling, not of literacy per se. A difference also emerged in the use of language to describe the tasks and their solutions. Much of this difference appears to be a result not of schooling versus nonschooling but of the form of schooling. Formal institutional schooling puts more emphasis on verbal formulations of general rules or generalized descriptions and competency in symbol systems.

In studies of the Vai, a West African people for whom schooling and acquisition of literacy are separate tasks, Cole and Scribner examined the extent to which the written word has distinct psychological qualities, "the dominant belief that literacy leads inevitably to higher forms of thought." They found that most research confounded literacy with schooling, and that none of the causal paths and factors suggested by proponents of that belief tested literacy as such. Literacy thus has been construed only in terms of that practiced in schools. In addition, "confusion stems from failure to differentiate the consequences of literacy over the course of human history from its consequences for the individual in present-day societies. It is a big jump from intellectual and cultural history to a theory of ontogenetic development in any present-day society."

Earlier studies led Scribner and Cole to skepticism about the "developmental" or "modernization" approach. "We did not assume that the skills promoted by schooling would necessarily be applied in contexts unrelated to school experience." The results of a number of tests focusing on concrete practices of literacy that had been held to produce behavioral changes (for example, sorting and verbal reasoning) indicated that improved test scores were associated with years of formal education, but that literacy did not provide a substitute for schooling. Literacy apparently was not the cause of these abilities; schooling had power of its own.

With regard to Goody's notion that with literacy skills comes an ability to analyze language, Scribner and Cole found that Vai literacy was associated with small improvement in the performances of some tasks, but not with any general evidence of better performance. That led them to a closer look at the place of writing in Vai culture. They found that although reading and writing were not prominent activities, Vai literates used their skills in numerous ways: for letter writing, recording and accounting, and other business, political, social, and cultural purposes. This literacy served many functions despite its failure to indicate "developmental" consequences on the tests.

The Vai almost always "contextualized" their written communications by giving general characteristics of the message and its sphere of relevance. Scribner and Cole were able to isolate some general skills involved in the acquisition and use of Vai literacy that are transferable to nonliterate behaviors. They found that analyzing oral speech and giving clearer instructions were important skills, in which Vai literates did differ from nonliterates. "These studies provide the first direct evidence that what an individual does with text, or with pencil and paper, can promote specific skills that are available to support these behaviors." As far as they could tell, these skills were associated with literacy rather than with general learning experiences. Yet, these consequences were not indicative of across-the-board abilities; they were highly specific to the Vai script.

Scribner and Cole urge that literacy be conceived more as "practice" than as "development." In terms of literacy, a technology of writing is central, as is knowledge of how to represent oral language in script in an understandable way. A variety of skills are needed to perform such a task, and with practice, the skills should become better organized, more efficient, less dependent on content, and more often transferable to new contents and contexts. Transferability, as well as other qualities, however, seems highly variable, and not automatic or inevitable. This conclusion leads to major questions about the environments in which literacy is learned, and about what else is taught there. Levels of generalization, as of expectations, must be sharply limited.

"We did not find that literacy in the Vai script was associated in any way with generalized competencies such as abstraction, verbal reasoning, or metalinguistic skills."[43] It is possible that the effects of literacy (and perhaps of schooling, too) are restricted to the practices actually engaged in or are generalized mainly to closely related ones, in contrast to the normative wisdom of general developmental changes in thinking and perhaps acting. An approach that begins with context—of learning, use, need, practice, and relationships—is the best method to which to tie a new research agenda.

As Olson reminds us, schooled literacy is a special use of literacy and language. Words not only are taken out of the "context of action," they are removed from other, nonschool uses, including much of oral language uses and some writing. Such literacy has become highly prized, and often rewarded. "To take explicit written prose as the model of a language, knowledge and intelligence has narrowed the conception of all three, downgrading the more general functions of ordinary language and commonsense knowledge," and much of speech, too. If school literacy is predominantly textually based and biased, most modes of verbal communications are cut off from it, made to suffer in comparison, and evaluated as inferior, although they may be more important to more persons' lives.

The many impacts include the structures of authority erected on these bases; the power of verbal manipulation; the uses of language and verbal ability for social differentiation and social stigmatization; and the reinforcement of inequality by lack of schooling and different uses of language. Whereas some children fare well in a system of structures that has elevated this form of specialized, explicitly textual literacy to its pinnacle, many more do not. That is not an independent result of success and failure, but one that relates closely to class, culture, family, and home environment.

The "literate bias" of schooling is another of literacy's legacies. It is the bias of the middle and upper middle classes and the dominant social groups and their conceptions of culture, order, norms, behavior, and values. Literacy, thus, is attached to structures of control and authority, and is itself, in the process of its transmission, neutralized. Its fullest potentials are not part of the instructional process or the expectations for its use. That kind of "practice" has not been part of the processes that made the West "a literate society." If we consider the kind and level of literacy typically taken from the schools today to be insufficient, inadequate, biased, or otherwise failing, then our conception of literacy, and the agencies that dispense it, should be reexamined.[44]

### 3. A Crisis in Literacy?

An international literacy crisis has been proclaimed for the late twentieth century. From all sides—newspapers, magazines, and television; educators, religious organizations, and legislators—we hear of the presumed decline and severe problems in popular literacy skills.[45] Typically, and reflexively, the schools, reading methods, liberalism, progressive education, government funding, the family, the mass media (especially television), parents, peers, youth, and popular culture are among the entities blamed for the low performance of students on tests of "competence" and achievement.[46]

There *are* problems with popular levels of skills and learning, and literacy abilities are not all that they might be; but that a "crisis-level" decline has taken place, which can be easily explained and for which responsibility can be meted out, has not been proved. Few of the tests and most severe worries relate directly to basic skills in reading and writing. Nor has a major, negative shift in the goals and methods of schooling been demonstrated. Given the easily overlooked fact that "crises" and "declines," in literacy as in other aspects of society, are recurrent throughout modern history, suspicions of other causes than changes in literacy abilities should be aroused. Today's debates are strikingly reminiscent of past discussions, although the contemporary context heightens the seriousness of perceptions and exacerbates fears.[47]

Many of the measures used as evidence of low American literacy levels are problematic and debatable, and do not receive the careful interpretation that they require. Changes over time are as often presumed as documented. Causes and effects are frequently confused; blame is assigned readily, whereas courses for improvement and constructive suggestions are not. Little effort is made to develop larger contexts for either the test score results or the analysis of causes.[48]

Equally important is the way in which social and cultural factors are "smuggled" in toward the end of discussions, which suggests that much more than literacy levels or test results is at stake. Literacy underlies progress; its lack represents decline. If literacy abilities—which probably have never been sufficient to meet the highest demands placed on them—are seen as lacking and declining, then other issues and fears come directly, if implicitly, into play.

The outcries did not become loud and constant until the mid-1970s, a time when concern was increasing about national standing, international status, power, productivity, well-being, inflation, security, energy supplies, and confidence in leadership and institutions. Fears of rising illiteracy came alive in a situation of growing social, economic, and political difficulties. As a central tenet of the "modernity syndrome," literacy was invested with great symbolic value; apparent changes in popular abilities only stimulated and reinforced other fears. As with other crises, that of literacy is fundamentally an outcome of historical development, and can be grasped only in terms of its history. Like the Reformations of the sixteenth century, the Enlightenment, and the nineteenth-century age of institution building, the current age is a key age of transition for literacy.

The relevance, reliability, and accuracy of the tests used to "prove" the "decline" in literacy are secondary, less important than literacy's pivotal place among the central crises of our age. The evidence of the tests only spreads and heightens concerns already present.[49] It is ironic that only in the recent movement to mandate competency testing as a legal requirement for high-school students have we attempted to institute and require a regular test of literacy (if literacy is what such examinations actually are testing). Only *after* "universal" literacy has been virtually achieved has it become necessary to test annually for such skills.

The tests themselves are problematic. Few are truly tests of the basic skills of reading and writing. Certainly those skills underlie the demands of the questions, but that is not the same as a test of or for literacy. Most test for very different kinds of knowledge, information, and abilities: "scholastic aptitutde," information acquired and retained, concrete and repeatable skills practiced in classrooms, or adult "life skills." As a consequence, the results are not always comparable.

Some commentators are not convinced of the presumed increase in illiteracy. According to Christopher Jencks, "Today's students are *not* doing worse than their predecessors on tests of truly basic skills." Many critics concede progress in the earlier years of schooling, but focus their attention on declines after the fourth or fifth grade. The problem, perhaps, is not literacy or basic skills:

> Where older students run into trouble is in making inference from what they read. They know what a passage says, but they do not understand what the author's point really is. When they write, they make no more spelling or punctuation mistakes than 17-year-olds made a few years ago, but they turn out less coherent paragraphs. The trouble, then, is not with "the basics" but with what for lack of a better term we might call complex skills.

That analysis confronts real problems in schooling and society. For skill problems, like literacy itself, may be symptomatic of other complications:

> But skills are not the only problem. Today's high school graduates have not read as widely as their predecessors, or at least they do not know as much about the kinds of things young people traditionally learned from reading. They do worse on tests that ask about literature, history, politics, and scientific subjects. And they do not seem to think as carefully about the problems testers set for them, even when the solution does not require external information.

A problem, not a "crisis," is an accurate description of the findings of test scores. Continuing progress in the early years indicates that neither preschool experiences or preparedness nor television watching, permissive childrearing, or instructional pedagogy for initial reading can be blamed. The schools or the family alone cannot be censured out of hand.[50]

These findings shift attention from literacy to other issues. That is more appropriate than attempting to change the working definition of literacy by loading it with new values and skills, which further confuses conceptual issues. Obsessions with literacy or "back to basics"—a mythical return to a past that never was—are inappropriate as a solution.

Changes in test scores usually indicate a change not in capacity or capability but in practice and interest. Tests such as SATs measure "relatively useless skills that schools do not try to teach": verbal analogies, sentence completion, puzzle solving. Tests of this sort are not appropriate for evaluating how well schools are instructing pupils in literacy or the basic literacy skill level of the students.

Despite the massive condemnation directed toward changing family structures and the impact of television, neither has been proved conclusively to account for the changes in test results. Greater significance than many have conceded should be accorded to "compositional" effects of changes in student bodies; similarly, in tandem with changes in school curriculum, perceptions of economic returns from school success have perhaps changed.

Changes in the schools are a commonly accepted contributor to declining test scores. The typically cited impacts of insufficient resources and expenditures, and of shifting from standard, prescribed curricula to electives and a diminution in reading-difficulty levels of textbooks are not borne out by the evidence. Grade inflation is another presumed cause that is not supported by studies. A major question relates to the *quantity* of academic work done in school. A new appeal to student interests in shaping the content of schooling has come about because of concern about student motivation. Declining belief in adult authority and the psychological pressures and changes of the times have also reduced pupils' interest.

> The problem is not so much declining test performance as the fact that millions of students are serving time in secondary schools without learning anything of importance. This is not a new problem, but the decline in test performance suggests that it has been getting worse. . . . Furthermore, the problem has been worse at the time [of] economic stagnation and the concomitant atmosphere of scarcity.[51]

A typical response has been the competency-testing movement. However, "if minimum standards have any effect, it will be to make high schools devote more attention to basic skills. But these are precisely the skills that have *not* declined in recent years." Nowhere have discussions focused on issues such as equity, opportunity, and equality—or critical definitions of literacy. The present confusions about the meanings of literacy are only worsened if literacy is defined primarily as a "competency" for compulsory examinations.[52]

The situation with respect to literacy is less serious than many believe. Egil Johansson suggests that this fear of loss and decline may be a feature of the historical moment of development. His analysis of Swedish literacy identifies real problems, but not a crisis. "The rumours of a new illiteracy are greatly exaggerated." Literacy is not a constant of the modern world; its levels rise and fall. The disadvantaged and non-native speakers remain the greatest challenge to the agencies that transmit literacy. Fundamentally, the issues are political and ideological.[53]

Literacy is often conceptualized as if it were a "consumer durable" to be purchased or invested in. In an economic study, John Bormuth showed that, contrary to public opinion, literacy's (narrowly) economic value is, and continues to be, worth far more than it costs to "produce" it, that literacy "is one of our nation's more important economic activities," and that "personal and social investment in literacy has been growing rapidly." Many people use reading and writing in their work; in this sense, literacy is undoubtedly productive. Shifts in the economy, from primary production to service and white-collar work, are one important reason. Bormuth also points to the enormous amount and "value" of literacy materials "consumed" annually.[54]

An inflexible view of literacy, without attention to contextual needs and uses, results only in disappointment. The most serious issues are not the test results but questions of definition and conceptualization and "the continuing inequality in literacy instruction and literacy accomplishments between the disadvantaged students in this country and the advantaged."[55] What illiteracy means to a society depends on how important literacy is considered to be by that society.

Modern societies tend to stress the importance of literacy without defining or understanding it. Consequently, literacy by itself is overvalued and taken out of meaningful contexts, creating pressures that increase the difficulties of learning useful skills. Shame and awareness of inferiority are two products of a racially and class-biased educational and social system. In this way, the very high social emphasis on the importance of literacy becomes counterproductive for many individuals.[56]

## 4. Literacy, Culture, and Society: Communications and the Future of Literacy

Despite rumors to the contrary, neither print nor literacy is "dying." Social thought and theory about literacy have progressed far more than the daily life practices of most persons, even in the advanced societies of the West. The relationships of print and literacy to other modes of communication, however, are changing.

Oral communications are said to have been declining at least since the advent of printing. Yet, they remain perhaps the major mode of communication between individuals: for the acquisition of news and information; the formation of opinion and influence; the maintenance of community, friendship, and family bonds; the formation of collective action; and the like. That does not lessen the importance of literacy; rather, it helps to put it into context. Historically, oral culture conditioned the reception and uses of the new media of literacy and print, which in turn have come to act reciprocally upon the other media. "New literacies" are not relegating older, "traditional" modes to the dustbins of the past.[57]

Examining literacy in specific contexts is the best approach to grasping the transformations and literacy's place in modern societies. Literacy acquisition is not universal; it varies across societies, and is frequently a "function of society-specific tasks, which are sometimes far removed from those of formal schooling."

A black working-class community studied by Shirley Heath in the southeastern United States provides a model. Preschool children there learned to read at a very young age, despite having no instruction from the adults. They found their own reading and writing tasks: trade names of bikes and cars, television messages, house and license plate numbers, etc. Stimuli and motivation came from the immediate environment, as did much of the skill learning and practice.

Reading in this community was a social, collective activity. Written materials were frequently used together with oral explanations, narratives, and jokes: "The authority of the materials was established through social negotiation by the readers." Neither communicative modes nor sources of information exist in isolation from one another; speech and print interact in determining each person's ongoing place in society and culture.

In this community, literacy gained its meaning from its context and practice. The common uses of literacy there—instrumental, social-interactional, news-related, memory-supportive, substitutes for oral messages, provisions of permanent record, and confirmation—differed from the uses emphasized in school-oriented discussion. Work was not literacy-centered. Oral and social relations shaped the uses of reading and writing. Literacy was important, but its roles differed from those elsewhere and from theoretical expectations. "The extent to which physiologically normal individuals learn to read and write depends greatly on the role literacy plays in their families, communities, and jobs." Just as formal instruction need not be the only path, literate-biased and "schooled" literacy are not the only way to understand literacy's place or its relationships with other media.[58]

Literacy no longer can be conceived in linear, progressive terms. Orality cannot be viewed as "traditional" or primitive. Indeed, neither can normally be grasped apart from the other. There is the print that we "listen to," the "voice" we hear when we read, and the "reading" we make of nonwritten things. With technological progress and governmental intrusion into our lives, literacy has lost some of its traditional associations. The type of literacy training linked to success in school is not needed to fill out basic forms and applications; television and radio can supply most of the information we need to know.[59] Most modern communities, notes Heath, "are neither preliterate, i.e., without access to print or writing of some kind, nor fully literate."

Walter Ong has noted the important, if shifting, relationships between the literate and the oral in modern societies. "Most Americans, even those who write miserably, . . . believe that what makes a word a real word is not its meaningful use in vocal exchange but rather its presence on the page of a dictionary. We are so literate in ideology that we think writing comes naturally." Writing, regardless of its central role in human existence, remains artificial, especially when compared to oral speech. Physiologically normal persons all speak; they do not all write.[60]

Western culture is at least as much an oral as a literate culture. Orality serves certain common functions for individuals and groups, but it also operates in new and different ways. Ong distinguishes between "primary" orality, that "untouched by writing or print," and "secondary" orality, which represents speech in modern societies: "the orality induced by radio and television," and totally dependent on them.[61]

The lack of comprehension of the relationships between the literate and the oral (and the visual, too) underlies controversies about the impact of electronic media; "youth culture"; ethnic subcultures; "standard English" and "black English"; bilingual education; oral skills; and the like. The failure of "literate" specialists, and to some extent literate cultures, to grant credibility to oral cultures is not new; it underlies these problems, complicates development of the sensitivities required to understand other cultural motifs and modes of communication, and leads to disparaging stereotypes. Herein lies another form of the "great divide." Until the biases of literate culture are altered, communicative interrelatedness will be obscured. If there is to be a "new literacy," it will develop *not* from the death of print, reading, or writing in the face of technology's electronic challenge, but from the changing relationships among communication technologies.[62]

Recent studies of the uses of literacy offer a contradictory picture. They illustrate both the necessity of a useful degree of literacy for most persons who live and work in advanced, technological societies, and the plight of those with no or less than useful skills. Feelings of inadequacy, humiliation, isolation, and dependence are commonly associated with the nonliterate. However, such psychological problems are also found among those with sufficient skills.[63] Literacy is vitally important in contemporary Western societies, but it does not result directly in personal competence or autonomy.

Contemporary research raises questions about the uses of literacy and the kinds of skills that are possessed. Contradictions remain largely unrecognized. For example, in Bormuth's attempt to prove the economic value of literacy, he used a survey that indicated that 87 percent of the gainfully employed had to read as part of their work. Reading, if such surveys can be trusted, is important to work, and should be seen as productive.

Averages, however, can be distorting. Reading needs, reading tasks, and time spent in required work-related reading vary across the occupational and class hierarchy; contributions through such reading differ in economic value, status, and rewards. Among the workers who rated reading tasks as very important were those who read nothing more than labels and writing on packages. These important status and occupational-level differences must be set in the context of changing occupational-force structures and changing job requirements, both of which are often misunderstood. The amount of money invested in work-related literacy activities is growing, but "since the size of the white-collar labor force has risen faster than the size of the total labor force and . . . white-collar workers perform more of this activity than blue-collar workers," that interpretation alone is incomplete and misleading.[64]

For many workers, the use of reading and writing is low-level, routine, and undemanding. A basic and practiced reading skill is all that is usually required, and the requisite skills likely are not those measured by tests of "functional" literacy. The important relationships are those among education, social class, income, and occupational level. Lower-class persons with minimal skills and low-level jobs not only have less demand for skilled literacy in their work but also tend to have a lesser degree of useful skills.

Equally important are the often declining requirements for higher-level job skills. Educational requirements have increased independently of changes in job requirements. Schooling involves more than job-related skills or cognitive abilities. More of the trends in the modernization and reorganization of work, including the use of advanced technologies and mechanization, have served to "de-skill," routinize, rationalize, and downgrade the level of learning or training needed to do the job. Studies of changing occupational distributions rooted in assumptions about the differential requirements of technologically oriented work or about "white-collar" work itself are sadly misleading, although they serve important functions for ideologies related to education, the schools themselves, and the control of the labor force.[65]

The literacy and skills transmitted by the schools have other relationships to work than are usually presumed. Despite the sociology and mythology of ever-increasing job requirements that include demands for more or "new" kinds of literacy, overall trends have been different. Automation and other impacts of technology and reorganization by and large have not had an upgrading effect on job requirements. In fact, they may have reduced skill requirements.[66] While most jobs demand some level of literacy ability, work is not increasing those needs for many persons.

Tests of competency and functional literacy are also beset with contradictions. A study by the Adult Performance Level project, for example, found that 20 percent of the U.S. population was less than "functionally competent." However, class, education, income, and job status related directly, and causally, to competency level, and in his analysis of this test, Fisher noted that test items were in fact selected because of their correlation with education, income, and job status. Those features invalidate the results.[67]

The U.S. Army conducted research to discern how much literacy training its charges required and at what levels its written materials should be aimed. The recruits did not have high educational levels, yet they were able to perform successfully in jobs where the reading difficulties of materials exceeded their average reading abilities by from four to eight grades. "The poor readers may be getting someone to do their reading. The general tests of reading comprehension could be poor predictors of job-specific reading achievement. Or the readability formulas may overestimate the difficulty of job-related tasks. There is good reason to believe that all three explanations are operating."

To counter some of these complications, job-related, task-reading tests were developed. In them, too, basic problems remain unsolved. "Many decisions, some more arbitrary than others, enter into the neatly packaged estimates of functional literacy that parade across the reader's desk."[68] The concept of functional literacy tests and their educational consequences are highly problematic. The results are often taken out of context, and their impact on literacy is limiting. Notions of competency are no answer to the presumed "crisis."[69]

Traditional print or alphabetic literacy, especially when denoted as "functional," pales alongside "new" literacies of electronic media, moving images, computers, or the arts and sciences. That works to the detriment of literacy, old and new, and of all persons concerned. It precludes serious studies of the impacts of and relationships between different "literacies" or communicative modes. The present crises obscure a longer view on change and the role of continuities. For example, it is seldom noted that the radio, long before television, was associated with less time spent in reading.[70]

In addition, most persons probably did little personal or "serious" reading even before the present century and the advent of competing media. Gluts of print and fears of low-level or improperly used reading skills are not novel. Few persons in the West today read more than one book a year, and most non-job-related reading is recreational. Newspapers and magazines dominate among the materials read. The uses of literacy in modern Western and advanced societies are important but often limited and relatively low-level.[71]

Most persons apparently are not all that interested in exercising their literacy more or improving it as a critical skill. The popularity of speed-reading training in North America suggests that many wish to read faster rather than at a higher level.[72] Genres of "pulp" (for example, Westerns and "Harlequin Romances") remain popular. Academicians fail to see the important social and psychological functions of this reading, and forget that serious and critical reading require training and practice, as well as encouragement and support.[73]

The schools have never attempted to provide more than "basic," "functional" literacy abilities. Literacy has never, in Western history, been concerned with providing a grounding in skills that were expected to be developed into higher, self-advancing critical tools. Serious questions should be addressed to the consequences that might follow from such abilities' becoming common. That would constitute a powerful "new" literacy. A literacy that sought to interrelate, integrate, and coordinate different communicative modes and abilities would be more powerful again.

Literacy and print undoubtedly are not dying. Nevertheless, communicative modes are changing. Any approach to literacy must be flexible and dynamic, and alert to the powerful roles of continuities and contradictions. This flexibility is one of conceptualization as well as action; it may move us from the *limits* of literacy for the *many* to the *potentials* of a newer literacy for *all*. Recognizing that there are many kinds of tools, many competencies, and many varieties of achievement is a requisite first step. Speech, sound, and visual sights surround us; communication and media reinforce them. They are more pervasive than print. Recognizing that need not diminish the sometimes exaggerated powers and import of alphabetic literacy.[74]

What is needed is a broader view of *reading and writing* that integrates and emphasizes the many human abilities in a context of a changing world that requires their development and use. Paths to learning individual literacy by the young must be made less rigid; more attention must be paid to different sequences and structures of learning; and more sensitivity must be shown toward cultural and class influences. New, empirical, and conceptual understanding of literacy must be gained, beyond the context of persisting inequalities and the dominance of the "literacy myth."[75]

The new approach to literacy, then, must link the past with the present; only then are new paths to the future thinkable. The passage from "old" to "new" literacies must combine with a solid intellectual grounding in traditional skills to form a new synthesis. Questions of class, culture, opportunity, equality, and increasing demands for new skills must be considered.

What would happen if the whole world became literate? Answer: not so very much, for the world is by and large structured in such a way that it is capable of absorbing the impact. But if the whole world consisted of literate, autonomous, critical, constructive people, capable of translating ideas into action, individually or collectively—the world would change.[76]

Literacy is only one of the factors linked to change and action. That is the role that it may play, if reformulated and reconceptualized. Perhaps a genuine new literacy will be available, needed, and sought. Literacy can then take its place among other fundamental human needs and rights.

# EMBLEMA XXIII.

## DURANT ÆQUA.

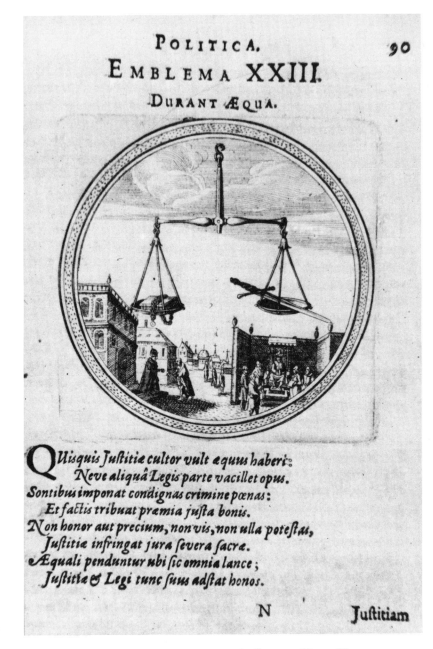

QUisquis Juſtitiæ cultor vult æquus haberi:
    Neve aliquâ Legis parte vacillet opus.
Sontibus imponat condignas crimine pœnas:
    Et factis tribuat præmia juſta bonis.
Non honor aut precium, non vis, non ulla poteſtas,
    Juſtitiæ infringat jura ſevera ſacrę.
Æquali penduntur ubi ſic omnia lance;
    Juſtitiæ & Legi tunc ſuus adſtat honos.

N                                    Juſtitiam

On balance: literacy/learning or lucre. . . . among the "legacies of literacy" from
Jacob a Bruck, *Emblemata politica*, 1618, p. 90. *Courtesy of The Newberry
Library, Chicago.*

# NOTES

## Introduction

1. David Olson, "Review: Toward a Literate Society," *Proceedings*, National Academy of Education, 1975–1976, pp. 111, 112.

2. Eric Havelock, *Origins of Western Literacy* (Toronto: Ontario Institute for Studies in Education, 1976), pp. 83, 18, 19.

3. Bruce G. Trigger, "Inequality and Communication in Early Civilizations," *Anthropologica* 18 (1976):39.

4. Kathleen Gough, "Literacy in Kerala," in *Literacy in Traditional Societies*, ed. Jack Goody (Cambridge: Cambridge University Press, 1968), p. 153.

5. Walter J. Ong, *The Presence of the Word* (New York: Simon and Schuster, 1970), p. 21.

6. Among a literature growing rapidly, see Harvey J. Graff, *Literacy in History: An Interdisciplinary Research Bibliography* (New York: Garland Publishing, 1981). Some of the most important historical writings are collected into an anthology entitled *Literacy and Social Development in the West*, edited by Harvey J. Graff for Cambridge University Press's Studies in Oral and Literate Culture series (1981).

7. See, for example, the interesting papers in Leon Bataille, ed., *A Turning Point for Literacy* (New York and Oxford: Pergamon Press, 1976); Harvey J. Graff, *The Literacy Myth* (New York: Academic Press, 1979); idem, "Literacy Past and Present: Critical Approaches to the Literacy-Society Relationship," *Interchange* 9 (1978):1–21: Jack Goody, *The Domestication of the Savage Mind* (Cambridge: Cambridge University Press, 1977); G. H. Douglas, "Is Literacy Really Declining?" *Educational Records* 57 (1977); 140–48; Egil Johansson, "The Post-Literacy Problem—Illusion or Reality in Modern Sweden?" in *Time, Space, and Man*, ed. Jan Sundin and Erik Soderlund (Stockholm: Almqvist and Wiksell, 1979), pp. 199–212; J. J. Micklos, Jr., "The Facts, Please, about Reading Achievement in American Schools," *Journal of Reading* 24 (1980): 41–45; Roger Farr, Leo Fay, and Harold H. Negley, *Then and Now: Reading Achievement in Indiana (1944–45 and 1976)* (Bloomington: Indiana University School of Education, 1978); Farr et al., *Then and Now: Reading Achievement in the U.S.* (Bloomington: Indiana University School of Education, 1974); John R. Bormuth, "Value and Volume of Literacy," *Visible Language* 12 (1978):118–61; Christopher Jencks, "What's behind the Drop in Test Scores," *Working Papers* 6 (1978):29–41. See also Epilogue, below.

8. Paul Copperman, *The Literacy Hoax* (New York: Morrow, 1978), among a large literature. See also Graff, *Literacy in History*, for a guide to this writing. For informed criticisms, see Manfred Stanley, "Literacy: The Crisis of a Conventional Wisdom," *School Review* 81 (1972):373–408; and Henry F. Dobyns, "Enlightenment and Skill Foundations of Power," in *Peasants, Power, and Applied Social Change: Vices as a Model*, ed. Henry F. Dobyns, P. L. Doughty, and H. D. Lasswell (Beverly Hills, Calif.: Sage, 1971), pp. 137–66. See also Epilogue.

9. See fig. I.2; Graff, *Literacy Myth*, Introduction, Appendixes; Roger S. Schofield, "The Measurement of Literacy in Pre-industrial England," in Goody, *Literacy*, pp. 311–25; Kenneth Lockridge, *Literacy in Colonial New England* (New York: Norton, 1974); M. T. Clanchy, *From Memory to Written Record* (Cambridge, Mass.: Harvard University Press, 1979); Francois Furet and Jacques Ozouf, *Lire et écrire* (Paris: les editions de minuit, 1977); David Cressy, *Literacy and the Social Order* (Cambridge: Cambridge University Press, 1980); *The History of Literacy in Sweden* (Umeå: School of Education, Umeå University, 1977);

Rab Houston, *Scottish Literacy and the Scottish Identity* (Cambridge: Cambridge University Press, 1985); for the most important examples.

10. See the studies cited in note 7 above, and Marshall McLuhan, *The Gutenberg Galaxy* (Toronto: University of Toronto Press, 1962) and *Understanding Media* (New York: McGraw-Hill, 1964); Elizabeth L. Eisenstein, *The Printing Press as an Agent of Change* (Cambridge: Cambridge University Press, 1979); Lawrence Cremin, *American Education: The Colonial Experience* (New York: Harper and Row, 1970); Alex Inkeles and David H. Smith, *Becoming Modern* (Cambridge, Mass.: Harvard University Press, 1974). See also the useful introductions in John Oxenham, *Literacy: Reading, Writing, and Social Organization* (London: Routledge and Kegan Paul, 1980); Havelock, *Origins*.

11. Howard Schuman, Alex Inkeles, and David H. Smith, "Some Social Psychological Effects and Non-effects of Literacy in a New Nation," *Economic Development and Cultural Change* 16 (1967):7; Inkeles and Smith, *Becoming Modern*; and a large body of literature including the well-known writing of David McClelland, Daniel Lerner, Mary Jean Bowman and Arnold Anderson, and Lucien Pye. For a summary, citations, and critique, see, for example, Graff, *Literacy Myth*, Introduction, chap. 5.

12. M. M. Lewis, *The Importance of Illiteracy* (London: Harrap, 1953), p. 16.

13. Sylvia Scribner and Michael Cole, "Literacy without Schooling," *Harvard Educational Review*, 48 (1978):449, 450, 452, 453; Goody, *Literacy, Domestication*; Jack Goody, Michael Cole, and Sylvia Scribner, "Writing and Formal Operations: A Case Study among the Vai," *Africa* 47 (1977):289–304; Sylvia Scribner and Michael Cole, "Studying Cognitive Consequences of Literacy" (Unpub. paper, 1976); idem, "Cognitive Consequences of Formal and Informal Education," *Science* 182 (1973):553–59; idem, *The Psychology of Literacy* (Cambridge: Harvard University Press, 1981); Michael Cole, "How Education Affects the Mind," *Human Nature*, April 1978, pp. 51–58.

14. Among a large and diffuse literature, see Ruth Finnegan, *Oral Literature in Africa* (Oxford: Oxford University Press, 1970); idem, *Oral Poetry* (Cambridge: Cambridge University Press, 1979); Havelock, *Origins*; Eric Havelock, *Preface to Plato* (Cambridge, Mass.: Harvard University Press, 1963); idem, "The Preliteracy of the Greeks," *New Literary History* 8 (1977):369–92; Birger Gerhardsson, *Memory and Manuscript: Oral Tradition and Written Transmission in Rabbinic Judaism and Early Christianity*, Acta Seminarii Neotestamentici Upsaliensis, vol. 12 (Uppsala, 1961); Clanchy, *From Memory*; F. L. Ganshof, *The Carolingians and the Frankish Monarchy* (Ithaca: Cornell University Press, 1971); E. LeRoy Ladurie, *Montaillou: Promised Land of Error* (New York: George Braziller, 1978); Natalie Z. Davis, "Printing and the People," in her *Society and Culture in Early Modern France* (Stanford: Stanford University Press, 1975), pp. 189–226; H.-J. Martin, "Culture écrite et culture orale, culture savante et culture populaire dans la France d'Ancien Régime," *Journale des Savants* (1975):225–82; Peter Burke, *Popular Culture in Early Modern Europe* (New York: Harper and Row, 1978); Margaret Aston, "Lollardy and Literacy," *History* 62 (1977):347–71; Carlo Ginzburg, *The Cheese and the Worms*, trans. John and Anne Tedeschi (Baltimore: John Hopkins University Press, 1980); Goody, *Domestication*; E. P. Thompson, "Eighteenth-Century English Society: Class Struggle without Class?" *Social History* 3 (1978): 133–65.

15. Havelock, *Origins*, p. 12.

16. For citations, see notes above, and Lawrence Stone, "Literacy and Education in England, 1640–1900," *Past and Present* 42 (1969):69–139; Carlo Cipolla, *Literacy and Development in the West* (Harmondsworth: Penguin, 1969). Readers may also wish to consult Eisenstein's series of articles that preceded the publication of her *Printing: History and Theory* 6 (1966); *Past and Present* 45 (1969); *Journal of Modern History* 40 (1968); *American Historical Review* 75 (1970); and *Annales; e, s, c* 26 (1971).

17. See, for example, Graff, *Literacy Myth*; Lockridge, *Literacy*; Schofield, "The Dimensions of Illiteracy in England, 1750–1850," *Explorations in Economic History* 10 (1973):437–54; Cressy, *Literacy*; David Cressy, "Educational Opportunity in Tudor and Stuart England," *History of Education Quarterly* 16 (1976): 301–320; idem, "Levels of Literacy in England, 1530–1730," *Historical Journal* 20 (1977):1–23.

18. Alexander Gerschenkron, "On the Concept of Continuity in History," in his *Con-*

*tinuity in History and Other Essays* (Cambridge, Mass.: Harvard University Press, 1968), p. 38, passim.

19. Goody, *Literacy*; Trigger, "Inequality"; William A. Bruneau, "Literacy, Urbanization, and Education in Three Ancient Cultures," *Journal of Education* (British Columbia) 19 (1973):9–22; Clanchy, *From Memory*; Cipolla, *Literacy*; among the relevant literature.

20. Lockridge, *Literacy*; LeRoy Ladurie, *Montaillou*; E. LeRoy Ladurie, *The Peasants of Languedoc* (Urbana: University of Illinois Press, 1975); Aston, "Lollardy"; Gerhardsson, *Memory*; Davis, "Printing"; Ginzburg, *Cheese*; Gerald Strauss, *Luther's House of Learning* (Baltimore: Johns Hopkins University Press, 1979); Mary Jo Maynes, "Schooling the Masses" (Ph.D. diss., University of Michigan, 1977); idem, "The Virtues of Anachronism: The Political Economy of Schooling in Europe, 1750–1850," *Comparative Studies in Society and History* 21 (1979): 611–25; Cipolla, *Literacy*; Johansson, *History*; Graff, *Literacy Myth*.

21. J. Kenneth Benson, "Organizations: A Dialectical View," *Administrative Science Quarterly* 22 (1977):4, 5, passim, and the literature cited there. See also Robert L. Heilbroner, *Marxism: For and Against* (New York: Norton, 1980), pp. 33–44.

22. For other examples, see Graff, *Literacy Myth*. A good recent example is Mary Ryan, *Cradle of the Middle Class* (New York: Cambridge University Press, 1981).

23. There is a large literature on these issues; see citations in the chapters that follow, esp. 6 and 7. On inventiveness, see Eugene Ferguson, "The Mind's Eye: Nonverbal Thought in Technology," *Science* 197 (1977):827–36; A. F. C. Wallace, *Rockdale* (New York: Knopf, 1978), pp. 237ff.; William M. Ivins, Jr., *Prints and Visual Communications* (Cambridge, Mass.: MIT Press, 1953); A. H. Mayor, *People and Prints* (Princeton: Princeton University Press, 1980).

24. "Literacy: Power or Mystification?" *Literacy Discussion* 4 (1973):389–414. See also Stanley, "Literacy"; Dobyns, "Enlightenment"; Goody, *Domestication*; Paolo Freire, *Pedagogy of the Oppressed* (New York: Herder and Herder, 1971); among a large literature.

25. On hegemony, see below. For an introduction to Gramsci's thought, see Walter L. Adamson, *Hegemony and Revolution: Gramsci's Political and Cultural Theory* (Berkeley: University of California Press, 1980); Graff, *Literacy Myth*; Raymond Williams, *Marxism and Literature* (Oxford: Oxford University Press, 1977); Stanley, "Literacy."

26. *Selections from the Prison Notebooks of Antonio Gramsci*, ed. and trans. Quentin Hoare and Geoffrey Nowell Smith (London: NLB, 1971), pp. 242, 12; John M. Cammett, *Antonio Gramsci and the Origins of Italian Communism* (Stanford: Stanford University Press, 1967), p. 204; Gwyn Williams, "The Concept of 'Egemonia' in the Thought of Antonio Gramsci," *Journal of the History of Ideas* 21 (1960):587; Adamson, *Hegemony*.

27. E. J. Hobsbawm, "Religion and the Rise of Socialism," *Marxist Perspectives* 1 (1978):22. My interpretation owes much to the writings of Adamson, *Hegemony*; Williams, *Marxism*; David B. Davis, *The Problem of Slavery in the Age of Revolution, 1770–1823* (Ithaca: Cornell University Press, 1975), pp. 348–62; Aileen S. Kraditor, "American Radical Historians on Their Heritage," *Past and Present* 56 (1972): 136–53; Eugene Genovese, "On Antonio Gramsci," in his *Red and Black: Marxian Explorations in Southern and Afro-American History* (New York: Pantheon, 1971), pp. 391–422; idem, *Roll, Jordan, Roll: The World the Slaves Made* (New York: Pantheon, 1974). See also Graff, *Literacy Myth*; R. W. Connell, *Ruling Class, Ruling Culture* (Cambridge: Cambridge University Press, 1977). For pioneering applications to educational history, see Michael B. Katz, "The Origins of Public Education: A Reassessment," *History of Education Quarterly* 16 (1976):381–407; idem, "The Origins of the Institutional State," *Marxist Perspectives* 1 (1978):16–22; Richard Johnson, "Notes on the Schooling of the English Working Class," in *Schooling and Capitalism*, ed. R. Dale, G. Esland, and M. MacDonald (London: Routledge, and Kegan Paul, 1976), pp. 44–54; E. P. Thompson, "Eighteenth-Century English Society."

28. Winchester, "How Many," p. 1; Johansson, *History*; Egil Johansson, "Literacy Studies in Sweden: Some Examples," in *Literacy and Society in a Historical Perspective: A Conference Report*, ed. Egil Johansson, *Educational Report*, Umeå, 2 (Umeå: University of Umeå and School of Education, 1973), pp. 41–66; Lockridge, *Literacy*; Strauss, *Luther's*. See also Bataille, *A Turning Point*.

29. See Graff, *Literacy Myth*, chap. 7; Cressy, *Literacy*; Johansson, "Literacy Studies," for some evidence and analysis. See also note 6 above.

# 1. The Origins of Western Literacy

1. Jack Goody and Ian Watt, "The Consequences of Literacy," in *Literacy in Traditional Societies*, ed. Jack Goody (Cambridge: Cambridge University Press, 1968), p. 38; on the issues dealt with in this chapter, see also Walter J. Ong, *The Presence of the Word* (New York: Simon and Schuster, 1970 [1967]).

2. Eric Havelock, *Origins of Western Literacy* (Toronto: Ontario Institute for Studies in Education, 1976), p. 18. See on sources Harvey J. Graff, *The Literacy Myth: Literacy and Social Structure in the Nineteenth-Century City* (New York: Academic Press, 1979), Introduction, Appendix A.

3. See Kathleen Gough, "Implications of Literacy in Traditional China and India" and "Literacy in Kērala," and Jack Goody, "Restricted Literacy in Northern Ghana" and "Introduction," in Goody, *Literacy in Traditional Societies*, pp. 69–84, 132–60, 198–264, 1–26.

4. I. J. Gelb, *A Study of Writing*, 2d ed. (Chicago: University of Chicago Press, 1963), p. 193, chaps. 1–6; Goody and Watt, "Consequences," pp. 35ff. In what follows I have drawn heavily on Gelb's major contribution.

5. Goody and Watt, "Consequences," pp. 36–37. The extent of literacy in China without alphabetic literacy, however, forces us to be cautious and to avoid alphabetic determinism; see Gough, "Implications of Literacy"; Evelyn Rawski, *Education and Popular Literacy in Ch'ing China* (Ann Arbor: University of Michigan Press, 1979). See also Gelb, *A Study*; David Olson, "Toward a Literate Society: Book Review," *Proceedings*, National Academy of Education, 1975–1976; idem, "From Utterance to Text," *Harvard Educational Review* 47 (1977): 257–81; William A. Bruneau, "Literacy, Urbanization, and Education in Three Ancient Cultures," *Journal of Education* of the Faculty of Education of The University of British Columbia, no. 19 (1973), pp. 9–22.

6. Goody and Watt, "Consequences," pp. 38–40. See below; see also Goody, "Introduction," pp. 11ff.

7. Havelock, *Origins*, pp. 3, 4; Bruce G. Trigger, "Inequality and Communication in Early Civilizations," *Anthropologica* 18 (1976): 27–52; Gelb, *A Study*; Gough, "Implications of Literacy"; Goody, "Introduction" and the references cited therein.

8. V. Gordon Childe, *Man Makes Himself* (London: Watts, 1963), p. 172; Bruneau, "Literacy"; Harold A. Innis, *Empire and Communications* (Toronto: University of Toronto Press, 1972 [1950]); idem, *The Bias of Communication* (Toronto: University of Toronto Press, 1951). Note, however, that both of these authors take overly deterministic stances, and that Bruneau especially confuses literacy with writing.

9. Gelb, *A Study*, pp. 230, 231; see also Bruneau, "Literacy"; Goody, "Introduction," "Restricted Literacy"; Gough, "Literacy," "Implications."

10. Bruneau, "Literacy," pp. 16, 14–16.

11. Childe, *Man*, p. 185.

12. Innis, *Empire*, p. 31, *Bias*, passim.

13. Goody, "Introduction," p. 21, quoting A. L. Oppenheim, *Ancient Mesopotamia* (Chicago: University of Chicago Press, 1964), pp. 230ff.; Goody, "Introduction," p. 21.

14. Gelb, *A Study*, pp. 197, 144ff.; Havelock, *Origins*; Eric Havelock, *Preface to Plato* (Oxford: Blackwell, 1963); idem, "Prologue to Greek Literacy," in *Lectures in Memory of Louise Taft Semple*, University of Cincinnati Classical Studies, vol. 2 (Norman: University of Oklahoma Press, for the University of Cincinnati, 1973); idem, "The Preliteracy of the Greeks," *New Literary History* 8 (1977): 369–92. For contemporary comparisons, see H. H. Youtie, "The Social Impact of Illiteracy in Graeco–Roman Egypt," *Zeitschrift fur Papyrologie und Epigraphik* 17 (1975): 202–221.

15. Gelb, *A Study*, p. 184; Goody and Watt, "Consequences," pp. 40–41.

16. Havelock, "Preliteracy," pp. 369–71; see also his *Preface*, "Prologue," and *Origins*.

17. Havelock, *Preface*, pp. 135, 134, 38–39; "Preliteracy."

18. Havelock, *Preface*, "Prologue," *Origins*, "Preliteracy"; but see also H. I. Marrou, *A History of Education in Antiquity*, trans. George Lamb (London: Sheed and Ward, 1956); F. A. Beck, *Greek Education* (New York, 1964); J. A. Davidson, "Literature and Literacy in Ancient Greece," *Phoenix* 16 (1962): 141–56, 219–33; F. D. Harvey, "Literacy in the Athenian Democracy," *Revue des Etudes Greques* 79 (1966): 585–636, for a variety of contrasting viewpoints.

19. Havelock, *Preface*, p. 106, chap. 5; pp. 120–21; "Preliteracy," p. 374; *Preface*, pp. 126, 190.

20. Havelock, "Preliteracy," pp. 371, 385–87; see also Marrou, *A History*; Kenneth J. Freeman, *Schools of Hellas: An Essay on the Practice and Theory of Ancient Greek Education from 600 to 300 B.C.*, ed. M. J. Rendall (London: Macmillan, 1908); M. I. Finley, *The Ancient Greeks* (New York: Viking Press, 1963).

21. Havelock, "Preliteracy," pp. 371–72, 372–73; Marrou, *A History*.

22. Havelock, *Origins*, pp. 22–24, 44, "Prologue."

23. On the abuse and limits of evidence, see Havelock, esp. "Preliteracy"; Alfred Burns, "Athenian Literacy in the Fifth Century B.C.," *Journal of the History of Ideas* 42 (1981): 371–88. For additional viewpoints on the material interpreted in this section, see Ong, *Presence*; Innis, *Empire*.

24. Davidson, "Literature," p. 147.

25. Chester Starr, *The Origins of Greek Civilization* (New York, 1961); Goody and Watt, "Consequences"; Gelb, *A Study*; Havelock, *Origins*.

26. See, for example, Frederic G. Kenyon, *Books and Readers in Ancient Greece and Rome*, 2d ed. (Oxford: Oxford University Press, 1951); George Haven Putnam, *Authors and Their Public in Ancient Times* (New York: G. P. Putnam's Sons, 1894); Havelock, *Origins*.

27. Havelock, "Preliteracy," *Preface*; Harvey, "Literacy"; Finley, *Ancient Greeks*; Davidson, "Literature."

28. Havelock, *Preface*, p. vii; *Origins*, p. 48.

29. For evidence and examples, see G. L. Hendrickson, "Ancient Reading," *Classical Journal* 25 (1929): 183–93; William Chase Greene, "The Spoken and the Written Word," *Harvard Studies in Classical Philology* 60 (1951): 23–59; Harvey, "Literacy"; Havelock, "Preliteracy," *Origins*, "Prologue," *Preface*; Finley, *Ancient Greeks*. Note also the example of Solon as "law–giver."

30. Harvey, "Literacy," pp. 593–97, 598; Havelock, "Preliteracy"; Davidson, "Literature." Note the parallels with the medieval context discussed below. Harvey notes that before the fourth century, there is good evidence that magistrates or their secretaries wrote down oral complaints.

31. Havelock, "Preliteracy."

32. Harvey, "Literacy," pp. 606–607, 608, 610, 611–15, 615–17. Parallels to the Middle Ages are very instructive.

33. See *Phaedrus* and *Seventh Letter*; Goody and Watt, "Consequences"; Havelock, *Preface*, "Preliteracy," *Origins*; Freeman, *Schools*; Greene, "Spoken"; Hendrickson, "Reading"; Finley, *Ancient Greeks*.

34. Havelock, *Origins*, p. 48; Putnam, *Books*; Kenyon, *Books*.

35. Havelock, "Preliteracy," p. 371; see also pp. 385–86; Marrou, *A History*; Freeman, *Schools*; Harvey, "Literacy"; Finley, *Ancient Greeks*; Goody and Watt, "Consequences"; Frank Pierrepont Graves, *A History of Education before the Middle Ages* (New York: Macmillan, 1909).

36. Marrou, *A History*; Finley, *Ancient Greeks*; Graves, *A History*; Harvey, "Literacy." On girls, see Sarah B. Pomeroy, "Technikai Kai Mousikai: The Education of Women in the Fourth Century and in the Hellenistic Period," *American Journal of Ancient History* 2 (1977): 51–68.

37. Marrou, *A History*, pp. 142, 145–46, 146, 147, 148; Pomeroy, "Technikai."

38. Freeman, *Schools*, p. 81.

39. Marrou, *A History*, pp. 155, 156, 157, 157–58, 163–68.

40. Freeman, *Schools*, pp. 43ff.; Harvey, "Literacy," pp. 617–33.

41. Marrou, *A History*, pp. 221–26, chap. 1.

42. Harvey, "Literacy," pp. 617–29; Freeman, *Schools*; Marrou, *A History*.

43. Havelock, "Preliteracy," *Origins*; Harvey, "Literacy"; Davidson, "Literature"; Putnam, *Books*; Kenyon, *Books*; Finley, *Ancient Greeks*; H. L. Pinner, *The World of Books in Classical Antiquity* (Leiden: A. W. Sijthoff, 1948).

44. Ong, *Presence*, pp. 56–58; Finley, *Ancient Greeks*, pp. 149–50. On memory, see Frances Yates, *The Art of Memory* (London: Routledge and Kegan Paul, 1966). See in general, for details but with caution, Innis, *Empire*. For a brief survey of developments in the Greek and Latin alphabets, see Havelock, *Origins*, chap. 4. Of course, later Greek philosophers such as Aristotle were probably oriented less toward the oral and more toward writing, but we should take care not to emphasize either to the exclusion of the other.

45. Kenyon, *Books*, pp. 75–80; quotation from p. 80.

46. Graves, *A History*, pp. 237–45; Marrou, *A History*.

47. Marrou, *A History*, pp. 268, 269–70; Graves, *A History*, pp. 246–49; Jérôme Carcopino, *Daily Life in Ancient Rome: The People and the City at the Height of the Empire*, trans. E. O. Latimer, ed. Henry I. Rowell (New Haven: Yale University Press, 1940), pp. 103–107; see also S. F. Bonner, *Education in Ancient Rome* (Berkeley: University of California Press, 1977).

48. Marrou, *A History*, p. 270; Graves, *A History*, p. 248; Carcopino, *Daily Life*, pp. 105–106.

49. Graves, *A History*, pp. 248–49, 264; Marrou, *A History*, pp. 268–73; Carcopino, *Daily Life*, pp. 105–107; W. Warde Fowler, *Social Life at Rome in the Age of Cicero* (London: Macmillan, 1908), chap. 6.

50. R. P. Bolgar, *The Classical Heritage and Its Beneficiaries* (Cambridge: Cambridge University Press, 1954), pp. 32–33.

51. Carcopino, *Daily Life*, p. 65; for the earlier period, see Fowler, *Social Life*.

52. Marrou, *A History*, p. 296.

53. Bolgar, *Classical Heritage*, pp. 32, 28–33; Fowler, *Social Life*, chap. 6; Marrou, *A History*, pp. 278–79; Carcopino, *Daily Life*, pp. 191–93.

54. Carcopino, *Daily Life*, p. 193; for good descriptions, see pp. 191–93.

55. Kenyon, *Books*, p. 85.

56. Carcopino, *Daily Life*, pp. 193–95, 195, 195–96, 197, 196–99, 113–21, 223–24; Kenyon, *Books*, p. 185.

57. Davidson, "Literature," pp. 228–31; Carcopino, *Daily Life*, pp. 193–95; Kenyon, *Books*; Putnam, *Books*; Davidson, "Literature."

58. Kenyon, *Books*, pp. 112, 114, 119, passim; Carcopino, *Daily Life*; Putnam, *Books*; Fowler, *Social Life*.

59. Carcopino, *Daily Life*, pp. 58–64; Fowler, *Social Life*, p. 265.

60. Innis, *Empire*, pp. 100, 102–103, chap. 5.

61. Fowler, *Social Life*, p. 205.

62. Carcopino, *Daily Life*, pp. 178–80.

63. See Goody, "Introduction," as well as the essays by Gough and Goody in *Literacy in Traditional Societies*. See also Ong, *Presence*.

64. See for one example Elaine Pagels, "The Gnostic Gospels," *New York Review of Books*, Oct. 25; Nov. 8, 22; Dec. 6, 1979, and her book of the same title.

65. Marrou, *A History*, pp. 330–33.

66. Graves, *A History*, pp. 278, 267–88.

67. Birger Gerhardsson, *Memory and Manuscript: Oral Tradition and Written Transmission in Rabbinic Judaism and Early Christianity*, Acta Seminarii Neotestamentici Upsaliensis, vol. 12 (Uppsala, 1961), pp. 21, 22, 26–27, 29.

68. Marrou, *A History*, pp. 336, 337, 339.

## 2. The Light of Literacy in the "Dark Ages"

1. See Michael Parkes, "The Literacy of the Laity," in *The Medieval World*, ed. David Daiches and Anthony Thorlby (London: Aldous Books, 1973), pp. 555–77; Michael T.

Clanchy, *From Memory to Written Record, England,* 1066–1307 (Cambridge, Mass.: Harvard University Press, 1979); Herbert F. Grundmann, "Literatus—Illiteratus. Der Wandel einer Bildungsnorme vom Altertum zum Mittelalter,"*Archiv fur Kulturgeschichte* 40 (1950):1–65.

2. See Roger S. Schofield, "The Measurement of Literacy in Pre-industrial England," in *Literacy in Traditional Societies,* ed. Jack Goody (Cambridge: Cambridge University Press, 1968), pp. 311–25; Kenneth A. Lockridge, *Literacy in Colonial New England* (New York: Norton, 1974); Francois Furet and Jacques Ozouf, *Lire et écrire* (Paris: les editions de minuit, 1977); Harvey J. Graff, *The Literacy Myth: Literacy and Social Structure in the Nineteenth-Century City* (New York: Academic Press, 1979).

3. Clanchy, *From Memory,* p. 183.

4. Eric A. Havelock, *Origins of Western Literacy* (Toronto: Ontario Institute for Studies in Education, 1976), p. 18.

5. Clanchy, *From Memory,* p. 184.

6. Parkes, "The Literacy," p. 1555.

7. See, for example, J. W. Thompson, *The Literacy of the Laity in the Middle Ages* (Berkeley: University of California Press, 1939); Robert Lerner, "Literacy and Learning," in *One Thousand Years,* ed. Richard DeMolen, (Boston: Houghton Mifflin, 1974), pp. 173, 165. See also Herlihy, "Ecological Conditions," in DeMolen, *One Thousand Years.*

8. Pierre Riché, *Education and Culture in the Barbarian West,* trans. from 3d French ed. by John T. Contreni (Columbia: University of South Carolina Press, 1976); Margaret Deansley, "Medieval Schools to c. 1300," in *The Cambridge Medieval History,* vol. 5, ed. J. R. Tanner (Cambridge: Cambridge University Press, 1926), pp. 765–79; Lerner, "Literacy"; among other secondary sources.

9. *The Letters of Sidonius,* ed. and trans. O. M. Dalton (Oxford: Oxford University Press, 1915), p. 409.

10. Thompson, *Literacy,* pp. 2–3, passim.

11. Riché, *Education,* pp. 3, 7.

12. Riché, *Education,* pp. 8–9; Lerner, "Literacy," pp. 171ff.

13. Lerner, "Literacy," p. 171; *Letters of Sidonius,* passim; *The History of the Franks, by Gregory of Tours,* ed. and trans. O. M. Dalton (Oxford: Oxford University Press, 1927), passim.

14. Riché, *Education,* p. 9; George Haven Putnam, *Books and Their Makers during the Middle Ages* (New York: G. P. Putnam's Sons, 1898), vol. 1.

15. See C. P. Wormald, "The Uses of Literacy in Anglo-Saxon England and Its Neighbours," *Transactions,* Royal Historical Society, 5th Series (1977), pp. 95–115; Jack Goody, "Introduction" and "Restricted Literacy in Ghana," in Goody, *Literacy.*

16. Riché, *Education,* pp. 11–13, 65 ff.; Thompson, *Literacy,* chap. 1.

17. Riché, *Education,* pp. 21–23; Thompson, *Literacy,* chap. 1; Lerner, "Literacy."

18. Thompson, *Literacy,* chap. 1; Riché, *Education,* pp. 74–75, passim; Dalton, *History of the Franks,* passim.

19. Riché, *Education,* p. 76.

20. Thompson, *Literacy,* pp. 8–10, 14–15; Dalton, *History of the Franks.*

21. Riché, *Education,* pp. 100–113.

22. See chap. 1, above; Riché, *Education,* pp. 113–21; Frank Davies, *Teaching Reading in Early England* (London: Pitman, 1973); Walter J. Ong, *The Presence of the Word* (New York: Simon and Schuster, 1970); Graff, *Literacy Myth,* chap. 7 and the literature cited there.

23. Riché, *Education,* pp. 124–35.

24. Frederick B. Artz, *The Mind of the Middle Ages,* A.D. 200–1500: *An Historical Survey* (New York: Knopf, 1953), p. 305; H. O. Taylor, *The Medieval Mind: A History of the Development of Thought and Emotion in the Middle Ages* (London: Macmillan, 1938), vol. 1, p. 249; Riché, *Education,* pp. 139–40; Dalton, *History of the Franks;* Thompson, *Literacy;* Lerner, "Literacy."

25. Riché, *Education,* pp. 156–57.

26. Riché, *Education,* pp. 177–83, 182–92, 196–203; Henri Pirenne, "De l'état de l'instruction des laiques à l'époque mérovingienne," *Revue Benedictine* 46 (1934): 165–77; Thompson, *Literacy.*

27. Riché, *Education*, pp. 206–209, 210–18, 226, 228–30; Thompson, *Literacy*.

28. Riché, *Education*, pp. 228–43, 247–65.

29. Riché, *Education*, pp. 266–73, 279, 280–89.

30. Riché, *Education*, pp. 290–302; Putnam, *Books*.

31. Riché, *Education*, pp. 307–311 R. B. Hepple, *Mediaeval Education in England* (London: The Historical Association, Leaflet no. 90, 1932), p. 4; Joan Simon, *The Social Origins of English Education* (London: Routledge and Kegan Paul, 1970).

32. Riché, *Education*, pp. 314–18, 318–22; Hepple, *Mediaeval Education*, pp. 4–6; F. M. Stenton, *Anglo-Saxon England* (Oxford: Oxford University Press, 1943), chap. 6.

33. Riché, *Education*, pp. 322–23, 328–34; Thompson, *Literacy*, for examples; Hepple, *Mediaeval Education;* see also Putnam, *Books*.

34. Riché, *Education*, pp. 337–45, 345–60.

35. Riché, *Education*, pp. 361–68; Putnam, *Books*.

36. On these points and what follows, see Riché, *Education*, pp. 369–99; Thomas Wright, *An Essay on the State of Literature and Learning under the Anglo-Saxons,* Introductory to the First Section of *Biographia Britannica Literaria* of the Royal Society of Literature (London: Charles Knight, 1839); Simon, *Social Origins*; Stenton, *England*; R. I. Page, *Life in Anglo-Saxon England* (London: Batsford, English Life Series, 1970); John Lawson, *Mediaeval Education and the Reformation* (London: Routledge and Kegan Paul, 1967); R. R. Bolgar, *The Classical Heritage and Its Beneficiaries* (Cambridge: Cambridge University Press, 1954); Hepple, *Mediaeval Education*; Deansley, ''Medieval Schools''; Wormald, ''The Uses.''

37. Riché, *Education*, pp. 394–99; Wright, *An Essay*; Stenton, *England*, chap. 6.

38. Riché, *Education*, pp. 399–404; see also Putnam, *Books*; Deansley, ''Medieval Schools''; Taylor, *Medieval Mind*; Artz, *The Mind*.

39. Riché, *Education*, pp. 404–413; see also Irving A. Agus, *Urban Civilization in Precrusade Europe: A Study of Organized Town-Life in Northwestern Europe during the Tenth and Eleventh Centuries Based on the Responsa Literature* (Leiden: E. J. Brill, 1965); Robert S. Lopez, *The Commercial Revolution of the Middle Ages* (Cambridge: Cambridge University Press, 1971); the works of Henri Pirenne; Thompson, *Literacy*, chap. 3; Artz, *The Mind*; Taylor, *Medieval Mind*.

40. Riché, *Education*, pp. 404–415, 415–21; Bolgar, *Classical Heritage*, p. 108.

41. Wormald, ''The Uses,'' p. 100; Riché, *Education*, pp. 421–27, 427–32; Thompson, *Literacy*; Putnam, *Books*.

42. Riché, *Education*, pp. 439–46; Thompson, *Literacy*; Wormald, ''The Uses''; Putnam, *Books*.

43. F. L. Ganshof, *The Carolingians and the Frankish Monarchy* (Ithaca: Cornell University Press, 1971), pp. 21, 28–29, passim; Lerner, ''Literacy''; Stenton, *England*; Hepple, *Mediaeval Education*; Thompson, *Literacy*; Bolgar, *Classical Heritage*, pp. 108–113.

44. Lerner, ''Literacy,'' pp. 182–88; Stenton, *England*; Hepple, *Mediaeval Education*; Putnam, *Books*. See also Thompson, *Literacy*.

45. Thompson, *Literacy*, pp. 27, 29, chap. 2; Wormald, ''The Uses,'' p. 100.

46. Lerner, ''Literacy,'' pp. 188–89; Thompson, *Literacy*, p. 35; Putnam, *Books*.

47. Ganshof, *Carolingians*, pp. 100, 127, 177 (emphasis added), 217, 134, 128–42. See also Thompson, *Literacy*, chap. 2; Wormald, ''The Uses.'' For parallels with a later period, 1066–1307, see Clanchy, *From Memory*.

48. Quoted in Riché, *Education*, p. 480.

49. Ibid., pp. 477–89; quoted in ibid., p. 489; ibid., pp. 489–94; Simon, *Social Origins*; J. W. Adamson, ''The Illiterate Anglo-Saxon,'' in his *''The Illiterate Anglo-Saxon'' and Other Essays on Education, Medieval, and Modern* (Cambridge: Cambridge University Press, 1946), pp. 1–20.

50. Riché, *Education*, p. 463.

51. Riché, *Education*, pp. 468, 476.

52. Quoted in Hepple, *Mediaeval Education*, p. 8.

53. Adamson, ''The Illiterate Anglo-Saxon,'' pp. 1–7.

54. Thompson, *Literacy*, p. 119; V. H. Galbraith, ''The Literacy of the Medieval English

Kings," *Proceedings*, British Academy, vol. 21 (1935), pp. 225, 216–20, 224–28 (Raleigh Lecture on History); Wormald, "The Uses"; Adamson, "Illiterate Anglo-Saxon"; Page, *Life*. For a later period, see Clanchy, *From Memory*.

55. Wormald, "The Uses," p. 107, passim.

56. Wright, *An Essay*; Stenton, *England*, chap. 6; Wormald, "The Uses"; Adamson, "Illiterate Anglo-Saxon"; Galbraith, "Literacy"; Page, *Life*; H. J. Chaytor, *From Script to Print* (Cambridge: Cambridge University Press, 1946); Putnam, *Books*; among a large and growing literature.

57. Wormald, "The Uses," pp. 110–11.

58. On these conclusions, see also Wormald, "The Uses"; Agus, *Urban Civilization*; Thompson, *Literacy*; Luitpold Wallach, "Education and Culture in Tenth Century," *Medievalia et Humanistica* 9 (1955):18–22.

## 3. New Lights of Literacy and Learning

1. See, for example, the essays in Richard DeMolen, ed., *One Thousand Years: Western Europe in the Middle Ages* (Boston: Houghton Mifflin, 1974); Robert Brenner, "Agrarian Class Structure and Economic Development in Pre-industrial Europe," *Past and Present* 70 (1976):30–75; Alan Macfarlane, *The Origins of English Individualism* (Oxford: Blackwell,1978). For a stimulating, if unconventional, study of the period, see Alexander Murray, *Reason and Society in the Middle Ages* (Oxford: Oxford University Press, 1978).

2. Robert Lerner, "Literacy and Learning," in DeMolen, *One Thousand Years*, p. 195. On the developments of this period, see the work of Carlo M. Cipolla, Robert S. Lopez, Henri Pirenne,and David Herlihy; *The Cambridge Economic History of Europe*, vols. 1–3; *The Cambridge Medieval History, Fontana Economic History of Europe*; Friedrich Heer, Marc Bloch, Georges Duby, R. H. Hilton, M. M. Postan, Susan Reynolds, Edward Miller and John Hatcher, R. J. Mols, Fritz Rorig. See also the bibliography in David Herlihy, "The Economy of Traditional Europe," *Journal of Economic History* 31 (1971):153–64; and idem, "Ecological Conditions and Demographic Change," in DeMolen, *One Thousand Years*, pp. 3–43, and the Cambridge and Fontana economic histories, as well as textbooks for the events of the three century period. Numerous local and regional studies might be consulted, as well.

3. Carlo Cipolla, *Literacy and Development in the West* (Harmondsworth: Penguin, 1969), pp. 41–46; see also Harvey J. Graff, *The Literacy* Myth: *Literacy and Social Structure in the Nineteenth-Century City* (New York: Academic Press, 1979), chap. 5, passim, and the literature cited therein.

4. J. K. Hyde, *Society and Politics in Medieval Italy* (London: Macmillan, 1973), p. 7; Cipolla, *Literacy*; Henri Pirenne, "L'instruction des marchands au Moyen Age," *Annales d'histoire économique et sociale* 1 (1929):13–28.

5. C. H. Haskins, *The Renaissance of the Twelfth Century* (Cambridge, Mass.: Harvard University Press, 1927), p. 63.

6. Hyde, *Society*, pp. 34–35.

7. Ibid., pp. 90–93, 167–77; see also David Nicholas, "Patterns of Social Mobility," in DeMolen, *One Thousand Years*, pp. 45–106. There is also a large literature on medieval Italian lawyers and legal education that can consulted.

8. See chap. 4 below for fourteenth-century developments. See also J. W. Thompson, *The Literacy of the Laity in the Middle Ages* (Berkeley: University of California Press, 1939), chap. 3; the works of Lauro Martines and Gene Brucker cited in chap. 4 below. For a case study, see Helene Wieruszowski, "Arezzo as a Center of Learning and Letters in the Thirteenth Century," *Traditio* 9 (1953):328, passim.

9. Hyde, *Society*, p. 87; J. K. Hyde, "Some Uses of Literacy in Venice and Florence in the Thirteenth and Fourteenth Centuries," *Transactions*, Royal Historical Society, 5th ser. 29 (1979):109–129.

10. Robert S. Lopez, *The Commerical Revolution of the Middle Ages* (Cambridge: Cambridge University Press, 1971), chaps.3–4; Henri Pirenne, *Economic and Social History of Medieval Europe* (New York: Harcourt, Brace, n.d.); idem, *Medieval Cities* (Princeton:

Princeton University Press, 1925); David Herlihy, "The Economy," *Pisa in the Early Re-naissance* (New Haven: Yale University Press, 1958); idem, *Medieval and Renaissance Pistoria* (New Haven: Yale University Press, 1967); Irving Agus, *Urban Civilization in Pre-crusade Europe* (Leiden: E. J. Brill, 1965).

11. See on this point, for example, Lawrence Stone, "Literacy and Schooling in England, 1640–1900," *Past and Present* 42 (1969):61–139; Walter J. Ong, "Latin Language as a Renaissance Puberty Rite," *Studies in Philology* 56 (1959).

12. Hyde, *Society*, pp. 168ff.; Graff, *Literacy Myth*.

13. Pirenne, *Economic History*, p. 15. See Cipolla, *Literacy*; Pirenne, *Economic History*, pp. 123-24ff., "L'instruction." See also Lopez, *Commercial Revolution*; Pirenne, *Cities*; Cipolla, *Literacy*, pp. 41–45, and the references cited therein.

14. Cipolla, *Literacy*, pp. 44–45, 42.

15. Pirenne, *Economic History*, pp. 124, 125–26; Sidney Painter, *Medieval Society* (Ithaca: Cornell University Press, 1951, pp. 87–91; Pirenne, *Cities*. On the development of the vernaculars, see, for example, Marc Bloch, *Feudal Society*, trans. L. A. Manyon (London: Routledge and Kegan Paul, 1961); C. W. Previté-Orton, *The Shorter Cambridge Medieval History* (Cambridge: Cambridge University Press, 1952), among a huge literature; see also below, this chapter and the next.

16. Thompson, *Literacy*, pp. 55–73.

17. For a brief summary, see Previté-Orton, *Shorter Cambridge*, chap. 17, passim. See also Hyde, *Society*; J. B. Russell, "Varieties of Christian Experience," in DeMolen, *One Thousand Years*; R. W. Southern, *The Making of the Middle Ages* (New Haven: Yale University Press, 1953), p. 144; idem, *Western Church and Society in the Middle Ages* (Harmondsworth: Penguin, 1970); *Cambridge Medieval History*, vols. 5, 6; Jean Danielou and Henri Marrou, *The First Six Hundred Years* (London, 1964); David Knowles and Dimitri Obolensky, *The Middle Ages* (London, 1969); Robert Brentano, *The Two Churches* (Princeton: Princeton University Press, 1968); Brian Tierney, *The Crisis of Church and State, 1050–1300* (Englewood Cliffs, N.J.: Prentice Hall, 1964); Geoffrey Barraclough, *The Medieval Papacy* (New York, 1968); Walter Ullmann, *The Growth of Papal Government in the Middle Ages* (London, 1962).

18. Previté-Orton *Shorter Cambridge*, pp. 475–76, 616, 617, 618. Note that similar de-velopments took place in the reform, administration, and organization of monasteries; these will not, however, be discussed here.

19. See Previté-Orton, *Shorter Cambridge*; Frederick B. Artz, *The Mind of the Middle Ages* (New York: Knopf, 1953); George Haven Putnam, *Books and Their Makers during the Middle Ages* (New York: G. P. Putnam's Sons, 1898). See also Frank Barlow, *The English Church, 1066–1154* (New York: Longman, 1979), chap. 6; JoAnn H. Moran, *Edu-cation and Learning in the City of York* (York: Borthwick Institute, 1979). Moran's *The Growth of English Schooling, 1340–1548: Learning, Literacy, and Laicization in Pre-Reformation York Diocese* (Princeton: Princeton University Press, 1985) appeared too late for inclusion here. See also Brian Stock, *The Implications of Literacy* (Princeton: Princeton University Press, 1982).

20. Margaret Deansley, "Medieval Schools to 1300," in *The Cambridge Medieval History*, vol. 5, ed. J. R. Tanner (Cambridge: Cambridge University Press, 1926), pp. 773, 777–78; Barlow, *English Church*.

21. Lerner, "Literacy," p. 196.

22. Putnam, *Books*; see below.

23. Lerner "Literacy," p. 203. Nicholas, "Mobility " pp. 80, 45–106.

24. R. R. Bolgar *The Classical Heritage and Its Beneficiaries* (Cambridge: Cambridge University Press, 1954), pp. 236–37, 214–15, 194–95. See Artz, *The Mind*; pp. 306–311; Southern, *Making*, pp. 97, 314–15; Haskins, *Renaissance*; Bloch, *Feudal Society*, chap. 7; David Knowles, *The Evolution of Medieval Thought* (Baltimore: Helicon Press, 1962), pp. 84–87; George C. Sellery and A. C. Krey, *Medieval Foundations of Western Civilization* (New York: Harper and Brothers, 1929), pp. 356–59; A. Clerval, *L'écoles de Chartres au Moyen Age* (Chartres: Libraire R. Selleret, 1895).

25. Deansley, "Schools," p. 778. In contrast to this view, see below; and Thompson,

*Literacy;* Wiersuzowski, "Arezzo"; Clerval, *L'écoles*; Artz, *The Mind*; Lynn Thorndike, "Elementary and Secondary Education in the Middle Ages," *Speculum* 15 (1940):400–408.

26. Thompson, *Literacy*, pp. 82, 85. See also Franz Bauml, "Varieties and Consequences of Medieval Literacy and Illiteracy,"*Speculum* 55 (1980):237– 65; Franz Bauml and Edda Spielmann, "From Illiteracy to Literacy: Prolegomena to a Study of the *Nibelungenlied*," in *Oral Literature: Seven Studies*, ed. J. J. Duggan (New York: Barnes and Noble, 1975), pp. 62–73. See also Stock, *Implications*.

27. Luitpold Wallach, "Education and Culture in the Tenth Century," *Medievalia et Humanistica* 9 (1955):18; Mother Frances Raphael Drane, *Christian Schools and Scholars, or, Sketches of Education from the Christian Era to the Council of Trent* (London: Burns, Oates, and Washburne, 1924), p. 254.

28. Gray Cowan Boyce, "Erfurt Schools and Scholars in the Thirteenth Century," *Speculum* 24 (1949):8, 9, 11, 18; Bauml, "Varieties"; Bauml and Spielmann, "From Illiteracy."

29. Wallach, "Education," p. 20; Bauml, "Varieties," p. 244; Bauml and Spielmann, "From Illiteracy" pp. 67–68.

30. Gerdes, quoted in Thompson, *Literacy*, p. 85.

31. Bauml and Spielmann, "From Illiteracy," pp. 67–68.

32. Bauml "Varieties," pp. 239–50. See also Roger Wright, "Speaking, Reading, and Writing Late Latin and Early Romance," *Neophilologus* 60 (1976): 178–89; Bauml, "Varieties"; Franz Bauml,"Medieval Literacy and Illiteracy: An Essay toward the Construction of a Model," in *Germanic Studies in Honor of Otto Springer*, ed. S. J. Kaplowitt (Pittsburgh: K and S Enterprises, 1978), pp. 41–54, for definitions and qualifications. For oral tradition, see the pioneering work of Albert Lord, Ruth Crosby, Milman Parry, Ruth Finnegan, and others (references in Bauml's articles).

33. Thompson, *Literacy*, pp. 87–88, 90–93, 97–98; Bauml, "Varieties"; Bauml and Spielmann, "From Illiteracy."

34. See Lopez, *Commercial Revolution*; Pirenne, *Economic History, Cities*, "L'instruction."

35. Thompson, *Literacy*, pp. 123–25, 126–27, 127–31. See, for example, Susan Noakes, "The Fifteen Oes, the *Disticha Catonis*, Marculfius, and Dick, Jane, and Sally," University of Chicago Library Society, *Bulletin* (Winter 1977), pp. 2–15; Wright, "Speaking."

36. Thompson, *Literacy*, pp. 133, 138ff., 135; Barlow, *English Church*, chap. 6; see also Bloch, *Feudal Society*; Previté-Orton, *Shorter Cambridge*; Edward P. Cheyney, *The Dawn of a New Era, 1250–1453* (New York: Harper and Brothers, 1936), chap. 8.

37. Thompson, *Literacy*, pp. 135–36.

38. L'Abbé Allain, *L'instruction primaire en France avant la Révolution* (Paris: La Librairie de de la Société Bibliographique, 1881), pp. 22–39; see also Clerval, *L'écoles*.

39. Pirenne, "L'instruction"; Sellery and Krey, *Foundations*; Artz, *The Mind*.

40. Cipolla, *Literacy*, pp. 44, 43; Pirenne, "L'instruction," pp. 24–25. George Huppert explores these antecedents in his *The Schools of Renaissance France* (Urbana: University of Illinois Press, 1984).

41. Pirenne, "L'instruction," pp. 23, 24.

42. See Thorndike, "Elementary"; Lopez, *Commercial Revolution*; Pirenne, *Economic History, Cities*; Cipolla, *Literacy*, p. 45.

43. Thompson, *Literacy*, p. 145; R. Wright, "Speaking"; Bauml, "Varieties," "Medieval Literacy."

44. Previté-Orton, *Shorter Cambridge*. There is, of course, a huge literature on the rise of the European vernaculars; see also Bloch, *Feudal Society*, chap. 6; Cheyney, *Dawn*, chap. 8; Putnam, *Books*; H. J. Chaytor, *From Script to Print* (Cambridge: Cambridge University Press, 1945); Bauml, "Varieties," "Medieval Literacy"; Bauml and Spielmann, "From Illiteracy."

45. Bloch, *Feudal Society*, pp. 81–87; see also John Bossy, "Blood and Baptism: Kinship, Community, and Christianity in Western Europe from the Fourteenth to the Seventeenth Centuries," in *Sanctity and Secularity: The Church and the World*, Studies in Church History, ed. Derek Baker, vol. 10 (Oxford: Blackwell, 1973), pp. 129–43; idem, "The Counter Reformation and the People of Catholic Europe," *Past and Present* 47(1970):51–70; Keith

Thomas, *Religion and the Decline of Magic* (Harmondsworth: Penguin, 1973), among an important and growing literature on the history of popular religion.

46. Bloch, *Feudal Society*, pp. 75, 76, 77; see also Bolgar, *Classical*, but see Wright, "Hearing"; Bauml, "Varieties."

47. See Eugen Weber, *Peasants into Frenchmen* (Stanford: Stanford University Press, 1976), for persistence into the nineteenth century, and later.

48. Bloch, *Feudal Society*, pp. 78–81; see above, and Thompson, *Literacy*; Cheyney, *Dawn*; Chaytor, *From Script*.

49. Thompson, *Literacy*, p. 166; V. H. Galbraith, "The Literacy of Medieval English Kings," *Proceedings*, British Academy, vol. 21 (1935), p. 210.

50. Thompson, *Literacy*, pp. 167–71, 171–80; Galbraith, "Kings"; see also Joan Simon, *The Social Origins of English Education* (London: Routledge and Kegan Paul, 1970); A. W. Parry, *Education in English in the Middle Ages*, Thesis Approved for the Degree of Doctor of Science in the University of London (London: W. B. Clive University Tutorial Press, 1920); A. F. Leach, *The Schools of Medieval England* (London: Methuen, 1915); Nicholas Orme, *English Schools in the Middle Ages* (London: Methuen, 1973); Barlow, *English Church*.

51. Thompson, *Literacy*, pp. 180–81; see also H. G. Richardson and G. O. Sayles, *The Governance of Medieval England from the Conquest to Magna Carta* (Edinburgh: University of Edinburgh Press, 1963).

52. M. T. Clanchy, *From Memory to Written Record* (Cambridge, Mass.: Harvard University Press, 1979); Richardson and Sayles, *Governance*.

53. Richardson and Sayles, *Governance,* pp. 119–20, 273, 274, 277–78, 165–279; see also Ralph V. Turner, "The *Miles Literatus* in Twelfth and Thirteenth Century England: How Rare a Phenomenon?" *American Historical Review* 83 (1978):928–45; Clanchy, *From Memory*; Galbraith, "Kings."

54. Richardson and Sayles, *Governance*, pp. 279–83; Clanchy, *From Memory*.

55. Clanchy, *From Memory*; see also Putnam, *Books*; Chaytor, *From Script*; Paul Saenger, "Silent Reading: Its Impact on Late Medieval Script," *Viator* 53 (1982):367–414.

56. Clanchy, *From Memory*, pp. 166, 173–74, chap. 6; see also Galbraith, "Kings"; Chaytor, *From Script*; Cheyney, *Dawn*; Previté-Orton, *Shorter Cambridge*; Bloch, *Feudal Society*, and above.

57. Clanchy, *From Memory*, chap. 7; Thompson, *Literacy*; Galbraith, "Kings;" Michael Parkes, "The Literacy of the Laity," in *The Medieval World*, ed. David Daiches and Anthony Thorlby (London: Aldous Books, 1973), pp. 555–77; Parry, *Education*; Leach, *Schools*; Simon, *Origins*; Richardson and Sayles, *Governance*; Barlow, *English Church*; see also below, esp. chap. 4.

58. Clanchy, *From Memory*, pp. 199–201, chap. 8, pp. 203, 204, 205, 211 (emphasis added), 212; see also pp. 220–57.

59. Clanchy, *From Memory*, pp. 214–20; see also W. J. Frank Davies, *Teaching Reading in Early England* (New York: Barnes and Noble, 1973); Walter J. Ong, *The Presence of the Word* (New York: Simon and Schuster, 1967); Chaytor, *From Script*.

60. Susan Reynolds, *An Introduction to the History of Medieval English Towns* (Oxford: Oxford University Press, 1977), pp. 44–45, 62, 64; see also Lopez, *Commercial Revolution*; Pirenne, *Economic History, Cities*; works of Hilton and Postan, Cambridge and Fontana economic histories, among a large literature.

61. Susan Reynolds, *An Introduction to the History of English Medieval Towns* (Oxford: Oxford University Press, 1977), pp. 83, 81, 84; George Unwin, "Mediaeval Gilds and Education," in *Studies in Economic History: The Collected Papers of George Unwin*, ed. R. H. Tawney (London: Macmillan, 1927), pp. 92–99; Georges Renard, *Guilds in the Middle Ages*, trans. Dorothy Terry, ed. G. D. H. Cole (London: G. Bel and Sons, 1918); Orme, *Schools*; Nicholas Orme, *Education in the West of England, 1066–1548* (Exeter: University of Exeter Press, 1976); Parry, *Education*; R. B. Hepple, *Mediaeval Education in England* (London: The Historical Association, Leaflet no. 90, 1932), and the literature cited above. See also the discussion in chap. 4 below.

62. Unwin, "Gilds," p. 97; Parry, *Education*, pp. 146–56; Reynolds, *Towns*, p. 86.

63. Reynolds, *Towns*, pp. 126–29, passim.

64. Orme, *Schools*; Turner, "*Miles Literatus*," p. 943.

65. Parkes, "Literacy," pp. 560, 561.

66. See Parry, *Education*; Hepple, *Mediaeval Education*, for an introduction to these issues. What follows is based on their studies and Barlow, *English Church*; Simon, *Origins*; Orme, *Schools, West*; Leach, *Schools*; Davies, *Reading*; John Lawson, *Mediaeval Education and the Reformation* (London: Routledge and Kegan Paul, 1967); Kenneth Charlton, *Education in Renaissance England* (London: Routledge and Kegan Paul, 1965); Rev. Edward L. Cutts, *Parish Priests and Their People in the Middle Ages in England* (London: Society for Promoting Christian Knowledge, 1898).

67. See the works cited above.

68. Hepple, *Mediaevel Education*, pp. 19–20; see also Parry, *Education*, p. 74; Orme, *Schools*; Barlow, *English Church*, chap. 6.

69. Orme, *Schools*, pp. 60–69; Hepple, *Mediaeval Education*, p. 20; Parry, *Education*, pp. 70–73; Leach, *Schools*; see also Foster Watson, *The English Grammar Schools to 1660: Their Curriculum and Practice* (Cambridge: Cambridge University Press, 1908), pp. 142ff.

70. Hepple, *Mediaeval Education*, pp. 20–22; Parry, *Education*, pp. 73–74; Leach, *Schools*; Orme, *Schools*; Barlow, *English Church*, chap. 6.

71. Parry, *Education*, pp. 74–75, passim; Clanchy, *From Memory*; Parkes, "Literacy"; Thompson, *Literacy*; Schofield, "Measurement"; Galbraith, "Kings"; Charles Sissons, "Marks as Signatures," *Library* 9 (1928):1–37.

72. Orme, *West*, p. 3, *Schools*; Parry, *Education*; Hepple, *Mediaeval Education*; Leach, *Schools*.

73. Leach, *Schools*, pp. 131–32, 167, 176, 178; Parry, *Education*; Orme, *Schools* (see his maps of school locations ca. 1300, p. 171). See also the work of JoAnn Hoeppner Moran, cited above and in chap. 4 below.

74. Hepple, *Mediaeval Education*, pp. 11–18; Parry, *Education*, pp. 84–87; Orme, *Schools*, chap. 8, passim; Leach, *Schools*.

75. Orme, *Schools*, pp. 64, 69, 70, 63.

76. Charlton, *Education*, pp. 15–16; Orme, *Schools*, pp. 60–62; Barlow, *English Church*, p. 238; Davies, *Reading*. Davies's book is very useful for examples, excerpts, and illustrations; its interpretation, however, must be read with great caution.

77. Barlow, *English Church*, p. 228; Noakes, "The Fifteen Oes," and her forthcoming book *The Historicity of Reading*.

78. Orme, *Schools*, 60, 52–53; Hepple, *Mediaeval Education*, p. 26; Barlow, *English Church*, chap. 6.

79. Orme, *Schools*, pp. 53–55, and the work of Eileen Power on women.

80. Parry, *Education*, pp. 102, 53, 54; see also Leach, *Schools*. This issue is considered at greater length in chap. 4 below.

81. Simon, *Origins*, p. 73; see also Cutts, *Parish Priests*; and above.

82. Bauml, "Varieties," p. 237.

83. J. Huizinga, *The Waning of the Middle Ages* (London: Edward Arnold, 1924), p. 48.

84. Bede Jarrett, O. P., *Social Theories of the Middle Ages* (Westminster, Md: Newman Book Shop, 1942), pp. 34, 35, 31–68.

85. Huizinga, *Waning*, p. 49, see also pp. 50–51, 136–51.

86. See also Ewart Lewis, *Medieval Political Ideas*, 2 vols. (London: Routledge and Kegan Paul, 1954); R. W. Carlyle and A. J. Carlyle, *A History of Mediaeval Political Theory in the West*, 6 vols. (Edinburgh and London: William Blackwood and Sons, 1903–1936); Previté-Orton, *Shorter Cambridge*; Charlton, *Education*. This topic obviously deserves more extended treatment.

## 4. Ends and Beginnings

1. For background literature on this paragraph and much of what follows, consult the literature cited in chap. 3 above. See also Denys Hay, *Europe in the Fourteenth and Fifteenth Centuries* (London: Longman, 1966); Harry A. Miskimin, *The Economy of Early Renaissance*

*Europe, 1340–1460* (Englewood Cliffs, N.J.: Prentice Hall, 1969); David Herlihy, "Ecological Conditions and Demographic Change," in *One Thousand Years: Western Europe in the Middle Ages*, ed. Richard DeMolen (Boston: Houghton Mifflin, 1974); Robert Brenner, "Agrarian Class Structure and Economic Development in Pre-industrial Europe," *Past and Present* 70 (1976):30–75; William McNeill, *Plagues and Peoples* (Garden City: Doubleday, 1976); E. LeRoy Ladurie, *Times of Feast, Times of Famine* (Garden City: Doubleday, 1971); the relevant works of Fernand Braudel and Immanuel Wallerstein on economic development. On educational impacts, see W. J. Courtenay, "The Effect of the Black Death on English Higher Education," *Speculum* 55 (1980):696–714; Robert Lerner, "Literacy and Learning," in DeMolen, *One Thousand Years*.

2. Herlihy, "Ecological"; see also Brenner, "Agrarian," and the debate stimulated by his article; Miskimin, *The Economy*, for national and regional details and variations.

3. Miskimin, *The Economy*; see also Harry A. Miskimin, "The Legacies of London, 1259–1330," in *The Medieval City*, ed. Harry A. Miskimin, David Herlihy, and A. L. Udovitch (New Haven: Yale University Press, 1977); Lerner, "Literacy," pp. 220, 223.

4. See, in general, Lerner, "Literacy"; C. W. Previté-Orton, *The Shorter Cambridge Medieval History* (Cambridge: Cambridge University Press, 1952); M. B. Parkes, "The Literacy of the Laity," in *The Medieval World*, ed. David Daiches and Anthony Thorlby (London: Aldous Books, 1973), pp. 555–77; G. R. Potter, "Education in the Fourteenth and Fifteenth Centuries," in *The Cambridge Medieval History*, vol. 8, ed. C. W. Previté-Orton and Z. N. Brooke (Cambridge: Cambridge University Press, 1936), pp. 688–717; Lynn Thorndike, "Elementary and Secondary Education in the Middle Ages," *Speculum* 15 (1940):400–408; J. W. Adamson, "Education," in *The Legacy of the Middle Ages*, ed. C. G. Crump and E. F. Jacobs (Oxford: Oxford University Press, 1926), pp. 255–85; Frederick B. Artz, *The Mind of the Middle Ages* (New York: Knopf, 1953); Hay, *Europe*; Friedrich Heer, *The Medieval World*, trans. Janet Sondheimer (London: Weidenfeld and Nicolson, 1962); Crump and Jacobs, *Legacy*; J. R. Hale, *Renaissance Europe* (London: Collins, 1971); Edward P. Cheyney, *The Dawn of a New Era* (New York: Harper and Brothers, 1936); Myron P. Gilmore, *The World of Humanism* (New York: Harper and Brothers, 1952).

5. John Larner, *Culture and Society in Italy, 1290–1420* (New York: Scribners, 1971), p. 26; see also Anthony Mohlo, ed., *Social and Economic Foundations of the Italian Renaissance* (New York: Wiley, 1969).

6. Charles T. Davis, "Education in Dante's Florence," *Speculum* 40 (1965):415, 415–35, citing Villani, *Cronica*, vol. 11, p. 94. See also David Herlihy and Christine Klapisch-Zuber, *Les Toscans et leur familles: une étude du catasto florentin de 1427* (Paris: Presses de la foundation nationale des sciences politiques, éditions de l'école des hautes etudes en sciences sociales, 1978 [English-language edition published by Yale University Press in 1985]), pp. 563–68; Carlo Cipolla, *Before the Industrial Revolution* (New York: Norton, 1976); idem, *Literacy and Development in the West* (Harmondsworth: Penguin, 1969); Gene Brucker, *Renaissance Florence* (New York: Wiley, 1969), p. 223; Larner, *Culture*, pp. 118–200; Peter Burke, *Culture and Society in Renaissance Italy* (London: Batsford, 1972). And see Potter, "Education"; Adamson, "Education"; Previté-Orton, *Shorter Cambridge*; Thorndike, "Elementary"; Parkes, "Literacy." Paul Grendler's current research on schooling in Renaissance Italy will add greatly to our understanding.

7. Davis, "Education," pp. 416, 420, 420–35; see also Larner, *Culture*; Potter, "Education"; Previté-Orton, *Shorter Cambridge* on friars et al.

8. Potter, "Education," p. 710.

9. See on this and related points Robert V. Wells, "On the Dangers of Constructing Artificial Cohorts in Times of Rapid Social Change," *Journal of Interdisciplinary History* 9 (1978):103–110; Norman Ryder, "The Cohort as a Concept in the Study of Social Change," *American Sociological Review* 30 (1965):843–61.

10. Cipolla, *Literacy*, arrives at a rate of school attendance above the 40 percent mark with Villani's data, pp. 45–46; Bonvecinus de Rippa, cited in Cipolla, *Literacy*, p. 45; Cipolla, *Literacy*, p. 46. See also J. K. Hyde, "Some Uses of Literacy in Venice and Florence in the Thirteenth and Fourteenth Centuries," *Transactions*, Royal Historical Society, 5th ser. 29 (1979):109–29; Larner, *Culture*, p. 189; Brucker, *Florence*, p. 223.

11. Brucker, *Florence*, pp. 223, 223–30; Davis, "Education"; see also below, and Eugene Ferguson, "The Mind's Eye: Nonverbal Thought in Technology," *Science* 197 (16 August 1977):328–36; A. F. C. Wallace, *Rockdale* (New York: Knopf, 1978); William Ivins, *Prints and Visual Communications* (Cambridge, Mass.: MIT Press, 1953); Thomas Kuhn, *The Structure of Scientific Revolutions* (Chicago: University of Chicago Press, 1962); Walter J. Ong, *Ramus, Method, and the Decay of Dialogue* (Cambridge, Mass.: Harvard University Press, 1958); idem, *Rhetoric, Romance, and Technology* (Ithaca: Cornell University Press, 1971); Marshall McLuhan, *The Gutenberg Galaxy* (Toronto: University of Toronto Press, 1962).

12. Larner, *Culture*, pp. 26–27; see also Burke, *Culture*; Herlihy and Klapisch-Zuber, *Les Toscans*; Mohlo, *Social and Economic*; David Herlihy, *Pisa in the Early Renaissance* (New Haven: Yale University Press, 1958); idem, *Medieval and Renaissance Pistoria* (New Haven: Yale University Press, 1967); Robert Lopez, *The Commercial Revolution of the Middle Ages* (Cambridge: Cambridge University Press, 1971). See also Cipolla, *Literacy*, pp. 56–58; on the economics of the decline, see Harry A. Miskimin, *The Economy of Later Renaissance Europe* (Cambridge: Cambridge University Press, 1977), chaps. 3, 4. Grendler's work will make an important contribution here.

13. Larner, *Culture*, pp. 27–28; see also Lopez, *Commercial Revolution*. On clocks, see Carlo Cipolla, *Clocks and Culture* (New York: Norton, 1977), and David Landes, *Revolution in Time* (Cambridge, Mass.: Harvard University Press, 1984). For a different view, see Elizabeth Eisenstein, *The Printing Press as an Agent of Change*, 2 vols. (Cambridge: Cambridge University Press, 1979).

14. Lauro Martines, *Power and Imagination: City-States in Renaissance Italy* (New York: Knopf, 1979), p. 191; for his definitions, see p. 209. On humanism more generally, the literature is vast; see below.

15. Larner, *Culture*, p. 149; see also Georges Duby, *The Foundations of a New Humanism* (Geneva: Éditions d'Art Albert Skira, 1966); Martines, *Power*, pp. 201–209.

16. Martines, *Power*, pp. 204, 205, 206. On the example of notaries in Genoa, see the useful essay by Benjamin Z. Kedar, "The Genoese Notaries of 1382," in Miskimin et al., *The Medieval City*, pp. 73–94.

17. Larner, *Culture*, pp. 122–24, 124–27, 127–33, 149.

18. Martines, *Power*, p. 191.

19. Larner, *Culture*, pp. 150–51, 152–53.

20. Larner, *Culture*; Martines, *Power*.

21. Martines, *Power*, pp. 199–200, 201.

22. Martines, *Power*.

23. Brucker, *Florence*, pp. 213, 214–15.

24. Brucker, *Florence*, pp. 216, 215–17, chap. 6; see also Lauro Martines, *The Social World of the Florentine Humanists* (Princeton: Princeton University Press, 1963); Burke, *Culture*.

25. Brucker, *Florence*, pp. 230–40; see also Larner, *Culture*; Burke, *Culture*; Martines, *Social World*; Potter, "Education"; Hans Baron, *The Crisis of the Early Italian Renaissance*, 2 vols. (Princeton: Princeton University Press, 1955).

26. Burke, *Culture*, p. 39, chap. 3.

27. Martines, *Social World*, pp. 263, 264, 265–66, 266–302, 280; see also J. G. A. Pocock, *The Machiavellian Moment* (Princeton: Princeton University Press, 1975); J. H. Hexter, *Reappraisals in History*, rev. ed. (Chicago: University of Chicago Press, 1979).

28. Eisenstein, *Printing Press*; McLuhan, *Gutenberg*; Larner, *Culture*, p. 158, passim; Denys Hay, ed., *The New Cambridge Modern History*, vol. 1 (1976), p. 8. See also Anthony Grafton, "The Importance of Being Printed," *Journal of Interdisciplinary History* 11 (1980):265–86.

29. Burke, *Culture*, pp. 39–40.

30. Burke, *Culture*, pp. 40–41, 40–43, 42, 43 (the example of Milan), 44, 43–53, for examples; for other examples, see above. See also the works of Ong, especially the essay cited above on Latin learning as a puberty rite; Eisenstein, *Printing Press*.

31. Burke, *Culture*, pp. 44–53, 46, 51, 53; Larner, *Culture*.

32. Ivins, *Prints*, pp. 158–59, passim.
33. Ferguson, "The Mind's Eye," pp. 827–36; see also Ivins, *Prints*; Wallace, *Rockdale*.
34. Larner, *Culture*, pp. 162–63, 164; see also Paul Saenger, "Silent Reading," *Viator* 53 (1982):367–414; Susan Noakes, "The Fifteen Oes," University of Chicago Library Society, *Bulletin* (Winter 1977), pp. 2–15, and her forthcoming *The Historicity of Reading*.
35. Ong, *Presence*, pp. 58–59, 59–60 (emphasis added), *Rhetoric, Ramus*; Frances Yates, *The Art of Memory* (London: Routledge and Kegan Paul, 1966); Adamson, "Education," pp. 278–79.
36. H. J. Chaytor, *From Script to Print* (Cambridge: Cambridge University Press, 1945), pp. 10–11, chap. 1; Ruth Crosby, "Oral Delivery in the Middle Ages," *Speculum* 11 (1936):88ff.
37. Chaytor, *From Script*, p. 19; Noakes, "Fifteen Oes." See also the recent work of Franz Bauml, cited in chap. 3 above.
38. Michael T. Clanchy, *From Memory to Written Record* (Cambridge, Mass.: Harvard University Press, 1979), notes that the power of memory may be greatly exaggerated. See also Larner, *Culture*, pp. 168–73.
39. Yates, *Memory*, pp. 4, 6–7, chaps. 3–4, pp. 77, 82, 84–85, 95, 103–104, 158. See also Eisenstein, *Printing Press*.
40. Yates, *Memory*, pp. 368–69, chap. 17. More generally, see Ong, *Presence*, pp. 60–63, passim.
41. Larner, *Culture*, pp. 164–165.
42. Richard Trexler, "Ritual Behavior in Renaissance Florence: The Setting," *Medievalia et Humanistica* 4 (1973):125; see also his "Florentine Religious Experience: The Sacred Image," *Studies in the Renaissance* 19 (1972):7–41; idem, "Ritual in Florence: Adolescence and Salvation in the Renaissance," in *The Pursuit of Holiness*, ed. Charles Trinkaus and H. A. Oberman (Leiden: Brill, 1974), pp. 200–64; idem, *Public Life in Renaissance Florence* (New York: Academic Press, 1980). Note also the forthcoming book on sixteenth-century Lyon by Natalie Davis, and other essays in Trinkaus and Oberman, *The Pursuit*, esp. those of Davis; and Natalie Davis, "The Sacred and the Body Social in Sixteenth-Century Lyon," *Past and Present* 90 (1981):40–70.
43. Marvin Becker, "Aspects of Lay Piety in Early Renaissance Florence," in Trinkaus and Oberman, *The Pursuit*, pp. 178–85, 177–85, 189, 193–95.
44. Trexler, "Ritual," pp. 204, 204–209. Paul Grendler's research also shows this aspect.
45. Cited in Trexler, "Ritual," pp. 209–210, 209–15, 216–18, 219–64, 239, 242, 243, 244. See also the studies by Potter, Bolgar, and Martines; and W. H. Woodward, *Vittorino da Feltre and Other Humanist Educators* (Cambridge: Cambridge University Press, 1905) and *Studies in Education During the Age of the Renaissance* (Cambridge: Cambridge University Press, 1906), among the literature.
46. Trexler, "Ritual," pp. 244–45, 245–64; see also Donald Weinstein, "Critical Issues in the study of Civic Religion in Renaissance Florence," in Trinkaus and Oberman, *The Pursuit*, pp. 265–70, esp. the first two points, and the papers by Oberman, Tentler, and Galperin in this volume.
47. Larner, *Culture*, pp. 158–59, 159–60, 161, 162. See Hale, *Renaissance Europe*, for the fifteenth century; see also below, and Hyde, "Some Uses."
48. George Haven Putnam, *Books and Their Makers During the Middle Ages* (New York: G. P. Putnam's Sons, 1898), p. 173. See also the above chaps.; Putnam, *Books*, passim; Chaytor, *From Script*, chap. 6; R. K. Root, "Publication before Printing," *Publications*, Modern Language Association, n.s. 21 (1913):417–31; for elsewhere in the West, see below. See also Larner, *Culture*, chap. 8.
49. Root, "Publication," pp. 418–19, 420–22, 423–24, 425, 426, 426–31.
50. Larner, *Culture*, pp. 178–80; Chaytor, *From Script*; Putnam, *Books*, chaps. 3, 4.
51. Larner, *Culture*, pp. 180–81; see also Chaytor, *From Script*; Lucien Febvre and Henri-Jean Martin, *L'apparition du livre* (Paris: Editions Alben Michel, 1958 [English translation, *The Coming of the Book* (London: New Left Books, 1976)]).
52. Larner, *Culture*, pp. 182–83, 186; Putnam, *Books* chap. 2.

53. Larner, *Culture*, pp. 165, 165–67, 167–68. See also, for these points and later, Heer, *Medieval World*; Crump and Jacob, *Legacy*; Bauml's articles.

54. Martines, *Power*, pp. 317–18; Hyde, "Some Uses." See also Paul Kristeller, "The Origin and Development of the Language of Italian Prose," in his *Renaissance Thought*, vol. 2 (New York: Harper and Row, 1965), pp. 119–41.

55. Martines, *Power* pp. 319, 320–21, 321, 321–22.

56. Martines, *Social World*, pp. 287, 286–88.

57. Louis Marks, "The Financial Oligarchy of Florence under Lorenzo," in *Italian Renaissance Studies*, ed. E. F. Jacob (New York: Faber, 1960), as cited in Martines, *Social World*, p. 289; Martines, *Social World*, p. 192. See also Burke, *Culture*; Baron, *Crisis*; Brucker, *Florence*; and other studies cited above for the implications of these developments.

58. Martines, *Social World*, pp. 292–302; David Herlihy, "Family and Property in Renaissance Florence," in Miskimin, et al., *The Medieval City*, pp. 3–24; Herlihy and Klapisch-Zuber, *Les Toscans*, pp. 563–83; Cipolla, *Literacy*, pp. 57–59; DeMolen, "Introduction," *The Meaning of the Renaissance and Reformation* (Boston: Houghton Mifflin, 1974), p. 5.

59. Miskimin, *Economy*, pp. 57–58, 101–102, passim; Lopez, *Commercial Revolution; Cambridge Economic History of Europe*.

60. Adamson, "Education," pp. 264–65; Lerner, "Literacy," p. 225; bibliography in Potter, "Education"; G. C. Boyce, "Erfurt Schools and Scholars in the Thirteenth Century," *Speculum* 24 (1949):1–18, provides one example. There are at present no good surveys of elementary education at this time, and very few good case studies. See also Bauml's articles.

61. Potter, "Education," p. 594; Thorndike, "Elementary," p. 407; Cipolla, *Literacy*, p. 49.

62. Miskimin, *Economy*; see chap. 3 above; Thorndike, "Elementary"; Cipolla, *Literacy*, p. 47.

63. See Albert Hyma, *The "Devotio Moderna" or Christian Renaissance* (Grand Rapids, Mich.: The Reformed Press, n.d.); idem, *The Christian Renaissance: A History of the Devotio Moderna* (New York: Century Co., 1924); idem, *The Brethren of the Common Life* (Grand Rapids, Mich.: Wm. B. Eerdmans, 1950); S. Harvey Gem, *Hidden Saints: A Study of the Brothers of the Common Life* (London: Society for Promoting Christian Knowledge, 1907); Potter, "Education"; Previté-Orton, *Shorter Cambridge*; R. R. Post, *The Modern Devotion: Confrontation with Reformation and Humanism*, Studies in Medieval and Reformation Thought, vol. 3 (Leiden: Brill, 1968).

64. Hyma, *Brethren*, chap. 1, pp. 31–34, 39, 44, 46, 27.

65. Potter, "Education," p. 694; Artz, *The Mind*, p. 312.

66. Gem, *Hidden Saints*, pp. 100, 104, chap. 5, pp. 104–106, 106–111; Hyma, *Brethren*.

67. Potter, "Education," pp. 694–95, 711; Hyma, *Brethren, The "Devotio Moderna"*; Gem, *Hidden Saints*; Post, *The Modern*.

68. Hyma, *Brethren*, pp. 86–87, 74–78, 92, 93, 93–97, 115–26; Potter, "Education," pp. 711–13; see also Hyma, *Brethren*, pp. 97, 109, 111; Putnam, *Books*, p. 282; Post, *The Modern*.

69. Putnam, *Books*, pp. 277–80, 280, 282, 283–86, 287, 296, 190–300.

70. E. LeRoy Ladurie, *Montaillou* (New York: George Braziller, 1978). After a period of uncritical acclaim, scholarly reviews that take issue with the author's method, use of sources, and interpretation are appearing; see, for example, David Herlihy in *Social History* 4 (1979):517–20; Natalie Z. Davis, "Les contours de Montaillou," *Annales: e,s,c,* 34 (1979):61–73. LeRoy Ladurie, *Montaillou*, pp. 234, 233, 235 (emphasis added), 235–36, 235–37, 237–38, 238–39, 239–40, 241–44, 244, 244–50, 247, 247–48, 249 (emphasis added), 250. Cipolla, *Literacy*, pp. 46–47. For English comparisons, see below. A *domus* was a household. According to Davis's research, in sixteenth-century French cities, peer groups were more important, as also in Trexler's Italian studies.

71. Miskimin, *Economy*, pp. 51–57, 121–22; see also Lopez, *Commercial*.

72. Potter, "Education," p. 694, passim; A. Clerval, *L'ecole de Chartres au moyen Age* (Chartres: Librarie R. Selleret, 1895), pp. 357–59, 426–27; Adamson, "Education," pp. 266, 263; Thorndike, "Elementary."

73. Previté-Orton, *Shorter Cambridge*, p. 1092; Cheyney, *Dawn*, p. 247.

74. Cheyney, *Dawn*, pp. 248–49, 254–55; for Italian parallels, see above; for Spain, see for an introduction Cheyney, *Dawn*, pp. 253–54; for England, see above and below, and the interesting John H. Fisher, "Chancery and the Emergence of Standard Written English in the Fifteenth Century," *Speculum* 52 (1977):870–89.

75. Cheyney, *Dawn*, pp. 255–56, 257. On the persistence of dialects, see, for example, the works of E. LeRoy Ladurie, especially his *Peasants of Languedoc* (Urbana: University of Illinois Press, 1974); Eugen Weber, *Peasants into Frenchmen* (Stanford: Stanford University Press, 1976).

76. Putnam, *Books*, pp. 255–76.

77. John Bossy, "Blood and Baptism: Kinship, Community, and Christianity in Western Europe from the Fourteenth to the Seventeenth Centuries," in *Sanctity and Secularity: The Church and the World*, Studies in Church History, vol. 10, ed. Derek Baker (Oxford: Blackwell, 1973), pp. 137, 141–43; see also the essays in Trinkaus and Oberman, *The Pursuit*.

78. See Lawrence Stone, "The Educational Revolution in England, 1560–1640," *Past and Present* 28 (1964):41–80; but see also David Cressy, *Literacy and the Social Order* (Cambridge: Cambridge University Press, 1980), and "Educational Opportunity in Tudor and Stuart England," *History of Education Quarterly* 16 (1976):301–320.

79. See, for example, Robert Brenner, "Agrarian Class"; idem, "The Origins of Capitalist Development," *New Left Review* 104 (1977):25–92; the work of Emmanual Wallerstein and Fernand Braudel.

80. Miskimin, *Economy*, pp. 28–51; see also the literature cited in this and earlier chaps. on English economic and social history, and Brenner, "Agrarian Class." Compare with Alan Macfarlane, *The Origins of English Individualism* (Oxford: Blackwell, 1978). For another perspective, see the work of Michael Postan.

81. Miskimin, *Economy*, passim; Susan Reynolds, *An Introduction to the History of English Medieval Towns* (Oxford: Oxford University Press, 1977); Miskimin, *Later Renaissance Europe*; and works of Wallerstein and Braudel, and also the scholarly criticism addressed to them.

82. Miskimin, *Later Renaissance Europe*, chaps. 2, 3, 4.

83. Reynolds, *Introduction*, pp. 168–69. See also Parkes, "Literacy"; Joan Simon, *The Social Origins of English Education* (London: Routledge and Kegan Paul, 1970). For good case studies, see JoAnn Hoeppner Moran, "Education and Learning in the City of York," Borthwick Institute, *Papers*, 1979, and her new book [Princeton University Press, 1985]. See also A. W. Parry, *Education in England in the Middle Ages* (London: W. B. Clives Tutorial Press, 1920); Clara P. McMahon, *Education in Fifteenth-Century England*, Johns Hopkins University Studies in Education, vol. 33 (Baltimore: Johns Hopkins University Press, 1947); Nicholas Orme, *English Schools in the Middle Ages* (London: Methuen, 1973).

84. Edwin Benson, *Life in a Mediaeval City, Illustrated by York in the Fifteenth Century* (London: Society for Promoting Christian Knowledge, 1920), pp. 45–49. On friars and education, see, for example, Potter, "Education"; on monasteries, Parry, *Education*; Orme, *Schools*. Moran's new work elaborates and extends these earlier discussions.

85. Moran, "Education," pp. 4–5, 15, 22, 38; JoAnn Hoeppner Moran, "Literacy and Education in Northern England, 1350–1550," *Northern History* 17 (1981):1–23.

86. Benson, *Life*, pp. 67–72, 314–17; see also below; L. F. Salzman, *English Life in the Middle Ages* (Oxford: Oxford University Press, 1926), pp. 139–45; Mary Dormer Harris, *Life in an Old English Town: Coventry* (London: Swan Sonnenschein and Co., 1898).

87. Sylvia Thrupp, *The Merchant Class of Medieval London* (Ann Arbor: University of Michigan Press, 1962 [1948]), pp. 155–56, 156–57; Cipolla, *Literacy*, pp. 56–57; see J. W. Adamson, "The Extent of Literacy in England in the Fifteenth and Sixteenth Centuries," *Library*, 4th ser. 10 (1930):162–93. Compare with a century later in Cressy, *Literacy*.

88. Thrupp, *Merchant Class*, pp. 158–59; see also Cressy, *Literacy*.

89. Thrupp, *Merchant Class*, pp. 159–60; see also Miskimin, "Legacies."

90. Thrupp, *Merchant Class*, pp. 166, 162–63, 164–69, 169–74.

91. See, in general, Parkes, "Literacy"; Potter, "Education"; Adamson, "Extent," "Education"; Artz, *The Mind*; Thorndike, "Elementary"; Orme, *Schools*.

92. Parkes, "Literacy," pp. 564–65, passim; Adamson, "Extent"; J. N. Miner, "Schools and Literacy in Later Medieval England," *British Journal of Educational Studies* 11 (1962–63):16–27.

93. See chap. 3 above and the literature cited therein; for overviews, see Orme, *Schools*; Nicholas Orme, *Education in the West of England* (Exeter: Exeter University Press, 1976); R. B. Hepple, *Mediaeval Education in England* (London: The Historical Association, Leaflet no. 90, 1932); A. F. Leach, *English Schools at the Reformation* (Westminster: Constable, 1896); idem, *The Schools of Medieval England* (London: Methuen, 1915); Foster Watson, *The English Grammar Schools to 1660* (Cambridge: Cambridge University Press, 1908); McMahon, *Education*; Parry, *Education*; Simon, *Origins*; Joan Simon, *Education and Society in Tudor England* (Cambridge: Cambridge University Press, 1966); John Lawson, *Mediaeval Education and the Reformation* (London: Routledge and Kegan Paul, 1967); Kenneth Charlton, *Education in Renaissance England* (London: Routledge and Kegan Paul, 1965); Woodward, *Studies, Educators*.

94. Orme, *Schools*, pp. 7, 192–93; Rev. Edward L. Cutts, *Parish Priests and Their People in the Middle Ages in England* (London: Society for Promoting Christian Knowledge, 1898), p. 133.

95. Parry, *Education*, pp. 127, 124–31. See also Moran, "Education," on this subject and what follows.

96. Hepple, *Mediaeval Education*, pp. 19–20.

97. See, for example, Potter, "Education"; such comments are legion. Peter Heath, *The English Parish Clergy on the Eve of the Reformation* (London: Routledge and Kegan Paul, 1969), pp. 19, 70, 73, 75, chap. 5, pp. 77–82, 81–86, 86–90, 91–92, chap. 6, passim. Heath's data on book possession should be compared with those presented in Margaret Deansley, "Vernacular Books in England in the Fourteenth and Fifteenth Centuries," *Modern Language Review* 15 (1920):349–58. See also Orme, *Schools*, pp. 12–21, passim; Bernard Lord Manning, *The People's Faith in the Time of Wyclif* (Cambridge: Cambridge University Press, 1919); H. Maynard Smith, *Pre-Reformation England* (London: Macmillan, 1938); Claire Cross, *Church and People, 1450–1660* (London: Harvester Press, 1976); Watson, *Grammar Schools*, and below.

98. Parry, *Education*, pp. 162, 167–69, 157–69; see lists of schools in Leach, *Schools*; Parry, *Education*. For one local study of the piety-education relationship, see M. G. A. Vale, *Piety, Charity, and Literacy among the Yorkshire Gentry, 1370–1480* (York: University of York Borthwick Institute of Historical Research, Paper 50, 1976). See also the literature on education in this period.

99. Hepple, *Mediaeval Education*, pp. 20; Watson, *Grammar Schools*, pp. 141–42; Parry, *Education*.

100. Hepple, *Mediaeval Education*, pp. 20–21; Watson, *Grammar Schools*, pp. 137–40; Adamson, "Education," p. 260; Watson, *Grammar Schools*, pp. 139–41, chap. 11.

101. Parkes, "Literacy"; Adamson, "Extent"; Clanchy, *From Memory*; Orme, *Schools*.

102. Hepple, *Mediaeval Education*; Watson, *Grammar Schools*, chaps. 8, 9, passim.

103. See Leach, *Schools*; Parry, *Education*; Orme, *Schools*; Watson, *Grammar Schools*.

104. W. J. Frank Davies, *Teaching Reading in Early England* (New York: Barnes and Noble, 1973), p. 123, passim, for descriptions of learning; Watson, *Grammar Schools*; Orme, *Schools*; Noakes, "Fifteen Oes."

105. Parry, *Education*, pp. 147, 146–56; see also McMahon, *Education*, pp. 146–61.

106. Parkes, "Literacy," pp. 564–65; H. S. Bennett, "Production and Dissemination," *Library*, 5th ser. 1 (1946–47):167–78; Deansley, "Vernacular"; see also Adamson, "Extent."

107. Cheyney, *Dawn*, pp. 249–53; see also Maynard Smith, *Pre-Reformation*; Salzman, *Life*; Heer, *World*; Fisher, "Emergence"; essays in Crump and Jacob, *Legacies*, esp. that by Cesare Foligno, "Vernacular Literature," pp. 173–96; the relevant volumes of the *Cambridge History of English Literature* and the *Oxford History*; the Paston Letters and other contemporary evidence; Deansley, "Vernacular"; Bennett, "Production"; *Cambridge History of the Bible*, vol. 2, and below; Beverly Boyd, *Chaucer and the Medieval Book* (San Marino, Calif.: Huntington Library, 1973).

108. V. J. Scattergood, *Politics and Poetry in the Fifteenth Century* (London: Blandford Press, 1971). I wish to thank Professor Barbara Hanawalt for calling this book to my attention. On Robin Hood and other bandits, in popular folklore and in reality, see the forthcoming essay by Hanawalt.

109. Parkes, "Literacy," pp. 568, 568–70; Bennett, "Production," p. 169, passim. See also Putnam, *Books*; Deansley, "Vernacular"; Boyd, *Chaucer* (this book contains a useful introduction and bibliography); Thrupp, *Merchant Class*; Ong, *Presence*, especially on commonplace books. For York examples, see Moran, "Education," and her new book.

110. Bennett, "Production," p. 172, 174; see also Boyd, *Chaucer*.

111. Putnam, *Books*, passim.

112. Cheyney, *Dawn*, pp. 218–19; see also Margaret Aston, "Literacy and Lollardy," *History* 62 (1977):347–71; Reynolds, *Introduction*; *Cambridge History of the Bible*, vol. 2; Parry, *Education*; Manning, *Faith*; Maynard Smith, *Pre-Reformation*; Margaret Deansley, *The Lollard Bible and Other Medieval Biblical Versions* (Cambridge: Cambridge University Press, 1920); Scattergood, *Politics*.

113. Cheyney, *Dawn*, pp. 219, 219–21.

114. Aston, "Lollardy," pp. 347–48, 349, 350–51, 351–54, 354–56, 356–58, 359–60, 360–61, 361–66, 366–70. For later examples, see Graff, *The Literacy Myth*, chap. 1. See also below, chaps. 6, 7, Epilogue; Cheyney, *Dawn*, for additional English evidence and German comparisons; Reynolds, *Introduction*, on religion and towns; Parry, *Education*, pp. 239–44, on Lollardy and educational development and the role of teachers; Scattergood, *Politics*, chap. 7.

115. Scattergood, *Politics*, p. 218; Salzman, *Life*, p. 112; see also Manning, *Faith*; Maynard Smith, *Pre-Reformation*; Cutts, *Parish*; for a later period, Keith Thomas, *Religion and the Decline of Magic* (Harmondsworth: Penguin, 1973).

116. Manning, *Faith*, pp. 1, 11, 16, 14–15, 17, 21, chap. 3, passim; see also Heath, *Clergy*.

117. Manning, *Faith*, chaps. 4, 5, p. 66, chap. 7, chap. 6, p. 49, chap. 8, pp. 94–95; see also Maynard Smith, *Pre-Reformation*, chap. 3; Cutts, *Parish*.

118. Hepple, *Mediaeval Education*, pp. 28–30; see also Parkes, "Literacy"; Reynolds, *Introduction*. See for implications and comparisons below, Epilogue, and the Introduction; for an important parallel, see Egil Johansson, *The History of Literacy in Sweden* (Umeå: School of Education, Umeå University, 1977).

119. In *Literacy and the Social Order*, David Cressy makes a similar case for the next two centuries; for the nineteenth century, see Graff, *The Literacy Myth*. Moran, "Education," makes a related case for York.

120. Orme, *Schools*, pp. 12–21; see also Heath, *Clergy*; Manning, *Faith*.

121. Orme, *Schools*, pp. 210–29; McMahon, *Education*; Parry, *Education*; Adamson, "Education," "Extent"; chaps. 2, 3 above.

122. Orme, *Schools*, pp. 29–36, and the references cited therein; chaps. 2, 3 above; Parkes, "Literacy"; Adamson, "Education"; Clanchy, *From Memory*; H. G. Richardson and G. O. Sayles, *The Governance of Mediaeval England from the Conquest to Magna Carta* (Edinburgh: University of Edinburgh Press, 1963).

123. Orme, *Schools*, pp. 36–43, and the literature cited therein.

124. Orme, *Schools*, pp. 43–50; see also above.

125. Orme, *Schools*, pp. 50–52; see also above.

126. On women's schooling and literacy, see above, Orme, *Schools*, pp. 52–55.

127. Orme, *Schools*, p. 56; Lerner, "Literacy," pp. 224–26, 228.

## 5. Print, Protest, and the People

1. See Elizabeth Eisenstein, *The Printing Press as an Agent of Change* (Cambridge: Cambridge University Press, 1979). See also Marshall McLuhan, *The Gutenberg Galaxy* (Toronto: University of Toronto Press, 1962).

2. The literature on the history of printing is too vast to cite here. In my sampling of

the field, I have benefited from the collections in the Newberry Library's excellent Wing Collection of the History of Printing, and from the guidance of Mr. James Wells.

3. Denys Hay, "Fiat Lux," in *Printing and the Mind of Man*, ed. John Carter and Percy J. Muir (London: Cassell, 1967), pp. xvii–xviii, xviii–xix, xx; see also Lucien Febvre and H.-J. Martin, *The Coming of the Book* (London: NLB, 1976; originally *L'apparition du livre* [Paris: Editions Albin Michel, 1958]).

4. Michael Clapham, "Printing," in *A History of Technology*, vol. 3, ed. Charles Singer, E. J. Holmyard, A. R. Hall, and T. I. Williams (Oxford: Oxford University Press, 1957), pp. 377–78, 381, 382; see also Febvre and Martin, *Coming*.

5. Hay, "Fiat Lux," p. xxi; see also Pierce Butler, *The Origin of Printing in Europe* (Chicago: University of Chicago Press, 1940); S. H. Steinberg, *Five Hundred Years of Printing* (Harmondsworth: Penguin, 1974); Colin Clair, *A History of European Printing* (London: Academic Press, 1976); Clapham, "Printing," pp. 383, 384, 385, 386–90, 387, 388; Febvre and Martin, *Coming*; James Thorpe, *The Gutenberg Bible* (San Marino, Calif.: Huntington Library, 1975), pp. 13–14, 10–14, among the literature.

6. Butler, *Origin*, p. ix.

7. McLuhan, *Gutenberg Galaxy*, pp. 164, 171; see also Harold Innis, *The Bias of Communication* (Toronto: University of Toronto Press, 1951); Archer Taylor and Gustave Arlt, *Printing and Progress: Two Lectures* (Berkeley: University of California Press, 1941); H.-J. Martin, *Livre, pouvoirs, et société à Paris* (Geneva: Librairie Droz, 1969); David Pottinger, *Printers and Printing* (Cambridge, Mass.: Harvard University Press, 1941); idem, *The French Book Trade in the Ancient Regime* (Cambridge, Mass.: Harvard University Press, 1958), among others. For cogent criticism, see Natalie Z. Davis, "Printing and the People," in her *Society and Culture in Early Modern France* (Stanford: Stanford University Press, 1975); Robert Darnton, "Reading, Writing, and Publishing in Eighteenth-Century France," in *Historical Studies Today*, ed. F. Gilbert and S. R. Graubard (New York: Norton, 1972); idem, "Le livre francais à la fin de l'Ancien Régime," *Annales: e, s, c* 43 (1971):112–32.

8. Febvre and Martin, *Coming*, pp. 10–11; see also the original French edition. This book is an essential but much neglected work, which deserves a better translation. See also Eisenstein, *Printing Press*, on the relations of intellectuals and publishing in the fifteenth through seventeenth centuries. Febvre and Martin, *Coming*, preface, addresses problems of study and organization in the history of books and printing.

9. Marcel Thomas, "Manuscripts," in Febvre and Martin, *Coming*, pp. 16, 17, 22–28; *Coming*, chap. 1; see also the literature cited above.

10. Febvre and Martin, *Coming*, pp. 46, 47, 49–76, 77–78; see also Eisenstein, *Printing Press*; Hay, "Fiat Lux"; and for the "invention of printing," see the literature cited above.

11. Hay, "Fiat Lux," p. xxii; see also Febvre and Martin, *Coming*, chap. 3; Rudolph Hirsch, *Printing, Selling, and Reading, 1450–1550* (Wiesbaden: Otto Harrassowitz, 1974); idem, *The Printed Word* (London: Variorum Reprint, 1978); L. V. Gerulaitis, *Printing and Publishing in Fifteenth-Century Venice* (Chicago: American Library Association, 1976); Curt Buhler, *The Fifteenth-Century Book* (Philadelphia: University of Pennsylvania Press, 1960); George Haven Putnam, *Books and Their Makers during the Middle Ages* (New York: G. P. Putnam's Sons, 1898); Sven Dahl, *History of the Book* (New York: Scarecrow Press, 1958); Clair, *European Printing*; Luigi Balsamo, "The Origins of Printing in Italy and England," *Journal of the Printing Historical Society* 11 (1976/77):48–63; Victor Scholderer, "Printers and Readers in Italy in the Fifteenth Century," *Proceedings*, British Academy 35 (1949):25–47.

12. Febvre and Martin, *Coming*, pp. 78–83, 84, 83–86, 87, 88–90; see also Hirsch, *Printed Word, Printing*; Eisenstein, *Printing Press*; Clair, *European Printing*; Putnam, *Books*; Paul Melotteée, *Histoire économique de l'imprimerie sous l'Ancien Regime* (Paris: Librairie Hachette, 1905); and French regional studies.

13. Febvre and Martin, *Coming*, pp. 90, 87–94, 91, 101, and other histories of printing. For some implications, see the interesting paper by Chandra Mukerji, "Mass Culture and the Modern World System," *Theory and Society* 8 (1979):245–68.

14. Hay, "Fiat Lux," pp. xxii–xxiii; Febvre and Martin, *Coming*, esp. chap. 7; Pottinger, *Printers*; and other related studies.

15. On costs, see, for example, the survey in Febvre and Martin, *Coming*, chap. 4; Melottée, *Histoire économique*; Clair, *European Printing*; Steinberg, *Printing*; Pottinger, *Printers*; and related works.

16. Hay, "Fiat Lux," p. xxiii. On authors, see Putnam, *Books*; Febvre and Martin, *Coming*, chap. 5; Eisenstein, *Printing Press*; Pottinger, *Printers, Book Trade*; other books cited above on printing and the book trade.

17. Hay, "Fiat Lux," p. xxiii.

18. Balsamo, "Origins," p. 50; see Eisenstein, *Printing Press*, for other examples. The secondary literature, it should be noted, is replete with data; missing is an interpretive emphasis, especially of a critical or questioning nature.

19. Davis, "Printing," pp. 191–92; see also the critical essays of Darnton. Compare these with the celebratory piece by Mandrou "Le livre," or H.-J. Martin's "Pour une histoire de 9la lecture," *Revue françaisec d'histoire du livre* 16 (1977):583–609; and other such examples.

20. Febvre and Martin, *Coming*, pp. 167–68, chaps. 6, 4, 5, 7.

21. Febvre and Martin, *Coming*, p. 179; Eisenstein, *Printing Press*; Balsamo, "Origins"; Albert Hyma, *The Brethren of the Common Life* (Grand Rapids, Mich.: Eerdmans, 1950); and other studies of this group, cited in chap. 4 above.

22. Febvre and Martin, *Coming*, pp. 170–71; for Italian examples, see Gerulaitis, *Printing*; Balsamo, "Origins"; for French, see *Coming*; Pottinger, *Book Trade*; in general, see Putnam, *Books*.

23. Febvre and Martin, *Coming*, pp. 171–72; see also the other works cited here, and for additional confirmation Anne Jacobson Schutte, "Printing, Piety, and the People in Italy," *Archive for Reformation History* 71 (1980):5–19; Susan Noakes, "The Development of the Book Market in Late Quattrocento Italy," *Journal of Medieval and Renaissance Studies* 11 (1981):23–55.

24. See, for example, Martin Lowry, *The World of Aldus Manutius* (Ithaca: Cornell University Press, 1979): Eisenstein, *Printing Press*; Febvre and Martin, *Coming*; Scholderer, "Printers"; Balsamo, "Origins"; Gerulaitus, *Printing*; and others.

25. Noakes, "Development"; see also Schutte, "Printing."

26. Febvre and Martin, *Coming*, pp. 177, 176–77, chap. 7; Harry Miskimin, *The Economy of Later Renaissance Europe* (Cambridge: Cambridge University Press, 1977); Paul Grendler, *The Roman Inquisition and the Venetian Press* (Princeton: Princeton University Press, 1977); and other references.

27. Febvre and Martin, *Coming*, pp. 181, 177–215; see the maps on pages facing p. 272 in the French edition and pp. 178–79, 184–85 in the translation. See also Clair, *European Printing*; Steinberg, *Printing*; Hirsch, *Printed Word, Printing*; Gerulaitis, *Printing*; Pottinger, *Printers, Book Trade*; Balsamo, "Origins"; Putnam, *Books*. Gerulaitis, *Printing*, p. 63; see his table on p. 60. For England, see H. S. Bennett, *English Books and Readers* (Cambridge: Cambridge University Press, 1952, 1965, 1970); Clair, *English Printing*; Balsamo, "Origins." See also R. F. Jones, *The Triumph of the English Language* (Stanford: Stanford University Press, 1953).

28. Gerulaitus, *Printing*, pp. 89, 92, 91–105; for fine distinctions over time and categories, see the tables in his chap. 4. See also Noakes, "Development"; Lauro Martines, *Power and Imagination* (New York: Knopf, 1979); Charles Trinkaus, *In His Image and Likeness* (London: Constable, 1970).

29. Schutte, "Printing," p. 9, passim.

30. Gerulaitus, *Printing*, p. 127, chap. 4. Compare this work with the standard texts, such as the *New Cambridge Modern History*, vols. 1, 2 or with Eisenstein, *Printing Press*. See also Curt Buhler, *The University and the Press in Fifteenth-Century Bologna* (Notre Dame: Medieval Institute, 1958), and note that Gerulaitus finds that in Florence, in sharp contrast to the other cities, almost 75 percent of books printed were in the vernacular. See also Hirsch, *Printed Word, Printing*.

31. Febvre and Martin, *Coming*, pp. 187, 186–92, chaps. 4, 7; Pottinger, *Book Trade*; and other relevant references from those presented above.

32. Hirsch, *Printing*, p. 1.

33. Jacob, "The Fifteenth Century," *Bulletin*, John Rylands Library 14 (1930):8; Hirsch,

*Printing*, p. 4, chaps. 1, 2; and see above chapters. For more on printing at this time, see Hirsch, *Printing*, chaps. 2–6.

34. Eisenstein, *Printing Press*, pp. xiii–xiv. This study of major proportions followed a number of years after her initial series of articles: "Clio and Chronos: An Essay on the Making and Breaking of Historical Book-Time," *History and Theory* 6 (Beiheft 6, 1966):36–64; "The Advent of Printing and the Problem of the Renaissance," *Past and Present* 45 (1969):19–89; "Some Conjectures about the Impact of Printing on Western Society and Thought: A Preliminary Report," *Journal of Modern History* 40 (1968):1–56; "The Advent of Printing in Current Historical Literature: Notes and Comments on an Elusive Transformation," *American Historical Review* 75 (1970):727–43; "L'avènement de l'imprimerie et la Réforme," *Annales: e, s, c* 26 (1971):1355–83. Among major critiques, see especially those by Anthony Grafton (*Journal of Interdisciplinary History* 11 [1980]:265–86), Michael Hunter (*The Book Collector* 28 [1979]:335–52), and Roger Chartier (*Annales: e, s, c* 36 [1981]:191–209).

35. Eisenstein, *Printing Press*, chaps. 1, 8, 10–11. She is, I think, unreasonably harsh in her treatment of scribal culture. For superb reviews, see those cited in note 34 above.

36. Eisenstein, *Printing Press*, pp. 88–89, 89, 91, 92–93, 101, 100–101, 105–106. On reading instruction and habits, see above chapters, Frank Davies, *Teaching Reading in Early England* (London: Pitman, 1973); Graff, *Literacy Myth*, chap. 7 and the literature cited there. See also below.

37. Eisenstein, *Printing Press*, pp. 108, 109 (one is reminded of James K. Murray's work on the *Oxford English Dictionary*, 111, 112, 111, cf. chaps. 3, 5, 6.

38. Febvre and Martin, *Coming*, pp. 319–22; Steinberg, *Printing*, pp. 120–26; Eisenstein, *Printing Press*, pp. 117–26, chap. 4; on development of English, see the early work of McLuhan, as cited in his *Gutenberg Galaxy*; Walter J. Ong, *Rhetoric, Romance, and Technology* (Ithaca: Cornell University Press, 1971); *Shakespeare Studies*; Martines, *Power*; Glanmour Williams, "Language, Literacy, and Nationality in Wales," *History* 56 (1971):1–16. This topic is obviously huge and extremely important, and requires sustained attention in relation to the development of capitalism, class, the state, and culture.

39. Eisenstein, *Printing Press*, pp. 126, 127.

40. Eisenstein, *Printing Press*, pp. 65–66, 67. See also Franz Bauml's studies cited in chap. 3 above. Eisenstein, *Printing Press*, pp. 67–68, 68, 69–70, cf. 129–59. See chap. 4 above and the citations there. Her quotation from Luther is from "Against the Heavenly Prophets in the Matter of Images and Sacraments" (1525), *Luther's Works*, vol. 40, pp. 99–100. See also R. W. Scribner, *For the Sake of Simple Folk* (Cambridge: Cambridge University Press, 1981).

41. Eisenstein, *Printing Press*, p. 130 (compare with Davis, "Printing." Robert Mandrou, *Introduction to Modern France* [New York: Harper and Row, 1977], *De la culture populaire* [Paris: Stock, 1964], whom Eisenstein cites in evidence), 131–36, 132, 159. See also Jack Goody, *The Domestication of the Savage Mind* (Cambridge: Cambridge University Press, 1977); Carlo Ginzburg, *The Cheese and the Worms* (Baltimore: Johns Hopkins University Press, 1980).

42. Hirsch, *Printing*, pp. 147–48, 149–51; for nineteenth-century parallels, see Graff, *Literacy Myth*, chaps. 1, 7. See also Schutte, "Printing."

43. Hirsch, *Printing*, p. 151; quotation from *An die Ratsherrn* (1524); see also Gerald Strauss, *Luther's House of Learning* (Baltimore: Johns Hopkins University Press, 1978), and below; *Die rechte Weis aufs Kurzest Lesen zu Lernen* (Marburg, 1534), quoted in Hirsch, *Printing*, pp. 151–52; see also Febvre and Martin, *Coming*, pp. 256–68; *Vives on Education*, ed. and trans. Foster Watson (Cambridge: Cambridge University Press, 1913); Hirsch, *Printing*, pp. 152, 153.

44. Febvre and Martin, *Coming*, pp. 252–58, 258–60; Eisenstein, *Printing Press*, vol. 2; Geneviève Bollème, *Les almanachs populaires* (Paris, 1969); idem, *La bibliotèque bleue* (Paris: Julliard, 1971); Mandrou, *De la culture*; Davis, "Printing"; Keith Thomas, *Religion and the Decline of Magic* (Harmondsworth: Penguin, 1973); Bernard Capp, *Astrology and the Popular Press* (London: Faber and Faber, 1979).

45. Ong, *Ramus, Method, and the Decay of Dialogue* (Cambridge, Mass.: Harvard

University Press, 1958), pp. ix, 240, 245–52, esp. chap. 11, *Rhetoric*; Eisenstein, *Printing Press*; Neal Gilbert, *Renaissance Concepts of Method* (New York: Columbia University Press, 1960).

46. Ong, *Ramus*, pp. 307–308, 308, 310, 313, 313–14; *Rhetoric*.

47. Ong, "Ramist Method and the Commercial Mind," in *Rhetoric*, pp. 165, 167, 171, 173–74, 178, 181, 182, 183.

48. Ong, "Ramist Method," pp. 184, 185, 186–87, see also pp. 187–89; Gilbert, *Method*.

49. Natalie Z. Davis, "Sixteenth-Century French Arithmetics on the Business of Life," *Journal of the History of Ideas* 21 (1960):20, 27, 43, 45–48, 48.

50. Richard Goldthwaite, "Schools and Teachers of Commercial Arithmetic in Renaissance Florence," *Journal of European Economic History* 1 (1972):420, passim.

51. Eisenstein, *Printing Press*, p. 168. The statistics on printed output certainly bear this conclusion out; see above; Hirsch, *Printing*; Gerulaitus, *Printing*; Febvre and Martin, *Coming*; other citations above.

52. Eisenstein, *Printing Press*, p. 169. Her evidence, I think, is more revealing than her emphasis. Paul Grendler's current study of Italian schooling promises to add much to our understanding of these issues.

53. Eisenstein, *Printing Press*, chaps. 3, 5–6, pp. 174, 177; P. S. Allen, *The Age of Erasmus* (Oxford: Oxford University Press, 1914); W. H. Woodward, *Vittorino da Feltre and Other Humanist Educators* (Cambridge: Cambridge University Press, 1905); idem, *Studies in Education during the Age of the Renaissance* (Cambridge: Cambridge University Press, 1906); Roberto Weiss, *The Spread of Italian Humanism* (London: Hutchinson, 1964); Franco Simone, *The French Renaissance*, trans. H. G. Hall (London: Macmillan, 1969); A. H. T. Levi, ed., *Humanism in France* (Manchester: Manchester University Press, 1970).

54. Eisenstein, *Printing Press*, chap. 3, sec. 2, pp. 181, 197, 192, passim, 208, 225, chap. 3, sec. 3, pp. 229, 230–31, 235; see also Jack Goody and Ian Watt, "The Consequences of Literacy," in *Literacy in Traditional Societies*, ed. Jack Goody (Cambridge: Cambridge University Press, 1968), pp. 27–68; Goody, *Domestication*; Graff, *Literacy Myth*, chap. 7; Ginzburg, *Cheese*; among the relevant literature. Other citations appear in the Introduction and Epilogue.

55. Eisenstein, *Printing Press*, pp. 242, 244, but see Davis, "Printing"; Carlo Cipolla, *Before the Industrial Revolution* (New York: Norton, 1976); idem, *Literacy and Development in the West* (Harmondsworth: Penguin, 1969).

56. Eisenstein, *Printing Press*, p. 245. See also Margaret Aston, "Lollardy and Literacy," *History* 62 (1977):347–71; Thomas, *Religion*; and below; Anne Yarborough, "Apprentices as Adolescents in Sixteenth-Century Bristol," *Journal of Society History* 13 (1979):69–70; Mark Curtis, "Education and Apprenticeship," *Shakespeare Survey* 17 (1964):53–72.

57. Eisenstein, *Printing Press*, pp. 249, 269. See also Davis, *Society*, chap. 8.

58. Eisenstein, *Printing Press*, p. 272, chap. 3, sec. 4, p. 279; Thomas, *Religion*; Frances Yates, *The Art of Memory* (London: Routledge and Kegan Paul, 1966).

59. Eisenstein, *Printing Press*, p. 290.

60. J. R. Hale, *Renaissance Europe* (London: Collins, 1971), pp. 282, 284–85; Woodward, *da Feltre*; Goldthwaite, "Schools"; Phillippe Ariès, *Centuries of Childhood* (New York: Vintage, 1962); Lawrence Stone, *Crisis of the Aristocracy* (Oxford: Oxford University Press, 1965); idem, *The Family, Sex, and Marriage in England* (London: Weidenfeld and Nicholson, 1977); Randolph Trumbach, *The Rise of the Egalitarian Family* (New York: Academic Press, 1978); Lawrence Stone, "The Educational Revolution," "Literacy and Education in England," and other references on education and schooling cited above and below. Studies in progress by Paul Grendler for Italy and George Huppert's new work on France (*The Public Schools of Renaissance France* [Urbana: University of Illinois Press, 1984]) enrich our understanding of Renaissance schooling.

61. Hale, *Europe*, pp. 296–97.

62. R. R. Bolgar, *The Classical Heritage and Its Beneficiaries* (Cambridge: Cambridge University Press, 1954), pp. 347, 350–51, 358–67, 360, 361. He may be, however, too negative. See Strauss, *Luther's*; see also Hale, *Europe*; Denys Hay, *The Italian Renaissance*

*in Its Historical Background* (Cambridge: Cambridge University Press, 1977, 2d ed.); idem, ed., *The Age of the Renaissance* (New York: McGraw-Hill, 1967); Richard L. DeMolen, ed., *The Meaning of the Renaissance and Reformation* (Boston: Houghton Mifflin, 1974); references in chap. 4 above and the studies of Wallace K. Ferguson; Herschel Baker, *The Dignity of Man* (Cambridge, Mass.: Harvard University Press, 1947); Martines, *Power*; Myron P. Gilmore, *The World of Humanism* (New York: Harper and Row, 1952); John Herman Randall, Jr., *The Making of the Modern Mind* (Boston: Houghton Mifflin, 1940); Peter Burke, *Culture and Society in Renaissance Italy* (London: Batsford, 1972); and below. See also Huppert, *Public Schools*; George Huppert, *Les Bourgeois Gentilshommes* (Chicago: University of Chicago Press, 1977), chap. 7; Helen Nader, *The Mendoza Family and the Spanish Renaissance* (New Brunswick, N.J.: Rutgers University Press, 1979).

63. DeMolen, *Meaning*, p. 5; Martines, *Power*, pp. 322–23, 323–37; Bolgar, *Classical*, p. 361; Burke, *Culture*, chap. 10; see also DeMolen, *Meaning*; Gilmore, *Humanism*; Hay, *Renaissance*; Hale, *Europe*; Donald Wilcox, *In Search of God and Self* (Boston: Houghton Mifflin, 1975); *Cambridge Modern History*, vol. 1; Brian Pullan, *Rich and Poor in Renaissance Venice* (Oxford: Blackwell, 1971); Richard Trexler, "Charity and the Defense of Urban Elites in the Italian Communes," in *The Rich, the Well Born, and the Powerful*, ed. F. Jaher (Urbana: University of Illinois Press, 1974), pp. 64–109; Woodward, *da Feltre*. According to Grendler, Venetian schooling in classics and the vernacular may have remained widespread by the second half of the sixteenth century.

64. Pullan, *Venice*, pp. 223–24, 223–28, 259–61, 268, 272, 379, 389, 401, 401–402, 401–404, 404, 404–411, 631, Conclusion; see also below; Trexler, "Charity," on Italian attitudes; Natalie Davis, "Poor Relief, Humanism, and Heresy," in her *Society and Culture*; Robert M. Kingdon, "Social Welfare in Calvin's Geneva," *American Historical Review* 76 (1971):50–69; Emanuel Chill, "Religion and Mendicity in Seventeenth-Century France," *International Review of Social History* 7 (1962):400–25; Paul A. Fideler, "Christian Humanism and Poor Law Reform in Early Tudor England," *Societas* 4 (1974):269–86; Harold J. Grimm, "Luther's Contribution to Sixteenth-Century Organization of Poor Relief," *Archiv für Reformationgeschichte* 61 (1970):222–33.

65. See, for example, John Bossy, "The Counter Reformation and the People of Catholic Europe," *Past and Present* 47 (1970):27–47.

66. Trinkaus, *Image*; Pullan, *Venice*; see also Hale, *Europe*; Gilmore, *Humanism*; Randall, *Modern*; DeMolen, *Meaning*; Wilcox, *Search*; Davis, *Society*; Peter Burke, *Popular Culture in Early Modern Europe* (New York: Harper and Row, 1978); Levi, *Humanism*; Weiss, *Spread*; H. G. Koenigsberger and G. L. Mosse, *Europe in the Sixteenth Century* (London: Longman, 1968); Bolgar, *Classical*; Lucien Febvre, *Life in Renaissance France* (Cambridge, Mass.: Harvard University Press, 1977); Mandrou, *Introduction*; G. Duby and R. Mandrou, *Histoire de la civilisation française* (Paris: Armand Colin, 1958); Simone, *French Renaissance*; see also Miskimin, *Later Renaissance*; Henry Kammen, *The Iron Century* (New York: Praeger, 1971); Jan de Vries, *The Economy of Europe in an Age of Crises* (Cambridge: Cambridge University Press, 1976); Cipolla, *Before*; Pierre Goubert, *The Ancien Regime* (New York: Harper and Row, 1969); Robin Briggs, *Early Modern France* (Oxford: Oxford University Press, 1977).

67. Hale, *Europe*, p. 298; Bolgar, *Classical*; see also references above, and Lionel Rothkrug's recent work.

68. Lewis Spitz, *The Religious Renaissance of the German Humanists* (Cambridge, Mass.: Harvard University Press, 1963); idem, "Humanism in the Reformation," in *Renaissance Studies in Honor of Hans Baron*, ed. A. Mohlo and J. A. Tedeschi (DeKalb: Northern Illinois University Press, 1971), pp. 640–62; Hajo Holborn, *A History of Modern Germany*, vol. 1 (New York: Knopf, 1969); Strauss, *Luther's*; Bolgar, *Classical*; Steven Ozment, ed., *The Reformation in Medieval Perspective* (Chicago: Quadrangle, 1971), esp. Mueller, "Piety in Germany around 1500," pp. 52, 53–54, 58, 59, 60, 61–62, 63–64; Steven Ozment, *The Reformation in the Cities* (New Haven: Yale University Press, 1975); Lionel Rothkrug, "Popular Religion and Holy Shrines," in *Religion and the People*, ed. James Obelkevich (Chapel Hill: University of North Carolina Press, 1979), pp. 20–86; idem, "Religious Practices and Collective Perceptions," *Historical Reflections* 7 (Spring, 1980); Rich-

ard Crofts, "Books, Reform, and the Reformation," *Archive for Reformation History* 71 (1980):21–36. See also Richard Gawthrop and Gerald Strauss, "Protestantism and Literacy in Early Modern Germany," *Past and Present* 104 (1984): 31–56; Gerald Strauss, "Lutheranism and Literacy: A Reassessment," in *Religion and Society in Early Modern Europe*, ed. Kaspar von Greyerz (London: Allen and Unwin, 1984), pp. 109–23.

69. Spitz, *Religious*; Strauss, *Luther's*.

70. Spitz, *Religious*, pp. 292–93, "Humanism"; Strauss, *Luther's*; Gerald Strauss, "Reformation and Pedagogy," in *The Pursuit of Holiness*, ed. Charles Trinkaus and H. A. Oberman (Leiden: Brill, 1974), pp. 272–93, with comment by Spitz, pp. 294–306; Hajo Holborn, *Ulrich von Hutten and the German Reformation*, trans. Roland Bainton (New Haven: Yale University Press, 1937); Bolgar, *Classical*; Harold J. Grimm, *The Reformation Era* (New York: Macmillan, 1954); idem, "Social Forces in the German Reformation," *Church History* 31 (1962):3–13; James Mackinnon, *The Origins of the Reformation* (London: Longman, 1939); and below.

71. On Erasmus, there is a large literature. J. K. Soward's introduction to the literacy and educational volume of the *Collected Works* (University of Toronto Press) is a fine exposition with references. I thank him for sharing a draft with me.

72. P. S. Allen, "Erasmus' Services to Learning," *Proceedings*, British Academy 11 (1924–25):350.

73. W. H. Woodward, *Desiderius Erasmus concerning the Aim and Method of Education* (Cambridge: Cambridge University Press, 1904), pp. 72, 73–74, 74–76, 83, 84, 63, 64–71, 85; see also Spitz, *Religious*; Eugene F. Rice, "Erasmus and the Religious Tradition," in *Renaissance Essays*, ed. P. O. Kristeller and P. P. Weiner (New York: Harper and Row, 1968), pp. 162–86.

74. Lucien Febvre, *Le problème* (Paris: Editions Albin Michel, 1962), *Renaissance*, chap. 1, pp. 5, 21, 27, 28–31, 31, 33, 37, 39–40, 72–73, 73, chap. 4, 77; see also *The Pursuit of Holiness*, esp. the papers by Davis, Galpern, Trexler, Tentler; Mandrou, *Introduction*; Bossy, "CounterReformation"; A. N. Galpern, *The Religions of the People in Sixteenth-Century Champagne* (Cambridge, Mass.: Harvard University Press, 1976); Thomas Tentler, *Sin and Confession on the Eve of the Reformation* (Princeton: Princeton University Press, 1977). Huppert's *Public Schools* is also relevant here.

110. Grimm, "Luther's," pp. 232–33; Gerald Strauss, *Luther's, Nuremberg in the Sixteenth Century* (New York: Wiley, 1966); Chrisman, *Strasbourg*; Kingdon, "Social Welfare"; Robert M. Kingdon, "The Control of Morals in Calvin's Geneva," in Buck and Zophy, *The Social History*, pp. 3–16; Monter, *Geneva*; Robert Jutte, "Poor Relief and Social Discipline in Sixteenth-Century Europe," *European Studies Review* 11 (1981):25–52.

*French Renaissance* (London: SPCK, 1919); Bolgar, *Classical*; R. R. Bolgar, "Humanism as a Value System with Reference to Budé and Vives," in A. H. T. Levi, ed., *Humanism in France* (Manchester: Manchester University Press, 1970), pp. 199–215. Margaret Aston, "The Northern Renaissance," in DeMolen, *Meaning*; Hirsch, *Printed Word*.

77. Bolgar, "Humanism," pp. 201, 203, 205, 211, see also *Classical*.

78. Huppert, *Bourgeois Gentilshommes*, pp. 60, 73, chap. 7, passim, and *Public Schools*.

79. Davis, "Poor Relief," pp. 18, 19–20, 24, 26, 29, 31, 34, 32–36, 37, 40, 41, 42–43, 45, 45–59; see also the citations above.

80. Roberto Weiss, *Humanism in England during the Fifteenth Century* (Oxford: Blackwell, 1957), pp. 1, 5, passim; see also L. Eisenstein, *The Italian Renaissance in England* (New York: Columbia University Press, 1902): Hay, *Renaissance*.

81. Denys Hay, "The Early Renaissance," in his *Italian Renaissance*, pp. 99, 99–110; see also Stone, "Educational Revolution," *Crisis*; Fritz Caspari, *Humanism and the Social Order in Tudor England* (Chicago: University of Chicago Press, 1954); Arthur Ferguson, *The Articulate Citizen and the English Renaissance* (Durham, N.C.: Duke University Press, 1965).

82. Aston, "Northern," pp. 77, 82, 101, 103, 105, 121; see also Bennett, *English Books*; Marjorie Plant, *The English Book Trade*, 2d ed. (London: Allen and Unwin, 1965); Davies, *Teaching*; Colin Clair, *A History of Printing in England* (London: Cassell, 1965); J. H.

Hexter, *More's Utopia* (Princeton: Princeton University Press, 1952); R. W. Chambers, *Thomas More* (New York: Harcourt, Brace, n.d.).

83. On the language question, see Joan Simon, *Education and Society in Tudor England* (Cambridge: Cambridge University Press, 1966); Kenneth Charlton, *Education in Renaissance England* (London: Routledge and Kegan Paul, 1965); R. F. Jones, *The Triumph of the English Language* (Stanford: Stanford University Press, 1953); Caspari, *Humanism*; McLuhan studies cited in his *Gutenberg*; Ong, *Rhetoric*; Muriel St. Clare Byrne, "The Foundations of Elizabethan English," *Shakespeare Survey* 17, ed. A. Nicoll (Cambridge: Cambridge University Press, 1964), pp. 223–40, among a larger literature. See also John H. Fisher, "Chancery and the Emergence of Standard Written English in the Fifteenth Century," *Speculum* 52 (1977):870–99 (I owe this last to Richard Venezky, University of Delaware.)

84. Caspari, *Humanism*, pp. 34–35; Woodward, *Erasmus, Humanist Educators*; Ferguson, *Articulate*; Stone, "Educational Revolution"; other studies of English education in this period; David Cressy, *Literacy and the Social Order in Early Modern England* (Cambridge: Cambridge University Press, 1980).

85. Caspari, *Humanism*, pp. 1–2, 6–7, 8, 9–10, 13–14; Ferguson, *Articulate*; Stone, *Crisis*, "Educational Revolution"; Lawrence Stone, "Social Mobility in England, 1500–1700," *Past and Present* 33 (1966), pp. 16–55. See also Robert Brenner, "Agrarian Class Structure and Economic Development in Pre-industrial England," *Past and Present* 70 (1976):30–75, and the ensuing series of responses and rejoinders; Richard Grassby, "Social Mobility and Business Enterprise in Seventeenth-Century England," in *Puritans and Revolutionaries, Essays in Seventeenth-Century History Presented to Christopher Hill*, ed. Donald Pennington and Keith Thomas (Oxford: Oxford University Press, 1978), pp. 355–81. This listing is but the tip of a larger literature.

86. Hexter, *More's*, pp. 116, 116–17, 117, 120, 123, 91, 91–93.

87. Caspari, *Humanism*, pp. 67–71, 71; see also Stone's work on this period; Ferguson, *Articulate*; Simon, *Education*; Charlton, *Education*; the works of Vives and Woodward cited above; R. M. Fisher, "Thomas Cromwell, Humanism, and Educational Reform, 1530–40," *Bulletin*, Institute for Historical Research 50 (1977):151–63; see also below.

88. David Cressy, "Educational Opportunity in Tudor and Stuart England," *History of Education Quarterly* 16 (1976):302–303; see also his other writings cited below and his *Literacy and the Social Order*; the aforementioned work of Lawrence Stone, to which Cressy's findings should be compared; Simon, *Education*; Caspari, *Humanism*; Woodward's writings; W. K. Jordan, *Philanthropy in England* (London: Allen and Unwin, 1959) and *The Charities of London* (1960), among his studies; the writings of Erasmus, More, Vives, Thomas Starkey, Thomas Elyot, J. A. Comenius, Richard Mulcaster, Roger Ascham, John Brinsley; other secondary literature is far too numerous to cite; see also below.

89. Fideler, "Christian Humanism," pp. 269–70, 273, 274, 276, 278, 279–80, 283, 284; for comparative perspectives, see the continental studies cited above; Richard Harvey, "Recent Research on Poverty in Tudor-Stuart England," *International Review of Social History* 24 (1979):237–52; the writings of Ferguson, Caspari, and Jordan, cited above.

90. Strauss, *Luther's*; Spitz, review of Strauss, *American Historical Review* 85 (1980):143; see also his comments on Strauss's earlier writing, *The Pursuit of Holiness*. See also Stone, "Literacy," pp. 78–79; Febvre and Martin, *Coming*; Eisenstein, *Printing Press*; Steven Ozment, *Reformation*, and his new *The Age of Reform* (New Haven: Yale University Press, 1980); Bossy, "Counter Reformation"; Jean Delumeau, *Catholicism between Luther and Voltaire* (London: Burns and Oats, 1977); Burke, *Popular Culture*; the eighteenth-century French studies by Michel Vovelle; W. J. Mommsen, ed., *The Urban Classes, the Nobility, and the Reformation: Studies in the Social History of the Reformation in England and Germany* (Stuttgart: Klett-Cotta, 1979), esp. R. W. Scribner's two contributions.

91. John Headley, "The Continental Reformation," in DeMolen, *Meaning*, pp. 131, 134, 141–42, 146–47, 147. See also Owen Chadwick, *The Reformation* (Grand Rapids, Mich.: Eerdmans, 1965); Grimm, *The Reformation*, "Social Forces," p. 6, passim; Bob Scribner, "Is There a Social History of the Reformation?" *Social History* 2 (1977):483–506; among the literature.

92. Headley, "Continental," pp. 150–51; see, in general, the literature on the German Reformation listed above and below; Richard Crofts, "Books, Reform, and the Reformation," *Archives for Reformation History* 7 (1980):21–36.

93. Louise Holborn, "Printing and the Growth of a Protestant Movement in Germany," *church History* 11 (1942):123; see also Richard Cole, "The Dynamics of Printing in the Sixteenth Century," in *The Social History of the Reformation*, ed. L. P. Buck and J. W. Zophy (Columbus: Ohio State University Press, 1972), pp. 93–105; Eisenstein, *Printing Press*; Crofts, "Books"; and most recently Miriam Chrisman, *Lay Culture, Learned Culture: Books and Social Change in Strasbourg, 1480–1599* (New Haven: Yale University Press, 1982).

94. Febvre and Martin, *Coming*, pp. 287–88, 288, 289, 289–95, 290, 291, 191–92, 292–93, 292–95; A. G. Dickens, *Reformation and Society in Sixteenth-Century Europe* (London: Thames and Hudson, 1966), p. 51. See also Cole, "Printing"; L. Holborn, "Printing"; Eisenstein, *Printing Press*, chap. 4; Scribner, *Simple Folk*. See also Egil Johansson, "Literacy Studies in Sweden: Some Examples," in *Literacy and Society in Historical Perspective*, ed. Egil Johansson (Umeåa: Umeåa University, 1973).

95. Manfred Hanneman, *The Diffusion of the Reformation in Southwestern Germany*, Department of Geography, Research Paper no. 167 (Chicago: University of Chicago, 1975), pp. 9, 7–9, chaps. 5–7, pp. 12, 9–13, 12–13, 13, 212, Conclusion; see also Eric Hobsbawm, "Socialism and the Rise of Religion," *Marxist Perspectives* 1 (1978):14–33; Antonio Gramsci, *Prison Notebooks*; Graff, *Literacy Myth*, chap. 1; Strauss, *Luther's*; idem, "Lutheranism"; Gawthrop and Strauss, "Literacy." Scribner's recent book *For the Sake of Simple Folk* adds much to our understanding.

96. Febvre and Martin, *Coming*, pp. 295ff; for a good case study, see Miriam U. Chrisman, *Strasbourg and the Reform* (New Haven: Yale University Press, 1967) and *Lay Culture*, among the literature. For France, see Febvre and Martin, *Coming*, pp. 295, 295–96, 296–319, 300, 300ff, 307. See also Ozment, *Cities*; E. LeRoy Ladurie, *Carnival at Romans* (New York: Braziller, 1979); idem, *Peasants of Languedoc* (Urbana: University of Illinois, 1974); compare with Aston, "Lollardy"; Davis, "Printing"; E. W. Monter, *Calvin's Geneva* (New York: Wiley, 1967); Robert M. Kingdon, "Patronage, Piety, and Printing in Sixteenth-Century Europe," in *A Festschrift for Frederick B. Artz*, ed. D. H. Pinckney and Theodore Ropp (Durham, N.C.: Duke University Press, 1964), pp. 19–36.

97. Eisenstein, *Printing Press*, chap. 4, pp. 310, 326, chap. 4, sec. 2, p. 333. An enormous amount of work needs to be done on this question. See Bossy, "Counter Reformation"; Egil Johansson, *The History of Literacy in Sweden* (Umeåa: Umeåa University, 1977); the work of David Cressy; Davis, "Printing."

98. Eisenstein, *Printing Press*, pp. 344, 348; see also Febvre and Martin, *Coming*; Paul Grendler, *Roman Inquisition*; Bossy, "Counter Reformation"; and related literature.

99. Eisenstein, *Printing Press*, p. 349, passim; Simon, *Education*; and other studies of English education; Johansson, "Literacy Studies," *The History*; Bill Widén, "Literacy in the Ecclesiastical Context," in Johansson, *Literacy and Society*, pp. 33–40; Eisenstein, *Printing Press*, pp. 350–52; Roger Chartier, Dominique Julia, and Marie-Madelein Compère, *L'éducation en France du XVIe au XVIIIe siècle* (Paris: Société d'édition enseignment supérieur, 1976); compare this argument with that of Eugen Weber, *Peasants into Frenchmen* (Stanford: Stanford University Press, 1976).

100. Eisenstein, *Printing Press*, p. 354; see also E. O. Evenott, *The Spirit of the Counter Reformation* (Cambridge: Cambridge University Press, 1968); Bossy, "Counter Reformation"; Kingdon, "Piety"; Robert M. Kingdon, *Geneva and the Coming of the Wars of Religion, Geneva and the Consolidation of the French Protestant Movement* (Geneva: Librairie Droz, 1956, 1967); Clair, *European Printing*; Putnam, *Books*; in general, see with caution Eisenstein, *Printing Press*, chap. 4, secs. 3–4.

101. Eisenstein, *Printing Press*, p. 428; see also Ariès, *Centuries*; Aston, "Lollardy"; Peter Laslett, *The World We Have Lost* (London: Methuen, 1971, 2d ed); Stone, *Family*; Christopher Hill, *Puritanism and the Revolution* (London: Secker and Warburg, 1958); Charlton, *Education*; Monter, *Geneva*; Strauss, *Luther's*; Louis B. Wright, *Middle-Class Culture*

*in Elizabethan England* (Chapel Hill: University of North Carolina Press, 1935); William Haller, *Liberty and Reformation in the Puritan Reformation* (New York: Columbia University Press, 1955); Edmund Morgan, *The Puritan Family* (New York: Harper and Row, 1965); Michael Walzer, *The Revolution of the Saints* (Cambridge, Mass.: Harvard University Press, 1965); Keith Thomas, "Women and the Civil War Sects," *Past and Present* 13 (1958):333; Levi Shucking, *The Puritan Family* (New York: Schocken, 1970); Bossy, "Counter Reformation."

102. See Johansson, *Literacy*; Kenneth A. Lockridge, *Literacy in Colonial New England* (New York: Norton, 1974).

103. Strauss, *Luther's*, pp. 1, 2; see also Spitz's comments in *The Pursuit of Holiness*; studies of Luther; Gerald Strauss, "Success and Failure in the German Reformation," *Past and Present* 67 (1975):30–63; Gawthrop and Strauss, "Literacy"; Charles E. Daniel, Jr., "Hard Work, Good Work, and School Work," in Buck and Zophy, *The Social History*, pp. 41–51; Chartier et al. *Education*; Goubert, *Ancien*; Francois Furet and Jacques Ozouf, *Lire et écrire: l'alphabètisation des francais de Calvin à Jules Ferry*, 2 vols. (Paris: Editions de Minuit, 1977); Davis, "Printing"; LeRoy Ladurie, *Romans, Langedoc*; M. Fleury and P. Valmary, "Les progrès de l'instruction élémentaire," *Population* 12 (1957):71–92; Stone, "Literacy"; Cressy, "Education"; David Cressy, "Literacy in Pre-industrial England," *Societas* 4 (1974); idem, "Levels of Literacy in England," *Historical Journal* 20 (1977):1–23; idem, "Literacy in Seventeenth-Century England," *Journal of Interdisciplinary History* 8 (1977):141–150; Johansson, *Literacy*; Lockridge, *Literacy*; Graff, *Literacy Myth*; for other references, see below, and to 1980 Graff, *Literacy in History*. The exceptions here are England and Sweden; for a useful introduction to related issues, see Michael B. Katz, *Class, Bureaucracy, and Schools* (New York: Praeger, 1975, 2d ed.).

104. Strauss, *Luther's*, pt. 1, pp. 4, 5, pts. 1 and 2, passim, p. 6, pt. 3, passim, pp. 7, 8, 9, 10, 11, 12. See also Spitz, comment.

105. Strauss, *Luther's*, pp. 13, 14, pt. 3, passim, pp. 15, 15–16, 17, 18, 19, 20, passim. See also the literature on literacy for comparisons.

106. Strauss, *Luther's*, pp. 22–23, 127, 128, chaps. 12–13, pp. 128, 129, 129–30, 160, 167, 168.

107. Strauss, *Luther's*, pp. 169, 170 and pt. 3, pp. 172, 172 and pt. 2, pp. 173–74, 189, 194, 195, 196. See also, and compare with Johansson, "Literacy Studies," *Literacy*; Graff, *Literacy Myth*, chaps. 1, 7. See, for a German example, Christopher Friedrichs, *rban Society in an Age of War: Nordligen, 1580–1720* (Princeton: Princeton University Press, 1978), chap. 8.

108. Strauss, *Luther's*, pp. 195, 97, 198; Friedrichs, *rban Society*.

109. Strauss, *Luther's*, pp. 200, 201, chap. 13, pp. 282, 288–91, 293; Friedrichs, *rban Society*; Lowell Green, "Education of Women, during the Reformation," *History of Education Quarterly* 19 (1979):93–116, see also the aforementioned work of Cressy, Stone, Johansson, Lockridge, Furet and Ozouf, Davis, LeRoy Ladurie.

110. Grimm, "Luther's," pp. 232–33; Gerald Strauss, *Luther's Nuremberg in the Sixteenth Century* (New York: Wiley, 1966); Chrisman, *Strasbourg*; Kingdon, "Social Welfare"; Robert M. Kingdon, "The Control of Morals in Calvin's Geneva," in Buck and Zophy, *The Social History*, pp. 3–16; Monter, *Geneva*; Robert Jutte, "Poor Relief and Social Discipline in Sixteenth-Century Europe," *European Studies Review* 11 (1981):25–52.

111. Kingdon, "Control." See also Norman Birnbaum, "The Zwinglian Reformation in Zurich," *Past and Present* 15 (1959):27–47; Stone, "Literacy," *Family*; Monter, *Geneva*; Robert C. Walton, *Zwingli's Theocracy* (Toronto: University of Toronto Press, 1967); Lockridge, *Literacy*; Cressy, "Educational," "Literacy," *Literacy*; Peter Clark, *English Provincial Society from the Reformation to the Revolution: Religion, Politics, and Society in Kent* (Hassocks, Sussex: Harvester Press, 1977); Keith Wrightson and David Levine, *Poverty and Piety in an English Village: Terling* (New York: Academic Press, 1979). See also Grimm, "Luther's"; Kingdon, "Social Welfare," "Control"; Chrisman, *Strasbourg*; Strauss, *Nuremberg*; Henry Barnard, *Memoires of Eminent Teachers and Educators . . . History of Education in Germany* (Hartford: Brown and Gross, 1878).

430 *Notes to Pages 143–147*

112. Andrez Wyczanski, "Alphabétisation et structure sociale en Pologne au XIVe siè-cle," *Annales: e, s, c* 29 (1974):705–713; W. Urban, "La connaissance de l'ecriture en Petite-Pologne dans la seconde moitié du XVIe siècle," *Przeglad Historyczny* (1977):257.

113. Headley, "Continental," p. 178; see also Birnbaum, "Zwinglian"; Walton, *Zwingli*; DeMolen, *Meaning*; Koeningsberger and Mosse, *Europe*; Dickens, *Reformation*; Grimm, *Reformation*; *New Cambridge Modern History*, vols. 2–3; Chadwick, *Reformation*; Mandrou, *Introduction*; Febvre, *Renaissance*; Simone, *French Renaissance*; Febvre, *Problème*; Febvre and Martin, *Coming*; LeRoy Ladurie, *Languedoc, Romans*; Furet and Ozouf, *Lire*; and related titles. Work in progress by Natalie Davis and others will help remedy some of the gaps in our knowledge. Mandrou, *Introduction*, pp. 74–75, passim; see also Ariès, *Centuries*; Furet and Ozouf, *Lire*; Chartier et al., *Education*; Duby and Mandrou, *Civilisation*; Bolgar, *Classical*; L'Abbé Allain, *L'instruction primaire en France avant de la Révolution* (Paris: Librairie de la Société Bibliographique, 1881); Davis, *Society*; LeRoy Ladurie, *Languedoc, Romans*; Bernard Bonin, "L'éducation dans les classes populaires rurales en Dauphine au XVIIe siècle," *Revue de Marseille* 88 (Supplément, 1972):63–69. The older literature, often ob-sessed with praise or censure of Jesuit activities, contains some useful information. See also Carlo Ginzburg, "High and Low: The Theme of Forbidden Knowledge," *Past and Present* 73 (1976):28–41; idem, "Cheese and Worms," in Obelkevich, *Religion and the People*, pp. 87–168; idem, *Cheese*; Huppert, *Public Schools*.

114. LeRoy Ladurie, *Languedoc*, pp. 161–64, 162–64, 164, and his *Romans*; see also Mandrou, *Introduction*, pt. 1, chaps. 3–4; Burke, *Popular Culture*; H.-J. Martin, "Culture orale, culture écrit," *Journal des Savants* (1975):255–89; Furet and Ozouf, *Lire*; Chartier et al., *Education*; Bonnin, "L'éducation."

115. Davis, "Printing," pp. 195, 195–96, 196–97, 197, 197–98, 197–99; see also Natalie Z. Davis, "Proverbial Wisdom and Popular Errors," in her *Society and Culture*; for English comparisons, see Margaret Spufford, "The Scribes of Villagers' Wills in the Sixteenth and Seventeenth Century and Their Influence," *Local Population Studies* 7 (1971):28–43; R. C. Richardson, "Wills and Will-makers in the Sixteenth and Seventeenth Centuries," *Local Population Studies*, 9 (1972):33–42; Matlock Population Studies Group, "Wills and Their Scribes," *Local Population Studies* 8 (1972):55–57; Wrightson and Levine, *Terling*, chap. 6; Mandrou, *Introduction*; Burke, *Popular Culture*. See now the original but unpersuasive views of Carlo Ginzburg, *Cheese*.

116. Davis, "Printing," pp. 201, 202, 202–203, 203, 208; see also LeRoy Ladurie, *Languedoc*; Martin, "Culture"; Mandrou, *De la culture*; Bollème, *Almanachs, Bibliotèque*.

117. Mandrou, *Introduction*, pp. 49–50, 50; on sight, see pp. 53–54; on sound and lan-guage, pp. 62–66; Galpern, *Religion*, p. 89, passim. See also *The Pursuit of Holiness*, especially essays by Davis, Trexler, Galpern, Tentler; Tentler, *Sin*. On rates of literacy, see Furet and Ozouf, *Lire*; LeRoy Ladurie, *Languedoc*; Bonnin, "L'éducation."

118. Davis, "Printing," pp. 209, 209–210; her *Society and Culture*, especially chaps. 1, 2, 3; LeRoy Ladurie, *Languedoc, Romans*; Furet and Ozouf, *Lire*; Chartier et al., *Education*; Allain, *L'instruction*; James B. Wadsworth, *Lyon, 1473–1503: The Beginnings of Cosmo-politanism* (Cambridge, Mass.: Mediaeval Academy of America, 1962); Huppert, *Bourgeois Gentilshommes, Public Schools*.

119. LeRoy Ladurie, *Languedoc*, pp. 163–64, 164; his *Romans*, pp. 27–28, passim; see also Cissie Fairchilds, *Poverty and Charity in Aix-en-Provence* (Baltimore: Johns Hopkins University, 1976); Furet and Ozouf, *Lire*, for parallels.

120. Natalie Z. Davis, "City Women and Religious Change," in her *Society and Culture*, pp. 79, 81–82, 82, 82–84; see also Elfreda T. Dubois, "The Education of Women in Sev-enteenth-Century France," *French Studies* 32 (1978):1–19; Carolyn Lougee's studies of seventeenth-century French women; among the relevant literature.

121. Davis, "Printing," pp. 210–11, 211, 212, 212–13, 213–14, 214, 214–18, 218, 219, 219–22, 222, 222–25; her "Proverbial"; compare with Peter Clark, "The Ownership of Books in England, 1560–1640," in *Schooling and Society*, ed. Lawrence Stone (Baltimore: Johns Hopkins University Press, 1976), pp. 95–113. See also Eisenstein, *Printing Press*; Febvre and Martin, *Coming*; Aston, "Lollardy"; Thomas Laqueur, "The Cultural Origins of Popular Literacy in England," *Oxford Review of Education* 2 (1976):255–75; Margaret

Spufford, *Contrasting Communities* (Cambridge: Cambridge University Press, 1974); idem, "The Schooling of the Peasantry in Cambridgeshire," *Agricultural History Review* 18 (1970), supplement:112–47; idem, "First Steps in Literacy: The Reading and Writing Experiences of the Humblest Seventeenth-Century Spiritual Autobiographers," *Social History* 4 (1979):407–436; the studies of Martin and Mandrou.

122. See, in general, the literature on literacy cited above; see also Harvey J. Graff, *Literacy in History: An Interdisciplinary Research Bibliography* (New York: Garland Press, 1981); the unpublished papers of the 1979 Bad Homburg conference on the history of literacy; R. P. de Dainville, "Effectifs des Collèges et scolarities aux XVIIe et XVIIIe siècles," *Population* 10 (1955):455–88; idem, "Collèges et frèquentation scolaire du XVIIIe siècle," *Population* 12 (1957):467–94; B. Bonnin, "L'education"; Jean Meyer, "Alphabétisation, lecture, et écriture: essai sur l'instruction populaire en Bretagne," *Congres national des sociétés savants* 1 (1970):333–53.

123. LeRoy Ladurie, *Languedoc*, pp. 304, 305, 306–307, 307–309; Fleury and Valmary, "Les progrès"; Furet and Ozouf, *Lire*; Chartier et al., *Education*; W. Frijhoff and S. Julia, *Ecole et société dans la France d'ancien régime* (Paris: Libraire Armand Colin, 1975); Allain, *L'instruction*; Huppert, *Bourgeois Gentilshommes, Public Schools*; others cited above. On the Counter Reformation, see among the literature the studies of Bossy, Delumeau, Evenott, Farrell, Olin, Kidd, Dickens, Janelle, deGuibert, Hughes, Jedin, and surveys; see also Goubert, *Ancien*; compare, however, with M J. Maynes, "Schooling the Masses: A Comparative Social History of Education in France and Germany, 1750–1850" (Ph.D. diss., University of Michigan, 1977; revised edition published by Holmes and Meier, 1985); Weber, *Peasants*; Roger Schofield, "Dimensions of Illiteracy, 1750–1850," *Explorations in Economic History* 10 (1973):437–54. See finally the regional studies of literacy, such as those cited above and those presented in vol. 2 of *Lire et ecrire*.

124. *Ministère de l'instruction publique et des beaux arts, Statistique de l'enseignement primaire* (Paris, 1880), vol. 2, pp. clxvi–clxxi, cited in Pottinger, *Book Trade*, pp. 13–14, also cited in Furet and Ozouf, *Lire*; Fleury and Valmary, "Les progrès," and elsewhere.

125. Bossy, "Counter Reformation," p. 52; see also Delumeau, *Catholicism*, and Philip Benedict, "The Catholic Response to Protestantism," in Obelkevich, *Religion and the People*; among the literature on the Catholic or Counter Reformation.

126. Bossy, "Counter Reformation," pp. 53, 64–65, 65–66, 66, 67, 67–70, 70 (quoting Hill, *Society and Puritanism*, p. 188); see also Delumeau, *Catholicism*; Thomas, *Religion*; Galpern, *Religions*; *The Pursuit of Holiness*; Bolgar, *Classical*; Furet and Ozouf, *Lire*; Johansson, "Literacy Studies"; Graff, *Literacy Myth*; Lockridge, *Literacy*. See also the studies of French and German women's education cited above; general surveys; Fernand Braudel's work; among the literature.

127. Marie-Christine Rodriguez and Bartolomé Bennasar, "Signatures et niveau cultural des temoins et accusés dans les procès d'inquisition du ressort du Tribunal de Tolède (1525–1817) et due ressort du Tribunal de Cordove (1599–1632)," *Cahiers du Monde Hispanique et Lusa-Brasilien* 31 (1978):17–46. On elites, see Helen Nader, *The Mendoza Family in the Spanish Renaissance* (New Brunswick: Rutgers university Press, 1979), pp. 77–80, 128–49.

128. Johansson, *Literacy*, pp. 2–3, 11, 15, 19, 20–25, 22–25, 28, 27–33, 32, "Literacy Studies"; R. F. Tommasson, "The Literacy of the Icelanders," *Scandinavian Studies* 57 (1975):66–93; references in note 122; for additional discussion of the Swedish example, see chaps. 6, 7, Epilogue, below.

129. C. S. L. Davies, *Peace, Print, and Protestantism* (London: Paladin, 1977), pp. 35; Laslett, *World*, p. 205; Ong, *Presence*; Aston, "Lollardy"; Dickens, *English*; Clark, *Provincial*; Wrightson and Levine, *Terling*; Spufford, *Contrasting*; Stone, "Educational Revolution"; Simon, "The Reformation and English Education," *Past and Present* 11 (1957):48, 53; her *Education and Society*; and related studies.

130. Davies, *Peace*, p. 134; Thomas, *Religion*, and his exchange with Hildred Geertz in *Journal of Interdisciplinary History* 6 (1975):71–110; B. Capp, *Astrology*; C. Hill, *Society and Puritanism* (New York: Schocken, 1964); idem, "Propagating the Gospel," in *Historical Essays, Presented to David Ogg*, ed. H. E. Bell and R. L. Ollard (London: Black, 1963), pp. 35–59; idem, "Puritans and the 'Dark Corners' of the Land," *Transactions*, Royal

Historical Society, 5th ser. 13 (1963):77–102; Alan MacFarlane, *Witchcraft in Tudor and Stuart England* (New York, 1970). Slavin, "English," pp. 219, 219–20, 220, 221, 222; see also Maynard Smith, *Pre-Reformation*; Claire Cross, *Church and People, 1450–1660* (London: Harvester Press, 1976); A. G. Dickens, *The English Reformation* (New York: Schocken, 1968); Peter Heath, *The English Parish Clergy on the Eve of the Reformation* (London: Routledge and Kegan Paul, 1969); and related works. Heath presents a well-balanced accounting of the clergy's strengths and weaknesses.

131. Quoted in Heath, *Parish*, p. 193; Davies, *Peace*, pp. 149, 154; see also the literature on the early Protestant movement in England, by Maynard Smith, Clebsch, Porter, Knappen, George, McConica, and others.

132. Davies, *Peace*, pp. 155, 182, 190, 191; Dickens, *English*, chap. 6; see also the studies of English literacy, readers, and books cited above. Dickens, *English*, p. 135; Ferguson, *Articulate*; Caspari, *Humanism*; Simon, *Education*; Fisher, "Cromwell"; J. K. McConica, *English Humanists and Reformation Politics* (Oxford: Oxford University Press, 1965).

133. Dickens, *English*, pp. 190–91, 191–93; see also Aston, "Lollardy"; Cressy's studies.

134. Simon, "Reformation," pp. 49, 53, 54, 56, 59–60, 62, *Education*; see also the aforementioned works by Caspari, Ferguson, Hexter, Charlton, Stone, Leach, Jordan, Orme, Watson, Thompson. Compare with Leach's seminal studies.

135. Cressy, "Opportunity," pp. 301, 302–303, 304, 306, his other studies, esp. *Literacy*, cited above; Simon, *Education*, p. 294; the works of Leach, Watson, Orme, Jordan, Hill, Greaves, Stone, Morgan, James Axtell, Walzer, Lockridge; Lawrence Cremin, *American Education: The Colonial Experience* (New York: Harper and Row, 1970); and other works on English and New English Puritans and Puritanism; the writings of Comenius and other contemporaries.

136. Jordan, *Philanthropy*, p. 297; Cressy, "Opportunity," pp. 396, 306–309, 309–313, 313, "Levels," "Pre-industrial," "Literacy in Seventeenth-Century England"; David Cressy, "Social Status and Literacy in North-east England," *Local Population Studies* 21 (1978):19–23; idem, "Occupations, Migration, and Literacy in East London," *Local Population Studies* 5 (1970):53–60; his debate with Stone, *Journal of Interdisciplinary History* 8 (1978):799–801; his 1972 Cambridge University dissertation; and *Literacy and the Social Order*. See also the other studies of English literacy cited above, and Roger Schofield, "The Measurement of Literacy in Pre-industrial England," in Goody, *Literacy in Traditional Societies*, pp. 311–25; Richard T. Vann, "Literacy in Seventeenth-Century England," *Journal of Interdisciplinary History* 5 (1974):287–94; Carole Shammas, "The Determinants of Personal Wealth in Seventeenth-Century England and America," *Journal of Economic History* 37 (1977):675–89; W. B. Stephens, "Male Illiteracy in Devon on the Eve of the Civil War," *Devon Historian* 9 (1975); idem, "Male and Female Adult Literacy in Seventeenth-Century Cornwall," *Journal of Educational Administration and History* 9 (1977):1–7. On the urban-literacy relationship, see Clark, *Provincial*; the work of Cressy; and the studies of Clark and Slack, Clark, and Patten. See also W. P. Baker, *Parish Registers and Illiteracy in East Yorkshire* (York: East Yorkshire Local History Society, 1961).

137. Cressy, "Pre-industrial," pp. 223 (see tables 1–5), 238–39, see also *Literacy*; E. A. Wrigley, "A Simple Model of London's Changing Importance in English Society and Economy," *Past and Present* 37 (1967):44–70; Stone, "Literacy"; and other articles on literacy in towns and cities.

138. Cressy, "Levels," pp. 1, 2, 4, 6, 7, 7–8, 8, 9, 9–14, 17, 17–23, 21, 23. His work is now summarized in *Literacy*. All his writings address issues of definition, sources, and methodology. See also the studies of literacy cited above by Stone, Laslett, Wrightson and Levine, Vann, Spufford, Schofield, Thomas, Laqueur, Lockridge, Furet and Ozouf, and Clark. See, on reading, F. Davies, *Teaching*; Cressy, *Literacy*, chap. 2; Charles Hoole, *A New Discovery of the Old Art of Teaching Schoole* (London, 1660); M. M. Matthews, *Teaching to Read Historically Considered*; Graff, *Literacy Myth*, chap. 7 and the references therein.

139. Cressy, "Social Status," p. 23; see also Stephens, "Cornwall"; Thomas, *Religion*; Hill, " 'Dark Corners.' "

140. Wrightson and Levine, *Terling*, pp. 15, 144, 144–45, 145, 145–46, 146, 149, 151, 152; see also Laqueur, "Origins"; Cressy, *Literacy*; Burke, *Popular Culture*; Peter Burke, "Popular Culture in Seventeenth-Century London," *London Journal* 3 (1977):143–62; Thomas, *Religion*; Capp, *Astrology*; Graff, *Literacy Myth*, chap. 7; Spufford, "First Steps," *Contrasting*; studies of scribes.

141. Laqueur, "Origins," pp. 255, 256, 259, 261; see also Graff, *Literacy Myth*, chap. 5; and chap. 7 below; Spufford, "First Steps," *Contrasting*. I am wary of interpretations such as Laqueur's, which lose sight of the social and economic, not to add political, contexts of popular actions. In general, see Graff, *Literacy Myth*; Goody, *Domestication*; Goody and Watt, "Consequences," among the literature.

142. See Laqueur, "Origins"; Shammas, "Determinants"; Cressy, *Literacy*; Dickens, *English*; Davies, *Peace*; Hill, *Puritanism*, "Propagating," " 'Dark Corners' "; Walzer, *Revolution*; H. C. Porter, *Puritanism in Tudor England* (London: Macmillan, 1970); William Haller, *The Rise of Puritanism* (New York: Columbia University Press, 1938); C. F. Richardson, *English Preachers and Preaching* (New York: Macmillan, 1928); M. M. Knappen, *Tudor Puritanism* (Chicago: University of Chicago Press, 1939); C. H. George and K. George, *The Protestant Mind of the English Reformation* (Princeton: Princeton University Press, 1961); Clark, *Provincial*; Wrightson and Levine, *Terling*; Bennett, *Books*; and related studies.

143. Wrightson and Levine, *Terling*, pp. 152–53, 153–54, 156, chap. 6, passim, 171–72, chap. 7, passim, p. 180; see also Timothy Breen and Stephen Foster, "Moving to the New World: The Character of Early Massachusetts Immigration," *William and Mary Quarterly* 20 (1973):189–222; Thomas, *Religion*; Walzer, *Revolution*; Hill, *Puritanism, Society, Century*, "Propagating," " 'Dark Corners' "; Peter Clark, "The Alehouse and the Alternative Society," in Pennington and Thomas, *Puritans and Revolutionaries*, pp. 47–72; Valerie Pearl, "Puritans and Poor Relief: The London Workhouse, 1649–1669," in Pennington and Thomas, *Puritans and Revolutionaries*, pp. 206–232.

144. Laqueur, "Origins," pp. 267, 267–68, 268; Laslett, *World*; see also, for later examples, E. P. Thompson, *The Making of the English Working Class* (New York: Vintage, 1967); Graff, *Literacy Myth*, chap. 5; chaps. 6–7, below; see on popular literature B. Capp, *Astrology*; the many works of Victor Neuberg, and related studies; Burke, *Popular Culture*; Margaret Spufford, *Small Books and Pleasant Histories* (London: Methuen, 1981).

145. Burke, "London," p. 149, 151, 154–57, passim; his *Popular Culture*; Laslett, *World*; Keith Thomas, "Work and Leisure," *Past and Present* 29 (1961):50–66.

146. Spufford, "Schooling," pp. 113, 120, 120–22, 123, 124 (map), 126–27, 127–30, 130, 131–41, 136, 136–37, 141–47, 144, 145, 146–47, her *Contrasting*, chap. 6, and pt. 3; see also the other studies of English literacy for comparisons; studies of contemporary education. Virtually all other studies reveal quite similar patterns. Clark, *Provincial*, pp. 187, 188–201, 189, 190, 191, 191–92, 199, 213–14, 214, 215, 209–212, 209, 210, 211, 212, "Alehouse," "Book Ownership," pp. 100, 104, 103; Pearl, "Workhouse"; studies of literacy, reading instruction, e.g., Cressy, *Literacy*; Bennett, *Books*.

147. See Simon, *Education*, pp. 196, 216, 218, 218–19, chap. 5, 222, 285; Cressy, *Literacy*; B. Simon, ed., *Education in Leicestershire* (Leicester: Leicester University Press, 1968); William Baldwin, *Shakespeare's Petty School* (Urbana: University of Illinois Press, 1943); Curtis, "Education"; F. Davies, *Reading*; Norman Wood, *The Reformation and English Education* (London: Routledge and Kegan Paul, 1913).

148. Simon, *Education*, p. 287; Stone, "Literacy," pp. 120–27; Lockridge, *Literacy*; James Scotland, *The History of Scottish Education*, 2 vols. (London: University of London Press, 1969); Ian J. Simpson, *Education in Aberdeenshire before 1872* (London: University of London Press, 1947); John Edgar, *History of Early Scottish Education* (Edinburgh: James Thin, 1893); Lockridge, *Literacy*; Cressy, *Literacy*; Johansson, *Literacy*, all attempt comparative views, as did Stone, "Literacy," earlier. Now, see the pioneering new work of Rab Houston, *Scottish Literacy and the Scottish Identity*.

149. Simon, *Education*, p. 291, chap. 12, p. 313, chaps. 14, 15; see also Foster Watson, *The English Grammar Schools of 1660* (Cambridge: Cambridge University Press, 1908); Stone, "Educational Revolution," *Crisis, Family*, "Social Mobility"; Lawrence Stone, *The*

*Causes of the English Revolution*, 1529–1642 (New York: Harper and Row, 1972); Cressy, "Opportunity."

150. See Simon, *Education*. On literacy in Italy and the Netherlands, see Cipolla, *Literacy*, as well as this book. More studies on the continent are badly needed.

151. Curtis, "Education," pp. 68–70, 66–67; Yarborough, "Bristol"; Stephen Smith, "The London Apprentices as Seventeenth-Century Adolescents," *Past and Present* 61 (1973):149–61. Mildred Campbell, *The English Yeomen under Elizabeth and the Early Stuarts* (New Haven: Yale University Press, 1942); Margaret Gar Davies, *The Enforcement of English Apprenticeship: A Study in Applied Mercantilism* (Cambridge, Mass.: Harvard University Press, 1956); Jocelyn Dunlop and R. D. Denman, *English Apprenticeship and Child Labor: A History* (London: Fisher Unwin, 1912); D. C. Coleman, "Labour in the English Economy of the Seventeenth Century," *Economic History Review* 8 (1956):280–95.

152. Richard L. Greaves, *The Puritan Revolution and Educational Thought* (New Brunswick: Rutgers University Press, 1969), esp. chap. 3; cf. W. A. L. Vincent, *The State and School Education* (London: SPCK, 1950), but compare with Cressy's findings for the period.

153. Pearl, "Workhouse," pp. 209, 219, passim; see also Hill, *Society, Puritanism*.

154. On the equation of modernity with literacy for this period, see Bernard Bailyn, *Education in the Forming of American Society* (Chapel Hill: University of North Carolina Press, 1960); Cremin, *American Education*; Richard D. Brown, "Modernization and the Formation of the Modern Personality in Early America, 1600–1865: A Sketch of a Synthesis," *Journal of Interdisciplinary History* 2 (1972):201–228; idem, *Modernization* (New York: Hill and Wang, 1976); E. A. Wrigley, "The Process of Modernization and the Industrial Revolution in England," *Journal of Interdisciplinary History* 3 (1972):225–59. For an opposite argument, see Lockridge, *Literacy*; Graff, *Literacy Myth*.

155. For useful introductions and evidence, see Bailyn, *Education*; Cremin, *American Education*; Kenneth A. Lockridge, *Literacy*; idem, "L'alphabétisation en Amérique," *Annales: e, s, c* 32 (1977):503–518; idem, "Studying the Literacy of Early America," in Johansson, *Literacy and Society*, pp. 22–32; T. H. Breen and Stephen Foster, "Moving to the New World: The Character of Early Massachusetts Immigration," *William and Mary Quarterly* 30 (1973):189–222; Carl Russell Fisk, "The English Parish and Education at the Beginning of American Colonization," *School Review* 23 (1915):433–99; Virgil V. Phelps, "The Pastor and Teacher in New England," *Harvard Theological Review* 4 (1911):388–99; Morgan, *Puritan Family*; John Demos, *A Little Commonwealth* (New York: Oxford University Press, 1970); Edward Eggleston, *The Transit of Civilization* (New York: Appleton, 1900); Samuel Eliot Morison, *The Intellectual Life of Colonial New England* (Ithaca: Cornell University Press, 1956); Philip Greven, Jr., *Four Generations* (Ithaca: Cornell University Press, 1970), among his writings; David D. Hall, "The World of Print and Collective Mentality in Seventeenth-Century New England," in *New Directions in American Intellectual History*, ed. John Higham and Paul Conkin (Baltimore: Johns Hopkins University Press, 1979), pp. 166–80; David D. Hall, "The Uses of Literacy in New England, 1600–1850," in *Printing and Society in Early America*, ed. W. L. Joyce, David D. Hall, R. D. Brown, and J. B. Hench (Worcester: American Antiquarian Society, 1983), pp. 1–47; Joyce et al., *Printing*; James Axtell, *The School upon a Hill* (New Haven: Yale University Press, 1974); Kenneth A. Lockridge, *A New England Town* (New York: Norton, 1970); T. H. Breen, "Persistent Localism," *William and Mary Quarterly* 32 (1975):361–84; among the literature.

On schooling, see R. R. Reeder, *The Historical Development of School Readers and of Method in Teaching Reading*, Columbia University Contributions to Philosophy, Psychology, and Education, vol. 8 (New York: Macmillan, 1900); Sanford Fleming; *Children and Puritanism* (New Haven: Yale University Press, 1933); Herbert Baxter Adams, *The Church and Popular Education*, Johns Hopkins University Studies in Historical and Political Science, vol. 28 (Baltimore, 1900); Daniel H. Calhoun, ed., *The Educating of Americans* (Boston: Houghton Mifflin, 1967); Brown, "Modernization," *Modernization*; Shammas, "Determinants"; Carole Shammas "Constructing a Wealth Distribution from Probate Records," *Journal of Interdisciplinary History* 9 (1978):297–308; Linda Auwers, "The Social Meaning of Female Literacy: Windsor, Connecticut, 1667–1775," Newberry Papers in Family and Community History, 77–4A, 1977; Jon Butler, "Magic, Astrology, and the Early American Religious Heritage, 1600–1760," *American Historical Review* 84 (1979):317–46; Lockridge, *Literacy*, "L'alphabétisation"; Thad W. Tate and David L. Ammerman, eds., *The Chesapeake in the Seventeenth Century* (New York: Norton, 1979); Aubrey C. Land et al., eds., *Law, Society, and Politics in Early Maryland* (Baltimore: Johns Hopkins University Press, 1977); Edmund Morgan, *American Freedom/American Slavery* (New York: Norton, 1976); James M. Smith, ed., *Seventeenth-Century America* (Chapel Hill: University of North Carolina Press, 1959); Richard Beale Davis, *Literature and Society in Early Virginia* (Baton Rouge: Louisiana State University Press, 1973); idem, *Intellectual Life in the Colonial South*, 3 vols. (Knoxville: University of Tennessee Press, 1978); Wesley Frank Craven, *White, Red, and Black* (Charlottesville: University of Virginia Press, 1971); and the relevant literature on early modern English education, literacy, society, and religion, again, among a much larger literature. See, for example, Peter Laslett and John Harrison, "Clayworth and Cogenhoe," in Bell and Ollard, *Historical Essays*; Peter Clark, "Migration in England during the Late Seventeenth and Early Eighteenth Centuries," *Past and Present* 83 (1979):57–90; Stone, "Social Mobility."

156. See, in particular, the work of Lockridge. David Cressy is now studying in comparative context the literacy and communications of migrants to New England. David Galenson has written about the literacy levels of servant migrants to the South: "Literacy and the Social Origins of Some Early American Colonists," *Historical Journal* 22 (1979):75–91; idem, " 'Middling People' or 'Common Sort?' The Social Origins of Some Early Americans Reexamined," with a reply by Mildred Campbell and a rejoinder, *William and Mary Quarterly* 35 (1978):499–540, 36 (1979):264–86; idem, "British Servants and the Colonial Indenture System," *Journal of Southern History* 44 (1978):41–66. See also David Souden, " 'Rouges, Whores, and Vagabonds'? Indentured Servant Migrants," *Social History* 3 (1978):23–43. On the literacy-migration relationship, see the writings of Barbara Anderson, Larry Long, Sune Akerman and Egil Johansson, and Harvey Graff, all cited in Graff, *Literacy Myth*, chap. 2. Lockridge, "L'alphabétisation," p. 505; see also Cressy, *Literacy*. See among the studies cited above those by Breen and Foster, Spufford, Clark, Wrightson and Levine, and Cressy.

157. Lockridge, *Literacy*, pp. 43, 99. Compare, however, with Cressy, *Literacy*, chap.8.

158. Lockridge, "L'alphabétisation," p. 509. See also Cressy, "Levels." For example, see Alex Inkeles and David H. Smith, *Becoming Modern* (Cambridge, Mass.: Harvard University Press, 1974); Goody and Watt, "Consequences"; for my comments, see *Literacy Myth*, Introduction, as well as the Introduction and Epilogue to this volume.

159. Louise Dechêne, *Habitants et Marchants de Montreal au XVIIIe siècle* (Paris and Montreal: Plon, 1974), pp. 465–67.

160. Lockridge, *Literacy*, pp. 49–50 (his quotation is from Bailyn, *Education*, p. 27); Morison, *Intellectual*, p. 59; Lockridge, *Literacy*, p. 50; see also Axtell, *School*; Cremin, *American Education*; Calhoun, *Educating*, for documents.

161. Lockridge, *Literacy*, p. 15; see also the aforementioned works of Cremin, Bailyn, Morison, Axtell. Note also that the measure of the signature does underestimate the number of readers who were not writers (again confirmed in unpublished research by John Waters, University of Rochester). See also the writings of Fisk, Phelps, Eggleston. Note Cremin's review of Lockridge in *Reviews in Education* 1 (1975):517–21, and Michael Zuckerman's of Cremin, *AAUP Bulletin* 57 (1971):18–20.

162. Lockridge, *Literacy*, p. 38, passim; Auwers, "Social Meaning," p. 9, passim. See David Levine's studies of intergenerational literacy transmission, cited in chaps. 6 and 7 below. See also Mary Beth Norton, *Daughters of Liberty* (Boston: Little, Brown, 1980); Linda Kerber, *Women of the Republic* (Chapel Hill: University of North Carolina Press, 1980).

163. Lockridge, *Literacy*, pp. 15, 17, 22, 29; Bailyn, *Education*, pp. 48–49; Cremin, *American Education*, pp. 546–50. See also the writings of Axtell, Hall, Morgan, Demos, and Shammas, and those on English literacy.

164. Lockridge, *Literacy*, pp. 33, 35–36. More recently, John Frye ("Class, Generation,

and Social Change: A Case in Salem, Massachusetts, 1636–1656," *Journal of Popular Culture* 11 [1977]:743–51) argues that a deviant subculture existed in New England communities, which included literates as well as illiterates.

165. Butler, "Magic"; Lockridge, *Literacy*, p. 37; Frye, "Class."

166. Hall, "World," pp. 167, 169; see also Cremin, *American Education*; Axtell, *School*; Morison, *Intellectual*. Compare with Lockridge, *Literacy*; Butler, "Magic."

167. Morison, *Intellectual*, pp. 113, 115, 115–27, 127–32, chap. 6.

168. Morison, *Intellectual*, p. 71; see also Morgan, *Puritan Family*; Demos, *Commonwealth*; Cremin, *American Education*; Axtell, *School*. A number of the papers presented at the American Antiquarian Society, Conference on Printing and Society in Early America, October 1980, amplify these points; see Joyce et al., *Printing*.

169. Morgan, *Puritan Family*, pp. 88, 98, 101; see also Morison, *Intellectual*; Axtell, *School*; Cremin, *American Education*; Phelps, "Pastor"; Paul Leicester Ford, *The New England Primer* (New York, 1897); Demos, *Commonwealth*.

170. Galenson, "Literacy," pp. 80–81; see also Lorena S. Walsh, " 'Til Death Us Do Part': Marriage and Family in Seventeenth-Century Maryland," in Tate and Ammerman, *Chesapeake*, pp. 126–52; Souden, " 'Rouges' "; Smith, *America*, esp. the essay by Campbell, and her debate with Galenson; Craven, *White*; Morgan, *American Freedom*. Lockridge, *Literacy*, pp. 49–51, 76, 77, 73–87, 83, 84–87; see also the literature on the Chesapeake cited above and Tate, "The Seventeenth-Century Chesapeake and Its Historians," in Tate and Ammerman, *Chesapeake*, pp. 3–50; Galenson, "Literacy." Walsh, " 'Til Death,' " pp. 148, 148–49, 149, 150; Shammas, "Determinants," p. 689. See also extracts from the laws in Calhoun, *Educating*; Carole Shammas, "English-Born and Creole Elites," in Tate and Ammerman, *Chesapeake*, pp. 274–96, for an instructive comparison; Morgan, *American Freedom*; Russell R. Menard's studies of mobility; Philip Greven, Jr., *The Protestant Temperament* (New York: Knopf, 1977); Davis, *Intellectual*, chap. 3; Russell R. Menard and Lorena S. Walsh, "Death in the Chesapeake," *Maryland Historical Magazine* 64 (1974):211–27; Russell R. Menard, "Immigrants and Their Increase," in Land et al., *Early Maryland*, pp. 88–110; Darrett R. and Anita H. Rutman, "Of Agues and Fevers: Malaria in the Early Chesapeake," *William and Mary Quarterly* 33 (1976):31–60; idem, " 'Now Wives and Sons-in-Law': Parental Death in a Seventeenth-Century Chesapeake County," in Tate and Ammerman, *Chesapeake*, pp. 153–82; Lois Green Carr and Lorena S. Walsh, "The Planter's Wife," *William and Mary Quarterly* 34 (1977):542–71; Daniel Blake Smith, "Mortality and Family in the Colonial Chesapeake," *Journal of Interdisciplinary History* 8 (1977–78):403–427. Davis, *Intellectual*, pp. 262–63, chap. 3, passim; Calhoun, *Educating*; Cremin, *American Education*; Davis, *Literature*; Lockridge, *Literacy*; and other relevant literature cited above.

171. Cremin, *American Education*, pp. 240–41, bk. 1, pt. 2, passim; Davis, *Intellectual*, chaps. 3, 4; Davis, *Literature*. Joyce, *Printing*, also includes useful materials.

## 6. Toward Enlightenment/Toward Modernity

1. James A. Leith, "Unity and Diversity in Education during the Eighteenth Century," in *Facets of Education in the Eighteenth Century*, ed. James A. Leith, *Studies in Voltaire and the Eighteenth Century*, vol. 167 (1977), p. 14; for parallels elsewhere, see Leith, *Facets*, passim; Harvey Chisick, *The Limits of Reform in the Enlightenment* (Princeton: Princeton University Press, 1981); Franco Venturi, *Italy and the Enlightenment*, ed. Stuart Woolf, trans. Susan Corsi (New York: New York University Press, 1972); Hajo Holborn, *A History of Modern Germany* (New York: Knopf, 1959–1963), vol 2; W. H. Bruford, *Culture and Society in Eighteenth-Century Germany* (Cambridge: Cambridge University Press, 1965); Helen Liebel, *Enlightened Bureaucracy versus Enlightened Despotism in Baden, 1750–1792. Transactions* of the American Philosophic Society 55, no. 5 (1965); Mary Jo Maynes, "Schooling the Masses: A Comparative Social History of Education in France and Germany, 1750–1850" (Ph.D. diss., University of Michigan, 1977) [published in 1985 as *Schooling for the People* (New York: Holmes and Meier)]; Harry C. Payne, *The Philosophes and the*

*People* (New Haven: Yale University Press, 1976); Peter Gay, *The Enlightenment: The Science of Freedom* (New York: Knopf, 1969); Nicholas Hans, *New Trends in Education in the Eighteenth Century* (London: Routledge and Kegan Paul, 1951); Lawrence A. Cremin, *American Education: The Colonial Experience* (New York: Harper and Row, 1970), for introductions. See also text and notes below.

2. Leith, "Unity," pp. 14, 15; J. H. Plumb, "The New World of Children in Eighteenth Century England," *Past and Present* 67 (1975):64–95; Philipe Ariès, *Centuries of Childhood* (New York: Vintage, 1962); Georges Snyders, *La pedagogie en France aux XVII^e et XVIII^e siècles* (Paris: Presses Universitaires de France, 1965): Charles Tilly, "Population and Pedagogy in France," *History of Education Quarterly* 13 (1973):113–28; the writings of John Locke (convenient editions are those edited by Peter Gay and James Axtell); John A. Passmore, "The Malleability of Man in Eighteenth-Century Thought," in *Aspects of the Eighteenth Century*, ed. Earl R. Wasserman (Baltimore: Johns Hopkins University Press, 1965), pp. 21–46; Gladys Bryson, *Man and Society: The Scottish Inquiry of the Eighteenth Century* (Princeton: Princeton University Press, 1945); Payne, *Philosophes*; Gay, *Enlightenment*; Leith, *Facets*; among a larger literature.

3. Leith, "Unity," p. 16; James A. Leith, "The Hope for Moral Regeneration in French Educational Thought, 1759–1789," in *City and Society in the Eighteenth Century*, ed. Paul Fritz and David Williams (Toronto: Hakkert, 1973), pp. 215–29; Leith, *Facets*; Payne, *Philosophes*; Gay, *Enlightenment*; Stanley Ballinger, "The Idea of Social Progress through Education in the French Enlightenment Period," *History of Education Journal* 10 (1959):88–99; J.-R. Armogathe, "Les catéchismes et l'enseignement populaire," in *Images du peuple an XVII^e siècle—Colloque d'Aix-en-Provence, 25 et 26 Octobre 1969* (Paris: Armand Colin, 1973), pp. 103–122.

4. Leith, "Unity," p. 18. On ambivalence and the like, see Payne, *Philosophes*; Chisick, *Limits*; Victor Neuberg, *Popular Education in Eighteenth Century England* (London: Woburn Press, 1972); Carl Kaestle, " 'Between the Scylla of Brutal Ignorance and the Charybdis of a Literary Education': Elite Attitudes toward Mass Schooling in Early Industrial England and America," in *Schooling and Society*, ed. Lawrence Stone (Baltimore: Johns Hopkins University Press, 1976), pp. 177–91; Klaus Epstein, *The Genesis of German Conservatism* (Princeton: Princeton University Press, 1966); Leo Gershoy, *From Despotism to Revolution, 1763–1789* (New York: Harper and Row, 1944); Leith, *Facets*.

5. See, for example, Harriet B. Applewaite and Darlene G. Levy, "The Concept of Modernization and the French Enlightenment," *Studies on Voltaire and the Eighteenth Century*, vol. 84 (1971), pp. 53–98; Arthur Wilson, "The Philosophes in the Light of Present Day Theories of Modernization," ibid., vol. 58 (1967), pp. 1893–1913; Gay, *Enlightenment*; and the writings of J. O. Appleby and Thomas Nipperdey, cited below; E. A. Wrigley, "The Process of Modernization and the Industrial Revolution in England," *Journal of Interdisciplinary History* 3 (1972):225–59. Compare with Charles Tilly, ed., *The Formation of National States in Western Europe* (Princeton: Princeton University Press, 1975); Raymond Grew, ed., *Crises of Political Development* (Princeton: Princeton University Press, 1978); Theda Skocpol, *States and Social Revolutions* (Cambridge: Cambridge University Press, 1979). For criticisms of this approach, see the recent writings of Charles Tilly, Joyce Appleby, Robert Nisbet, and Dean Tipps.

6. Wilson, "Philosophes," p. 1908, quoting David Apter, *The Politics of Modernization* (Chicago, 1965), p. 1909.

7. Gay, *Enlightenment*, pp. 497–99; Payne, *Philosophes*; Chisick, *Limits*; Roland Mortier, "The Philosophes and Public Education," *Yale French Studies* 40 (1968):62–78; Ballinger, "Social Progress"; Leith, *Facets*; Liebel, *Enlightened*; Venturi, *Enlightenment*; E. A. J. Johnson, "The Place of Learning, Occupational Training, and 'Art' in Pre-Smithian Economic Thought," *Journal of Economic History* 24 (1964):129–44; Payne, *Philosophes*, p. 94; Chisick, *Limits*; Mortier, " 'Philosophes.' "

8. Payne, *Philosophes*, pp. 95, 96, 97, quotations from Payne; see also Epstein, *Genesis*; Chisick, *Limits*; Leith, *Facets*; M. G. Jones, *The Charity School Movement* (Cambridge: Cambridge University Press, 1933); Brian Simon, ed., *Education in Leicestershire* (Leicester: University of Leicester Press, 1968); Liebel, *Enlightened*; K. M. Baker, "Scientism, Elitism,

438 Notes to Pages 175–178

and Liberalism: The Case of Condorcet," *Studies on Voltaire and the Eighteenth Century*, vol. 55 (1967), pp. 129–65; Karl Weintraub, "Towards the History of the Common Man: Voltaire and the Condorcet," in *Ideas in History*, ed. Richard Heer and Harold T. Parker (Durham, N.C.: Duke University Press, 1965), pp. 39–64. Compare with Condorcet, see below.

9. Payne, *Philosophes*, p. 97. See also, for examples, Gershoy, *From Despotism*; William Doyle, *The Old European Order* (Oxford: Oxford University Press, 1978); Pierre Goubert, *The Ancien Regime* (New York: Vintage, 1974); Maynes, "Schooling"; Olwen Hufton, *The Poor of Eighteenth-Century France* (Oxford: Oxford University Press, 1974); Cissie Fairchilds, *Poverty and Charity in Aix-en-Provence* (Baltimore: Johns Hopkins University Press, 1976); Steven Kaplan, *Bread, Politics, and Political Economy in the Reign of Louis XV*, 2 vols. (The Hague: Martinus Nijhoff, 1976).

10. On earlier developments in England, see Johnson, "Learning"; for the eighteenth century, see Charles F. Mallett, "Community and Communication" in *City and Society in the Eighteenth Century*, ed. Paul Fritz and David Williams, pp. 125–47; Thomas Laqueur, *Religion and Respectability* (New Haven: Yale University Press, 1976), among his studies; Jones, *Charity*; Simon, *Education*; Michael Sanderson's articles cited below.

11. Payne, *Philosophes*, p. 100. See also Johnson, "Learning"; studies on and works of John Locke; Ariès, *Centuries*; Snyders, *Pedagogie*; Hans, *New Trends*; studies on French education cited below. The gap is the theme of Chisick's work.

12. Payne, *Philosophes*, pp. 97–98; Leith, *Facets*; Liebel, *Enlightened*; Epstein, *Genesis*; Chisick, *Limits*; Maynes, "Schooling"; H. C. Barnard, *The French Tradition in Education* (Cambridge: Cambridge University Press, 1922); idem, *Education and the French Revolution* (Cambridge: Cambridge University Press, 1969).

13. Payne, *Philosophes*, pp. 98, 99. See also, in general, Gay, *Enlightenment*; Chisick, *Limits*; Ballinger, "Social Progress"; Snyders, *Pedagogie*; Roger Chartier et al., *Education et Société en France* (Paris: Société de l'éducation Superieur, 1976); K. Martin, *French Liberalism*; Lester G. Crocker, *Nature and Culture* (Baltimore: Johns Hopkins University Press, 1963); Elizabeth Fox-Genovese, *The Physiocrats* (Ithaca, N.Y.: Cornell University Press, 1976); and other references on England, Spain, and Germany. On opposition in Germany, see, for example, Epstein, *Genesis*.

14. Douglas Dakin, *Turgot and the Ancien Régime in France* (London: Methuen, 1939), pp. 274–75. See also Snyders, *Pedagogie*; Payne, *Philosophes*; Gay, *Enlightenment*; Ballinger, "Progress"; W. H. Wickwar, *Baron D'Holbach* (London: Allen and Unwin, 1935), pp. 135, 135–36. See also Gay, *Enlightenment*; Payne, *Philosophes*; Arthur M. Wilson, *Diderot* (New York: Oxford University Press, 1972); Crocker, *Nature*; Snyders, *Pedagogie*; studies of Rousseau.

15. Payne, *Philosophes*, p. 100. See also Liebel, *Enlightened*; Chisick, *Limits*; Frederick Hertz, *The Development of the German Public Mind* (London: Allen and Unwin, 1962); Jones, *Charity*; Venturi, *Enlightenment*; Leith, *Facets*; Maynes, "Schooling," among the relevant literature.

16. Payne, *Philosophes*, p. 101, quoted p. 101, p. 102.

17. Payne, *Philosophes*, p. 102. See also Liebel, *Enlightened*; Holborn, *Germany*; Maynes, "Schooling"; Leith, *Facets*; Payne, *Philosophes*, p. 104; G. Bollème, *Les Almanaches populaires* (Paris: 1969); and the work of H.–J. Martin cited below. Payne, *Philosophes*, pp. 104–105, 105. See also Liebel, *Enlightened*; Leith, *Facets*.

18. See, for example, Condorcet quoted in Weintraub, "Towards," p. 56.

19. Olwen Hufton, "Review Article," *Historical Journal* 20 (1977): 975; Payne, *Philosophes*, pp. 106, 106–108. See also the works of Gay, Wade; and Weintraub on Voltaire; James A. Leith, "Modernisation, Mass Education, and Social Mobility in French Thought, 1750–1789," *Eighteenth Century Studies* 2 (1973): 223–38; Ballinger, "Social Progress."

20. Leith, "Moral," p. 215, passim; Norman Suckling, "The Enlightenment and the Idea of Progress," *Studies in Voltaire and the Eighteenth Century*, vol. 58 (1967), pp. 1461–80; Charles Frankel, *The Faith of Reason* (New York: King's Crown Press, 1948); Ballinger, "Social Progress"; Chisick, *Limits*; Gay, *Enlightenment*; Leith, "Moral," p. 218; see also Passmore, "Malleability," the works of Locke; Snyders, *Pedagogie*.

21. Quoted in Leith, "Moral," p. 226; see also James A. Leith, "The Idea of the Inculcation of National Patriotism in French Educational Thought," in *Education in the Eighteenth Century*, ed. J. D. Browning (New York: Garland, 1979), pp. 59–77; Ballinger, "Social Progress," pp. 90, 92–93. See also the works of Bury, Frankel, Manual, Tuveson, Randall, Smith, K. Martin, and Weintraub, and below.

22. Quoted in Payne, *Philosophes*, pp. 109, 110, 110–11. See also Leith, "Modernisation" and *Facets* for comparisons. But see Chisick, *Limits*.

23. Quoted in Payne, *Philosophes*, p. 111.

24. Payne, *Philosophes*, p. 114. See also Chisick, *Limits*.

25. Payne, *Philosophes*, p. 115; Gay, *Enlightenment*. On the actual fate of French experiments, see Chisick, *Limits*.

26. J. S. Schapiro, *Condorcet and the Rise of Liberalism* (New York: Harcourt Brace, 1934), pp. 106, 198, quoted p. 199, pp. 200, 201. See Chisick, *Limits*. See also works of Ballinger, Koyre, and Weintraub.

27. Schapiro, *Condorcet*, pp. 201, 203, 205, 206, 209–210. Note parallels with More's Utopia. See also Arthur Wilson, " 'Treated Like Imbecile Children' (Diderot): The Enlightenment and the Status of Women," in *Women in the Eighteenth Century*, pp. 89–104; Chisick, *Limits*.

28. S. T. McCloy, *The Humanitarian Movement in Eighteenth-Century France* (Lexington: University of Kentucky Press, 1957), pp. 233–34. See also Maynes, "Schooling"; François Furet and Jacques Ozouf, *Lire et écrire* (Paris: les séditions de Minuit, 1977); Gershoy, *From Despotism*; Barnard's studies; Leith, *Facets*; Chisick, *Limits*; D. N. Baker and P. J. Harrigan, eds., *The Making of Frenchmen* (Waterloo, Ontario: Historical Reflections, 1980).

29. See, for example, Joan Simon, "Was There a Charity School Movement? The Leicestershire Evidence," in Simon, *Education in Leicestershire*, compare with Jones, *Charity*; Laqueur's interpretation should also be compared with Sanderson's, Chisick's, and Maynes's.

30. Mary Jo Maynes, "The Virtues of Anachronism: The Political Economy of Schooling in Europe," *Comparative Studies in Society and History* 21 (1979): 613, "Schooling," and *Schooling in Western Europe* (Albany: State University of New York Press, 1985).

31. See, for example, Louise Tilly and Joan Scott, *Women, Work, and the Family* (New York: Holt, Rinehart, and Winston, 1978); David Levine, *Family Formation in an Age of Nascent Capitalism* (New York: Academic Press, 1977).

32. Thomas Nipperdey, "Mass Education and Modernization—The Case of Germany, 1780–1850," *Transactions*, Royal Historical Society 27 (1977): 157; Christopher Friedrichs, *Urban Society in an Age of War: Nordligen, 1580–1720* (Princeton: Princeton University Press, 1979), p. 234, chap. 8, passim. See also Gerald Strauss, "Lutheranism and Literacy: A Reassessment," in *Society in Early Modern Europe*, ed. Kaspar Von Greyerz (London: Allen and Unwin, 1984), pp. 109–123 and Strauss and Richard Gawthrop, "Protestantism and Literacy in Early Modern Germany," *Past and Present* 104(1984): 31–56.

33. Goubert, *Ancien Regime*, p. 263. See also Jean Delumeau, *Catholicism between Luther and Voltaire* (Philadelphia: Westminster Press, 1977); and M. Vovelle's work on Christianization; G. Bolleme, *La Bibliothèque Bleue* (Paris, 1971); R. Mandrou, *De la culture populaire* (Paris, 1964); Bollème, *Almanaches*; Peter Burke, *Popular Culture in Early Modern Europe* (New York: Harper and Row, 1978).

34. Bruford, *Eighteenth Century*, pp. 122–23, 123–24, 230, 232, 233–34. See also A. Ward, *Book Production, Fiction, and the German Reading Public* (Oxford: Oxford University Press, 1974); A. Pinloche, *La réforme de l'éducation en Allemagne* (Paris: Armand Colin, 1889); Eugenie Rendu, *De l'education populaire dans l'Allemagne du Nord* (Paris: Hachette, 1855); Thomas Alexander, *The Prussian Elementary Schools* (New York: Macmillan, 1918).

35. Holborn, *Germany*, p. 276; work of Brunschweig, Krieger, Rosenberg, Epstein, Hartung.

36. Fritz Hartung, *Enlightened Despotism* (London: Historical Association, 1957), pp. 17, 18; Bruford, *Eighteenth Century*; Henri Brunschweig, *Enlightenment and Romanticism in Eighteenth-Century Prussia*, trans. Frank Jellinek (Chicago: University of Chicago Press, 1974); Ward, *Book Production*.

37. Holborn, *Germany*, p. 276.

38. Epstein, *Genesis*, pp. 78–79, 78–81, 81.
39. Alexander, *Prussian*, pp. 8, 10, 13, 14, 16, 17, 17–21.
40. Gershoy, *From Despotism*, pp. 276, 276–77; Hartung, *Enlightened*; Leith, *Facets*, Holborn, *Germany*.
41. B. Becker-Cantario, "Joseph von Sonnenfels and the Development of Secular Education," in Leith, *Facets*, pp. 29–48; Maynes, "Schooling."
42. Maynes, "Virtues," pp. 613–14, 616, 614, 617, 620; "Schooling," vol. 1, passim.
43. Maynes, "Schooling," chaps. 2, 4, 5. See Peter Petschauer, "Improving Educational Opportunities for Girls in Eighteenth-Century Germany," *Eighteenth-Century Life* 3 (1976): 56–62.
44. Maynes, "Schooling," quoted on pp. 273, 285, 292, 294, chap. 6, pp. 331–32, passim. See also Ward, *Book Production*; on literacy and its acquisition, see articles by Margaret Aston and Margaret Spufford cited in earlier chapters; on changes in the family and work, see Tilly and Scott, *Women*; Hufton, *The Poor*; Olwen Hufton, "Women and the Family Economy," *French Historical Studies* 9 (1975): 1–22; and chap. 5 above.
45. Etienne François, "Die Volksbildung am Mittelrhein in ausgehenden, 18. Jahrhundert," *Jahrbuch für est-deutsche Landesgeschichte* 3 (1977): 277–304.
46. Ward, *Book Production*, p. 149; Rolf Englesing, *Der Burger als Leser: Lesergeschichte in Deutschland, 1500–1800* (Stuttgart, 1974), among his work.
47. On Eastern Europe, see, in Leith, *Facets*, the studies by Matyas Bajko, pp. 191–222, and Grzegorz Leopold Seidler, pp. 337–58; C. F. Cushing, "Books and Readers in Eighteenth Century Hungary," *Slavonic Review* 47 (1969): 57–77.
48. G. Ricuperati and M. Roggero, "Educational Policies in Eighteenth-Century Italy," in Leith, *Facets*, pp. 223–24, 224, 225, 228–29, 235, 239, 257–58, 258–59, 261, 262, 265, 268, 269. See also, for decline of communes, chap. 5 above; Venturi, *Enlightenment*, passim, and esp. pp. 203–204; Franco Venturi, *Alfabetismo e cultura scritta* (Perugea: Università Degli Studi, 1978); Cipolla, *Literacy*, p. 63; M. R. Duglio, "Alfabetismo e societa a Torino nel secolo XVIII," *Quaderni storici* 17 (1971): 485–509, esp. the tables. See also "Alfabetismo e cultura scritta," *Quaderni Storici* 38 (1978).
49. See chap. 5 below, and tables there; M. C. Rodriguez and B. Bennessar, "Signatures et niveau culturel . . . ," *Cahiers du Monde Hispanique et Lusa-Brasilien* 31 (1978): 17–46.
50. See especially Furet and Ozouf, *Lire*; Michel Fleury and Pierre Valmary, "Les progrès de l'instruction élémentaire de Louis XIV à Napoleon III," *Population* 12 (1957): 71–99; Jacques Houdaille, "Les signatures au mariages de 1740 à 1829," *Population* (1977): 65–89; Chartier et al., *Education*, chap. 3.
51. See, for example, Michel Vovelle, "Y-a-t-il une revolution culturelle au XVIII$^e$ siècle?" *Revue d'Histoire moderne et contemporaine* 22 (1975): 89–141; idem, "Maggiolo en Provence," *Revue Marseille* 88 (1972); or Jean Queniart's books and articles; on limitations of experiments, see Chisick, *Limits*.
52. Goubert, *Ancien Regime*, pp. 262–64. For a related attempt at a balanced account, see William Sewell, Jr., *Work and Revolution* (Cambridge: Cambridge University Press, 1980).
53. For the strengths and limitations of these data, see Fleury and Valmary, "Progrès"; Chartier et al., *Education*; Furet and Ozouf, *Lire*; Jean Queniart, "Les Apprentissages scolaires élémentaires," *Revue d'histoire moderne et contemporaine* 24 (1977): 3–27; Jean Meyer, "Alphabétisation, lecture, et écriture . . . en Bretagne," *95$^e$ Congres National des sociétés savantes*, Reims, 1970, vol. 1, pp. 333–53; among others.
54. Major source for this survey is the review by Fleury and Valmary. See their maps and tables, and also those in the above cited studies of Chartier et al. and Furet and Ozouf, among dozens of local and regional studies.
55. On this point and what follows, see Furet and Ozouf, *Lire*; Francois Furet and Vladimir Sachs, "La croissance de l'alphabétisation en France," *Annales, e, s, c* 29 (1974): 714–37.
56. Houdaille, "Signatures," pp. 70, 75, passim. See also Chartier et al., *L'Education*;

Maynes, "Schooling"; Vovelle, "Y-a-t-il"; E. LeRoy Ladurie's and Lutz Berkner's studies of inheritance.

57. Chartier et al., *Education*, p. 90. "Une France double" is their phrase. See also Goubert, *Ancien Regime*; Mandrou, *Modern France*.

58. Chartier et al., *Education*, chap. 3; Furet and Ozouf, *Lire*, passim, esp. their departmental graphs; for examples, see Vovelle, "Y-a-t-il"; and see below.

59. Chartier et al., *Education*, pp. 97–98; Furet and Ozouf, *Lire*, Francois Furet and Jacques Ozouf, "Literacy and Industrialization," *Journal of European Economic History* 5 (1976): 5–41; for England, see below, and chap. 7.

60. Chartier et al., *Education*, p. 98, and references there for Garden and other local-regional studies. See also Furet and Ozouf, *Lire*, and Harvey J. Graff, *Literacy in History: An Interdisciplinary Research Bibliography* (New York: Garland, 1981) for citations for French local and regional studies.

61. J. C. Perrot, *Génèse d'une ville modern: Caen au XVIII^e siècle* (Paris: Mouton, 1975). See chap. 7 below and chap. 5 above for more on literacy and migration. See also Graff, *Literacy Myth*, chap. 2.

62. Chartier et al., *Education*, pp. 99–100; Bernard Bonnin, "L'éducation dans les classes populaires rurales en Dauphiné," *Revue de Marseille* 88 (1972): 63–93, 65; Vovelle, "Y-a-t-il"; Furet and Ozouf, *Lire*; Maynes, "Schooling," among others, and below.

63. Chartier et al., *Education*, pp. 101, 100–101, 102, 103, 104, 105, 106, and the references given there. See also E. LeRoy Ladurie, *Peasants of Languedoc* (Urbana: University of Illinois Press, 1974); Bonnin, "L'éducation," pp. 64–65; Vovelle, "Y-a-t-il," "Maggiolo." See in general: bibliographies in Furet and Ozouf, Chartier et al., Graff, *Literacy in History*. See also as examples: Sylvie Cadieu-Sabatier, *Les protestants de Pont de Veyle au 17^e siècle* (Editions de Trevoux, 1975); Queniart, "Les apprentissages": Jean Queniart, "Deux Exemples d'alphabétisation: Rouen et Rennes à la fin du XVII^e siècle," *95^e Congrès des sociétés savantes*, Reims, 1970, histoire modern, vol. 1, pp. 355–66; Jean Nicolas, *La Savoie au 18^e siècle, Noblesse et bourgeois* (Paris: Maloine, 1979), pp. 930–31; Jacques Solé, "Lecture et classes populaires à Grenoble, " *Images du peuple au XVIII^e siècle*—Colloque d'Aix-en-Provence, 25 et 26 Octobre 1969 (Paris: Armand Colin, 1973), pp. 95–102; Harvey Chisick, "School Attendance, Literacy, and Acculturation," *Europa* 3 (1980): 185–220.

64. Maynes, "Schooling," pp. 37, 38, 38–40, 43, 54–55, 59, 72, 74ff., 100–101, 102ff., 103, 109–110, 116, 253–62, table 17—p. 267, pp. 287, 291, 294, 301, 305, 328, 329–30, 343, 384–85, 386, 387, quoted p. 391, pp. 392–93, 395–96, 399ff., 402ff.; passim, "Virtues." See also Vovelle, "Y-a-t-il"; Goubert, *Ancien Regime*; D. Julia and W. Frijhoff, *Ecole et Société* (Paris: Librairie Armand Colin, 1975); Chartier et al., *Education*; George Huppert, *Les Bourgeois Gentilshommes* (Chicago: University of Chicago Press, 1977), and his book on schools; Baker and Harrigan, *Making*, esp. pt. 2; F. de Dainville, "Effectifs des Collèges et scolarité." *Population* 10 (1955): 55–88; idem, "Collèges et fréquentation scolaire," *Population* 12 (1957): 467–94. In addition to other educational studies cited, see Albert Bourgeois, "Le clerc d'église et l'enseignement en Artois avant La Révolution," *Bulletin de la Société Academique des Antiquaires de Morinie* 18 (1954): 193–239; D. Julia, "L'enseignement primaire dans la diocèse de Reims," *Annales historiques de la révolution française* 200 (1970): 233–86; M. Laget, "Petites écoles en Languedoc," *Annales, e, s, c* 26 (1971): 1398–418; L'Abbé Allain, *L'Instruction Primaire en France* (Paris: Librairie de la Société Bibliographique, 1881); D. Julia and P. Pressly, "La population scolaire en 1789," *Annales, e, s, c* 30 (1975): 1516–61; Robert R. Palmer, "The Old Regime Origins of the Napoleonic Educational Structure," in *Vom Ancien Regime zur Französischen*, ed. Albert Cremer (Gottingen: Vandenhoeck and Ruprecht, 1978); L. Burnier, *Histoire Littéraire de L'éducation morale et religieuse en France* . . . 2 vols. (Lausanne: Georges Bridel, 1864); C. E. Elwell, *The Influence of the Enlightenment on the Catholic Theory of Religious Education in France* (Cambridge, Mass.: Harvard University Press, 1944); F. E. Farrington, *The Public Primary School System of France* (New York: Teachers College, 1906); Comte E. Fontaine de Resbecq, *Histoire de l'enseignement avant 1789* (Lille, 1878); Geraldine

Hodgson, *Studies in French Education* (Cambridge: Cambridge University Press, 1908); J. Morange and J.-F. Chaissing, *Le mouvement de réforme de l'enseignement en France* (Paris: Presses Universitaires de France, 1974); Charles Muteau, *Les écoles et collèges en Provence* (Dijon: Imprimèrie Darantière, 1882). On family economy, see Tilly and Scott, Hufton, Goubert.

65. Vovelle, "Y-a-t-il," pp. 98, 106, 108, 108–109, 111, 109–114, 114–32, 118, 121, 132–33, 140. See also Vovelle, "Maggiolo"; Furet and Ozouf, *Lire*, esp. chap. 6; Maynes, "Schooling"; Queniart, "Les apprentissages."

66. See Dominique Julia, "L'enseignement primaire dans le diocèse de Reims à la fin de l'Ancien Régime," *Annales historiques de la revolution francaise* 200 (1970): 233–86.

67. Jean Vassort, "L'enseignement primaire en Vendômis," *Revue d'histoire moderne et contemporaine* 25 (1978): 625–55. See also studies in Furet and Ozouf, *Lire*, vol. 2; Maynes, "Schooling"; Baker and Harrigan, *Making*; Vovelle, "Y-a-t-il"; Dainville, "Effectifs," "Collèges."

68. Harvey Chisick, "Institutional Innovation in Popular Education in Eighteenth Century France," *French Historical Studies* 10 (1977): 41, 46; see his *Limits*.

69. René Tavenaux, "Les écoles de campagne en Lorraine au XVIII siècle: à-propros d'une étude recente," *Annales de l'est* 52 (1970): 166, passim; Leith, "Moral Regeneration," p. 225, passim. See also Julia, "L'enseignement"; Maynes, "Schooling"; Furet and Ozouf, *Lire*. This question is in special need of more study.

70. For printing, see citations in earlier chapters. Robert Darnton, "Reading, Writing, and Publishing in Eighteenth-Century France," in *Historical Studies Today*, ed. F. Gilbert and S. R. Graubard (New York: Norton, 1972), p. 249.

71. Citations for Bollème and Mandrou are provided above. A new, realistic view of the sociocultural context is sketched in Eugene Weber, "Fairies and Hard Facts: The Realities of Folktales," *Journal of the History of Ideas* 42 (1981): 93–113. On colporteurs, see Pierre Brochon, *Le livre de colportage en France* (Paris, 1954); J. J. Darmon, *Le colportage de libraire en France* (Paris, 1972); Albert Labarre, *Histoire du livre* (Paris, 1970). For one summary, see G. Bollème, "Littérature populaire et littérature de colportage," in *Livre et Societe* 1 (Paris: Mouton, 1965): 61–92.

72. H.-J. Martin, "Bibliotèque Bleue," *Publishing History* 3 (1978): 74, 77, 78, 81, 82, 85, 86, 87–88, 88. See also the studies on book dealers by Robert Darnton: "Trade in the Taboo," in *The Widening Circle*, ed. Paul J. Korshin (Philadelphia: University of Pennsylvania Press, 1976), pp. 11–84; idem, *Business of Enlightenment* (Cambridge, Mass.: Harvard University Press, 1979).

73. Martin, "Bibliotèque," p. 88, 90 On language issues and problems, see the next chapter. See also, for France, Maynes, "Schooling"; Furet and Ozouf, *Lire*; Chartier et al., *Education*, chap. 3; Eugene Weber, *Peasants into Frenchmen* (Stanford: Stanford University Press, 1976).

74. Martin, "Bibliotèque," pp. 89, 90; Mandrou, *De la culture populaire*; Bollème, "Littérature populaire," pp. 75, 80; see also her *La Bibliotèque bleue, Almanaches.*

75. A. M. Van der Woude, "De alfabetisering," *Algemene Geschiedenis der Nederlanden*, vol. 7 (1980), pp. 257–64; Joseph Ruwet and Yves Wellemans, *L'Analphabétisme en Belgique* (Louvain: E.J. Brill, 1978).

76. H. A. Barton, "Popular Education in Sweden," in Leith, *Facets*, pp. 535, 536. See also B. J. Hovde, *The Scandinavian Countries, 1720–1860*, 2 vols. (Boston: Chapman and Grimes, 1943); Egil Johansson, *The History of Literacy in Sweden* (Umeå: University of Umeå, School of Education, 1977); idem, "Literacy Studies in Sweden," in *Literacy and Society in a Historical Perspective*, ed. Egil Johansson (Umeå: University of Umeå and School of Education, 1973), pp. 41–66; idem, "Reading and Writing Ability in Sweden and Finland" (unpub. ms.); idem, "Literacy and Popular Education in Sweden" (unpub. ms., 1972); Kenneth A. Lockridge, *Literacy in Colonial New England* (New York: Norton, 1974); idem, "Notes on the Definition, Quantity, and Quality of Literacy in Sweden" (unpub. ms., 1974).

77. Quoted in Egil Johansson, "Studying Literacy in Sweden in the Church Examination Registers" (unpub. ms., 1973), p. 7.

78. Barton, "Popular," pp. 527, 536, 537, 537–38, 539.

79. Johansson, *History*, p. 34, passim, "Literacy Studies"; for Finnish parallels, see Bill Widén, "Literacy in the Ecclesiastical Context," in Johansson, *Literacy and Society*, pp. 33–40; for Denmark, see Carol Gold, "Educational Reform in Denmark, 1784–1814," in Leith, *Facets*.

80. Richard F. Tommasson, "The Literacy of the Icelanders," *Scandinavian Studies* 57 (1975): 66–93.

81. Thomas Laqueur, "The Cultural Origins of Popular Literacy in England, 1500–1850," *Oxford Review of Education* 2 (1976): 255–75; idem, "Working-Class Demand and the Expansion of English Elementary Education, 1750–1850," in Stone, *Schooling and Society*, pp. 192–205; *Religion*.

82. See for introductions J. H. Plumb, "The Public, Literature, and the Arts in the Eighteenth Century," in Paul Fritz and David Williams, eds., *The Triumph of Culture* (Toronto: Hakkert, 1972), pp. 27–48; "New World"; Richard Altick, *The English Common Reader* (Chicago: University of Chicago Press, 1957); C. A. Cranfield, *The Press and Society* (London: Longman, 1978); E. P. Thompson, "Eighteenth-Century English Society: Class Struggle without Class?" *Social History* 3 (1978): 133–65.

83. Bernard Mandeville, *The Fable of the Bees*, 2 vols. (Oxford: Clarendon Press, 1924).

84. David Cressy, "Levels of Literacy in England, 1530–1730," *Historical Journal* 20 (1977): 9, 11, 22, 23. See also Jones, *Charity*; Simon, "Was There," pp. 55–100.

85. Lawrence Stone, "Literacy and Education in England, 1640–1900," *Past and Present* 42 (1969): 109. See also Levine, *Family Formation*; David Levine, "Education and Family Life in Early Industrial England," *Journal of Family History* 4 (1979): 368–80; Thomas Laqueur, *Religion and Respectability* (New Haven: Yale University Press, 1976), "Working-Class Demand;" Hans, *New Trends*, pp. 5, 6. See also Neuberg, *Popular Education*.

86. Roger Schofield, "Dimensions of Literacy, 1750–1850," *Explorations in Economic History* 10 (1973): 445–46, 446, 447, 449, 450–51, 453; idem, "The Measurement of Literacy in Pre-industrial England," in *Literacy and Traditional Societies*, ed. Jack Goody (Cambridge: Cambridge University Press, 1968), pp. 311–25. These articles outline his project, and explain and defend the methods. See also Stone, "Literacy"; Laqueur's writings; Rab Houston, "The Literacy Myth?: Illiteracy in Scotland, 1630–1760," *Past and Present* 96 (1982): 81–102; idem, "Illiteracy in the Diocese of Durham, 1663–89 and 1750–62," *Northern History* 18 (1982): 239–51; idem, "The Development of Literacy: Northern England, 1640–1750," *Economic History Review* 35 (1982): 199–216; W. P. Baker, *Parish Registers and Illiteracy in East Yorkshire* (York: East Yorkshire Historical Society, 1961); Victor Hatley, "Literacy in Northamptonshire," *Northamptonshire Past and Present*, 1966–1976. For the industrial revolution and nineteenth-century developments, see chap. 7 below; Michael Sanderson "Education and the Factory in Industrial Lancashire, 1780–1840," *Economic History Review* 20 (1967): 266–79; idem, "The Grammar School and the Education of the Poor, 1786–1840," *British Journal of Educational Studies* 11 (1962): 28–43; idem, "Social Change and Elementary Education in Industrial Lancashire, 1780–1840," *Northern History* 3 (1968): 131–54; idem, "Literacy and Social Mobility in the Industrial Revolution in England," *Past and Present* 56 (1972): 75–104; and debate with Laqueur, ibid. 64 (1974): 96–112; W. B. Stephens, "Illiteracy and Schooling in the Provincial Towns, 1640–1870," in *Urban Education in the Nineteenth Century*, ed. David Reeder (London: Francis and Taylor, 1977), pp. 27–48; Graff, *Literacy Myth*, chap. 5; E. G. West, "Literacy and the Industrial Revolution," *Economic History Review* 31 (1978): 369–83; idem, *Education and the Industrial Revolution* (London: Batsford, 1975); Levine, *Family Formation*, "Education" Rab Houston, *Scottish Literacy and the Scottish Identity* (Cambridge: Cambridge University Press, 1985).

87. Levine, "Education," pp. 368, 372, 375, 377, 378–79. *Family Formation* provides the background and context. Compare, however, with Neuberg, *Popular Education*; Laqueur's writings; Jones, *Charity*; Simon, "Was There." See also chap. 7 below.

88. Thompson, "Eighteenth"; E. P. Thompson, "Patrician Society, Plebian Culture," *Journal of Social History* 7 (1974): 382–405; idem, "The Moral Economy of the English

Crowd," *Past and Present* 50 (1971): 76–136; idem, *The Making of the English Working Class* (New York: Vintage, 1967); Robert Malcolmson, *Popular Recreations in English Society* (Cambridge: Cambridge University Press, 1973); Levine's work.

89. Laqueur, "Cultural Origins," pp. 255, 256, 259, 265, 267. See also Stuart MacDonald, "The Diffusion of Knowledge among Northumberland Farmers," *Agricultural History Review* 27 (1979): 30–39; chap. 5 above; Keith Thomas, *Religion and the Decline of Magic* (Harmondsworth: Penguin, 1973); Bernard Capp, *Astrology and the Popular Press: English Almanacs, 1500–1800* (London: Faber and Faber, 1979).

90. Thompson, "Eighteenth Century," pp. 155, 153, *Making*.

91. Laqueur, "Cultural Origins," p. 268; Leslie Shepard, *The History of Street Literature* (Detroit: Singing Tree Press, 1973); Robert Collinson, *The Story of Street Literature* (London: Dent, 1973); Neuberg, *Popular Education*; Victor Neuberg, *Popular Literature* (Harmondsworth: Penguin, 1977); idem, *The Penny Histories* (Oxford: Oxford University Press, 1968).

92. Plumb, "New World," pp. 65, 69, 70. See also Lloyd DeMause, ed., *The History of Childhood* (New York: Psychohistory Press, 1974); Lawrence Stone, *The Family, Sex, and Marriage in England* (London: Weidenfeld and Nicolson, 1977); Randolph Trumbach, *The Rise of the Egalitarian Family* (New York: Academic Press, 1978); Plumb, "The Public"; Hans, *New Trends*; Mallett, "Education"; the works of John Locke, esp. the editions of James Axtell and Peter Gay; John Money, "The Schoolmasters of Birmingham and the West Midlands," *Histoire sociale* 9 (1976): 129–58; Jones, *Charity*; Richard Thompson, "English and English Education in the Eighteenth Century," in Leith, *Facets*, pp. 65–84.

93. Thompson, "English," pp. 69, 71; Plumb, "New World"; Mallett, "Community and Communication," pp. 77–97.

94. Plumb, "New World," pp. 72, 80; Thompson, "English"; Money, "Schoolmasters." Laqueur, "Demand," pp. 196, 192, "Cultural Origins"; Plumb, "New World"; J. H. Higginson, "Dame Schools," *British Journal of Educational Studies* 22 (1974): 166–81; D. P. Leinster-MacKay, "Dame Schools," *British Journal of Educational Studies* 24 (1976): 33–48; Neuberg, *Popular Education*; J. Simon, "Was There."

95. Jones, *Charity*, p. 4, quoted on p. 76. See the interesting evidence of Griffith Jones, *Welsh Piety* (London: J. and W. Oliver, 1760); Sam Chandler, *Doing Good Recommended from the Example of Christ*, A Sermon Preached for the Benefit of the Charity-School in Gravel-Lane, Southwark, Jan., 1728 (London: John Gray, 1728); idem, *An Account of Charity-Schools in Great Britain and Ireland* (London: Joseph Dowling, 1711); idem, *An Account of Charity-Schools Lately Erected in England, Wales, and Ireland* (London: Joseph Dowling, 1706); idem, *Methods of Erecting, Supporting, and Governing Charity-Schools: With an Account of the Charity-Schools in Ireland* (Dublin: J. Hyde, 1721); George Lord William Broke, *The Blessings of The Poor*, A Sermon . . ., June 12, 1712 (London: Joseph Dowling, 1712); and, of course, the infamous position of Mandeville, *Fable*. See also Dorothy George, *London Life in the Eighteenth Century* (New York: Capricorn Books, 1965), pp. 218ff.; Mallett, "Education"; Charles Birchenough, *History of Elementary Education in England and Wales* (London: University Tutorial Press, 1938); H. C. Barnard, *A History of English Education* (London: University of London Press, 1961). On the limits of charity schools, see Laqueur, "Demand"; J. Simon, "Was There."

96. Laqueur, "Cultural Origins," pp. 257–58, 258–59, 259. See also his "Demands," pp. 257–58; Neuberg, *Popular Education*, chaps. 2–3, for examples. I disagree with Neuberg's interpretation. See my review in *History of Education Quarterly* 15 (1975).

97. Plumb, "The Public," pp. 27, 31, 34, "New World"; Cranfield, *Press*; A. S. Collins, "The Growth of the Reading Public during the Eighteenth Century," *Review of English Studies* 2 (1926): 284–94, 428–38; Hilda Hamlyn, "Eighteenth-Century Circulating Libraries in England," *Library*, 5th ser. 1 (1946): 197–222; James Sutherland, "The Circulation of Newspapers and Literary Periodicals, 1700–1730," *Library*, 4th ser. 15 (1934): 110–24; R. L. Walters, "Voltaire, Newton, and the Reading Public," in Fritz and Williams, *The Triumph of Culture*, pp. 133–55; R. M. Wiles, "Middle Class Literacy in Eighteenth Century England: Fresh Evidence," in *Studies in the Eighteenth Century*, ed. R. F. Brissenden (Canberra: Australian National University Press, 1968), pp. 49–66; idem, "Provincial Culture in Early Georgian England," in Fritz and Williams, *The Triumph of Culture*, pp. 49–68;

F. E. Compton, *Subscription Books* (New York: New York Public Library, 4th Bowker Lecture, 1939); Paul Kaufman, *The Community Library*, *Transactions* of the American Philosophical Society 57, no. 7 (1967); idem, "Readers and Their Reading in Eighteenth-Century Lichfield," *Library* 28 (1973): 108–115; idem, "Reading Vogues at English Cathedral Libraries," *Bulletin*, New York Public Library, vol. 62–63 (1963–64); idem, "English Book Clubs and Their Social Import," *Libri* 14 (1964); Michael Harris, "London Printers and Newspaper Production," *Journal of the Printing Historical Society* 12 (1977/78): 33–51; David Stoker, "The Establishment of Printing in Norwich," *Transactions*, Cambridge Bibliographic Society 7 (1977): 94–111; John Feather, "Cross-Channel Currents: Historical Bibliography and *L'histoire du livre*," *Library*, 6th ser. 2 (1980): 1–15 and *The Provincial Book Trade in Eighteenth-Century England* (Cambridge: Cambridge University Press, 1985); Alan Dugald McKillop, "English Circulating Libraries, 1725–50," *Library* 14 (1933/34): 477–85; E. S. Siebert, *Freedom of the Press in England* (Urbana: University of Illinois Press, 1952).

98. Wiles, "Middle Class," pp. 51, 52. Kaufman, *Community Library*, p. 37, and his other studies cited above. Wiles, "Middle Class," p. 55. See also Marjorie Plant, *The English Book Trade*, 2d ed. (London: Allen and Unwin, 1965); Colin Clair, *A History of Printing in Britain* (London: Cassell, 1965); F. A. Mumby, *The Romance of Book Selling* (London: Chapman and Hall, 1910); F. A. Mumby and Ian Norrie, *Publishing and Bookselling*, 4th ed. (London: Jonathan Cape, 1956); other relevant literature cited above. Raymond Williams, *The Long Revolution* (New York: Harper and Row, 1961), p. 181; Sutherland, "Circulation," for an early attempt at counting; Michael Harris, "London"; Cranfield, *Press*; George Boyce et al., *Newspaper History* (Beverly Hills, Calif.: Sage, 1978); Altick, *English Common*; among the literature. Wiles, "Middle Class," pp. 61, 59, "Provincial Culture"; Plumb, "The Public"; Collins, "Growth"; Williams, *Long Revolution*; Altick, *English Common*; Cranfield, *Press*.

99. Plumb, "The Public," p. 35; Malcolmson, *Recreations*; Graff, *Literacy Myth*, chap. 7.

100. Plumb, "New World," pp. 80, 81, "The Public," See also Altick, *English Common*; Cranfield, *Press*.

101. Neuberg, *Popular Literature*, pp. 105–106, *Popular Education*; Victor Neuberg, "Literacy in Eighteenth Century England," *Local Population Studies* 2 (1969): 44–46; idem, "Popular Education and Literacy" 4 (1972): 55–57.

102. Peter Laslett, "Scottish Cobblers, Weavers, and Miners Who Bought Books in the 1750s," *Local Population Studies* 3 (1969): 7, 8, 10, 10–11. R. E. Jones, "Book Owners in Eighteenth-Century Scotland," *Local Population Studies* 23 (1979): 34, 35.

103. Neuberg, *Popular Education*, p. 98, quoted p. 101, chap. 4, passim for examples, *Popular Literature*, *Penny Histories*. See also Weber, "Fairies."

104. Neuberg, *Popular Literature*, pp. 103, 105, 116, passim.

105. Neuberg, *Popular Education*, pp. 137–38, 118, 119–20, chap. 6, passim. For related studies of popular politics, see articles published in *Past and Present*; see also Thompson, "Eighteenth-Century," *Making*; Robert K. Webb, *The British Working Class Reader* (London: Allen and Unwin, 1955); John Brewer, *Party Ideology and Popular Politics* (Cambridge: Cambridge University Press, 1976). There is an obvious need for more detailed studies of working-class uses of literacy and print.

106. Malcolmson, *Recreations*, p. 1, passim. See also Keith Thomas, "Work and Leisure," *Past and Present* 29 (1966): 50–66.

107. See in general E. P. Thompson's writings. Thompson, "Eighteenth Century."

108. Lockridge, *Literacy*, pp. 99, 100. On the earlier period, see chap. 5 above. See also work of Houston, cited above, especially *Scottish Literacy*; T. C. Smout, "New Evidence on Popular Religion and Literacy in Eighteenth-Century Scotland," *Past and Present* 97 (1982): 114–27; Ian J. Simpson, *Education in Aberdeenshire before 1872* (London: University of London Press, 1947); James Scotland, *The History of Scottish Education*, 2 vols. (London: University of London Press, 1969); H. M. Knox, *Two Hundred and Fifty Years of Scottish Education, 1696–1946* (Edinburgh: Oliver and Boyd, 1953); Jones, *Charity*; John McFarlan, *Inquiries concerning the Poor* (Edinburgh: Longman and Dickson, 1782); John Edgar, *History*

*of Early Scottish Education* (Edinburgh: James Thin, 1893). See other secondary literature cited above.

109. Quoted in Scotland, *Education*, pp. 56, 57; Scotland, *Education*, p. 57, quoted on p. 57; see also McFarlan, *Inquiries*; Jones, *Charity*. Houston, *Scottish Literacy*, is now the place to begin.

110. McFarlan, *Inquiries*, pp. 235, 237, 237–45, 245–46, 247; see also pp. 247–70.

111. Knox, *Two Hundred and Fifty*, p. 3; Jones, *Charity*, pp. 167, 167ff. See also V. Durkacz, "The Source of the Language Problem in Scottish Education," *Scottish Historical Review* 57 (1978): 28–39.

112. Durkacz, "Source," pp. 28, 33, 38. See also Jones, *Charity*, esp. chap. 6. Jones's final sentence in this chapter is wholly unsupported.

113. See, in general, Donald H. Akenson, *The Irish Education Experiment* (London: Routledge and Kegan Paul, 1970), esp. chap. 2; James Johnston Auchmuty, *Irish Education* (Dublin: Hodges Figgis and Co., 1937), chaps. 1, 3, 4; Patrick John Dowling, *The Hedge Schools of Ireland* (London: Longmans, Green, 1935); Jones, *Charity*, chap. 7. For the nineteenth century, from and for which there is better evidence, see chap. 7 below.

114. Lockridge, *Literacy*, pp. 13, 15, 18, 21, 21–22, 22, 23, 27; see also Kenneth Lockridge, "Social Change and the Meaning of the American Revolution," *Journal of Social History* 6 (1973): 403–439; idem, "The American Revolution, Modernization, and Man: A Critique," in *Tradition, Conflict, and Modernization: Perspectives on the American Revolution*, ed. Richard M. Brown and Don E. Fehrenbacher (New York: Academic Press, 1978), pp. 103–119. Compare with Lawrence Cremin, *American Education: The Colonial Experience* (New York: Harper and Row, 1970); Bernard Bailyn, *Education in the Forming of American Society* (Chapel Hill: University of North Carolina Press, 1960); Samuel Eliot Morison, *Puritan Pronaos* (New York, 1936); David Hall, "The World of Print and Collective Mentality in Seventeenth-Century New England," in *New Directions in American Intellectual History*, ed. John Higham and P. K. Conkin (Baltimore: Johns Hopkins University Press, 1979), pp. 166–80.

In support of the interpretation presented here, see below, and Alan Tully, "Literacy Levels and Educational Development in Rural Pennsylvania," *Pennsylvania History* 39 (1972): 301–312; Harry S. Stout, "Culture, Structure, and the 'New' History," *Computers and the Humanities* 9 (1975): 213–30; idem, "Religion, Communications, and the Ideological Origins of the American Revolution," *William and Mary Quarterly* 34 (1977): 519–41; Rhys Issac, "Evangelical Revolt: The Nature of the Baptists' Challenge to the Traditional Order in Virginia," *William and Mary Quarterly* 31 (1974): 345–68; idem, "Preachers and Patriots: Popular Culture and the Revolution in Virginia," in *The American Revolution: Explorations in the History of American Radicalism*, ed. Alfred Young (DeKalb: Northern Illinois University Press, 1976), pp. 125–56; idem, "Dramatizing the Ideology of Revolution: Popular Mobilization in Virginia, 1774 to 1776," *William and Mary Quarterly* 33 (1976): 357–85; A. G. Roeber, "Authority, Law, and Custom: The Rituals of Court Day in Tidewater Virginia, 1720 to 1750," *William and Mary Quarterly* 37 (1980): 29–52. See also the study in progress of late-eighteenth-century Vermont by William Gilmore. Gilmore's literacy study is to be published in the *Proceedings*, American Antiquarian Society. A major book is forthcoming. For a novel perspective, see Daniel Calhoun, *The Intelligence of a People* (Princeton: Princeton University Press, 1973), and his unpublished studies of educational development. In their new book, Lee Soltow and Edward Stevens present original data for this period: *Literacy and the Rise of the Common School* (Chicago: University of Chicago Press, 1982).

115. Lockridge, *Literacy*, pp. 28 (and graph 6, p. 39), 42. On women's education, see the comments in Mary Beth Norton, *Liberty's Daughters* (Boston: Little, Brown, 1980); Linda Kerber's recent articles and book. John Waters, Rochester University, reports to me cases of reading but not writing literacy among women in historical studies.

116. Linda Auwers, "The Social Meaning of Female Literacy: Windsor, Connecticut, 1660–1775," *Newberry Papers in Family and Community History*, 77–4A, 1977, pp. 2, 9, 19, 25, 27, 27–28 (now published in *Historical Methods* 13 (1980): 204–214). See also the unpublished work of Kathryn Sklar, and Ross Beales, "Studying Literature at the Community Level: A Research Note," *Journal of Interdisciplinary History* 9 (1978): 100, 100–101.

117. Lockridge, *Literacy*, pp. 73–75, 75, 77, 78. See also David Galenson, "Literacy and the Social Origins of Some Early Americans," *Historical Journal* 22 (1979): 75–91; idem, " 'Middling People' or 'Common Sort'?: The Social Origins of Some Early Americans Reexamined," with a rebuttal by Mildred Campbell, *William and Mary Quarterly* 35 (1978): 449–540, and 36 (1979): 264–86; idem, "British Servants and the Colonial Indenture System in the Eighteenth Century," *Journal of Southern History* 44 (1978): 41–66. For a brief Canadian comparison, see Alan Greer, "The Pattern of Literacy in Quebec, 1745–1899," *Histoire Sociale* 11 (1978): 293–335; and my comment, ibid., 12 (1979); Louise Duchêne, *Habitants et Marchands de Montréal* (Paris and Montreal: Plon, 1974).

118. Lockridge, *Literacy*, pp. 36–37, 36, "Social Change," "American Revolution." See also Stout, "Culture," p. 224.

119. Lockridge, *Literacy*, pp. 33, 34, 35, 36, 86, 86–87, 95, 97ff.; see also Kenneth A. Lockridge, "The Modernization of Attitudes in Pre-industrial Anglo-America," Edinburgh Conference on Anglo-American Society, 1973; idem, "L'aphabétisation en Amerique, 1650–1800," *Annales, e, s, c* 32 (1977): 503–18.

120. Lockridge, *Literacy*, pp. 93–94; for England, see also the studies of Schofield, Cressy, Stone, and Laqueur, all cited above.

121. Stout, "Culture," p. 224, for his suggestions on linguistic analysis, pp. 225–27. See also James Axtell, *The School upon the Hill* (New Haven: Yale University Press, 1974); R. D. Davis, *Intellectual Life in the Colonial South*, 3 vols. (Knoxville: University of Tennessee Press, 1978); Carl F. Kaestle, "The Public Reactions to John Dickinson's *Farmer's Letters*," *Proceedings*, American Antiquarian Society 78 (1968): 323–59; Allan Raymond, "To Reach Men's Minds: Almanacs and the American Revolution," *New England Quarterly* 51 (1978): 370–95.

122. Roeber, "Authority," pp. 30, 31, 34, for his reconstruction of the ritual and examples, pp. 36–52, passim.

123. Stout, "Religion," pp. 520, 526, 527, 527–28, 530–31, 532, 534, 535, passim. See also Cremin, *American Education*; Axtell, *School*; Walter J. Ong, *The Presence of the Word* (New York: Simon and Schuster, 1970); idem, *Interfaces of the Word* (Ithaca: Cornell University Press, 1977); Gary Nash, *The Urban Crucible* (Cambridge, Mass.: Harvard University Press, 1979); Kaestle, "Reactions"; Raymond, "Almanacs"; Eric Foner, *Tom Paine and His America* (New York: Oxford University Press, 1976). It should be noted that Stout's analysis is controversial.

124. Isaac, "Dramatizing," pp. 360, 361–62, 358–60 for examples. See also his other articles, cited above. Isaac, "Preachers," pp. 132, 137, 138. See also Davis, *Intellectual*; Louise J. Hienton, *Prince George's Heritage* (Baltimore: Maryland Historical Society, 1972). On popular religion and popular mentalities, see Jon Butler, "Magic, Astrology, and the Early American Religious Heritage, 1600–1760," *American Historical Review* 84 (1979): 317–46; James Henretta, "Families and Farms: Mentalités in America," *William and Mary Quarterly* 35 (1978): 3–32. Kaestle, "Reaction"; Isaac, "Preachers"; see also Cremin, *American Education*; Bernard Ballyn and John Hench, eds., *The Press and the American Revolution* (Worcester, Mass.: American Antiquarian Society, 1980), esp. Weir's chapter on the press in the South.

125. Isaac, "Dramatizing," pp. 365–66, 366, 369, 370–78, 379–85. See also Bailyn and Hench, *Press*. For Clanchy and other earlier parallels, see chap. 3 above.

126. Isaac, "Preachers," pp. 142–43. See also William L. Joyce et al., eds., *Printing and Society in Early America* (Worcester, Mass.: American Antiquarian Society, 1983).

127. Kaestle, *Evolution*, pp. 1, 1–2, 5, 7, 9. See Cremin, *American Education*, pt. 5; Richard Morris, *Government and Labor in Early America* (New York: Columbia University Press, 1941); Marcus W. Jernagan, *Laboring and Dependent Classes in Colonial America* (Chicago: Chicago University Press, 1931).

128. See also Cremin, *American Education*; and compare with Leonard Woods Labaree, *Conservatism in Early American History* (New York: New York University Press, 1948). On the Enlightenment in America, see Cremin, *American Education*; Henry May, *The Enlightenment in America* (New York: Oxford, 1976); Henry Commager, *The Empire of Reason* (Garden City: Doubleday, 1977); Donald Meyer, *The Democratic Enlightenment* (New York:

Capricorn, 1976); David Lundberg and Henry May, "The Enlightened Reader in America," *American Quarterly* 28 (1976): 262–71; Allen O. Hansen, *Liberalism and American Education in the Eighteenth Century* (New York: Macmillan, 1926); Charles F. Arrowood, ed., *Thomas Jefferson and Education in a Republic* (New York: McGraw-Hill, 1930); Frederick Rudolph, ed., *Essays on Education in the Early Republic* (Cambridge, Mass.: Harvard University Press, 1965); the studies of Norton and Kerber, cited above; John C. Henderson, *Thomas Jefferson's Views on Public Education* (New York: Putnam's Sons, 1890); Roy J. Honeywell, *The Educational Work of Thomas Jefferson* (Cambridge, Mass.: Harvard University Press, 1931); Adrianne Koch, *The Philosophy of Thomas Jefferson* (New York: Columbia University Press, 1943); idem, ed., *American Enlightenment* (New York: Braziller, 1965); Francis N. Thorpe, *Franklin's Influence in American Education* (Washington, D.C.: U.S. Bureau of Education, 1903); Thomas Woody, ed., *Educational Views of Benjamin Franklin* (New York: McGraw-Hill, 1931). See the references on colonial education provided above. Cremin's survey provides an excellent bibliography to 1970, but it is not a satisfactory account itself. See also Bailyn and Hench, *Press*.

129. Cremin, *American Education*, p. 388.

130. Arthur Benedict Berthold, *American Colonial Printing as Determined by Cultural Forces* (New York: Burt Franklin, 1970 [1935]), pp. 31, 29, chap. 4, for examples. For reading on "enlightened readers," see Lundberg and May, "The Enlightened Reader in America," *American Quarterly* 28 (1976): 262–71. See also Bailyn and Hench, *Press*, esp. Tanselle's chapter, and papers from the 1980 "Printing and Society" Conference.

131. Lawrence C. Wroth, in Hellmut Lehmann–Haupt, *The Book in America*, 2d ed. (New York: Bowker, 1951), pp. 17, 26; Frederick Hamilton, *A Brief History of Printing in America* (Chicago: United Typothetae, 1918), p. 24; other relevant literature cited above; Bailyn and Hench, *Press*.

132. Cremin, *American Education*, p. 547.

133. Hamilton, *Printing*, pp. 24, 25; Cremin, *American Education*, esp. chap. 18; Kaestle, "Reaction"; Richard Merritt, *Symbols of American Community* (New Haven: Yale University Press, 1966).

134. Cremin, *American Education*, p. 389, passim; Raymond, "Almanacs"; Butler, "Magic"; Frank Luther Mott, *A History of American Magazines*, 5 vols. (Cambridge, Mass.: Harvard University Press, 1930–68); idem, *American Journalism*, rev. ed. (New York: Macmillan, 1950); Jesse Shera, *Foundations of the Public Library* (Chicago: University of Chicago Press, 1949); H. W. Boynton, *Annals of American Bookselling* (New York: Wiley, 1932); Paul L. Ford, ed., *The New England Primer* (New York, 1897).

135. Stout, "Culture," p. 225; Cremin, *American Education*, pp. 548–50, see also pp. 544–61, passim. For analogous interpretations, see Richard D. Brown, *Modernization: The Transformation of American Life, 1600–1865* (New York: Hill and Wang, 1976); Bailyn, *Education*; James Lemon, "Early Americans and Their Social Environment," *Journal of Historical Geography* 6 (1980): 115–31; Joseph J. Ellis, "Culture and Capitalism in Prerevolutionary America," *American Quarterly* 31 (1979): 169–86. For criticisms, see above; Lockridge, *Literacy*; Tully, "Literacy"; Michael Zuckerman, review of Cremin in *Bulletin*, American Association of University Professors 57 (1971): 18–20.

136. Kaestle, "Reaction."

137. Dirk Hoerder, *Crowd Action in Revolutionary Massachusetts, 1765–1780* (New York: Academic Press, 1977); Nash, *Urban*.

138. Lockridge, *Literacy*, "Social Change," "American Revolution"; Michael Zuckerman, "The Fabrication of Identity in Early America," *William and Mary Quarterly* 34 (1977): 183–214; Joyce Appleby, "Modernization Theory and the Formation of Modern Social Theories in England and America," *Comparative Studies in Society and History* 20 (1978): 259–85; Henretta, "Families and Farms."

139. Lockridge, "Social Change," pp. 427–28.

140. Henretta, "Families and Farms," pp. 15, 25; see also Lockridge, "American Revolution"; Lockridge, "American Revolution," p. 118.

## 7. The Nineteenth-Century Origins of Our Times

1. Carlo Cipolla, *Literacy and Development in the West* (Hardmonsworth: Penguin, 1969); Robert Nisbet, *History and Social Change* (New York: Oxford, 1969); Dean C. Tipps, "Modernization Theory and the Comparative Study of Societies," *Comparative Studies in Society and History* 15 (1973): 199–266; Ian Weinberg, "The Problem of Convergence," *Comparative Studies in Society and History*, 11 (1969): 1–15; the writings of Charles Tilly; Syzmon Chodak; Manfred Stanley; E. A. Wrigley, "The Process of Modernization and the Industrial Revolution," *Journal of Interdisciplinary History* 3 (1972): 225–59; Joyce Appleby, "Modernization Theory and the Formation of Modern Social Theories in England and America," *Comparative Studies in Society and History* 20 (1978): 259–85. For one view of nineteenth-century literacy development, see Harvey J. Graff, *The Literacy Myth: Literacy and Social Structure in the Nineteenth-Century City* (New York: Academic Press, 1979). See also M.J. Maynes, *Schooling in Western Europe* (Albany: State University of New York Press, 1985).

2. See Peter Meyers, *The Modernization of Education in Nineteenth Century Europe* (St. Louis: Forum Press, 1977). This example is merely one representative case.

3. Recent writings on institutional development include David Rothman, *The Discovery of the Asylum* (Boston: Little Brown, 1971); Michael B. Katz, "The Origins of Public Education: A Reassessment," *History of Education Quarterly* 16 (1976): 381–408; idem, "Origins of the Institutional State," *Marxist Perspectives* 1 (1978): 6–23; Graff, *Literacy Myth*; among others. See also Peter Flora, "Historical Processes of Social Mobilization, Urbanization, and Literacy, 1850–1965," in *Building States and Nations*, vol. 1, ed. S. N. Eisenstadt and Stein Rokken (Beverly Hills, Calif.: Sage, 1973), pp. 213–58; Wolfram Fischer, "Social Tensions at Early Stages of Industrialization," *Comparative Studies in Society and History* 9 (1966): 64–83. The following sketch is an expansion and an amendment of the interpretation offered in Graff, *Literacy Myth*, esp. chap. 1, passim.

4. See, for example, Victor Neuberg, *Popular Education in Eighteenth Century England* (London: Woburn Press, 1971); *Papers* of such groups as the London Central Society of Education.

5. Susan Houston, "The Victorian Origins of Juvenile Delinquency," *History of Education Quarterly* 12 (1972): 259.

6. For development of this concept, see Graff, *Literacy Myth*, chap. 1. E. P. Thompson, "The Moral Economy of the English Crowd," *Past and Present* 50 (1971): 79, 78. On moral economy, see also Louis Tilly on bread riots, Steven Kaplan on eighteenth-century France; Charles Tilly, ed., *The Formation of National States in Western Europe* (Princeton: Princeton University Press, 1975).

7. Allison Prentice, "The School Promoters," (Ph.D. diss., University of Toronto, 1974), p. 200; see also her book *The School Promoters* (Toronto: McClelland and Stewart, 1977).

8. Katz, "Origins," p. 391, Mary Jo Maynes, "Schooling the Masses," (Ph.D. diss., University of Michigan, 1977); Richard Johnson, "Notes on the Schooling of the English Working Class," in *Schooling and Capitalism*, ed. Roger Dale, Geoff Esland, and Madeleine McDonald (London: Routledge and Kegan Paul, 1976), pp. 44–54; among the literature.

9. *Selections from the Prison Notebooks*, ed. and trans. Q. Hoare and G. N. Smith (London: NLB, 1971), p. 242. We should note the parallels with much of schoolmen's and reformers' writing during the period.

10. Hoare and Smith, *Selections*, p. 12; John Cammett, *Antonio Gramsci and the Origins of Italian Communism* (Stanford: Stanford University Press, 1967), p. 204; Gwyn Williams, "The Concept of 'Egemonia,' " *Journal of the History of Ideas* 21 (1966): 587. See also Introduction above. E. J. Hobsbawm, "Religion and Socialism," *Marxist Perspectives* 1 (1978): 22. This interpretation is indebted to the pioneering work of David B. Davis, A. S. Kraditor, Raymond Williams, Walter Adamson, Eugene Genovese, R. W. Connell, Richard Johnson, and Michael Katz.

11. See Michel Fleury and Pierre Valmary, "Les progrès de l'instruction élémentaire de Louis XIV à Napoléon III d'après l'enquête de Louis Maggliolo," *Population* 12 (1957): 71–99. See, in general, the survey presented in François Furet and Jacques Ozouf, *Lire et écrire* (Paris: Les éditions de Minuit, 1977), and other citations in chap. 6 above, and below. In general, see Donald N. Baker and Patrick J. Harrigan, eds., *The Making of Frenchmen* (Waterloo, Ontario: Historical Reflections Press, 1980). Jacques Ozouf, "Le peuple et l'école: note sur la demand populaire d'instruction en France au XIX^e siècle,' *Melanges d'Histoire Sociale Offerts à Jean Maîtron* (Paris: Les editions Ouvrières, 1976), p. 167. Cipolla, *Literacy*, table 25, pp. 117–18; Furet and Ozouf, *Lire*.

12. Cipolla, *Literacy* table 28A, pp. 121–23, table 26, p. 119.

13. Cipolla, *Literacy*, table 28B, pp. 123–25.

14. Cipolla, *Literacy*; François Furet and V. Sachs, "La croissance de l'alphabètisation en France, XVIII^e-XIX^e siècle," *Annales: e,s,c* (1974): 714–37; Furet and Ozouf, *Lire*; John Shaffer, "Family, Class, and Young Women," *Journal of Family History* 3 (1978): 62–77.

15. See Fleury and Valmary, "Les progrès"; Jacques Houdaille, "Les signatures au mariage de 1740 à 1829,' *Population* (1977): 65–89; Furet and Ozouf, *Lire*.

16. Houdaille, "Les signatures"; Furet and Ozouf, *Lire*; Raymond Oberlé, "Etude sur l'analphabètisme à Mulhouse an siècle de l'industrialisation," *Bulletin*, Musée Historique de Mulhouse 67 (1959): 99–110; Alain Corbin, "Pour une étude sociologique de la croissance de l'analphabètisation (au XIX^e siècle)," *Revue d'histoire économique et sociale* 53 (1975): 99–120; Michel Vovelle, "Y-a-t-il eu une révolution culturelle au XVIII^e siècle? A propos de l'éducation populaire en Provence," *Revue d'historie moderne et contemporaine* 22 (1975): 89–141; Dominique Julia, "L'enseignement primaire dans le diocese de Reims à la fin de l'Ancien Régime," *Annales historiques de la Révolution français* 200 (1970): 233–86; M. Laget, "Petites écoles en Languedoc au XVIII^e siècle," *Annales: e, s, c* 26 (1971): 1390–418; René Tavenaux, "Les écoles de campagne en Lorraine au XVIII siècle," *Annales de L'Est* 62 (1970): 159–71; Maynes, "Schooling"; R. Chartier, M. M. Compère, and D. Julia, *L'Education en France* (Paris: Société d'edition d'enseignement supérieur, 1976), esp. chap. 3; Jean Vassort, "Enseignement primaire en Vendômois à l'Epoque Révolutionnaire," *Revue d'Histoire Moderne et Contemporaine* 25 (1978): 625–55; D. Julia and P. Pressly, "La population scolaire en 1789," *Annales: e, s, c* 20 (1975): 1516–61; Jean Meyer, "Alphabètisation, lecture et écriture: essai sur l'instruction populaire en Bretagne du XVI^e au XIX^e siècle," *Congrès national des sociétés savantes* 95 (1970): 333–53; Robert Gildea, "Education in Nineteenth-Century Brittany: Ille-et-Vilaine, 1800–1914," *Oxford Review of Education* 2 (1976): 215–30; J.-P. Aron, P. Dumont, and E. LeRoy Ladurie *Anthropologie du Conscripts français* (Paris–The Hague: Mouton, 1972); M. Fresel-Lozey, *Histoire démographique d'un village en Bearn* (Bourdeaux: Bière, 1969); Le Roy Ladurie's several papers on nineteenth-century French recruits.

17. Furet and Sachs "La croissance," as reprinted in *Historical Methods Newsletter* 7 (1974), summary of French original, p. 146. Furet and Sachs, "La croissance," p. 726 and map; see also Furet and Ozouf, *Lire*, maps, passim.

18. Furet and Sachs, "La croissance," p. 730.

19. Furet and Ozouf, *Lire*, esp. chap. 2; Houdaille, "Les signatures."

20. H. C. Barnard, *Education and the French Revolution* (Cambridge:. Cambridge University Press, 1969), pp. 210, 211, 212–13, chap. 16, passim.

21. See, for example, the studies of Furet and Ozouf, Gontard, Barnard, Julia and Pressly, Vassort, and Vovelle, among others.

22. James A. Leith, "Modernisation, Mass Education, and Social Mobility in French Thought, 1750–1789," in *Studies in the Eighteenth Century*, vol. 2, ed. R. F. Brissenden (Canberra: Australian National University Press, 1973), pp. 263, 238. See also idem, "The Hope for Moral Regeneration in French Educational Thought, 1750–1789," in *City and Society in the Eighteenth Century*, ed. Paul Fritz and David Williams (Toronto: Hakkert, 1973), pp. 215–29; Furet and Ozouf, *Lire*; Maurice Gontard, *L'enseignement primaire en France de la Révolution à la loi Guizot* (Paris: Société d'édition des belles lettres, n.d.), for

early nineteenth century; Maynes, "Schooling"; among others. Furet and Ozouf, *Lire*, p. 113.

23. Ibid., pp. 97, 97–98, 108, 108–109, 110; Gontard, *L'enseignement*.

24. Furet and Ozouf, *Lire*, esp. chap. 3; Gontard, *L'enseignement*; Antoine Prost, *L'enseignement en France* (Paris: Armand Colin, 1968).

25. Maynes, "Schooling," chaps. 1, 2; p. 68. See also Mary Jo Maynes, "The Virtues of Archaism: The Political Economy of Schooling in Europe, 1750–1850," *Comparative Studies in Society and History* 21 (1979): 611–25 and *Schooling the People* (New York: Holmes and Meier, 1985). See other local studies cited above, and Furet and Ozouf, *Lire*, passim.

26. Maynes, "Schooling," pp. 76, 78, 84–85, 86, 91, 132, 134, 147, 152–54, 180, 181–82. See also Furet and Ozouf, *Lire*; Gontard, *L'enseignement* among others. Quoted in Maynes "Schooling," pp. 193, 193–94.

27. Maynes "Schooling" pp. 209, 212, 239, chap. 5 pp. 270, 279. For graphs on literacy, see Maynes "Schooling," pp. 290ff., and chap. 6 above. See also Furet and Ozouf, *Lire*, among other references.

28. Maynes "Schooling," pp. 295–300; figures 12a-h, pp. 296ff. See also Furet and Ozouf, *Lire*, esp. chap. 6.

29. Maynes, "Schooling," p. 303; Shaffer, "Family." Maynes, "Schooling," p. 331, chap. 6; see also Furet and Ozouf, *Lire*; Ozouf, "Le peuple." For a later period, compare with Louise Tilly, "Individual Lives and Family Strategies in the French Proletariat," *Journal of Family History* 4 (1979): 137–52 among her studies. Maynes "Schooling," pp. 384–85; the works of Corbin, Oberlé, Furet and Ozouf, Shaffer, and Tilly cited above; Alain Darbel, "Inégalités régionales ou inegalités sociales? Essai d'explication des taux de scolarisation," *Revue française de sociologie* 8 (1976): 140–66; Lenard R. Berlanstein, "Growing Up as Workers in Nineteenth-Century Paris," *French Historical Studies* 11 (1980): 551–76.

30. Maynes, "Schooling," pp. 396, 296–397, 409–410, chap. 6, passim. Recent studies of the French working class are highly relevant in these respects. For the more recent period, important studies are those of Pierre Bourdieu and Fritz Ringer.

31. Furet and Ozouf, *Lire*; Maynes, "Schooling," chap. 7, pp. 442–54.

32. Charles Tilly "Population and Pedagogy in France," *History of Education Quarterly*, 13 (1973): 113–28; Maynes, "Schooling,"chap. 7, p. 459; Philippe Ariès, *Centuries of Childhood* (New York: Vintage, 1962); Harvey J. Graff, "Literacy, Education and Fertility, Past and Present," *Population and Development Review* 5 (1979); the papers of John Caldwell.

33. Charles Tilly "Did the Cake of Custom Break?" in *Class Consciousness and Class Experience in Nineteenth-Century Europe*, ed. John Merriman (New York: Holmes and Meier, 1979), pp. 17–44; Flora, "Historical Processes"; Graff, *Literacy Myth*, passim.

34. François Furet and Jacques Ozouf, "Literacy and Industrialization: The Case of the Departement du Nord in France," *Journal of European Economic History* 5 (1976): 5, 15, 18, 24, 25, 25–26, 26. This article is included as a chapter in *Lire*, chaps. 5, 6. See also Flora, "Historical Processes"; Corbin, "Pour une étude"; Oberlé, "Etude"; L. Tilly's articles on family strategies; Graff, *Literacy Myth*, chap. 5; Roger Schofield, "Dimensions of Illiteracy," *Explorations in Economic History* 10 (1973): 437–54; and the studies of Michael Sanderson and W. B. Stephens, cited in chap. 6. Furet and Ozouf, "Literacy," p. 28. See also the writings of Louise Tilly and Joan Scott on women and the family. Compare with Edward Shorter, *The Making of the Modern Family* (New York: Basic Books, 1975) Furet and Ozouf, "Literacy," pp. 34–35, 35. See also L. Tilly's several studies; Raymond Oberlé, "Etude." Furet and Ozouf, "Literacy," p. 40; see also their *Lire*. For a relevant English comparison, see David Levine, *Family Formation in an Age of Nascent Capitalism* (New York: Academic Press, 1977), and his articles on literacy and family life, cited in chap. 6. For French comparisons, see the work of Oberlé, Corbin, and L. Tilly, cited above. More generally, on urbanization, industrialization, and literacy, see Furet and Ozouf, *Lire*, passim.

35. Eugen Weber, *Peasants into Frenchmen* (Stanford: Stanford University Press, 1976), pp. 302, 303, 304ff., 306. For useful critiques, see Tilly, "Did the Cake." See also work of Furet and Ozouf, Maynes, and others on the schools. Weber, *Peasants*, pp. 310, 308, 318, 319, 320ff., 321, 322. See also Furet and Ozouf, *Lire*; J. Hébrard, "Ecole et alphabètisation au XIX^e siècle," *Annales; e, s, c* 35 (1980): 66–80. Corbin, "Pour une étude," p. 115, passim. See also Furet and Ozouf, *Lire*, esp. chap. 5.

36. Weber *Peasants*, p. 323, quoted on pp. 325, 325–26, 326. For my tastes, his chap. 18 is far too narrow. For interesting comparisons with North America, see Graff, *Literacy Myth*, pt. 1; Lee Soltow and Edward Stevens, *The Rise of Literacy and the Common School* (Chicago: University of Chicago Press), 1981).

37. William H. Sewell, Jr., "Social Mobility in a Nineteenth-Century European City: Some Findings and Implications," *Journal of Interdisciplinary History* 7 (1976); 222–23, 224, 228, *Structure and Mobility: The Men and Women of Marseille, 1820–1870* (Cambridge: Cambridge University Press, 1985). See also Mary Lynn McDougall, "Consciousness and Community," *Journal of Social History* 12 (1978): 129–45. Compare with Teresa McBride, "Social Mobility for the Lower Classes: Domestic Servants in France,' *Journal of Social History* 8 (1975): 63–78; idem, *The Domestic Revolution* (New York:. Holmes and Meier, 1976); Weber, *Peasants*; Oberlé, "Etude." See also Graff, *Literacy Myth*, and references cited there.

38. E. LeRoy Ladurie, "The Conscripts of 1868," in his *Territory of the Historian* (Chicago: University of Chicago Press, 1979), pp. 33–60; Weber, *Peasants*, p. 288.

39. Weber, *Peasants*, pp. 288–89, 289, 328, 293, 298–99, 302, 297, chap. 16 passim. On recruits' literacy, see the work of LeRoy Ladurie and his colleagues. In general, see the studies of Abel Chatelain, Alain Corbin, Teresa McBride; Furet and Ozouf.

40. Weber, *Peasants*, p. 328; Robert Thabault, *Education and Change in a Village Community* (New York: Schocken, 1971); Teresa McBride, "A Woman's World," *French Historical Studies* 10 (1978): 664–83; idem, "The Modernization of 'Woman's Work'," *Journal of Modern History* 49 (1977): 231–45; Furet and Ozouf, *Lire*; Raymond Boudon, *Education, Opportunity, and Social Inequality* (New York: John Wiley, 1974); Pierre Bourdieu                                                                                                          and J.-C. Passerson, *Reproduction in Education, Society, and Culture* (Beverly Hills, Calif.: Sage, 1977); Darbel, "Inégalité"; Fritz Ringer, *Education and Society in Modern Europe* (Bloomington: Indiana University Press, 1979).

41. Weber *Peasants*, pp. 329, 330, 329–30, 330–31, 331–32, 332, passim, pp. 332–38; cf. pp. 336–38 for examples of negative and/or mixed results.

42. Weber *Peasants*, pp. 336–37, 338. See also Baker and Harrigan, *Making*.

43. Tilly, *From Mobilization to Revolution* (Reading, Mass.: Addison-Wesley, 1978). Compare with the work of David McClelland, Karl Deutsch, Samuel Huntington, Alex Inkeles, and David H. Smith. See also Flora, "Historical Processes."

44. Tony Judt, *Socialism in Provence* (Cambridge: Cambridge University Press, 1979), pp. 187, 187–88, 188, 190–93, 192, 193, 194, 194–95, 195, 197, chap. 9 passim. See also recent studies of French urban working-class development. See below for English comparisons.

45. Furet and Ozouf, *Lire*, p. 348, passim; Patrice Higonnet, "The Politics of Linguistic Terrorism and Grammatical Hegemony," *Social History* 5 (1980): 49, 57, 59, 62, 62–65, 66, 67, 68, 69. See also Maynes, "Schooling," esp. chap. 3; Chartier et al., *L'Education*; Gildea, "Brittany"; Weber, *Peasants*. See also related papers in *History Workshop* 10 (1980).

46. Maynes, "Schooling," pp. 162, 166, 168. See also Gildea, "Brittany"; Weber, *Peasants*; Furet and Ozouf, *Lire*; Vovelle, "Y-a-t-il"; Meyer, "Alphabètisation"; Chartier et al., *L'Education*.

47. Weber, *Peasants*, esp. chaps. 6, 18, 24, 25 for introductions; for eighteenth and nineteenth centuries, see the studies cited in notes 64–65, above; for Third Republic, see the work of Lawrence Wylie; P.-H. Hélias, *The Horse of Pride* (New Haven: Yale University Press, 1978), as examples.

48. Weber, *Peasants*, p. 337. See also his chap. 18 and his appendix on language; Furet and Ozouf, *Lire*, chap. 7.

49. Furet and Ozouf, *Lire*, pp. 330–32, 331–32, 334–35, 335, 335ff., 340, 341, 343–44, 348; compare with Gildea, "Brittany"; Weber, *Peasants*.

50. Colin Clair, *A History of European Printing* (London: Academic Press, 1976); Roger Schofield, "The Measurement of Literacy," in *Literacy in Traditional Societies*, ed. Jack Goody (Cambridge: Cambridge University Press, 1968), pp. 311–25; James Smith Allen, "Toward a Social History of French Romanticism," *Journal of Social History* 13 (1979): 253–76; Geneviève Bollème, *La Bibliothèque bleue* (Paris: Julliard, 1971); Pierre Brochon, *Le livre de colportage* (Paris: Librairie Grund, 1954); A. Clandin, *Histoire de l'imprimerie en France* (Paris, 1900–1914); J. J. Darmon, *Le colportage de librairie en France sous le Second Empire* (Paris: Plon, 1972); Paul Dupont, *Histoire de l'imprimerie*, 2 vols. (Paris, 1883); Albert Labarre, *Histoire du livre* (Paris: Presses Universitaires de France, 1970); H.-J. Martin, *Le livre et la civilisation écrite*, 3 vols. (Paris: Ecole nationale superière des bibliotèques, 1968–1970); Ph. Renouard, *Imprimeurs Parisiens, librairies, fondeurs de caractères et correcteurs d'imprimerie depuis l'introduction de l'imprimerie a Paris* (Paris: Librairie A. Claudin, 1898); Weber, *Peasants*; Robert Escarpit, Pierre Orrecchioni, and Nicole Robine, "La lecture," in *Les Loisirs: La vie populaire en France du Moyen Age à nos jours*, vol. 2 (Paris: Editions Diderot, n.d.), pp. 277–352; Priscilla P. Clark, "The Beginnings of Mass Culture in France," *Social Research* 45 (1978): 277–91.

51. Escarpit et al., "La lecture," p. 297; Weber, *Peasants*, pp. 452, 453.

52. Escarpit et al., "La lecture," pp. 297–98, passim; Allen, "Toward," pp. 255, 265–67; Clark, "Mass Culture."

53. McDougall "Consciousness," p. 132; See also the works of Furet and Ozouf, L. Tilly, R. Bezucha, R. Oberlé, A. Corbin, and W. Sewell, and the recent work of Charles Tilly, William Sewell, Ronald Aminzande, Michael Hanagan, J. Harvey Smith, Richard Price, and others for uses of literacy and, especially, for contexts.

54. Weber, *Peasants*, chap. 27, pp. 455, 459, 460, 461, quoted on pp. 462, 465, 469. See also studies cited above; Gildea, "Brittany", J. Hébrard, "Ecole."

55. See Furet and Ozouf, *Lire*; Shaffer, "Family"; Boudon, *Education*; Bourdieu and Passeron, *Reproduction*; Ringer, *Education and Society*; L. Tilly, "The Family Wage Economy," *Journal of Family History* 4 (1979). Other citations are found above. See also, for local studies, Furet and Ozouf, *Lire*, vol. 2, and the bibliography in that volume. Local studies include Aquitaine, Languedoc, Rouen, Champagne, Seine-et-Marne.

56. Cipolla, *Literacy*, p. 85, table 11, pp. 86–87. See, in general, on German education and literacy: Karl A. Schleunes, "The French Revolution and the Schooling of European Society," *Proceedings*, Consortium on Revolutionary Europe, 1977, pp. 140–50; idem, "Enlightenment, Reform, Reaction: The Schooling Revolution in Prussia," *Central European History* 12 (1979): 315–42; Thomas Nipperdey, "Mass Education and Modernization—The Case of Germany, 1780–1850," *Transactions*, Royal Historical Society, 5th ser. 27 (1977): 155–72; Flora, "Historical Processes"; Meyers, *Modernization*; Etienne François, "Die Volksbildung am Mittelrheim im ausgehenden 18. Jahrhundert. Eine Untersuchung über den vermeintlichen 'Bildungsrückstand' der Katholischen Bevolkerung Seutschlands im Ancien Regime," *Jahrbuch fur est-deutsche Landesgeschichte* 3 (1977): 277–304; Thomas Alexander, *The Prussian Elementary School* (New York: Macmillan, 1918); Hajo Holborn, *A History of Modern Germany*, 3 vols. (New York: Knopf, 1959–1963); Friedrich Paulsen, *German Education, Past and Present* (New York: Scribners, 1912); A. Pinloche, *La réforme de l'éducation en Allemagne au dix-huitième siècle* (Paris: Armand Colin, 1899); Eugene Rendu, *De l'éducation populaire dans l'Allemagne du Nord* (Paris: Librairie de L. Hachette, 1855); Hans Rosenberg, *Bureaucracy, Aristocracy, and Autocracy* (Cambridge, Mass.: Harvard University Press, 1958); Calvin Stowe, *Report on Elementary Public Instruction in Europe. . . .* (Columbus, Ohio: Samuel Medley, Printer to the State, 1837); Maynes, "Schooling"; Klaus Epstein, *The Genesis of German Conservatism* (Princeton: Princeton University Press, 1966).

57. Maynes, "Schooling, pp. 34ff., 40, 56, 58, 79, 82, 100, 115, 122, 132, 135, 172–73, 180, 180–81, quoted on p. 189, pp. 190, 197, 219–21. See also work of Schleunes, Nipperdey, cited above, among other sources. See, too, Maynes, "Virtues." On language, see Maynes, "Schooling," pp. 169ff.; Cipolla, *Literacy*, has statistics on language. See also David Crew, *The Social History of a German Town* (New York: Columbia University Press, 1979).

58. Maynes, "Schooling," chap. 5, table 17, pp. 267, 269, table 18, pp. 271, 278, 287, 305.

59. Crew, *Social History*, pp. 88–89, passim.

60. Maynes, "Schooling," p. 316, chap. 6, pp. 357–61, 365, 377, 379, 409–410, 425–26. See also Crew, *Social History*; Ringer, *Education*; Tilly and Scott, *Women*.

61. Crew, *Social History*, pp. 122–23, 90–95.

62. Peter Lundgren, "Educational Expansion and Economic Growth in Nineteenth-Century Germany," in *Schooling and Society*, ed. Lawrence Stone (Baltimore: Johns Hopkins University Press, 1976), pp. 20, 25, 32–34, 34, 35, 42, 47; idem, "Industrialization and the Educational Formation of Manpower in Germany," *Journal of Social History* 9 (1975): 64, 73, 77, 78. See also W. O. Henderson's and Lawrence Schofer's works on German economic development; Crew, *Social History*; Barrington Moore's seminal works. More generally, see the normative viewpoints expressed in the work of M. J. Bowman and C. A. Anderson, and E. G. West, the critique in Graff, *Literacy Myth*, chap. 5, and the literature cited there.

63. Ronald Fullerton, "Creating a Mass Book Market in Germany: The Story of the 'Colporteur Novel', 1870–1890," *Journal of Social History* 10 (1977): 265, 266, 267, 276; R. Schenda, *Volk ohne Buch* (Frankfurt, 1970); R. Engelsing, *Analphabetentum und Lekture* (Stuttgart, 1973); idem, *Der Bürger als Leser* (Stuttgart, 1974).

64. H.-J. Steinberg, "Workers' Libraries in Germany before 1914," *History Workshop* 1 (1976): 167–73, 173, 174.

65. See the literature on German education and book production, cited above, and in chap. 6.

66. Schleunes, "Enlightenment," pp. 339–40; Nipperdey, "Mass Education," p. 157, passim. See James Sheehan, *German Liberalism in the Nineteenth Century* (Chicago: University of Chicago Press, 1978).

67. Cipolla, *Literacy*, pp. 80–81, 14, 93. See also chap. 6 above; Holborn, *Modern Germany*. Compare with Vovelle, "Y–a–t–il"; Furet and Ozouf, *Lire*.

68. Cipolla, *Literacy*, pp. 14, 19, 83, quoted on pp. 33, 35, 93, 94, appendices 2, 3, pp. 129, 128, 93. Gramsci's writings are relevant here. For an introduction, see Walter Adamson, *Hegemony and Revolution* (Berkeley: University of California Press, 1980).

69. Rudolph Bell, *Fate and Honor, Family and Village* (Chicago: University of Chicago Press, 1979), pp. 156, 157, quoted on pp. 157–58, 158, tables 24–25, pp. 159–60, 158–59, 159, 160, 160–61. See also John Briggs, *An Italian Passage* (New Haven: Yale University Press, 1978).

70. Cipolla, *Literacy*, Appendix; Francine Van de Walle, "Education and the Fertility Transition in Switzerland" (unpub. ms., 1976; revised version published in *Population and Development Review* 6 [1980]: 463–72). See also Graff, "Education, Literacy, and Fertility."

71. Roger Girod, "Le recul de l'analphabétisme dans la région de Genève de la fin du XVIIIᵉ au milieu du XIXᵉ siècle," *Mélanges d'histoire économique et sociale Antony Babel* (Geneva, 1963), p. 179, table 1, pp. 183, 185–89, 188–89.

72. See, in general, A. Van de Woude, "Schrift en culture," *Spiegel Historiael* (1972): 130–33; section in *Algemene Geschiedenis der Nederlunden* 7 (1980): 257–63; Yves Wellemans, "L'analphabétisme en milieu urbain Belge au XIXe siècle," *Revue Belge d'histoire contemporaine* 10 (1978): 183–87; Herman Boon, *Enseignement Primaire et alphabétisation dans l'agglomeration Bruxelloise de* 1830 à 1879 (Louvain: Publications Universitaires de Louvain, 1969); Joseph Ruwet and Yves Wellemans, *L'Analphabétisme en Belgique* (Louvain: Bibliotèque de l'Université Louvain, 1978); Michel Fournaux, "L'analphabétisme à Liège au XIXᵉ siècle," *Annuaire d'histoire Legeoise* 16 (1975): 151–216; Micheline Soenen,

"Un élément d'information sur le taux d'alphabétisation en Brabant à la fin du XVIII<sup>e</sup> S.: La Declaration du Peuple Belgique de Janvier–Fevrier 1790," *Archives bibliotèques et musées de Belgique* 42 (1971): 224–40; Ron Lesthaeghe, *The Decline of Belgian Fertility* (Princeton: Princeton University Press, 1977).

73. Van de Woude, *Algemene Geschiedenis*, pp. 262, 258, 260, 263.

74. Cipolla, *Literacy*, p. 91, Appendices, pp. 127, 93; see also the urban studies cited in note 93 above.

75. Van de Woude, *Algemene Geschiedenis*, pp. 259–60; Wellemans, "L'analphabétisme," p. 185; see also the work of Wellemans and Ruwet and Fournaux.

76. Wellemans, "L'analphabétisme," pp. 186, 186–87; see also the studies cited in this article, Ruwet and Wellemans, Boon, cited above.

77. Ruwet and Wellemans, *L'Analphabétisme*, table 25, p. 80, table 30, p. 96, passim. See also the case studies of Boon, Fourneaux, Soenen.

78. Boon, *Enseignement*, p. 87. See also Lesthaege, *Decline*. For a revealing discussion of the cultural politics of Flemings and Walloons, see Aristide R. Zolberg, "The Making of Flemings and Walloons: Belgium, 1830–1914," *Journal of Interdisciplinary History* 5 (1974): 179–235. Language is a major issue; literacy is mentioned on p. 199, where the author draws attention to the educational gap and postulates that it may have been due to the high incidence of child labor fostered by the household–based Flemish economy. Regional differences continued over time, he also notes.

79. Lesthaeghe, *Decline*, pp. 190, 191–93, 193, 194; see also p. 189 and his chap. 6. For revealing comments especially useful to the cultural historian, see Luc Danhieux, "Literate or Semi–Literate?" *Local Population Studies* 18 (1977): 52–53.

80. Cipolla, *Literacy*, pp. 155, 76–77, 71n. On criminality, see Graff, *Literacy Myth*, chap. 6 and below. See also Egil Johansson, "Literacy Studies in Sweden: Some Examples," in *Literacy and Society*, ed. Egil Johansson (Umeå, 1973); idem, *The History of Literacy in Sweden* (Umeå, 1977); idem, "Reading and Writing Ability in Sweden and Finland" (unpub. ms.); idem, "Studying Literacy in Sweden in the Church Examination Registers" (1973); idem, "Literacy and Popular Education in Sweden" (1972); idem, "Literacy in Sweden," among his seminal works; the unpublished work of Kenneth A. Lockridge; Carol Gold, "Educational Reform in Denmark," and H. A. Barton, "Popular Education in Sweden," in *Facets of Education*, ed. James A. Leith, *Studies on Voltaire and the Eighteenth Century*, vol. 167 (1977), pp. 49–64 and 523–42; B. J. Hovde, *The Scandinavian Countries, 1720–1860*, 2 vols. (Boston: Chapman and Grimes, 1943), among others, for developments and context.

81. Hovde, *Scandinavian*, p. 604, chap. 15, passim.

82. Johansson, *History*, pp. 43, 61, 62, 64, 58–60, 65–66; pp. 65–73 present an international comparison. See also Bill Widén, "Literacy in the Ecclesiastical Context," in Johansson, *Literacy and Society*, pp. 33–40.

83. Johansson, "Literacy Studies," pp. 52–54, 55–56. For an original formulation of this argument, see Graff, *Literacy Myth*, chap. 7 and evidence presented there. For additional Swedish evidence, from the example of Tuna, see Johansson, *History of Literacy*, p. 49.

84. Johansson, "Literacy Studies," pp. 58, 61, 63, 62, 63–64, as well as Johansson's and Lockridge's other studies cited above.

85. For a general discussion of this relationship, see Graff, *Literacy Myth*, chap. 2. On imagery of mobility, see Anselm Strauss, *The Contexts of Social Mobility* (Chicago: Aldine, 1971). On Sweden, see the work of Sune Åkerman, especially "Mobile and Stationary Populations: The Problem of Selection," in Johansson, *Literacy and Society*, pp. 67–81; idem, with Per Gunnar Cassel and Egil Johansson, "Background Variables of Population Mobility," *Scandinavian Economic History Review* 22 (1974): 32–60; idem, "Internal Migration, Industrialisation, and Urbanization," ibid. 23 (1975): 149–85; idem, "Splitting Background Variables: Aid–Analysis Applied to Migration and Literacy Research," *Journal of European Economic History* 8 (1979): 157–92; idem, "Swedish Migration and Social Mobility: The Tale of Three Cities," *Social Science History* 1 (1977): 178–209, among his work on this topic. See also Hans Norman and Harald Ranblom, *From Sweden to America*

(Minneapolis: University of Minnesota Press, 1976). Åkerman, "Mobile," pp. 76, 77, 78, 79; "Background," p. 59, passim. See also Graff, *Literacy Myth*, chap. 2, and the citations to the studies of Barbara Anderson and Larry Long presented there. See in general the Introduction and Epilogue to this book, and the pioneering studies of literacy and the context of learning by Michael Cole and Sylvia Scribner.

86. Richard F. Tomasson, "The Literacy of the Icelanders," *Scandinavian Studies* 57 (1975): 68, passim. Quotation from Cipolla, *Literacy*, pp. 73–74. Tomasson includes other examples and interesting data on contemporary reading patterns.

87. See, for example, Richard Johnson, "Educational Policy and Social Control in Early Victorian England," *Past and Present* 49 (1970): 96, among his writings; Carl F. Kaestle, "Between the Scylla of Brutal Ignorance and the Charybdis of a Literary Education: Elite Attitudes toward Mass Schooling in Early Industrial England and America," in Stone, *Schooling and Society*, pp. 177–91; J.-G. Daigle, "Alphabétisation et culture populaire dans l'Angleterre victorienne," *Histoire sociale* 10 (1977): 5–23; John Vincent, *Bread, Knowledge, and Freedom* (London: Europa, 1981). There is a large, if sometimes unwieldy, body of writing on the history of English education, and a growing literature on literacy.

88. Schofield, "Dimensions," pp. 443, 446, 449–50, 451–52. See also Lawrence Stone, "Literacy and Education in England, 1640–1900," *Past and Present* 39 (1969): 61–139; Cipolla, *Literacy*. Among local studies, see Levine, *Family Formation*; David Levine, "Education and Family Life in Early Industrial England," *Journal of Family History* 4 (1979): 368–80; idem, "Illiteracy and Family Life during the First Industrial Revolution," *Journal of Social History* 14 (1980): 25–44; W. B. Stephens, "Illiteracy and Schooling in the Provincial Towns, 1640–1870," in *Urban Education*, ed. David Reeder (London: Francis and Taylor, 1977), pp. 27–48; idem, "Literacy in Devon during the Industrial Revolution," *Journal of Educational Administration and History* 8 (1976): 1–5; idem, "An Anatomy of Illiteracy in Mid-Victorian Devon," in *Education and Labour in the South-West*, ed. Jeffrey Porter (Exeter: University of Exeter Department of Economic History, 1975), pp. 7–20; Roger Smith, "Education, Society, and Literacy: Nottinghamshire in the Mid–Nineteenth Century," University of Birmingham, *Historical Journal* 12 (1969): 42–56; Victor A. Hatley, "Literacy at Northampton, 1761–1900," *Northamptonshire Past and Present* 4 (1966): et seq.; W. P. Baker, *Parish Registers and Illiteracy in East Yorkshire* (York: East Yorkshire Local History Society, 1961); Michael Sanderson, "Literacy and Social Mobility in the Industrial Revolution in England," *Past and Present* 56 (1972): 75–104, and exchange with T. W. Laqueur, ibid. 64 (1974): 96–112; R. K. Webb, "Working Class Readers in Early Victorian England," *English Historical Review* 65 (1950): 333–51; idem, "Literacy among the Working Classes in Nineteenth Century Scotland," *Scottish Historical Review* 33 (1954): 100–114; idem, *The British Working Class Reader* (London: Allen and Unwin, 1955); Richard Altick, *The English Common Reader* (Chicago: University of Chicago Press, 1957); Vincent, *Bread*; John Hurt, *Elementary Education and the Working Classes* (London: Routledge, 1979); E. P. Thompson, *The Making of the English Working Class* (New York: Vintage, 1967). See also the *contrasting views* of E. G. West, and the work of Bowman and Anderson, cited above. Thomas Laqueur, *Religion and Respectability* (New Haven: Yale University Press, 1976); idem, "Working Class Demand and the Growth of English Elementary Education," in Stone, *Schooling and Society*, pp. 192–205; idem, "The Cultural Origins of Popular Literacy in England, 1500–1850," *Oxford Review of Education* 2 (1976): 255–75.

89. Kaestle, "Between," pp. 178, 179, 180, 180–81. See among a larger literature D. C. Eversley, *Social Theories of Fertility and The Malthusian Debate* (Oxford: Oxford University Press, 1959); E. G. West, "The Role of Education in Nineteenth-Century Doctrines of Political Economy," *British Journal of Educational Studies* 12 (1964): 161–73; idem, *Education and the State* (1970); idem, *Education and the Industrial Revolution* (London: Batsford, 1975); Mark Blaug, "The Economics of Education in English Classical Political Economy: A Re-examination," in *Essays on Adam Smith*, ed. Andrew S. Skinner and Thomas Wilson (Oxford: Clarendon Press, 1975), pp. 568–99; Barry Supple, "Legislation and Virtue: An Essay on Working Class Self–Help and the State in the Early Nineteenth Century," in *Historical Perspectives in English Thought and Society in Honour of J. H. Plumb* (London: Europa, 1974), pp. 211–54; Peter Dunkley, "Paternalism, the Magistry,

and Poor Relief in England, 1795–1834," *International Review of Social History* 24 (1979): 371–97; J. H. Higginson, "Dame Schools," *British Journal of Educational Studies* 22 (1974): 166–81; D. P. Leinster-Mackay, "Dame Schools: A Need for Review," ibid. 24 (1976): 33–48; Brian Simon's several books; Harold Silver's studies; Neuberg, *Popular Education*; James Lawes, "Voluntary Schools and Basic Education in Northampton, 1800–1871," *Northamptonshire Past and Present* 6 (1979): 83–91, among others in this vein. See also David Mitch, "Subsidized Schooling and the Spread of Popular Literacy in Nineteenth Century England," and "The Impact of the Demand for Literate Workers on the Spread of Literacy in Nineteenth Century England" (unpub. ms., now completed as "The Spread of Literacy in Nineteenth–Century England" [PhD. diss., University of Chicago, 1982]). Compare with studies cited above and U. Henriques, *Before the Welfare State* (London: Longman, 1979). See also below, and Michael Sanderson, "The Grammar School and the Education of the Poor," *British Journal of Educational Studies* 11 (1962): 28–43; idem, "Education and the Factory in Industrial Lancashire, 1780–1840," *Economic History Review* 20 (1967): 266–79; idem, "Social Change and Elementary Education in Industrial Lancashire, 1780–1840," *Northern History* 3 (1968): 131–54; A. C. O. Ellis, "Influences on School Attendance in Victorian England," *British Journal of Educational Studies* 21 (1973): 313–26; G. F. A. Best, "The Religious Difficulties of National Education in England, 1800–70," *Cambridge Historical Journal* 12 (1956): 155–73; T. R. Phillips, "The Elementary Schools and the Migratory Habits of the People," *British Journal of Educational Studies* 26 (1978): 177–88; Alexander James Field, "Occupational Structure, Dissent, and Educational Commitment: Lancashire, 1841," in *Research in Economic History* 4 (1979): 235–87; Gillian Sutherland, *Elementary Education in the Nineteenth Century* (London: The Historical Association, 1971); Harold Silver and Pamela Silver, *The Education of the Poor* (London, 1975); Reeder, *Urban Education*; Philip McCann, ed., *Popular Education and Socialization in the Nineteenth Century* (London: Methuen, 1977); J. M. Goldstrum, *The Social Context of Education* (Shannon: Irish Universities Press, 1972).

90. Eversley, *Social Theories*, p. 144, passim; see also William Petersen, *Malthus* (Cambridge, Mass.: Harvard University Press, 1980), among others. Compare with the recent writings on fertility and family and literacy by David Levine and Harvey J. Graff.

91. Blaug, "Economics," p. 568, quoted on p. 573, p. 579. See also the work of E. G. West.

92. Richard Johnson, "Notes on the Schooling of the English Working Class, 1780–1850," in *Schooling and Capitalism: A Sociological Reader*, ed. Roger Dale, Geoff Esland, and Madeleine MacDonald (London: Routledge and Kegan Paul, 1976), pp. 44, 45, 47, 48; see also his "Educating the Educators: Experts and the State, 1833–9," in *Social Control in Nineteenth Century Britain*, ed. A. P. Donajgradzki (London: Croom Helm, 1977), pp. 77–107, "Educational Policy." Vincent, *Bread*; Richard Johnson, " 'Really Useful Knowledge': Radical Education and the Working–Class Culture, 1790–1848," in *Working–Class Culture: Studies in History and Theory*, ed. John Clarke, Charles Critcher, and Richard Johnson (London: Hutchinson, 1979), pp. 75–102; I. J. Prothero, *Artisans and Politics in Early Nineteenth–Century London: John Gast and His Time* (Baton Rouge: Louisiana University Press, 1979). See also, among the works cited above, those in Reeder, McCann, Hurt, West, Sutherland, Laqueur, Webb, Altick, Mitch; Brian Harrison, "State Intervention and Moral Reform," in *Pressure from Without*, ed. P. Hollis (New York: St. Martins Press, 1974), pp. 289–322. North American case studies are good comparisons; see below and references in Graff, *Literacy Myth*, passim. See also Robert Malcolmson, *Popular Recreations* (Cambridge: Cambridge University Press, 1973); J. F. C. Harrison, *The Early Victorians* (London: Weidenfeld and Nicolson, 1971); idem, "Education in Victorian England," *History of Education Quarterly* 10 (1970): 485–91. See the literature on the working class cited below. Roger Gilmour, "The Gradgrind School," *Victorian Studies* 11 (1967): 207–244. Contemporary writings on morality and the social purposes of schooling are especially relevant; they are too voluminous to cite.

93. Laqueur, "Cultural Origins," p. 265, passim; Vincent, *Bread*. See also the work of E. G. West. For an introduction to issues and contexts, see Gareth Stedman Jones, *Outcast London* (Oxford: Oxford University Press, 1971); John Hurt, *Schooling and the Working*

*Class*; John Foster, *Class Struggle and the Industrial Revolution* (London: Weidenfeld, 1974); Michael Anderson, *Family Structure in Nineteenth Century Lancashire* (Cambridge: Cambridge University Press, 1971); Thompson, *Making*; Graff, *Literacy Myth*, esp. chaps. 7, 5; among others.

94. Laqueur, "Working Class Demand," pp. 192, 201, *Religion*. See also Sutherland, *Elementary*; Vincent, *Bread*; and the literature on Sunday and dame schools cited above; and Supple, "Legislation and Virtue," and Neil McKendrick, "Home Demand and Economic Growth: A New View of the Role of Women and Children in the Industrial Revolution," in *Historical Perspectives*, pp. 211–54, 152–210. But compare with the work of Field and Sanderson, cited above.

95. Anderson, "Literacy and Schooling on the Development Threshold: Some Historical Cases," in *Education and Economic Development*, ed. C. A. Anderson and M. J. Bowman (Chicago: Aldine, 1965), pp. 347–62; M. J. Bowman and C. A. Anderson, "Concerning the Role of Education in Development," in *Old Societies and New States*, ed. Clifford Geertz (New York: Free Press, 1963), pp. 247–69; idem, "Education and Economic Modernization in Historical Perspective," in Stone, *Schooling and Society*, pp. 3–19. The latter contains the best summary of their work. The roots of the human capital school of economists, largely dominated by Gary Becker and Theodore Schultz, are found in these approaches. For a useful critical analysis of approaches in the economics of education, see W. G. Bowen, "Assessing the Economic Contribution of Education," in *The Economics of Education*, vol. 1, ed. Mark Blaug (Harmondsworth: Penguin, 1968), pp. 67–100.

96. Bowman and Anderson, "Education," pp. 7, 8. See also the work of E. G. West, cited above. See Jack Goody, *The Domestication of the Savage Mind* (Cambridge: Cambridge University Press, 1977); Introduction and Epilogue, above and below.

97. Schofield, "Dimensions," pp. 452–53, 454; John Talbott, "The History of Education," *Daedalus* 100 (1971): 141. See also Furet and Ozouf, *Lire*, and above; Flora, "Historical Processes"; Lundgren's work, discussed above; Graff, *Literacy Myth*, chap. 5. Compare with Anderson and Bowman, West.

98. Bowman and Anderson, "Education," p. 4, see also pp. 14–16. See also Harold Perkin, "The Social Causes of the British Industrial Revolution," *Transactions*, Royal Historical Society 18 (1968): 123–43; idem, *Origins of Modern English Society* (London: Routledge, 1969); the work of Eric Hobsbawm; M. W. Flinn, "Social Theory and the Industrial Revolution," in *Social Theory and Economic Change*, ed. T. Burns and N. Saul (London: Tavistock, 1967), pp. 9–34; Stephen Marglin, "What Do Bosses Do? Origins and Functions of Hierarchy in Capitalist Production," *Review of Radical Political Economics* 6 (1974): 60–112, 7 (1975): 20–38; William Lazonick, "The Subjection of Labour to Capital: The Rise of the Capitalist System," ibid. 10 (1978): 1–31, among other important studies of industrialization. For hints of the limited role of literacy, see A. F. C. Wallace, *Rockdale* (New York: Knopf, 1978); William Ivins, *Prints and Communications* (Cambridge, Mass.: MIT Press, 1969). See also David McClelland, "Does Education Accelerate Economic Growth?" *Economic Development and Cultural Change* 11 (1966): 262, 266; David Landes, *The Unbound Prometheus* (Cambridge: Cambridge University Press, 1969). See, too, George Sturt, *The Wheelwrights Shop* (Cambridge: Cambridge University Press, 1923); John Burnet, ed., *Useful Toil* (Harmondsworth: Penguin, 1974); Edward Shorter, ed., *Work and Community in the West* (New York: Harper and Row, 1973). See the works of E. P. Thompson, R. K. Webb, T. W. Laqueur, and Vincent, and below.

99. Schofield, "Measurement," p. 312. E. G. West's recent work does not persuasively refute this case.

100. Stephens, "Illiteracy," pp. 27, 28–29, 30, 32–33, 33. See also the local and case studies of literacy and schooling cited above, and Alan Armstrong's and Frances Finnegan's recent books on York and social conditions therein. Marsden's article, found in McCann, *Popular Education*, stresses the important role of intraurban variation.

101. Sanderson, "Social Mobility," pp. 75, 102. See his other articles cited above, the studies of Richard Johnson, David Levine, and David Vincent.

102. Levine, "Education," pp. 373, 377, 378, 379; "Illiteracy," pp. 26, 31, 38, 39,

40, 41–42. For background, see his *Family Formation*. More generally, see Graff, "Literacy, Education, and Fertility," *Literacy Myth*, chap. 2.

103. Sanderson, "Social Mobility," pp. 75, 80, 89, sec. 3, pp. 91, 96, 97–98, 99, 99–101, 101–102. See also his other articles cited above. See Laqueur's *Past and Present* debate with Sanderson and West, "Literacy." In support, see Mitch's study.

104. See in general Graff, *Literacy Myth*, chap. 5; Cipolla, *Literacy*; Schofield, "Dimensions," "Measurement"; Johnson, "Notes," among other relevant literature.

105. E. G. West, *Education and the Industrial Revolution* (London: Batsford, 1975), p. 256; Johnson, "Notes," p. 47; Sidney Pollard, "Factory Discipline in the Industrial Revolution," *Economic History Review* 16 (1963): 225. See also his *Genesis of Modern Management* (Harmondsworth: Penguin, 1968), esp. chap. 5; Keith Thomas, "Work and Leisure in Pre-industrial Societies," *Past and Present* 29 (1964); Malcolmson, *Popular Recreations*; Herbert Gutman, "Work, Culture, and Society in Industrializing America, 1815–1919," *American Historical Review* 78 (1973): 531–88; Harrison, *Early Victorians*; Alexander J. Field, "Educational Reform and Manufacturing Development in Mid-Nineteenth-Century Massachusetts (Ph.D. diss., University of California at Berkeley, 1974); Johnson, "Notes"; Marglin, "Bosses"; Inkeles and Smith, *Modern*, chap. 11. Richard Awkwright, quoted in Pollard, "Factory Discipline," pp. 258, 258, 268; Johnson, "Notes," provides additional examples.

106. Harrison, *Early Victorians*, pp. 135–36; Johnson, "Notes"; McCann, *Popular Education*; Donajgradzki, *Social Control*. For contemporary opinion, see the writings of Kay and Kay-Shuttleworth and quotations in Johnson's articles. For important recent approaches, see Gareth Stedman Jones, "Working-Class Culture and Working-Class Politics in London, 1870–1890: Notes on the Remaking of a Working Class," *Journal of Social History* 7 (1974): 460–508; the works of Patrick Joyce, Johnson, J. F. C. Harrison, Brian Harrison, E. P. Thompson, Malcolmson, John Foster cited above; R. Q. Gray's studies of artisans; Geoffrey Crossick, *An Artisan Elite in Victorian Society* (London: Croom Helm, 1978); idem, ed., *The Lower Middle Class* (London: Croom Helm, 1977); Trygre R. Tholfsen, *Working Class Radicalism in Mid-Victorian England* (New York: Columbia University Press, 1977); Alan Anderson's work on clerks; Robert Colls, *The Collier's Rant: Song and Culture in the Industrial Village* (London: Croom Helm, 1977); Caroline Reed, "Middle Class Values and Working Class Culture in Sheffield," in *Essays in Economic and Social History of South Yorkshire*, ed. Sidney Pollard and Colin Holmes (Sheffield: South Yorkshire County Council, 1976), pp. 275–95. On literacy's course, see the work of Schofield, West, Laqueur, and Mitch.

107. Johnson, "Notes," p. 50; quotation is from Gramsci, *Selections from the Prison Notebooks*, p. 242. See also Introduction and Section 1, above; Graff, *Literacy Myth*, chap. 1, passim. On lack of connection in some places between literacy and schools, see Roger Smith's Nottingham study; see also the work of T. W. Laqueur; A. J. Field; John Vincent; W. Lazonick; studies in Donajgradzki, *Social Control*. R. P. Dore, *Education in Tokugawa Japan* (London: Routledge and Kegan Paul, 1967), p. 292. On crime, see below; J. J. Tobias, *Crime and Industrial Society in the Nineteenth Century* (Harmondsworth: Penguin, 1972); David Phillips, *Crime and Authority in Victorian England* (London: Croom Helm, 1977); W. B. Hodgson, *Exaggerated Estimates of Reading and Writing as Means of Education* (London, 1868) [I have reprinted this text, with an introduction, in *History of Education Quarterly* 26 (1986); Graff, *Literacy Myth*, chap. 6; George Rudé and E. J. Hobsbawm, *Captain Swing* (New York: Pantheon, 1969). Laqueur, "Cultural Origins," p. 270. See also Stone, "Literacy"; Webb, *Reader*; Vincent, *Bread*; Tholfsen, *Working Class*; Thompson, *Making*; among the related literature.

108. Laqueur, "Cultural Origins," pp. 269, 270. On the press, see Webb, *Reader*; Thompson, *Making*; Stanley Harrison, *Poor Man's Guardians* (London: Lawrence and Wishart, 1974); G. A. Cranfield, *Development, The Press, and Society* (London: Longman, 1978); Louis James, *Fiction for the Working Man, 1830–1850* (London: Oxford University Press, 1963); Alan J. Lee, *The Origins of the Popular Press in England, 1855–1914* (London: Croom Helm, 1976); George Boyce, James Curran, and Paul Wingate, eds., *Newspaper*

*History* (London: Constable, 1978). See also the working-class cultural and political studies cited above, and for the later eighteenth and early nineteenth centuries, see the recent studies of John Brewer and articles in *Past and Present*. See also Graff, *Literacy Myth*, chap. 5; Patrick Keane, "Adult Education and the Cornish Miner," *British Journal of Educational Studies* 22 (1974): 261–91.

109. Thompson, *Making*, pp. 711–12, 712, 712–13, 713; Vincent, *Bread*. See also Webb, *Reader*; Graff, *Literacy Myth*, chap. 7; Thompson, "Eighteenth-Century English Society: Class Struggle Without Class?" *Social History* 3 (1978): 133–65; Hobsbawm and Rudé, *Captain Swing*.

110. Webb, *Reader*, pp. 34, vii, chap. 4, passim, pp. 158, 158–59, 160; Vincent, *Bread*, pp. 140, 155. See also Neuberg, *Popular*; idem, "The Literature of the Streets," in *The Victorian City*, ed. H. J. Dyos and Michael Wolff (London: Routledge and Kegan Paul, 1973), vol. 1, pp. 191–209; titles cited above. But see Alec Ellis, "Influences on the Availability of Recreational Reading for Victorian Working Class Children," *Journal of Librarianship* 8 (1976): 185–95; A. R. Thompson, "The Use of Libraries by the Working Class in Scotland in the Early Nineteenth Century," *Scottish Historical Review* 42 (1963): 21–29; Victor Kiernan, "Labour and the Literate in Nineteenth-Century Britain," in *Ideology and the Labour Movement*, eds. D. E. Martin and David Rubinstein (London: Croom Helm, 1979), pp. 32–61; Alvar Ellegard, "The Readership of the Periodical Press in Mid-Victorian Britain," *Gotesbourgs Universitets Årsskrift* 63 (1957): 3–25; idem, "Directory," *Victorian Periodicals Newsletter* 12 (1971): 3–22. More general and very suggestive is Steven Marcus, "Reading the Illegible," in Dyos and Wolff, *The Victorian City*, pp. 257–76. See also the studies of elementary education and reform, and working-class culture, as well as Peter Bailey, *Leisure and Class in Victorian England* (Toronto: University of Toronto Press, 1978).

111. Mitch, "Subsidized Schooling," pp. 1, 2, 23–24, 34. See also the work of Richard Johnson, John Hurt, John Vincent, Alec Ellis, Richard Altick, Roger Smith, T. R. Phillips, and David Rubinstein, articles in Reeder, *Urban Education*, and McCann, *Popular Education*, among others. Compare specifically with views of West and Laqueur. For contemporary opinion, see the writings of Henry Brougham, Kay-Shuttleworth, and their peers.

112. J. M. Goldstrum, "The Content of Education and the Socialization of the Working-Class Child," in McCann, *Popular Education*, pp. 93–110, *Social Context*, pp. 1, 2, passim, pp. 67, 68, chap. 2, pp. 80, 104, 129. See Gilmour, "Gradgrind"; Ruth M. Elson, *Guardians of Tradition* (Lincoln: University of Nebraska Press, 1964); Sherwood Fox, "School Readers as an Educational Force," *Queen's Quarterly* 39 (1932): 688–703; Graff, *Literacy Myth*, chap. 7; Donald Akenson, *The Irish Education Experiment* (New Haven: Yale University Press,, 1969).

113. Alex Inkeles, "Making Men Modern," *American Journal of Sociology* 75 (1969): esp. p. 213; idem, "The School as a Context for Modernization," *International Journal of Sociology* 14 (1973): 163–79; Robert Dreeben, *On What is Learned in School* (Reading, Mass.: Addison-Wesley, 1968), pp. 144–45, passim; Samuel Bowles and Herbert Gintis, *Schooling in Capitalist America* (New York: Basic Books, 1976); Herbert Gintis, "Education, Technology, and the Characteristics of Worker Productivity," *American Economic Review* 61 (1971): 266–79.

114. The Rev. Moseley in *Minutes of Committee of Council of Education* (1851–1852), vol. 1, p. 288, as quoted in Goldstrum, *Social Context*, p. 148; Commission, Popular Education, pp. 239, 244, 248, 243. In general, see Graff, *Literacy Myth*, chap. 7; Daniel Calhoun, *The Intelligence of a People* (Princeton: Princeton University Press, 1973). More specifically, see the writings of W. B. Hodgson, Goldstrum, Altick, Rubinstein, Hurt; Carl Kaestle, ed., *Joseph Lancaster and the Monitorial School Movement* (New York: Teachers College Press, 1973); McCann, *Popular Education*; Reports of Inspector James Fraser in the 1860s.

115. Commission, Popular Education, pp. 246–61.

116. *Report*, Committee, Council of Education, 1865–1866, p. 23, quoted in Goldstrum, *Social Context*; Hodgson, *Exaggerated Estimates*, pp. 4–5. See also M. M. Lewis, *The Importance of Illiteracy* (London: Harrap, 1953), pp. 40–43.

117. Altick, *Common Reader*, pp. 150, 151, 151–52. See also studies of Hurt, Rubinstein, Phillips; McCann, *Popular Education*.

118. Hurt, *Working Class*, pp. 210, 211–12, 212, passim. See also W. E. Marsden, "Social Environment, School Attendance, and Educational Achievement," in McCann, *Popular Education*, pp. 193–230; articles in Raphael Samuel, ed., *Village Life and Labour* (London: Routledge and Kegan Paul, 1975); Stedman Jones, "Working Class," *Outcast*; John C. Holley, "The Two Family Economies of Industrialism: Factory Workers in Victorian Scotland," *Journal of Family History* 6 (1981): 57–69; studies of the labor aristocracy by Gray, Tholfsen, Crossick, Foster, and others; Robert Roberts, Richard Hoggart, and Paul Willis on working-class culture. See also Calhoun, *Intelligence*, pp. 80, 85, chap. 2; Graff, *Literacy Myth*, chap. 7, and below.

119. See, in general, Mitch, "Spread"; Graff, *Literacy Myth*, p. 216, chaps. 5, 7, p. 217; Stedman Jones, *Outcast*; E. J. Hobsbawm, "The Tramping Artisan," in his *Labouring Men* (Garden City, N.Y.: Doubleday Anchor, 1967), pp. 41–74. Skilled, literate, and organized working men could, of course, read about economic conditions, and therefore employment opportunities, in the working-class press. The development, circulation (including oral transmission of news, group and shop reading aloud), and impact of the labor press in this period are critical and require separate detailed study. See also Thompson, *Making*; Prothero, *Artisans*; Webb, *Reader*; Harrison, *Early Victorians*.

120. Mitch, "Impact of the Demand," pp. 1–2, 4, 5, 6, quoted on p. 8, p. 14, quoted on p. 56, quoted on p. 27, quoted on pp. 27–28, pp. 48, 52, 55, 56, quoted on p. 56. For servants, see John Gillis, "Servants, Sexual Relations, and the Risk of Illegitimacy," *Feminist Studies* 5 (1979): 142–73. See also Laqueur, "Working Class Demand"; Raphael Samuels, "The Workshop of the World," *History Workshop* 3 (1977): 6–72; Marglin, "Bosses." See, too, recent historical studies of women's work.

121. Laqueur, "Cultural Origins," p. 269, passim. See also Graff, *Literacy Myth*; and work of Altick, Neuberg, Webb, and others, above. See James Walvin, *Leisure and Society* (London: Longman, 1978); Vincent, *Bread*.

122. Neuberg, "Literature," p. 191. See also the work of Lee and James; Leslie Shepard, *The History of Street Literature* (Detroit: Singing Tree Press, 1973); Robert Collison, *The Story of Street Literature* (London: Dent, 1973); Patrick A. Dunae, "Penny Dreadfuls: Late Nineteenth-Century Boy's Literature and Crime," *Victorian Studies* 22 (1979): 133–50. Compare with Alec Ellis, "The Users and Uses of Public Libraries at the Outbreak of the First World War," *Journal of Librarianship* 11 (1979): 39–44; Phillip Corrigan and Val Gillespie, *Class Struggle, Social Literacy, and Idle Time* (Brighton, Sussex: John L. Noyce, 1978); J. R. Allred, "The Purposes of the Public Library: The Historical View," *Library History* 2 (1972): 185–204; Altick, *Common Reader*; Helen Meller, "Cultural Provision for the Working Classes in Urban Britain," *Bulletin* of the Society for the Study of Labour History 17 (1968): 18–19; Standish Meacham, *A Life Apart: The English Working Class* (Cambridge, Mass.: Harvard, 1977); Paul Thompson, *The Edwardians* (Bloomington: Indiana University Press, 1975); Hugh McLeod, *Class and Religion in the Late Victorian City* (Hamden, Conn.: Archon, 1974); Stuart MacDonald, "The Diffusion of Knowledge among Northumberland Farmers, 1780–1815," *Agricultural History Review* 27 (1979): 30–39; Lynn Lees, "Getting and Spending: Family Budgets of English Industrial Workers in 1890," in Merriman, *Class Consciousness*, pp. 169–86.

123. Walvin, *Leisure*, pp. 57, 56–57. Altick, *Common Reader*, p. 364. See also studies of Hurt and Ellis.

124. For two recent and revealing attempts to evaluate modern literacy, which end in accepting more of the "literacy myth" than they reject, see David R. Olson, "Toward a Literate Society: Book Review," *Proceedings*, National Academy of Education, 1975–1976, pp. 109–178; H. S. Stout, "Culture, Structure, and the 'New' History," *Computers and the Humanities* 9 (1975): 223–25. See also the essays in Léon Bataille, ed., *A Turning Point for Literacy* (New York: Pergamon Press, 1976); Joyce Appleby, "Modernization Theory and the Formation of Modern Social Theories in England and America," *Comparative Studies*

*in Society and History* 20 (1978): 269–85. In general, see Graff, *Literacy Myth*, chap. 7, for a first approach. See also Geoffrey Best, *Mid-Victorian Britain* (London: Weidenfeld and Nicolson, 1971); Bailey, *Leisure*; Peter Bailey, " 'A Mingled Mass of Perfectly Legitimate Pleasures': The Victorian Middle Class and the Problem of Leisure," *Victorian Studies* 21 (1977): 725.

125. Cipolla, *Literacy*, for example, reflects the normative view. See, for example, Stout, "Culture"; Thomas Cochran, *Social Change in America* (New York: Harper and Row, 1972); David R. Olson, "From Utterance to Text," *Harvard Educational Review* 47 (1977): 257–81; Jack Goody and Ian Watt, "The Consequences of Literacy," in *Literacy in Traditional Societies*, ed. Jack Goody (Cambridge: Cambridge University Press, 1968), pp. 27–68; G. H. Bantock, *The Implications of Literacy* (Leicester: Leicester University Press, 1968); the works of Walter J. Ong, Eric Havelock, Harold Innis, Elizabeth Eisenstein, and Marshall McLuhan; David Riesman et al., *The Lonely Crowd* (New Haven: Yale University Press, 1961 ed.); the writings of Peter Berger and his associates; Jean Chall and J. S. Carroll, eds., *Toward a Literate Society* (New York: McGraw-Hill, 1975). For further discussion and citations, see Graff, *Literacy Myth*, chap. 7; Epilogue, below.

126. Thompson, "Eighteenth Century," p. 153; Richard Hoggart, *The Uses of Literacy* (Boston: Beacon, 1960); idem, *On Culture and Communication* (Oxford: Oxford University Press, 1971); Henri-Jean Martin, "Culture écrit et culture orale, Culture savante et culture populaire, dans la France d'Ancien Régime," *Journal des Savants* (1975): 225–82; Natalie Davis, *Culture and Society in Early Modern France* (Stanford: Stanford University Press, 1975), pp. 189–269; David Riesman, *The Oral Tradition, the Written Word, and the Screen Image* (Yellow Springs, Ohio: Antioch Press, 1955); Stout, "Culture"; Gerald Suttles, *The Social Order of the Slum* (Chicago: University of Chicago Press, 1968); Charles Tilly, *An Urban World* (Boston: Little, Brown, 1974); Alejandro Portes, "Rationality in the Slum," *Comparative Studies in Society and History* 14 (1971–1972): 268–86; the works of Michael Young and Peter Wilmott; that of Elizabeth Bott; Howard H. Irving, *The Family Myth* (Toronto: Copp Clark, 1972); Graff, *Literacy Myth*, chaps. 2, 5, 7; Epilogue, below; the writings of Edmund Carpenter; David Riesman, "The Oral and Written Traditions," *Explorations* 6 (1956): 22–28. See Brian Harrison's studies of pubs and drink; Jon Kingsdale, "The 'Poor Man's Club': Social Functions of the Urban Working-Class Saloon," *American Quarterly* 25 (1973): 472–89; Daniel Calhoun, "The City as Teacher," *History of Education Quarterly* 9 (1969): 313, 319, passim; Marcus, "Reading." The latter two offer brilliant, original suggestions for new interpretations. See Rhys Isaac, "Dramatizing the Ideology of Revolution: Popular Mobilization in Virginia, 1774 to 1776," *William and Mary Quarterly* 33 (1976): 357–85; H. S. Stout, "Religion, Communications, and the Ideological Origins of the American Revolution," ibid. 34 (1977): 519–41; Calhoun, "City"; Graff, *Literacy Myth*, chaps. 5, 7; Vincent, *Bread*; Prothero, *Artisans*, among the literature. Nathan Hatch, "The Communication Strategy of Elias Smith," Paper presented to the Conference on Printing and Society in Early America, American Antiquarian Society, Oct. 1980; Colls, *Collier's Rant*.

127. Michael Anderson, *Family Structure in Nineteenth Century Lancashire* (Cambridge: Cambridge University Press, 1971), esp. chap. 10. I do not accept Anderson's theoretical orientation, however. See also Neuberg's work; Stedman Jones's studies; Lynn Lees, "Patterns of Lower Class Life," in *Nineteenth-Century Cities*, ed. Stephan Thernstrom and Richard Sennett (New Haven: Yale University Press, 1969), pp. 359–85; idem, "Mid-Victorian Migration and the Irish Family Economy," *Victorian Studies* 20 (1976): 25–44; idem, *Exiles of Erin* (Ithaca: Cornell University Press, 1979); Thompson, *Edwardians*.

128. See, for example, Marsden, "Social Environment"; Hurt, *Elementary Education*; essays in Geoffrey Crossick, ed., *The Lower-Middle Class in Britain* (New York: St. Martins, 1977); G. Anderson, *Victorian Clerks* (Manchester: University of Manchester Press, 1976).

129. Geoffrey Crossick, "The Emergence of the Lower Middle Class," in his *Lower-Middle Class*, pp. 38, 39; Anderson, *Clerks*; Bailey, *Leisure*. R. Q. Gray, "Religion, Culture, and Social Class," in Crossick, *Lower-Middle Class*, pp. 149–50. See also works of Bailey and Crossick, Gray's other studies; Best, *Mid-Victorian*.

130. Stedman Jones, "Working Class Culture," p. 489; see also studies of Tholfsen, Crossick, MacLeod, Gray, among the relevant literature.

131. Raymond Williams, "The Press," in Boyce, Curran, and Wingate, *Newspaper History*, p. 47. See also works of Dunae, Altick, Bailey, and Stedman Jones. For examples of exaggerations, see Walvin, *Leisure*, pp. 52–53; Walvin, *Leisure*, pp. 53–54.

132. Lynn H. Lees, "Getting and Spending: The Family Budgets of English Industrial Workers in 1890," in *Class Consciousness and Class Experience in Nineteenth-Century Europe*, ed. John M. Merriman (New York: Holmes and Meier, 1979), pp. 183–85; Vincent, *Bread*; Thompson, *Edwardians*, pp. 273, 274; Tholfsen, *Radicalism*, quoted on p. 106. See also the studies of Altick, Stedman Jones, Bailey, Meacham, McLeod, Kiernan, Laqueur, Brian Simon; D. W. Davies, *An Enquiry into the Reading of the Lower Classes* (Pasadena: Grant Dahlstrom, 1970). Tholfsen, *Radicalism*, pp. 108–109, 109. See also studies of Simon, Laqueur, J. F. C. Harrison.

133. See Stedman Jones, "Working Class Culture," pp. 471, 499. See also the studies of P. Thompson, Tholfsen, Crossick, Bailey, Joyce, Ellis, Meacham, Hurt, among others.

134. R. Q. Gray, *The Labour Aristocracy in Victorian Edinborough* (Oxford: Oxford University Press, 1976), pp. 130, 102; Crossick, *Artisan Elite*, p. 251. See also articles in Crossick, *Lower-Middle Class*; Tholfsen, *Radicalism*, and studies by Bailey, Reid, Marsden, Hurt, and others.

135. See especially the works of Brian Simon, Thomas Laqueur, J. F. C. Harrison, John Vincent, and Robert Webb, among others.

136. Stan Shipley, "The Libraries of the Alliance Cabinet Makers' Association," *History Workshop* I (1976): 181, 181–82; listing of holdings is on pp. 182–84. See also the work of Ellis, P. Thompson, P. Keane, and A. R. Thompson—compare with the latter.

137. Bailey, *Leisure and Class*, pp. 59–61. See also Walter Houghton, "Victorian Periodical Literature and the Articulate Classes," *Victorian Studies* 21 (1979): 389–412; works of Neuberg and Altick. There is a large, if not always useful, literature on the middle class, its values and culture.

138. Sally Mitchell, "Sentiment and Suffering: Women's Recreational Reading in the 1860s," *Victorian Studies* 21 (1977): 29, 34, 40, 45; Ann Douglas, *The Feminization of American Culture* (New York: Knopf, 1977), pp. 61–63.

139. On street literature, see Shepard, *History*; Neuberg, "Literature"; Martha Vicinus, *The Industrial Muse* (London: Croom Helm, 1975); Hoggart, *Uses*; Altick, *Common Reader*; Webb, *Reader*. On the middle class, see Bailey, " 'A Mingled Mass,' " *Leisure*. See also Graff, *Literacy Myth*, esp. chap. 7; Neuberg, *Popular Literature*; Walvin, *Leisure*.

140. Houghton, "Victorian Periodical," pp. 389, 391, passim.

141. Bailey, " 'A Mingled Mass,' " *Leisure*; Best, *Mid-Victorian*; Crossick, *Lower-Middle Class*. See also Geoffrey Crossick, "The Labour Aristocracy and Its Values: A Study of Mid-Victorian Kentish London," *Victorian Studies* 19 (1976): 301–328; Gray, *Labour Aristocracy*; H. J. Perkin, *The Origins of Modern English Society* (London: Routledge and Kegan Paul, 1969); M. R. Marrus, ed., *The Emergence of Leisure* (New York: Harper and Row, 1974); Harrison, *Early Victorians*; S. G. Checkland, *The Rise of Industrial Society in England* (London: Longman, 1964); Patricia Branca, *Silent Sisterhood* (Pittsburgh: Carnegie Mellon University Press, 1975). For comparisons, see Edward Pessen, *Riches, Class, and Power before the Civil War* (Lexington, Mass.: D. C. Heath, 1973); Rush Welter, *The Mind of America* (New York: Columbia University Press, 1975); F. C. Jaher, ed., *The Age of Industrialism in America* (New York: Free Press, 1968); John Cawalti, *Apostles of the Self-Made Man* (Chicago: University of Chicago Press, 1965); Irwin G. Wyllie, *The Self-Made Man in America* (New York: Free Press, 1966).

142. For an important contemporary opinion, see Hodgson, *Exaggerated Estimates*, pp. 3, 3–4, 4, 4–5, 5, 6, 7, 8, 9.

143. Ibid., pp. 6–7. For the normative view, see Tobias, *Crime*. For a contrasting view, see Graff, *Literacy Myth*, chap. 6; Phillips, *Crime*; R. D. Storch's studies of policing and working-class culture and those of Roger Lane and Eric Monkkonen, among the literature. I have reprinted Hodgson's essay in *History of Education Quarterly*.

144. Phillips, *Crime*, p. 154, passim, p. 160. See also Thomas Wyse, *School Reform*, as quoted in Egerton Ryerson, "Report on a System of Public Elementary Instruction for Upper Canada," in *Documentary History of Education in Upper Canada*, ed. J. G. Hodgins, vol. 6 (Toronto, 1899), p. 151; Henry Maynew in *The Morning Chronicle*, March 29, 1850, quoted in Tobias, *Crime*, p. 207. And see M. Hill and C. F. Cornwalles, *Two Prize Essays on Juvenile Delinquency* (London, 1850), p. 220, quoted in Tobias, *Crime*, p. 207; Stedman Jones, *Outcast London*. See also Graff, *Literacy Myth*, pp. 250–51, for data, and passim. Tobias, *Crime*, has excellent quotations of contemporary opinion. Hodgson, *Exaggerated Estimates*, pp. 11, 13, 14, 14–15. For a superb fictional but extraordinarily accurate view, see Robert Tresell, *The Ragged Trousered Philanthropists* (New York: Monthly Review Press, 1978 [1914]). I discuss this subject in "Literacy, in Literature as in Life," *History of Education Quarterly* 23 (1983): 279–96; Scotland has not been treated separately in this chapter. There is no direct evidence respecting literacy and its meanings. In general, see Stone, "Literacy"; Ellen Alwall, *The Religious Trend in Secular Scottish School-Books, 1850–1861 and 1873–1882* (Lund: C. W. K. Gleerup, 1970); H. M. Knox, *Two Hundred and Fifty Years of Scottish Education, 1646–1946* (Edinburgh: Oliver and Boyd, 1953); James Scotland, *The History of Scottish Education*, 2 vols. (London: University of London Press, 1969); Ian J. Simpson, *Education in Aberdeenshire before 1872* (London: University of London Press, 1947). See also Holley, "Two Family"; Houston, *Scottish Literacy*.

145. On transformations in nineteenth-century Irish society, see Joseph Lee, *The Modernisation of Irish Society* (Dublin: Gill and Macmillan, 1977); Oliver Macdonagh, "The Irish Famine Emigration," *Perspectives in American History* 10 (1976): 357–446; Robert Kennedy, *The Irish: Emigration, Marriage, and Fertility* (Berkeley: University of California Press, 1973); Lynn Lees, *Exiles*, and her articles; Lynn Lees and John Modell, "The Irish Countryman Urbanized," *Journal of Urban History* 3 (1977): 391–408. On education, see Goldstrum, *Social Context*; Akerson, *Irish Education Experiment*; James J. Auchmuty, *Irish Education: A Historical Survey* (Dublin: Hodges Figgis and Co., 1937); Patrick J. Dowling, *The Hedge Schools of Ireland* (London: Longmans, Green, 1935).

146. T. W. Freeman, *Pre-famine Ireland* (Manchester: Manchester University Press, 1957), pp. 133, 134, 136, 135, 133. See also the work of Lynn Lees, cited above.

147. Kevin O'Neill, "Some New Insights into Pre-famine Irish Emigration," paper presented to the Social Science History Association, Cambridge, Mass., 1979, p. 4. See also his 1979 Brown University diss. See Webb, "Reader"; Graff, *Literacy Myth*, chap. 2; Lees, *Exiles*, and her articles; Anderson, *Family Structure*; Freeman, *Pre-famine Ireland*.

148. Lees, *Exiles*, pp. 34–35. See also O'Neill, "New Insights"; for data and arguments, Barbara Anderson, "Internal Migration in a Modernizing Society: The Case of Late Nineteenth Century European Russia" (Ph.D. diss., Princeton University, 1973), published as a book by Princeton University Press in 1980.

149. Freeman, *Pre-famine Ireland*; Webb, "Working Class Readers"; Lees, "Patterns"; *Exiles*. See also Anderson, "Internal Migration"; Larry H. Long, "Migration Differentials by Education and Occupation," *Demography* 10 (1973): 243–58; Akerman, "Mobile and Stationary Populations"; Graff, *Literacy Myth*, pp. 65–66.

150. See the studies by Goldstrum and Akenson.

151. Akenson, *Irish Education*, pp. 376, 378, 380–81, 387, chap. 1, p. 235. Compare with Auchmuty, *Irish Education*. See also, on demographic consequences, Kennedy, *Irish*. On language issues, see Glanmour Williams, "Literacy and Nationalism in Wales," *History* 56 (1971): 1–16. See also Lees, *Exiles*; Graff, *Literacy Myth*, chap. 1; Goldstrum, *Social Context*.

152. Lawrence A. Cremin, *American Education: The National Experience* (New York: Harper and Row, 1980), p. 485. Cremin's recent history, of which I shall be critical at times, remains magisterial; it also contains by far the best bibliography for this period. See also Kenneth A. Lockridge, *Literacy in Colonial New England* (New York: Norton, 1974), and Lee Soltow and Edward Stevens, *The Rise of Literacy and the Common School* (Chicago: University of Chicago Press, 1981), as well as chaps. 5 and 6 above, for colonial background. Carl Kaestle's study of U.S. education, 1780–1850, *Pillars of the Republic* (New York: Hill and Wang, 1983), advances our understanding.

153. Cremin, *American Education: National*, p. 497.

154. See, among many studies, Kaestle, "Between the Charybdis"; Carl F. Kaestle, *The Evolution of an Urban School System* (Cambridge, Mass.: Harvard University Press, 1973), Pillars; Stanley Schultz, *The Culture Factory* (New York: Oxford University Press, 1973); Cremin, *American Education: National*; Henry F. May, *The Enlightenment in America* (New York: Oxford University Press, 1976); Donald Meyer, *The Democratic Enlightenment* (New York: Capricorn, 1976); Henry S. Commager, *The Empire of Reason* (Garden City, N.Y.: Doubleday, 1977); Frederick Rudolph, ed., *Essays on Education in the Early Republic* (Cambridge, Mass.: Harvard University Press, 1965). On eighteenth-century educational thought, see the relevant references in chap. 6 above.

155. Quoted in Louis B. Nye, *The Cultural Life of the New Nation* (New York: Harper and Row, 1960), p. 150. See also John C. Henderson, *Thomas Jefferson's Views on Public Education* (New York: Putnam's Sons, 1890); Allen O. Hansen, *Liberalism and American Education in the Eighteenth Century* (New York: Macmillan, 1926), among the relevant literature.

156. Nye, *Cultural Life*, pp. 154–55, 156. See also selections in Rudolph, *Essays on Education*; Hyman Kuritz, "Benjamin Rush: His Theory of Republican Education," *History of Education Quarterly* 7 (1967): 432–51; Cremin, *American Education: National*; Rush Welter, *Popular Education and Democratic Thought in America* (New York: Columbia University Press, 1962); idem, ed., *American Writings on Popular Education* (Indianapolis: Bobbs-Merrill, 1971); the works of Kaestle and Schultz; Raymond Mohl, "Education as Social Control in New York City," *New York History* 51 (1970): 219–37, among his work; David Rothman, *The Discovery of the Asylum* (Boston: Little Brown, 1971); John Alexander, *Render Them Submissive* (Amherst: University of Massachusetts Press, 1980). For women, see Ruth Bloch, "American Feminine Ideals in Transition," *Feminist Studies* 4 (1978): 92–99; Linda Kerber, *Women of the Republic* (Chapel Hill: University of North Carolina Press, 1980); Mary Beth Norton, *Liberty's Daughters* (New York: Knopf, 1980); Nancy Cott, *Bonds of Womanhood* (New Haven: Yale University Press, 1977).

157. Kaestle, "Between the Charybdis," pp. 177–78, 178, 181–82, 182, 183, 184, 185, 187. See the literature on blacks cited below, especially William R. Taylor, "Toward a Definition of Orthodoxy," *Harvard Educational Review* 36 (1966): 412–26.

158. Alexander, *Render* pp. 142, 145, 145–46, 149, 150, 151, 152, 153, 156, 157, 158–59. See also the works of Kaestle and Mohl on New York City, Schultz on Boston, cited above; Kaestle, *Joseph Lancaster*; Michael B. Katz, *The Irony of Early School Reform* (Cambridge, Mass.: Harvard University Press, 1968); idem, *Class, Bureaucracy, and Schools* (New York: Praeger, 1975); idem, "The Origins of Public Education: A Reassessment," *History of Education Quarterly* 16 (1976): 381–407, Cremin, *American Education: National*, pt. 1, passim. Recent studies by Bruce Laurie, Paul Faler, and Gary Nash are also are useful. Too little is known about rural schooling at this time. But see Carl F. Kaestle and Maris Vinovskis, *Education and Social Change in Nineteenth-Century Massachusetts* (Cambridge: Cambridge University Press, 1980); Kaestle, *Pillars*; David Tyack, "The Spread of Public Schooling in Victorian America," *History of Education* 7 (1978): 173–82. See also Gilmore's forthcoming study; Mary Ryan, *Cradle of the Middle Class* (New York: Cambridge University Press, 1981). Quoted in Kurtiz, "Rush," p. 435; ibid., p. 437; Cremin, *American Education: National*, passim. On educational implications of the Northwest Ordinance, see Dennis Dennenberg, "The Missing Link: New England's Influence on Early National Educational Policies," *New England Quarterly* 52 (1979): 219–33. Kaestle's *Pillars* fills many gaps. There is a large literature on the place of morality in schooling; see Graff, *Literacy Myth*, chap. 1.

159. Lockridge, *Literacy*, passim; Soltow and Stevens, *Literacy*, pp. 34, 35–36, 105, 113, chap. 4, chap. 5 (pages refer to a manuscript version the authors kindly shared). See also, on regional patterns, Albert Fishlow, "The American Common School Revival: Fact or Fancy?" in *Industrialization in Two Systems*, ed. H. Rosovsky (New York, 1966), pp. 40–67; Taylor, "Orthodoxy"; Kaestle and Vinovskis, *Education*; reports of the U.S. Census; Maris Vinovskis and Richard Bernard, "Beyond Catherine Beecher," *Signs* 3 (1978): 856–69. For a Canadian comparison, see Graff, *Literacy Myth*. On criminality, see, for example,

Katz, "Origins"; Graff, *Literacy Myth*, chap. 6; Susan Houston, "Victorian Origins of Juvenile Delinquency," *History of Education Quarterly* 12 (1972): 254–80. See also John W. Meyer, David Tyack, Joane Nagel, and Audri Gordon, "Public Education as Nation–Building in America," *American Journal of Sociology* 85 (1979): 591–613.

160. For women, see the citations to the writing of Kerber, Norton, Cott, and Bloch, above. See also Vinovskis and Bernard, "Beyond"; Maris Vinovskis and Richard Bernard, "The Female School Teacher," *Journal of Social History* 10 (1977): 332–45; Kathryn Sklar, *Catherine Beecher* (New Haven: Yale University Press, 1973); special issues of the *History of Education Quarterly*; Allison Prentice, "The Feminization of Teaching," *Histoire Sociale* 8 (1975): 8–20; Thomas Dublin, *Women at Work* (New York: Columbia University Press, 1979); Clyde Griffen and Sally Griffen, *Natives and Newcomers* (Cambridge, Mass.: Harvard University Press, 1978); Jill Conway, "Perspectives on the History of Women's Education," *History of Education Quarterly* 14 (1974): 1–12; Soltow and Stevens, *Literacy*, passim; Ryan, *Cradle*; among a growing literature. Soltow and Stevens, *Literacy*, p. 155. See, in general, Graff, "Literacy, Education, and Fertility," for a discussion of these issues and for a historical bibliography. See also Michael B. Katz and Mark J. Stern, "Fertility, Class, and Industrial Capitalism," *American Quarterly* 33 (1981): 63–92.

161. Soltow and Stevens, *Literacy*. See, for example, Stephan Thernstrom, *Poverty and Progress* (Cambridge, Mass.: Harvard University Press, 1964); Michael B. Katz, *The People of Hamilton* (Cambridge, Mass.: Harvard University Press, 1975); James Henretta, "Families and Farms," *William and Mary Quarterly* 35 (1978): 3–32; Graff, *Literacy Myth*, pt. 1, among others; David Hogan, "Education and the Making of the Chicago Working Class," *History of Education Quarterly* 18 (1978): 227–70.

162. Horace Mann, *Fifth Annual Report of the Secretary of the Board of Education* (Boston, 1842), p. 89. See also, for the stress on collective benefits rather than individual, John Eaton, *Illiteracy and Its Social, Political, and Industrial Effects* (New York, 1882). Edward Stevens's study of illiteracy and judicial proceedings is relevant here. See Graff, *Literacy Myth*, chaps. 2, 3, 5, and below.

163. Stevens and Soltow, *Literacy*, pp. 160, 160–62. See their "Economic Aspects of School Participation in Mid–Nineteenth–Century United States," *Journal of Interdisciplinary History* 8 (1977): 221–43; Lee Soltow, *Men and Wealth in the United States* (New Haven: Yale University Press, 1975); idem, "Economic Inequality in the United States, 1790–1860," *Journal of Economic History* 31 (1971): 822–39; Graff, *Literacy Myth*, pt. 1.

164. Dublin, *Women*, pp. 149, 150, 150–51, 151, 153, chap. 9 passim, chap. 10 passim. See also, for background and comparisons, Thomas Bender, *Toward an Urban Vision* (Lexington: University of Kentucky Press, 1975); Kaestle and Vinovskis, *Education*; Katz, *Irony*; Alexander J. Field, "Educational Expansion in Mid-Nineteenth-Century Massachusetts," *Harvard Educational Review* 46 (1976): 521–52; idem, "Economic and Demographic Determinants of Educational Commitment," *Journal of Economic History* 39 (1979): 439–59; Graff, *Literacy Myth*, esp. chap. 5.

165. Bender, *Toward*, p. 121, passim; Carl F. Kaestle, "Social Change, Discipline, and the Common School in Early Nineteenth-Century America,"*Journal of Interdisciplinary History* 9 (1978): 1–18; Dublin, *Women*. See also Paul Faler, "Cultural Aspects of the Industrial Revolution," *Labor History* 15 (1974): 367–94; R. D. Gidney, "Elementary Education in Upper Canada," *Ontario History* 65 (1973): 169–85; Kaestle and Vinovskis, *Education*. See, too, G. R. Stetson, *Literacy and Crime in Massachusetts* (Boston: Blair and Hallett, 1886); Katz, *Irony*, among the literature on crime. Barbara Brenzel's study of the state reform school for girls is important in this respect.

166. Graff, *Literacy Myth*, esp. chaps. 2, 4. On Quebec, see Allan Greer, "The Pattern of Literacy in Quebec," *Histoire Sociale* 11 (1978): 293–335, and my comments, ibid., 12 (1979): 444–55. See also Soltow and Stevens, *Literacy*; Harvey J. Graff, "Literacy and Social Structure in Elgin County, 1861," *Histoire sociale* 6 (1973): 25–48; Graff, *Literacy Myth*, chap. 7; research in progress on illiteracy and the law in nineteenth–century America by Stevens supports these conclusions. Calhoun, "City as Teacher," pp. 313, 319, *Intelligence*, and above discussion. See the recent work of Donald Scott on print and the public lecture system, unpublished paper presented to the American Antiquarian Society Conference

on Printing and Society in Early America, October 1980. See also Jennifer Tebbe, "Print and American Culture," *American Quarterly* 32 (1980): 259–79.

167. Soltow and Stevens, *Literacy*, chap. 7. On the development of education in this period, see the previously cited work of Katz, Kaestle, Kaestle and Vinovskis, Tyack, Cremin, and Fishlow, and Bowles and Gintis, *Schooling*. See also the many relevant local and case studies.

168. See above and below, and *Literacy Myth*, chap. 7; Calhoun, *Intelligence*.

169. Soltow and Stevens, *Literacy*, chap. 7, passim. See also Taylor, "Orthodoxy"; Robert Church and Michael Sedlak, *Education in the United States* (New York: Free Press, 1976) for the South.

170. Soltow and Stevens, *Literacy*, pp. 216, 218, 218–19, chap. 8. On attendance and its determinants, see Katz, *People*, chap. 5; Michael B. Katz, "Who Went to School?" *History of Education Quarterly*, pp. 432–54; Ian Davey, "Education Reform and the Working Class" (Ph.D. diss., University of Toronto, 1975), among his studies; Haley Bammen, "Patterns of School Attendance in Toronto," *History of Education Quarterly* 12 (1972): 381–410; Selwyn Troen, "Popular Education in Nineteenth Century St. Louis," *History of Education Quarterly* 13 (1973): 23–40; Kaestle and Vinovskis, *Education*, among their studies; Selma Berrol, "Who Went to School in Mid–Nineteenth Century New York?" in *Essays in the History of New York City*, ed. Irwin Yellowitz (Port Washington, N.Y.: National University Publications, 1978), pp. 43–60; Graff, *Literacy Myth*, chap. 4; among a growing literature. Soltow and Stevens, *Literacy*, p. 231, chap. 6. See also Meyer, Tyack et al., "Public Education," among the other relevant literature cited above.

171. Elson, *Guardians of Tradition*; Barbara Finkelstein, "The Moral Dimensions of Pedagogy," *American Studies* 15 (1974): 79–89; idem, "Pedagogy as Intrusion," *History of Childhood Quarterly* 2 (1975): 349–78; Graff, *Literacy Myth*, esp. chap. 1; Katz, *Irony*; Kaestle, *Evolution*; Tyack, "Spread"; David Tyack, "The Kingdom of God and the Common School," *Harvard Educational Review* 36 (1966): 447–69; Timothy L. Smith, "Protestant Schooling and American Nationality," *Journal of American History* 53 (1967): 679–95; George R. Stetson, *Literacy and Crime in Massachusetts and the Necessity for Moral and Industrial Training in the Public Schools* (Boston: Blair and Mallett, 1886); Charles Bidwell, "The Moral Significance of the Common School," *History of Education Quarterly* 6 (1966): 50–91; Carol Billman, "McGuffey's Readers and Alger's Fiction," *Journal of Popular Culture* 11 (1977): 614–19; Robert Lynn Wood, "Civil Catechetics in Mid-Victorian America," *Religious Education* 68 (1973): 5–27; Steven L. Schlossman, "The 'Culture of Poverty' in Ante–bellum Social Thought," *Science and Society* 38 (1974): 150–66; Janet A. Miller, "Urban Education and the New City: Cincinnati's Elementary Schools, 1870 to 1914," *Ohio History* 88 (1979): 152–72; Clifford S. Griffen, "Religious Benevolence as Social Control," *Mississippi Valley Historical Review* 44 (1957): 423–44; W. David Lewis, "The Reformer as Conservative: Protestant Counter-Subversion in the Early Republic," in *The Development of an American Culture*, ed. Stanley Coben and Lorman Ratner (Englewood Cliffs, N.J., 1970), pp. 64–91; Prentice, *School Promoters*, among a larger literature.

172. Finkelstein, "Moral Dimensions," pp. 79, 80; see also her "Pedagogy"; Stetson, "Literacy," p. 10. See also Edward Mansfield's writings in *Reports* of the U.S. Commissioner of Education; Prentice, *School Promoters*; Graff, *Literacy Myth*, chaps. 1, 6; Katz, *Irony*; Michael Hindus, *Prison and Plantation* (Chapel Hill: University of North Carolina Press, 1980).

173. Barbara Finkelstein, "Reading, Writing, and the Acquisition of Identity in the United States," in *Regulated Children/Liberated Children*, ed. Barbara Finkelstein (New York: Psychohistory Press, 1979), p. 133, and her other essays; see also Graff, *Literacy Myth*; Katz, "Origins," Tyack, "Spread," Kaestle, "Social Change"; Calhoun, *Intelligence*.

174. Soltow and Stevens, *Literacy*, pp. 237–38, 238–39, 243, 244, 245. Troen, "Popular Education"; Selwyn Troen, *The Public and the Schools* (Columbia: University of Missouri Press, 1975); Kaestle, *Evolution*; Kaestle and Vinovskis, *Education*; Patricia K. Good, "Irish Adjustment to American Society," *Records* of the American Catholic Historical Society of Philadelphia 86 (1975): 7–23; Griffen and Griffen, *Natives*; Thernstrom, *Poverty*; Stephan Thernstrom, *The Other Bostonians* (Cambridge, Mass.: Harvard University Press, 1973);

468 *Notes to Pages 350–351*

Graff, *Literacy Myth*, esp. pt. 1; Carol Schumacher, "School Attendance in Nineteenth-Century Pittsburgh" (Ph.D. diss., University of Pittsburgh, 1977); Soltow, *Men and Wealth*; Katz, *People*; Davey, "School Reform"; Jay Dolan, *The Immigrant Church* (Baltimore: Johns Hopkins University Press, 1975); James Sanders, *The Education of an Urban Minority* (New York: Oxford University Press, 1977); Marvin Lazerson, "Understanding American Catholic Educational History," *History of Education Quarterly* 17 (1977): 297–317; Timothy Walsh, "Catholic Social Institutions and Urban Development," *Catholic Historical Review* 64 (1978): 16–32; Kathleen Conzen, *Immigrant Milwaukee* (Cambridge, Mass.: Harvard University Press, 1976); Jo Ellen Vinyard, *The Irish on the Urban Frontier* (New York: Arno Press, 1976); the work of Vincent Lannie, among the literature. See also, for presumed economic implications, Eaton, *Literacy*; Gavin Wright, "Cheap Labor and Southern Textiles before 1880," *Journal of Economic History* 39 (1979): 665–80. For "new immigrants" of the late nineteenth and early twentieth centuries, see below.

175. Soltow and Stevens, "Economic Aspects," pp. 242–43, *Literacy*; Graff, *Literacy Myth*, pt. 1; Katz, "Origins"; Michael B. Katz, "Origins of the Institutional State," *Marxist Perspectives* 1 (1978): 6–23; Roger Lane, *Violent Death in the City* (Cambridge, Mass.: Harvard University Press, 1979).

176. Griffen and Griffen, *Natives*, pp. 80, 81, 82, 83, passim. See also Katz, *Irony*, "Origins." For relevant comparisons, see the useful studies of Conzen, *Immigrant Milwaukee*; Dublin, *Women*; Ryan, *Cradle*; Jo Ellen Vinyard, "Inland Urban Immigrants: The Detroit Irish, 1850," *Michigan History* 58 (1973): 121–39; Hogan, "Education"; the studies cited above; Richard Griswold de Castillo, "Literacy in San Antonio, Texas, 1850–1860," *Latin American Research Review* 15 (1980): 180–85; Michael Weiss, "Education, Literacy, and the Community in Los Angeles in 1850," *Southern California Quarterly* 60 (1978): 117–42. Additional data are found in the empirical work of Easterlin, Haines, Goldin, and Leet, and in the emerging literature on immigrants and the working class in specific localities. It should be noted, too, that some immigrants did not accept the public schools, on the grounds of religion and/or language. It could be a divisive issue. Their own moral bases, however, often shared much with the consensus. See, for example, studies in Theodore Hershberg, ed., *Philadelphia* (New York: Oxford University Press, 1980).

177. Katz, "Origins," p. 383. See also his "Institutional State." See the literature on educational development in general, especially Kaestle and Vinovskis, *Education*; Cremin, *American Education: National*; Lawrence A. Cremin, *American Education: The Colonial Experience* (New York: Harper and Row, 1970).

178. Meyer and Tyack et al., "Public Education," p. 591. See also David Tyack, *The One Best System* (Cambridge, Mass.: Harvard University Press, 1974); Edward Eggleston, *The Hoosier Schoolmaster* (various editions). But see J. H. Ralph and Richard Rubinstein, "Immigration and the Expansion of Schooling," *American Sociological Review* 45 (1980): 943–54.

179. Katz, "Origins," p. 384; Tyack, "Spread," pp. 178–79. See also the literature cited in note 220 below.

180. Katz, "Origins," pp. 386, 391, 383; his "Institutional State," *Class, Bureaucracy, and Schools*. On crime and literacy, see Graff, *Literacy Myth*, chap. 6; Katz, *Irony*; Hindus, *Prison*; writings of Stetson, Horace Mann, Francis Lieber, and other contemporaries; Prentice, *School Promoters*; Houston, "Victorian," among her work. See also S. L. Schlossman, *Love and the American Delinquent* (Chicago: University of Chicago Press, 1977); Rothman, *Discovery*; among the literature. On women, see the literature cited above.

181. *Annual Report of the Secretary of the Board of Education* 5 (Boston, 1842): 81, 87–89, 90, 100. On the biases inherent in Mann's survey, see the *Annual Report*, passim; Maris Vinovskis, "Horace Mann on the Economic Productivity of Education," *New England Quarterly* 43 (1970): 550–71. Soltow and Stevens, "Economic Aspects," provide other examples. See also, Marglin, "Bosses"; Alexander Field, "Industrialization and Skill Intensity: The Case of Massachusetts," *Journal of Human Resources* 15 (1980): 149–75. See above for comparisons. Mann, *Fifth Annual Report*; Vinovskis, "Mann," p. 568. This discussion is indebted to the work of Vinovskis, pt. 2, and the literature cited above. See also Frank

Tracey Carleton, *Economic Influences upon Educational Progress in the United States, 1820–1850* (Reprinted: New York: Teachers College Press, 1965), chap. 4; the work of Alexander Field. On the relationship between literacy and inventiveness, so prized by Mann, see Eugene Ferguson, "The Mind's Eye: Nonverbal Thought in Technology," *Science* 197 (1977): 827–36; Wallace, *Rockdale*, pp. 237ff. Alexander Field, "Educational Reform and Manufacturing Development in Mid–Nineteenth Century Massachusetts" (Ph.D. diss., University of California, Berkeley, 1974), esp. chaps. 8, 9; Gintis, "Education"; Bowles and Gintis, *Schooling*, pt. 2; Dreeben, *On What Is Learned*. See also Edward Jarvis, M.D., "The Value of Common-School Education to Common Labour," *Report of the U.S. Commissioner of Education* (Washington, D.C., 1872), pp. 572–85, 577, 574, 585. See also Eaton, *Illiteracy*. For the South, see Wright, "Cheap Labor"; Roger L. Ransom and Richard Sutch, *One Kind of Freedom* (Cambridge: Cambridge University Press, 1977). In general, see E. Verne, "Literacy and Industrialization," in *A Turning Point for Literacy*, ed. Leon Bataille, pp. 211–28; Ivar Berg, *Education and Jobs* (Boston: Beacon Press, 1971); G. C. Squires, "Education, Jobs, and Inequality," *Social Problems* 24 (1977): 436–50; Inkeles and Smith, *Becoming Modern*; James Bright, "Does Automation Raise Skill Requirements?" *Harvard Business Review* 36 (1958): 85–98; idem, "The Relationship of Increasing Automation and Skill Requirements," in *Report* of the U.S. National Commission on Technology, Automation, and Economic Progress Appendix, vol. 2 (Washington, D.C.: GPO, 1966), pp. 203–221. See also Epilogue, below. Eaton, *Illiteracy*, pp. 18–19, 4. For the South, see also Wright, "Cheap Labor"; Ransom and Sutch, *One Kind*.

182. Katz, "Origins," pp. 395, 398, 400, 401, 402. See also Graff, *Literacy Myth*, esp. pt. 1, chap. 1. See in general Kaestle, "Social Change"; Kaestle and Vinovskis, *Education*; Davey, "School Reform"; Tyack, "Spread"; David Tyack, "Ways of Seeing," *Harvard Educational Review* 46 (1976): 335–89; W. M. Landes and L. C. Solomon, "Compulsory Schooling Legislation," *Journal of Economic History* 32 (1972): 36–91; R. B. Everhart, "From Universalism to Usurpation," *Review of Educational Research* 47 (1977): 499–530; Charles Burgess, "The Goddess, The School Book, and Compulsion," *Harvard Educational Review* 46 (1976): 199–216. On teaching jobs, see Vinovskis and Bernard, "Female School Teacher"; Keith Melder, "Women's High Calling," *American Studies* 12 (1972): 19–32; Sklar, *Beecher*; Prentice, "Feminization."

183. Graff, *Literacy Myth*, chap. 1; Dreeben, *On What Is Learned*; Michael W. Apple, *Ideology and Curriculum* (London: Routledge and Kegan Paul, 1979); Bowles and Gintis, *Schooling*.

184. Meyer and Tyack, "Public Education," pp. 599, 600, 601. See also the literature on morality and on school development cited above, and Harriet Friedmann, "World Market, State, and Family Farm," *Comparative Studies in Society and History* 20 (1978): 545–86, among her studies; Greer, "Sunday Schools"; Cremin, *American Education: National*; Anne M. Boylan, "Sunday Schools and Changing Evangelical Views of Children in the 1820s," *Church History* 48 (1979): 320–33; idem, "The Role of Conversion in Nineteenth-Century Sunday Schools," *American Studies* 20 (1979): 35–48; idem, "Evangelical Womanhood in the Nineteenth Century," *Feminist Studies* 4 (1978): 62–80; Prentice, *School Promoters*.

185. Cremin, *American Education: National*: pp. 301, 302, and the literature cited above; Soltow and Stevens, *Literacy*; papers by Hatch, Scott, Gilmore at the Printing and Society Conference. Louis B. Nye, *Society and Culture in America*, (New York: Harper and Row, 1974), p. 367, and the literature cited above. The following is an interpretive synthesis of material found in the above literature.

186. Soltow and Stevens, *Literacy*, p. 55; among many examples.

187. Michael H. Harris, "Books on the Frontier: The Extent and Nature of Book Ownership in Southern Indiana, 1800–1850," *Library Quarterly* 42 (1972): 416–17, 426, 428, passim. See also, among the literature, Howard H. Peckham, "Books and Reading on the Ohio Valley Frontier," *Mississippi Valley Historical Review* 44 (1958): 649–66; H. H. Dugger, "Reading Interest and the Book Trade in Frontier Missouri" (Ph.D. diss., University of Missouri); and titles in Michael H. Harris and Donald G. Davis, *American Library History: A Bibliography* (Austin: University of Texas Press, 1978). Edward Stevens, "Wealth and

Culture on the American Frontier: (unpub. ms., 1977), pp. 17, 22, 24, passim. See also Soltow and Stevens, *Literacy*, passim, and the work of Boylan on Sunday schools and the publishing histories cited above.

188. Joseph Kett, "The American Family as an Intellectual Institution, 1780–1880" (unpub. ms., 1977), appendix, pp. 42, 44, passim. For finer comparisons, see his tables. Now published as Joseph Kett and Patricia A. McClung, "Book Culture in Post-revolutionary Virginia," *Proceedings*, American Antiquarian Society 94 (1984): 97–147.

189. Quotation is from issue of December 29, 1855; it is commonly quoted. J. W. Tebbel, *A History of Book Publishing in the United States*, 3 vols. (New York: Bowker, 1972–75—vols. 1, 2), for example, includes a number of similiar statements.

190. Cremin, *American Education: National*, p. 311. See, for example, Graff, *Literacy Myth*, chap. 7; Calhoun, "The City," *Intelligence*; Cremin, *American Education: National*; Marcus, "Reading," among others.

191. Tebbel, *History*, vol. 1, p. 508, vol. 2, passim. See also Nathan Hatch's study of religious dissemination, in progress; Cremin, *American Education: National*; Boylan on Sunday schools, among others.

192. See for examples Kett, "American Family," among the above-cited literature, and Allan Horlick, *Country Boys and Merchant Princes* (Lewisburg, Pa.: Bucknell University Press, 1975).

193. Tebbel, *History*, vol. 1, pp. 228–29, 545.

194. Douglas, *Feminization*, pp. 61–62, 62–63, 63, 60. See also Mitchell, "Sentiment and Suffering," and above. On classes of literature for women, see Tebbel, *History*; Frank Luther Mott, *A History of American Magazines*, 5 vols. (Cambridge, Mass.: Harvard University Press, 1930–68). More generally, see Cott, *Bonds of Womanhood*; Barbara Welber, "The Cult of True Womanhood," *American Quarterly* 18 (1966): 151–74, and the proliferating literature on American women's culture.

195. See also the works of Kerber, Sklar, Dublin, Cott, Vinovskis and Bernard, and Ryan, among other relevant references. Recent economic studies, such as those by Claudia Golden, Elyce Rotella, and Mark Aldrich, are also germane.

196. Quoted in Tebbel, *History*, vol. 2, p. 28; ibid., vol. 2, p. 171, passim. See also below, and Calhoun, *Intelligence*. See Mott's studies of magazines and newspapers, and Michael Schudson, *Discovering the News* (New York: Basic Books, 1978). Figures are from Schudson, *Discovering*, p. 13.

197. Schudson, *Discovering*, pp. 18, 46, 49; Mott, *Magazines, Journalism* provides other examples, as does Tebbel, *History*, vols. 1 and 2.

198. Cremin, *American Education: National*, pp. 196, 201, 205, 208, 212, 213–14, 217. See also, on religious publishing, works of Hatch, Boylan, Mott, Tebbel. On voluntarism, see Richard D. Brown's studies. See also Donald Scott's work in progress on lyceums and cultural development; Robert Weir's comments at the American Antiquarian Society Conference on Printing and Society in Early America, October 1980; Graff, *Literacy Myth*, esp. chaps. 1, 7, and above. On conflict, the work of Alan Dawley, Michael Feldberg, Paul Faler, Bruce Laurie, Ian Davey, Bryan Palmer, Gregory Kealey, and David Montgomery is particularly useful.

199. See Graff, *Literacy Myth*, chap. 8, passim. For the working class, see as key examples William G. Shade, "The 'Working Class' and Educational Reform in Early America: The Case of Providence, Rhode Island," *Historian* 39 (1976): 1–23; Katz, *Irony*; Bender, *Urban Vision*; Alan Dawley, *Class and Community* (Cambridge, Mass.: Harvard University Press, 1976); Paul Faler, *Mechanics and Manufacturers* (Albany: SUNY Press, 1981): Alan Dawley and Paul Faler, "Working-Class Culture and Politics in the Industrial Revolution: Sources of Loyalism and Rebellion," *Journal of Social History* 9 (1976): 466–80; Bruce Laurie, *Working People of Philadelphia* (Philadelphia: Temple University Press, 1980); idem, " 'Nothing on Compulsion': Life Styles of Philadelphia Artisans, 1820–1850," *Labor History* 15 (1974): 337–66; Paul Faler, "Cultural Aspects of the Industrial Revolution: Lynn, Massachusetts, Shoemakers and Industrial Morality, 1826–1860," ibid., pp. 367–94; Susan Hirsch, *Roots of the American Working Class* (Philadelphia: University of Pennsylvania Press, 1978); Herbert G. Gutman, "Work, Culture, and Society in Industrializing America," *Ameri-*

*can Historical Review* 78 (1973): 531–88; Wallace, *Rockdale*; Paul Johnson, *A Shopkeeper's Millennium* (New York: Hill and Wang, 1978); John Modell, "Patterns of Consumption, Acculturation, and Family Income Strategies in Late Nineteenth-Century America," in *Family and Population in Nineteenth-Century America*, ed. T. K. Hareven and Maris Vinovskis (Princeton: Princeton University Press, 1978), pp. 206–240, among the literature.

200. See, for example, the work of Graff, Kaestle, Katz, Faler, and Laurie.

201. Dawley and Faler, "Working-Class Culture," p. 468; Faler, "Cultural Aspects," pp. 384–85. See also work of Laurie, Bender, Montgomery, Gutman, Hirsh, Katz.

202. Faler, "Cultural Aspects," pp. 386, 387; Kaestle, "Social Change," p. 15. See also Davey, "School Reform".

203. Dawley and Faler, "Working-Class Culture," p. 469.

204. Laurie, *Working People*, p. 95.

205. Faler, "Cultural Aspects," p. 392; Dawley and Faler, "Working-Class Culture," p. 470. See also Dawley, *Class*; Laurie, *Working People*.

206. Faler, "Cultural Aspects," p. 392, and work of Katz, Laurie, Dawley.

207. This discussion draws upon Graff, *Literacy Myth*, chap. 5, esp. pp. 211ff. Citations are provided there. See also Modell, "Patterns"; Dublin, *Women*.

208. The following draws upon Graff, *Literacy Myth*, chap. 7, pp. 272–78. Citations are provided there. See also above for comparative perspectives. See also Ralph Connor, *Glengarry Schooldays* (Toronto: McClelland and Stewart 1968 [1902]), Eggleston, *Hoosier Schoolmaster*, for descriptive accounts presented as fiction.

209. On reading instruction, see H. B. Lamport, "A History of the Teaching of Beginning Reading" (Ph.D. diss., University of Chicago, 1935); M. M. Matthews, *Teaching to Read Historically Considered* (Chicago: University of Chicago Press, 1966); N. B. Smith, *American Reading Instruction* (Newark, Del.: International Reading Association, 1934); F. Adams, L. Gray, and D. Reese, *Teaching Children to Read* (New York: Ronald Press, 1949); E. B. Huey, *The Psychology and Pedagogy of Reading* (New York, 1980, reprinted; Cambridge, Mass.; MIT Press, 1968); W. J. F. Davies, *Teaching Reading in Early England* (New York: Barnes and Noble, 1974); W. S. Gray, *The Teaching of Reading and Writing* (Paris: UNESCO, 1956); Jean Chall, *Learning to Read* (New York: McGraw-Hill, 1967); Chall and Carroll, *Literate Society*; Jean Chall and J. S. Carroll, "Reading, Language, and Learning," *Harvard Educational Review* 47 (August 1977); Calhoun, *Intelligence*. Calhoun's work is particularly valuable, although my conclusions about reading instruction in the nineteenth century were formed before his volume was published. See also Jose Ortega y Gasset, "The Difficulty of Reading," *Diogenes* 28 (1959): 1–17. We should note also the persisting problems and controversies over reading methods.

210. Ryerson, "Report on a System," pp. 167, 163, 168. See George Combe, *The Constitution of Man* (Hartford, Conn., 1845), on the philosophical bases of the new pedagogy, as well as Katz, *Irony*. See also Nelson Sizer, *How to Teach According to Temperament and Mental Development* (New York, 1877). For England, see Richard Johnson, "Notes on the Schooling of the English Working Class," in *Schooling and Capitalism*, ed. R. Dale, G. Esland, and M. MacDonald (London: Routledge, Kegan Paul, 1976), p. 48. On the fallacies in such approaches, see Frank Smith, "Making Sense of Reading," *Harvard Educational Review*, special issue pp. 386–95. William Russell, "The Infant School System of Instruction," *Proceedings*, the American Institute of Instruction 1 (1830): 98; Thomas Palmer, "Evils of the Present System of Primary Instruction," ibid. 8 (1837): 211, 212, 214, 216. *Second Annual Report of the Secretary of the (Massachusetts) Board of Education* (Boston, 1839), pp. 37, 39. *Second Annual Report*, pp. 39–40.

211. *Lectures*, American Institute of Instruction, 1843 (Boston, 1844), pp. 143–84; 144, 159, 153, 157–58, 149–53, 156, 160–61. On problems with this approach, see Smith, "Making Sense," pp. 388ff. *Seventh Annual Report . . .* (Boston, 1844), pp. 86–90, 93, 99. See also Ryerson, "Report on a System"; "City of Kingston," Excerpts from Local Superintendent's Reports, *Annual Report of the Chief Superintendent*, 1851, 1852.

212. See Association of Masters of the (Boston) Public Schools, *Remarks on the Seventh Annual Report of the Honourable Horace Mann, Secretary of the Massachusetts Board of Education* (Boston, 1844), pp. 56–103; Samuel Greene, "On Methods of Teaching to Read,"

American Institute of Instruction, Lectures, 1844 (Boston, 1845), pp. 211, 213–16, 207–235. See also Smith, "Making Sense"; Chall, *Learning*, on the problems associated with these common, as well as continuing, failings today. Masters, *Remarks*, pp. 77–78; Greene, "Methods," p. 233. See Katz, *Irony*, esp. pp. 139–46, for larger pedagogical implications of the debate. Greene, "Methods," pp. 220, 221; Masters, *Remarks*, pp. 56, 83–87, 99. The debate continued; see Mann, *Reply to the "Remarks of Thirty-one Schoolmasters"* (Boston, 1844), *Answer to the "Rejoinder" of Twenty-nine Boston Schoolmasters* (Boston, 1845); Masters, *Rejoinder to the Reply* . . . (Boston, 1845).

213. See Ryerson, *Annual Report*, 1871; William Russell, "On Teaching the Alphabet," *Massachusetts Teacher* 15 (1862): 209–212; idem, "Methods of Teaching to Read," ibid. 16 (1863): 87–90; idem, "Reading Made Easy," ibid. 17 (1864): 328; Calhoun, *Intelligence*, chap. 2; "The Cultivation of the Expressive Faculties," *American Journal of Education* 3 (1857): 328; "City of Kingston."

214. Calhoun, *Intelligence*, pp. 80, 85, chap 2; Ryerson, "Report on a System," *Annual Report*, 1871; N. A. Calkins, "Primary Reading," *New York Teacher and American Educational Monthly* 8 (1870): 34–35; T. P. D. Stone, "Reading in Common Schools," New York Regents, *Annual Report*, 1871; "City of Kingston", Calhoun, *Intelligence*; Ryerson, *Annual Report*, 1877, "Report on a System." See also Katz, *Irony*. "City of Kingston," 1852; *Journal of Education* 18 (1965): 152; *Annual Report*, 1871. The Rev. John May repeated these criticisms a decade later, revealing the continuing failure to teach good reading and the stress on articulation. Reading was not taught as it "deserved" to be; the result was "a sort of cross between reading and a Gregorian chant." Moreover, "good reading is not only a pleasing and elegant accomplishment, but also an excellent intellectual exercise." The issue of intelligence, of understanding, continued to be confused with articulation: "You must understand a passage and enter into its spirit before you can read it in public," as if that were a goal for all pupils. *Essays on Educational Subjects* (Ottawa, 1880), p. 21. Present-day problems and practices should be compared; see Chall, *Learning*; Smith, "Making Sense"; *Harvard Educational Review*, passim.

216. Prentice, "School Promoters," p. 120; May, *Essays*, p. 20. Cf. Cremin, *American Education: National*; Soltow and Stevens, *Literacy*.

217. "Letters to a Young Teacher, XIII," *American Journal of Education* 4 (1857–1858): 226. Prentice, "School Promoters," esp. chap. 4; *Journal of Education* 6 (1853): 175; Mann, *Second Annual Report*, p. 40.

218. On literacy and nationalism, see among a large literature Glanmour Williams, "Language, Literacy, and Nationality in Wales," *History* 56 (1971): 1–16. On the language differences of class and culture and their contributions to "learning problems," see D. R. Entwhistle, "Implications of Language Socialization for Reading Models and for Learning to Read," *Reading Research Quarterly* 7 (1971–1972); Basil Bernstein, "Determinants of Perception," *British Journal of Sociology* 9 (1958): 159–74; idem, "Social Class, Language, and Socialisation," *Current Trends in Linguistics* 12 (1973); and the work of William Labor and Shirley Heath.

219. Calhoun, *Intelligence*, p. 78, quoted on p. 80, pp. 130–31, 70–133, passim; see also his "The City as Teacher"; current research of Donald Scott; Cremin, *American Education: National*; Graff, *Literacy Myth*, chap. 7; Otis W. Caldwell and Stuart A. Courtis, *Then and Now in Education* (1925, reprinted: New York: Arno Press, 1971). On Canada, see Frederick Grove, *A Search for America*; (reprinted; Toronto: McClelland and Stewart, 1971); Ryerson, *Annual Report*, 1871. While there is no reason to consider illiterates disadvantaged in basic skills or in the ability to communicate, there are grounds to find them less able in higher verbal skills, and especially in formally learned cognitive skills, perhaps useful (if not required) for gaining responsible work, performing some jobs, conducting themselves in formal settings, such as courtrooms, etc. See the work of Scribner and Cole and Greenfield, cited in Epilogue; D. R. Entwhistle, "Developmental Sociolinguistics: Inner City Children," *American Journal of Sociology* 74 (1968): 37–49.

220. Among the relevant literature, see Lawrence Levine, *Black Culture and Black Consciousness* (New York: Oxford University Press, 1977); Thomas Webber, *Deep Like the Rivers* (New York: Norton, 1978); Eugene Genovese, *Roll, Jordan, Roll* (New York: Pan-

theon, 1974); Herbert Gutman, *The Black Family* (New York: Pantheon, 1976); Ransom and Sutch, *One Kind*; Taylor, "Orthodoxy"; Jay Mandle, *Roots of Black Poverty* (Durham, N.C.: Duke University Press, 1978); Elizabeth Pleck, "The Two Parent Household," in *The American Family in Social Historical Perspective*, ed. Michael Gordon (New York: St. Martins, 1973), pp. 152–78; idem, *Black Migration and Poverty: Boston* (New York: Academic Press, 1979); Edward Magdol, *A Right to the Land* (Westport, Conn.: Greenwood Press, 1977); Leon Litwak, *Been in the Storm So Long* (New York: Knopf, 1979); Vernon Burton, "Race and Reconstruction," *Journal of Social History* 12 (1978): 31–56; Ira Berlin, "The Structure of the Free Negro Caste in the Antebellum United States," *Journal of Social History* 9 (1976): 297–318; idem, "Time, Space, and the Evolution of Afro-American Society in British Mainland North America," *American Historical Review* 85 (1980): 44–78; idem, *Slaves without Masters* (New York: Vintage, 1975); James McPherson, *The Abolitionist Legacy* (Princeton: Princeton University Press, 1976); Jacqueline Jones, *Soldiers of Light* (Chapel Hill: University of North Carolina Press, 1980); William P. Vaughn, *Schools for All* (Lexington: University of Kentucky Press, 1974); James O. Horton and Lois E. Horton, *Black Bostonians* (New York: Holms and Meier, 1979); Leon Litwak, *North of Slavery* (Chicago: University of Chicago Press, 1961); Henry Bullock, *A History of Negro Education in the South* (New York: Praeger, 1970); the studies of Horace Mann Bond; R. E. Butchart, *Northern Schools, Southern Blacks* (Westport, Conn.: Greenwood Press, 1980); R. C. Morris, *Reading, 'Riting, and Reconstruction* (Chicago: University of Chicago Press, 1981); Louis Harlan's books and articles; the numerous studies of August Meier and Elliott Rudwick; R. F. Engs, *Freedom's First Generation* (Philadelphia: University of Philadelphia Press, 1979); J. J. Mohraz, *The Separate Problem* (Westport, Conn.: Greenwood Press, 1979); R. K. Goodenow and A. O. White, eds., *Education and the Rise of the South* (Boston: G. K. Hall, 1980); the articles of James Anderson; those of Arthur White; the studies of Theodore Hershberg; those of William and Jane Pease; the important studies of ghetto life by Alan Spear, Kenneth Kusmer, David Katzman, Gilbert Osofsky, James Borchart; Pete Daniel, "The Metamorphosis of Slavery," *Journal of American History* 66 (1976):88–99; the seminal work of Robert Fogel and Stanley Engerman; Robert Higg's economic and demographic studies; Edward Meeker, "Mortality Trends of Southern Blacks," *Explorations in Economic History* 13 (1976): 13–42; idem, "Freedom, Opportunity, and Fertility," *Economic Inquiry* 15 (1977): 397–412; Edward Meeker and James Kau, "Racial Discrimination and Occupational Attainment," *Explorations in Economic History* 14 (1977): 250–76. This listing, of course, is but a sampling of a booming literature. See also, for attempts at comparisons, Timothy L. Smith, "Native Blacks and Foreign Whites: Varying Responses to Educational Opportunity in America," *Perspectives in American History* 6 (1972): 309–335.

221. Cremin, *American Education: National*, p. 228. See also the antebellum studies cited above.

222. Genovese, *Roll, Jordan, Roll*, 561–62, 562, 563, 563–64, quoted on p. 564. See also Webber, *Deep*; Magdol, *Right to the Land*; the literature on Reconstruction; the unpublished research of Herbert Gutman; Taylor, "Orthodoxy."

223. Webber, *Deep*, pp. 136, 137, quoted on p. 193, pp. 193, 215; chap. 11, passim. See also the *Autobiography of Frederick Douglass*; Genovese, *Roll, Jordan, Roll*; Albert Robateau, *Slave Religion* (New York: Oxford University Press, 1978); Gutman, *Black Family*; the work of Kenneth Stampp; Levine, *Black Culture*; John Blassingame, *The Slave Community* (New York: Oxford University Press, 1972, 1980). Levine, *Black Culture*, pp. 158, 159, 161, 166–67, passim.

224. Genovese, *Roll, Jordan, Roll*, p. 565. Many other sources speak to the same point. Willie Lee Rose, *Rehearsal for Reconstruction* (Indianapolis: Bobbs-Merrill, 1964), pp. 238, 80. See also Jones, *Soldiers*; Magdol, *Right to the Land*; unpublished research of Gutman. Washington, quoted in Webber, *Deep*, p. 138; quoted in Cremin, *American Education: National*, p. 518; Higginston quoted in Levine, *Black Culture*, p. 155; the latter source includes a number of other examples.

225. Levine, *Black Culture*, pp. 155, 156.

226. Ibid., pp. 177, 157. See also the large and growing literature on postbellum black life and culture.

227. Lois E. Horton and James Oliver Horton, "Race, Occupation, and Literacy in Reconstruction Washington, D.C." (unpub. ms., 1979), quoted on p. 3, pp. 7–8, 9, 10, 12–13. This work is usefully compared with the work of Hershberg on Philadelphia. See also Eaton, *Illiteracy*; Ransom and Sutch, *One Kind*; G. Wright, "Cheap Labor"; Smith, "Native Blacks."

228. Ransom and Sutch, *One Kind*, pp. 23, 30–31, see also p. 181, passim. See also writings on Reconstruction and postbellum Southern education and society.

229. Litwak, *Been in the Storm*, pp. 472, 474, 475, 476, 477, 479, 480, 480–81, 482, 483, 486, quoted on p. 486, passim. See also Louis Harlan, *Separate and Unequal* (New York: Atheneum, 1968); J. Morgan Kousser, "Separate but *Not* Equal," *Journal of Southern History* 46 (1980): 17–44; Magdol, *Right to the Land*; unpublished research of Gutman; Jones, *Soldiers*; Ransom and Sutch, *One Kind*.

230. Ransom and Sutch, *One Kind*, p. 25, quoted on p. 25, pp. 25–26, 26–27, 27, 28–30; on occupations and literacy, p. 35; farmers, pp. 180–81. Ransom and Sutch write: "It is also likely, as we have pointed out, that many slave 'artisans' were illiterate. While not a serious disadvantage to the slaveowner, the skilled freedmen probably found illiteracy a major obstacle to pursuing artisan trades independently. The need in these occupations to communicate with distant suppliers and customers, to keep books, and to make financial arrangements meant that those who could not read and write would, in most cases, have to work for others. Even then, illiteracy would hinder artisans from attaining great proficiency. That such was the case is suggested by the postwar literacy rates reported in Table 2.7 for black workers in various occupations. The literacy rate among artisans was four times higher than that among farm laborers," p. 35.

## TABLE 2.7 (Ransom and Sutch)
### Literacy rates of gainfully occupied black males: 1870

| Occupation | Sample | Sample Size | Percentage Literate |
|---|---|---|---|
| Farmer | Rural | 151 | 8.2 |
| Farm laborer | Rural | 1,997 | 5.0 |
| Laborer | Rural | 392 | 7.1 |
| Laborer | Urban | 399 | 12.0 |
| Servant | Urban | 185 | 7.0 |
| Other unskilled | Urban | 284 | 16.2 |
| Artisan | Urban | 335 | 21.8 |
|   Carpenter | Urban | 143 | 18.9 |
|   Blacksmith | Urban | 41 | 19.5 |
| Commercial | Urban | 70 | 30.0 |
| Professional | Urban | 25 | 80.0 |
| All occupations | Rural | 2,642 | 5.7 |
| All occupations | Urban | 1,582 | 14.9 |

"While a white laborer would not be viewed as obviously unskilled, a white who had previously been a sharecropper might have a difficult time arguing for more independence from a new landlord. The landlord would reason that, had the white laborer actually possessed managerial skills, he would have rented for a fixed fee. There is some evidence, which we offer in Table 9.3, that white sharecroppers were as a class less skilled than other white farm operators. White operators of small-scale family farms were generally able to read and write: only about 15 percent of the white owners, for example, were illiterate. Yet among white sharecroppers the illiteracy rate exceeded 25 percent. In sharp contrast is the pattern of illiteracy displayed by black operators of family-sized farms. Among blacks illiteracy was lowest among sharecroppers. As we noted in Chapter 5, and the figures in Table 9.3 reflect, sharecropping attracted the most able black workers,'' pp.180–81.

TABLE 9.3 (Ransom and Sutch)
**Percent of operators of family farms who were illiterate, by race and tenure, Cotton South: 1880**

| | Percent Illiterate | |
| Form of tenure | White | Black |
| --- | --- | --- |
| Owners | 15.1 | 84.9 |
| Renters | 7.7 | 82.6 |
| Sharecroppers | 25.6 | 76.6 |
| All operators | 18.0 | 79.5 |

231. Burton, "Race and Reconstruction," pp. 32, 33, 36, 45, 46, passim.
232. Magdol, *Right to the Land*, pp. 84, 83, examples on pp. 84–89. See also the unpublished work of Gutman.
233. Pleck, *Black Poverty*, pp. 53–54, 50, 52, 67, 103, 118, 119, chap. 5, pp. 128, 140, 138, 141, 142, 150, 151, 135, 144, chap. 6. Compare with studies of Kusmer, Katzman; Graff, *Literacy Myth*, chap. 2. See also Pleck, "Two Parent"; Thernstrom, *Other Bostonians*.
234. For additional demographic and economic data on blacks related to literacy, see the work of Edward Meeker, Robert Higgs, and Gavin Wright. See also Eaton, *Illiteracy*; Ransom and Sutch, *One Kind*; Graff, "Literacy, Education, and Fertility."
235. Among recent studies, see Smith, "Native Blacks"; Timothy L. Smith, "Immigrant Social Aspirations and American Education," *American Quarterly* 21 (1969): 523 –43; idem, "Religion and Ethnicity in America," *American Historical Review* 83 (1978): 1155–85; John Briggs, *An Italian Passage* (New Haven: Yale University Press, 1978); John Bodnar, *Immigration and Industrialization* (Pittsburgh: University of Pittsburgh Press, 1977); idem, "Immigration and Modernization: The Case of Slavic Peasants in Industrial America," *Journal of Social History* 10 (1976): 44–71; idem, "Materialism and Morality: Slavic-American Immigrants and Education, 1890–1940," *Journal of Ethnic Studies* 3 (1976): 1–19; idem, "Socialization and Adaptation: Immigrant Families in Scranton, 1880–1890," *Pennsylvania History* 43 (1976): 147–62; Virginia Yans McLaughlin, *Family and Community* (Ithaca, New York, 1977), and her articles; Judith Smith's unpublished work on Italians; Kristian Hvidt, *Flight to America* (New York: Academic Press, 1975); Runblom and Norman, *From Sweden*; Thomas Kessner, *The Golden Door* (New York: Oxford University Press, 1977); Joseph Barton, *Peasants and Strangers* (Cambridge, Mass.: Harvard University Press, 1975); Thernstrom, *Other Bostonians*; Gutman, "Work, Culture"; Hogan, "Educating"; David Hogan, "Capitalism and Schooling" (Ph.D. diss., University of Illinois, 1978); Marvin Lazerson and Michael Olneck, "The School Achievement of Immigrant Children," *History of Education Quarterly* 14 (1974): 453–82; Marvin Lazerson, *Origins of the Urban School* (Cambridge, Mass.: Harvard University Press, 1971); David Cohen, "Immigrants and the Schools," *Review of Educational Research* 40 (1970); special issues of the *Journal of Urban History*; work of Maxine Sellers; Selma Berrol, "Education and Economic Mobility: the Jewish Experience in New York City, 1880–1920," *American Jewish Historical Quarterly* 45 (1976): 257–71; idem, "Immigrants at School: New York City, 1900–1910," *Urban Education* 4 (1969): 220–30; Moses Rischin, *The Promised City* (Cambridge, Mass.: Harvard University Press, 1962); Nathan Glazer and Daniel Moynihan, *Beyond the Melting Pot* (Cambridge, Mass.: MIT Press, 1970); Stephen Steinberg, *The Academic Melting Pot* (New York: Carnegie Foundation, 1974); idem, *The Ethnic Myth* (New York: Atheneum, 1981); Leonard Covello's books on Italian immigrants; Humbert Nelli's and Rudolph Vecoli's studies; Robert Higgs, "Race, Skills, and Earnings: American Immigrants in 1909," *Journal of Economic*

*History* 31 (1971): 420–28; W. G. Smith, *A Study of Canadian Immigration* (Toronto, 1920), esp. chap. 12; Nelson R. Beck, "The Use of Library and Educational Facilities by Russian-Jewish Immigrants in New York City, 1880–1914," *Journal of Library History* 12 (1977): 128–49; Babette Inglehart, "The Immigrant Child and the American School: A Literary View," *Ethnicity* 3 (1976): 34–52; Clarence J. Karier et al., *Roots of Crisis* (Chicago: Rand McNally, 1973); Clarence J. Karier, *Shaping the American Educational State* (New York: Free Press, 1975); Paul Violas, *Education and the American Working Class* (Chicago: Rand McNally, 1978); Lawrence Cremin, *The Transformation of the School* (New York: Vintage, 1962).

236. Higgs, "Race," passim. See also Hogan, "Education"; Barton, *Peasants*; Briggs, *Italian*; the work of Bodnar; Thernstrom, *Other Bostonians*.

237. Smith, "Aspirations," pp. 523, 525. See also the work of Briggs, Higgs, Kessner, Yans McLaughlin, Bodnar, Thernstrom, Hogan. Note the important interpretive differences among them.

238. Bodnar, "Materialism," pp. 1, 8, 13, 14, passim. See also his other studies, and those of Yans McLaughlin, Steinberg, Kessner, and Nelli on Italians. Compare with Briggs and Smith. See also Hogan's work.

239. Bodnar, "Immigration and Modernization," p. 50. See also Hogan's studies, and Gutman, "Work, Culture"; Gabriel Kolko, *Main Currents in American History* (New York: Harper and Row, 1974).

240. See the literature cited and the evidence presented in Graff, *Literacy Myth*, and Epilogue, below.

241. See, on the mobility debate, in addition to the recent social science literature, the work of Steinberg, Thernstrom, Yans McLaughlin, Bodnar, Kessner, Briggs, and Barton, and Michael Weber, "Residential and Occupational Patterns of Ethnic Minorities," *Pennsylvania History* 44 (1977): 317–34; idem, *Social Change in an Industrial Town* (University Park: Pennsylvania State University Press, 1976); Michael Weber and A. E. Boardman, "Economic Growth and Occupational Mobility," *Journal of Social History* 11 (1977): 52–74; Dean Esslinger, *Immigrants and the City* (Port Washington, N.Y.: Kennikat, 1975); Bodnar et al., "Migration, Kinship, and Urban Adjustment," *Journal of American History* 6 (1879): 548–65; G. W. Kirk, Jr., *The Promise of American Life*, Memoirs, American Philosophical Society, vol. 124 (Philadelphia, 1978). The significance of place of origin and place of settlement has not been sufficiently appreciated; that is one focus of Yans McLaughlin's interpretation. This issue is by no means settled; the mental and methodological gyrations of students on these questions are depressingly instructive. See also Hogan, "Making"; Michael Piore, *Birds of Passage* (Cambridge: Cambridge University Press, 1979); R. C. Edwards, Michael Reich, and D. M. Gordon, eds., *Labor Market Segmentation* (Lexington, Mass.: D. C. Heath, 1975).

242. Bodnar, "Socialization," pp. 159, 161, passim. Compare with Berrol, "Education"; Graff, *Literacy Myth*, esp. chap. 4; Yans McLaughlin, *Family*; Kessner, *Golden Door*; Barton, *Peasants*; Briggs, *Italian*; Olneck and Lazerson, "Immigrant."

243. Hogan, "Education," pp. 230–31, 231–32, 234, 236, 245, 248, 249, 253. See also work of Olneck and Lazerson, Yans McLaughlin, Briggs, Nelli, Kessner, Berrol, Graff, Rischin, Steinberg, and earlier studies of the working class and schooling such as those of Davey. See also Paul Osterman, *Getting Started: The Youth Labor Market* (Cambridge, Mass.: MIT Press, 1980).

244. Berrol, "Education," pp. 264, 264–65, 271, passim. See also work of Hogan, Steinberg, Kessner, among others.

245. Hogan, "Making," pp. 256–57, 257, 259. See also Gerd Korman, *Industrialization, Immigrants, and Americanizers* (Madison: State Historical Society of Wisconsin, 1967); examples in Daniel Calhoun, ed., *The Educating of Americans* (Boston: Houghton, Mifflin, 1967); Karier et al., *Roots of Crisis, Shaping*; Cremin, *Transformation*; Violas, *Education*; Miller, "Urban Education"; Gutman, "Work, Culture"; Kolko, *Main Currents*; work of Bodnar, Yans McLaughlin, Barton, Kessner, Nelli, Smith, and others.

246. Korman, *Industrialization*, p. 137, chap. 6, passim, for nonschool approaches and the important efforts of Peter Roberts. On hereditarian assumptions in contemporary social

thought, see Charles Rosenberg, "The Bitter Fruit: Heredity, Disease, and Social Thought in Nineteenth-Century America," *Perspectives in American History* 8 (1974): 189–238.

247. See excerpts in Calhoun, *Educating*, pp. 418–420.

248. Yans McLaughlin, *Family*, pp. 47, 47–48, 172, passim. See also the studies of Nelli, Olneck and Lazerson, Kessner, Briggs, Barton, and Berrol, among the relevant literature.

249. See, for example, the studies of Smith, Kessner, Briggs, and Barton. They suffer from a tendency to "massage" their evidence to show the promise of mobility.

250. Bodnar, *Immigration*, p. 92, chaps. 5–6, passim. See also studies of Yans McLaughlin, Hogan, Bodnar's other work, Gutman.

251. Miller, "Urban Education," p. 164, is one example. See also the literature on school reform and progressivism, a selection of which is cited above.

252. Calhoun, "The City," p. 319.

## Epilogue

1. See Shirley Heath, "The Functions and Uses of Literacy," *Journal of Communications* 30 (1980): 123; John Bormuth, "Value and Volume of Literacy," *Visible Language* 12 (1978): 118–61; idem, "Literacy Policy and Reading and Writing Instruction," in *Perspectives on Literacy: Proceedings of the 1977 Conference*, ed. Richard Beach and P. David Pearson (Minneapolis: College of Education, University of Minnesota, 1978), pp. 13–47.

2. Numerous authors have attempted in recent years to develop new definitions of literacy. For a representative listing, see citation in Harvey J. Graff, *Literacy in History: An Interdisciplinary Research Bibliography* (New York: Garland Publishing, 1981). As examples, see Sam V. Dauzat and Jo Ann Dauzat, "Literacy: In Quest of a Definition," *Convergence* 10 (1977): 37–41; Robert L. Hillerich, "Toward an Assessable Definition of Literacy," *English Journal* 65 (1976): 50–55; Manfred Stanley, "Literacy: The Crisis of a Concept," *School Review* 80 (1972): 373–408; John Oxenham, *Literacy: Writing, Reading, and Social Organization* (London: Routledge and Kegan Paul, 1980); among countless others. An enormously important nineteenth-century view is W. B. Hodgson, *Exaggerated Estimates of Reading and Writing as Means of Education* (London: 1868). See also Harvey J. Graff, *The Literacy Myth: Literacy and Social Structure in the Nineteenth-Century City* (New York: Academic Press, 1979).

3. Johansson, *The History of Literacy in Sweden* (Umeå: School of Education, Umeå University, 1977), p. 71; italics added. See also Carlo Cipolla, *Literacy and Development in the West* (Harmondsworth: Penguin, 1969); numerous UNESCO publications; Rudolph Binion, "Observations sur la disparition de l'analphabétisme," *Population* 8 (1953): 121–28. Questions of definition, measurement, and comparability are severe and often limiting; see the literature cited above and in Graff, *Literacy Myth* and *Literacy in History*.

4. Johansson, *History*, p. 73.

5. On U.S. censuses, see, for example, John K. Folger and Charles B. Nam, *Education of the American Population* (Washington, D.C.: GPO, 1967), Appendix C; Carroll B. Wright, *The History and Growth of the United States Census* (Washington, D.C.: GPO, 1900); Daniel Calhoun, *The Intelligence of a People* (Princeton: Princeton University Press, 1973). On nineteenth-century censuses and literacy, see Harvey J. Graff, "What the 1861 Census Can Tell Us about Literacy," *Histoire sociale* 8 (1975): 337–49. Among other writings on definitions and measures, see articles in John B. Carroll and Jean S. Chall, eds., *Toward a Literate Society: Report of the National Academy of Education* (New York: McGraw-Hill, 1975). Other approaches, including that of "functional" literacy, are considered below.

6. *Current Population Report*, series P-20, no. 99, Feb. 4 1960. See also Carroll and Chall, *Toward*; Carman St. John Hunter and David Harmon, *Adult Illiteracy in the United States: A Report to the Ford Foundation* (New York: McGraw-Hill, 1979); Jonathan Kozol, *Prisoners of Silence: Breaking the Bonds of Adult Illiteracy in the United States* (New York: Continuum Publishing, 1980) and *Illiterate America* (Garden City, N.Y.: Doubleday, 1985).

7. Hunter and Harman, *Adult Illiteracy*, p. 56; see also sec. 3, below, and writings in Carroll and Chall; Bormuth; Kozol, among others. It is Kozol, of course, who calls for the

Americanization of the Cuban approach, both in his *Prisoners* and in Jonathan Kozol, "A New Look at the Literacy Campaign in Cuba," *Harvard Educational Review* 48 (1978): 341–77. Exportations of "modernization" schemes with literacy as a central element have not stopped.

8. Rose-Marie Weber, "Adult Illiteracy in the United States," in Carroll and Chall, *Toward*, p. 148; see also John Bormuth's writings, including "Reading Literacy: Its Definition and Assessment," in Carroll and Chall *Toward*, pp. 61–100, among others.

9. Hunter and Harman, *Adult Illiteracy*, p. 31, chap. 2 for their data. There is a voluminous and growing literature in sociology and economics on inequality, education, stratification, and labor markets that influences my views. It is simply too large to cite here; important examples through 1979 are cited in Graff, *Literacy in History*.

10. David Olson, "Toward a Literate Society: Review," *Proceedings*, National Academy of Education 2 (1975): 148–49; Heath, "Functions," p. 132.

11. Johansson, *History*, p. 75. See also Paolo Freire, *Pedagogy of the Oppressed* (New York: Herder and Herder, 1971); idem, *Education for Critical Consciousness* (New York: Seabury Press, 1973); Kozol, as cited above; Léon Bataille, ed., *A Turning Point for Literacy: Adult Education for Development. The Spirit and Declaration of Persepolis* (Oxford: Pergamon Press, 1976); Richard Jolly, "The Literacy Campaign and Adult Education," in *Cuba: The Economic and Social Revolution*, ed. Dudley Seers (Chapel Hill: University of North Carolina Press, 1963), pp. 190–219; Richard Fagen's writings on Cuba and Nicaragua; many UNESCO publications; Robert Arnove, "The Nicaraguan National Literacy Campaign of 1980," *Comparative Education Review* 25 (1981); Jack Goody, ed., *Literacy in Traditional Societies* (Cambridge: Cambridge University Press, 1968); J. R. Clammer, *Literacy and Social Change: A Case Study of Fiji* (Leiden: E. J. Brill, 1976); Stanley, "Literacy"; USSR, "The Abolition of Adult Illiteracy," *UNESCO Journal of Fundamental and Adult Education* 11 (1959); P.L.M. Serrys, *Survey of the Chinese Language Reform and the Anti-illiteracy Movement in Communist China*, Studies in Chinese Communist Terminology, no. 8 (Berkeley: Institute for Chinese Studies, Institute of International Studies, University of California, 1962); M. Zinovyev and A. Pleshakova, *How Illiteracy Was Wiped Out in the USSR* (Moscow: Progress Publishers, n.d.); Gerald Duverdier, "La pénétration du livre dans un société de culture orale: le cas de Tahiti," *Revue française d'histoire du livre* 1 (1971): 25–53; Hendrik Thomas, "Literacy without Formal Education: A Case Study in Pakistan," *Economic Development and Cultural Change* 22 (1974): 489–95; Alex Inkeles and David H. Smith, *Becoming Modern* (Cambridge, Mass.: Harvard University Press, 1974); Henry F. Dobyns, "Enlightenment and Skill Foundations of Power," in *Peasants, Power, and Applied Social Change: Vicos as a Model*, ed. Henry F. Dobyns, Paul L. Doughty, and Harold D. Lasswell (Beverly Hills, Calif.: Sage Publications, 1971), pp. 137–66; Christopher J. Lucas, "Arab Illiteracy and the Mass Literacy Campaign in Iraq," *Comparative Education Review* 25 (1981): 74–84; Brian Street, "The Mullah, the Shahname, and the Madrasseh, " *Asian Affairs* 62 (1975): 290–306; and *Literacy in Theory and Practice* (Cambridge: Cambridge University Press, 1984); Anthony Burton, "The Submerged and the Seers: Adult Literacy in Peru, 1973–1974," *Anthropology and Education Quarterly* 11 (1980): 235–54; idem, "Education as Transformation: Identity, Change, and Development," Special Issue, *Harvard Educational Review* 51 (February 1981). Arnove and I have collaborated on an analysis of the idea, past and present, of literacy campaigns.

12. Ian Winchseter, "How Many Ways to Universal Literacy?" Unpub. paper, presented to the Ninth World Congress of Sociology, Uppsala, Sweden, 1978 and the Leicester Conference on the History of Literacy, 1980, p. 1. See also Mark Blaug, "Literacy and Economic Development, " *School Review* 74 (1966): 393–417; articles by Levin, Walter, and Fry in *Harvard Educational Review*, Special Issue, "Transformation"; papers in Bataille, *Turning Point*; sec. 2, below, and citations herein.

13. UNESCO Secretariat, "Literacy in the World since the 1965 Teheran Conference," in Bataille, *Turning Point*, pp. 5, 7, 13, 13–14; Harvey J. Graff, "Literacy, Education, and Fertility—Past and Present: A Critical Review," *Population and Development Review* 5 (1979), and John Caldwell, "Mass Education as Determinant of the Timing of the Fertility Transition," ibid. 6 (1980): 225–55, as examples. See also Harvey J. Graff, "Literacy Past

and Present: Critical Approaches in the Literacy-Society Relationship," *Interchange* 9 (1978): 1–21. In the political modernization approach, the many writings of Pye, Huntington, Inkeles, and Lerner are most important.

14. Johan Galtung, "Literacy, Education, and Schooling—For What," in Bataille, *Turning Point*, pp. 98–99. This important paper is conveniently reprinted in Harvey J. Graff, *Literacy and Social Development in the West: A Reader* (Cambridge: Cambridge University Press, 1981).

15. See Freire's work, cited above, and Stanley, "Literacy," and other references on Third World Developments cited above. Citations in text are: Kozol, "New Look," pp. 363–64; Burton, "Submerged," p. 245.

16. References not found in this book appear in either or both *The Literacy Myth* and *Literacy in History*. For an example of the newly appearing criticisms, see Henry Levin, "The Identity Crisis of Educational Planning," *Harvard Educational Review* 81 (1981): 85–93.

17. Jack Goody, *The Domestication of the Savage Mind* (Cambridge: Cambridge University Press, 1977); Ruth Finnegan, "Literacy versus Non-literacy: The Great Divide? Some Comments on the Significance of Literature in Non-Literate Cultures," in *Modes of Thought: Essays on Thinking in Western and Non-Western Societies*, ed. Robin Horton and Ruth Finnegan (London: Faber and Faber, 1973), pp. 112–44. Examples of the "divide" or "dichotomy" are legion. See, for example, the works of McLuhan or the classic paper of J. C. Carother, "Culture, Psychiatry, and the Written Word," *Psychiatry* 22 (1959) : 309–320. Citation is Finnegan, "Great Divide?" pp. 112–13. See also the works of Shirley Heath, including a number of forthcoming papers, a book, cited above, and "Protean Shapes in Literacy Events: Ever-Shifting Oral and Literate Traditions," in *Spoken and Written Language*, ed. Deborah Tannen (Norwood, N.J.: Alex, 1982); the writings of David Olson.

18. G. H. Bantock, *The Implications of Literacy* (Leicester: Leicester University Press, 1966), pp. 5, 13, 14. He is, of course, no exception in either his stance or his confusions and contradictions. A review of the literature quickly shows that.

19. Goody, *Domestication*, p. 41.

20. Jack Goody and Ian Watt, "The Consequences of Literacy," in *Literacy and Traditional Societies*, ed. Jack Goody (Cambridge: Cambridge University Press, 1968), pp. 29, 33, 38, 39, 43, 48–49, 53, 55, 56, 57, 57–58, 58. This seminal paper was originally published in *Comparative Studies in Society and History* in 1963. Goody's introduction to *Literacy and Traditional Societies* should also be consulted in terms of the changes in his thinking on this subject. This work has influenced many scholars. Olson is one prominent example; Bantock is another. See their works cited above. See also Carothers, "Culture"; Ihsan Al-Issa, "Effects of Literacy and Schizophrenia on Verbal Abstraction in Iraq," *Journal of Social Psychology* 71 (1967): 39–43; W. Watson and C. L. Hunt, "The Neuropsychiatric Implications of Illiteracy," *U.S. Armed Forces Medical Journal* 2 (1951): 365–69; works of McLuhan and Harold Innis.

21. The literature here is mammoth and growing daily. See, for introductions, the many studies of W. H. Sewell, R. M. Hauser, and David Featherman; Peter Blau and Otis D. Duncan, *The American Occupational Structure* (New York: Wiley, 1967); Christopher Jencks et al. *Inequality* (New York: Basic Books, 1972) and *Who Gets Ahead?* (New York: Basic Books, 1979); Raymond Boudon, *Education, Opportunity, and Social Mobility* (New York: Wiley, 1974); Ivar Berg, *Education and Jobs* (Boston: Beacon Press, 1971); Gregory Squires, *Education and Jobs* (New Brunswick, N.J.: Transaction Books, 1979); the recent studies of A. H. Halsey, John Goldthorpe, and Eric Wright, among numerous others.

22. Blau and Duncan, *American Occupational*, passim; Robert Mare, "Change and Stability in Educational Stratification," *American Sociological Review* 46 (1981): 72. See also Michael R. Olneck and James Crouse, "The IQ Meritocracy Reconsidered: Cognitive Skill and Adult Success in the United States," *American Journal of Education* 87 (1979): 1–31.

23. Blau and Duncan, *American Occupational*. See the literature cited above, and Pierre Bourdieu and Jean-Claude Passerson, *Reproduction in Education, Society, and Culture* (Beverly Hills, Calif.: Sage Publications, 1977); works of Goldthorpe, Halsey, Boudon; and Henry Levin, "Educational Opportunity and Social Inequality in Western Europe," *Social Problems*

24 (1976): 148–72. Much of the voluminous and contentious literature is cited in Graff, *Literacy Myth* and *Literacy in History*.

24. Berg, *Education*, chap. 1, pp. 40–41, 59, 80–83, chap. 5, pp. 87, 104. See also studies of Squires and Jencks cited above; Harry Braverman, *Labor and Monopoly Capital* (New York: Monthly Review Press, 1974); James Bright, "Does Automation Raise Skill Requirements?" *Harvard Business Review* 36 (1958): 85–98, among the literature.

25. Levin, "Educational," pp. 148–72; Gerald W. Fry, "Schooling, Development, and Inequality: Old Myths and New Realities," *Harvard Educational Review* 51 (1981): 115, 107–116; Barbara Jacobson and John M. Kendrick, "Education and Mobility: From Achievement to Ascription," *American Sociological Review* 38 (1973): 439–60; John Meyer et al., "The World Educational Revolution," *Sociology of Education* 50 (1977): 242–58.

26. Levin, "Identity Crisis," pp. 86, 87–88.

27. Goody and Watt, "Consequences," pp. 58–59, 59, 59–60; Heath, as cited above; E. M. Rogers and W. Herzog, "Functional Literacy among Columbian Peasants," *Economic Development and Cultural Change* 14 (1966): 190–203, is one empirical example. See also Olson, "Toward."

28. Goody and Watt, "Consequences," pp. 60, 61–63.

29. Goody, "Introduction," pp. 1–2, 16, passim.

30. Goody, *Domestication*, p. 9, chap. 1, passim, pp. 12, 37, chap. 3, passim, pp. 48, 51, for examples, chaps. 4–7. Similar discussions and critical comparative reviews are also required for the major works of Innis and McLuhan. See, for example, James Carey, "Harold Adams Innis and Marshall McLuhan," *Antioch Review* 27 (1967): 5–39; Gerald E. Stearn, ed., *McLuhan Hot and Cool* (New York: New American Library, 1967). David Olson attempts some of this revision; see his "Toward," "From Utterance to Text: The Bias of Language in Speech and Writing," *Harvard Educational Review* 47 (1977): 257–81, and "The Languages of Instruction: The Literate Bias of Schooling," in *Schooling and the Acquisition of Knowledge*, ed. Richard C. Anderson and William E. Montague (Hillsdale, N.J.: Lawrence Erlbaum Associates, 1977), pp. 65–98.

31. See, among the studies, Inkeles, Howard Schuman; and David J. Smith, "Some Social Psychological Effects and Noneffects of Literacy in a New Nation," *Economic Development and Cultural Change* 16 (1967); 1–14; Alex Inkeles, "Industrial Man," *American Journal of Sociology* 66 (1960): 1–31; idem, "The Modernization of Man," in *Modernization*, ed. Myron Weiner (New York: Basic Books, 1966), pp. 138–50; idem, "Making Men Modern," *American Journal of Sociology* 74 (1969): 208–225; idem, "The Fate of Personal Adjustment in the Process of Modernization," *International Journal of Comparative Sociology* 11 (1970): 81–114; idem, "The School as a Context for Modernization," *International Journal of Comparative Sociology* 14 (1973): 163–79; Alex Inkeles and David H. Smith, "The OM Scales," *Sociometry* 21 (1966): 353–77; Alex Inkeles and Karen A. Miller, "Modernity and Acceptance of Family Limitation," *Journal of Social Issues* 30 (1974): 167–88; Inkeles and Smith, *Becoming Modern*. The writings of Lucien Pye, Samuel Huntington, and Daniel Lerner are relevant here.

32. Inkeles, "Making," pp. 212, 213. This and the larger study, it should be noted, included only men. On hidden curriculum, see Michael Apple, *Ideology and Curriculum* (London: Routledge and Kegan Paul, 1979).

33. Inkeles and Smith, *Becoming Modern*, pp. 83, 133, 138, 14, 143, 246. See also Charles Tilly's important review in *Peasant Studies* 6 (1977).

34. Smith, "Some Social Psychological," pp. 3, 7, 10–12.

35. Inkeles, "School as Context," p. 175, and Tilly review. For example of fertility, see Graff, "Literacy, Education, and Fertility." This formulation might be compared with Richard Easterlin's surprising presidential address to the Economic History Association, "Why Isn't the Whole World Developed?" *Journal of Economic History* 41 (1981): 1–19.

36. For Daniel Lerner, see "Towards a Communication Theory of Modernization," in *Communication and Political Development*, ed. Lucien Pye (Princeton: Princeton University Press, 1963); idem, "Literacy and Initiative in Village Development," MIT Center for International Studies, *Rural Development Research Project* (Cambridge, Mass.: MIT Press, 1964); idem, *The Passing of Traditional Society* (New York: Free Press, 1958).

37. Rogers and Herzog, "Functional Literacy," pp. 197, 201.

38. J. E. de Young and C. L. Hunt, "Communication Channels and Functional Literacy in the Philippine Barrio," *Journal of Asian Studies* 22 (1962): 71.

39. Lerner, "Literacy," pp. 4, 5.

40. Dobyns, "Enlightenment and Skill," pp. 137, 150, 150–51, 151. This article gives some background information on the Cornell project. This approach, we are now recognizing, is supported by a growing and increasingly persuasive amount of data and interpretation, historical and more contemporary. Much of it is cited in this book or in Graff, *Literacy Myth and Literacy in History*. See as examples, however, *The Literacy Myth*; Roger Schofield, "Dimensions of Illiteracy, 1750–1850," *Explorations in Economic History* 10 (1973): 437–54; Levin, "Identity Crisis"; Fry, "Schooling"; Pamela Barnhouse Walters, "Educational Change and National Economic Development," *Harvard Educational Review* 51 (1981): 94–106, Blaug, "Literacy"; David McClelland, "Does Education Accelerate Economic Growth?" *Economic Development and Cultural Change* 14 (1966): 257–78; Manfred Stanley, "Social Development as a Normative Concept," *Journal of Developing Areas* 1 (1967): 301–316. Compare such recent approaches with the normative perspectives of Bowman and Anderson, H. H. Golden, and V. Bonac, for example. Walters, "Educational Change," pp. 104, 104–105; and see the literature cited above and in *Literacy in History*.

41. Dobyns, "Enlightenment and Skill," pp. 152, 154–55, and work in progress. McClelland, "Does Education"; see also the large literature on education as human capital and the increasingly powerful criticisms of it. One introduction is Samuel Bowles and Herbert Gintis, "The Problem with Human Capital Theory," *American Economic Review* 65 (1975): 74–82. For an instructive perspective, compare Dobyns's work with James Howe, "The Effects of Writing on the Cuna Political System," *Ethnology* 18 (1979): 1–16, or with the normative psychological literature.

42. Sylvia Scribner and Michael Cole, "Literacy without Schooling: Testing for Intellectual Effects," *Harvard Educational Review* 48 (1978): 448. See also their "Cognitive Consequences of Formal and Informal Education," *Science* 182 (1973): 553–59, a number of unpublished papers, and *The Psychology of Literacy* (Cambridge, Mass.: Harvard University Press, 1981); Michael Cole, "How Education Affects the Mind," *Human Nature*, April 1978, pp. 51–58; and Jack Goody, Michael Cole, and Sylvia Scribner, "Writing and Formal Operations: A Case Study among the Vai," *Africa* 47 (1977): 389–404.

43. Scribner and Cole, "Cognitive Consequences," pp. 554, 558; idem, "Literacy," pp. 449, 451, 452, 453, 454, 456–57, 457. See also Sylvia Scribner and Michael Cole, "Research Program on Vai Literacy and Its Cognitive Consequences," *IACCP Cross-Cultural Psychology Newsletter* 8 (1984): 2–4; Cole, "How Education"; Edward de Bono, "Disturbing Thoughts about Thinking," *Times Literary Supplement*, May 5, 1981. David Olson, for one, follows in the McLuhan tradition of failing to note the difference between literacy in everyday life and its place in intellectual history. Their approach should be compared, for similarities and differences, with those of both Olson and Goody.

44. Olson, "Languages of Schooling," pp. 75, 86, passim. This perspective also draws upon the rich but justly criticized work of Basil Bernstein on sociolinguistic patterns in England; William Labov's many studies in the United States, as well as those of D. R. Entwhistle; Richard Hoggart's classic *The Uses of Literacy* (Boston: Beacon Press, 1961); Bourdieu and Passerson, *Reproduction*; Paul Willis, *Learning to Labour* (Farnborough: Saxon House, 1977), among his own and other studies of the Centre for Cultural Studies, University of Birmingham. In these respects, studies of the family and its relationships respectively with schooling and with stratification have much to tell us, as do the newly developing fields of educational and communicative ethnographies.

45. See Stephen Judy, *The ABCs of Literacy: A Guide for Parents and Educators* (New York: Oxford University Press, 1980), p. xii. His calm tone, if not his full analysis, is a welcome relief from the outcries of so many. By contrast, see the shrillness of Paul Copperman, *The Literacy Hoax: The Decline of Reading, Writing, and Learning in the Public Schools and What We Can Do about It* (New York: William Morrow, 1978), and Joseph Gold, ed., *In the Name of Language!* (Toronto: Macmillan—Maclean-Hunter, 1975).

46. These quotations come from the *Dallas Times Herald*, August 23, 1978, August 17,

1977, November 13, 1977, and April 15, 1976 respectively. They are representative of any major daily newspaper and other organs.

47. David H. Smith, "The Perennial Problem of Illiteracy," *Modern Age* 17 (1973): 33–39; see also Graff, *Literacy Myth*, chap. 7; George H. Douglas, "Is There a Decline in Literacy?" *English Journal* 65 (1976): 140–48; Judy *ABCs*; Roger Farr et al., *Then and Now: Reading Achievement in Indiana* (Bloomington: School of Education, Indiana University, 1974); idem, *Reading Achievement in the United States: Then and Now* (Bloomington: School of Education, Indiana University, 1974), among other reports; Richard Ohmann, "The Decline in Literacy Is a Fiction, If Not a Hoax," *Chronicle of Higher Education*, October 25, 1976; Bormuth, as cited above; Egil Johansson, "The Postliteracy Problem—Illusion or Reality in Modern Society?"in *Time, Space, and Man: Essays on Microdemography* (Stockholm: Almqvist and Wiksell, 1979), pp. 199–212; among others. The continuing cries of Rudolph Fleisch on reading methods are one good example. Now see Bruno Bettelheim and Karen Zela, *On Learning to Read* (New York: Knopf, 1981).

48. Vance Packard, "Are We Becoming a Nation of Illiterates?" *Readers Digest*, April 1974, p. 82.

49. See, for example, Diane Ravitch, "The Schools Are for Learning," *Journal of Current Social Issues* 13 (1976): 3–9; idem, "Minimum Competency Testing: The Consumer Movement in Education," *Journal*, Institute for Socioeconomic Studies 3 (1978): 1–9; William Van Til, "What to Expect If Your Legislature Orders Literacy Testing," *Phi Delta Kappan* 59 (1978): 556–57; Seymour Yesner, "Let's Not Return to Basic Skills," *English Journal* 62 (1973): 892–95; idem, "The Basics and the Basic Value of Human Beings," ibid. 67 (1978): 15–17; Barbara Lieb-Brilhard, "What If Johnny Could Read and Write? . . . Another Look at the Literacy Issue," *Communication Education* 26 (1977): 251–53; idem, "U.S. Literacy Level Not Bad," *Intellect* 104 (September 1977): 104–115; Bormuth, "Value and Volume"; C. A. Bowers, "Cultural Literacy in Developed Countries," *Prospects* 7 (1977): 325–35; Joseph Collignon, "Why Leroy Can't Write," *College English* 39 (1978): 852–59; Harvey Daniels, "Is There a Decline in Literacy?" *English Journal* 65 (1976): 17, 19–20; Robbie G. Davis, "Needed: Functional Literacy Skills Curricula and Tests," *Educational Technology* 17 (1977): 52–54; Thomas J. Farrell, "Literacy, the Basics, and All That Jazz," *College English* 38 (1977): 443–59; Walt Haney and George Madaus, "Making Sense of the Competency Testing Movement," *Harvard Educational Review* 8 (1978): 462–84; Annegret Harnischfeger and David E. Wiley, "The Marrow of Achievement Test Score Declines," *Educational Technology* 14 (1976): 5–14; idem, "Explosion of a Myth: Quantity of Schooling and Exposure to Instruction," *Educational Researcher* 3 (1974): 7–12; Christopher Jencks, "What's behind the Drop in Test Scores?" *Working Papers for a New Society* 6 (1978): 29–41; L. Fisher, *Functional Literacy and the Schools* (Washington, D.C.: National Institute of Education, 1978); John J. Micklos, Jr., "The Facts, Please, about Reading Achievement in American Schools," *Journal of Reading* 24 (1980): 41–54; Patrick Lynch, "Public Policy and Competency Testing," *Education and Urban Society* 12 (1979): 65–80; Otis W. Caldwell and Stuart A. Courtis, *Then and Now in Education, 1845–1923: A Message of Encouragement from the Past to the Present* (Yonkers-on-Hudson, N.Y.: World Book Co., 1923; Reprinted, New York: Arno, 1971). The recent outpouring of writings on definitions and measures of literacy, too numerous to cite here, is another aspect of this contemporary situation. Daniel P. Resnick, Carnegie-Mellon University, is preparing a history of the origins of the minimum competency testing movement; one portion has recently appeared in the *Review of Educational Research* 8 (1980).

50. Jencks, "What's behind," pp. 29, 29–30. See also the above-cited works of Wiley and Harnischfeger; Fisher; Micklos; Douglas; Farr; R. A. Dentler and M. E. Warshawer, *Big City Drop-Outs and Illiterates* (New York: Praeger, 1965); Kozol, *Prisoners, Illiterate*; Hunter and Harman, *Adult Illiteracy*; Fisher, *Functional Literacy*, pp. 16–19, and Appendix for his analysis of the various tests. See also Dentler and Warshawer, *Big City*.   51. Jencks, "What's behind," pp. 31–32, 38, 39, 40. See also papers of Wiley and Harnischfeger; Fisher; Douglas; Judy; Farr; Graff, *Literacy Myth*, and the literature cited there.

52. Jencks, "What's behind," p. 41; Haney and Madaus, "Making Sense," p. 481. See also the comments on the competency testing movement by Lynch, Lieb-Brilhard, Yesner,

Farrell, Wiley and Harnischferger, Micklos, and Fisher in studies cited above, note 55.

53. Johansson, "Postliteracy," pp. 199, 207; Richard Venezky, "Fantasy and Realism," in Beach and Pearson, *Perspectives on Literacy*, p. 43; see also work of John Bormuth cited above; Douglas; Graff, *Literacy Myth*; and for earlier examples, see the interesting views of M. M. Lewis, *The Importance of Illiteracy* (London: Harrap, 1953); H. R. Huise, *The Illiteracy of the Literate* (New York: Appleton-Century, 1933).

54. Bormuth, "Value and Volume," p. 122, passim.

55. Venezky, "Fantasy," pp. 43, 47, 49. See also Bormuth, "Literacy Policy"; Patricia A. Graham, "Whither Equality of Educational Opportunity?" *Daedalus* 109 (1980): 115–32; idem, "Literacy: A Goal for Secondary Schools," *Daedalus* 110 (1981): 119–34.

56. Lewis, *Importance*, pp. 7, 10, 16, 9, 126–27, 98.

57. These statements are based on my reading of and thinking on a large, somewhat ungainly, and growing literature. Much of it was cited in my *The Literacy Myth*. See, for example, the works of David Riesman, Gerald Suttles, Charles Tilly, Alejandro Portes, Michael Young and Peter Wilmott, Elizabeth Bott, Howard Irving, cited in *The Literacy Myth*, chap. 7, n. 54. For historical patterns, see the studies of Franz Bauml, Natalie Davis, Ruth Finnegan, and Peter Burke, among others cited in above chapters. The rich sociological and anthropological studies of "street corner society" and daily life interactions are very relevant here; see, for example, the work of Richard Hoggart and Shirley Heath cited in the chapter. Dell Hymes has much to offer in this respect, too. A number of other ethnographies are in progress. Walter Ong's writings, cited below, are especially provocative. In terms of education, see also Thomas J. Farrell, "Literacy, the Basics"; Barbara Lieb-Brilhard, "What If Johnny." Naturally, McLuhan should be consulted, as should Donald R. Gordon, *The New Literacy* (Toronto: University of Toronto Press, 1971).

58. Heath, "Functions," pp. 126, 127, 129, 130, 131. Her "Protean Shapes" gives many of the details, as other papers do. A full, book-length treatment has been completed.

59. Heath, "Protean Shapes," pp. 35, 35–36. On issues of work, skills, and literacy, see, as leading examples, Harry Braverman, *Labor and Monopoly Capital* (New York: Monthly Review Press, 1974); Bright, "Does Automation"; James Bright, "The Relationship of Increasing Automation and Skill Requirements," in *The Employment Impact of Technological Change*, Appendix, vol. 2, *Report* of the U.S. National Commission on Technology, Automation, and Economic Progress (Washington, D.C.: GPO, 1966), pp. 203–221; the new historical and contemporary sociology of the workplace and labor process, in particular the work of Michael Burawoy, David Noble, or Richard Edwards; Berg, *Education*; Fisher, *Functional Literacy*; Duane M. Nielsen and Howard F. Hjelm, eds., *Reading and Career Education*, Perspectives in Reading, no. 19 (Newark, Del.: International Reading Association, 1975); Oscar Hall and Richard Carlton, *Basic Skills of School and Work: The Study of Albertown*, Ontario Economic Council, Occasional Paper 1 (Toronto, 1977); the work of Thomas G. Sticht. On the larger issues, and the common confusion over them, see Walter J. Ong, as cited below; Oxenham, *Literacy*; David Riesman, "The Oral and the Written Traditions," *Explorations* 6 (1956): 22–28; idem, *The Oral Tradition, the Written Word, and the Screen Image* (Yellow Springs, Ohio: Antioch University Press, 1956); Marshall McLuhan, *The Gutenberg Galaxy* (Toronto: University of Toronto Press, 1962); idem, *Understanding Media* (New York: McGraw-Hill, 1964); Gordon, *New Literacy*; Natan Katzman, "The Impact of Communication Technology: Promises and Prospects," *Journal of Communication* 24 (1974): 47–59; James W. Carey, "A Cultural Approach to Communication," *Communication* 2 (1975): 1–22; Garth S. Jowett, "Toward a History of Communication," *Journalism History* 2 (1975): 34–37; idem, "Communications in History: An Initial Theoretical Approach," *Canadian Journal of Information Science* 1 (1976): 5–13; E. D. Hirsch, Jr., *The Philosophy of Composition* (Chicago: University of Chicago Press, 1977); Stuart Ewen, "The Bribe of Frankenstein," *Journal of Communication* 29 (1979): 12–19; J. R. Holz and C. R. Wright, "Sociology of Mass Communications," *Annual Review of Sociology* 5 (1979): 193–217; Jennifer Tebbe, "Print and American Culture," *American Quarterly* 32 (1980): 259–79; Michael R. Real, "Media Theory: Contributions to an Understanding of American Mass Communications," ibid., pp. 238–58; Edmund Carpenter and Marshall McLuhan, eds., *Explorations in Communication* (Boston: Beacon Press, 1960);

John D. Stevens and Hazel Dicken Garcia, *Communication History* (Beverly Hills, Calif.: Sage Publications, 1980); Colin Cherry, *On Human Communication* (Cambridge, Mass.: MIT Press, 1966 ed.); George A. Miller, *The Psychology of Communication* (New York: Basic Books, 1975); Richard Hoggart, *On Culture and Communication* (New York: Oxford University Press, 1972); Raymond Williams, *Communications* (Harmondworth: Penguin, 1976); idem, *Culture* (London: Fontana, 1981); James Curran, et al., eds., *Mass Communication and Society* (London: Edward Arnold, 1977).

60. Persisting, indeed perennial, debates over reading pedagogy are perhaps the best example.

61. Walter J. Ong, "Literacy and Orality in Our Times," *Journal of Communication* 30 (1980): 200, 200–201; idem, "The Literate Orality of Popular Culture Today," in his *Rhetoric, Romance, and Technology* (Ithaca: Cornell University Press, 1971), pp. 284, 296, 297. See also his *Rhetoric*, passim; idem, *Interfaces of the Word* (Ithaca: Cornell University Press, 1977); idem, *The Presence of the Word* (New York: Simon and Schuster, 1970); idem, "Literacy and Orality in Our Times," *Profession* (Modern Language Association) (1979): 2–13; Elizabeth McPherson, "The Significance of the Written Word," ibid. (1977): 22–25; Hirsch, *Philosophy*; Finnegan, "Literacy," in Ruth Finnegan, *Oral Poetry* (Cambridge: Cambridge University Press, 1977); Bauml, as cited in earlier chapters; the classic studies of Millman Parry and Albert Lord; the writings of David Olson.

62. Ong, "Literacy and Orality," *Profession*, pp. 4, 6. See also the literature cited above, especially notes 67 and 69. On nonalphabetic print, see, for example, the important work of William Ivins, Jr., *Print and Visual Communication* (Cambridge, Mass.: MIT Press, 1953); and A. Hyatt Mayor, *Prints and People* (Princeton: Princeton University Press, 1980). On the relationships with "inventiveness," for which some evidence suggests that literacy is often less crucial, see, as examples, Ivins, *Print*; A. F. C. Wallace, *Rockdale* (New York: Knopf, 1978). Obviously these issues are enormously complex but inordinately important. I can do no more than introduce them here, given that complexity, the domination of dichotomized thinking about them in isolation from other media, and our gross lack of knowledge. See, for example, the work of McLuhan, Riesman, and Gordon, cited above, as well as studies of television that appear, for example, in the *Journal of Communications*; John Culkin, "The New Literacy: From the Alphabet to Television," *Media and Methods* 14 (1977): 64–67, 78–81, 58–61.

63. See in this respect the work of Kozol, Hunter and Harman, and the "underground" critical literature on adult basic education. Good examples of the latter are found in articles by J. Berland and D. McGee in the *Working Teacher* (Vancouver) and in unpublished work by David Wallace, Simon Fraser University.

64. Bormuth, "Value and Volume," pp. 122, 129–31, see also pp. 129–33, 133, and the well-known work of Sticht, Sharon, and Nielsen and Njelm. See, however, Fisher, *Functional Literacy*, for a methodological critique of much of this work. Sylvia Scribner has been studying some of these issues.

65. Braverman, *Labor*, pp. 336, 340–41, 435, 436, 439. See also the work of Bright and Berg, cited above; Herbert Gintis, "Education, Technology, and the Characteristics of Worker Productivity," *American Economic Review* 61 (1971): 266–79; Samuel Bowles and Herbert Gintis, *Schooling in Capitalist America* (New York: Basic Books, 1976); Graff, *Literacy Myth*, esp. chaps. 1, 5; above, chap. 7; Robert Dreeben, *On What Is Learned in School* (Reading, Mass.: Addison-Wesley, 1969).

66. Bright, "Does Automation," p. 86. See also Fisher, *Functional Literacy*. See evidence in Hall and Carlton, *Basic Skills*.

67. Adult Performance Level Project, *The Adult Performance Level Study* (Austin: University of Texas, Division of Extension, 1973), *Adult Functional Competency: A Summary* (1975), *Adult Functional Competency: A Report to the Office of Education Dissemination Review Panel* (1975). But see Fisher, *Functional Literacy*, for important criticisms and qualifications. In this respect, see also, among a larger literature, Mark Blaug, "Literacy and Economic Development," *School Review* 74 (1966): 393–417; papers in Bataille, *Turning Point*.

68. Fisher, *Functional Literacy*, pp. 55, 64, 65, 72.

69. Wide-ranging and highly relevant discussions include Stanley, "Literacy"; Galtung, "Literacy."

70. For example, see JoAnn Vanek, "Work, Leisure, and Family Roles: Farm Households in the United States, 1920–1955," *Journal of Family History* 5 (1980): 422–31, and the references provided there.

71. Amiel Sharon, *Reading Activities of American Adults* (Princeton: Educational Testing Service, 1972). Sharon's results are summarized in Bormuth, "Value and Volume." See also Fisher, *Functional Literacy*; Robert Escarpit, *The Book Revolution* (Paris: UNESCO, 1965); Heinz Steinberg, "Books and Readers a Subject of Research in Europe and America," *International Social Science Journal* (1972); Douglas Waples and Ralph W. Tyler, *What People Want to Read About* (Chicago: American Library Society and University of Chicago Press, 1931); Roger Smith, ed., *The American Reading Public: What It Reads, Why It Reads*, (New York: R. R. Bowker, 1963); idem, "Reading of Books," *Daedalus* 92 (1963): 5–20; R. A. Hintz and C. J. Couch, "Writing and Reading as Social Activities," *Sociological Quarterly* 14 (1973): 481–95; Leonard Shatzkin, "The Book in Search of a Reader," in Smith, *American Reading Public*, pp. 127–37; Dieter Richter, "Teachers and Reading: Reading Attitudes as a Problem in Teaching Literature," *New German Critique* 7 (1976); C. A. Bowers, "Cultural Literacy in Developed Countries," *Prospects* 8 (1977): 323–35; José Ortega y Gasset, "The Difficulty of Reading," *Diogenes* 28 (1959): 1–17.

72. Steinberg, "Books," p. 746.

73. Ortega y Gasset, "Difficulty," p. 1, passim. See also Richter, "Teachers"; Bowers, "Cultural Literacy," among other writings on critical reading.

74. Olson, "Toward a Literate Society," p. 147. See also, as cited above, Graff, *Literacy Myth*, chap. 7 and citations therein; Gordon, *New Literacy*; works of McLuhan; and articles by Lieb-Brilhard and Farrell.

75. Galtung, "Literacy," p. 100. See also Patricia A. Graham, "Whither," "Literacy: A Goal"; Venezky, "Fantasy and Realism"; Stanley, "Literacy."

76. Galtung, "Literacy," pp. 93, 99, 97, 105.

# INDEX

Alcuin, Archbishop of York: educational reform, 47–48

Alfred, King of England: development of education, 50–52

Almanacs: eighteenth-century France, 218, 220; seventeenth- and eighteenth-century American colonies, 256; nineteenth-century France, 281, 282. *See also* Franklin, Benjamin; Literature, popular

Alphabet: origins, 17; development in Greece, 19–26; and literacy in China, 404n. *See also* Syllabary; Writing

Americanization: and education in late nineteenth-century United States, 370–71, 372. *See also* Immigrants and immigration

*Ancient Regime*: continuity into eighteenth century, 182–83, 192; literacy as sign of status, 201

Apprenticeship: as education in eighteenth-century France, 210. *See also* Guilds

Armed Forces Qualifying Test: inadequacy as test of literacy, 3

Artists: education of in Renaissance Italy, 84

Athens: and development of literacy, 22–26; origin of equation of literacy with democracy, 23. *See also* Greece

Atticus: and production of books in Rome, 28

Augustine: on education in the Dark Ages, 36

Austria: education in the eighteenth century, 185, 187; literacy in the nineteenth century, 294–97

Belgium: plan for education of the poor in sixteenth century, 131–32; literacy in eighteenth century, 220, 222–23; literacy in nineteenth century, 304–308. *See also* Flanders; Literacy rates; Low Countries

Bible: translation into English in fourteenth century, 103; typesetting of Gutenberg Bible, 109; controversy over use of vernacular, 135–36; use of vernacular in sixteenth-century France, 144; Church approval of translation into French, 147; sixteenth-century England, 151, 152

*Bibliotheque bleue*: availability and subject matter of popular literature in eighteenth-century France, 218–19

Black Death: effect on literacy, 75–76

Blacks: literacy in nineteenth-century United States, 361–66; literacy in twentieth-century United States, 375–76; occupation and literacy in nineteenth-century United States, 474n–475n. *See also* Literacy rates; Slavery

Books: production in Rome, 28; production and circulation in ninth century, 48; in ninth- and tenth-century England, 52; production and distribution in fifteenth-century Germany and the Netherlands, 92–93; availability of in fourteenth- and fifteenth-century York, 96; trade in fifteenth-century England, 103; demand for before printing, 108–109; early printing of, 109–20; early development of markets, 113–14; ownership of in sixteenth-century France, 146; seventeenth-century New England, 169; eighteenth-century France, 218–20; eighteenth-century Iceland, 230; eighteenth-century American colonies, 254, 255. *See also* Manuscripts; Literature, popular

Boston: literacy in the seventeenth century, 249; literacy and economic position of blacks in nineteenth century, 365–66

Brethren of Common Life: influence on literacy in the Low Countries in the fourteenth and fifteenth centuries, 91–92; education of Erasmus, 125

Brittany: use of French languague in nineteenth century, 278

Bude, Guillaume: and humanism in sixteenth-century France, 127

*Cabinets de lecture*: availability of popular literature in nineteenth-century France, 280. *See also* Libraries

Caesar, Augustus: establishment of state library, 28

Canada: literacy of French settlers in Quebec, 164; literacy of Irish immigrants in nineteenth-century Ontario, 338; literacy in nineteenth century, 347–48; homogenization of language in nineteenth century, 360–61; inadequacies of reading instruction in nineteenth century, 472n

Capitalism: control of labor through education in the nineteenth century, 261–62; and education in nineteenth century, 263–64. *See also* Industrialization; Working class

Catholicism: early medieval France, 64–65; approval of French vernacular Bible, 147; and education in seventeenth-century France, 148; educational efforts outlawed in eighteenth-century Ireland, 248; and adult literacy in nineteenth century, 286; and literacy in nineteenth-century Switzerland, 302; and illiteracy in nineteenth-century Ireland, 339. *See also* Christianity; Church; Religion

Chapbooks: availability and subject matter of popular literature in eighteenth-century England, 244–45. *See also* Literature, popular

Charlemagne: educational reform under, 47–48

HARVEY J. GRAFF is Associate Professor of History and Humanities at The University of Texas at Dallas, author of *The Literacy Myth*, *Literacy in History*, and *The Labyrinths of Literacy*, and editor of the publication series *Interdisciplinary Studies in History*.